student-centered language arts and reading, k-13

student-centered language arts and reading, k-13

a handbook for teachers

second edition

JAMES MOFFETT
BETTY JANE WAGNER

Houghton Mifflin Company • Boston

Atlanta   Dallas   Geneva, Illinois   Hopewell, New Jersey   Palo Alto   London

The preparation of the first edition of this book was principally supported by a two-year grant from Carnegie Corporation of New York. The statements made and views expressed are solely the responsibility of the authors.

Cover photos courtesy of Ingbert Grüttner and National Educational Association Communications Services, Joe Di Dio.

Printed in the U.S.A.

Library of Congress Catalog Card Number: 76-11920

ISBN: 0-395-20630-8

contents

how to use this book

This is a textbook for teachers when they are in training and a handbook for use when they are on the job. It covers curriculum and methods of language arts and reading for both elementary and secondary school and applies also to teaching English in basic college courses.

We offer the book as a basic text for courses in elementary language arts methods, reading methods, secondary English methods, and secondary reading methods. We believe that whatever the emphasis of the course, it will benefit considerably from the context of integrated school language learning that the book aims to provide. Most educators today agree that the elementary and secondary years should be fused into a strong educational continuity and that reading should be interwoven with the other language arts. In fact, past efforts have shown the practical impossibility of drawing a line between elementary and secondary levels or between reading and other language work. Furthermore, the recent increase in this country of literacy problems has made the teaching of "basic skills" an issue that even a high school or college teacher may have to deal with. So this book contains the ideas and information needed to teach beginning or remedial reading and writing.

Whatever the age of one's students, a teacher today must be able, we believe, to individualize learning and to do justice to the depth and complexity of language growth. All this requires knowing a lot more than if one is merely to follow teacher's guides as verbatim scripts or to become an usher in a mechanized, teacher-proof system. We have gone far, on one hand, into the psychology of language and development and far, on the other, into the nuts-and-bolts details of classroom practices. We hope the book will serve in many ways and at different times during the owner's training and career.

The book was written so as to offer course instructors and readers as much flexibility as possible. We assume that instructors will assign some portions to discuss in class or otherwise work over in the course, assign other portions to assimilate on one's own, and leave still other material for reference when the student-teacher goes into a classroom. We expect that instructors will vary in how much they want to play up or play down the sections on literacy (Part Three), rationale (Part One), and aims and assessment (Part Five). The five main parts stand in enough expository independence of each other so that they might be read in another order, though their printed order has the value of gradual orientation. After the lead chapter in each part, chapters also permit skipping about. The index, the appendixes, the topical chapter titles, and considerable textual cross-referencing should further facilitate getting at what one is most interested in and using the book flexibly to make one's own emphasis and sequence.

Parts of some chapters may not apply to the growth stage of a teacher's students, so he may want to skim at times. In order to allow readers to determine, rather than the authors to guess, which stage of development their students have reached, we have described developmental differences by students' capacities, experiences, and interests rather than by age or grade. Given the tremendous range of variation within any single classroom between primary school and senior high school, we judged that breakdowns not only by grades but even by grade blocs would be impractical.

The more some works grow, the more they owe. The body of ideas and practices that make up this book have represented the thought and practice of an increasingly large number and broad range of persons. Acknowledging individual indebtedness becomes impossible, though we would at least like to thank specifically those who read the manuscript and offered us their valuable criticism: Tom Barton, Washington State University, Pullman; Rose Feinberg, University of Lowell; Kenneth Goodman, University of Arizona, Tucson; Floren Harper; Robert Hillerich, National College of Education; Prentiss Hosford, University of Georgia, Atlanta; Elizabeth Kelly; Joel Weinberg, Simmons College; and Richard Whitworth, Ball State University.

The widening circles of indebtedness began among people whom we met where we taught or did research—Phillips Exeter Academy, the National College of Education, the Harvard Graduate School of Education—and spread nationally when the first version of this book became widely known and widely used and when we collaborated with the other coauthors of the *Interaction* series, benefitting not only from the expertise of these colleagues but also from the feedback to our joint work. We have made some specific acknowledgments in footnotes to the text, but footnotes could never cover the myriad of teachers, language arts coordinators, reading specialists, students, education professors, and other school or university people from whom we have learned what we feel we know. Our experience necessarily incorporates the experience so gained during countless workshops, consultations, professional meetings, teacher-supervision sessions, experiments with students, collaborations on school materials, responses to our work, and so on. This incorporation is so massive that anyone writing a methods book from our position must indeed be considered to some extent as only a spokesperson for accumulated professional experience, no matter how original or idiosyncratic his ideas may be in some respects. While neither claiming nor necessarily desiring consensus, we do feel once again, in expressing indebtedness, just how much we have drawn from others to synthesize our "own" ideas. To all those who see their ideas in what we say, thank you.

James Moffett
Betty Jane Wagner

Note: Throughout this book the words "he," "him," and "his" are used in their generic sense to refer to both males and females. The coauthors—one male, one female—agreed to this policy because so many readers, both male and female, object to the cumbersomeness of "he/she" or "(s)he."

preface

In the original introduction to this book, I said that I hoped to offer a way of teaching not incarnated in textbooks, "an alternative to the installation of a prepackaged curriculum." I still feel strongly that organic English is killed by special books for writing, speaking, spelling, skill-building, and so on, and that it is far too basic ever to be embodied in textbooks, especially those committed to this or that concept of literature or rhetoric. But I have directed a new program of school materials called *Interaction: A Student-Centered Language Arts and Reading Program* (Houghton Mifflin, Boston, 1973). To readers who have not seen the program this may appear to contradict the stand in this book. Actually, *Interaction* came about as an effort to offset some limitations of the first edition of this text.

Interaction adheres faithfully to the philosophy of the first edition by making available the reading material, recordings, activity cards, games, and films that would implement the book's ideas and render textbooks unnecessary. It goes beyond the first edition, however, toward a greater individualization, now advocated in this edition, that allows different students to do different things at the same time, and frees the teacher from lesson-planning and direction-giving to do all the things that really make education work—coaching, counseling, and consulting.

This book may be used in two ways with *Interaction*. Those who purchase that program will find this book extends the teacher's guides and gives more detail about both method and rationale. Those who will not have *Interaction* can look at its materials to see examples of the sorts of materials and practices recommended herein. Asterisks have been placed in this text beside those kinds of materials or those titles that can be found in *Interaction*. This is handy, because one frustration of a handbook is that it can only describe materials, and rather inadequately sometimes, especially unfamiliar things. *English Through Interaction* films are cited by title, since they are classroom documentaries for teacher education.

Interaction is consistent with this book because the school program came into existence itself as one kind of revision of the methods text. But each is independent of the other. Illustrated by *Interaction*, this book can serve those people who would like more background and detail for *Interaction* as well as the more general audience in the profession for whom it was originally written.

James Moffett
Berkeley, California
1976

student-centered language arts and reading, k-13

rationale

A useful idea for thinking about language learning is embodied in the story of Tweedledum and Tweedledee, the boyish twins Alice meets in the looking-glass world. Like their names, they resemble each other to a point and then diverge. Tweedledum and Tweedledee represent all of us. We are similar in a general way and different in particular ways. And our differences, like theirs, emerge from the similarity itself. Only things that share a common origin can diverge. Our common humanity is like white light that, passing through the prism of heredity and experience, separates itself into the colors of individual variation. Out of one, many.

But at any time, the possibility remains of emphasizing the similarity and becoming one again. Tweedledum and Tweedledee *agreed* to have a battle, but when a "monstrous crow" flew down and frightened them, "they quite forgot their quarrel." Pushed to essentials, we forget our differences. The democratic slogan *e pluribus unum* emphasizes this reversal toward similarity. Out of many, one. We have the choice to stress similarity and unity or difference and multiplicity. Likeness and unlikeness are in the eye of the beholder and hence at the center of conceiving and verbalizing. For this reason, the rationale of this student-centered curriculum will invoke again and again this concept and this choice.

The value of theory

Such a general concept may seem far removed from the perennial teacher concern about "What do I do Monday morning?" Faced with thirty or so wrigglers in a room, you may grow quickly impatient with theory. But good theory should serve as a blueprint for action so that you *know* what to do Monday and any other time. It should provide a basic framework that indicates what to do in any situation and why to do this rather than that. It does not guide, however, by spelling out action as specifically as a musical score or a recipe. It gives you a comprehensive and integrated perspective within which all problems can be placed, a consistent way of thinking so that you can think what to do *as you go*. This is critical, because all that you can plan definitely for a class is something general enough to encompass all students. Running a classroom cannot be like following a script. Panic comes from forgetting your lines and not being able to improvise. Trying to stick to a script causes more difficulty than playing by ear. But playing by ear works only when you have thought out well what you are about. If you understand deeply enough what you are doing, you don't need to keep asking, "What do I do Monday morning?"

Let's apply the concept of similarity and difference to the traditional daily lesson plan. You try to think of a detailed activity that twenty to forty youngsters will be ready and able to do Monday morning. But there isn't any such thing. You can't have it both ways—to be so specific and so general at the same time. Any task specific enough to be done on a certain day cannot be appropriate for two or three dozen students, because people differ more than that. In fact, the more specific the level of action we're talking about, the more different people will be. Any need general enough, on the other hand, to apply to a whole class will translate into action far too long-range to fit even a weekly or a monthly lesson plan. This is, of course, no argument against planning, but if the planning is to accommodate both similarities and differences in students, it must be a *general way of individualizing,* not one assignment for all at the same time. Teaching can be planned for a group only to the point where similarity leaves off. Planning must take the form of a lessons plan, a plan for how to specify different lessons for different youngsters at the same time.

The rationale for this curriculum starts with such fundamental ideas as like/unlike and general/specific, and progresses down to practices. The chapters in Parts One and Two of this book move the same way, from general to specific. *The chief purpose of this rationale is to enable you to run a classroom without one lesson plan for all each day and one sequence for all each year,* because you will be a far more effective teacher if you can operate a Tweedle process that permits Dee and Dum activities to go on simultaneously within it. First, the rationale aims to stimulate an understanding of what you are doing that will enable you to work within a *general* plan in which details are worked out with different working parties as you go. Second, some activities, like analyzing dummy sentences, should not be done at all, and other activities, like show-and-tell, work well only when done certain ways. For good judgment in choosing activities and deciding how they are to be done, you need to relate decision-making to a philosophy of language learning and language growth. Third, although most of what is taught in a traditional curriculum is taught in the one proposed here, some things may not be named or classified in a way you are looking for or taught in a way you expect. You need to know what the goals are and how the proposed activities may teach them in unfamiliar ways. Finally, when a program calls for strenuous innovation, you need to know why you should abandon some time-honored activities and go to the trouble of starting new ones.

If you don't like the sound of this and want to skip ahead to parts of the book that get down to nuts and bolts, go ahead—and don't feel guilty. You may even put this curriculum into effect without reading the rationale for it. More power to you. But be prepared to return to the rationale if you don't understand how improvisation can teach essay writing or how peers can teach each other something when no one of them knows more than the others. If a certain practice does not work well, the problem may be that you don't understand what you are attempting. To act without understanding is never practical. Too often, teachers do not know why they are doing what they do, and an alarming number admit that they don't believe in what they are doing. Sooner or later you simply have to think about what you are up to. Otherwise you never really know what to do Monday morning and therefore search constantly for nuts-and-bolts answers.

A model of mental growth

Because teachers of composition and comprehension necessarily deal with the putting of thought into speech and the interpreting of speech into thought, they need a model of mental growth. They are not concerned with language alone. Problems of composition and comprehension have to be resolved *between* thought and speech as students try to match one with the other. The model of growth educators choose makes a critical difference in how everyone involved thinks about learning.

The growth model assumed in traditional schooling is based on nineteenth-century physics and the industrial assembly line. According to this mechanical model, an educated student is a "product" issuing from one end of a closed system into which he and some other inert materials were fed. Knowledge structures are assembled by putting small parts together to make subassemblies that are in turn put together to make the finished product. The upshot is that students can't see the woods for the trees. They are usually working on parts, without knowing why, and too seldom experience fully functioning communication in school. One falsity in this model is that in reality a child is more maker than made.

It is important, whatever the model, that it depict growth sequence as cumulative, not linear. Don't picture growth as a ladder or a series of stepping-stones, because these metaphors imply that the learner leaves behind old learning as he acquires new. Most learning is never shed but, rather, becomes assimilated or transformed into more advanced skills and knowledge. Imagine growth as a circle that becomes filled with more and more detailed and interfused figures. Only a moving picture could show this succession properly, but we'll have to settle for a series of still pictures (Figure 1.1, page 4). Imagine this figure as a single circle becoming increasingly complicated within.

Biology is the most appropriate field from which to draw a model of education, because mental growth parallels the growth of the total organism, in which it occurs. The best model of mental growth is the human embryo. It grows from a single cell to an extraordinarily intricate organism without ever

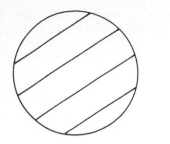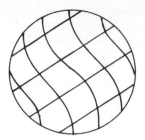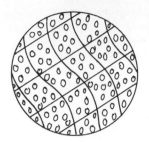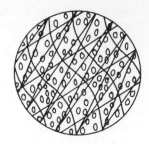

FIGURE 1.1 DEPICTION OF GROWTH

being anything less than a whole and without ever functioning any other way than as a whole (Figure 1.2). A fertilized human egg is a human being before elaboration. What it is to become is already coded genetically within and will unfold through interaction with the environment. As the French expression says, "The more it changes the more it is the same thing"—that is, the more it fulfills what it has always been latently. It effects change by differentiating itself into limbs and organs, and it sustains itself across change by interrelating these parts by nerves and blood vessels as fast as they become articulated. The beauty of embryonic—and of mental—development lies in the great biological principle of simultaneous *differentiation and integration.*

At birth the mind of a child is simple, like a cell, and one with the world, because it has never had to deal with the world. Just as the child's body par-

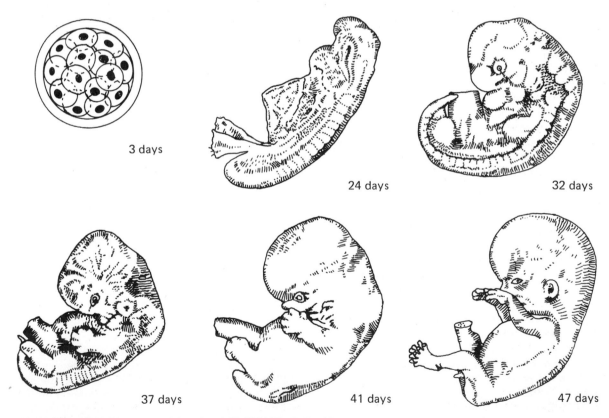

3 days

24 days

32 days

37 days

41 days

47 days

FIGURE 1.2 STAGES OF GROWTH IN THE HUMAN EMBRYO

took of the mother's body, his mind partook of surroundings with no consciousness of separation. Marvelous faculties of reason like classifying and inferring exist already in potential state but lie dormant, pending the environmental exchanges that will activate them. Cut off from the mother, the child begins to become conscious of himself. Thrust up against physical and social realities, the child begins to construct an ego to negotiate with the things and people he is now starting to feel separate from. Distinguishing one's organism from one's environment—perhaps the real trauma of birth—is the archetype of all differentiating. As he differentiates self from world, the child also differentiates the mind into thoughts that match the way the physical and social worlds are broken down. For safety and satisfaction, he has to learn to make distinctions, to tell the difference between one thing and another. He learns to analyze, in other words, or, more accurately, his experience activates his inborn ability to analyze.

Humpty Dumpty's fall symbolizes this breakup of the egg's primal unity and simplicity into the inevitable differentiation an organism must undergo if it is to survive. The higher the animal the more its survival depends on acting differently toward different things—on flexibility—and hence the more it must differentiate its own insides into specialized parts. Growth means moving away from an initial lumping together, which in the mental realm some psychologists call global thinking. (Vestiges of it will hound students and teachers for years to come in the form of undiscriminated, undetailed, unrelated, unexplained ideas.)

Humpty Dumpty's problem is not that he broke himself down but that all the king's horses and all the king's men cannot put him back together again. The other half of growth is integration. As an *egg* Humpty Dumpty indeed cannot be put back together. An egg has to change into something else, and integrating new parts is actually *re*integrating. The differences emerging because of the breakdown must be constantly restructured. After a certain stage nutrients no longer diffuse directly throughout protoplasm; gastrointestinal organs evolve to specialize in processing nutrients, and these must form a sequence among themselves, so that each does its job successively, and must form other appropriate relations with heart, lungs, brain, and so on to coordinate functions.

As the embryo must integrate the organs and vessels it articulates for fending and foraging in the environment outside the womb, the mind must organize the concepts and statements into which it is breaking thought down for matching it to material and social realities. The mind must synthesize parts into wholes at the same time it analyzes the whole into parts. Recent brain research suggests, in fact, that the reason for the brain having two hemispheres is so that it can specialize in both functions at once. Usually the left hemisphere (in most right-handed people) undertakes to analyze and the right to synthesize. The more differences the mind distinguishes, the more relating it must conceive in order to coordinate the parts as a whole. The mind must see the unlikeness of things existing in their unique state of concreteness and yet see likeness among things as reordered out of time and space into the abstract realm of thought. In his original global state of mind, the child was no more aware of similarity than of difference, because perception of one depends on perception of the other. Analysis and synthesis together create the complexity, the higher organization, that characterizes growth.

Abstracting

The matching off of thought with the forms of language cannot be done on a one-to-one basis. An idea may be said many ways. The myriad options for matching thought with speech create, in fact, all the glories and problems of comprehension and composition. Working in the gap, then, between invisible thought and visible language, you the teacher need a concept applying equally to both. The concept of abstracting serves this purpose.

Abstracting is mentally mapping reality. It comprises two opposite processes, analysis and synthesis, working together simultaneously. By virtue of analysis, the mind is able to elaborate global wholes into their particulars. By virtue of synthesis, the mind is able to generalize otherwise disparate particulars into wholes. Elaboration emphasizes differences and leads into the world. From it we gain discrimination and detailed fidelity to reality. Generalization emphasizes similarity and leads into the mind. From it we gain increased scope and the power of mental relating. Neither can function without the other, for just as generalizing presupposes some prior breakdown into particulars from which generalities can be drawn, elaborating presupposes some prior generalities that can be broken down into particulars. Abstraction is a tension between the two processes. It binds mind to world.

This tension stretches across any effort to speak, listen, read, or write. In composition, teachers constantly urge students to be specific, to add concrete details to narrative and description or to give examples to illustrate their ideas in an essay. On the other hand, teachers push students to relate ideas to other ideas and to details, to give emphasis and unity, to "tie things together." All of these are classic issues in relating generality to instance so as to convey meaning. For comprehension, a reader must relate an author's little facts to his main point, draw conclusions from cues and clues, put examples and evidence in proper relation to statements they support, and "pull together" the various big and little things the author has said into an understanding that focuses on the general and subordinates the particular in the ratio an author intends.

GENERALIZING

To *abstract* is to draw off. A trait is that which is drawn off. The abstracter selects a trait that for one purpose or another he deems an important aspect of an object, event, scene, or experience. Doing this presupposes some analysis: in order to select out *spotted* as a trait of some things, one first has to differentiate figures from backgrounds and spots from other figures—that is, break down reality. A trait is drawn off to reduce and reorder the world. The speckles on fruit, the spots on some animals, the freckles on people, the dots on a blouse, the ground pattern of sunlight through leaves, knotholes in paneling, the dark and bright places in someone's "checkered career"—all become mentally digested in such a way that the spottedness of each dissociates itself from the concrete context in which it was embedded. This stripping off of local and detailed circumstances isolates the trait. Then once singled out, a trait is ordered in the mind. It joins with the spottedness of the others to form a concept based on a common denominator, a vaguer image that can include sets of spots of different contexts, origins, purposes, colors, regularity. What is drawn from different sources is distilled to make a new mental entity. In this way, synthesis accompanies analysis.

Generalizing is a process of putting mind over matter. People don't draw off traits of things as they do broth from beef, of course, because broth contains actual molecules of beef, whereas an abstrac-

tion can only *symbolize*—code from a physical to a mental medium—and hence must partake of mental qualities. The mind codes reality within its own medium of bioelectrical circuitry the way a television receiver recapitulates original action electronically on its screen—by forming itself to match the form it is simulating. Whereas the television receiver can recapitulate only temporal and spatial forms of matter in motion, the mind can make logical forms as well because it is a far more complex medium having ocular representation as only one of its submedia.

All that can be abstracted from something is *form*. The basic idea of informing is to put into form, and that's exactly what happens in matching experience with thought. Form is not a something but a relation—succession in time, direction and position in space, conjunction of circumstances or conditions. Relations are intangible, like mind itself. So thought can consist only of relating. Concepts result from sorting things into classes, and sorting is relating different things according to a common trait like spottedness. The traits themselves have to be formal in order to be drawn off—either an aspect of physical form such as spottedness or a relation such as that of owing in the concept of duty.

Abstracting spottedness shows at work the logical faculty responsible for generalization—*analogy*. (*Analogic* is thinking of things as like.) This is the same faculty responsible for metaphor. (The poet Gerald Manley Hopkins "drew off" spottedness in "Pied Beauty," which begins, "Glory be to God for dappled things....") Generalizing is a form of thought that may take several language forms, as we will show later; it is not just a class concept in noun or adjective form, as in the example above.

ELABORATING

To *elaborate* means to work out. Nothing can be elaborated that is not already contained as germ in the whole or generality to be elaborated. Elaboration is the flowering of an idea; seed differentiates into stem, root, leaves, and blossoms—all of which come from within. Elaboration is unfolding a given, whether the given is an object to be descriptively detailed, a summary of action to be filled in, a statement to be exemplified, or a premise from which corollaries are to be deduced. Buried in someone's use of *spotted* are concrete, remembered instances—fruit, fabric, or face—that he "has in mind" and could summon for elaboration. Elaborating particulars makes explicit ("unfolded") the referents of words, whereas generalizing leaves instances implicit, assumed. When the referent of a word is not a physical thing but an idea itself, then elaborating brings out the ramifications ("branchings"), the hidden implications.

Whatever the level, elaborating works by reversing generalization. Generalizing achieves scope by extending the referent over time and space—over all spotted things anywhere, any time. Elaborating achieves discrimination by narrowing the compass of time and space covered—down to some spotted animals at some times and places, for example, or one freckled child at one time and place. Elaborating localizes, puts things back into time and the concrete circumstances from which generalizing drew them. This leads to multiplicity, of course, for as generalizing subsumes many instances into one concept or statement—"uses up" raw material at a great rate, so to speak—specifying particulars restores their original quantity, as well as quality, of particulars.

It also turns up instances one had not thought of before. It is a tool for finding out fully what one means. Once armed, for example, with the concept of a spectrum one could look for instances other than the orderly arrays of color shades and musical tones by which one may have first come to understand the concept and thus think of scaling metals by their degree of tensile strength or scaling people by their degree of patience. Or one might check how broadly a statement like "Opposites attract" applies by thinking of as many instances of it in different domains as one can. So it is that elaboration leads back from mind to world in a reversal of analogy.

THE DUAL FUNCTION OF ABSTRACTING

The function of abstracting is to enable the individual to match his mind to the world, on the one hand, and to fellow minds, on the other. *Abstracting from* experience makes information, to accommodate oneself to external realities. *Abstracting for* other people makes communication, to benefit from community. (One of the benefits is receiving other people's information.) The dual functions of informing oneself and communicating to others interact with each other, because the same abstracting apparatus is serving both. The habit of communicating one's information influences how a person informs himself. Thought is private and speech public, but

constantly matching thought with speech inevitably causes thinking to become somewhat public and stereotyped. This influence can be reciprocal; thought can cause speaking to become somewhat private and original.

THE PARTIALITIES OF ABSTRACTING

The very function of abstracting biases it toward personal desire or public conventions (which represent communal desire). Mapping is always for a purpose, if only a playful one, and this purpose necessarily makes abstracting partial. Mental maps always specialize, like geographic maps, which may show mineral resources or air routes or ethnic distribution or temperature zones but never everything. No abstraction can render justice to all aspects of something, in its totality, because selective reduction is the point of abstracting. People can't deal with all aspects of all things. They have to choose traits according to their values. This is why content is a factor of intent. One trades a loss of reality for a gain in control, to get a mental handle on reality toward certain ends. Abstracting is decision-making. This is necessary for survival, but the great and haunting danger of boomeranging always remains: one may exclude from his maps aspects of reality more vital to him than those his desires or his society's conventions direct him to single out.

Abstractions can be true, then, only relative to some given value system and frame of reference guiding the selective reduction. They may be useful or beautiful but never true except in a partial way. Raw phenomena present themselves, and thought can only *re*present them in one or another biased way. This relativity unnerves many people, who simply cannot believe that the maps they and their fellows hold to be self-evident are not *the* maps. Or even if our own maps are not quite correct and complete, surely some maps somewhere are. But it is in the very nature and function of the abstracting process that it should fail to yield the absolute truth some part of a human being seems to hunger for.

Earlier eras made a distinction between human truth and divine truth. Religious beliefs aside, this distinction is necessary to remind us that no human being is desireless and unconditioned by his society and that no human being has a vantage point of universal scope or impartiality. No matter how brilliant his mental faculties, his mind works in the service of a mortal bound to a certain time and space and inheritance. This is why spiritual leaders have always said, "If you wish to know divine truths, you must link up with the divine, not seek to know in this way with the brain." To claim that one's utilitarian, scientific, and aesthetic statements about the world correctly and completely describe the world is to claim omniscience for reason.

Both mystics and scientists repudiate such intellectual arrogance. They agree that the world is too big for words, that if absolute knowledge comes, it comes by total illumination, not by putting back together with one faculty of reason what we have torn down with another, admirable as this dual process of synthesis and analysis is for its biological purpose. We cannot experience all of reality, cannot render all we experience into thought, and cannot render all we think into words. This may be why Hamlet tells Horatio that there are more things in heaven and earth than are dreamt of in philosophy.

ABSTRACTING AS COMPOSING AND COMPREHENDING

Human beings are born composers. By drawing off traits of the world and rearranging them according to some mental order, people constantly compose reality, for composition literally means putting together, selecting and arranging the elements of a medium. Everybody puts together his own world, more or less like other people's because of social influences and similarities in basic equipment, more or less different because of individual variations in background and heredity. Our mental maps are compositions.

The root idea of *comprehension* resembles remarkably that of composition, despite the fact that they are supposed to be opposing sender and receiver viewpoints. To comprehend means to take together. The difference between "put together" and "take together" is the difference between composing and comprehending. *Put* suggests that one has wider choice of what to select than *take,* which suggests that one is given a previously selected set of things from which to abstract for some purpose. This is in fact exactly the case in reading, for example, where one must make sense of someone else's writing, just as the writer has to make sense of the matter he confronts. If a person runs up against either a text or an experience that he cannot fit into his previous mental maps, he says he doesn't know what "to make of it." Similarly, we say of a speaker or writer, "He doesn't make sense." The common

idea that people *make* sense, create meaning, seems to acknowledge that whether composing something themselves or comprehending someone else's composition, people are in the same basic position. Whether faced with physical events or a book, one has to interpret. Interpreting is one kind of abstracting. Within this similarity of *making* sense, then, composing and comprehending differ in whether one is abstracting from raw reality or from another's abstraction of it. Listening or reading is digesting someone else's digestion. This is a difference in the *level* at which one is abstracting.

LEVELS OF ABSTRACTION

Actually, no reality is truly raw by the time people become conscious of it. All that the nervous system can do is simulate in the medium of the body those phenomena it registers. A retinal image, for example, is the body's equivalent of the artist's conception. So the sensory impressions from which people abstract concepts are themselves abstractions. There are higher and lower orders of abstraction within both perception and conception, as we will explain farther on. Moreover, as we just said, people make some of their information by comprehending other people's compositions in various media—that is, by abstracting from others' abstractions. Any such successive abstracting creates higher levels from lower ones. People not only make the reality they know, they make it by abstracting higher abstractions from lower ones. Knowledge-making is hierarchical.

Processing matter into mind comprises several stages that relate to degrees of growth. The nervous system codes external reality from the outside in, first with the muscles or motor apparatus, then with the senses, then with memory, and finally with reason. Stages may be bypassed, as when we learn about something from pictures only or as when we read about something, but when we abstract for ourselves from the ground up, each of these four knowledge-making organs abstracts from the abstraction created by the organ below. Reason doesn't go directly to work on raw external reality; it operates on what the senses represent to it of external reality, most of which has been filed away in the memory. And memory depends completely on sensory reports for the material it files away. Sensory perception abstracts information from external reality on the basis of body placement, position, movement, and interaction with environmental objects. What we see is limited to where the body takes the head and which way the head directs the eyes, so that abstracting begins with the organism's own selective action. (Moreover, some sensors report what is going on just within the body itself.)

It is imperative, however, to understand the two-way nature of abstracting. The case is not that reason is the victim of wayward sensorimotor apparatus and memory. To a point it is fair to say that the muscles, the senses, and the memory have minds of their own, because each is a specialized organ made to function a certain way, and the information created by each is unique. But the overriding fact is that these organs are told what to report on. The mind executes the orders of the will and the emotions by *organ*izing all functions around these orders. Orders are to screen reality according to declared priorities. So the muscles, senses, memory, and reason all abstract under constraints imposed from above at the same time that they report upward. This compares to personnel at different echelons of a social organization sending reports to their superiors about what their superiors want to be informed of, not just about anything they might take it into their head to say. Each organ gives form to what it receives according to both its own form and the shaping directions it operates under.

The report at each echelon summarizes the reports submitted to it from echelons below, in pyramidal fashion, so that information becomes more reductive and further removed from original sources the higher it goes. The final report placed on the president's desk or sent to trustees or shareholders has the virtue of being pertinent to what they want most to know about, but the successive abstractions risk loss of fidelity to the original external reality. More and more the organism or organization is processing previous processing. This is how the abstracting *for* cannot in practice be separated from abstracting *from*, and this principle of mind over matter reaches down to the very lowest level of abstracting.

Communication

Like Tweedledum and Tweedledee, people communicating must share a common base—the same language and some similar assumptions, values, and motives. But if their minds do not differ in some way, they have nothing to communicate to each other. *Communicating is overcoming a differential,* some imbalance of knowledge between the two parties,

whether the knowledge is public information or private feeling. The idea is to match minds—to share. The better the minds match to begin with, the easier communication is, but the less there is to communicate. The more there is to communicate, the harder it is, because the minds share less initially. Thus it is easier to talk with someone sharing interests, values, and style, but we learn more from someone different. Critical matters arise from such simple truths. For example, we don't *know* how like or unlike our minds are except by communicating in the first place. Comprehending and composing concern nothing so much as trying to match private minds by means of a public vehicle called language.

LEVELS OF CODING

Language is a medium of communication and follows the general principles of all communication. This means, for one thing, that its superstructure is the set of relations among sender, receiver, and message. For another thing, it means that language shares common characteristics with other media of communication—down to the point where media differentiate, according to the unique characteristics of each, into graphics, electronics, music, body movement, and so on. All media communicate something from beyond themselves, some raw experience that has to be coded into the medium. Thus the content or messages of language are themselves nonverbal. People code their as yet unsymbolized experience ("raw") into one or another medium according to the graphic, acoustical, electronic, or other material traits of the medium. But before they can code into any medium they have to think the experience in some way, not consciously perhaps, not yet in words, but abstract it and organize it in some form in the mind (see Table 1.1, page 10).

Conceptualization

The first level at which we encode experience, then, is that of conceptualization. But who is doing the sending and who the receiving? Thinking is self-communicating. Sender and receiver are different parts of the same nervous system, and so we don't have names for them. Thinking is so reflexive that we don't know how to separate a sender and a receiver, but still we know that experience is being registered, processed, and transmitted. Let's just say that the thinking represents the communication trinity of sender, receiver, and message at its genesis, as it is differentiating itself from the primordial unity of raw experience.

Verbalization

At the second level, people encode thought into speech and decode speech into thought. This level of coding we may call verbalization. It involves how to put things and how to take things—what teachers call composition and comprehension. Verbalization is oral but not necessarily external, since one verbalizes to oneself while writing. Learning at this level is developmental; that is, it grows as people grow.

Literacy

At the third level, people encode from oral speech to writing and decode from writing into oral speech. What is called literacy comprises these activities. This level is derivative, because it is an overlay of printed symbols upon vocal symbols. Coding between oral and written words is what teachers call the basic skills or the two Rs, reading and writing. On the reading side, literacy covers what teachers call decoding and word recognition; and on the writing side, it covers the transcription skills of handwriting, spelling, and punctuation. (Interestingly enough, the term *decoding* acknowledges some communication model even though the symmetrical term *encoding* has no currency in schools, and the term *word recognition* acknowledges that reading is recognizing words in a secondary medium.)

Throughout this book we will use the term *literacy* to indicate the activities of this level. Though it is not a common school term, *literacy* designates at once both reading and writing skills and thus captures the whole of this level of coding in a single word. Literacy is not developmental beyond the age of about eight, when the necessary sensory and muscle development has been reached: a person may learn to read and write at any time thereafter, but nothing in later growth will make this learning significantly easier or different than it is for the child.

Contrasting Verbalization with Literacy

Teachers habitually think of literacy as first or basic, as reflected in the misnomer "basic skills," because the two Rs occur early in the school career and lay the foundation for book learning. But we do well to remind ourselves that reading and writing actually occur last—that is, not only after the acquisition of oral speech but also after considerable nonverbal experience. The three levels of coding, summarized in Table 1.1, mean that experience has to be encoded into thought before thought can be encoded into speech, and thought encoded into speech before speech can be encoded into writing. Each is basic to the next, so that far from being basic itself literacy depends on the prior codings. It merely adds an optional, visual medium to the necessary, oral medium.

Much confusion in language teaching has resulted from the fact that anyone reading or writing necessarily merges all three levels of coding. Teachers have too often assumed that when a student is performing at the level of literacy, the difficulties he has must be of that level, whereas the difficulties may be of any one of the three levels or of all at once. When composing and comprehending are done orally, then word recognition and transcribing can be ruled out, and the difficulties can be seen to be in the conceptualizing of experience or in the verbalization of thought. Despite all the hue and cry about basic skills, most problems facing language teachers do not concern spelling, punctuation, and word recognition nearly so much as they do thinking and speaking, which are the true basic skills. But because the problems *manifest* themselves at the coding level that students are asked to perform on—that is, in reading and writing—the problems *look* as if they are problems of literacy.

If communicating is overcoming a differential between sender and receiver, then we can see that the really difficult learning issues will be at the level of verbalization, where meaning is involved, not at the level of literacy. Matching speech with print requires

TABLE 1.1 THE THREE LEVELS OF CODING

		CODING	
(1)	CONCEPTU-ALIZATION	experience into thought	NON-VERBAL
(2)	VERBAL-IZATION	thought into speech	ORAL
(3)	LITERACY	speech into print	WRITTEN

little intellectual work. It requires some information —spellings, punctuation marks, and the spatial conventions of print—but literacy is conventional and cut-and-dried. It is not difficult or developmental but seems so because it drags on for years for reasons of inefficiency to be discussed later.

By contrast, matching off words with the world, and one mind with another, requires little information but the utmost in intellectual activity. Communicating, in fact, requires *making* information—symbolizing experience—or *interpreting* the information someone else has made. The intrinsically difficult learning problems that students and teachers have to deal with are those entailed in composition and comprehension. These can be practiced orally. This has the great advantages of affording plentiful practice and of concentrating directly on the manifold problems of verbalizing without confusing them with the stereotyped problems of literacy. Perceptual pairing of oral sounds with written words is of itself easy. School should focus on thinking, to match thought with speech, and verbalizing, to match mind with mind. Literacy represents the Tweedle part that remains the same for all, whereas verbalization represents difference and creativity.

"Language Arts" *is* what the language arts *are*—speaking, listening, reading, and writing. There are four activities because people encode and decode language at two levels—oral and written. We have to keep in mind the fifth activity, thinking, which grounds the other four. (See Table 1.2.)

THE COMMUNICATION STRUCTURE

As a medium of communication, language has for its superstructure the fundamental structure of communication, which is the set of relations among sender, receiver, and message. This triad translates readily into language arts terms:

1. Oral speech—speaker, listener, subject
2. Literacy—writer, reader, text
3. Narrative—narrator, auditor, story
4. Drama—performer, audience, script
5. Grammar—first person, *I;* second person, *you;* third person, *it*

This common concept helps to interrelate various aspects of language arts.

The *fundamental formula of communication* is:
I to *you* about *it*

TABLE 1.2 THE TWO LEVELS OF VERBAL CODING

	EN-CODING DE-CODING	
VERBAL-IZATION (basic)	speaking —— listening	ORAL
LITERACY (derived)	writing —— reading	WRITTEN

The *to* relation is very different from the *about* relation, and the two should not be thought of as on the same plane. This is because sender and receiver exist on the flesh-and-blood plane, whereas anything or anybody communicated *about* exists only on a symbolic plane. The *to* relation of sender and receiver is social and hence subject to virtually all the truths of other social relations. Sender and receiver can reverse roles, for example, as in conversation and correspondence. The *about* relation between sender and message or receiver and message, on the other hand, is an abstractive relation in which a person does not deal directly with other people or things but with some representation of them. As Figure 1.3 on page 12 depicts, the social relation governs the abstractive relation, for intent determines content. The I-you relation is drawn solid to indicate this primacy of the flesh-and-blood plane, whereas the other is dotted to indicate it is symbolic and dependent.

COMBINING PLANES OF COMMUNICATION WITH LEVELS OF CODING

These two planes of the basic communication structure correspond to the first two levels of coding. The raw experience with which coding begins corresponds to the flesh-and-blood plane of sender and receiver. A sender is not only trying to act on a receiver in the nonverbal world, he is also coding some message out of the nonverbal world. When he codes his experience to the level of verbalization, he has a message on the symbolic plane. The reason the literacy level has no counterpart is that it is peculiar to language and not common to all communication. Let's merge now the two communication planes with the three levels of coding:

1. *Nonverbal experiencing*—the world of human and material phenomena

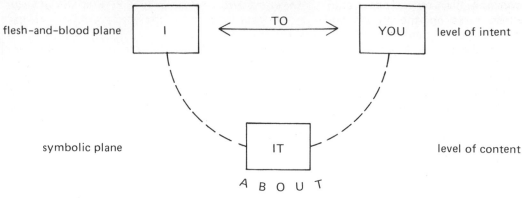

flesh-and-blood plane   I   ←—— TO ——→   YOU   level of intent

symbolic plane   IT   level of content

A B O U T

FIGURE 1.3 PLANES OF COMMUNICATION

2. *Verbalization*—the symbolic plane, making messages *from* experience *for* other people
3. *Literacy*—a second layer of symbols, written words for spoken words

Or, in short form:

1. Things and people
2. Symbols for things and people
3. Symbols for symbols for things and people

Each level is a governing context for the level below—an important order to keep in mind; that is, raw experience and human socializing are the ground from which verbalization and literacy are successively derived. Without the level before, the next level is impossible. The first two can exist without what follows. People can experience without verbalizing, and they can verbalize without reading and writing, so literacy is the most dependent and the least necessary. That fact may well be the most important of all for teaching literacy. The less necessary, the less motivation. Then it's true too that reading and writing require much prior speaking, which in turn requires much prior experiencing as food for thought. If literacy depends on its antecedents, how far can we get teaching literacy directly and by itself? On the other hand, how much can school learning be made to include oral verbalizing and the nonverbal experience to verbalize about? These are far-reaching questions of curriculum and methods. They have to be answered, however, for language learning must go beyond and beneath language itself—into social contexts and psychological processes.

DISCOURSE

It is handy to have a term that covers at the same time all four of the basic language arts—speaking, listening, reading, and writing. For this reason we will use throughout this book another term not common in schools—*discourse*. It designates all communication in the medium of language, oral or written. As *literacy* catches the two-way nature of coding between spoken and written words, *discourse* catches the four-way nature of verbal communication: we may send or receive, orally or in writing. A single instance of discourse is any complete communication having a sender, receiver, and message bound by a purpose. A discourse, for example, would be a conversation, a lecture, a letter or journal, poem or short story, ad or label. It is critical to understand that a discourse is a whole, not a part. Because it is staked out by the superstructure of language—sender-receiver-message— it is the largest unit of language and hence the only unit of language that is not partial. A complete discourse is the only language unit worthy of being made a *learning* unit, a point that will recur in this book.

By embracing at once both oral and written speech, the concept of discourse encourages us to deal at either level with comprehension and composition, the two main parts of a language arts course. Comprehension and composition can be, and are, practiced more often orally than in writing. They are, in fact, basic to *all* communication media and thus do not belong, as literacy does, only to language. When we receive, we are comprehending. When we send, we are composing. Some difficulties of each stance are common to all media, some are peculiar to each medium. Learning to comprehend and compose in any medium should help to do those things in other media. To discourse is to compose with language, to verbalize, whether one is at the same time writing down the verbalization or not. Figure 1.4 is intended to pull together schematically what has been said up to here about verbal communication.

Differences in Discourse

Issues of composition and comprehension vary with the kind of discourse. You need to know what all the kinds of discourse are and how they relate to each other so that you can help students to practice composing and comprehending in a variety of ways and eventually to cover the whole universe of discourse.

Differences in discourse derive essentially from differences among sender, receiver, and subject. Distance, in one sense or another, often makes the difference. The basic shift, for example, from speaking to writing occurs when speaker and listener are removed from each other in time and space. A conversation is defined by the fact that communicants occupy the same space-time (are face to face) or at least occupy the same time (are connected by telephone) and hence can reverse roles as sender and receiver to exchange unplanned speech. A letter is a letter, by contrast, because the correspondents are not face to face. Time-space distance

FIGURE 1.4 THE TWO DIRECTIONS AND TWO LEVELS OF VERBAL COMMUNICATION

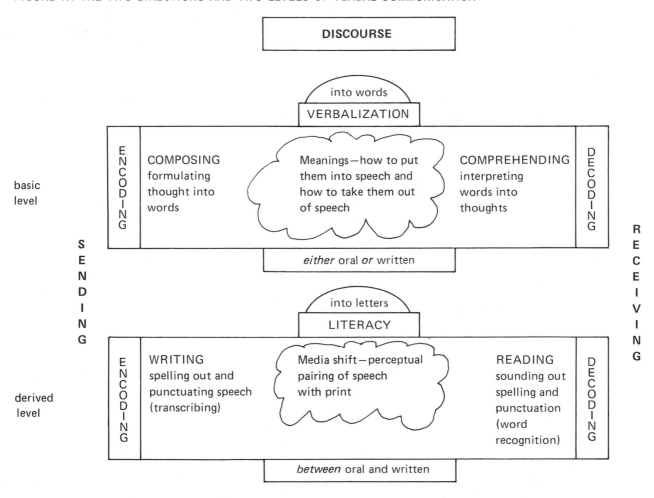

forces a shift from oral to written discourse and hence from immediate, spontaneous exchange to more pondered, long-range dialogue-at-a-distance. Entailed in this shift is the replacement of all vocal characteristics by some written equivalents.

Various kinds of discourse differ according to whether the speaker is also the subject (autobiography) or whether a true third person is the subject (biography). Similarly, the distinction between soliloquy and dialogue depends on whether first and second persons are the same or different actual persons (talking to oneself or to another). Not only may one communication "person" coincide with another, but each person may be singular and plural. When the sender is *we,* the discourse is some committee report or joint memo. The difference between biography and chronicle or history is the difference between *he* or *she* and *they.* The difference between the physical sciences and the social sciences, however, is the gender difference between *it* and *he* or *she,* between humankind verbalizing about things, to which it has no inner access, and verbalizing about fellow human beings, to which it has access by both empathy and speech itself. How shifts in relations of the three persons generate differences in discourse is a topic to be pursued on page 454 in connection with growth and sequence. Here we will develop the point only a bit more by taking each relation at a time in suggestive fashion.

Sender's Relation to Receiver

In the relation of *I* to *you* lie all the issues of rhetoric, the first of which is the form of the whole communication, not just whether it shall be a poem or a report or a label—for each of these might have a different form from others of its kind—but how to pattern ideas and images by sequence, subordination, repetition, and so on, to create what English teachers call organization. Binding sender and receiver is purpose. Intent governs not only content but also, to a great degree, form, because the communication motive initiates a discourse and gives it overall shape. A poet is not trying to do the same things to his receiver as a short-story writer, an ad man, or a labeler. And imagine how differently ideas or events might be organized in a personal letter than in a public lecture.

This I-you relation governs style too, the choice of words and the construction of sentences. Aiming at a small, known audience, a sender knows better what to assume, what needn't be said, which words and sentences will work best; but in aiming at a large, anonymous audience he has to name and phrase ideas in a way that some average member of the audience can understand and respond to. A sender has to verbalize his thought in an organization and style designed to fit his receiver, no matter how plural—or how *singular!* This we have called abstracting *for,* and it makes up about half of the composition process.

Sender's Relation to Subject

The distance between sender and subject differentiates, as we said, true narrative into autobiography, memoir, biography, and chronicle or history. This distance relates also to first-person and third-person narrative point of view and to firsthand and secondhand sources of information. Taking time distance now, firsthand reportage alone may range between recounting events from within the middle of the sequence (letters and diaries) to recounting events some time after the whole sequence is over (autobiography and memoir).

Consider now that any of these variations in telling true stories may be *simulated* in fiction. These same varying distances between sender and subject are employed to create the repertory of fictional techniques that includes omniscient third-person, single-viewpoint third-person, subjective first-person, journal and epistolary fiction, interior monologue, dramatic monologue, and so on.

Verbalizing the subject at different removes from oneself works out to be approximately the same thing as verbalizing experience at different levels of abstraction. Compare, for example, a police log of events on a certain evening with that station's annual summary of crime in its precinct. Now compare both in turn with a theoretical essay generalizing about trends in kinds of crime in the United States. Let's say that the essay digested many such local summaries and that each local summary had in turn digested many such daily logs. Each of these three ways of digesting the original raw material corresponds to a familiar type of discourse—log, summary report, and essay. Together they make a hierarchy of levels of abstraction. So distance and abstraction are related in ways significant for composition.

A sender abstracts *from* experience at the same time he abstracts *for* his receiver. Herein lies the other half of the composing process. The coordination of these two kinds of abstracting accounts for how the sender verbalizes his thought into speech; it affects the differences in discourse. Abstracting *from* is the half of the composing process usually called *logic;* abstracting *for* is the half usually called *rhetoric.*

Receiver's Relations to Sender and Subject

So far we have taken the point of view of the sender, which is to say that we have been charting discourse from the composition side. The receiver's relations to sender and subject cover comprehension as the reverse of composition. What the receiver must comprehend is the fusion of rhetoric and reference that we have just described as resulting in composition. He must interpret the abstracting *for* and the abstracting *from.* "Consider the source" means "Be aware of who the sender is and of what he is trying to do to you." An effective listener or reader takes into account the communication circumstances or, to draw on a more recent saying, knows to what extent "the medium is the message." Form speaks, whether it is a traditional literary form like myth or whether it is the boss's office memo. The receiver must understand the rhetoric that is being used on him even when it consists not of loaded words but of the framework itself. And for good comprehension he has to understand the nature of the information he is receiving— at what distance the original raw experience stood from the sender and to what level of abstraction the sender has verbalized the material.

The best way for the receiver to learn to comprehend is to compose. Communication is a game like any other in some respects. To play well you have to play all roles in it. You cannot be a good fielder in baseball if you are not also a base runner, because to know which team mate to throw the ball to you must know what the runner is most likely to do. This is why a good theory of language arts should make clear that composition and comprehension are equal and reciprocal. Chess players role-play each other in order to read each other's mind, and that is what readers and writers have to do. Most communication problems come down to similarity and difference among the three "persons." A learner needs to practice all roles and relations of the communication structure. This amounts to being sender, receiver, and sometimes even subject in all kinds of discourse. (See Figure 1.5.)

FIGURE 1.5 RELATIONSHIPS AMONG SENDER, RECEIVER, AND SUBJECT

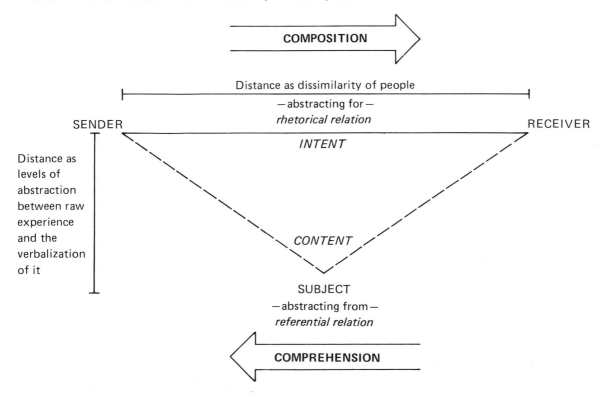

If the communication triad of sender-receiver-message is the superstructure of discourse, what are the substructures contained within it? As we have said, the first step from communication in general to language in particular brings us to the overall form or organization of a given discourse—letter, fable, dialogue, analytical essay. Each utilitarian, literary, or scientific form may of course be given any number of organizations. But whatever the organization, so long as it frames a complete discourse, it is the primary language structure for learning.

The Paragraph

The next unit after the structure of a discourse is the paragraph or stanza. Like all other language structures, it is nested within the one above it, which governs it. This means that the number, sequence, and make-up of paragraphs depend on the kind of discourse in which they occur and on the particular organization determined by the intent and content of the communication situation. As regards intent, whether a writer structures a certain paragraph from details to large view or from large view to details depends on which strategy seems best to orient his reader or would best lead in and out of neighboring paragraphs. As regards content, the structure of a narrative paragraph may follow chronology; that of an essay paragraph, some logical relation such as cause and effect or statement plus instance.

The Sentence

The next unit is sentence structure, which is the set of relations among words making a statement, question, or command. Now we are in the domain of grammar, which consists of word function, word order, and word endings. The structure of a sentence governs the structure of each word in it. One cannot assign a plural or tense ending to a word without knowing the rest of the sentence in which it plays its part. Whether *read* is pronounced with a long or short *e* depends on whether the rest of the sentence makes it past or present. A choice among synonyms like *demur, disagree,* or *deny* depends on the sense and style of the rest of the sentence. Sentence structure also governs punctuation, which in fact has no meaning without sentence structure. Punctuation groups and relates words as cues to their function in the sentence.

The Word

Any single word is itself a structure, since it also contains parts related to each other—letters, syllables, phonemes, morphemes, prefixes, and suffixes. Again, the whole word governs choice within it. A spelling may relate two or more letters into a blend of sounds (*che*), but we do not know which sound values until we know what the whole word is (*ache* or *chess*). Phonics rules operate within the word structure, as for the short-vowel-to-long-vowel transformation of *mad* to *made*.

For curriculum, what is important is the chain of governance reaching all the way down to the lowliest particle of a word from the ultimate structure that is the final authority—the communication relations among sender, receiver, and message. Therefore composing and comprehending words, sentences, and paragraphs can be done intelligently only within the framework of a complete discourse. Except in those relatively rare cases, noted in Chapter 12, Word Play, and Chapter 19, Ideas, where an isolated paragraph, sentence, or word constitutes a complete discourse unto itself, none of these substructures should ordinarily be used as learning units, because as fragments they have no context on which to base judgments.

Defining language arts

Defined by communication concepts, language arts is a set of two productive and two receptive activities—speaking and listening, reading and writing—one pair for the verbalization of experience (comprehension and composition) and the other pair for the transcription of speech (literacy). Verbalizing implies thinking, of course, since it is putting thought into, and taking it out of, language. So thinking inevitably grounds all four language activities and hence must be considered part of language arts. (This is not to say that thinking and verbalizing are one and the same. Not all thinking is verbal, but all verbalizing contains thought.)

A communication definition of language arts has three assets: (1) It places the medium of language in a general frame alongside the other media so that language can be understood in a comparative perspective. (2) It is *generative*. From the concepts of coding and the triad, for example, as we have indicated in this chapter, one can generate the levels and dimensions and kinds of discourse that students and teachers have to deal with every day in the classroom. (3) It is impartial—whole and unbiased. It delineates fully and equally the fundamental structure of the subject without regard for dated trends, historical happenstance, or this or that school of thought.

COMPARING CONVENTIONAL AND COMMUNICATION DEFINITIONS

Compare now the communication definition of the language arts with the definition we can infer from school conventions, which we are happy to say are changing. Most striking are the bias and incompleteness of what schools have called language arts or English. Despite some innovations it is still not four-way. It is heavily biased against the productive activities of speaking and writing, against oral comprehension and composition, and against nonliterature. Not only does it favor receptive activities—in particular, reading and literature—but it fills the curriculum with information *about* language that cannot be justified in teaching speaking, listening, reading, and writing. In short, much is left out, added, and thrown off-balance, thereby violating the processes of verbalization and literacy as we have just been discussing them. Wholeness and purposeful order are lost. The substructures of the language that have meaning only when framed by their contexts—the word, the sentence, the paragraph—are sprung out of relation and treated as isolated learning units. Comparing school language arts to the communication model is like comparing some ancient ruins with the original, rediscovered blueprint. Parts are missing, other parts misaligned, so that proportions are off; and foreign matter drifting in has obscured the main lines even more. The chief force eroding the edifice is institutionalism.

The Bias Toward Reception

Although composing and comprehending, encoding and decoding, are equal as goals, they are not treated as equals in the conventional language arts curriculum. One obvious reason for this imbalance is that students' production of discourse cannot be uniformly programmed, processed, and tested the way that material fed into students can be. Producing language is more difficult to learn to do because it is more creative than receiving language. By the same token schools find it harder to teach.

Not only are creative writing and journalism given low priority but "composition" is not, as one might naively suppose, writing. It is, rather, a body of prescriptions and proscriptions *about* writing—rules and formal grammar, assemblage and diassemblage of dummy sentences and paragraphs, and sometimes a thin kind of expository writing (usually a test of the reading). "Creative writing" is too often reserved for kids and teachers who have served time doing regular composition and have earned an elective as time off for good behavior. Composition, furthermore, virtually never includes oral composition such as improvisations and small-group discussions, which may provide more opportunities for practicing how to put thought into language and may be just as effective as writing itself.

A critical part of the bias against student language production has been the exclusion or slighting of activities allowing students to use oral language. Like creative writing and journalism, speech and dramatics are gaining ground today as elective courses, sometimes in lieu of a required English course, but in many places they are still exotic options, and seldom are they ever matter-of-factly incorporated into basic language arts at the elementary level or into English at the secondary level. Dramatics is too often oriented toward play production rather than toward student language production (improvisation, as discussed in Chapter 5, Dramatic Inventing). Small-group discussion has yet to be established as a serious and staple process. In many quarters talking is still bad behavior. Few teacher-training institutions offer preparation in how to run improvisations, rehearsed readings of texts, and the variety of small-group vocalizing such as topic discussion, task talk, brainstorming, panels, and so on.

Fortunately, many educators have been working hard, with some success, to reverse this picture. It is important, however, for new teachers to understand the traditional background into which this reform is making welcome inroads. And if a teacher locates in a school system untouched by such changes, he should be prepared for language schooling not to fit the communication definition.

The Double Standard About Literature

A kind of double standard operates whereby reading is defined as literature at the same time that writing is defined as exposition. So not only is comprehension limited to *reading* comprehension but reading is limited to literature, as least at the secondary level. But the universe of discourse comprises utilitarian and informative matter too. Now a reasonable point can be made that this bias toward literature in high school English, and to some extent in elementary language arts, balances out throughout the total school curriculum, if social studies and science periods are considered too. Some English teachers argue, fairly, that if they don't teach literature, no one else will.

But why, then, are students not allowed to *write* literature? Why is literature the special province of "English" as a receptive but not a productive activity? Smart elementary teachers have always let children write stories, poems, plays, fables, riddles, and so on, but except for this poignantly brief love affair that some lucky children are allowed to have with "creative" writing in the early years, the majority of schoolchildren go all the way through elementary and secondary language arts without ever writing literature.

Fortunately again, something is being done about this bias also, at least as regards reading content. More and more conferences and workshops are being held on the theme of "reading in the content areas," partly perhaps because of the across-the-board decline in reading ability. At any rate, this trend points up both the past bias and the acknowledgment today that reading content should embrace the nonliterary as well as the literary.

Language Arts as Mere Information

Another form of the bias toward student intake is the tendency to convert the realistic use of language into information *about* language. This makes of language arts a history or science course—the chronological development of English language and literature, formal grammatical analysis or modern linguistics, and literary-critical terms and analysis.

Teaching the history and science of either language or literature cannot be justified in elementary courses and in required secondary courses. It is based on a false analogy with other subjects. A native language is a very different subject from others in the curriculum. It is a symbol system, not a topic, and when someone learns a symbol system, he learns how to operate it. To learn to operate it well, over the whole range of its possibilities, takes a long time, because it involves the intricate relations of thought to speech. By not including information

about language, the English teacher can concentrate on teaching youngsters how to speak, listen, read, write, and think about *any* subject. Languages are to say things with. They have no particular content because everything is their content.

Terms, concepts, and generalities about language and literature should have no priority over terms, concepts, and generalities in other domains of interest. No evidence exists, either practical or scientific, that learning generalizations about language will improve speaking or writing. Experience shows that concepts and precepts fail to teach comprehension and composition. What students need is not formulations about how English has been and is used, much of which they observe for themselves if allowed to talk, read, and write enough. What they need is *practice* and *awareness*. The real problem is to think clearly and to say what one means.

But if the science of language can't help students learn the arts of language, then can linguistics and literary criticism still be justified for their own sake? Why not teach language as history, science, *and* art? We could shrug at this point and say, "Why not?" We could rationalize teaching the native language as a foreign object if we wished. But if learning to operate the language is really the main goal, then art has to have priority over science. Besides, is there time to do both, given the difficult, developmental nature of thought and speech? Students might choose to pursue linguistics or literary history as they would any other topic. Wouldn't the history and science of language and literature be more likely candidates for electives than journalism, creative writing, or drama?

Finally, the main case against teaching language arts as information may be that, for youngsters, the science interferes with the art. Canned intellectualizations short circuit the intellectual work that the learner should be doing. Defining myth or satire for students merely closes their minds before they have had a chance to think. Fancy formulations give an intellectual glamour to the curriculum's appearance, but in fact students are doing rote learning and hardly need think at all. The crux of language education is to confront directly the problems of putting one's own experience into words and of interpreting someone else's words into experience. The hollowness of the informational approach may be seen in the fact that far too many youngsters in this country can name the parts of speech but can't put them together to say what they mean, can tell you what onomatopoeia is but hate poetry.

The Case of Grammar

In this country grammar teaching has been so closely identified with English teaching that we must dwell a bit on it as a special case of converting language arts into mere information. If *grammar* were rightly understood as nothing more than what it is —word function as indicated by word ending and word order—much unnecessary confusion and controversy could be eliminated. But in the popular mind, and to a lesser extent in the teaching profession, the term often means nothing less than a "solid education." So smothered in mystique is real grammar that it can hardly be approached rationally.

Actually, whether to learn word form and sentence construction should not be controversial, since no one can compose and comprehend without them. The only question is *how* to learn them. Can children learn how to interrelate words into statements from oral exchange only, or do they have to be taught to analyze sentences into parts, name the parts, and memorize as rules the dos and don'ts of English grammar?

The question is mostly academic at the outset, so far as school is concerned, since linguists generally agree, and one can see for himself, that children know how to comprehend and compose the word forms and word order of English before they come to school. The misunderstanding persists, however, that students are "making mistakes" when they speak and write. Now, in fact, the only way a native speaker can make a mistake of grammar is by using word form and word order in some way peculiar to himself. At an intermediary stage of language acquisition, for example, children will often overgeneralize the rules they are inferring by saying "I bringed," but this sort of deviation always disappears without special teaching as the child hears and practices more and thence infers exceptions to and refinements of the rules. But no child makes mistakes of word order in his native language. He does not say, "A car blue in street the is." What are the mistakes children are making that appear to justify teaching as information the grammatical rules they already know how to use and understand in speech?

What Are Grammatical Mistakes?

The plain fact is that most language failures attributed to grammatical ignorance are not grammatical mistakes. Poor punctuation, illogicality, ambiguous pronoun reference, run-on or rambling sentences, inaccurate vocabulary, lack of transition or coherence or subordination, and generally ineffectual expression—none of these are grammatical mistakes. One can speak perfectly correct sentences and commit all of these faults. The confusion comes from equating grammar with effective expression or with a literacy issue such as punctuation (comma splices and sentence fragments being errors a person makes in writing down his speech, not in speaking itself).

But aren't there still real grammatical mistakes that both children and adults can make? That depends on whether a speech habit shared throughout a whole speech community can be sensibly considered a mistake. "Grammatical mistakes" such as "Dress like you should" or "Everyone took their time" are "mistakes" made throughout the whole standard-English-speaking community and raise the question: What is meant by "correct" in this case? We know, for instance, that distinguishing *as* from *like* seldom if ever increases clarity. (In French, the same word *comme* is used in all situations where English uses either *as* or *like*. Likewise, while "It's me" may be considered an error in English, its direct counterpart *"C'est moi"* is perfect in standard French.) And the fact is that *everyone* means all and hence seems to require the plural pronoun. Psychologically, such "mistakes" make some sense and will no doubt persist, especially if the grammatical distinctions serve no purpose or suffer from ambiguity. Drills on rules have no effect, in any case, on such widespread and long-standing habits.

But what about "He go walking" and "I ain't got no use for it" and "Three brother be driving down the street"? Surely these are pure and simple grammatical mistakes. Yes, if judged against the grammatical usage of the standard or majority dialect, but if millions of people speak these things in strict conformity with their language heritage, are we to say they are all making mistakes? These can be deemed mistakes only if we accept the idea that an entire speech community can be wrong. The notion of *group* error, in other words, raises a totally different issue from that of individual error. Since speech is communal, it is right to expect the individual to line up with others, but can we rightly expect a member of a minority community speaking a nonstandard dialect to "correct" his speech to the standard dialect of the majority?

Most "errors" that people advocating formal grammar have in mind are simply dialectical variations in usage. The prevailing view of linguists, which again you can corroborate from your own experience, maintains that one dialect is logically and rhetorically as good as another. By far, most dialectical variations in grammar consist of changed or missing word endings, not of changes in word order or syntactic relations. A missing verb ending is simply made up for by something somewhere else in the predicate or sentence, and "three pig" is no less clear than "three deer." (The difference between "sick at my stomach" and "sick to my stomach" is a dialectical difference in idiom, not in grammar at all, and both versions are equally good.)

It is true, of course, that though equally good, the minority dialect may cause its speaker to suffer because of current prejudice. Inasmuch as this affects the awarding of jobs and other social treatment, a minority dialect speaker may well find a motive to want to learn the grammar of the majority dialect— not really a difficult feat anyway for the very reason that dialectical differences in the United States seldom go beyond word endings into patterns of words.

What Is the Effect of Formal Grammar Instruction?

Returning to the question, though, of *how* grammar is learned, and assuming that a nonstandard speaker wants to learn standard grammar, let's look at the conclusion of a survey of research based on efforts to correct grammatical errors:

> In view of the widespread agreement of research studies based upon many types of students and teachers, the conclusion can be stated in strong and unqualified terms: the teaching of formal grammar has a negligible or, because it usually displaces some instruction and practice in actual composition, even a harmful effect on the improvement of writing.[1]

So regardless of the kind of grammatical deviation —whether of standard speakers interchanging *like* and *as,* small children overgeneralizing rules, or nonstandard speakers differing from the majority dialect—formal grammar teaching will not correct the deviation. Actually, this finding should come as no surprise, since naming parts of speech and analyzing sentence constructions have little to do with the main kind of dialectical variation—verb and noun endings. Drill on conjugations may work sometimes for people learning a second language, but for native speakers such abstract rules can hardly compete against years of speech habits. If an additional

dialect is to be annexed, it will be learned the same way as the first, by speaking with and hearing those who already speak it.

Error correction is only one aim of grammar teaching. To speak and write correctly is a paltry thing alone. Dick and Jane can do it splendidly. Correctness is easy and is mostly acquired before school. Dialectical variations are superficial, and anyone motivated to do so can adopt standard usage if he can gain access to speakers of the standard dialect. What is hard is to use grammar *effectively,* to take advantage of the resources of English constructions to say what one means and to say it in ways that have the desired effect on the receiver. A sentence having a single word or simple phrase as subject ("*Such an idea* never occurred to him.") is neither more nor less correct than one having a clause for a subject ("*What other people might think of his actions* doesn't concern him."), but only more mature users of the language are capable of the latter. Of the three main measures of sentence growth identified by Kellogg Hunt (see page 452), none involve correctness and all involve greater versatility in phrasing and stating ideas *within* the limits of English grammatical acceptability. All improve with general growth anyway, so that all *any* treatment can do is accelerate or enhance this growth.

What effect does formal grammar study have on effective expression? Besides the negative conclusion already quoted, experimental evidence comes from two recent pieces of research availing themselves of the latest theory from transformational grammar and aiming directly at increasing versatility in sentence construction according to the growth norms of Kellogg Hunt. John Mellon[2] and Frank O'Hare[3] have both shown that students' grammatical facility can increase by practice in combining simple sentences into complex ones without their knowing grammatical analysis or terminology. Mellon showed, further, that when before-and-after writing samples of students undergoing a course in one of the most widely favored grammar books in Warriner's series[4] were compared with those of students who did not undergo any grammar treatment,

---

[1] Richard Braddock, Richard Lloyd-Jones, and Lowell Schoer, *Research in Written Composition,* National Council of Teachers of English, Urbana, Ill., 1963, pp. 37–38.

[2] John Mellon, *Transformational Sentence-Combining: A Method for Enhancing the Development of Syntactic Fluency in English Composition,* National Council of Teachers of English, Urbana, Ill., 1969.

[3] Frank O'Hare, *Sentence Combining: Improving Student Writing Without Formal Grammar Instruction,* National Council of Teachers of English, Urbana, Ill., 1973.

[4] John E. Warriner et al., *English Grammar and Composition,* Harcourt Brace Jovanovich, New York, 1959.

no difference in sentence construction could be detected.

It is not at all surprising that decades of experimental research and of classroom experience should show overwhelmingly that formal grammar instruction is a waste of time. Can anyone seriously believe that theorizing about habits as deep and automatic as those of speech will alter practice? It is a great fallacy to think that merely shifting knowledge from intuition to intellect improves performance, or that it even increases knowledge. From much common experience with other kinds of skills, musical and athletic, for example, we know in fact the opposite —that thinking directly about complex internal operations throws them off. Composing words into sentences by grammatical rules is extremely complex and must be allowed to operate automatically. Grammatical processing will change and improve through speech and writing practice as students undertake challenging new tasks in discourse that entail modifying, elaborating, and styling their sentences and that motivate revision. No, what is surprising is that schools should persist so long in pursuing a dead end in the face of such negative evidence from all sides. Students are taught formal grammar year after year, but they never seem to learn it, and their speech and writing do not improve from it, because the instruction is nonfunctional, whether based on traditional or recent linguistics.

Other rationales are sometimes offered for teaching formal grammar. One hears, for example, "Shouldn't grammar be taught as an aid to learning foreign languages?" But a decision to teach grammar for this reason amounts to taking sides in an important controversy among foreign-language teachers, many of whom abhor the grammar-translation approach and espouse a more "direct method" based on conversation and oral pattern drills and avoidance of grammar and translation. At any rate, if foreign-language teachers want students to know formal grammar, let them teach it and teach it in the way most fitting for their purpose.

"But a knowledge of grammatical terms helps the teacher discuss composition with his students." If a teacher feels such a need for vocabulary for parts of speech, kinds of clauses, and types of construction —*adverb, subordinate,* and *appositive,* for example —then let him set aside one class period to name and illustrate these things, supplying a handout sheet or two for reference. No need for a course, a textbook, and so on. Actually, discussing composition with students requires no grammatical terms and may well be more effective if the teacher makes

points about sentence construction by illustrating alternatives rather than by introducing into the composition situation an extra element to contend with.

We hear still another voice: "Grammar disciplines the mind—it teaches students to think logically." The answer to this is that ordinary language is far too ambiguous for training in logic, and if teachers are serious about this, they should instead introduce symbols and concepts from symbolic logic. (See pages 448–449 for both of these points.)

The reasons given to justify teaching formal grammar are as weak as the evidence against its effectiveness is strong. What is one to make of so little warrant for so entrenched a part of the curriculum? We can only assume that, again, institutional reasons blind some educators and overpower others. Formal grammar is easy to administer and test, and huge numbers of textbooks, curricula, and teacher-training programs are committed to it. Although the public's distance from the learning site inclines them to cling longer to the grammar mystique, we have found from many frank discussions with groups of teachers that the majority of experienced teachers today know that teaching formal grammar is merely rationalized, not rational, but they seldom dare to say so before administrators and parents.

We strongly recommend that grammar as information and analysis be supplanted in the curriculum by more active practice of the language arts. Functional grammar-in-action will be taught very effectively by the means listed on page 464, which includes also some games that will even teach some grammatical terms on an optional and secondary basis. But doing away with formal grammar teaching will require some re-education of the public, to the extent that many citizens think it teaches standard usage and effective expression and equate it with some vague notion of "high standards."

In summary, grammar may be taught for two good reasons—"correctness" and effectiveness. Since personal mistakes correct themselves by school age, correctness can mean only the annexing of standard dialect and applies only to speakers of minority dialects. Other so-called mistakes are errors of judgment or logic owing to some psychological factors or to language inexperience, neither treatable by grammatical analysis. Grammar may be taught in two main ways—by experience with discourse that entails the varieties of word forms and sentence constructions, or by analyzing dummy sentences and naming parts. Plentiful discursive experience is what really teaches grammar, for it exercises judgment and provides language intake, whereas formal grammar study has been proved irrelevant. Politics more than pedagogy retards the changing of the curriculum to fit this truth.

Fragmentation

Institutions naturally find it convenient to compartmentalize; and without a unifying theory to resist this, the various language activities have been cut off from each other, even when taught in the same room by the same teacher. In elementary school, reading and language arts are traditionally treated as separate subjects with separate budgets, materials, times, and sometimes teachers. In secondary school, literature and composition usually bear no relation to each other except for the use of writing as a test of the reading. But it is enormously inefficient to split off the target activities. Students need to bring one to bear on the other. Just as an organic gardener grows different plants mixed together so they feed and protect each other, the language teacher needs to interweave all the language arts so that each will stimulate, follow up, and develop the other. Reading and writing are to some degree the reverse of each other, which means that youngsters can learn decoding through spelling and comprehension through composition. Creative dramatics is one of the best ways to deepen and check reading comprehension. Creative writing teaches literature. Discussing and improvising teach how to take things and how to put things—the real basics of reading and writing.

Institutional Reasons Versus Educational Reasons

Surely all this biasing serves a purpose. Yes, but the reasons and purposes are *institutional,* not *educational.* More or less unconsciously the emphases over the years have settled in favor of those who work in educational institutions, not those required to attend them. A lot of honest soul-searching is needed to improve the teaching of language arts.

Schools tend to standardize and simplify to deal with large numbers. Making kids write what a reading selection means has become a school norm from the primary grades through college, in the form of comprehension quizzes, literary-critical essays, and so on. The old grade-school book report becomes dignified as a "term paper." Writing to test reading is popular because it kills two institutional

birds with one stone. It readies the student for college "composition" (even though he may not be on a college-bound "track"!), and at the same time it tests reading comprehension. Secondary-school English is a service course for college term papers and essay questions, like the college's own composition courses. Not having written much else themselves, and pressured a great deal to "prepare" kids for college, English teachers ride herd on a narrow kind of exposition. This applies pressure in turn on the elementary teacher, so that this sort of exposition becomes, along with reading comprehension scores, the main measure of school language learning. Testing is essentially the only kind of writing colleges and hence schools have usually been interested in. In fact, the institution's obsessive self-monitoring for results accounts for much of the strange bias of schooling.

The university is also implicated in school institutionalism because teachers look to it for guidance. Its research focus on language as an object dominates over practical learning facts, and composition becomes decomposition—dissection of the art into a science. So kids study about morphemes and determiners and transitions and "direction of modification" but never learn to write. Too easily it is assumed that teachers should turn right around and teach university information to their charges. They are tempted to do so because in institutional formats it is easier to teach and test comedy and subordination by defining one and explaining the other than it is to let kids write comedies and abstract raw material into hierarchical knowledge structures of their own. This tendency to read about writing matches the other tendency to write about reading.

Good education is not easy to administer and to assess. So just as neither the university professor nor the schoolteacher is eager to open up the can of worms involved in changing *composition* from a placid noun to a squirmy verb, the managerial technocrat abhors untidy subjects because they foul up his "systems" approach to cost accounting. Harmony reigns.

CHANGING CONVENTIONAL DEFINITIONS

Symptomatic of the problem is the waning but still influential definition of secondary-school English called the tripod—language, literature, and composition. The tripod has no central concepts that can generate useful ideas for the profession. It limits reading to literature. By a kind of quiet coup, the word *language* tends to rationalize the teaching of formal grammar or linguistics. Typically, the definition consists of three *nouns*—things, bodies of content—and that indeed fits with the traditional way literature and composition are taught.

Comparing conventional definitions with the purely rational communication model helps you to match what you are doing against what you ought to be doing. You need to liberate your thinking from convention enough to envision what teaching the language arts ought to be like. This is the first step toward getting institutions to conform to their mission, instead of the mission conforming to the institutions. Even if you can do nothing to change your institution, you need to carve out your subject clearly enough at least once to know what it really is.

Language arts or English should be a kind of intellectual "homeroom," where a student can see the totality of his symbolic life. It is the one place where all forms and contents can be learned in relation to each other—the fictional and the actual side by side, comprehension and composition as reverses of each other, spoken and written speech interplaying, language competing with and complementing other media. If the rest of the curriculum is to be divided up mostly by topics, then language arts must be not only the guardian of literature but the patron of general communication process. Students need this intensive but comprehensive focus on symbolization so that they will be generally sophisticated speakers, listeners, readers, and writers in the topical subjects. In this broader sense, language arts might indeed act as a service course to other courses.

You need not fear you have no subject and try to manufacture one by making kids read about writing and write about reading. Words on words strengthen nothing but doubts, because they merely shadow what you're trying to teach, which is words on world. The special province of the language teacher, and therefore the main definition of language arts, is communication consciousness.

Goal statements

Another way of defining language arts, and a way that moves us nearer to practices, is to frame statements of goals. The following aims proceed from the more comprehensive to the more specific. This progression also shifts from the conceptual level of coding to the verbalization and literacy levels.

COMMUNICATION GOALS

It is at this level that goals can interrelate media, subject areas, language arts, and other arts to create a common ground for an interdisciplinary curriculum.

1. Heed signals from all sources.
2. Gain access to all sources of information, inside and outside oneself.
3. Overcome the amnesia toward the past and the anesthesia toward the present caused by pain and socialization and open all channels to memory, perception, and feeling.
4. Find out what the environment shows, what other people know, what records store, and what media convey.
5. Discriminate different sources and abstraction levels of information and understand what each is worth.
6. Enlarge to its fullest the range of *what* one can conceive, transmit, and respond to and of *how* one can conceive, transmit, and respond.
7. Find out what various media can and cannot do—language, body expression, graphic arts, movies, and television, competing with and complementing each other.
8. Become familiar with all roles—sender, receiver, subject—and with the varying distances and relations among them—communicating to oneself, to known individuals, remote audiences, for example, or communicating about oneself, firsthand subjects, abstract subjects, and so on.

LANGUAGE ARTS GOALS

These goals further specify, in the medium of language only, what many of the goals for information and communication stated more comprehensively. At this point, traditional curriculum might rely on the categories *language, literature,* and *composition* for secondary school and *reading* and *language arts* for elementary. The breakdown of curriculum proposed in this book, on the other hand, will begin with a division between discourse and literacy, each of which will then be separately specified.

Discourse Goals

These cover the verbalization level and hence composition and comprehension.

1. Make language choices wisely—how to put things and how to take things (*composition* and *comprehension*).
2. Expand to the maximum the repertory of language resources one can employ and respond to—from vocabulary and punctuation, phrasing and sentence structure, to style and dialect, points of view and compositional form.
3. Extend to the maximum the fluency, facility, pleasure, and depth with which one can speak, listen, read, and write (the target activities of language learning).
4. Expand to the maximum the range, depth, and refinement of the inborn thinking operations—classifying, generalizing, inferring, and problem-solving.

These are very compactly stated and so might be parceled out into a larger number of separate statements. Note that they emphasize the individual nature of learning by taking a learner where he is and moving him as far as he can go.

DISCOURSE OBJECTIVES

We shift now to a critical level of generality where statements of aims must break down language learning into some categories practical for organizing curriculum. The following objectives divide all discourse into nine kinds. Each kind can be practiced by speaking, listening, reading, and writing. Each kind is defined and detailed in a chapter of its own in Part Four that proposes specific practices for attaining it. Since this division yields only authentic discourses as assignments, the learning units are never less than a whole discourse of some sort (except for some games, for reasons discussed on page 41). The chief effect of dividing this way is to specialize comprehension and composition so that they can be practiced in nine different ways. Each kind of discourse can then suggest specific assignments and materials.

Students should be able to send and receive effectively in oral and written form:

1. Word Play (riddles, puns, tongue twisters, much poetry)
2. Labels and Captions (language joined with pictures or objects, graphs, maps, and so on)
3. Invented Dialogue (improvisation and scripts)
4. Actual Dialogue (discussion and transcripts)

5. Invented Stories (fiction, fables, tales, much poetry, and so on)
6. True Stories (autobiography, memoir, biography, reportage, journals, and so on)
7. Directions (for how to do and how to make)
8. Information (generalized fact)
9. Ideas (generalized thought)

These discourse objectives include and go beyond traditional English and reading objectives. Traditionally, a language arts curriculum aims to get comprehension and composition up to reasonably high proficiency. Discourse objectives break down this aim into the nine areas in which comprehension and composition occur outside of school and which should therefore be practiced inside of school.

Each kind of discourse has traits of its own that will involve students in different ways of informing, communicating, thinking, and using language. Basing curriculum on this nine-way breakdown ensures that students will cover all discourse and extend their initial range of listening, speaking, reading, writing, and thinking. Each kind presents students with different issues of comprehension and composition, oral and written. Since students work in all areas at all ages, they aim continually at nine different objectives for comprehension and composition. This way of specifying keeps restating the main aims but does so by useful differentiations.

The nine areas are such that while working in them students will also be fulfilling the larger humanistic and communication goals. The discourse areas are multimedia, for example, which means that true stories might be told not just with words but with a combination of words and drawings or on film with a cued narration. For another example, the data-gathering required to produce discourse in all of these areas will necessitate students opening all channels of information—observing, interviewing, experimenting, consulting sources—and activating all their inborn logical capacities.

These kinds of discourse cover the three grammatical modes—declarative, interrogative, and imperative—and the four traditional types of discourse—description, narration, exposition, and argumentation. True Stories and Invented Stories are narrative. Description distributes itself under several of the objectives—as Captions, stage directions for Invented Dialogue, details for Invented Stories and True Stories, and as Information. Poetry stretches across many of the goals, being not an area of discourse but a way of discoursing about many things. It may be, for example, a joke in verse (Word Play), a rhyming epitaph (Labels and Captions), an Invented Dialogue, a ballad (Invented Story), or lyric (Ideas). This shows its variety and offers many opportunities to come upon it. The other three genres of literature —drama, fiction, and essay—are directly covered by Invented Dialogue, Invented Stories, and Ideas respectively.

This list of discourse objectives corresponds roughly to a developmental sequence of growth. For explanation see "Growth in Kinds of Discourse" starting on page 454.

LITERACY OBJECTIVES

In order to read and write at all in *any* kind of discourse, students need to learn to spell out speech sounds and to sound out spellings—the old two Rs. For reading, this means recognizing spoken words when written. For writing, this means spelling, punctuation, and handwriting. So undergirding the discourse objectives are two for basic skills. In contrast to the discourse objectives on page 24, which break down comprehension and composition of oral *and* written language into areas of discourse, literacy objectives aim at bridging *between* oral and written language, whatever the type of discourse.

1. The student will be able to sound out with normal intonation any text that he can understand if read to him.
2. The student will be able to transcribe whatever he can say or understand orally. (*Transcribe* covers both spelling and punctuation.)

These in a nutshell are the so-called basic skills. By stating them in this way, relative to a student's general development in thought and speech, the goals can apply at any age and keep us focused on the central issue, which is getting back and forth between the auditory medium of vocal speech and the visual medium of print.

For reasons explained at length in Chapter 20, Setting Goals, we recommend that objectives for language arts not be stated more specifically than those here. It is certainly possible and desirable, however, to specify further the details of learning to comprehend and compose, read and write. Indeed, the rest of this book does precisely that. Part Three, Literacy—"The Basic Skills," treats literacy in particular, Part Four, Developmental Reading, Speaking, and Writing, takes up each of the nine kinds of discourse one at a time, and Part Five, Aims and Assessment, sets forth ways of evaluating.

From the experience of many English and reading teachers in many places we have concluded that learners must have three things—individualization, interaction, and integration. Together these three *I*'s constitute a general formula for an effective school language program. They also define *student-centered* in a triple way. Student-centered teaching

1. arranges for each learner to select and sequence his own activities and materials (individualization).
2. arranges for students to center on and teach each other (interaction).
3. interweaves all symbolized and symbolizing subjects so that the student can effectively synthesize knowledge structures in his own mind (integration).

Discussion of the three *I*'s will outline the main methods of this curriculum, and much of this book will elaborate details of the methods.

Individualization

Learning language is *personal*. We start learning it in the first year of life within the family circle, and for the rest of our lives it permeates everything we feel, think, and do. It is intimately connected to our individuality. Because individuals vary a great deal, we must expect them to go about learning the specifics of language in very different ways.

VARIATION

Individual variation is no doubt the toughest fact of life in the classroom. If students were all ready to learn to read and write the same things at the same time in the same way, some major problems would dissolve overnight. But they are not. They vary enormously in many different dimensions, even in so-called homogeneous groups. In actual fact, *every* class is heterogeneous.

People vary because of two main human givens—group background and individual make-up. They come from different racial and ethnic communities, where they may even have learned first a different language than English or may have grown up speaking a nonstandard dialect; in any case they will have inherited the language habits of a particular social and economic class. Some groups use language mostly for social communion, some for sport, some for problem-solving, and some for intellectual analysis. Group attitudes toward language vary from contempt to worship.

Different individuals have dominances toward the physical, the emotional, the intellectual, or the intuitive. Some gravitate toward visual media, some toward auditory, some toward manipulatory, and some toward the kinesthetic (the body itself as medium). Some learn better from peers, some from elders, some from the same sex, some from the other sex, some from certain personality types, and so on. Each has learned the same words in different connections and has private as well as public meanings for them. Each has a different notion about what language, especially written language, is worth and what it can do for him. Youngsters the same age want to read very different things, and any one class may have a spread of reading maturity ranging over six to ten grades as measured by standardized reading tests.

Another critical variation in individuals is *timing.* People not only differ in *how* they learn the same things but in *when* they can or want to learn them. Something that may seem uninteresting or impossible to a child at one time suddenly seizes him and is easily learned when it comes up in another connection. Such right connections are the triggers of learning and often have nothing to do with *child development,* the predictable growth from one level of difficulty into the next. These connections are simply personal, which makes them unpredictable.

The longer youngsters have been in school, the more they vary. They know different facts, have read different books, misspell different words, have mastered different vocabulary and sentence structures, and have had different writing experience. Families move a lot in this country, so a locally standardized curriculum can't control this. We can try to erase differences by standardizing more on a national scale and standardizing in more and more detail, as with specific objectives. However, trying to eradicate differences not only goes obviously in the wrong direction for learning, but also violates the basis of a free society.

THE POWER TO CHOOSE

Accommodating individual variation is only part of true individualization. The other part concerns *will.* Will is the energy that drives learning. It is personal force taking the direction of some intent. If it is lined up behind an activity, it will sooner or later realize itself even if handicapped by bad circumstances. If it is missing, no approach seems to work, and teachers are forever shopping among methods and materials and asking, "How can I motivate so-and-so to do such-and-such?" Asking the question at all shows that the learner has not been allowed to exercise his will. (*Motivate* should not be a transitive verb, for it makes no sense to speak of someone motivating somebody else.)

So individualization means not only accommodating differences in learners but allowing the individual to make decisions about how he is to spend his time. In other words, if other people or diagnostic tests habitually make the decisions for him, he does not take on the responsibility for his own education and put his will behind his efforts. Results then are poor, and educators think that it is necessary to program his schedule even more rigorously. The problem is that he feels he doesn't belong to himself and takes the attitude that since "they" want me to

read, let them worry about it. As soon as others want the results of learning more than the learner, the game is over. Even if a youngster means to comply with the arbitrary tasks others assign him, he will sabotage his own efforts unconsciously. Personal integrity must be preserved by whatever means.

The argument against student choice is usually that youngsters don't know what there is to choose from or how to make wise decisions. This is truer than it should be because schools seldom teach students to choose. The longer a student has been in school the harder it is to help him make decisions. He is conditioned to obey, not to exercise his will and hence practice decision-making. He will even resist doing what he wants to do, so painful is it to decide. But to use crippling conditioning as an argument for further infantilizing students compounds the problem and fulfills its own prophecy. The point is that decision-making is the very heart of education. It can occur only from practice in making daily decisions about how to spend one's time. This is what exercises the will so that motivation ceases to be a problem and activities succeed.

It is the essence of the school's job to show learners what there is to choose from and to give them every opportunity to understand how wise decisions are in fact made. Personal choice is at the center, not only so that the learner *cares* about what he is doing, but so that good judgment will develop— whether the option is which book to turn to next, which activity to select, which medium to say something in, whom to ask for help, which phrasing to express an idea in, or which way to interpret a line of poetry. But personal choice does not operate in a vacuum; in school or outside, it is influenced by peers, elders, the environmental array, and intrinsic connections among things and actions. Thus, the student-centered curriculum is never "permissive" or "unstructured." It is not based on some empty and faddish notion of "doing your own thing." Any individual anywhere is always a force in a field of other forces and very hard put indeed to tell inside from outside.

It is absolutely essential to understand that placing individual choice at the center is not merely a bleeding-heart or sentimental liberal stance. Learning to operate a language simply demands constant choosing, and if students cannot make decisions, they will fail. From the lowest to the highest levels of language, ability depends on *selection* of some sort or another. Decoding and transcribing are choosing, that is, choosing which sounds or spellings or punctuation marks are correct for a given situation. Comprehending and composing are choosing—how to take this, how to put that. The mind must be active and questioning. It must be aware of alternatives and of what difference it will make to select this rather than that. There is more than one spelling of the long *a* sound, more than one meaning of many words, and more than one way to cast an idea.

Furthermore, the options go even deeper. People have choice about what to perceive and what to value. These choices underlie their language choices. Abstracting takes place throughout the whole of human experiencing. Our behavior is very dependent on our information, on what we think is so and on what we think the meaning of something is. The job of schools is to open for the young the array of options among what can be seen, what can be made of what can be seen, and what, consequently, can be done. Choice cannot be confined to the small things of language but must encompass all thought, speech, perception, and action. Subtract choice from behavior and you subtract it from perception, thought, and speech as well, because these all operate in circular continuity. Don't expect good judgment in reading comprehension if you're not willing to grant decision-making in daily activity. Exercise of the will and an active intelligence strengthen with habit and go together.

NOT ONE BUT MANY STRUCTURES

Among the false and negative notions there always crops up the fearful idea that when the teacher steps out of the "nervous host" role, the classroom becomes unstructured. Nothing can be "unstructured." When we use that word, we mean that we don't see in what we are observing a structure that we recognize or expect or want. Disorder is a structure we don't like. Preschool prattle, for example, does not lack structure; we just don't know what it is, not at least until we have lived with the prattle awhile (like a psychoanalyst listening daily to his patient's free associations and gradually picking up patterns). A bystander observing a truly individualized classroom in action may not at first know what each student is doing, what he has been doing, and what structuring and restructuring is going on within him, but a teacher coaching and counseling daily in small groups can see the individual patterns of those

students as they select and sequence different activities accomplishing the same general goals.

Our traditional classroom has not had *enough* structure, in the sense of enough structure*s*. One lesson plan for all each day, one sequence for all each year—that is not to structure *more;* that is simply to let a single structure monopolize the learning field. This monopoly prevents individualization and makes it difficult for learners to develop judgment, which requires that they be structur*ing* in school, not structur*ed* by school. Structuring is choosing. Judgment is choosing. Comprehending, composing, making sense of the world—these are structuring. For one thing, we can't *stop* a child from structuring. (We have already tried that way.) The wisest choice for educators to make is to place student structuring at the center of school life. School should be harder and more fun.

It should be clear that truly *individualizing* means helping each student build his own curriculum day by day. Most uses of the term individualization are trivial and duck the issue. It is much talked about and seldom done. Most teachers know it is necessary and want to feel they are doing it, but very few know how. It is not hard to understand the difficulty: it's just hard to face it. Honest individualizing requires nothing less than abandoning one lesson plan for all each day and one sequence for all each year. It means planning for the unpredictable, because individuals will not only be going different ways, they will do so in patterns of decision you may influence but may not predetermine.

SEQUENCING

One error of traditional curriculum planning has been to assume that specific sequences can apply to all students. What is the sense of trying to predict the right sequence of reading matter and the right sequence of writing for some mythical third-grade or tenth-grade class when you are certain to be wrong for the majority of its members? The kinds of talking, reading, and writing that twenty to forty youngsters of the same age are capable of and ready for range over six to ten years of any regular school sequence. This is a tough truth, because it frustrates any efforts to write a single sequence for all students so specific as to span a period as lengthy as even a year. But, however painful, we simply have to abandon the year, or any shorter period, as a workable time unit of a common sequence for all. For this reason, the concept of the yearly "grade" levels remains a severe obstacle to curriculum development, because it implies a similar learning advance for all students for each year. One sequence for all is possible but only over a much longer span of time and only in a general way.

It is stages, not ages, that are important for sequence. Trying to anchor stages to grades or ages only creates illusion. Different students pass through stages at different chronological times. What holds for different people is the *order,* regardless of the timing. So growth descriptions can only say when some learning will occur in relation to when other learning occurs for the same individual. Most classrooms throw together people undergoing different stages of physical, social, or mental development.

Programmed learning has made a show of trying to individualize—and sometimes it looks good, compared to bad teaching—by at least leaving kids alone. But its solution is also its problem: programmed learning is isolated rather than individualized learning and hence lacks utterly the *interaction* so vital to learning language. The whole point of individualization is to allow for differences among individuals in how and when they need to learn things. A system that puts everybody off in a corner with a machine or workbook, that sends everybody through the same sequence, allowing only minor variations in things such as pace, hardly comes to grips with the real issue. Programmed learning, in fact, usually delivers the learner into the hands of the enemy, partly because it fits only too well some of the political and commercial interests that hamstring public institutions, and partly because the learner is so pleased at the paltry but new control he is allowed in manipulating materials that he mistakes it for real power and real decision-making and thus seriously mislearns what choosing is all about. See also pages 407 and 427 ("Computers").

MAJOR MEANS OF INDIVIDUALIZING

In addition to the other two *I's* themselves, individualization requires (1) the widest possible array of options to choose from, (2) some way to learn how to make good choices, and (3) some way of getting personal tutoring.

Maximum Accessibility

In order for students to put together unpredictable language courses while interacting with others doing the same, it is essential to allow each student to gain access at any time to any activity, book, person, medium, materials, and methods. Let's call this the principle of maximum accessibility. Different schools and teachers will approximate the ideal more or less, depending on many local circumstances. Accessibility may be gained by various kinds of pooling—pooling students, teachers, materials, time, and space. Certain kinds of team teaching and some newer building arrangements such as "pods" of rooms can help. Scheduling language and language-related classes in the same time block permits pooling. So does allowing students to pass from one room to another to get to certain material or human resources.

It may be hard for someone accustomed to the traditionally overcontrolled classroom to conceive the variety, richness, and breadth of activities and materials required to implement honestly the principle that any student should be able to find at any time something to read or write or otherwise practice language with that is right for him at that moment. An individualized classroom must have at least the equivalent of three or four ordinary grades' worth of things to do and things to do them with. And these choices must represent the broader definition of language arts that we gave in Chapter 1, Basic Concepts. Providing the variety of human resources entails the use of aides and community people, the mixing of students of different abilities and even ages, and thoughtful deploying of general and specialized teaching staff.

A Logging and Counseling System

A student who has access to many possible activities and materials must have some way to learn to make good choices among them. He needs to keep track of what he is doing and of what he still needs so that the teacher can help him and he can learn more about helping himself. The idea is for teacher and student to chart the past together so that they can plan the future. The student keeps some kind of record of which activities, materials, and people he has worked with. Periodically, the teacher looks at this and talks it over with the student, translating his record into coverage of the discourse and literacy objectives and pointing out to the student which areas he is weak and strong in. Thus a teacher might say, "Most of your work so far has been in reading. I think you should try more writing now." Or, "You've been reading for a long time in adventure and mystery stories. I think you would enjoy some science fiction and some sports stories." Or the counsel might be to do certain activities to improve spelling or punctuation. See page 423 for details about such a system.

A one-to-one relationship with individual students seems an unheard-of luxury in a conventional classroom. To believe it, you have to realize that what usually prevents this is the traditional emcee or host role of the teacher when locked into one lesson plan for all each day and one sequence for all each year. When students are all doing the same activity at the same time under your direction, you are never free to work one-to-one, whereas real individualization frees you to give attention to small working parties and individuals. Important changes in management must free teacher as well as student, for students learning how to take over their own learning will need more personal help than those just slogging their way through a cut-and-dried sequence. When free to circulate, you can closely observe individuals daily and feel confident of being able to offer good counsel when it is needed.

Coaching

The other major part of the one-to-one relating now opened up is coaching. You can listen to a student read aloud to you and make suggestions about his pronunciation or decoding problems. Or you can read with him something he has written and offer your personal responses, including whatever suggestions for improving his writing that you feel he can accept favorably. You can show individuals how to diagnose and correct their own spelling and punctuation errors. As students become truly involved in activities they have chosen, they invite advice and coaching because they care about results. During rehearsal of a reading or preparation of some media presentation you can coach them on technique. You can sit in on their discussions and improvisations and writing workshops and feed back to them what you think they are doing and what you think alternatives might be.

The beauty of all this is that the more self-directing you help them become, the freer you are to counsel and coach them to higher realms of language learning. A common misunderstanding about self-directed individualization and peer interaction is that the teacher becomes suddenly bereft of function. Letting students choose and letting them interact requires a great deal of skill and work from

the teacher. The difference is that you commonly work with small groups and individuals rather than a whole class at once. Coaching, counseling, consulting are really what make education work. They are precisely the roles that teachers have always wanted but have seldom found a way to arrange for.

In terms of the communication triangle of sender, receiver, and message, individualization considers the sender or the receiver alone for a moment. It emphasizes the variation among *I*'s and *you*'s. It insists that learners are coming from different ethnic, social, geographic, emotional, and intellectual places. This distance between learners is a good thing as well as a problem. Individual variation is not just something to put up with. It is a potent means of learning. The fact is that people learn from their differences, whereas their similarity merely sets up the possibility of their learning from each other. Having to communicate across differences in style, attitude, knowledge, point of view, dialect, and so on develops all aspects of thought and language, from vocabulary, grammar, and pronunciation to clarity, comprehension, and intellectual sophistication. The exploitation of differences, then, is the bridge between individualization and the second concept in the prescription, interaction.

Interaction

Learning language is *social,* because language is social in origin and in purpose. It is learned *through* people in order to communicate *with* people. Like the personal nature of language, this is an inescapable fact that often becomes invisible for the very reason that it is so obvious. It is all well and good to look at mature reading and writing and say that those are solo activities. But reading and writing entirely on one's own represent ends, not means. Soloing rises out of collective effort. Monologue, the basic act of writing, is born of dialogue. Comprehending what someone said hundreds of years ago in Greece comes about from understanding first what some contemporary is telling you face to face.

THE ORAL BASE

Social interaction is necessary in the classroom to develop vocal speech into an instrument of communication both for its own sake and for the sake of reading and writing. Practice in vocalizing will develop pronunciation, enunciation, fluency, confidence, and expression—all those skills usually called *speech* in school. And reading and writing can progress little further than the limits of their oral base. If a learner cannot understand something said to him, he will probably not comprehend it in a book. If he cannot say something to himself at least, he will not be able to write it. Hard pressed to teach apparently reluctant students to write, some teachers question an oral emphasis, saying, "Oh, they'll talk all right—that's not the problem." But most speech remains very undeveloped, however talkative a person may be, and until it becomes a more worthwhile instrument of communication many students will be both unwilling and unable to read and write.

Like dramatic play, conversing is something the child does before he comes to school, a fact that implies two things. First, it is something that the school can build on from the outset, a familiar medium to extend and use as a substratum for reading, writing, and thinking. Second, since children learn to talk out of school, their talk within school should provide additional learning not easily acquired anywhere else.

School should be a place where children talk at least as much as outside, for fostering speech is the business of the language classroom. Too often there is the hidden inscription above the door that says, "Abandon all speech ye who enter here." The kids get the message: "Speech is not wanted. Here you sit quietly and don't socialize; paperwork is what they care about except when they want you to read aloud or answer a question. Talking to other children is bad behavior." So long as talking is excluded from the curriculum and not utilized within, peer conversation can only appear as a disciplinary problem, whereas actually it can become one of the mainstays of the curriculum through processes described in Chapter 4, Talking and Listening, and Chapter 5, Dramatic Inventing.

POOLING KNOWLEDGE

It may not be obvious how peer youngsters can learn from each other when none of them seems to know any more than his fellows. First, it's not true, as we said before, that peers share the same knowledge and ignorance. Interaction is necessary in order to pool what kids do know, to exchange phonics

understanding, spellings, factual information, views on a subject, or know-how in various skills. The value of letting kids pool what they know is obvious. What is harder to see is how unskilled readers or writers can help each other improve. They can do so in several different ways.

PLAYING GAMES OF LANGUAGE AND LOGIC

One of the best ways to sharpen logical powers is through games, as we know from either playing or being told about chess. Games theory is a whole area of advanced modern mathematics, because the strategies of games depend on combining logical steps or "moves." As described on page 471, games can embody splendidly the logic of classes and hierarchies. And a game context can permit focusing on substructures of the language such as phonics, vocabulary, and grammar without violating communication integrity, because games frankly substitute rules for the sender-receiver-message relations as a basis for making decisions. Most games are social, of course, and require students to interact. The interaction entailed in playing such valuable games for their own sake also generates a lot of very good discussion along the way as students follow directions, interpret rules, and bring out the game's possibilities.

STIMULATING AND SUPPORTING EACH OTHER

Many youngsters who would never crack a book or write something alone will do so with pleasure if they have partners. Partners give language tasks a social incentive until the individuals get involved enough to find their own reasons for wanting to do it later alone. This gets some learners over a hump posed by fear, timidity, dependence, lack of confidence, bad previous experience, and other negative attitudes. Problems that would overwhelm any one of them alone can be solved together. If not, no one of them feels like a failure, and they can more easily seek outside help together. Partners stimulate, complement, and sustain one's own ideas. Part of what makes this work is the sheer pleasure of socializing, but part of the trick is the support kids give each other. Many students get through homework this way who would otherwise be daunted or unmotivated. The same reciprocal support should operate routinely inside the classroom.

In order to put their will behind what they are doing, senders and receivers must have authentic audiences for speaking and writing and must become authentic audiences for hearing and reading. The more often outsiders such as adults or younger children can serve as audience the better, but practicing discourse constantly requires more audiences and feedback than can be arranged with outsiders. Classmates must serve for each other. This fits an individualized classroom because if different parties are doing different things at the same time, they have reason to be interested in receiving each other's activities. Performers can do a rehearsed reading of a text for the rest of the class. But even members of a group writing together serve as audience when they exchange and read each other's papers or take turns reading them aloud. Without handy audiences for one's language productions, little reason can be found to do them, and language practice lacks the force that should drive it.

If students produce language only for the teacher, they lack motivation or they substitute grades and pleasing the teacher for authentic reasons to talk and write. Lack of authentic audience is in fact a major cause of school language difficulty. An authoritative adult, parental substitute, and dispenser of grades simply cannot suffice alone for audience, because he is a loaded figure about whom youngsters have too many attitudes irrelevant to composition. This perverts the sender-receiver relation into an entirely too particular case of "trying to get effects on an audience." Other human resources have to be called on as well, inside and outside the classroom. Interaction may be with other classes, community people, teacher aides, and so on, but must rely as a staple on classmates. This allows all students constantly to reverse roles of sender and receiver and to learn from both sides.

COOPERATION TO OPERATION

The *cooperation* of groups becomes internalized as the mental *operation* of individuals. Thus, in keeping with the emphasis on the oral base, talking provides far more exercise in trying to formulate thought than actual writing does and permits speaker and listener to identify and work out communication problems together. Eventually individuals internalize the reader's needs and amend thought and speech without external aid. Similarly, performing becomes the chief means of deepening and checking reading comprehension: enacting, reading aloud, and translating reading matter into another medium become internalized so that individuals "play out" and visualize any text in their heads to actively "grasp" it when they are reading solo and silently.

Internalization works in many ways that will be detailed in later chapters. As a general process it works by imitating physical or social behavior on an inner, mental level. The developmental psychologist Jean Piaget has described how children gradually internalize concrete operations into logical operations. In this way, manipulating weights on a balancing scale prepares for "manipulating" algebraic equations. Internalizing group exchanges into individual habits of thought and speech also illustrates Piaget's concept.

Members of a group think and discourse separately in the same way they have done collectively. This internalization is in fact the main way everybody becomes socialized and acculturated. It may work for good or ill. If a group spends its time heaping scorn on outsiders, its members will tend to think in simple additive accumulation and to project their feeling into other people. If a group splits constantly into win-lose conflicts of teams, the thinking of its individuals will tend to dichotomize issues into simplistic either-or polarities. The first group is stuck with "and . . . and," the second with "but . . . but." Another group may pick up each other's ideas, images, and wit and build on them—pursuing, testing, elaborating, amending. Their process of *expatiating* is obviously very desirable for helping the individual to become thoughtful in both the intellectual and social senses and to think alone with more logic, imagination, and wit. Expatiation encourages the qualifying use of "although," "if," "unless," "whenever." It alone would justify small-group process, but consider too that when members of a group challenge and qualify within a sustained spirit of collaboration this teaches the individual to entertain differing ideas and viewpoints within himself alone, without resorting to simple-mindedness to keep peace of mind.

FEEDBACK

If we think of the main way human beings learn to do skilled activities we realize it is by practice, coaching, and trial-and-error. Think of learning to

What your students need is not information (beyond the facts of literacy) but awareness of their egocentricity. In the final chapter, we say that a major dimension of growth is toward decreasing egocentricity, which we define as assuming too much about the similarity and difference between one's own mind and that of other people. See page 438 for examples and further discussion. Years of analyzing language learning have convinced us that egocentricity is the biggest single cause of problems in comprehension and composition. For speaking, reading, and writing, egocentricity manifests itself in very practical ways that conventional teaching has noted in its own way but has not done much about because it has not afforded the student enough means of *comparing* his understanding of a test, or his way of saying something, or his way of seeing something, with that of another.

Believing that lack of information or advice is the cause of comprehending and composing problems may be the greatest mistake of all language teaching. A reader failing to put together all the meaning cues of a text cannot be told what to do because he already *thinks* he is doing that. He is unaware of what he is omitting or how he is distorting or tuning out. You can score him wrong as often as you like on comprehension tests, but he will continue to misread, despite even phonics mastery and good vocabulary, if he is unwittingly adding and subtracting the text. A writer failing to lead his reader, to give information in the needed order, to elaborate detail, to tie things together, to emphasize and subordinate, to put punctuation where he would if he were vocalizing, and otherwise neglecting to guide the reader with cues will never improve merely from being told to avoid these things or from studying rules and models for good sentences. He too *thinks* he is doing these common-sense things. The reason conventional reading and writing programs are usually so ineffectual is that students don't learn from the dos and don'ts of prescribing and proscribing. The problem is somewhere else utterly. What they need is insight about their own outlook.

How do they get this? By constant comparison. Because the problems of composing and comprehending are problems of matching minds, the main solution to egocentricity is to do something together and compare results. Comparing is matching. A light goes on in the head of a youngster who discovers that his peers understood a story differently from the way he did or that they don't agree about some idea he believed everyone took for granted. *The youngster doesn't realize that what he said or read could be taken another way.* He is unconscious of alternatives. How do we know what to assume people share and what to assume they don't?

We know people are alike to a point, but where is that cutoff point? *That* is the information the learner needs to know. And the only way he can find it out is to *try* to understand or express something and heed others' reactions—to compare. Even if he decides that a whole group is wrong except himself, at least he now knows he can't assume they share his mind set. And that breaks his egocentricity. The basic *I* is not reduced of course. Rather, to broaden understanding is to enlarge the *I* from a point to an area. The learner can stay centered, as he should, but centered in a larger field than the isolated ego.

Undoing egocentricity occurs best with peers. If students match understanding and expression with more advanced people, as happens when comprehension is tested or compositions marked, they too often just feel wrong and attribute the discrepancy to the maturity gap. This is a common way of dismissing adult responses or standards and defending against loss of self-esteem. It follows that to correct the problems they should try to figure out what the adults have in mind. But the main issue is not matching their minds to those more advanced but to those of their own maturity.

Anything a student misunderstands or expresses badly should be perceivable as such to peers. If peer consensus sides with the student—if the student and his peers misunderstand a text together or do *not* have trouble following what one of them has said—then you have to question whether the text is inappropriate for the group or whether the composition can in fact be fairly called unclear. So interaction with peers will provide the most useful comparison for breaking egocentricity. Where you as teacher help is to get them comparing and to open up alternative solutions when the peers establish the mismatching. This takes you out of the negative role of judge, where you can be discounted, and puts you in the positive role of expert consultant, where you will be sought for help. Make *them* judge. Constant comparison ties in with good judgment about language, because knowing one's own mind in relation to others guides decisions about how to put and take things.

Yet, interaction is not limited to peers. Although

ride a bike, play a guitar, throw a ball. We practice through trials and get coached on the errors. If language arts are actions that we *learn to do* and not information that we merely *learn,* then they are not basically different from musical and sports skills. But how does practice cause improvement? Practice provides feedback.

Feedback is any information a learner receives as a result of his trial. This information usually comes from his own perception of what he has done: the bicycle falls over, the ball goes over the head of the receiver, or the guitar notes sound untrue. The learner heeds this information and adjusts his next trial accordingly, and often unconsciously. But suppose the learner cannot perceive what he is doing—does not, for example, hear that the notes are wrong—or perceives that he has fallen short of his goal but does not know what adjustments to make in his action. This is where the coach comes in. He is someone who observes the learner's actions and the results and points out what the learner cannot see or figure out how to correct for himself. He is a human source of feedback who supplements the feedback from inanimate things.

But, you may say, learning to write is different from learning to ride a bicycle or even learning to play the guitar, which are, after all, physical activities. Writers manipulate symbols, not objects, and they act on the minds of other people, not on matter. Yes, indeed. But these differences do not make learning to write an exception to the general process of learning through feedback. Rather, they indicate that in learning to use language the only kind of feedback available to us is human response.

Let's take first the case of learning to talk, which is a social activity and the base for writing. The effects of what we do cannot be known to us unless our listener responds. He may do so in a number of ways—by carrying out our directions, answering our questions, laughing, looking bored or horrified, asking for more details, arguing, and so on. Every listener becomes a kind of coach. But of course a conversation, once launched, becomes a two-way interaction in which each party is both learner and source of feedback. Learning by heeding feedback depends on plentiful trials and accurate, timely feedback. Paramount, of course, are the quantity and quality of response a student receives to his speaking and writing and to his expression of what he understands others to mean. The teacher's job is

to arrange for both trials and feedback—*to teach the students to teach each other.* This is where teacher expertise comes into play.

TRIAL-AND-ERROR

Now, trial-and-error sounds to many people like a haphazard, time-consuming business. Trial-and-error is by definition never aimless, but without help the individual alone may not think of all the kinds of trials that are possible, or may not always see how to learn the most from his errors. And if it is a social activity he is learning, like writing, then human interaction is in any case indispensable. So we have teachers to propose meaningful trials (assignments) and to arrange for a feedback that insures the maximum exploitation of error.

The teacher does not try to prevent the learner from making errors. He does not preteach the problems and solutions (and of course by "errors" we mean failures of vision, judgment, and technique, not mere mechanics). The learner simply plunges into the assignment, uses all his resources, makes errors where he must, and heeds the feedback. In this action-response learning, errors are valuable; they are the essential learning instrument. They are not despised or penalized. Inevitably, the person who is afraid to make mistakes is a retarded learner, no matter what the activity in question.

In contrast to the exploitation of error is the avoidance of error. The latter works like this: the good and bad ways of carrying out the assignment are arrayed in advance, are pretaught; then the learner does the assignment, attempting to keep the good and bad ways in mind as he works. Next, the teacher evaluates the work according to the criteria that were laid out before the assignment was done. Even if a system of rewards and punishments is not invoked, the learner feels that errors are enemies, not friends. Avoiding error is an inferior learning strategy to capitalizing on error. It's like the difference between looking over your shoulder and looking where you are going. Nobody who intends to learn to do something wants to make mistakes. In that sense, avoidance of error is assumed in the motivation itself, and this is why exercise of will is critical. But if the learner is allowed to make mistakes with no other penalty than the failure to achieve his goal, then he knows why they are to be avoided and wants to find out how to correct them. Errors take on a different meaning. They define what is good.

comparison within the peer groups proves to be the most important and practical, youngsters need to compare across age differences as well. Younger children should know what older students think and how they react. This is one good argument for arranging buddy systems of tutoring between students of different ages. Comparison should extend to adults also in situations where older people's views are not forced on youngsters or used to judge them but are simply asserted. Youngsters really do want to know what their elders think because they want to exploit their knowledge for growing up.

Teachers, teacher aides, parents, visitors, and other community people should have occasions to influence young people who are not their own children. Nonparental adult opinion is very valuable. It helps bring to youngsters the viewpoints of the world beyond the home and the immediate peer group. Many activities suggested in later chapters, such as polling and interviewing, direct students to seek out the views of adults. *Anyone* can help deliver people from egocentricity, and everybody should be used. So the wise teacher does not jealously guard the teaching role for himself. This merely shows insecurity. A real teacher is someone who can show people how to learn from everything and everybody.

SMALL-GROUP PROCESS

The means that most facilitates interaction is small-group process. Most group work in conventional schooling fails to foster exchanges between peers because the group is too large or the teacher dominates. A tradition in elementary school, for example, is for the teacher to take one group aside at a time and to direct it so that all interaction occurs between the teacher and one student at a time. Meanwhile, the rest of the class is doing "seat work" or "busy work." In secondary school, teachers often lead discussion by an entire class at once, a practice that fails to allow enough participation for each student. Both procedures tie up the teacher and put off the day of self-direction. For most effective classroom management you should shift more direction to groups and make students address their words and deeds to each other. Then when you want to coach or counsel individuals, do so one-to-one, and when you want to consult with a group, just move in and out of it. In this way all students get maximum benefit of both you and each other.

Sheer volume of participation is a critical feature of small-group process that may be overlooked in emphasizing how peers can learn from each other's differences and from collaboration. The inborn human faculties for abstracting raw experience into orderly symbols must have huge quantities of data, as the infant has when he infers basic grammar from hearing thousands and thousands of other people's sentences and their emendations of his own sentences. School has to offer equivalent quantities of grist for the intellectual mills. Whether the youngster is still working on auditory and visual discrimination, spelling and punctuation, or ideas and forms, he needs *volume.* He must have both variety and volume of intellectual and language experience. Individualizing provides much of the variety. What provides most of the volume is the high participation that small groups afford.

If learners don't process each other's work in groups, they cannot gain enough experience with the language arts to become good at them. When a teacher has to process everything that's written, students can't possibly write enough. And when the teacher has to monitor and read everything the students read, they don't read nearly as much as they might. This problem of control and management of numbers keeps students from practicing sending and receiving language enough. Since large quantities of reading are the main means of acquiring correct spellings and larger vocabulary, these skills suffer along with the more basic matter of learning to decode, which requires numberless occasions for hearing and seeing words at the same time. With the amount of writing held down, students have little chance to practice composition, spelling, and punctuation, and consequently all those skills loom as gigantic problems for which special methods of teaching have to be devised.

The only limit to how much kids can talk, read, and write in small groups is the amount of time in a day, because a teacher who only oversees the processing of talk, reading, and writing facilitates it instead of becoming a bottleneck! Volume of practice is simply more effective in the long run than controlling the flow of language to a rate you can handle alone. Besides, your other role of coaching and counseling, made possible partly by the self-direction of collaborative groups, counters very well any likelihood of students not getting the benefit of your expertise.

In a small group an individual can talk more and can get more response to what he says or writes, because the group can take plenty of time for each member. He can read more because the small group he is reading with does not have to pace itself by the lowest common denominator of a whole class and does not have to hold back to accommodate the ponderous administration of a large group. The individual can also play more learning games, improvise more, and perform texts more in small groups. The give-and-take of small groups goes further faster, handles tasks more efficiently, and gets more work done. Each member is motivated to be more active because he is more involved and has more control over the direction the group takes. Eventually, each student can take advantage of the whole class membership, for he will belong to many different groups in one year, and groups can exchange ideas and feed back to each other. Yet a whole class can always meet as such when it makes sense. The strategy is to take advantage of both large numbers and small focus by constant flexible subgroupings.

In sum, interaction furthers the main language arts goals because it exploits individual variation and employs social resources to solve what are social problems when correctly understood. Pooling knowledge, playing learning games together, stimulating and supporting each other, using each other as audience—these are all practical ways to give individuals the advantage of numbers. Internalizing, feeding back, and comparing mental sets go deeper. They are three major learning methods. By means of them we all learned to speak and to master other skills as well.

Integration

Language learning is integrative. We build interior knowledge structures as we grow, drawing on all sources and kinds of knowledge. Since integrity of the organism is a biological necessity, we must always remain whole no matter how much we may change as we grow and no matter how incoherent the environment may be. A human being is made to synthesize all forms of experience into one harmoniously functioning whole. If experience is too incoherent to integrate, we may mentally or physically negate what we can't assimilate, as when some students tune out or drop out of school because they cannot fit it into the rest of their life. Or we may structure our knowledge to fit the incoherence, a desperate strategy that "integrates" only by overlooking at one level of consciousness what at another level we know is not so. An individual is meant to be indivisible.

Language learning is different from other school subjects. It is not a *new* subject, and it is not even a *subject.* It permeates every part of people's lives and itself constitutes a major way of abstracting. So learning language raises more clearly than other school courses the issue of integration.

INTEGRATING SCHOOL WITH HOME

Since people learn language outside of school and before they enter school, you should think of it as a continuity that you will try to help youngsters develop while they are passing through your hands. The best teaching strategy is to extend language learning as much as possible from what youngsters already know and can do. This is why goals should be stated as expansions of and elaborations of language facility, and this is why the oral base is all-important.

More specifically, school must accept widely varying dialects, lifestyles, values, and ethnic heritages. A student takes both home and school seriously. If they are made to conflict, he is caught in the middle and has to reject one or disguise the conflict from himself. Either choice is terrible education. America is and has always been a pluralistic nation made up of mixed cultures. Its strength has been to appreciate and accommodate differences. This was a necessity from exploration and colonial times through immigration days to the present assertion of minority identities. School should foster the interplay of differences so that youngsters will come to know, among other things, what other lifestyles, values, and dialects there are. Order, harmony, and efficiency are not achieved by putting kids in uniforms of either cloth or thought. They are achieved by helping individuals stay undivided. Whole people make a harmonious community, no matter how different they are.

Even if the school does not try to force a student to abandon his heritage and way of life, a student of a minority culture may find little to identify with if the books and other materials are drawn excessively from the majority culture. Or if the methods and media available to learn through do not accommodate the learning modes of his ethnic group, then the student still feels when he comes to class that he is entering a foreign land. Much of the reading material, for example, that youngsters like to read depends for interest on the reader identifying with the figures and settings in stories. The less a youngster has been around, the harder it is for him to identify across differences of culture and lifestyle and language style. If someone comes from a heritage that sings and dances its poetry, he may find it very hard to get involved in silent reading of poetry followed by discussion of imagery. A classic cause of neurosis in American Indians is said to be the conflict between their native tendency to collaborate and the white schools' emphasis on competition. Certainly every minority member finds himself living in two cultures at once, one at home and one at school. This is unavoidable by the very definition of being in a minority, but whether this double life enriches the student or splits him down the middle depends on whether the classroom contains enough breadth to include methods and materials he can build a bridge with.

For students who first learned a language other than English but are embedded in an English-language culture, the problem is naturally more acute, so in addition to suitable content and approaches they may need to use or at least sometimes hear their first language in an English context until they become bilingual. See page 473 for teaching English as a foreign language.

INTEGRATING CLASSROOMS

It should be very clear from the needs of individualization and interaction that different students must be mixed, not separate. A main way to do this is to avoid so-called tracking and ability grouping in favor of heterogeneous classes. When segregated, slower students tend to get a negative image of themselves that makes them actually perform worse than they might and advanced students get an elitist inflated feeling. But more serious, each suffers from lack of variety and ends getting a standardized curriculum. The fact is that few youngsters are uniformly good or bad at *all* the many possible language activities involved in speaking, reading, writing, and performing the whole variety of possible discourse.

Homogeneous grouping is usually based on test scores in reading comprehension and grammar or on facility with limited kinds of expository writing. But when taught and evaluated over a broader range of language activities that include oral comprehen-

sion and oral composition, performing and improvising, and the full gamut of types of reading and writing, then different students prove to be good at different things. Based on this bias, homogeneity is more apparent than real.

Segregating by "ability levels" is actually designed to make feasible one lesson plan for all each day and one sequence for all each year. Crudely, it allows for variations among students by recognizing, say, two or three levels of achievement in a couple of high-priority areas. This actually thwarts individualization, since segregation drowns differences in a limited similarity and fails to *utilize* even the acknowledged differences in ability. Homogeneity, then, maintains the inefficiency of the conventional approach to classroom management and limits severely the options of teachers and students.

Grouping by ability, and by ability in only a couple of kinds of language learning, has also undone in both Northern and Southern communities most of the benefits that might come about from racial integration. One such benefit would surely be improved communication among different racial groups. Aside from elemental moral issues, racial integration serves the best interests of language learning for all. The youth of today's world will surely have to "speak each other's language" in more ways than one. Not only must they understand each other's lifestyles and viewpoints, but they should annex each other's dialects and language styles and literature.

Many adults worry that mixing their pupils or offspring with children who speak little English or nonstandard English will "corrupt" their language. This is a needless fear, for neither party loses the language learned in the family. Youngsters exposed to peers of other cultures and languages simply know more than youngsters restricted to their own kind. Again, it is *difference* that teaches, not similarity. Having to talk across language differences, to accommodate differences in thought and speech, is excellent education. And growing together will certainly ensure domestic tranquility and law and order better than growing apart.

Children of minority groups usually do not score as high as middle-class white children for a number of reasons. English may be their second language, whereas the exams test English. They may speak a nonstandard dialect, whereas most reading matter is written in standard dialect, and the grammar tested for is that of standard dialect. In fact, "errors" in grammar are almost by definition deviations from standard usage. Fewer minority families have enough money to belong to the middle class and consequently benefit less from the "hidden curriculum" of the middle class—the at-home language experiences such as being read to and talked with a lot by parents who are well educated. Middle-class children often learn to read at home, not at school, and they usually acquire from home many of the words, concepts, and sentence structures they might encounter on reading comprehension tests.

Poor or minority families often provide a very rich language environment at home too, but its assets are not the sort schools usually test for. Their language is mostly oral, but ability grouping depends strictly on paper and pencil tests of literacy. Furthermore, their language may be directed more toward verbal games than analyzing, more toward poetic figures of speech than toward higher abstractions. Again, school tests do not attempt to measure what poor or minority children may do best. Considering all these factors, we can't avoid concluding that so-called ability grouping works specifically against racial integration as well as against more general integration of language resources.

Most schools that claim to be "integrated," North or South, run segregated schools in fact by tracking —tracking that is mostly on the basis of literacy skills. Being under the same roof but kept apart makes youngsters cynical and causes eruptions of hostility between races that parents and administrators take as proof that integration is a bad idea. This friction shows just the opposite, that if the adults themselves feel that racially different children should not mix, then children infer they must be enemies and should act toward each other accordingly.

It's unfair to say that "ability" grouping was designed to sabotage racial integration. Clearly, it has been a mainstay of conventional teaching even in all-white schools for decades. In fact, we think most teachers really believe in racial integration but believe also in tracking. One reason they do not see the contradiction in their beliefs is that racial integration creates problems for them as teachers that conventional classroom organization and methods are impotent to solve. Suddenly the room is whirling with kids varying so much in language background, learning style, and cultural bent that the teacher may stagger back, feeling flabbergasted, frightened, and inadequate. Nothing in pre-service or in-service experience has prepared a teacher to help such different people all learn at once and learn from each

other. Caught in this plight, many a "liberal" teacher harbors secret disliking for minority children and finds easy rationalization for ability grouping. But the dislike may really not be prejudice so much as sheer dismay about not knowing how to handle the situation. Indeed, a teacher should not have to make a haunting choice between his professional survival and what he knows in his heart to be the welfare of those children he is charged with. To say that ability grouping is a cop-out on racial integration is merely to say it is a cop-out on *all* handling of difference.

Students of like interest or ability should sometimes group together. This is allowed for in the freedom to form any kind of subgroups—homogeneous or otherwise—within the total heterogeneous group. If you envision small working parties forming, breaking up when finished with a book or other activity, and re-forming on some other basis for some other activity, then you can see how it is possible to have the best of both worlds—to enjoy at once the advantages of both similarity and difference. There is no reason to settle for less.

INTEGRATING "SUBJECTS"

Language is not a subject like history, science, geography, or social studies because it comprises all these. It is a symbol system. It is the medium into which these other subjects are cast. So we must distinguish between symbolizer and symbolized. The real kinship is between English and math, because both are symbol systems by means of which we encode experience, math being a special notation that purifies and extends ordinary language. This kinship is rightly expressed in the three Rs. The native language codes experience qualitatively, in words, whereas mathematical symols encode it quantitatively, in numbers. As with other languages, we can translate between math and English. We can read equations out loud in English, for example, even though none of the symbols are in English, and sometimes when no equivalent symbol exists for a concept in math we have to talk around it until we explain it, just as we have to do for some Russian or Chinese expressions. And math, like English, can be applied to any subject matter. So a language is not just one more garment hanging among others on a rack. It is the weaving principle by which garments come into existence. This makes it the warp and woof of the whole academic curriculum.

Content

But what does integrating all "subjects" through language amount to practically? First, it means including as part of language arts materials many reading selections, periodicals, games, and visuals that draw subject matter from history and the behavioral and physical sciences. This does not have to be "presented" but merely made available within an individualization system. Without such content all goal areas of discourse cannot be covered and all students cannot find what they need to read, write, and talk about.

History and science can really be defined by the level of abstraction to which material is symbolized. History is *what happened,* or True Stories. Science is *what happens,* or Information. Abstracting further from either of these produces Ideas, higher-level generalizations and theories about people and things that carry history and science into philosophy. In other words, some "subjects" are just different areas of discourse, different levels of abstracting into language. These can be further subdivided into geography, civics, ancient history, American history, biology, chemistry, and physics, but these all just specialize *what happened* and *what happens* into more local focuses such as the workings of democratic government or forms of life versus forms of inanimate matter.

All of these are the content of English just as much as literature (covered in Chapter 12, Word Play; Chapter 14, Actual and Invented Dialogue; and Chapter 15, Invented Stories). Students learning to operate their language must learn to send and receive any sort of message, regardless of which level it has been abstracted to or which mode of abstraction was employed (fictional or factual). Furthermore, comparisons of one level or mode with another is the main way to learn about each. It is with subjects as with students: differences teach.

Singling subjects out for separate study in elementary school seems rather pointless. Unless the teacher is a specialist, he cannot add expertise to what materials might offer. All that separating subjects can do is obstruct individualization by programming large-group instruction. In secondary school teachers can presumably add expertise, but by then such subjects are mostly optional. In any case, students should practice these areas of discourse continually from primary school on, because history and science grow with the students. Biology, physics,

chemistry, astronomy, archaeology, government, geography, economics, psychology, sociology, anthropology—these must be open to learners every year of school. Any subject is a good one if youngsters want to talk or read or write about it. This range would serve English by helping to ensure interest for very different learners. And the language teacher can best help them acclimate to various discourse. Then when they do take a specialized course later, students will benefit far more from the specialist teacher's expertise, which usually has to be held in check to deal first with the students' language problems!

Process

The social studies and science are not just inherited information. They are also processes or "disciplines" by means of which people today continue to create information and ideas in those fields. These are data-gathering and abstracting processes that are the same for the social studies and science as they are for all other information and ideas that are put into language.

Polling and interviewing are important data-gathering tools in the social sciences. Historians and biographers have to sift and assimilate memoirs, journals, correspondence, archives, and other records. Both behavioral and physical scientists have to observe a great deal and take notes. They may have to set up special situations to observe, which we call experiments. They may have to collate others' observations with their own and hence have to poll, interview, or ransack documents. Charting, graphing, labeling, and captioning may figure into any of these. There isn't one of these processes that should not be part and parcel of the language arts curriculum. In fact, if youngsters do not do these same activities themselves, they will have no opportunity to produce much discourse in the range of True Stories, Information, and Ideas. (Plagiarizing doesn't count!) In short, practicing the roles of sender and receiver means, among other things, role-playing historian, scientist, and philosopher.

Certain realistic activities naturally integrate both the contents of different subjects and the processes of different fields. Let's take the example of a consumer study on flashlight batteries. It can entail shopping, computing price comparisons by some measures of dollar efficiency, analyzing the batteries physically, polling people for battery-buying habits, making charts and diagrams, taking photos, reading up on relevant information, discussing findings, writing up the data and conclusions, and presenting results as an illustrated book or a slide show with narration or a labeled and captioned exhibit. Such interweaving of processes and subject areas allows each subactivity to act as lead-in or outcome of another and hence to bring each to bear on all. Effects are far more powerful than when these activities are singled out and separately scheduled. Pooling of people and materials will do it, but you must change your notions of where boundaries are.

INTEGRATING LANGUAGE ARTS WITH OTHER ARTS AND MEDIA

A sad recent trend has been to devalue and even eliminate the arts from schools in order to ride herd on "basic skills." This is one of the reasons the basic skills often do not come along very well. We cannot pluck language out and place it under glass. It is integrally related to a host of nonverbal activities that set it up, accompany it, or follow it up. Think of some sports, lively arts, and media. Some, like dance or pantomime, may only parallel language by encoding experience in the medium of the body, but even when totally disjoined from language, such alternative forms teach about language precisely by doing what it does but doing it differently. But from song lyrics to slide-tape narrations, most arts and media relate rather directly to language. The relation is usually a complementing or competing one. Many students need these ties to have reasons for learning language, including basic skills, and to have interesting forms of it to practice with.

Composition

Besides being expressive and communicative, the arts share a common process—composition. Making something that means something is composing. Composing a poem or story, a dance, a piece of music, a film, a painting, a sculpture, or mobile always consists of putting together some elements of the medium into original relationships. Selecting and patterning elements are similar processes whether one is working with words, body movements, images, or strokes and colors. The common denominator for these processes is form.

Those arts that move in time, like language, dance, music, and motion pictures, all share issues of sequence and pace. Many terms on musical scores, like *accelerando* and *crescendo,* apply equally well to dance, literature, and moving pictures. Whereas the lively arts move in time, serially, the graphic arts of painting, drawing, sculpture, and still photography present their elements simultaneously. But part of the art of lively arts is to create some feeling of simultaneity while moving in time, and part of the art of graphics is to create some feeling of dynamics through the static. Thus people speak of direction, depth, rhythm, and animation in a painting or photo, and cubistic painting and sculpture get a time dimension by giving several views of the same objects. Forms come from nature—its cycles, rhythms, and repetitions, its "variations on a theme" and motifs, its ordering of elements.

Comprehension

Comprehending the nonverbal arts requires the receiver to do many of the same things he does in receiving language. He must put things together for himself in his own mind—"grasp" what is there. He must pay attention to the elements of the medium and how they have been ordered and become sensitive to the total effect that the parts create as they accumulate into a whole, by either the action of the medium moving in a sequence or by his own viewing action as he scans. He must open himself to another's composition and let all the cues work on him in combination with each other. All of this is required for reading comprehension, whether the text is a great work of art or merely a how-to-do-it set of instructions.

The classic elements of verbal composition—organization, emphasis, unity—that figure so much in problems of writing and reading, are not peculiar to the language arts. By practicing the lively arts and graphic arts students can work with the same issues of composing and comprehending, and they can perceive language as one instance of basic forms of nature.

TOTAL IMMERSION

The strategy that most facilitates integration is immersion of the learner in language by leaving intact the natural relations among different language activities, different subjects, different forms, different media, and different arts. If every learner cannot find for himself these multiple points of entry into language use and multiple pathways to general goals, then individualization is a hollow slogan. A classroom has to be a cornucopia of opportunities so that no matter which way he looks a student can see interesting connections among things, words, ideas, and people. The reason free choice is sure to work in a total-immersion environment is that it makes little difference what a student chooses on any one occasion. The main thing is to keep practicing language with involved care. So saturating the learner with language reinforces the strategy of going for volume and variety.

A group fascinated by animals can track them for weeks with great interest across folk tales, fables, true memoirs, poems, encyclopedic entries, newspaper and magazine articles, statistics, charts and graphs and maps, photos, animal card games, films, and so on. At the same time they can interweave play-acting of animals, observing and note-taking, journals, keeping pets, telling and writing animal stories and fables, photographing and drawing and captioning, discussing, arithmetical calculation, rehearsed reading of animal stories, and so on. The secret of all this is the timely connection, and it can't be scheduled. But the constant possibility of timely connections can be arranged by making all sorts of language use available all the time.

This constant possibility depends in turn partly on tying language to other subjects, arts, and media. Various current movements in education may help teachers trying to integrate in the ways we have been describing here. One of these is the humanities movement. A strong force in it is the National Humanities Faculty, which operates from Concord, Massachusetts. Another is the Association of Humanistic Psychology in San Francisco. The Educational Arts Council in Boston supports efforts to link language arts with the other arts.

FRAMING WORK IN WHOLE COMMUNICATION STRUCTURES

Only when people have a complete communication structure can they authentically practice literacy, composition, and comprehension and hence profit from volume and immersion. Context governs text.

Failure of the Particle Approach

Vocabulary drills, dissection of dummy sentences, labeling grammatical parts, and writing isolated sample paragraphs do not teach how to write. If they did, colleges would not be frantically increasing their remedial writing enrollments. Vocabulary lists actually misteach, because without context the learner has to ignore connotation, style, tone, and other aspects of good word usage in favor of absolute synonymy and abstract dictionary definitions. Words learned in context are better understood and better remembered. Similarly, practicing clause subordination or other sentence construction in a vacuum teaches students that clause subordination is somehow good for its own sake and that how one constructs a sentence has no relation to the logical and rhetorical demands of what one is trying to express. Neither of these inferences is true. And how can one learn to paragraph the flow of ideas when limited at the outset to a single paragraph? There is no such thing as a well-constructed paragraph when the paragraph is a fragment stripped of point and purpose or when the writer is forced to say what he has to say in one paragraph. Faced with form for its own sake, a student rightly concludes that content is unimportant and fills the form with tripe. As for reading, many children test out on all the isolated parts—the separate sound-spellings and "reading skills"—but cannot or will not read.

When wholes are disintegrated and doled out to students, it becomes an academic point as to whether they *cannot* put them back together on their own or whether they simply don't care enough to try, since the approach can prevent either cognition or motivation from working.

But you may ask, isn't it enough to surround a word with a sentence, or a sentence with a paragraph—each substructure with the one above instead of *all* those above? What's wrong, for example, with teaching vocabulary by using a word appropriately in a sentence? Though obviously better than word lists, this is still deficient to the extent that the unsituated sentence remains itself ambiguous as to intent, connotation, style, and so on. Furthermore, since this compromise approach affords neither the alleged advantage of lists nor the real advantage of full context, it just isn't practically worthwhile.

Acceptable Cases of Focusing on Substructures

Some single sentences and single paragraphs are of course real wholes unto themselves, complete discourses. A proverb is an example of a single-sentence discourse. Some captions are complete in either a sentence or a paragraph. Entries in dictionaries and encyclopedias legitimately call for isolated words, sentences, and paragraphs. But the task must be to say something, not to tailor language and thought so as to come up with a paragraph when done. It should be the communication situation that calls for a single paragraph.

Another exception to our stance against particle learning may be certain kinds of games in which phonemes, syllables, words, phrases, and isolated sentences are treated entirely as play tokens, frankly as fragments not intended to communicate. Such games we recommend in the spirit of the Word-Play goal. Phonics, spelling, vocabulary, and sentence construction can be very effectively learned by board and card games or social games, for example, without misteaching or making language arts seem dull and pointless. The difference is that we openly substitute for the communication structure a game structure, so that kids understand we are not playing by communication rules but by arbitrary game rules. But it's essential that teachers not rationalize drills by calling them games. A game must have its own, noncommunicative rules. Most of all, it must be perceived *by students* as a game. Another caution is to make the playing of such games an individual option. Don't assume all youngsters need a phonics or vocabulary game but rather suggest them for *some* students as *one* learning avenue to the goal. Chapter 10, An Integrated Literacy Program; Chapter 11, Decoding and Encoding Separated; Chapter 12, Word Play; and Appendix A treat games in detail.

This curriculum exploits both games and single-word, single-sentence, single-paragraph discourse as ways of "getting specific" without violating the integrity of language learning. In this connection perhaps the importance of the goal Labels and Captions may now be more apparent.

Wholeness is the key. The great principle of nature is unity—the harmony of many things in oneness, of parts within wholes. In both Western and Eastern civilizations unity has always been the highest ideal of education. In our own age of increasing fragmentation it takes a special effort to offset disintegration and compartmentalization. So it is critical to integrate language schooling in every possible way—the learner, the learning, and what is to be learned. The individual's state of mind necessarily reflects in some measure the state of his surroundings. The environment for language learning must preserve the truth about language: as the main ingredient in our symbolic life it not only operates within every aspect of our lives but part of its very function is to integrate the diversity of experience into a harmonious whole. Keeping this always in mind makes teaching language far more successful.

Making schooling more effective

If one were asked to name three things that are the hardest for schools to bring about, the answer would most likely be individualization, interaction, and integration. This is because the trend of any institution, not just of schools, goes the other way—toward standardization, isolation, and compartmentalization. These are chronic problems of governments, corporations, and every other sort of private and public institution. Much of the present hue and cry about accountability just expresses the citizen's frustration with the diminishing "payoff" of his institutions, which have rapidly grown larger and hence even more inefficient.

The whole purpose of an institution is to gain the advantage of doing things as a large group over doing things alone. But it is precisely the large numbers that cause institutions always to drift toward standardization, isolation, and compartmentalization. Is this a hopeless bind? In order to run schools at all, we must assume that a way out can be found. Any discussion of methods must take account not only of how children grow in thought and speech, but of how the individualization, interaction, and integration required for their growth can be instituted in schools.

It is first necessary to acknowledge that in combating failure or inefficiency in basic language skills we are not dealing with learning problems but with institutional problems. Practically speaking, there is no mystery about how people learn to read and write. It occurred successfully centuries before public schools existed, and it occurs frequently nowadays at home. But in the old days or in a modern middle-class home a tutorial situation explains the difference—no large numbers to teach at once. The fact is that learning to read and write, despite the awful fracas it causes in schools, is easier than learning to speak and requires little intelligence. This is a critical point, because it means we have to quit ascribing failure to learners, or shopping around for new technical innovations in learning, and start changing schoolroom management.

Let's contrast home learning and school learning, for a very important and universally successful kind of learning takes place at home that schools should emulate. Learning to talk is far harder than learning to read and write, and yet every child who is not defective learns to speak even before his nervous system is fully developed and regardless of any so-called underprivileged environment. Children learn to speak with no special instructor or curriculum or learning site—and also with no dropouts, under-achieving, or failure. If you doubt that learning to speak is considerably harder than learning to read and write, you should consider for a moment what it entails.

First, the infant must distinguish human speech from all the other environmental sounds. Then he must classify together those speech sounds that are alike. At the same time, he is pairing off speech sounds with those things they stand for. But in order to pair words with things he has to analyze the heretofore indivisible world and conceptualize these things that people talk about. That is, he is master-ing at once both of the first two levels of coding. To utilize his growing stock of words and meanings, he infers from others' sentences the grammatical laws of the language so he can make up and inter-pret sentences he has never heard before. Deducing for himself the basic grammar is itself nothing short of marvelous, but if we consider all the analyzing, classification, and deduction that must go on for a child to speak, we have to admit that what he did before school was an astounding intellectual feat surpassing anything normally asked of him in school.

We don't usually think of literacy as easy, or of learning to speak as difficult. More likely, we have the reverse impression. The home learning of speech occurs very spontaneously and successfully compared to school literacy learning, which seems to occur only by dint of tremendous strain, if indeed it occurs at all. We mustn't be deceived by the ease of one and the strain of the other. The difference is not that reading and writing are harder but that they are attempted under what we can only call, com-paratively speaking, adverse conditions. If it hap-pened that human beings learned to write first and to speak second, in school, then we would be hav-ing crash programs in learning to speak, such as The Right to Speak, along with feverish search and research about how to improve instruction in speak-ing. The only serious problem of learning to read

and write is that it comes second and in an institu-tion. This is quite different from a *learning* problem.

All the faculties that a child needs for learning to read and write have been well exercised in learning to speak—the very same abilities to analyze, clas-sify, and infer. For literacy a child has to pair spoken words with written words—a relatively easy task, since the stock of meanings is already attached to the spoken words, and the grammatical model has already been generated within. (In neither case is the learning explicitly formulated, nor would explicit formulation help operate the language.) If literacy learning then drags out interminably over elemen-tary and even secondary school, that is entirely a matter of institutional inefficiency except for one other factor that results from literacy coming second —weaker motivation. Once able to communicate through speech, a youngster at ease in his small circle of family and friends feels no need to acquire a second medium. But the compelling reasons in our culture for wanting to read and write are pre-cisely what should become apparent as the child moves out of the home into the larger world beyond.

A language teacher could do no better than study how speech is learned at home, because schools will beat their own institutionalism only if they build methods of language teaching on the home model. Besides having the great advantage that the infant is powerfully motivated to join the human race through speech, the home has the very assets of individualization, interaction, and integration.

A child learns language through everything, all the time, and with everybody. Learning is not thought of as a specialized activity and is not restricted to a certain time, place, people, and circumstance. The child constantly initiates speech efforts and gets feedback, on the basis of which he modifies his speech. Such parent-child interactions have been recorded and studied and demonstrate beautifully the action-response-revision model of learning that a warm, spontaneous, responsive environment gives. The child himself sequences his activities and ma-terials from whatever array he can avail himself of. People don't shame him if he speaks ineptly, so he dares to try over and over until he gets good. There is no penalty for error, and the total immersion allows him to get all the powerful benefits of feed-back and trial-and-error. His trials are constant and copious and relatively uninhibited. No anxiety is in-duced by pressure for achievement and by incessant monitoring for progress—the notorious hallmarks of the institution, which has to ascertain who is doing his job well and which materials work best and which kids aren't getting their due. The reason home learning succeeds is that the natural learning processes of the growing child are not disrupted by extraneous factors.

WHAT MAY REDEEM SCHOOLS

Large numbers are not all negative, and the home has its limitations. School could in fact supply exactly what is missing at home—a larger volume and variety of human and material resources to interact with. Learning through differences certainly means getting out and mixing with the world. And wherever large numbers congregate, there too can accumulate larger amounts of materials, equipment, and facilities than most families could afford. Further realization, in fact, of individualization, interaction, and integration can never come about within the physical and psychological constraints of the home. Its limits remind us indeed of why we bother with institutions in the first place. Their function is to take advantage of numbers without succumbing to the disadvantages. The current "crisis in the classroom" indicates that schools have not found how to make themselves pay off in human returns under the conditions of mass education that a democracy requires. The methodology offered in this book aims at *utilizing* numbers instead of being done in by them.

LEARNING BY DOING

We advocate learning to do a thing by doing it rather than by doing something else that is *assumed* to teach it. Learning to do A by doing A is a direct method of learning as opposed to learning B in order to do A, which is an indirect method. Examples of indirect methods are diagramming sentences in order to learn to speak or write better, or memorizing definitions of lists of words in order to read better. In both cases the first activity, B, is significantly different in kind from the second or target one, A. Furthermore, there is no evidence that learning B results in learning A. On the other hand, there is evidence from all sorts of human experience other than language that doing A leads to improving skill in A. A direct method of learning justifies *itself,* whereas an indirect method has to be *proved* effective. In language arts, indirect methods have not led to improved skills; they have only been proved to lead to the mastery of B or the indirect process itself.

Practice of the activities of speaking, writing, listening, performing, and reading is not only the means to the goal but also the goal itself. All five processes are goals, and yet each can be a means to the others. People can learn to write by talking, to read by listening, to spell by reading, and so on. Transference of this sort does occur; it is a way of learning A by practicing another A, but since both A's are goals in themselves, neither is *merely* a means to another end, as a B activity would be in the indirect-learning model presented above. It is precisely this fact of transference that justifies integrating all language activities with one another.

Speaking and writing are so much alike in process that for learning purposes they should be considered alternative modes of composition, both translating thought into language. Listening, performing, and reading likewise can be considered the same processes for learning purposes because in each, language is converted into perception and thought. The generality of the communication triangle presented in the first chapter illustrates the way in which certain activities are similar when considered as either sending or receiving. Similarly, the concepts of decoding and encoding help us see how reading and writing might both teach spelling, punctuation, word attack, or recognition, since these are the very things that constitute literacy, and literacy is the very stuff of both reading and writing, which are just reversed vectors of each other.

On the other hand, isolated words, sentences, or paragraphs have no such relationships to the main aims. The relation of a sentence to a piece of writing, for example, is that of part to whole. It remains to be proved that exercising with a part will teach the target activity of which it is a part.

The relations among performing, speaking, listening, reading, and writing are relations of equals, of whole to whole. Their differences are differences of either distance (speaking and writing) or of direction (reading and writing), which are important differences indeed, but they do not impair the learning of literacy, composition, or comprehension. Rather, they enhance this learning, for distance and direction are themselves dimensions of the learning that must be understood by varying the form of the activity. Indirect learning has no such justification.

PROOF OF THE METHODS

No school program can truthfully claim to be proved by scientific fact. It is impossible to control scientific experiments in school. Claims for this or that method or program that it produces a certain rise in test scores cannot be replicated and often fade within a year or two anyway. In "An Assessment of the Michigan Accountability System,"[1] the authors say, "Test results are not good measures of what is taught in school, strange as it may seem." Proof, then, of the effectiveness of methods must come from massive accumulation of experience in and out of school. This is really more objective and reliable anyway, because it distills greater quantities of evidence and distributes judgment over more assessors.

Traditional practices, especially of the indirect sort, have been tried for years by this test and found drastically wanting, as evidenced by the great discontent of the public, the declining literacy rate, and the decrease in general reading, writing, and thinking skills. The whole national school system has been the lab for this bit of experimentation. Direct learning, by doing, is so basic that evidence for it exists on every hand. Practice of target activities under conditions of awakened will, copious and various trials, and plentiful, relevant, nonthreatening feedback has been validated by centuries of successful learning in other areas, such as sports, arts, crafts, and government. And in the activity closest to reading and writing—speaking—we have the best evidence of all for the approach advocated in this book. We all learned to talk this way.

THE DIRECTION FOR THE FUTURE

Change is considered risky and radical, but when traditional approaches have clearly failed, it is riskier *not* to change, to cling to proven failures. Furthermore, the kind of change proposed through this curriculum could be characterized as reactionary rather than radical. Individual programs, different working parties doing different things at the same time, kids teaching kids, nongraded heterogeneity— these all went on in the one-room schoolhouse. Such "innovations" would in fact be a return to an

[1] Ernest R. House, Wendell Rivers, and Daniel L. Stufflebeam, "An Assessment of the Michigan Accountability System," *Phi Delta Kappan,* June 1974, 668.

earlier American tradition. It is a great irony that learning should have got so misshapen that the old tried-and-true methods appear new and risky while newer and failing methods are considered safe and traditional.

Maximum accessibility, logging and counseling, coaching and consulting, small-group process, total immersion, trial-and-error-with-feedback, and learning by doing—all work together to turn around the school's institutional problem of numbers. They make the three *I*'s possible (not to mention the three Rs!). They convert a curse to a blessing. The large numbers and the individual variation that teachers usually despair of can further the very goals that these factors seem to impede. But it is necessary to jettison negative attitudes that have arisen from frustration. One is the notion that basic skills and individual creativity stand in opposition so that you have to choose one or the other. Actually, nothing is more certain than that you will never get one without the other. "Basics first, frills later" needlessly splits schools and communities into warring camps. Basics are whole, human things within which basic skills flourish. Personal will is no frill.

The classroom should be a microcosm of what is most positive about America—its diversity and flexibility. The hybrid strength that comes from continual synthesis seems to be humanity's chief adaptation now for survival in a very rapidly changing world. The youth of the nation that serves as the growing edge of that world culture cannot afford to be hung up at a rudimentary level of language development by unnecessary problems. There are simply too many other things that schools have got to start teaching that teachers don't now have time for because of the inefficiency in teaching basic language skills. This curriculum is meant to overcome this inefficiency and to get on to the more sophisticated symbol usage that the future will require of children of the last quarter of the twentieth century.

An ancient Chinese doctor is supposed to have said: "There is only one diagnosis—congestion— and only one remedy—circulation." This applies remarkably well not only to problems of digestive, pulmonary, cardiovascular, glandular, and nervous systems, but also to vocabulary, spelling, grammar, reading comprehension, and composition.

A classroom in which the student-centered curriculum we are advocating is in full swing may resemble classrooms that are implementing other current methods of organization. Before we explain just how to set up a student-centered classroom, let us look at how the approach described in this book is like certain other similar ones.

Current educational trends

Some trends—classroom learning centers, elective courses, and contracts —have been preparing for the student-centered approach and have made as much headway as they have, no doubt, because many researchers see the necessity of arranging for students to take different paths toward the same goals. As steppingstones, all three of these trends are useful, but teachers need to take them to their logical conclusions. As for multiage groupings and team teaching, they may or may not support this approach. Programmed learning looks like individualizing, as we said on page 29, but actually flies in the face of the kind of student interaction and structuring of one's own learning that we are presenting. On the other hand, open education is a trend that very closely resembles our approach.

LEARNING CENTERS

A *learning center* is a station learners go to that has directions posted and materials stocked for carrying out alone or as a small group some learning activity without teacher guidance. The choice and the self-direction make learning centers valuable for moving a curriculum toward individualization and for freeing the teacher to coach, counsel, and consult. Depending on the nature of the activities the teacher is letting students choose among, however, learning centers may limit the range of activities because they are limited by space. The average classroom can hold only about twelve to twenty such stations along with all else the room must contain, whereas a fully individualized classroom should offer a couple of hundred activities. The idea of learning centers is excellent, but in order to ensure a very wide range of activity choices, it must be extended and supplemented. A major way is to put directions on activity cards and to cross-reference these to other materials. Or activity cards may be combined with learning centers, the latter being one good way to ease students into an activity-card system.

ELECTIVE COURSES

Electives also introduce some choice, permitting students to follow interests and assume some responsibility for their own education. They are a stepping-stone to individualization, but carrying them to their logical conclusion would remove several drawbacks. Electives still suffer from the old notion of bound-aries—of putting a special group off by themselves with a certain teacher at a certain time and place. An individualized language classroom com-prises at any moment a number of instant electives, since exactly this situa-tion results when different working parties choose their own activities. Whereas an elective course has an arbitrary time length set in advance by school or departmental policy, projects chosen within a general class may start and stop when appropriate. Electives are limited to what a given faculty can undertake and divide up among themselves, but students should not be limited to faculty specialties or talents. Teachers do not have to know all about an area students want to explore; what they should do is help students to find materials and sources and perhaps outside experts for the pursuit of virtually any sort of language-related interest.

It is highly desirable for students to rub elbows with those doing different projects in the same time and space, because many get interested in and learn about other activities that they would not have thought of or dared at first to choose. This cross-fertilization is too powerful to imagine until you have seen it at work. Finally, students going different ways need to do so within a framework of guidance that safeguards against fragmentation, imbalance, and serious omissions. It is far better to do this through weekly counseling by a language teacher who knows a student's work very well from having him in a general English class than through a remote course counselor or an abstract departmental "coverage" requirement. Many students have picked a shallow way through an elective system, avoiding some basic activities like writing, and failing to get a balanced education.

CONTRACTS

A contract is an agreement between a student and a teacher about individual work that the student is going to do. Whether the agreement is student-centered or teacher-centered depends very much on how a teacher sets it up. Contracting can be an effective way to individualize a classroom, especially for a teacher making the transition from a traditional teaching style into student decision-making. It is truly unfortunate, however, that the idea of working out with a student what he is to do next should take on the legal and commercial connotations associated with the word *contract*. After all, a student owes the teacher nothing. (From the legal and commercial point of view, it would more likely be the other way around!) Contracting may imply that the work is not something a student would want to do anyway for intrinsic learning reasons, or it may be used by some teachers to induce guilt or anxiety in students so that they will do some task that otherwise they would be unable to summon motivation for. Sometimes contracts may be noth-

ing more than district or departmental behavioral objectives assigned to students entirely by the teacher's decisions.

Contracting should be just a way of counseling students about their work on the basis of what they have done, want to do, and need to do. In this vein a contract is a statement of what the learner aims to do and of the plans he has worked out with the teacher for achieving his aim. This formalization of a counseling session seems to help some students and teachers understand and remember more definitely what the learner is going to try to do and how he is going to go about it. It may include the setting of a schedule or deadline and may make younger or less independent students feel that they are still being told what to do when they are really being helped toward self-reliance.

MULTIAGE GROUPINGS

If multiage groupings—or nongradedness—are instituted to achieve greater diversity among students, then they are consistent with this approach. We suspect, however, that multiage groupings have frequently been used to facilitate homogeneous grouping across grades. Used in this way, they will, of course, fail to exploit the interaction of individuals who are different and will lull teachers into a false notion that they have students whose "abilities" are the same and therefore who can all be expected to learn in the same way at the same time.

The great value of multiage grouping, a benefit widely demonstrated in the development of informal education in the British schools, is that learners grow best as they help or get help from students of different ages and abilities. They benefit by temporarily grouping with students who are different. They can also find learners who are like them in some ways or are well suited to work with them despite age differences. In other words, if it is to support this curriculum, nongradedness should foster maximum accessibility to other people.

TEAM TEACHING

This too may or may not support the kind of curriculum we are presenting. If team teaching is used as a way to divide up students or time blocks, it can inhibit rather than facilitate accessibility. If, on the other hand, team teaching is seen as a way for students to share the same teachers, it can be an excellent means for achieving maximum integration of both the subject matters and the processes of different disciplines. Naturally, the special abilities of different teachers are better used if they are made available to all students in a pool. This could occur if the teachers circulated among several classrooms of students during the same time period; if students were permitted to circulate over several classrooms during a given time period to locate a teacher; or even if students were allowed to carry out the same work partly in one teacher's class and partly in another's when the classes occur at different time periods. Youngsters writing song lyrics should be able to get help with the music from the music teacher without having to get special dispensation and go through red tape. The best ways to find a teacher are for the student to go from one room to another or to hail a teacher as he walks around. Another way is for teachers to permit interclass activities between classes meeting at different times.

OPEN EDUCATION

The trend that most closely resembles what we are advocating is open education. Like its counterpart in Britain, the "integrated day," this mode of classroom operation puts student choice at the center of the learning process. Valiant efforts toward open education have been made in recent years, but all too often the process has ended at the discussion stage for the very reason that strategies and methods for implementing the process were lacking. Though not derived from the open education movement, our curriculum parallels it in many ways and should lend support to those teachers trying to implement it. Open education seeks to achieve what we have termed *maximum accessibility* as a means toward individualizing, arranges for small working parties to pursue different things at the same time, fosters interaction, and promotes integration by breaking down rigid divisions between subjects. Both open education and this curriculum aim at a thoroughgoing humanistic individualization that so far has remained marginal in this country.

Individual sequencing of activities

To understand the processes of this curriculum, visualize a classroom where students are working in various small groups or alone. The small working parties are doing different activities at the same time with the aid of activity cards and other self-directing materials they have chosen. For example, the activities may be reading stories; reading a script aloud, each student taking the part of a different character; writing; reading their own writing to each other and getting feedback; listening to tapes; developing a group drama to be performed later for the class; talking about stories read earlier; playing language games; or making their own tape recordings. Each student selects among a wide range of activities and thus has a different set of experiences, though often he is choosing to work with others. With your counseling, he determines the sequence of his pursuits and keeps track of what he does. Because many different pathways lead to the same ends, all students do not need to cover the same material. Many different activities teach the same language arts skills. The precise routing makes little difference for the ultimate goal but makes a critical difference for the individual learner in how he reaches that goal.

It is hard to imagine how this operates until you have seen it. The routing is not haphazard, however, because students usually don't stay with something they know so well that it no longer interests them, nor do they choose an activity they are not yet ready to be successful at. When the learner controls what he does, being influenced rather than ordered, he feels positive and powerful. With that and a rich array of materials, one can do a lot. If the materials in the classroom attract and impel, reinforce and interrelate, students will be lured into using them.

How then does a student decide which activity to pursue? He may move into a project in any number of ways:

1. His own interest may prompt him to seek out the materials or directions that will enable him to do what he wants. If he does not already know where to find these, he looks or asks. Some materials may attract his eye, and he finds directions for using them attached to the materials.

2. Classmates may ask him to join in an activity someone else has already selected. In most classrooms there are some students who seem to lack self-direction, who "drift" from one thing to another. Simply because they are "not busy," these students are likely to be solicited by the more self-directing students to help with a project, drama, or game calling for another participant. In every classroom there are also students with special abilities, such as reading or drawing skills. These students might

frequently be chosen for the special contribution they can make, and they may, in effect, function as tutors for others while continuing to learn themselves. If picked at random or as friends, students may be introduced to activities they otherwise might not have thought of or have preferred. This is one safeguard against the limitation of personal choice.

3. A youngster may be introduced to an activity by seeing the product of another individual or group, something shared with the class. One of the values of audience sessions is that the spectators get ideas for activities they might enjoy. Every teacher knows the value of having charismatic classroom leaders pioneer into hitherto untried activities, providing a stimulus for others who might otherwise consider such activities "stupid" or "silly."

4. The classroom materials themselves should be cross-referenced to one another so that, for example, when a student finishes playing a card game he can choose, with the aid of optional routings printed on or attached to the game, another activity that is related to it.

5. A student may be counseled by you when he seems to need advice or guidance about what to do. See "A Logging and Counseling System" on page 29 in Chapter 2, Means, and page 423 in Chapter 21, Evaluating. Since you are free from the demanding role of directing the whole class at once, you can help match up learners with activities that seem a best next step for them. Your conferences can be in conjunction with evaluation sessions when students themselves are encouraged to assess what they have done and what types of activities they might move into. Whenever possible, give the learner a choice of what to do so he accepts as the norm that the responsibility of deciding is his own. Simply help him become aware of his options. Your goal is always to help a student become more "in charge" of his own learning. Of course, you must begin where the learner is, rooting your suggestions firmly in an acceptance and understanding of what he is interested in and what the limits of his awareness about the potential of language really are. At the same time your goal is to help him see how to break through those limits.

Small groups in the classroom

Except for whole-class sessions set aside for sharing projects, students are constantly interacting in subgroups, some formed for a short activity, some for a long-range project. Groups start and stop at different times. A student should get experience working alone, in small groups, in large groups, and in groups structured for different activities.

Small-group process is the matrix for all the activities in this curriculum—discussion, reading, dramatic play and interplay, writing for real purposes and audiences, and active, spontaneous response to both books and the writing of other students. Learning through group process starts in the home, goes on outside of school, continues into college, and will continue throughout the learners' lives, for it is the main means of "adult education." Youngsters learn to use language in natural social exchanges. Group learning fosters motivation and confidence leading to independence and initiative. As students regularly work together, they mature in their capacity to share responsibility for the welfare of the group, little by little making your direction and consultation less necessary to their ongoing activities. Your response, however, will always be needed.

WAYS OF FORMING GROUPS

Groups may be formed most simply by allowing students to choose each other, especially if they are unused to small-group process. In most classes there will be students for whom working together with a friend is more important than choosing any particular activity, and this fact has to be respected while you also influence them to venture with new partners. When students choose each other, there is the problem of unselected people. Instead of putting all these together into a new group, it is usually advisable to approach the groups already formed and ask them if they will work with one more person. The unselected youngster might be given a special role such as that of observer or recorder for a group. Students with social or emotional difficulties would not usually be grouped together by themselves but distributed over groups that can deal with them. Dividing a class into small groups minimizes the power of emotionally ill or disruptive individuals who might otherwise impede the functioning of an entire class. In small groups they are more likely to find a socially valued role and thereby get the attention and feedback they seek. You are also freer to deal with them.

Normally, groups would be forming on different bases and at different times. The following guidelines may be helpful for setting up working parties:

1. Put together an effective working party that contains people with different abilities and skills (including leadership qualities) for the activity they're setting out to do.
2. Put students together randomly when they happen to be looking for partners or small groups at the same time or want to do the same activity.
3. Deliberately mix students of different temperaments or complementary personality traits or of different backgrounds in such a way that they can better utilize the human resources by meshing together in certain effective ways or by having to talk across differences in outlook, background, or dialect.
4. Put together long-range groups whose members might become over a period of weeks or months a semipermanent writing workshop in which strong trust grows and members become familiar with each other's needs, habits, and ways of expression.

A student may well be in more than one kind of group in the same time period. For example, one of the groups, such as a newspaper editing and proof-reading group or a writing workshop, might not need to meet every day and can run concurrently with a student's other activities. One of your responsibilities is to pick up on and counsel a student who has competing responsibilities that preclude his effective participation in any one group.

GROUP SIZE

The number of persons a group needs depends largely on the activity they pursue. Experienced students will often know how to group themselves, but you may need to help some groups determine an appropriate size, given their activity or purpose.

For most discussions or panels, around five is an ideal number, providing enough variety of viewpoint to stimulate interaction but at the same time minimizing the risk of shy individuals dropping out because the group is too large. Five can be a good size for some writing groups if the kind of discourse they are writing is fairly short, like limericks or fables, but since some kinds of writing take more time and thought for group members to examine each other's compositions, size might better be limited to around three members. For improvising, except for the crowd-scene type, it is best to keep the

groups down to two or three so that interaction is tight and close and the action keeps moving and does not get confused, or you risk dropouts. Very experienced improvisors, however, can take a larger group and still be effective.

Some students may need to work into the small-group process by participating in pairs or trios first. The classic problems of groups—inattention and dropping out, interrupting each other, not responding pertinently, not sticking to the subject, becoming distracted—are sharply reduced when only two or three are interacting. The price, of course, is a loss of ideas and stimulation afforded by more minds; but if the priority is getting inexperienced kids into small-group process, follow a general principle of starting small and building up. The larger the group, the greater the risk of a shy learner withdrawing and a more aggressive one taking over most of the responsibility. If you circulate and listen in, you can often head off this tendency. When students are choosing an activity card and forming up a working party for it, check out group size according to what you know about how groups function and about the maturity of your students.

Flexible Groups

At times, it may be necessary to leave the size of a group open to change in the middle of an activity. For example, let's say that five youngsters have finished reading a story and have decided to act it out, but the drama calls for only three players. What do the others do? Perhaps they can be involved in production as set designers, musicians, or creators of special effects; or they may decide to leave the others and do something else.

Sometimes you may decide to combine two groups of two or three into a larger discussion group. This technique is one way to get boys and girls to work together in the same group but still provide each student with at least one other person with whom he wants to work.

If a small group seems to lose focus or energy—to "go weak" on an activity—you may join them and help them see how to proceed. Sometimes the solution will be to break the group down into smaller units, at least temporarily. Avoid shifting individuals from group to group as this may cause bad feeling, and the new group may regard another individual as an intruder.

Dynamics of Small Groups

Generally, each group size up to six has a different basic dynamic that makes it appropriate for certain tasks. Two people are good for activities that might also be done alone but that some youngsters are not yet ready to do by themselves; or for two-part reading aloud together, as with riddles, brain teasers, and other question-and-answer texts. Sometimes a highly skilled independent worker chooses to work and share with only one other person.

Trios are better than pairs for discussion, but they tend to pit two against one, which is a problem unless used as a way to balance a strong personality. They also provide a minimal number for vocal interaction among students who would "fall apart" in a larger group. Groups of four tend to split into pairs, and this dichotomizing often hurts discussion by polarizing it and pitting two against two, but it fits well many game formats and other tasks not featuring discussion. A group of five allows many internal relationships to develop, and it also provides maximum stimulation without being so large that it is inefficient.

DURATION OF GROUPS

Ad hoc or temporary task forces can operate for as long as they need to in order to accomplish their group-defined task. These groups might stay together as short a time period as ten minutes or as long as several weeks. How long a group stays together depends on the nature of the task and the maturity of the participants. After finishing one activity together, a group may choose to do another together, or perhaps some members will so choose but others will decide to do something else or to join another working party. Short-term random groups have the advantage of getting students used to working with all sorts of people, providing the communication challenge of differences. Long-term groups have the advantage of both developing a deeper familiarity of members with each other and experiencing the kinds of group dynamics that can evolve only over a long period of time.

Fostering small-group process

Many teachers feel that it won't work just to start in but that they should train groups one at a time until they are ready to do without the teacher. This seems reasonable, but in practice what usually happens—and this is the classic problem of inaugurating small-group process—is that in the very effort to show youngsters how it's done, the teacher only succeeds in making them more teacher-centered. As both adult and teacher you are a powerful figure; and though this varies a lot with age and personality, most youngsters have great difficulty not talking to and for you if you are in their group, even if you try to take only an overseer role. Those learners who most need initiation into peer interaction are the ones who will focus most on you.

The only way to avoid this trap is to assume nothing, play it by ear, and be ready to operate in any of several different ways. If beginning groups are limited to two or three members, you may never have any trouble—if the task, topic, or whatever really involves the group. You may cruise by rather than sit in; that is, just stand near and listen in. This way your presence may not interfere with the interplay among group members but still enable you to make observations or suggestions about their functioning. If you feel a group *must* have you because you have tried other ways unsuccessfully, then your sitting in may be worth the risk, especially if you play a role expressly aimed at weaning them from you. That is, you would do best to refrain from leading the group in the usual sense or trying to get ideas across; rather you should attempt to model a typical-member kind of participation.

Setting a model for good interaction means listening alertly and responding pertinently. This often means questioning a previous speaker, but it is critical that the questions be honest efforts to have the speaker clarify or elaborate what he has said, *not* answer-pulling to get him to say something you may have thought of. Remember that the goal here is purely to initiate a process of exchanging and expatiating between learners.

You may find that with very young children you have little difficulty getting them to operate in small groups. With older students who have been in school a long time but have never participated in small groups you may have more problems. These students need to be thoroughly persuaded that small-group process is a serious and staple part of the whole language curriculum and not just a chance to fool around. They will not believe this for a while and may therefore test your seriousness sometimes by seeming not to make it work. If you take over the leadership, you only delay the day they can operate by themselves.

Activity cards with directions for group projects are actually substitute teachers, providing the information and directions students need to launch their activities together. If you have not operated in an activity card system, you may not be able to imagine how much cards can structure and maintain group process. As soon as possible you want the learners to be able to take off from the activity card alone without your help. If you set a pattern of reading activity-card directions to a group or telling them how to interpret the directions when this is not necessary, you have trapped yourself into a "teaching" role that will swamp small-group process because you will never have time to lead several small groups at the same time.

A PLAY-IT-BY-EAR TEACHING STYLE

Your job is not to lead small groups but rather to move from group to group and help set up, observe, counsel, assist, suggest strategies or materials, tutor, trouble-shoot, join as a participant in a game, respond, evaluate, and so on. If a group of students is having trouble using a tape recorder, you either show them how to do it or ask an experienced youngster to do so; if another group of students is arguing over the rules of a game, you suggest that one of them reread the rules to the others, but you do not arbitrate the dispute lest you make the group even more dependent on you. If, as you watch a group doing an improvisation, you notice that one of the participants seems to misunderstand the point of the scene, you may ask the others how they see his role. At a later time you may discuss the improvised selection with him to find the elements that interfered with his comprehension or recollection of the reading. What you do not do is to set yourself up as sole problem-solver. You note problems, keep your own record of the kinds of experiences each student is having, and then guide him into new areas when he is ready. Your goal is to keep the process alive, not necessarily to intervene to improve the end products that the students are working on.

This play-it-by-ear teaching style is an involved interaction with students that takes energy, patience, interpersonal awareness, and courage. When you respond rather than direct, the students are the active users of language. On the other hand, the minute you set yourself up as the explainer or presenter of information students need, you make the written matter useless to the students. They are thrust into the role of the uninitiated—the persons who passively receive from you what you know. The invigorating and bracing task of choosing and responding for themselves is lost. Anything they read will be explained by you, so why read it? Your formal explainer stance has constituted a barrier rather than a doorway to information. This is no less true if you have arranged for small-group process herein described and are using the most student-centered of materials. Your stance is what makes the difference, and if you go from group to group as an explainer and director, small-group process will be inhibited, not facilitated.

When working spontaneously you may not look as organized as a teacher who is working with a lesson plan for the whole class that casts him as the star. As you play it by ear, what you know best you may be deliberately keeping to yourself while you patiently watch the learner falter toward his own discovery.

This is not to imply that you will never impose your will; you will, whenever behavior by a student becomes not only unproductive but destructive of the responsible group process that is the goal for all. A student should not have the choice of whether or not he can destroy the work of another, whether the destruction be physical (tearing up a display or messing up a learning area) or psychological (booing or ridiculing a presentation by another child or group). Teachers set limits of acceptable behavior in student-centered classrooms just as they do in any classrooms. This function is not inconsistent with student-centering.

Small-group process is *no panacea* for behavior problems. If you have trouble establishing your own authority, keeping a calm and friendly manner, or regularly working with students without shouting at or arguing with them, this program will not alleviate your problems. If, on the other hand, you welcome honest interaction with students and respect their values and judgments, this curriculum will work well for you. The limits of behavior that you set should not preclude honest verbal interaction. Teachers who demand polite but phony behavior may plant seeds of rebellion or withdrawal. Communication is most valuable when honest; honest communication is not always pleasant. To avoid it because of this fact is to buy an outward conformity and pretense of "working together" with the currency of honest motivation and expression of feeling. This is seldom worth the price in the classroom or outside it.

AIDES

In building toward student independence even as you give help, you can use teacher aides, other paraprofessionals, parents, older students, or student teachers in a natural and relaxed way never before possible in teacher-centered classes. Since the role of the teacher aide is not to share the spotlight with you but to join small working parties and perhaps help them read activity directions, play a card game, listen to an oral reading, watch an improvisation, or write down a dictated story, any adult with minimum reading skills and a warm, responsive personality will be an asset in a student-centered classroom. Some elderly people make excellent aides. The aide or student teacher does not have to nervously "take over the class" and face that supreme challenge of establishing authority so fraught with disaster and so dreaded by inexperienced paraprofessionals or student teachers. Instead, those adjunct teachers supplement your advisory role by focusing on student needs, sharing their insights with you, and eventually perhaps coaching individuals in reading or spelling and making helpful suggestions to drama or writing groups.

There is no way to get around the hard fact that when immature, egocentric learners are working on different projects, their needs for adult response can often exceed what any one teacher can provide at any one time. Activity cards and learning centers allow aides to enter at any time and start helping right away, without your having to stop and explain activities and give directions, though you will want to lay down guidelines for aides helping with coaching and counseling. Figure 3.1 on page 54 illustrates what a teacher or aide may do, with time freed by self-directing materials.

If the teacher and aide can be part of a teacher team that can occasionally meet and discuss problems of small-group process, they will find this extremely valuable. Talking over what has happened in your class in groups of various types, or discussing audio and video tapes of group operations will help you get insights on how to improve the processes. See "Interaction Analysis" on page 420.

Materials and equipment

A classroom needs the widest possible array of materials and activities for students to choose among. Such variety becomes possible in an individualized, small-group curriculum because only a few copies of each book title are needed and only one copy of each game or activity card. Also, teachers can share the same materials by letting the learners go from one room to another or to a common center to get what they need. Materials should initiate and facilitate every language-related activity you and coworkers can imagine that your students might have the ability and interest to do and benefit from. Cross-reference materials to each other if they are not already made that way, so that each item mentions as optional routing at least two other items from which a student can choose a follow-up activity.

You may inherit, of course, traditional textbook series and workbooks that are inappropriate for individualization and generally inefficient—basal readers, language and composition textbooks, literature series, speller series, and other books for which most school districts have special adoption categories. For literacy mastery, you need other materials besides books—bimedia materials and manipulables. For composition, the only materials needed are stimulants and activity directions, both of which are far more effective when not in book form. Composition textbooks, furthermore, convert writing into an informational subject to be read about, because they rely on a concepts-precepts approach. For literature, stock all the books you can get hold of but ignore the pedagogical paraphernalia contained in textbook readers—the questions at the end of selections, the thematic organization, the definitions of literary types, and the terminology of literary criticism. Some series that are bad from this standpoint still contain good or excellent selections, so just consider them as miscellaneous anthologies that your students can browse through or be directed to for certain reading material.

The drawbacks of these textbook series arise from the misconceptions of language arts discussed in Chapter 1, Basic Concepts, and from the bias of the whole educational-industrial complex toward books as the medium of learning even when they are patently less practical than other sorts of materials. If you do not have the money or the choice to

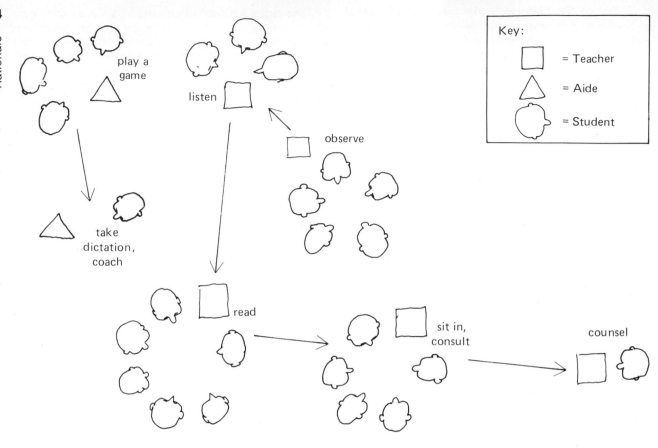

play a
game

listen

observe

take
dictation,
coach

read

sit in,
consult

counsel

Key:

□ = Teacher

△ = Aide

= Student

FIGURE 3.1 ROLES OF THE TEACHER OR AIDE

Source: Adapted from James Moffett *Interaction,* Level 3 Teacher's Guide, Houghton Mifflin, Boston, 1973, p. 30.

obtain the materials we recommend, you can often salvage parts of these series. Buried in some composition texts, for example, may be good photos for writing stimulants and directions to the student for good writing activities that you can put onto activity cards.

FOUR BROAD LEVELS

Among the many traits that make textbooks and workbooks undesirable is that they are often broken down into yearly grades. The students in any one classroom span a far greater range of difficulty and interest than can be included in materials designed to cover one year and to cover it at the standardized pace of an "average" student. The only way to individualize is to give each class access to far more

materials than any one student can work through in a year. This means that students live with the same materials for several years' running. The breakdown must not be by the year but by a much larger time unit such as a block of years constituting a growth phase, and even then the units will have to overlap. So aside from the fact that no third- or tenth-grade class is standard enough to fit manufacturers' designations, even materials not designated by grades are inadequate if calculated to last only a year.

We suggest breaking down materials and activities for the whole of elementary and secondary school into four levels, each of which spans several years. Place your own class within one of these levels, and put together for it a set of materials covering the whole range of capacity and interests that may arise during those years for any student in the class.

1. During this "primary" or "infant school" period of age five or six to seven or eight, the child
   - is still closely tied to parents and home.
   - is not much allied with peer group yet.
   - is still developing small-muscle control and perceptual discrimination.
   - is very given to communicating with the body.
   - thinks very concretely.

2. During this prepubic "elementary" period of age seven or eight to eleven or twelve, the child
   - is rather well socialized and fairly independent of home.
   - still complies with adults but has consolidated a peer group.
   - acquires main physical and mental competencies.
   - has strong drive to get good at what the society values.
   - is most suggestible and receptive to others' ideas and influences, hence most highly absorbed in reading.
   - objectifies thought more into significant imagery and into concepts.

3. During this period of initial adolescence of age twelve and thirteen to fifteen or sixteen or later, the youth
   - vacillates between lingering dependence on adults and real independence, creating a second version of "the terrible twos," or self-contradictory, "irrational" behavior.
   - attaches tightly to the peer group and follows its criteria, treading a delicate way between peer-group conformity and compliance with adult demands.
   - shows interest in the wider world beyond immediate locality.
   - develops sexual powers and feelings.
   - uses abstract logic disjunct from physical operations and from imagery.

4. During this period of virtual adulthood, which only some youths reach while still in high school, the student
   - still values highly his peer group, but his peer group more nearly coincides with the general adult public.
   - reaches full physical growth.
   - focuses seriously on mate and career selection.
   - possesses full human mental capacity but suffers the limitations in thought of early conditioning and of inexperience *as* an adult.

The breakdown of materials and activities into four levels gives maximum assurance that students will go as far each year as they are truly able. At the same time, less advanced students will not be constantly humiliated or have their confidence eroded by being expected to move along with "the others." All students have access to at least three times the range of difficulty and variety found in a conventional classroom and so will be able to find both their level of development and the particular points of entry into speaking, reading, and writing that are necessary for them.

Another extremely important advantage of the broad four-level breakdown is the fact that it can accommodate the basic human need to rehearse what one has learned and to circle back to it from time to time. One can see this easily in youngsters who like to reread the same book, months or years apart, or in other students who seem to have learned something but who resist rather strenuously the efforts of adults to tear them away and push them onto some other, newer learning. There is always a real reason why youngsters want to rehearse learning or mark time or circle back. While on occasion it may be something negative (which can be brought out and overcome), usually the desire to return to a book already read or an activity already performed means that the learner needs to strengthen his confidence or reassure himself of his mastery. Sometimes he is simply tired of challenge and feels the need for the security of doing something he knows how to do well.

At other times the learner may be engaging in an entirely new type of process or reading a kind of literature he has never touched before, in which case he may ease himself into it by choosing material that in a conventional classroom might be considered "beneath his reading level." With so many options, a student may at any point experiment— may challenge himself with very difficult material without having to wait until he has "graduated" into it. If he finds it too hard, he can pull back. There isn't the sense of failure that comes when a student is moved lock-step with his class to the next assignment before he is ready. You should expect that your students will rotate among materials in a somewhat spiral fashion, reading parts of certain books one year, then returning to read other more challenging parts later on. They can circle, advance, return to touch base, and venture forth once more.

Each class set of materials should comprise

reading matter, recordings of some reading selections, language games, activity directions on cards and posters, photos and films, media equipment, and raw materials for making things. Students will create a second set of books, recordings, games, activity cards, photos, and films using the media equipment and raw materials, so the supply of classroom materials is continually augmented with student-produced ones. No school can afford all the materials needed if schooling is really successful. The students will feel the need to make or find things they don't have. For example, once students are really hooked on books, no classroom library will be adequate. The stock has to be replenished by their own writing and by bringing in other reading matter.

Although multimedia materials and a rich classroom environment are desirable, a resourceful teacher can do a great part of what is suggested in this curriculum with just paper, pencils, old literature textbooks, magazines, newspapers, a few paperbacks, and books borrowed from a library. If there is a cassette recorder, the teacher and students can make their own recordings. Often parents can contribute games and magazines with pictures; local businesses are good sources of reams of paper blank on one side, outdated and inexpensive photographic paper, free cardboard boxes, wallpaper samples, yard-goods remnants, and so on. Activity cards made by you can direct students to make new materials—games, booklets, recordings, directions for projects, props, photographs, films, posters, or other activity cards.

The minimum requirements for this curriculum are a set of books and teacher- or student-produced activity cards. As a matter of fact, most of the activities presented in this book were first created by teachers and students in actual classrooms. They were written onto cards that could be used over and over. The following specification of materials may serve as a guide for the optimum, which you may approach by some combination of buying, making do with old stuff, making things yourself, getting students to make them—as *well* as begging and borrowing. (The *Interaction* program was meant to be such a roundup, as complete as cost allows.)

BOOKS AND PERIODICALS

The reading matter should be thought of as a classroom library and can consist of any sort of books or periodicals—textbook anthologies, trade books, paperbacks, and magazines loaned or donated from outside, and books made by students. Since reading is individualized as soon as children start to read at all, single copies are fine. Five or six copies of any one title usually suffice for members of a small group to discuss, act out, or otherwise share reading material. As a general strategy in procuring books, trade off number of copies for number of titles so long as enough multiple copies of a few titles exist to sustain small-group process. Class sets of one title are a waste and a contradiction of individualization.

Try for a variety of reading matter that covers all kinds of students of your class's level and all areas of discourse listed on page 24 and dealt with chapter by chapter in Part Four, Developmental Reading, Speaking, and Writing. In representing types like fables, reportage, and haiku, or topics like sports, mystery, and science fiction, try to do so by books that contain nothing but the one type or topic. This not only teaches literary forms by example but can be used to organize the classroom library. Especially, it facilitates using a certain kind of reading, such as myths, in conjunction with writing, acting, and other activities with myths, because an activity card can refer to the book, which can be taken out and used for the activity without removing other matter from circulation, as happens when myths, say, are bound into an omnibus reader. Indeed, the more modular all the materials, the more things you and the students can efficiently do with them.

Organize the library, with the help of your students perhaps, according to categories that will themselves teach as class members go about searching and replacing books, and that will still be practical for the actual collection of books and periodicals you have on hand. Mixed anthologies make this hard, of course, and if students are to search among them for types and topics, you and they will have to make a list of individual selections and write in next to each title the location of the book where it may be found. Actually, working out and maintaining with your students a cataloguing and placement system may be a kind of blessing, because they will learn a lot about books and libraries from this. To some extent you can mesh your class system with that of the school and local libraries as a lead to the use of those. Subscribing to periodicals or taking in donations of them is a fine way for students to become acquainted with the kinds of magazines and newspapers available and to learn how to store and index them.

For suggestions about criteria of selection and for other descriptions of reading matter, see "The Classroom Library," starting on page 142 in Chapter 7, Reading.

RECORDINGS

Recordings are allotted a large role in this curriculum for reasons explained on page 131 regarding general reading, on page 201 for beginning reading and writing, and on page 240 for punctuation. Professional recordings serve also as a model for the performing activities described in Chapter 6, Performing Texts.

Buying Recordings

Some commercial reading programs now sell recordings of texts along with the texts. Such a combination is certainly a major factor to consider in selecting books. Though more expensive than making your own recordings, commercial ones may offer the advantages that professional readers can bring to the rendering of a text. Look for whether:

1. The reading matter itself is truly first-rate.
2. The oral interpretation is appropriate for the kind of text and really interesting *to youngsters* (and avoids the conventional saccharine and condescending tone).
3. The reading is deliberate enough for learners to follow without spoiling absorption.
4. The stress, pausing, and intonation indicate punctuation clearly.
5. Different voices are used for variety and identification.
6. Different dialects are represented.
7. Texts indicate which selections are recorded.
8. A recorded signal indicates bottom of page in texts for small children.
9. Format facilitates searching for a cassette and for a selection on a cassette.

Take time, perhaps with other teachers, to listen to a lot of the recordings and to deliberate over their value for teaching both literacy and literature and also for the performing of texts.

Making Recordings

The advantages are saving money (though the cost of even blank tapes can mount up) and having recordings for texts you prefer but that are not commercially recorded. Also, making the recordings can be a fine learning activity for students. For making your own recordings, follow the nine guidelines just enumerated for commercial recordings. As much as you can, get students to make recordings. See Chapter 6, Performing Texts, for procedures in rehearsing readings. Knowing in advance that their rehearsed reading can be added to the classroom listening library provides excellent motivation for students to work up and tape a reading of some selection from the classroom book library. You want to have your students contributing to the stock of recordings even if you buy commercial recordings, or if you and other adults are also making recordings. (Some of what they record will be student writing.) Explain that certain standards of clarity and expression have to be met in recording for the classroom listening library, because other students will be using their work to learn from.

Mixing professional, adult, and student recordings makes sense. Not all selections in a commercial program of any size can be recorded, which leaves a real need for local supplementation, and besides, a classroom should always have additional texts, acquired a number of ways, other than the main reading program. Professional renditions will set standards, while student renditions will foster identification and encourage other class members to try recording. To get especially talented adult readers, recruit among school staff members, parents, and actors in local theater groups. Recording is a fine chance for community people to help schools.

Set up together the classroom book library and listening library so that it is easy and attractive for students to browse among both or find a selection in either when given a title. Label the tapes and organize them by whatever system you organize the books—alphabetically within types or topics, and so on. Or, if tape-browsing doesn't seem likely for your students, attach tape to book, or place in the book a simple directive for locating the tape. Books that have selections recorded might be flagged some way on the outside so that nonreaders will know which to consider. Near the books and tapes should be inviting chairs or carpets and the tape player. A small group might listen and look at once.

Headphones help keep down noise, but bookcases, screens, and carpets all baffle sound too.

ACTIVITY CARDS

One reason for not putting activity directions in books is that books lock them into one order, whereas most language arts activities should be unsequenced so that individuals can put together their own sequences according to need. Also, if not posted already at an activity center, directions should be separately portable and in a durable form so that they can be carried to and propped along-side materials one needs. An activity card or poster serves as a focal and reference point for a working party. Students can look back at it from time to time, and you or an aide can stop and help without having to ask what the party is doing or having to recall what the directions are. Activity cards array the tasks that a student may choose from in addition to games or other materials bearing their own directions. Through cross-referencing, they lead students to books, recordings, games, and other materials either needed for the activity or suggested as follow-up.

These activity charts or cards can be either commercially produced or made by students and teachers. Cardboard laminated with plastic is durable, but if that is too expensive, any five-by-seven-inch or larger cards will do. Posters work well for younger children. Each activity card, poster, or chart could list the materials needed for the project, the number of people who can do this at one time (ranging from a single individual to a whole class), and the step-by-step procedure. Illustrations are highly desirable and often necessary for the activity. Cards can be grouped by categories such as "Bookmaking," "Finding Out," or "Acting Out," and different categories placed in different parts of the classroom. Please study the sample activity cards in Figure 3.2 (pages 60-61) before reading on.

Activity cards replace teacher-presented lessons and conventional textbooks in language, composition, spelling, and so on. They may be thought of as pages from a teacher's manual or lesson plans—enlarged, made more durable, and laid out where students can get at them directly without having to wait for the teacher to translate them. These suggested activities are the single most important means of individualizing a classroom, because they enable different students to choose from a wide range of activities at any given moment. These cards also

free you to work closely with individuals and small groups. Activity cards are the major stimuli for composition. Most commonly, a written task is embedded in an attractive small-group social process, thereby providing an easy pathway from familiar oral activity into writing. The cards also provide *reasons* for reading in each of the nine areas of discourse. We suggest that you set up an activity so that it can be usefully repeated by the same party. If each card covers an activity so specific that it can't be usefully repeated, you will have thousands of cards.

Activity cards or posters present a problem, of course, to nonreaders or poor readers, but they are also a prime kind of reading matter and a way to learn to read. They are of high interest because they are geared to action and tell students how to run their environment. You or an aide or classmate can read the directions sometimes to real beginners, pointing to words as you read. Then later the illustrations, the action cues, the student's memory of the first reading, and the collaboration of partners will enable him to figure out the words again. Members of a working party can usually read directions together even if they could not alone, and parties who cannot should ask for help, but give only minimal help, so that students will try for themselves as much as is feasible.

GAMES

Some games require no special materials and can be conveyed on an activity card alone, but some require card decks, game boards, or other manipulable gear. Many of these latter games teach phonics* (see page 206), grammar* (see page 464), vocabulary* (see page 468), and logic* (see page 469). Many "creative" or educational toy companies put out good learning games. Browse in toy stores, look through ads in teaching magazines, and look in toy catalogues (some of which apply to secondary students also), because school marketing itself does not get many games into the classroom.

The problem with games in schools is that too many parents, teachers, and administrators still do not understand how serious very entertaining games can be. Powerful prejudices keep game materials, for example, from being adopted or otherwise allotted funds in many localities. The terrible difficulties schools have had with literacy make it seem so grim that the idea of learning it through games may seem fanciful and frivolous. Books are at least sober —we all know that—and even in an age of great technological advances, widespread application of game theory, and sophistication about media, many people still don't believe learning can occur without books. But the fact is that if you analyze virtually any old folk game, you can see how it may have originated as a learning practice for some skill. Public schools were not established until very recent times, before which much important learning of skills and knowledge was embodied in games for both children and adults. Professional educators have a deep obligation to use in schools whatever works well, to fit the right means to the right tasks, even if this requires the self-discipline to overcome their own prejudice and the patient courage to deal with that of other people. The importance of games for language arts is that they permit about the only practice with word particles, single words, and single sentences that does not violate communication principles. Other games are based on principles of classification, serialization, and inference that directly exercise logical faculties.

CONSUMABLE BOOKLETS

Be very wary of most consumable booklets. The traditional workbooks build in many misguided approaches that should be abandoned or replaced. Other discussions in this book should make clear which ones to avoid. Booklets of crossword puzzles*, word-find mazes, and other language games are fine. Very helpful also for some students are comics with empty balloons to fill in with dialogue* and open-ended read-and-write booklets designed to stimulate writing*. See descriptions on pages 157 and 277.

LITERACY MATERIALS

For beginning or weak readers appropriate phonics materials may be needed. See Part Three, Literacy —"The Basic Skills," for an extended discussion of these. Manipulable letters and other physical word-making materials are important. Look-say stimuli such as card games, bingo, or other word-matching activities should be available. To develop manuscript and cursive writing skills, appropriate models and letters to trace are useful.

EQUIPMENT

If you teach beginning or remedial reading and writing, you may want some kind of phonoviewer or sound film-loop projector or television cartridge player for presenting the sound-symbol system of English. See Chapter 10, An Integrated Literacy Program. At all age levels photographs, slides, and movies provide a provocative stimulus to speak, read, and write. Empty cassettes with recorders are useful for developing oral language skills. When possible, a movie camera and a videotaper should be on hand. Inexpensive or homemade still cameras can be used by children to make photographs for caption or narrative writing. Sometimes people in the community can be called on to help supply media materials and ideas and also to work with students using them. See "Media" in Appendix A, for more on this.

Since most student writing is for sharing with peers and others, you should be prepared to duplicate it for distribution. If the school has access to a ditto machine, or, better yet, if one can be brought to the classroom where students may be taught how to use it, the problem is solved inexpensively. Even very young children can be taught how to make ditto masters, and the process provides a natural pressure for accurate lettering and spelling. A Thermofax copying machine that makes ditto masters directly from pages written by students is a great boon.

A raised platform for drama production is useful but not essential. A puppet theater and materials for making puppets are desirable in elementary classes. A corner for house or store play is good in the early years. Students can make many drama props themselves.

Art materials of all sorts need to be available at all levels. Painting easels, finger and other paints, colored paper, tagboard, porous pens, and poster paper are popular materials. In general, the wider the array of art media, the better. Not only art supplies but art objects—paintings, sculpture, designs —all can stimulate language production. Materials for physically making and binding books—cardboard, dry mount, and cloth—provide a powerful motive for writing.

CARE, STORAGE, AND DISTRIBUTION

Good organization before the students arrive in the class is one of the keys to smooth group process. Materials and equipment are often expensive, and their value needs to be appreciated by students. One way to build this appreciation is to have the materials easily accessible and clearly displayed in an orderly way. Most students need to be guided in caring for and storing materials. Games composed of

Source: From James Moffett *Interaction*, Level 2 Activity Cards, in the "Making Up" category, Houghton Mifflin, Boston, 1973.

number of students

title of activity

category of activity

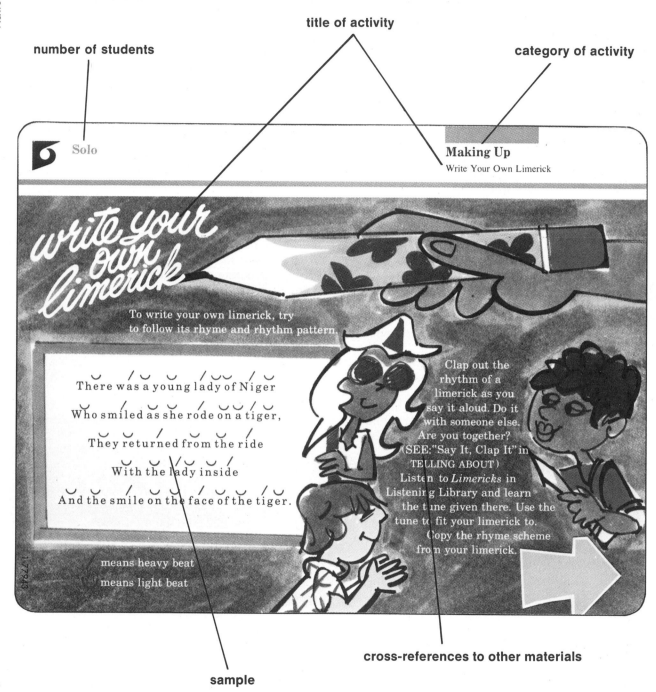

sample

cross-references to other materials

directions

Read the limerick begun below—
Using the limerick rules, see if you can finish
it by finding your own 4th and 5th lines.

> An astronaut flying in space
> was always forgetting his place.
> Was it page sixty-eight
>
> –
>
> –

Put in the beat marks where they sound right.

Write a whole limerick yourself now.

Make a collection of limericks
you write as well as those by others.
Sing them. Tape them in funny or
surprising voices, as on the
Limerick recording.

Put a limerick or
two on a display
board and invite
others to put up
theirs.

Organize
a limerick
contest.

Try: "Story Poems"
and "New Words,
Old Tune" in
MAKING UP

follow-up options

many small pieces must be put back before the students leave a game center, recorders stored where they won't fall, booklets closed with flat markers rather than left open or bent backwards. Because other learners are frustrated when one student fails to care for materials, these orderly details are important. Too many of the alternative schools organized in recent years have faltered in part because no one wanted to hamper the students' freedom long enough to impose reasonable standards of housekeeping. An orderly arrangement of materials and time set aside for students to care for and put them away is not only consistent with, but a prerequisite to, a workable class where students have real choices and freedom to pursue their learning tasks at their own pace and in their own way.

You must decide before the students ever arrive just which decisions the learners will have and which ones they will not, such as a decision as to whether or not to clean up after their projects. Individualized learning makes great demands on you as a teacher because you have to be wholly alive and responsive all day. Your task may well become overwhelming if you also have to spend time each day rearranging and cleaning up the classroom. This responsibility simply must be the learners'.

You need to decide how materials are to be stored so students can find and return them to their storage spaces without having to move a great deal of other equipment. In a student-centered classroom it is inappropriate to have supplies in a teacher's desk or closet to be distributed by you alone, to have materials such as books issued permanently to specific students and thus unavailable for others, or to have you spending a great deal of time appointing monitors to distribute materials. Small-group process gets hopelessly bogged down if students have to stand in line for materials they need. One of the advantages of having small groups of learners doing different things at the same time is that each child can go to the appropriate center and get what he needs; supplies don't have to be passed out to a whole class at once, and thus fewer materials of any one kind are needed.

Each student will need a place to store his personal supplies and work-in-progress, but this need not be a desk. A cubbyhole, bin, plastic washbasin, or cardboard box stored along a wall or on a shelf will do. Younger children who do not carry their own paper and pencils into the classroom will need a place to find these and other supplies. Tracking charts of student progress and folders of written and other completed work can be alphabetized and stored in a box or file where students and teachers can find them.

Appropriate work areas

In a school where a teacher is free to arrange furniture, you can set up and equip a learning environment providing areas for several different types of activity—reading, listening to recordings, acting out, writing, playing games, or watching films or slides. An area does not have to be a "corner"; there are not enough of these in any classroom. An area is simply a place where a small group of students can find the materials they need and a place to work on a certain type of activity. In some schools you will be limited to what you can do with furniture that has to remain stationary. However, even bolted-down desks or the floor can be used for card games. In schools where you are free to rearrange furniture, you can move bookcases perpendicular to the wall thus dividing space for small group work and gaining for your students added display space by using the backs of the bookcases as bulletin boards. One teacher set up a small teacher's office as a quiet reading room, covering a child's crib mattress with furry material and putting it on the floor with pillows and a lamp above to make an attractive "couch" for individual or small-group reading.

In the early elementary years classrooms may look very much like well-equipped preschool or kindergarten classes with a variety of centers set up and labeled with appropriate signs. Activity cards to be used at each center can best be stored there. Signs listing the rules for keeping the center efficiently organized and orderly are useful for students of all ages. Students can refine the classroom order by making up filing systems for such things as cassettes or making up lists of directions for the use of various items of equipment, such as filmstrip viewers. Starting by following the suggestions the teacher posts at various learning centers, students can proceed to move beyond these into a full-scale activity card system whereby each student gets an idea for a way to proceed, engages in an activity, refines it according to his own purposes, writes up directions for what he has done, and leaves these directions on an activity card for another student to follow later. A chart where a youngster can sign up or hang his name tag for a particular activity at a certain time might be hung near each set of materials. This is especially helpful when the number doing a particular thing at any one time has to be limited. Also, a list of youngsters who have already done a particular activity can be useful to students who might want to call on them for help.

At all grade levels you may find the following types of areas convenient for small-group work. As you read these descriptions, you need to keep in mind how you might vary them in order to meet your own students' needs and work within the limitations of the school. Each classroom will look different, but most of these suggestions can be implemented to some degree. For a sample arrangement, see Figure 3.3.

READING AREA

This is a place where a large part of the classroom library is displayed and where students can sit comfortably to read. This can be a depressed floor area, a grouping of comfortable chairs or a couch, a round table with chairs, or if nothing else, a group of school desks. For individual reading or other work, study carrels are desirable. Large refrigerator cartons can serve if equipped with desks, lamps, and even curtains for privacy.

LISTENING AREA

Here are stored a record player or cassette recorder —ideally one equipped with earphones—and discs or cassettes. Youngsters can bring to this area books that are recorded and watch the words as they listen to the recordings.

DRAMA AREA

Here a small group of students can improvise or act out a text in preparation for performance. A school hallway or empty classroom will serve well; a screened-off area within the class is good, and a raised platform with either empty floor space or room for chairs around it when an audience is needed is the best of all. Simple costumes or props are welcome but not necessary accoutrements. Much can be done with only brightly colored squares of cloth that students can use in imaginative ways. The drama center in a primary classroom may well be the same as the playhouse center since so much of the acting out at that age calls for household props anyway. A puppet theater or roll-a-story box could be part of the drama center. Of course, for play performances there is nothing better than a full-blown stage with lights and curtains.

ART AND SCIENCE AREA

A classroom sink can serve as center of both an art and science area. A great many language activities from kindergarten through high school are stimulated and followed up by illustration and other graphic arts. Dramatic productions are enhanced with sets, masks, and costumes; and books, newspapers, and magazines students produce can be illustrated using various art media. A sink, counter or table space, and storage space for a wide range of art supplies are very desirable in secondary as well as elementary classrooms.

Unless the school has a room or rooms equipped as laboratories, each classroom needs a place where various scientific experiments may be set up, watched closely, and recorded in a variety of ways. The area can have growing plants, live animals, and other physical objects for observation, manipulation, and experimentation. A table where classroom museums and collections can be assembled is important.

GAME AREA

Here language and logic games of all sorts are stored. If space is a problem, the clutter of furniture can be avoided here and a carpet used instead. Students often prefer playing on the floor anyway. All that is needed is a place to keep the games. If holes are made in game boards, they can be hung and their parts stored in hanging bags beside them. Since many of the basic skills materials recommended in this book are games and manipulables, this game area might be combined with what is often called a skills center or reading lab.

FILM AREA

If the classroom can be provided with a movie or slide projector and films, an area for viewing these should be set up. This need be nothing more elaborate than a small expanse of white wall and a cart for the projectors.

Here is one way to arrange a student-centered classroom. The screen can be removed to arrange for audience sessions with the stage as a focus. Games may be played on the floor or at a table.

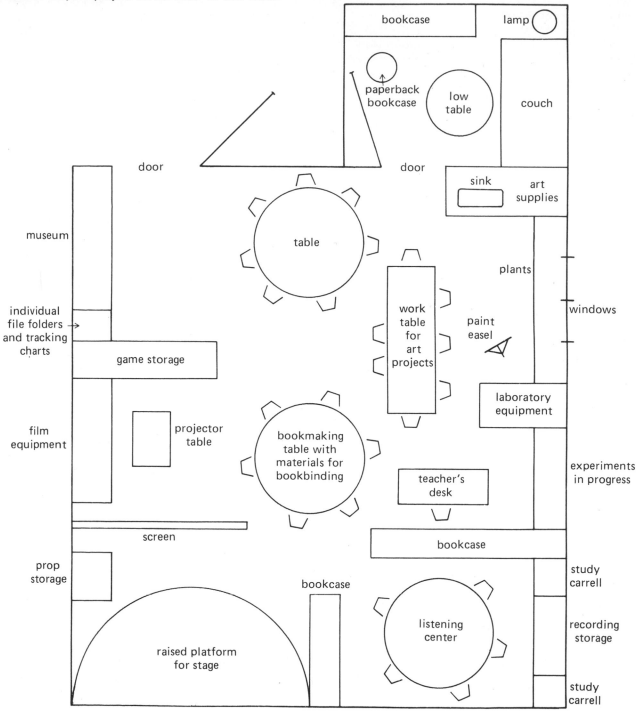

TRAVELING LEARNING CENTERS

In many schools, especially at the junior and senior high school level, teachers do not have a stationary teaching room where they can set up places for students to do small-group work. They move from room to room. If you are one of these, you will have to rely on activity cards to play a much greater part in creating different learning centers quickly. You may have cards and other materials in boxes or large envelopes, each container complete with all that the students need for a set of activities of a specific type. These can be put in various spots throughout the room. Tape recorders and books can be kept on a rolling cart to go from room to room with the teacher. A prop basket, art materials, or other items not used every day may be stored in a place where students who need them can get them to bring to the class. More reliance will be placed on students to bring in their own materials and quickly set up their own work centers. Also, students will have to store more of the "in-process" work such as books they are making or newspaper copy in their lockers rather than in the classroom. If bulletin board space is limited or unavailable, halls and display cases can be used.

POD, RESOURCE CENTER, AND OTHER CROSS-SCHOOL ARRANGEMENTS

An increasing number of school buildings are being constructed to facilitate a flow of students from one area to another rather than to separate students into different classrooms all opening onto a hallway. These pod or open-space arrangements can be equipped to provide for maximum accessibility to adults, other students, and materials. This curriculum is ideally suited for such physical arrangements. Because teachers, like students, differ in their interests, areas of expertise, and styles of leadership, cross-school movement by both learners and teachers is highly desirable in any setting.

Scheduling will become a big problem unless you let the learners themselves assume some responsibility here. For example, when a small group needs an art teacher, they can leave their names in her mailbox or on a special hook beside her desk and tell her what they need and when they will be assembled for work. Ideally, learners should feel that all adults are there to confer with, and they can learn how to arrange to share the teachers in an orderly way, making their own appointments, and

sequencing their own consultations in relation to the job they have chosen to do. In high school, ad hoc pooling of learners with teachers would have the effect of providing "instant electives." The goal at all levels should be to minimize the scheduling problems and maximize the flexibility for each student.

SHARING AREA

At all grade levels there needs to be one large space where all the students can gather as an audience for a presentation—film, slides, drama, interpretive reading or whatever. This could be in or out of the classroom. Better in, if out discourages arranging for it. If students get used to gathering on a carpet in a part of the room that is used for small-group work at other times, moving of furniture can be minimized and arranging for performances simplified. In one small classroom a student committee made a map showing where each desk was to be moved to make room for an audience. These sessions for presenting something to the whole class can be scheduled at a regular time or arranged impromptu whenever a small group or individual has something ready to present.

An emphasis on small-group process by no means excludes whole-class activities. Flexible dynamics are the key, after all—from solo to pair to small-group to whole-class. Figure 3.4 illustrates some of the whole-class activities and the arrangements they call for.

Because all writing is to be shared, you need to plan for ample display space for student writings, charts, graphs, art products, museums, and so on. When the bulletin board and wall space is used up, students can string up cord and hang their displays from the ceiling. We won't discourage you now with the problems you may have with the janitor!

Getting started

Gearing to the level of your students, explain at the beginning of the year the gist of how the class will operate and briefly why. To older students say that some activities that they expect may be missing, but that the new ones are meant to teach the same things, only better (vocal interaction and certain card games, for example, rather than formal grammatical analysis). Take them on a tour of the different areas and show materials so that they know generally what the resources are and how activities

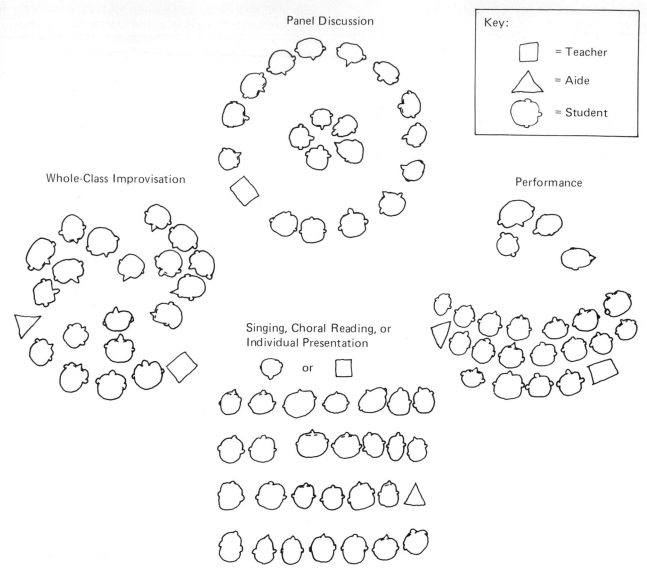

Panel Discussion

Whole-Class Improvisation

Performance

Singing, Choral Reading, or
Individual Presentation

FIGURE 3.4 CLASSROOM ARRANGEMENTS FOR WHOLE-CLASS ACTIVITIES

Source: From James Moffett *Interaction,* Level 3 Teacher's Guide, Houghton Mifflin, Boston, 1973, p. 31.

are organized. Give them some time to poke around while you just observe who gravitates to what and how they react—joyously or fearfully, for example—to the environment you have prepared.

People not used to this sort of curriculum need to ease into it—both teacher and students. This means some degree of compromise at first. One general way of easing in is to limit for a while the quantity of materials, activities, and choices put into play,

then to open up gradually to full volume and variety. Another is to direct students more about what to do. This is tricky, because if you do not direct them toward self-reliance, they will get in or remain in dependent habits. A third general way is to do more large-group or whole-class work until students get to know the materials and the system. Try not to assume too much dependence and to compromise more than you need to, and be sure to allow for much individual variation in youngsters' readiness to operate this way. We hope the following list will serve usefully as a set of strategies that you can combine in your own way.

• Plunge in with the full system of individualizing and small groups but make available for a while only a subset of the materials and activities so that students are not overwhelmed by choice nor you by counseling. The subset might comprise some of the more basic and repeatable activities and those materials most attractive to your students.

• Set up five or six groups such that each student knows or chooses some but not all of the other members; then give each group an activity card to do in a class period and to describe afterwards to the other groups. In this way, working parties will do different things at the same time, share their products afterward, and acquaint everyone with all the activity cards. Next, each group can choose an activity from those the other groups did. Repeat this procedure with activity cards that entail the use of books, recordings, and other materials to which they are cross-referenced. Then repeat with games and let each group tell the others what their game is like. Next, groups choose a book or card and, when finished, follow one of its routings to other materials.

• Set up several groups and give each a number of activity cards to look over and choose one from. After they have finished, ask each group to tell and show what they did, then list the activities and let anyone sign up for any activity or choose from among the unselected cards. Attach to each card the names of those who did it the first round so that the second crew can consult with them.

• Do one activity at a time with the whole class, projecting the activity card as you read from it and referring to it frequently as students do the steps together. Use the occasion to point out all the typical features of the card as we did on pages 60 and 61. After several activities have accumulated, let students choose one of those and help them to form up working parties. Sample some of the books one at a time for the whole class by projecting the selected pages on an opaque projector while you read aloud or play a recording of the text they are looking at. Then again let students choose among these and form groups. Next, project two or three activity cards for reading follow-up or let them choose from routings at the end of the book, if it has any.

• If you have a lot of aides, form up small working parties and let the aides help each group to choose an activity, book, or game and to counsel them, when finished, about following optional routing or otherwise choosing a follow-up. Keep the same groups constant for a while; then have aides help students change groups or go solo as they choose a new activity.

• Allow students who appear self-reliant to choose and form their own working parties while you take others aside a group at a time to stick with them through enough activities that they get the idea and can start working without you. Teach a group to play a game; then replace yourself in that group with a student new to the game and let old hands teach him, until eventually most of the class knows most of the games. This will start some dependent children to doing group work without you. In the meantime, ask the more self-reliant ones to lead a couple or so of the others through an activity they have already done.

However you start, you want to make sure, of course, that individuals start some time to do different things, to work alone sometimes, and to work with a variety of classmates. Use the launching process to give all students experience with all components—books, activity cards or areas, recordings, games, and other materials. Start the logging and counseling system as soon as students have got beyond merely getting acquainted with the materials and the system and are starting to individualize enough so that you can differentiate their different experience records and their future needs.

The secret is to avoid paralyzing students with too much choice or too difficult choices and yet keep them making decisions. Some teachers without activity cards simply write on the board a list of activities that students can choose from. Even if the choice is only one out of two or three alternatives, that is a beginning and would threaten only the most extreme cases. Another chronic sort of immaturity that must be dealt with is the tendency to lump all activity cards together and say, "I've *done* activity cards," as if the similarity in the form of the directions means that the activities themselves are alike. Such a student will flip through cards and be unable to find anything to do or go through activities like popcorn. Try to head off such problems by making this student slow down and really pay attention. His growth will consist of learning to discriminate differences, so help him do this with the cards themselves by taking him or his group step by step through at least a couple of cards so that he dwells on the steps and options and cross-references along the way. He needs to do a few activities with such loving care, and so enjoy the fruits of his labors, that thereafter he understands that each activity feels different.

Newcomers to school have no more problems working in a curriculum of individual choice and small-group process than they would starting off in any other kind of curriculum, whereas the longer students have been in school, the harder it is for them to make *any* significant change. If you teach older students, you can expect some to resent and resist being asked to do things differently. They need to be reassured that all this new stuff is really "English" and that it isn't just your personal "trip."

They may test your own conviction and steadfastness about it. Some will not thank you for requiring them to make decisions and to rouse out of their familiar school stupor. But if while understanding the reluctance to have the game changed on them midway, you hold a steady course toward their personal responsibility and deep involvement with their own learning, you will see resurrections as gratifying as anything a teacher can experience.[1]

---

[1] The *English Through Interaction* film "A Pupil-Centered Classroom" shows first graders operating in the manner described in this chapter but without special materials. Its counterpart at the secondary level, "A Student-Centered Language Arts Curriculum," shows tenth graders operating this way with the *Interaction* materials, which are especially designed for it.

PART TWO

basic processes

4

talking & listening

This chapter covers task talk and topic talk, considering the learner as both speaker and listener. Chapter 5, Dramatic Inventing, covers other spontaneous talk, of a fictitious sort.

Listening is developed by many activities in this curriculum—by playing games, listening to recordings, viewing films and slide-tapes, serving as audience for other students' performances, participating in writing workshops, and so on—but talking and improvising differ from these in calling for an immediate response, in making the listener and speaker constantly change roles. Having something to listen *to* is not all that is needed for exercising listening skill. The learner must have something to listen *for*—a good reason to listen. Purely as audience for a performance, he may respond only inwardly, and inner responses may be enough, for the moment. But listening often prepares for action, either now or later. And when the listener takes outward action right away as the result of what he hears—as in conversing and improvising—he learns to attend carefully and respond relevantly so that on those occasions when he does *not* take action immediately, his inner responses are better.

To listen well one must truly *receive,* not jam the channel by transmitting at the same time. On the other hand, the perpetual sound issuing from electronic media and urban bustle numb many children to the point of simply tuning out sound. Classroom experience calling for responses by listeners acts as a corrective. The reason we do not isolate the treatment of listening in this book is that activities that *entail* attention, as a preparation for action of one's own, teach listening skills far better than special drills focusing on listening alone.

When peer conversation is valued, it can be practiced and given form and validity, providing learning of a sort that seldom occurs in casual out-of-school conversation. Because conversing requires the listener to comprehend and the speaker to compose, it is a good way to get voluminous, timely, and well-motivated practice in getting and giving meaning. This process transfers readily to reading and writing. Comprehending ideas, relations, and styles presented orally helps a person understand these in a book. Listening skill is the foundation for reading skill at all ability levels of comprehension, just as talking skill is the foundation for writing skill at all levels of composition.

Because constant practice and good interaction are the best teachers of speaking and listening, peer talk in small groups should be a staple learning activity for all grades, allotted a large amount of time in this curriculum. Students will need teachers committed to making small-group process work, a sense of seriousness about the experience, and repeated opportunities to see what can be achieved through this means. Students new to small-group talk may have difficulty at first, no matter what their age. They may need adult presence, but not necessarily adult leadership, in order to focus so that serious and involved participation will occur. Otherwise, they may get disgusted with an unproductive or silly interchange and thus not want to repeat the process.

When talk teaches, the speakers are picking up ideas and developing them —substantiating, qualifying, and elaborating; building on, amending, and varying each other's sentences, statements, and images. All these are part of an external social process that each member of the group gradually internalizes as a personal thought process: he begins to think in the ways that the group talks. Not only does he take unto himself the vocabulary, usage, and syntax of others and synthesize new creations out of their various styles, points of view, and attitudes, he also structures his thinking into mental operations resembling those of the group interactions. Good discussions by groups build toward good thinking by individuals. See pages 32 and 465 for examples of thinking as an internalized conversation.

Your job is to establish those small-group interactions that, when internalized by individuals, will most enhance the growth of thought and speech. For students the purposes for conversing need not, and in most cases, should not be to improve their listening and speaking skills, but rather to solve a problem, explore a topic, play a game, complete a group-chosen project, and so on. Although the most mature may appreciate the skills for their own sake, most youngsters need more practical and satisfying goals. Conversing activities should allow for this. The practices presented in this chapter aim to accommodate both their motivation and yours.

A major issue for the teacher concerns how much to lead and how much to leave alone. The more you lead, the more those who have most to learn about conversing will speak to and for you only and be lost without you. And yet without some guidance from you, many youngsters will simply fall back on old habits and learn little. So you will have to play by ear as we suggested for all small-group process. Do allow, however, for the tremendous help that activity cards and other self-directing materials can afford in focusing and structuring group talk when you aren't there, especially to the extent that talk interweaves with other activities. The more talk shifts from tasks to topics, the more difference the activity directions themselves make in setting up and guiding good conversation. Please keep this in mind as you read the following activities. You play your part in peer talk as much when you make or choose activity directions as when you influence their talk directly while it is occurring.

Task talk

An easy way to gain interactive experience toward topic discussion arises naturally as a by-product of doing other things. This "incidental" talk actually teaches a great deal about vocal exchange and often exercises thought and speech as much as discussion having only that goal.

GIVING DIRECTIONS

Whenever a small group of students is collaborating, a natural situation exists for giving and taking directions. The classroom should provide repeated opportunities for a member who knows how to do something to share what he knows with others, giving them step-by-step instructions. For example, a knowledgeable student might show others how to work audiovisual equipment, how to make an art project, how to set up a science experiment, how to work a puzzle, or how to play a game. Giving directions poses one of the most challenging kinds of communication problems. See Chapter 17, Directions.

PROJECTS

Any committee work calls for discussion—deciding on goals, determining who is to do what, suggesting how each person is to go about his job, and arranging a time schedule so members can get together to work or share ideas. Rather than focusing on the process of discussion itself, a group of inexperienced learners can focus on a concrete goal, such as making a magnet; planning a white-elephant, bake, or other sale; setting up a laboratory for research; organizing a class party; or writing a group poem or song. Putting together a collection such as a museum, collage, bulletin board display, or anthology involves selecting, ordering, and arranging items—a process that provides an important stimulus for task-oriented language. A group-produced TV show, radio broadcast, slide presentation, newspaper, book, literary magazine, encyclopedia with pictures, or catalogue of information, such as a telephone or address book or consumer's guide, requires considerable planning plus later maintenance talk. Older learners can coordinate their research projects on a topic such as organic gardening so that a variety of information-gathering techniques like interviews, case studies, surveys, eyewitness reporting, library research, experiments, or journals might all contribute to final information-sharing, significant discussion, and a full-scale report. Such multigroup projects entail frequent exchanges to coordinate, compare, and otherwise interrelate.

Disagreements arise during play of card and board games because players interpret or remember rules differently, so players have to remind each other, discuss their varying understanding of the rules, and refer to the rules as evidence. Then some games deliberately call for a refinement of the rules, and this refinement is one of the strongest motivational forces for meaningful, concentrated discussion. Most folk games such as charades, Password, "Twenty Questions," or "Button, Button, Who's Got the Button?" are known by different rules, and one of the valuable problems players face is agreeing on some version or compromise of versions of how to play.

BRAINSTORMING

Much task talk centers on solving practical problems. Brainstorming is a technique for bringing forth from a group a great number of different and stimulating ideas for solving a problem. Instead of weighing ideas as they come up, members "storm their brains" for further possibilities, withholding judgment for the sake of amassing as many solutions to the problem as they can think of.

A recorder who can write fast should put all suggestions on a blackboard or large paper where the group can see them. Each participant sitting in a semicircle can call out his thought or suggestion as soon as there is an opening, and the recorder should write it immediately. Participants should be encouraged to give off-the-top-of-the-head, rapid-fire, unreflective thoughts, not apologizing for the wildness or silliness of any suggestion. Evaluation will come later. No analysis, editorial comment, or negative criticism of anyone else's ideas should be allowed. At this point, the more ideas the better. If a participant is reminded of something by another person's suggestion, he can add to it or take off from it in any way he likes. The recorder puts down everything, whether sensible or "silly." Keep the time for brainstorming short—six to ten minutes.

The goal is for the group to concentrate fully and build toward as intense an experience as possible.

Wait a while for the evaluation of the ideas—a day or so for older students. The next session can begin with the recorder reading all the ideas, and the group can list them in categories, such as:

- Good ideas that can be tried right away
- Long-range projects or projects that need some rethinking
- Unusable ideas

At this point, but not before, critical thinking is allowed. It is in this second session that a true discussion occurs. The wealth of suggestions must be organized, reflected upon, and evaluated.

Any problem of interest to the students is good grist for a brainstorming session. Problems may be personal ones, broad social issues, subjects related to other studies in school, or ways to do something:

- Ways to improve the classroom
- Uses for a hundred left-over milk cartons
- Materials to do rubbings of
- Ways to reduce litter or pollution
- Things to do for class assembly
- Ways to extend the readership of student writing outside the classroom
- Ways to overcome poverty
- The best way to make friends
- Ways to cut down on drug abuse
- Ways to avoid the problem of unwanted children
- A good place to go on a class trip
- Inventions that are needed
- Kinds of machines that could be made

Older students may want to refine their consideration of a problem by spreading it over five brainstorming sessions. Using this analytic structure, they can list in columns their responses to what amounts to an alternating series of three positive and two negative questions. Each session deals with only one question.

1	2	3	4	5
What is the issue, problem, or goal?	What has caused this situation or keeps us from accomplishing our goal?	What might we do to solve the problem or reach our goal?	Is there anything that will prevent us from doing this?	What should be our next steps?

Brainstorming quickly generates a number of ideas to look at, and it builds facility and confidence in the participants. Licensed to think rapidly without fear of criticism and to freely take off from the ideas of others, students develop their imaginations and have an experience that will serve them in good stead when faced with improvising or writing tasks that call for quick-witted facility and abundance of concrete ideas. The critique and ordering of the suggestions that follow the initial brainstorming session provides valuable experience in analytical thinking and categorizing. Brainstorming was first used by industry as a strategy for overcoming obstacles, solving difficulties, or finding more efficient or effective production procedures. It minimizes conflict among group members and builds communal commitment to the ideas generated. The participants tend to view all suggestions as the property of the group as a whole.

Like all other small-group activities, brainstorming becomes internalized as an individual process. As a problem-solving tool focused on a question, it combines task talk with topic talk.

Topic talk

Topic talk exists primarily to deal with a relatively disembodied subject and is not merely a by-product. Just as students may bridge into it by means of problem-solving that focuses on a well-defined question, they may also use talk about physically present objects or pictures as a concrete approach to the abstractness of topic discussion.

SHOW-AND-TELL

A natural avenue to topic discussion is show-and-tell —if listeners are encouraged to participate and if the group is small (three to six). Although a fine transition from play prattle to speech modified for an audience, talking while showing belongs no more to small children than to adults, who do exactly this when they demonstrate appliances, explain exhibits, chat about a "conversation piece" on the coffee table, or use a skeleton to teach anatomy. As a school practice, talking while showing is very sound at all ages, but you should avoid ticking off one child after another around a big circle. Large groups intimidate those who would most benefit from show-and-tell and discourage questioning, without which the main value is lost.

The main value for the undeveloped child, whose utterances tend to be short, egocentric, and undetailed, is to encourage elaboration. For the more developed learner, small-group, interactive show-and-tell gives help in stating and organizing better the material he has begun to elaborate. The trick for both is to use dialogue to make the monologue fuller and better verbalized for an audience. This experience will improve written composition without pen ever touching paper.

Show-and-tell allows the speaker to take off from a familiar or loved object that he feels and knows more about than his audience does and that, by prompting ideas, helps him to find and sustain and maybe even organize a subject. But the very personal nature of the object challenges his egocentricity, for outsiders do not share his feeling and knowledge.

As he talks, he can look at the object and do things with it, which will suggest things to say, but his speech continuity can no longer merely follow the blow-by-blow continuity of his play. What he does is tell stories about how he got the object or what he has done with it, or give information about what it is and how it works. His speech diverges somewhat from the ongoing action, becomes more independent, and necessarily becomes more abstract. While pointing, he inevitably talks of some things that cannot be pointed to—the past, feelings, purpose, function, and certain general information. But to be an important kind of learning, show-and-tell must be taken seriously and shaped into a distinct process, good for any age.

Procedure

Help students to come together in groups small enough to reduce shyness, encourage interaction, permit listeners to examine the object, and afford everyone a long enough turn without tiring the group.

Second, make clear through activity directions and by your own example that listeners should question and otherwise contribute. Let the shower-teller begin as he will. When he has said all that initially occurs to him, encourage the audience by solicitation and example to ask natural questions: "When did they give it to you?" "What happened to the wing there?" "What's the red button for?" "What do you do if you want to get the money out again?" "Where do you keep it?" "Do you let your brother use it?" These questions call for anecdote, explanation, and information. They are asked at first by the teacher and then by the other listeners as the other children grasp the possibilities. Questions act as prompts that replace play as a cue for ideas. They cause the speaker to sustain his subject, to elaborate. With experience, the speaker will be more likely to anticipate questions and supply more information and background without waiting for questions to prompt him. Thus the monologue element will grow. A lot of practice in oral explaining can even influence the order of information—the mentioning of certain items first so that later items will be clearer. Questioning, then, is fixed as part of the procedure. It allows the needs of the audience to influence the speaker.

Another sort of contribution from the audience can take the form of similar anecdotes or information summoned to mind in the listeners by what the speaker is saying. A good session can, in fact, produce a spontaneous "thematic unit" in this way that could lead to making a booklet or display together featuring the similar objects and experiences.

Third, the talk might be given a special focus by directions asking students to bring, on different occasions, something that (1) has a good story behind it, (2) they made or grew, (3) means a great deal to them, or (4) moves or works in a funny or interesting way. This is how show-and-tell can become something of a composition assignment. Narrative, exposition, and explanation are emphasized in turn by calling for objects that are associated with memories or that have certain characteristics. Some objects were acquired in an interesting way or have had curious things happen to them; thereby hangs a tale (narrative), so the speaker must grapple with sequence and continuity. Drawings and paintings that he has done also contain stories—fantasies or real events—that the artist can relate as he explains his picture. If the object was made or grown, the speaker tells how he made or grew it (description of a process). If it has special meaning for him, he tells how he feels about it (personal essay). Gadgets, machines, and other apparatus elicit explanation of purpose and operation.

Show-and-tell will grow as students grow, for their meaningful objects will reflect their maturing amusements, crafts, thoughts, and feelings. But for older students, call show-and-tell by another name to avoid suggesting that they are continuing a childish activity. Talking while displaying or pointing can blend with activities described in Chapter 13, Labels and Captions, which features the coordination of words with things. Thus, show-and-tell not only parallels the juxtaposition of words and pictures in a book but also prepares for such monologues as slide-show and film narrations, display and exhibit explanations, and sales pitches, all of which are activities to make available also. The television talk-show format provides a more mature-seeming occasion for older students to combine show-and-tell presentation with other dialogue. To make the connection with composition, show-and-tell activity directions should include an option to write up the presentation, after it has benefited from audience interaction, and print it with others as a book of memories or how-to-do-it or whatever.[1]

SMALL-GROUP DISCUSSION

By *discussing* we mean small-group peer interaction, not what has generally been called class discussion, which is rarely a real discussion. The sheer size of a classroom of students precludes enough attention, participation, and interaction—three essentials for authentic discussion. The teacher invariably talks too much to maintain continuity. You may resort to prompting by questions to keep the discussion going, and most class members may play only the very restricted role of answering these questions, unless they are the loquacious few who carry on long monologues. Serial exchanges between you and pupil A, then you and pupil B, and so on, may serve another purpose, such as checking information or soliciting scattered opinions, but this is not discussion.

Small-group discussion should be a staple, significant classroom process given the same kind of importance and commitment afforded reading or writing activities. It is through discussing that learners face the challenge of defining, clarifying, qualifying, elaborating, analyzing, and ordering experiences, concepts, opinions, or ideas, thereby developing their thinking and verbalizing skills for reading and writing.

Your basic job as the teacher is to create a good climate for talk and listening to talk—relaxed but concentrated. The tone must be warm and friendly but not saccharine. You do not have to revere children's words; but everything you do should show you truly value what your students say. You need to

---

[1] See the *English Through Interaction* film, "Do and Talk," for illustrations of show-and-tell and task talk in an elementary classroom; it also shows examples of listeners contributing similar experiences.

see to it that the class members do the same. The art of conversing is a profound cognitive activity, not an application of etiquette like practicing table manners. Mere polite attention is not what you are aiming for; relevant, perceptive, insightful response to one another is.

You may also have to train at least some of your students to talk seriously to peers in small groups. Your hardest job will probably be to determine who needs training and how best to help those without keeping them dependent on you. See pages 49 to 53 in Chapter 3, Organization and Materials, for general suggestions on forming and running groups. It is very easy to conclude erroneously that students don't know how to converse seriously and effectively, for many factors other than discussion ability can account for bad discussion. Aside from the number and personalities of the particular people forming the group, a major factor is motivation, which depends in turn on the nature of the topic, how it was chosen, why the topic is to be discussed in the first place, whether results will lead to other action, and what sort of warm-up, if any, preceded discussion.

Embedded Discussion

Until students have become seasoned discussants in small-group peer situations, they may not see the value of discussion for its own sake. To choose first to discuss, then to choose a topic—with no warm-up or follow-up activities—presupposes either very sophisticated students or those who have got used to peer discussion and know that it has its own rewards. Before reaching this point, most students of any age will need for the discussion to be built into a continuity of other activities leading in and out of it. We do not mean now merely task talk that accompanies other action, for it has no crystallized topic.

An example of topic talk embedded in a bigger framework would be a discussion of what the moral of a fable should be after reading it without its moral. Activity directions say to listen to the fable, write down on a slip of paper what one thinks the moral should be, then read aloud the morals, then either choose one or fashion a new one that group members think expresses the moral best, and finally reveal what the author's moral was. The activity really just specifies how to go about discussing the meaning of a reading selection—or a fellow member's composition—in a way pertinent to the

fable form. In effect, the activity directions provide warm-up and follow-up for discussion and program the structure of it to the extent, for example, of forcing a summary statement—the moral the group members choose. The suspense about what the author's moral is adds interest to their own discussion, but the main motivation is to compare their understandings of the fable and to work out one that fits best. Revealing the author's moral may, in fact, provoke further discussion if they disagree with it, as they are especially likely to do when a classmate has written the fable.

As this example suggests, various activities embedding discussion within other language arts activities may well set up successful discussion so that training may not be necessary. Discussion of both reading selections and each other's writing will often naturally center on topics. Members of a group reading a selection in common can follow the practice on page 138 of writing down questions or other topics and bringing these to the discussion. And whenever a writing-workshop group tries to work out just what the main idea of a member's composition is, there automatically is a good discussion focus (what the author's "theme" was). Both reading and writing serve well also in furnishing knowledge common to all group members to which they can refer for evidence, namely, the text itself.

Other good embedded discussions occur when activity directions say to write personal problems (real or made-up) as a letter to an advice column, then to answer these for each other. That is, each writes a problem letter and after these are read one at a time in the group, the members discuss the best solution to each. For one thing, this activity solicits topics from students themselves, and this ensures a lot of motivation. If directions say for all to draft a response or to write separate responses, these can be posted along with the problem letter for other students to read and judge. Part Four, Developmental Reading, Speaking, and Writing, contains many other examples of interwoven reading, speaking, writing, drawing, or viewing photos, and so on, that frame well and structure small-group discussion of topics. Before you conclude that certain of your students don't know *how* to discuss, try some such activities.[2]

[2] For examples of both embedded and other topic discussion, see the secondary-level film "Small-Group Discussion" in the *English Through Interaction* series. See "Discussing Topics" for discussion at the elementary level.

Letting students discuss topics drawn from social studies, science, or math will extend the possibilities of involved, purposeful talk. It is not the purpose of a discussion to *convey* information; that should be done elsewhere—through trips, reading, classroom pets, films, and life experience outside as well as inside the classroom. But subject-matter studies can supply in other contexts the information that students can put into meaningful frameworks of ideas by means of discussion, at the same time sharpening their communication skills. The best topics have no factually correct answer. Sharing common facts as *background* for discussion is important, however, and makes it easier to get in the habit of backing up statements.

Establishing Conditions

If student talk is to be valued, it must first be heard, and one of the things you need to do is to set up a place where a small group of students can attend to one another. The younger the participants, the more difficult it is for them to concentrate on a single subject and to adapt their talk to partners. Attunement to the group is, in short, the main quality. And the main problem is distraction, whether it comes from outside the group, from irrelevant private associations of ideas, or from entanglements of personalities. So, at first, you exert an influence against distraction and for concentration.

This need not and should not be done in a disciplinary way. Physical distraction from outside the group should be minimized by setting aside for such groups a quiet corner of the room (carpets help), preferably partitioned off, or ideally, another room, so that the rest of the class can be doing something else. Members of the group are seated in a circle, perhaps around a table. A specific visual focus may help: write the subject on a placard or chalkboard close by, or place the picture or object within easy view. Small-group discussions may be noisy and thus may pose the problem of disturbing the rest of the class. One teacher solved the noise problem in a ninth-grade class by placing a group in a corner of the classroom with a microphone and an interconnected set of headphones. An interesting advantage of this ingenious makeshift arrangement is that students listen more closely to each other and concentrate better.

The basic conditions for small-group discussion are matters of common sense. Group members need to agree on a topic, say what they think about it, listen to what others say about it, respond to what others say, and stick to the topic. The question, about which teachers may disagree, is whether these common-sense conditions, which in fact define small-group discussion, need to be stated and taught to students as rules.

An initial presentation of rules may help some less mature children to conceptualize discussion behavior, which may, in turn, help them to achieve the behavior. The purpose is to induce certain speaking habits, such as listening and responding, and certain conceptual habits, such as defining and summarizing. Once the habits have been formed, the rules can be dropped. Rules about participating, listening, and sticking to the subject are appropriate for beginners only and should be discontinued once youngsters have learned to do these things. Small children may like rules and rituals, but this aspect should be emphasized no more than is necessary to induce the habits. It may very well be that you need not set up rules at all, depending on the development of your students, but can let them remind each other of common sense as they criticize taped playback of their own discussions. At any rate, the issue is not whether to hold each other to paying attention, contributing, sticking to the topic, and so on, but whether *formulations as rules* will help discussants to do this. While not assuming that students do need rules, we concede that sometimes even those who can already conceive discussion behavior adequately may still be helped to achieve it by using ready-made formulations as handy reminders as they learn to point out their lapses to each other.

If you decide to have discussion rules, below are some that may be placed on a card or wall chart and referred to before and during discussion and again afterwards, when group members evaluate their interaction. These were formulated by Dr. Babette Whipple in the course of her experimentations with what she calls Grouptalk, "a conversation in which a leader, using a recorder, helps a small group of people to follow rules while they talk together trying to answer a discussion question."

STARTING RULES
1. *Read* today's question.
2. *Understand it:* tell yourself what it means.
3. *Discuss its meaning:* tell others what you think the question means.
4. *Decide on one meaning:* agree on the meaning before you start answering the question.

1. *Contribute:* give your answer to the question.
2. *Be relevant:* stick to the subject.
3. *Listen:* try to understand what someone else is saying.
4. *Respond:* comment on what others have said.

ENDING RULES

1. *Sum up:* help in the summary by trying to remember the main ideas discussed.
2. *Evaluate:* listen to the playback and comment on how well the Grouptalk rules were followed.[3]

The Ending Rules go beyond common sense, of course, and build into discussion procedure two final steps that while generally optional for discussion are very useful indeed for training. It is important to keep in mind that both the presence of a leader and the use of rules do aim at training only.

Some teachers who have tried small-group discussion and been disappointed have concluded too readily that poor results meant that rules and a leader were necessary. This may be true, but if students are using the small-group discussion time to "get away with stuff" because you are not close by, or if certain personalities deadlock the group, or if an inept attack on a topic leads to a dead end, it may well *appear* that the problem is the students' lack of understanding of how to interact. Since rules for good discussion are just common sense, though, you have to ask why a group is breaking them. Students' departures from the rules will have more to do with distraction, impulsiveness, poor motivation, and egocentricity than with ignorance of common-sense discussion principles, and you would do better to gain insight into these causes, as you will through experience, than to harp on the rules.

If well convinced from trials and observation that your students truly cannot discuss well without some training with you, then we recommend that you help them in ways described in the next section, which owes something to Dr. Whipple's work. Even students who can discuss without you might well benefit from your sitting in and guiding them occasionally. But before you make judgments about what they need, let them try topic discussion when it is embedded in integrated language arts activities, such as the fable example mentioned earlier, or

[3] See the book from which this definition and set of rules are drawn: Babette Whipple, *Dynamics of Discussion: Grouptalk,* Porthole Press, Belmont, Mass., 1975.

such as the captioning of photos and other activities in Part Four, Developmental Reading, Speaking, and Writing. Most efforts like those of Dr. Whipple and of teachers trying out small-group discussion tend to isolate it as a relatively separate activity, at least in comparison with discussion occasions that we recommend, which aim to parlay one language arts activity continuously into others and to sustain such learning chains as long as possible. The degree to which small-group discussion is isolated or integrated makes enormous difference in how well students go about it. Furthermore, many groups that fall apart or fail to follow common-sense principles will discuss well when following activity directions, which to some extent can build in the focus, the reminding, and the strategies that a teacher might provide. Habits of autonomous peer interaction in all other activities, finally, do wonders for small-group discussion because the heart of the matter is social collaboration anyway.

Teaching the Process

A major reason youngsters may not listen to each other is that they assume that they can learn only from adults, not from other minor critters like themselves. If you attend to and value their peer talk, they will also. As in many other matters, real attention establishes value. If you praise and blame, or otherwise make yourself the motive center of the group, students will talk to and for you, not to and for peers, and consequently will listen only to you and use the time while another member is talking to prepare their next bright remark for you to praise. Listening to peers, then, is directly related to honoring peer ideas, and the problem of inattention decreases as the peer-to-peer nature of the group becomes real to youngsters. (They may not believe it at first.)

When students are not listening to one another, you can stop them and ask one to repeat what another has just said. You should resist the temptation to repeat what a soft-spoken child has contributed, thus focusing the attention of the group on you. Ask him or a classmate to do that so you build toward independence of your leadership even as you exert it. You can do a great deal to establish a positive tone by accepting the ideas and feelings the youngsters contribute, supporting the participation of each even when the only contribution a shy member might be capable of is a repetition of what someone else has said. Attentive listening on your part provides a model for the concentration of attention that good group process demands.

As trainer you do not participate in discussion of the subject matter; you participate at the level of process, not of content. The measure of your success is how well the discussion goes without you, how soon the children can take over your role of getting the process going and can function autonomously. You may have to help groups get started, but your goal is to enable them to exchange with their peers in learning ways. By so doing you will give them a great educational gift for the rest of their lives. After all, any teacher's ultimate goal is to become unnecessary. If you need too much to feel needed, you unconsciously keep the students dependent on you.

Establishing the Meaning of the Topic

At first you may need to help see to it that all the participants understand the question or topic in the same way. You may begin by asking someone to say what it means to him and asking the others if they agree. They may need to define certain key words. If they define *animals* so as to exclude birds and fish, let that definition stand, though it is incorrect. If all agree, it will serve at this point for the purpose of discussion. Correction can take place at other times, and if you use your role to give information, you will succeed in making the learners dependent on you. Try not to do anything as you start a group off that they won't later be able to do very easily for themselves.

Discussion sessions give you important insights into students' concepts and knowledge so you can better fit other learning into the frameworks they already have. Discussing key words is a good way for learners to acquire vocabulary and sharpen concepts. Having some members in the group who don't know what certain words mean poses the valuable problem for the others of having to explain them. You should not assume this prerogative by supplying needed definitions yourself. The agreement on the meaning of the topic at the beginning provides a touchstone throughout the discussion when the teacher or pupil remarks that some utterance is off the subject. After settling on the sense of the topic, the discussion itself can begin.

Keeping the Focus

Usually all that an off-subject utterance requires is a neutral reminder. But try to be aware of why students digress. If too many discussants wander frequently from the topic, you had better ask if the subject really interests them, or determine what else the matter might be. They might discuss what would be a better topic. Digressing is, after all, mostly a matter of involvement. Think of how difficult it is to divert even a small child from something he wants to do very badly. But digression may also arise because of involvement. Something just said may remind a child that "Daddy locked himself out of the house yesterday" or set him to wondering, "What would happen if a locomotive got too hot and started to turn red all over?" Though irrelevant to the group's present focus, these are legitimate private associations and should not appear as enemies to the teacher or as mistakes to the child. You simply say, "That might be a good incident to act out next time" or "You can suggest that for a later topic." No remark is ultimately inappropriate, only immediately inappropriate. All ideas will get their time; another idea has the floor now.

Repetitions and Non Sequiturs If a participant has a high percentage of repetitions or non sequiturs, he may not be listening well. In that case, simply say, "Joan has already mentioned that," or "Did you hear Joan say that before?" This lets the repeater know that he may have missed something, and also shows that you are setting an example of listening.

One characteristic of immature discussants is abrupt change in topic. Your first assumption might be that the speaker has not been listening. Some non sequiturs, however, are not born of inattention; a learner may be breaking new ground in another aspect of the topic. When you feel that the abrupt switch shows that the speaker did not hear his predecessor, you might ask him if he heard, then ask that previous speaker to repeat what he said, then let the present speaker continue. Occasionally, when you feel that a certain remark is especially fruitful or difficult or deserving of thought, ask someone to paraphrase what was said. Such feeding back can help the speaker to know how well he was understood as well as sharpen listening among peers. Part of your role is to influence pace so that ideas are given their due and the discussion thickens and thins at appropriate places.

The Impulsive Interrupter If someone seriously interrupts another's sentence, say, "Brad hasn't finished yet," in a factual rather than accusing tone of voice, or "Remember about waiting your turn";

or make a simple gesture that says, "Hold off a moment." In extreme cases, when a chronically impulsive child habitually interrupts, you may as well focus the group momentarily on this problem and discuss it before proceeding, if the group seems mature enough. Ask what they all might do to help the interrupter listen more and wait for his turn. The point is that when an individual problem impairs group functioning, it is then a group problem also, and time should be taken to restore functioning. Turning in annoyance on the individual culprit makes him defensive and makes matters worse; he needs rational help. If the group can think of no solution, ask the interrupter to act as recorder for several minutes, listening only, and perhaps taking notes, and then, when the time is up, to tell in his own words the gist of what the group said, and to voice what he thinks of what they said. If this is done to help the individual and not to punish him, we think it may bring him around. At the same time as it causes him to delay his responses and to become involved in listening during this delay, it also assures him that he in turn will have a definite and full hearing.

The interrupter's difficulty in waiting usually stems from one or more of these three things—impulsive inability to delay responses, egocentric disregard for what others say, or overanxiety about having a chance to get attention. Small-group rather than whole-class discussions will at least provide the interrupter with more opportunity for the attention from others that he needs.

Encouraging Participation

To encourage participation by everyone without calling attention to shyer members, training rules can include the understanding that each member will say in turn at the outset what he thinks about the topic. Then after everyone has said what he thinks initially, members can comment on each other's openings. Groups discussing without the teacher may still want to agree to do this if members feel it useful.

The understanding should be that a discussant who wants to talk does not raise his hand; his cue to speak is someone else's stopping. One of the main problems of teacher-led discussion is that children tend to talk to the teacher instead of to each other. If you call on members who raise their hands, you inevitably become the focus of the group, which is difficult to avoid in any case. A rule about hearing out the last speaker and then starting to

speak without signaling will help students focus on each other and reinforce the rule about listening.

If someone does not participate for a long time, you can say, "We haven't heard from you yet," or "What comes to your mind about this?" Sometimes just looking at a person will draw him out. Students who habitually withdraw may need a skillful alternation of encouraging and letting alone.

Questioning

One of your roles is to make a discussion more sophisticated by sparely interjecting questions calling for elaboration, clarification, or qualification. These questions are not mere conversation prompters; they should express your real feeling that what a speaker has said is incomplete, unclear, exaggerated, or overgeneralized. Whereas a declarative statement to that effect sounds critical and omniscient, a question or request makes the speaker think a little more and sets an example of questioning for the listeners, who may well have found the statement incomplete or unclear too but were not aware that they did, or, with childish acceptance, did not realize that questioning might relieve their uncertainty. You might say: "Will you explain that a little more?" (clarification); "*All* animals?" or "Is there a time when that is *not* true?" (qualification); "Tell us some more about what they do because I'm not sure yet how that fits in." "Can you give some examples?" "What other possibilities are there?" or "What would happen if you did that?" (elaboration). Since you are in the same role of listener as the other children, each question suggests what they too might have asked, or could ask in the future.[4] At the same time, the speaker is given feedback to help him come more on his true course by adding to or adjusting his first statement.

Helping with Hang-ups

Dr. Whipple has classified disagreements that arise in discussion into three categories—disagreements of definition, information, and value. Certainly you need to be adept at spotting mere definitional hang-ups, where discussants are attaching different meanings to the same word or concept. The initial agreement about what the topic means should head off some definitional misunderstandings, but, of

---

[4] A good discussion of clarifying questions can be found in Louis E. Raths, Merrill Harmin, and Sidney B. Simon, *Values and Teaching,* Charles E. Merrill Books, Inc., Columbus, Ohio, 1966.

course, as new words and concepts are introduced into discussion, the problem may crop up again. For example, you might say, "Leon, I think when you say 'power' you are including a lot of things Anne isn't thinking about." Or ask another member if he thinks those two students mean the same thing by the word. Either you or another student should try to say what Leon means and what Anne means. Leon and Anne can be asked if that is in fact what they do mean. In other words, hang-ups should come under discussion until, again, the group process continues unimpaired.

Definitional disagreements should make way for more important ones. If you believe a disagreement stems from different information—Alice has seen so-and-so and Elmer has heard or read something different—you may ask, "How do you know?" or "Where did you learn that?" or "What do you think proves what you say?" Partly, this questioning is intended to establish the habit of asking for, and giving, evidence. Identifying and documenting factual statements is something that small-group discussion should pursue eventually in many ways. Mainly, at first, you help the students to see how some disputes may be resolved by getting more or better information, or at least to see that different information is the source of the dispute. This could lead to research that could be brought into the next session. For disagreements founded on different values, you can only remark, "Jeff and Carol seem to be arguing over a difference in what they like. He considers machines very important, and she doesn't because she cares a lot more about live things." This does not, of course, resolve the disagreement—but it serves to clarify the basis of the disagreement.

Often blockages reflect personal relations among the participants. If doing so does not embarrass them too much, you might remark, "Ed and Rick always seem to disagree, no matter what the subject is," or ask, "Do you always agree with Julia?" Another person may say, "Sure, they like each other" (giggles). "Do you think you can like each other and still disagree sometimes?" It is true that an adult cannot meddle much with students' interrelationships without creating fear of exposure. You can say, however, that when feelings they have about each other interfere with the activities of the group, the group may need to talk about them. Ganging up, jeering, or chronic arguing for the sheer sake of contest play havoc with discussion.

Since the whole purpose of the group is to learn how best to talk together, no malfunction can be ignored, whatever the reason for it. If members do not seem aware that discussion is being determined by personal feelings, you should at least say that you think that it is. How far you should go beyond that is too difficult to say here; playing by ear is wisest in such sensitive matters. If the group want to get on with their discussion, they will have a good reason for wanting to improve their group interaction. In some cases personality clashes cannot be lessened by group attention, and what is needed is a change of the make-up of the group so that these students do not have to work together. Sometimes one student will so dominate the others that the best thing to do is to add new members who might challenge the dominant one.

Sometimes when discussants get blocked because they have exhausted all the ways they know how to think about a subject, you can encourage them to think about the topic from a fresh point of view. If they are discussing shoplifting, for example, and they reach an impasse, you might ask them to consider the problem from the point of view of a store owner or law-enforcement officer or insurance adjuster.

As soon as feasible, a discussion group should meet without you. You should merely walk by or observe at a distance, making clear that you are available and on call for problems but that you trust them to function effectively on their own. See page 420 for more on evaluating discussions. You want them to learn to talk to each other, not to you. If the small-group discussions are leading to the achieving of a group project, they will have a built-in structure, and your availability for counseling will be all that is called for.

Topics

Whether you are training a group or not, you may help members to find and to frame topics. As students mature, topics can be stated so as to call for increasingly difficult thinking tasks. The following broad types of topics come in order of increasing difficulty.

Enumeration

The kind of topic most appropriate for beginning conversationalists calls for listing or enumeration: "How many different ways does an animal get food?" First, listing is a simple kind of thinking but an important one, and we know that small children can do it and learn from it. Cognitively, the process is one of furnishing positive instances of a category, "Animal Ways of Food-Getting" or "Uses of the Magnet." This relates to concept formation. Disagreement occurs when an instance is offered— say, birds flying south to get food—and another child objects, in effect, that the instance is negative, not positive. (Birds fly south, he says, for reasons other than to get food.) If the category is "Vehicles," "sled" may be disputed as an example. These disputes lead to precision of concepts and finer discrimination, to more analytical thinking.

Second, listing requires the least interaction among learners. Essentially, it is a piling of ideas like brainstorming. One pupil influences another mainly by thought association: a suggestion by one makes another think of something along the same line. Disagreement over instances, however, does represent greater interaction and a step upward from mere influence by association.

Enumerative topics may be of different sorts that can be roughly scaled to form a progression. For the youngest children the topics should be concrete, such as: "If you were going on a space trip, what would you need to take?"; "How many ways can you think of to use a Ping-Pong ball? A brick? A coat hanger? A paper clip?" and so on; "How many things can you think of that can carry things?" For more mature learners at level two and above, the enumerative topics can call for categories that are more abstract, complex, or novel, such as: "How do people get other people to do what they want?" or "How do people decide who owns what land?" Finally, enumeration topics can call for dividing items into more than one list, such as: "How can you tell what things will cost a dollar or more and what will cost ten cents or less?"; or making decisions according to a system of priorities of importance, such as: "If you were leaving your home forever and could take only three things with you, what would you choose and why?"

Comparison

Enumeration can lead to definition and comparison topics by making the category one of similarities or differences but taking only one or the other at a time at first: "In what ways are cars and boats alike?" or "How are you different from a chimpanzee?" Dealing simultaneously with both similarities and differences—full comparison—is rather advanced and should come after experience with just one at a time.

Chronology

Another kind of topic for beginners calls for chronological ordering—making up a group story, planning an action, or telling how something is made. Such topics could be interspersed with the enumerative kinds. Most often they will relate to other activities such as drama, writing, and making things. The purpose of discussion is to work out an order of events that is going to be carried out in some way. The process is one of building, act by act or step by step, which is relatively simple in itself but usually entails reasons for choosing one suggestion over another. Thus, the main form is easy but invites some more complex kinds of thinking. Undoubtedly, children will leap ahead and then later think of things that should have gone before. This backtracking and readjusting is something a summary could help put to rights.

Stories are usually built chronologically and provide good experience with ordering ideas. Serial stories, for which one person begins, another adds on, and then another continues, provide a valuable experience in narrative composition, a task that can begin orally and later be taken to paper. Answers to questions such as "When were you the most afraid?" or "What was the most fun you ever had?" evoke personal narratives.

Planning an action also calls for chronological ordering. Questions such as "How are we going to arrange for the class to get here and not suspect our surprise?" or "How are we going to get John's bicycle back?" call for chronologically ordered steps. To deal with a question such as "How should we go about making a bird feeder?" both enumerative and chronological orderings may be needed. For example, a listing of things that birds will be attracted to and will peck at might have to precede a session on construction, in order to settle on the type of feeder.

Analysis or Illustration

These topics call for analyzing, explaining causes, or furnishing some sort of evidence such as anecdote, logical reasons, or facts and figures. Topics may be stated as questions of several sorts—yes or no, which or what, how or why, and so on. Some may be put as propositions to accept, modify, or reject: "Hunting should be allowed," "Kids our age should be required by law to attend school," or "Everybody should be allowed to own a gun." The problem with such yes-or-no topics, however, is that they may be answered in an overbinding either-or fashion and thus may block qualification and refinement of thought. "When should . . .?" and "Who should . . . ?" are sometimes better.

Some topics, like international affairs, are so remote and make participants so dependent on secondhand sources that students often merely parrot what they have read or heard. A topic that has proven very successful at many age levels, on the other hand, is "Do you think it is better to be the oldest child in a family, the youngest, the middle, or an only child?" The topic is of universal interest, allows participants to draw evidence from their real-life experience as well perhaps as from literature and factual reading. It staves off crude dichotomy because it has more than two alternatives, and yet the alternatives are concrete and finite. The degree of truth in a selected proverb can make a good topic for analysis—for example, "Is it always true that the early bird gets the worm?"

Ranking in order of priority is another valuable discussion problem, calling for clarification of individual values as group members share aloud their opinions about which is the best, the most pleasant, the most morally right of a set of alternative actions. See page 384. Whenever the discussion leads to a conflict in values, the goal is to clearly recognize why the individuals differ and to respect these differences rather than to push all members to "agree." In these cases, differences are not something to be resolved, but rather a source of further exploration and individual commitment. It sometimes helps to ask group members what sort of proof it would take to persuade them of the other person's point of view. A small group is an appropriate place to make sure that the minority or individual opinion is respected and valued even if it is held by only one person.

See Chapter 19, Ideas, for more suggestions for discussion and writing topics.

Optional Procedures

One way for students to take over the trainer's role is to listen to themselves after a discussion. Though generally optional, tape-recording the sessions of beginners can help them considerably to become aware of how much they participate, how they interact, when they interrupt, and when they get off the topic. Procedure consists of letting the recorder run as they talk, then playing back and discussing their discussion, stopping the player whenever they want to point out something. Even very young children just becoming socialized can often spot such things as all talking at once or getting off the subject, when they listen to themselves. (They also enjoy hearing themselves.) Older learners can become more aware of the individual ways they interact. The feedback they give each other as they listen to the tape is often preferable to outsider commentary, including that of the teacher, or to rule-setting before the discussion, because it accomplishes the same thing without inhibiting talk and without making discussion seem like a totally new invention of schools.

Summarizing their own discussion gives group members extra learning benefits and frequently proves useful for a following activity. Everyone simply tries to say what he remembers that is important of the ideas they expressed, and individuals amend or add to what the others remember. Activity directions may require a summary so that some conclusion can become the basis of further action, but even without follow-up, discussants will get satisfaction sometimes from feeling either some resolution of their topic or some advancement of it over where they started with it.

Sometimes groups may find that members disagree about which points were made, or the effort to recall and pull together their ideas may stimulate further ideas. Occasionally the act itself of summarizing helps members clarify what they did say or decide. Sometimes new ideas occur as previous ideas are reassembled, thrown in a different order, paraphrased, and checked for omissions. Once all the returns are in, perspective is sometimes different. Summarizing is important for developing thought because it is abstracting. Younger children will content themselves with selective recollection, but as they grow, their manner of summarizing will also grow; it will approach the drawing of conclusions.

If its task calls for a summary record, the group can appoint a scribe to write down its conclusions. In fact, it may want a scribe to take notes throughout the discussion as well. In this case, the scribe reads back the notes and the other members amend if necessary and dictate a summary as they thrash it out. As routine, the procedure will pall, but if members have a reason to want to remember the items they enumerated, the arguments they brought forth, or the conclusions they came to, then using a scribe will seem natural and necessary. A common use for both scribing and summarizing is to report to classmates the ideas a small group comes up with in connection with a broader project. Often, then, the scribes may become spokesmen, and if several groups are reporting to each other, the spokesmen might form a panel to feed the ideas of small groups into the large group. This would be appropriate when the class wants to pool ideas or to know what other groups have thought on some subject. The scribes can meet in a semicircle before the rest of the class, each reporting on what his group has said, commenting on each other's reports, and then inviting the class to comment.

Of course, some students are not able to write well enough or fast enough to act as scribes, but even a few key words would be a good beginning. With young children who are taking notes on a discussion for the first time, you may do well to choose a more verbally able child. Later, scribes may be volunteers, and, finally, the role can be rotated.

Panel Discussion

Small-group discussion may evolve into panel discussion, which is discussion held before an audience and unplanned except for the designation of a topic. Panels become one of the options open to students who have had small-group discussion experience and are mature enough to take an audience. One kind of panel may be constituted simply by making a group out of the scribes who are reporting to the class from their respective groups. As each reports, the others can question him, then they can proceed to full discussion. If the groups have been discussing the same topic at the same time, as "buzz groups," the scribe-panelists or spokesmen can bring to bear on a topic the ideas of a whole class. If the groups have been conducting different investigations related to a common theme or project, panelists can interplay these varying points of view. The only necessary preparation for a panel is deciding on a topic. Discussants need not be assigned positions in advance nor directed to prepare what each will say. On some occasions participants might prepare by reading something about the topic beforehand.

The benefits of discussing before an audience are twofold. The participants in the discussion have the advantage of feedback on their ideas from the other panelists and feedback on the quality of their interaction from the audience. A discussion before an audience takes on the qualities of a workshop, whereby the discussion process itself can become a focus of evaluation as well as the subject under discussion. The audience benefits by becoming aware of aspects of discussion dynamics that are hard to remain sensitive to when they are participating—things that make and break communication, advance or block ideas. For example, a panel may circle repetitiously, become lost in trivialities, get distracted from a good line of thought by an irrelevance, fail to pick up and develop each other's points, or get hung up unwittingly on a hidden problem of definition; some members may dominate or contend with certain others out of personal opposition, or stubbornly reiterate just for the sake of defense. Somehow students must become aware of poor interactions without feeling badly criticized.

One way to become aware of problems is to observe them take place among another group of people who are discussing a topic together. Another way, requiring some skill and delicacy, is for spectators to reflect the discussants back to themselves after the panel is over. The tone is important, and you must set it to preclude severely negative or sarcastic criticism that would inhibit rather than help the panelists. This positive tone must have been set before in small-group discussion, of course. What is important is that students get used to having both their ideas and the way they talk about them responded to by the audience. You ask for such reactions, or, once the procedure is familiar, simply wait for the response. Part of the task of the audience should be an effort to summarize the main ideas that were brought out and the areas of agreement and disagreement.

Since one purpose of panel discussions is to help students think new thoughts, they should be encouraged to abandon pre-established opinions and turn over ideas open-mindedly. Listening carefully to one another and responding relevantly and thoughtfully should be encouraged. Students need to learn to value questioning one another in ways that sharpen definitions and clarify opinions without polarizing the discussion into paralyzing conflict or personal attacks on one another. Dividing panelists into teams, setting up debates, and choosing dualistic yes-or-no topics all promote dogmatism rather than flexibility. Panelists bring personal biases to a discussion anyway; they should not be prevented, by a prior commitment, from changing their minds, making concessions, or finding areas of agreement with other panelists.

Exploiting Audience Response

A common experience for spectators is that they find themselves itching to get into the fray. While listening, they think of counter-arguments, points left out, other sorts of ideas stimulated by the panelists. This is an excellent educational moment that can be exploited in three ways. One is simply to turn the pent-up reaction into a class-wide discussion, in which case the panel will have served as the springboard. Another is to let some of the more aroused spectators form a second panel. The last way is to take the discussion to paper while it is hot. The audience can put down what they think about what has been said, the point being not to recapitulate the panel discussion but to express further thoughts stimulated by it. Part of the later aftermath of the panel may be to pick up the issues in small-group discussion and to read aloud in class the papers written in repsonse to the panel.

The Inner-Outer Circle

One format is very useful. The participants can sit facing each other in a circle with the audience in a larger concentric circle around the outside. One way to arrange this is to have the concentric circles nearly equal in number. The outer circle can observe the quality of the interaction of the inner circle, noting who contributes, who seems to want to contribute but does not, who listens and adds on to what others say, who interrupts and who is interrupted, who sticks to the subject and who does not, and who comments on what someone else has said. Observers can either take notes or fill in a check sheet and share these with the participants. Then the inner circle and outer circle can exchange places, and the observers carry on a discussion while the others watch. After these observers share their notes, an evaluation of the entire procedure can take place.

Mock Panels

Discussion and improvisation meet in the form of mock panels, for which students play roles—that is, pretend to be certain people or kinds of people engaged in turning over an issue. They can play roles from an imagined situation or those of characters from fiction, improvising a discussion of an issue according to how they think the characters would have talked about it. On a more abstract level, each discussant may be assigned a certain family, social, or professional role that would be expected to furnish him with a particular bias, point of view, or investment. For example, he could be the president of a white property owner's organization facing the first sale in his neighborhood to a black family. See page 99 for more on mock panels.[5]

Monologues

The continuity of a monologue must come from within the speaker, from his perception of how to string his utterances together to develop a subject. He does this spontaneously, of course, without thinking ahead, but practice in holding forth in this way can improve what he does spontaneously. Monologuing is an important step toward the development of sustaining composition on paper, which is what writing actually is—a sophisticated form of monologue. Because of this closeness to writing, monologues are dealt with in Part Four, Developmental Reading, Speaking, and Writing, especially in Chapter 19, Ideas. But monologue arises out of dialogue. Questions prompt the shower-teller or the interviewee, or a small group sends its spokesman to report its ideas or findings to the whole class, or one person takes over a "talk show" and holds forth. From dialogue the speaker learns to objectify and organize his thoughts, to accommodate and interest a listener. Using this experience, he practices monologuing further with announcements, storytelling, media narrations, and speeches.

[5] For some activity guides containing very good discussion strategies and topics for preschool through grade six, oriented toward personal and social awareness, see: Geraldine Ball and Uvaldo Palomares, *Human Development Program (Magic Circle),* Human Development Training Institute, Inc., 7574 University Ave., La Mesa, Calif. 92041.

In this chapter we suggest dramatic activities that are largely improvisational. We reserve for the next chapter the rendering of texts. Dramatic inventing covers the "creative dramatics" of elementary school, the "improvising" of secondary, and the "role-playing" of both. The activities these terms usually refer to hold good in most cases for a wide range of school years. The actors invent all or most of the dialogue, action, and characterization, drawing material sometimes from the surrounding culture but, if so, always remaking it in their own way. Improvising is making up the particulars as one goes along. This creative process is at the heart of all oral language development, for any speaker plays the options of the language and makes up new sentences he has never heard before. But drama is not all verbal. Actors practice also the repertory of "body English" that accompanies speech or simply speaks for itself.

Drama is not necessarily theater. Theater concerns performance for an audience, whose point of view is accommodated and for whose benefit effects are calculated. Theater is a secondary effect of drama, an outgrowth appropriate in school only for experienced players who ask for an audience. Dramatic invention may or may not be presented before an audience.

The following activities represent different ways in which students of all ages can be stimulated to act out without using a script. They include not only dramatic scenes of tension and conflict but also certain warm-up movements, acting games, play with objects, role-playing, and other inventive expression through gesture, words, and action. These take place concurrently in the curriculum but might be begun by students in a staggered fashion, following roughly the order of their presentation in this chapter. Any one may be returned to at any point as a warm-up for a more demanding activity or as another way of coming at an experience. For example, pantomime is never "outgrown"; it continues to play an important part in developing one's communication skills even into adulthood. The important thing is that dramatic inventing not be considered appropriate only for young children. The older students become, the harder it is to introduce them to dramatic work if they have never had it before, but it is important to do so, if for no other reason than to help them empathize with others in reality as well as in literature. Whatever their age, improvising helps people respond to others relevantly and spontaneously. Some of the processes presented first below may give students of any age the experience they need to undertake more mature improvisations. Unison actions, for example, will help students feel comfortable with one another and get used to conscious body expression. Newcomers of any age will probably need to develop their acting powers within the safety of whole-class or small, unwitnessed groups.

Dramatic invention begins in play with objects and shifts to movement-to-sound, other unison movement activities, guessing games such as charades, acting out stories, putting on puppet shows, role-playing in crowd scenes and small groups, leading finally for experienced students into improvisation from minimal situations. All of these experiences hold the key to the performance and writing of scripts, both of which may be carried on concurrently with improvising. All have the primitive element of group participation in a here-and-now event. Because there is minimal delay of response or abstracting and categorizing, the experience is close to the natural mode of both the young child and the openly involved adult; thus dramatic inventing is appropriate from kindergarten into adulthood.

dramatic inventing 5

Play with objects

The first dramatic activity of the young child is solitary play, spontaneous acting out not so much to deliberately imitate what he sees about him as to become it. This early drama wells up from a passion to understand, to find one's identity through action. In this sense the root meaning of the Greek word δρᾶμα—deed or action—is realized. At first, toys are the stuff of drama. For the small child, they automatically imply some words and deeds; they provide a point of departure. Grasping a stuffed animal, Dorothy-of-Oz puppet, wand, sword, stethoscope; donning a feather, cap, mustache, kerchief, or cape; standing before a moon rocket or counter or gate of gold—all these suggest to a child what to do, by evoking a host of associations in which the item is embedded in his mind. (Of course, these associations vary somewhat among cultures; a Southern black or a Harlem Puerto Rican may find meaning in different objects than a middle-class white would.)

The stimulus of objects doesn't end with the early years, however. Even adults are eased into drama by concrete points of departure or stimulants that both suggest and limit the dramatic idea. Few persons, no matter how experienced, plunge right in when asked to "make up a drama." Often just one prop or object will start them off. For example, if a player places a crown on his head, his action is both stimulated and to an extent determined. Certain acts such as hammering an anvil no longer seem appropriate, but at the same time other things are suggested. A student with a crown can then grasp an imaginary scepter, project a tone of command, assume a stance of authority. By limiting action and feeling to that appropriate for the role, a child becomes a player, assuming behaviors that are not customary. His imagination determines the extent to which the new role can move him into new awareness, into hitherto unrealized experience.

Classrooms need to contain many objects that can stimulate drama. For primary children this can be a playhouse center with dolls, furniture, toy phones, a cash register, career uniforms and equipment, and so on. For older students a prop box with bits of costumes will do. The equipment need not be elaborate. Young children can make wooden or cardboard boxes into crude furniture, cars, store counters, operating tables, or castles. For all grades rostrum blocks (small, portable platforms), if avail-

able, permit players to work with vertical space. An inexpensive, colored spotlight or two clamped on the back of a chair or onto a shelf help establish mood. An inexpensive light dimmer can quickly create a similar magic. The classroom needs window shades to control light for mood as well as for projections. As performers gain experience, they will increasingly be able to imagine the properties they handle instead of actually having to have them on hand.

Costumes are never necessary, but inexperienced students seem to invent more freely and feel more comfortable when a token of dress or property is provided. Too complete costuming can impede a novice's movement, and sheer realism can stultify creativity. Thus a "costume" may be something as simple as a paper bag mask or a picture hung around the neck or pinned on the front of the actor's shirt. We suggest that dramatic work begin within a framework of conventions of the sort children like—familiar props and settings, stock characters, and symbolic pieces of costume. They want to "be" an ogre, a fox, or a fireman. They seem to have to be themselves by being something else. In primitive fashion, they wish to take on—to invest themselves with—the qualities and powers of some object, animal, or fantasy figure. Or they wish to test out adult roles symbolizing powers they wish to have. They work out realities through fantasies and thus prefer the symbolic and ritualistic to the actual and original. This does not mean, however, that play-acting conventional roles in borrowed situations is learning to be unoriginal and stereotyped. It is simply that young actors require masking and stereotyping as conditions for being creative. They are less interested in what they are—weak, fearful, dependent—than in what they want to be—powerful, fearless, and self-providing. Sometimes they act out both roles at once by assigning to a toy or a puppet the weaker role and assuming the more powerful role themselves. Realistic role-playing, imitating various kinds of adults, may be both an assumption of power roles and also an effort to understand adults. No matter what our age, we never outgrow this need to role-play. All of us project what we would like to be into roles we enjoy or need to assume—if only in our minds or our dreams. As we stand in another's shoes, we begin to understand and develop empathy.

Props or bits of costume may be put in groups of three to five in separate paper bags. Then each small group in the class may be given the challenge of making up a skit using all the props in the bag. Any object may serve any of a number of functions: for example, a cane may be a shepherd's crook, a railing of an ocean liner, a bar to a locked door, a trapeze, an umbrella, Neptune's trident, and so on; the only stipulation is that each of the objects in the bag must be used in the skit. Then bags of props can be exchanged, or their contents shuffled, new skits performed, and then these compared with the first ones. The skits can then be taken to paper and turned into scripts or stories.

All you need do at first is to provide a few materials and a time and climate for acting out. For young children the play process usually takes care of itself if there are plenty of fantasy objects and playmates. An audience should be provided only when the participants ask to share what they have done.

Experience suggests that a natural sequence is from playing alone to playing in pairs to playing in larger groups. Children will vary, of course, in their social growth. An advantage of acting out at school rather than at home is that individual play soon becomes group play as children become interested in and influenced by what others are doing. A child may begin by monologuing his fantasy as he plays, or by making up a conversation between two puppets, and end by playing doctor to several patients. Certain props, such as play money or a pair of telephones or walkie talkies, naturally call for social play and promote interaction; they also promote the specific social play of talking.

Puppet play

Toys and costumes as props can be supplemented by various types of puppets and a puppet stage, which, however crude, are for most learners an irresistible stimulus to dialogue. Because improvising actions and dialogue for a puppet is for many youngsters a less threatening way to act out something, many children will work with puppets before they are willing to engage in other dramatic activities. Their own person is masked in the puppet they are playing, but the same challenge of improvising and inventing that is present in any acting-out process is there.

You and the students can find in books* some directions for how to make a puppet stage and all

kinds of puppets—stick, Styrofoam, papier-mâché, mitten, sock, glove, finger, paper-bag, box, paper-plate, or yarn puppets, and so on.

If possible, a puppet theater should be available where inexperienced puppeteers may improvise without an audience if they prefer and where the more experienced may stage a performance, inviting a small group or the whole class to watch. This type of performance is an appropriate first-one-with-an-audience because the puppets, not the puppeteers, are the focus. Youngsters will use their voices more boldly because they think of them as issuing from the puppets. (The children's feeling of identity with the puppets is especially strong when they have made the puppets themselves.) Despite the common belief that small children are born showoffs and have unfettered imaginations, we think the fact is that premature performing can spoil the very important evolution of play into other dramatic activities. You need to watch patiently for the moment when the performers are truly ready for and not inhibited or exploited by an audience. Because the focus is on the puppet, the reaction of the audience is likely to be taken less personally than it would be in another kind of drama.

Work with puppets generates task talk focusing on who will make the puppets and how they will be made, who will act each part, who will announce, who will do the scenery, and so on. Puppeteers face a strong challenge to effective oral composition and cooperative verbal interaction.

Movement to sound

Movement to sound, including rhythm and music, has some advantages over play with toys; it leaves more to the imagination, and it prompts the youngster to use his body more. We recommend movement-to-sound sessions two or three times a week for younger children.

Underlying all language is sensitivity to the experiences of the senses and to mood and feeling; music has power to evoke these and provides a strong impetus first to bodily expression and then to language development. Live or recorded instrumental music or songs can stimulate expressive movement and pantomime not only of action but also of the more subtle elements of feeling and mood.

Simple rhythms provided by clapping the hands

or beating a drum, tambourine, sticks, cans, or boxes; or playing other instruments, such as gongs, bells, pipes, recorders, or whistles, can be a good beginning, followed by recorded marches or dances. A piano, autoharp, or guitar can stimulate movement well.

The important thing is to diversify the sound for perceptual discrimination, emotional range, and bodily articulation. Play with all the possibilities, no matter what instrument you use: shift the stress in rhythms, speed up and slow down tempo, raise and lower or shorten and lengthen the notes, widen and narrow the intervals between notes, make the sound skip or trip or drag or slide, alternate quiet and turbulence. Isolate one at a time the various dynamics of music—staccato, glissando, crescendo, accelerando, ritardando—then join them later into little sequences for the children to respond to with bodily movement.

In responding to these diverse sounds students will have the opportunity to build a wide repertory of body movements. Upon this repertory depends the ability to act with the body—to pretend to be a frog or an old man climbing a snowy mountain. As in all other matters, access to a broad spectrum of possibilities directly increases one's creative invention. Enlarging the repertory, in this case, need not be done through systematic exercises; if frequent enough, diverse stimulation will eventually lead children to find the whole range. Learning to discriminate various auditory dynamics will sensitize children to pattern and structure in other media, including literature. And running the sound spectrum is running the emotional gamut—exercising feeling in a controlled, communal fashion.

Unlike play with objects, which best begins with solitary play and gradually moves to interaction among a larger group, movement-to-sound best begins, even for very young children, as a whole-class simultaneous activity. This can progress from movement in concert (not unison) to individual movement and thence to interaction among individuals. We suggest this because personal invention comes slowly, and because many children are shy of bodily exposure, which is minimized when everyone is doing the same sort of thing together. Confidence comes from identifying with a large group such as a class. But as is true in many other areas, the individual develops by shedding his dependence on the group. Once he is able to express himself somewhat in his own way, he can learn to interact with other individuals in a more truly social way than when he was merely a herd member. The following procedural suggestions reflect the progression from concert to individualized movement. The three stages are for convenience, but herd movement continues to be a good warm-up for any group, no matter how experienced.

HERD MOVEMENT

As for most drama work, a large floor area is needed, preferably a special room set aside and equipped with piano, record player, and other sound instruments, but a classroom will do if the desks can be moved. Cafeterias and gymnasiums will also serve well but may not be available for enough hours of the day and often overstimulate by acting as acoustical echo chambers. One of the side benefits of the birth decline is the existence in many school buildings of unused classrooms and other space where movement-to-sound can take place.

Since you make the sounds while the children react, a controlled activity of the whole class becomes possible. This gives each child a chance to act out his feelings in a creative way without the embarrassment of having an audience.

Begin by beating a strong, simple rhythm that children will take as a cue to either skip, run, tiptoe, slide-step, leap, jump, or hop, directing them only to "move the way the sound tells you to." Groups almost always fall into a circular movement, often following one or two leaders. Both this ritual and your control of the sound production impose order on this mass energy. Try out many of the variations mentioned above, gradually complicating the sound sequences by producing different dynamics in succession, but hold each pattern long enough for students to work into it. It is important to slow the pace and lower the volume whenever the group is not listening carefully. Have everyone stop and freeze when the music stops.

INDIVIDUAL INVENTION

Begin to alternate these locomotions with movements-in-place by sometimes directing the children to move each in a small area of his own, and occasionally even telling them not to move their feet. But first make the sound while they are resting and ask for ideas about how to move to it. Experiment with moving just one part of the body (finger, heels, toes, head, elbows, shoulders, and so on) at a time or with sitting and moving only from that position. Try motions that are twirling, angular, smooth, jerking, gliding, striking, shaking, bouncing, pushing, pulling, stretching, thumping, or swinging. Let the class try out these various motions one at a time in concert. The question would be: What is happening? Who are you? Where are you? This helps the children verbalize or demonstrate the movement idea in dramatic terms.

Then dispense with the practice of asking for ideas and just tell the children to move in place as the sound tells them to. Those who still have to imitate will do so, and those who are ready will invent. Occasionally repeat a sound sequence and tell them to do a different movement to it than they did the first time. Continue the sound variations. Encourage the children to imagine a setting, an action there, and a personage. Have them be that person or thing doing that action in that place. Introduce more extended pieces of music, especially music suggestive of mood and action. Let them know that they may speak as they move. Let them move about, each in his own area.

SMALL-GROUP INTERACTION

Place the class in pairs, trios, and quartets (gradually increasing the number in each group) and direct them to share space with their partners. The point is not to make children act or dance together but simply to clump them for spontaneous interaction, to let them influence each other in a group-defined space. They may move in place or move about, but in either case they should remain in their group areas. Recompose the groups on each occasion. Continue sound variations.

These three stages are cumulative; to enter a new stage is not to abandon previous ones but to add to them.

Warming-up and concentration activities

It is well to begin any drama session with some activities involving the entire group to help them feel comfortable, relaxed, and in the mood to improvise and act expressively. Talking about an activity, trying it, then discussing feelings, actions, and qualities of performance help performers assimilate and evaluate the experience.

RELAXATION EXERCISES

To loosen up the body, try singing games such as "Hokey Pokey" that call for kinesthetic experience, or exercises like these:

- Roll the head clockwise and counterclockwise.
- Hunch up one shoulder and then the other in quick succession.
- Pretend to yawn several times until you actually do yawn.
- Stretch tall, then to each side; bend over, unlock the knees and bounce gently. Repeat several times.
- Start at one end of the room and move forward in a relaxed stupor, allowing your body to be tipped off balance in a forward direction, but don't fall; just keep moving forward, unbalanced and loose. When you get to the end of the space, reverse the balance and walk backward; then fall and lie flat on the floor and close your eyes.
- Get as low as possible and scrunch up into a tiny space, tightening each muscle; then, slowly, open up, taking as much space as you can.
- On the floor take each part of the body in turn, beginning with the toes, and tense and release all the muscles; go all the way up to your forehead; then lie still for a few moments, eyes closed. Open your eyes; take a deep breath.

CONCENTRATION ACTIVITIES

To help young children concentrate and listen discriminately, games such as "Simon Says" serve well as a starter. The leader dictates a series of actions, and only when the direction is prefaced with the words "Simon says" does the group follow. When the leader gives a direction without this preface, anyone who then does that action is out of the game. Games such as those below demand more concentration.

Toss Imaginary Objects

- Arrange yourselves in a circle or in two lines facing each other. Begin by throwing out an imaginary ball, telling a particular person to catch it, while all eyes watch it.
- After everyone is involved, change the size or weight of the ball, saying, for example, "Watch

the ball; it is getting tinier and heavier. It is like a tiny marble made of lead. It is very, very heavy."

- Later you can again change the ball to a big ball, and then into a big beach ball, a hot potato, a porcupine, a pillow, a feather, and so on.

Mirrors

- Work in pairs, one to be the actor, and the other, the mirror.
- Face your partner. If you are the actor, start moving any way you choose, moving slowly and with concentration. You may either pretend to do something such as combing your hair, or you may move abstractly in straight or curved lines with different parts of your body.
- If you are the mirror person, try to pick up your partner's actions so exactly that no one is able to tell who is the actor and who is the mirror.
- Then change so the actors are mirrors and the mirrors, actors.
- For a more challenging activity, have teams of two initiate an action such as winding a ball of yarn, and have the other team mirror the action.
- At another time have a person convey an emotion and the other person mirror the feeling as well as the action.

Pantomime

To pantomime is to render feeling, idea, and story wordlessly in gesture and action. It is but a step from moving to music and is often effectively combined with it. After movement to sound has become a regular activity and has reached the stage of individual invention, it may easily be combined with pantomime. Instead of toys or sounds, the stimulant now is an *idea* of an action. As with other processes described above, it is usually less threatening to begin as a whole class working simultaneously to eliminate the potential threat of an audience and to help participants feel comfortable. Whole-class activities give students a background of experiences they can draw on later in smaller groups. The progression, as with movement to sound, is two-fold— toward individuals doing different things at the same time and toward individuals forming small groups that do different things at the same time.

UNISON

The best way to initiate your students into pantomime will probably be to give the whole class one action at a time to do together.

Walk in a Circle as a Whole Class

As students walk, you or a student leader feed in suggestions, starting with simple sensory experience and moving at a later time to names of times or places that evoke a more imaginative response for which students supply more of the sensory details for themselves. Keep the pace slow to allow time for belief. Here are some suggestions; you or the children can provide others:

- As you walk, you are slowly getting taller and taller. You are seven feet tall, now twelve feet. How do you feel? Now you shrink back to your own size.
- You are walking through tall grass. Is it smooth, slippery, prickly? What color is it? Is it dry and brittle or fresh and supple? Now you are walking over hot sand, on egg shells, in a swampy, muddy marsh, through water, through molasses, in deep snow, over fallen leaves, on slippery ice, along the edge of a cliff, through cobwebs, in a dense fog, in quicksand.
- You are very hot, very cold, floating on air, frozen into an icicle, now melting bit by bit, caught in the heavy gravity of Jupiter.
- You are lost in a dark tunnel; you are walking at night under bright stars; you are fighting with an octopus; you are entering a strange school for the first time; you are carrying a heavy fish tank full of water to the brim; you are skating fast; you are leading a lumbering camel across the desert.

Pretend to Be

Ask pantomimists to pretend to be all sorts of things, at first selecting simple acts: a giant striding, a hobbled prisoner, someone hauling on a rope or pulling a sled, someone opening a door or window or umbrella or difficult bottle, someone drinking something pleasant or unpleasant, a salesperson demonstrating a product. Typical actions can be combined with simple characterizations at this point. Young children particularly delight in assuming the role of an animal such as a frog, fish, elephant, butterfly, or duck and acting out its characteristic behavior. This activity can begin with unison actions, then individuals can choose an animal, and, finally, they can pantomime different animals and guess each other's. Anything that can be experienced with the senses can be pantomimed.[1]

Pretend to Do

When ordinary acts such as washing hands, swimming, eating a meal, peeling an orange, playing a game such as baseball, or riding a bicycle are pantomimed, students are pressed to rely on kinesthetic and sensory memory, making explicit previously unnoticed details of an action and performing steps in chronological sequence. The feel of the experience is re-created in a process that is very demanding of concentration and memory. Pantomiming an action in slow motion can help learners re-create through remembered sensing of shape, size, color, texture, weight, temperature, odor, and so on.

Select actions that will continue to enlarge the repertory of movements—bending, twisting, contracting, stretching—with all parts of the body, and in all directions. Tell students, for example, to imagine that they are standing close to a building, facing it, and straining to look up at someone in a very high window; then the person at the window throws something out that curves slowly over their heads and falls behind them; they follow it with their eyes, bending back until, as it nears the ground behind them, they finally have to twist around. Or station them all along the walls and tell them to try to push the wall over in as many different ways as they can think of without *striking* the wall.

Once the children are familiar with the process, ask them for suggestions, and from then on merely relay individual ideas to the group, which can try them out one at a time in concert. Continue to select the ideas, however, both for muscular and dramatic variety. Then give the children an action made up of a series of acts, such as entering a window, taking something from a chest, hiding it on one's person, and leaving. Then add different motives for doing the action, such as to play a joke on a friend or to commit a burglary.

[1] A very helpful book for combining pantomime and yoga exercises, illustrated with photos of preschool to junior high children, is: Rachel Carr, *Be a Frog, a Bird, or a Tree*, Doubleday & Co., Inc., Garden City, New York, 1973.

Pantomime a Story

As soon as children have had some experience with pantomime, they can do whole-class unison action while someone narrates or reads aloud. As you read the story step by step, slowly and expressively, allow the children to pantomime each new act and to "be" each new character that comes up. All pupils play all roles, including those of objects. Next, help them make up together a verbal story that they can then proceed to act out in the same step-by-step manner as you tell or read it. Student compositions provide considerable material for both pantomime and verbal dramas. See page 299 for more suggestions.

SMALL GROUP

Small-group work can begin after students are well experienced with unison pantomimes and after they have acquired some social maturity. Some directions might tell them how to do such things as the following, any of which may be done as a whole class prior to small-group work.

Create a Contraption

- Have one person (possibly the teacher for inexperienced groups) step into an open space and start a movement, such as rotating a gear, making his body into a part of a machine. He keeps this movement going.
- Have another person join him, adding a different motion but relating himself to the moving part in some way. For example, he might alternately squat and stand to represent a piston.
- While the first participants keep up their motion in pantomime, the rest of you, one by one, attach yourselves to the "contraption," each adding a different motion.
- When everyone is participating, have your leader call for a slowing down or speeding up of the contraption's operation, and, finally, push the "off" button to stop it.
- The next time, each of you can add an appropriate sound such as a "bddddt" or a screech as your part goes into action. You may want to expand this to phrases or incipient characterizations for each part of the machine.

- Sit in a circle so you can all see each other. Pretend to open an imaginary present in front of you. Each of you finds inside your package something you have wanted for a long time. Then take turns opening each of the gifts, pantomiming its shape, texture, weight, uses, and so on. See if the others can guess what it is. If they cannot, describe how the gift feels, smells, and so on but still don't tell what it is.
- As a variation of this, one at a time, open your gift, pantomime its qualities, use it, and then pass it on to the person on your right, who in turn uses it in the same manner and then changes it into something else which he then uses and passes on. For example, you may receive a wrist watch, which you wind, listen to, set, fit onto your wrist, and so on, and then you may take it off and stretch it into a tennis racket and start practicing backhands.

Get Out of a Trap

- As a group, pretend to lie down to sleep. When you awake, you find yourself in some kind of enclosure—a box, a dome-shaped plastic bell, a large ball, a metal machine, or some such thing.
- Then slowly examine its limits in pantomime. Feel the texture, temperature, dimensions, and strength of this container.
- Finally, after thoroughly exploring it, find a way out and escape.[2]

Create an Environment

- Meet as a group in a large space.
- One at a time, in slow-motion pantomime, put something in the space. For example, you may pretend to push in a large harp and bench and then sit down and play it so everyone will know what you have brought in.
- If you are next, decide in your own mind where this place is and introduce another object that belongs in such a place. For example, you might bring in a music stand and set it up, shaping it

[2] For warm-up exercises "Mirrors," "Pantomime a Story," "Create a Contraption," and "Get out of a Trap," see the *English Through Interaction* elementary-level film, "Creative Dramatics."

with your hands as you do so. Then you move it near the harp, stopping to play on the strings before you leave.
- Each of you then goes into the space and puts a new thing in it and uses one other thing that someone else put there. You must be careful to walk around or take account of everything that has been put in the space. For example, you cannot open a window at the same place where a previous actor has pantomimed a cupboard.
- Be sure that the dimensions and shape of whatever you put in the space are clearly revealed. Do the pantomime slowly and in detail. Discuss afterward what actions were the most believable and what everyone thought each of the others was pantomiming.
- You may decide to do an improvisation in the environment you have created, using all the things you have put there.

Experienced students meet in small groups, choose a story, cast themselves in the various roles, and improvise a pantomime. Then they rotate roles and repeat the pantomime, discussing the two versions and determining which was better and why. Make sure players keep in mind that pantomime is played without words and without props; their bodies alone tell the story. Objects are suggested by movement in feigned relation to them or can be played by other children (rock, tree, revolving door, and so on). Good pantomime demands concentration, belief, and memory. All players must know what things are in which places.

When the students have been through a pantomime once, they can discuss any changes they might make, rotate roles, and then do it again. Both the revisions and the role reversals are important. Doing different versions of the same basic action is a form of composition and also draws some attention to technique (the commentary coming from the participants, not from the teacher or any other audience). Recasting roles establishes early the principle of flexibility and point of view in role-playing and breaks any typecasting based on traits of personality and physical build that children by themselves are apt to institute. Again, the main value is in the acting itself and in the pupil discussion entailed by it; the teacher should not ask one group to perform for others. Let the students decide they want to do this.

GUESSING GAMES

Any pantomime can be a focus for a guessing game. After students have acquired some confidence and ease from earlier pantomimes, they can take turns pantomiming characterizations, actions, and places to be, and have a partner or a small group guess who they were, what they were doing, and where they were. The feedback that comes from the guessers who tell the actor what they saw shows him any discrepancies between what was actually shown and what he had in mind. This is enough for the pantomimist to learn from. Quick, constructive suggestions for making explicit what he had in mind help too.

Ideas for pantomimes might come at first from suggestions by others: each member writes in advance on a slip of paper something that one person could act out alone—such as a small boy trying to walk a big, strong dog on a leash—and these slips are shuffled and passed around. Writing the directions has a value, too: the author of a slip sees his words translated into action and gets a sure-fire indication of whether his written speech is understandable or not. Pupils are reminded of the possibility of getting their own directions to act out. In fact, this possibility prepares for making up one's own act impromptu. The one who wrote the slip should not guess when he recognizes his action, however. After the pantomime and the guessing have ended, the actor reads aloud to the group the directions he received.

What Am I Doing?

Here is another guessing game you might put on activity cards; you and your class will think of others:

- Each of you thinks of an activity you perform at least once a week. Recall exactly what takes place and where the action goes on. Then work out a pantomime.
- Take turns doing your pantomimes while the others watch. Guess what the actor is doing.
- The next time you might write out what you are going to do, describing each motion in detail. Then have the others write what they see as they watch your pantomime, and compare their versions with yours.

- Another time onlookers might guess the time of day or where the action takes place. You might choose actions associated with an occupation, such as putting out a fire with a fire hose or producing an oil painting.
- Rather than individually showing actions you might do pantomimes in pairs, such as washing both sides of a window.
- You might pantomime an action that is appropriate for a given place, such as a doctor's office, a beach, a supermarket, or a space rocket, and have the audience guess where you are.

Antonyms

- Form pairs. Each pair of students thinks of two words that mean the opposite of each other.
- Pantomime, a pair at a time, in slow motion, one person doing one word, and the partner doing the other. The group guesses what both words are.
- Vary this game by having pairs pantomime two homophones, words that sound the same but mean different things, such as *right* and *write* or *fare* and *fair*; or homographs, words that are the same but differ in origin and meaning and sometimes in pronunciation, such as *wind, pen,* or *bear.*

Dramatic Skits

This will work best with students who have had some previous experience with pantomime:

- Form a group; then think of a problem and plan a way to pantomime it, showing the characters frustrated in some way and then working their way to a solution. Act this out for another group, which guesses what happened. The problem can be made up or selected from a poem, story, or song that other students are familiar with, in which case the guessing involves the recognition of it in nonverbal form, and the acting out is translating. If the material is original, the spectators' guesses translate action into words.
- Hold off guessing until the entire skit is over. Disagreements over interpretation should be parlayed into discussion, after which the situation or scene is revealed, that is, verbalized by the actor or actors. Ask the spectators to say

specifically which gestures and movements made them construe the action as they did.

- After the spectators have compared their interpretations, your group states what you were trying to do as actors. Discussion can then center on discrepancies between what you intended and what others inferred. This feedback can now become a joint effort to think about which gestures and movements communicated and which did not and how to better match deeds to intentions.

Charades

Within small groups the guessing game can be extended into the more adult form of charades—the acting out of verbal phrases, titles, and quotations. In this case, what the audience tries to guess are not the actions themselves but certain words that the actions merely evoke. This feature, of course, makes the game more sophisticated and more abstract, since actions must be linked with particular words for them, not with just any words for them (*steed,* not *horse*), and often, via purely verbal associations such as puns, the right word is arrived at secondarily (*I* by pointing to one's *eye*). Also, instead of holding off the answer until the end of a whole presentation, the actor makes the audience guess at each act, each word. This makes for intense audience participation and fast feedback.

Thus, the actor learns very soon if he is communicating. In fact, before he can continue he must adjust his body English until he does communicate. When he fails, he tries another action. At the same time, his audience must keep offering words until *his* feedback lets them know that they have hit on the one wording that will do. Both are learning communicative precision, one by trying out gestures and the other by trying out words. The audience develops flexibility in interpreting and in wording because they must offer alternatives—a wholly different ''reading'' of the action, a one-word synonym, or a variant phrasing. The essential skill required of the actor is to play on associations he and the audience share, associations between things and words and between some words and other words. A fundamental part of writing is knowing which associations are in fact shared and can therefore be counted on for communicating. The art is to evoke one thing by means of another. Private associations will not work. The best way to sort private from public, to put oneself in the place of the audience, to discover a com-

mon coinage, is by playing precisely this sort of game, verbally and nonverbally.

Here is the procedure for charades:

- Divide into small groups and either take individual turns acting out for the rest of the group, or form groups to take turns pantomiming for the rest of the class.
- Use agreed-upon signals to indicate whether the words represent the title of a movie, TV show, song, book, quotation, proper name, or famous person.
- Show how many words by holding up that many fingers.
- Act out each word or syllable. The number of syllables can be indicated by placing that many fingers against the inner arm.
- The first person or group to guess wins and is the next one to perform.

SLIDE SHOW OR MOVIE

Pantomime lends itself to presentation in a series of slides or a movie. In order to depict a story in pictures without recorded sound, actors need to rely on their skills in gesturing and body English they have learned in pantomime. Several different versions of the same scene might be tried before filming the best one. After a series of slides or a movie has been made, a student may tell or record a story to accompany it.

PANTOMIME AND DANCE DRAMA

Combining movement to music with pantomime opens interesting possibilities. It stimulates all players to respond to the same stimulus at the same time, but they may respond in very different ways. Either individual pantomimes can take place simultaneously or small-group interaction can take place as the music is played. All three ways of responding —unison, individual, and small-group—may be combined in planning a group pantomime after listening to a piece of music once or twice; or, if known story-music such as *Peter and the Wolf* is used, roles can be simply assigned; or grouped individuals can invent movements in relation to, say, three partners, the directions being to move as one feels but to stay aware of the others, to share the group space, and to let oneself be influenced. (Reciprocal influence adds a social stimulant to the musical one.)

For students having considerable experience with movement, pantomime to music can lead to dance drama in which the feelings stirred by music act as a more open, more subjective stimulant than words, while at the same time the ongoing rhythm and melody create a series of quite specific stimuli that can be readily translated to movement. The actions of pantomime tend to mimic recognizable outward gestures, whereas dance drama tends to express less explicit inner moods given form by the music. So movement to music offers more opportunity for personal, free improvisation. Story music makes a good bridge at first between these two kinds of body English; then later students can explore other ways to fuse the prior verbal directions behind a pantomime with the ongoing stimulus of melody, rhythm, and musical mood.

Enactment and improvisation

DRAMATIZING STORIES

Play with objects, movement to sound, and pantomime may be combined with speech to act out a borrowed or original story. This can begin in the primary grades. First the children choose a story, read or listen to it being read (unless it is already well known), and then talk about it. At this time they recall the story together and decide: when and where the story takes place, which character each of them is to play, what they are going to be doing as the scene begins. Then they can begin the action, improvising the dialogue, and stop when they need to decide such things as whether or not some inanimate things should be played by people, which props if any are needed, whether musical or rhythmic accompaniment is wanted, and whether individual or choral singing seems to be called for (as in enacting some story songs).

In small groups the children act out the main actions of the story in their own way, filling it in, making up some of the details and dialogue, and using some details and dialogue that they remember. They improvise their parts. They need not refer back to the source at this point, for they can change and add things to extend and expand the original material. They should feel free to enlarge or eliminate the role of any character or add a character if they like. They can change events in the plot or make up different endings to the story.

Once a group develop a version they like, they may decide to put on a performance for an audience. The important distinction between an improvised play and a scripted one is that in the improvisation every rehearsal will be somewhat different; the players will have to listen to each other's dialogue and respond spontaneously to the different versions. This demand for relevant response makes improvised drama a particularly valuable stimulus to language development.

The purpose of this freewheeling handling of a story is to provide an opportunity for a group to expand and develop a story in a way that interests *them,* much in the same way that a minimal situation is used. See page 96.

Another purpose of enacting a story is to reinforce literature. For this it is best to enact the story just after reading it, thereby tying the printed word to the physical world of behavior and sharpening reading comprehension by translating the subject into another medium. For example, during preparatory discussion, children might need to refer to the book when making decisions about how to act out the story. This task talk focuses on an analysis of the text to determine meaning, characterization, tone, style, and so on.[3]

Stories can be rehearsed and acted out several times, of course. In this case the dialogue continues to vary from one performance to the next, but the cues and sequence of action are quickly "jelled" or solidified through rehearsal so that such improvised performances are sometimes called jelled or structured improvisation.[4] Acting out stories leads easily into Story Theater, described on page 111.

CROWD-SCENE IMPROVISATIONS

Large-group improvisation attunes players to the presence and actions of many people at once and lets individuals experience the collective energy of large numbers.

Large-group improvisations are best done in a group of fifteen to thirty students, which is large enough for each person to feel comfortable in the "crowd" yet not so large that the teacher cannot be aware of individual performance. There must be

---

[3] See the *English Through Interaction* film, "Creative Dramatics," for a dramatization of part of *The Wizard of Oz.*

[4] See the treatment of this kind of improvisation in Elizabeth Flory Kelly, "Curriculum Dramatics, " in *Children and Drama,* ed. Nellie McCaslin, David McKay Co., Inc., New York, 1975, p. 109.

sufficient room to move about freely. As with small-group improvisations, warm-up routines before and discussion after the drama build confidence and stimulate student experimentation.

One way to get started is to dramatize a setting in which a crowd of people would ordinarily be gathered—each carrying on his own business. Favorite settings for crowd-scene improvisations are marketplaces (usually either foreign or historical), airports, public beaches, prison camps, parks, street corners, carnivals, or circuses. The class talks together about the scene, and players make up roles and typical actions for themselves, suggesting things that might happen in that setting. Then the drama begins, and each student acts the way his chosen character would, interacting with the others when appropriate. After a few minutes you may create an incident, perhaps by capitalizing on some bit of action going on in one part of the scene. You might suggest, for example, that someone was cheated in a purchase. By this means you can extend actions and sustain the scene, focusing the attention of the group and pushing them to solve this problem. The spontaneous behavior of the players will suggest to you a sequence of events. Experienced students can supply ideas for the plot from the outset. Your role is to see to it that the students' ideas are developed in a satisfying way.

If you see that a group seems to be losing energy, you can stop the drama and either suggest a new "What if . . . ?" or ask them for a decision that will revitalize their commitment. "Should we have something exciting happen now?" If the answer is "yes," then, "What will it be?" "Do you want me to begin it, or should you?" and so on. The question "How does it seem to be going?" will often help the group focus on what they feel they must do to get on with the drama. You can pose options such as "Should we all go to the hospital, or do you want to stand here and wait for the stretchers to come?" [5]

An alternative is to side-coach or feed in directions as stimuli without breaking the action, as was described earlier for whole-class pantomime. Players should not pause or look at the coach but should simply react in role to the stimulus. You might talk the whole group into a mood, using your voice itself to induce a particular state: "It's getting toward quitting time now, and you're getting weary and feeling hungry. Your movements slow down, and you begin to think about going home and settling in, but you have to keep going and you fight the temptation to give in early. You don't feel very patient, but you try to pay attention and keep working." The idea of this mood may come to the coach because the scene needs slowing down or simply would benefit from a change of action level. Create changes to see what happens. Later players can discuss how they were affected by these directions. Give play to your own inspiration; students will respond in kind, and some will learn to coach too. You might side-coach just one individual or a subgroup. Given, for example, the mood just induced, you could say: "You two by the door, you're gossiping, it looks like. You're gossiping about some of the others. You look around, and you smile as if there's a secret between you. You're setting yourselves apart, drawing attention, and you seem up while everybody else is running down." [6]

THE MINIMAL SITUATION

A minimal situation is the briefest statement of character and event for players of a given experience to get an improvisation under way. This is the "given" on which the players build. The difference between improvisation and enactment is necessarily a matter of degree only, since there are always some "givens," suggestive ideas that are the starting point for acting out. In improvising, one makes up more of the story as he goes along; when enacting, one has more details specified in advance. Since young children's inventions tend to be drawn so much from familiar stories anyway, the distinction breaks down even more at this age. The younger the child, the more givens there will need to be. Nevertheless, launching even young children from a minimal situation rather than from a known story does place them further along the way toward individual creativity. Since they have less to go on, they must heed carefully the actions and words of others, because these cue their responses.

There are several sources of minimal situations: (1) an idea presented on an activity card or by the teacher; (2) an action to be elaborated from a previous reading selection (in which case the improvisation is a kind of free enactment); (3) a situation abstracted by the teacher from a play, a story, or a

[5] For more ways to keep large-group drama going, see Betty Jane Wagner, *Drama as a Learning Medium*, National Education Association, Washington, D.C., 1976.

[6] See the secondary-level *English Through Interaction* film "Large-Group Improvisation."

poem soon to be read; (4) an original student idea drawn from life or imagination; and (5) a situation embodying a moral, social, or psychological issue that arises from group discussion or reading.

An Idea Presented on an Activity Card or by the Teacher

The main reason for presenting a minimal situation this way is to give beginners the main idea so that they will think up situations of their own later. Suggest situations calling for dialogue but encourage use of pantomime as well.

For students of any age, a good beginning in dialogue is to role-play any two people, such as an interviewer and a politician, a parent and a teacher having a conference about a pupil, brothers arguing, two persons pictured talking together in a photograph or series of photographs.

Dialogue may be evoked by imagining meeting in unusual ways such as coming together as spies who recognize each other by subtle clues, running into each other unexpectedly on the same tight rope or on another planet or in the same apartment for which both of you have just signed a lease. Activity cards may present situations posing conflict, such as: a high school student who has just borrowed the family car without permission, has had an accident, and is arriving home; a shoplifter who is getting caught; a couple who, for no reason they can divine, are surrounded by a crowd of neighbors who want them to sell their home; a child who has just discovered he is different from other children.

An improvisation may begin with the students writing on three separate slips of paper a setting, a problem, and a character. Then the papers are mixed up, and each small group draws one setting and one problem for the group, and one character for each player, and improvises a drama. Mature students can replay each improvisation as a comedy, a serious drama, a dance presentation, an operetta, a melodrama, and so on. They may begin by writing more elaborate character profiles, such as "you are an aging dancer depressed by the death of your one close friend." The setting and action can be spelled out more elaborately as well.

Mature improvisers can start with almost no givens. They may even get to the point where they can simply get together and be two people with a specific problem; they pick up clues from one another as to who they are and why they are together.

This represents the freest stage of spontaneous invention. Here is an example of this type of minimal situation, which one of us was once given in an acting class: "Tom wants the chair here and *Susan* wants it over *there*." The understanding is that whatever setting, circumstances, and identities the actors establish for themselves as they go along must be maintained from then on. (The two of us became interior decorators who disagreed over the arrangement of a client's room.) The audience notes what ploys each person uses to get his way and discusses these afterward. If the actors become physically deadlocked over the chair, or otherwise run out of invention, another pair takes the floor for a while, or other group members stop them and make suggestions or side-coach. At the heart of this type of minimal situation is conflict, the essence of drama.

Another form of spontaneous invention, one that even elementary children can succeed at, despite its obvious difficulty, is rhetorical practice at its most elemental. Send one actor out of the room and give a brief direction to the other actor that the rest of the class can also hear. The direction simply stipulates the effect one actor is to produce on the one who is out of the room, using any means except physical violence: "Make her laugh"; "Make him sad (or unfriendly)"; "Startle (or cheer) him." The person who was sent out of the room simply returns and reacts spontaneously. The means of getting the effect may be many—making up anecdotes, asking questions, flattering, launching into commentary, drawing the other into an exchange about a certain topic, and, of course, physical maneuvers. In the ensuing discussion, students can talk about which kinds of things actors did or did not do that worked or did not work.

This sort of very free improvisation develops fluent invention that will help many activities—writing, conversing, acting out scripts, and perhaps even reading. It is a high point of creative expression. To succeed, a student needs to choose his gestures and words for a specific objective, to affect another person. This is a touchstone for developing empathetic social relationships.[7]

[7] We are much indebted to Viola Spolin for many of the ideas presented in this chapter. See the excellent sourcebook: Viola Spolin, *Improvisation for the Theater*, Northwestern University Press, Evanston, Ill., 1963. See also her *Theater Game File*, 1975, a set of 204 activity cards and a handbook, from CREMEL Institute, 3120 59th St., St. Louis, Mo., 63139.

Improvising, either before or after the reading, is an effective way of stimulating an interest in literature and working with it in a way that will probably also improve silent reading skill. The students are asked to pick a scene or piece of action from a short story or to select a whole poem. They may choose scenes they like very much or ones they do not understand well. The latter should be encouraged. They then cast themselves into the appropriate roles, drop the text, and start improvising. They may recapitulate some of the action and dialogue as they remember it and at the same time invent changes. If they cannot recall the text, they may either refer back to it or invent a new interaction. Synoptic versions of fairy tales, legends, historical events, myths, and Bible stories can be elaborated by making up dialogue and the particularities of the action. For any narrative, what improvisation does is to translate *what happened* into *what is happening,* thus making the abstraction of the story come alive in the present moment. For older students, converting narratives into drama demonstrates the relationship between the two. For younger ones, the process provides another stimulus to invention and language production.

A scene merely alluded to in a play or piece of fiction (an off-stage action) can be improvised from the slight references made to it, the students drawing on their understanding of the rest of the work in order to create the scene the author did not present directly.

Exploring other possibilities of a text makes the author's choices meaningful. And players have to think about motivations and relationships in order to act their roles. Discussions of interpretation inevitably arise en route, and these discussions are practical, not arbitrary. The hunt for hidden meanings that students resist so strongly when the teacher probes with question after question is replaced by the effort of trying to understand what one is trying to do. Changing roles and replaying a scene is another way to deepen that understanding.

Improvising a historical event is a potent way of picking up the past and charging it with vitality and significance. After students have read the facts surrounding an event such as Archimedes' discovery of the displacement of water or the Norman conquest of Britain, they play a scene that brings to life what it must have been like in those times when that hap-

pened. At the moment of the drama, unknown facts are ignored, and the students imagine from what they do know. After the improvisation anachronisms can be noted and new facts sought so that the next version is more authentic. Again, improvising stimulates reading to find out. As students assimilate and make historical material their own, they cannot help but enhance their communication skills at the same time. Each time a new version of the improvisation is played, taking account of newly found facts, it has a fresh focus.

Before the students have seen a text, you can abstract in advance a key scene, such as the scene in *Julius Caesar* in which Cassius tries to persuade Brutus to join the conspiracy to kill Caesar. The situation can be stated in more or less detail, depending on how much of it the students seem to need or to be able to use. These details would be facts and circumstances, not character traits, since giving the latter would force the teacher to pre-interpret the play for the students and perhaps lead to stereotyping. Mainly, A is trying to talk B into helping to kill a friend of B's for the good of the group. A number of scenes from *Julius Caesar* could be improvised in this way before knowing the play.

Situations Originating with the Students

These open up the way to writing plays. There are two stages in this development. In the first, a group improvising an original situation composes it by doing different versions until it is wrought to the members' satisfaction; then they collaborate in writing it down in play format, as dialogue and stage directions, or in transcribing it if they have recorded it. You may need to help them find an appropriately dramatic conflict or moment of tension around which to develop an improvisation.

After some experience in this group composition, they are ready for the second stage: individuals choose a minimal situation, either of their own or from a list of class suggestions, and write a playlet based on it. This amounts to improvising a scene alone on paper. (See Chapter 14, Actual and Invented Dialogue, for a script-writing sequence.)

Sometimes an idea comes up in discussion, and the students turn it into a concrete reality by improvising it. Then as they discuss their improvisation, they build a new generalization from their own concrete example. Through improvising they "live through" the experience and gain insights about it.

Situations Embodying Moral, Social, or Psychological Issues

Improvising scenes with characters drawn from real life is often called role-playing. "Playing the Problem" is improvising a problem situation drawn from the real life of one of the students or from an advice column or from imagination, such as having personal mail read by another family member, having a relative treat one child as a favorite, having a parent blame you for everything, having a family member who is becoming an alcoholic or facing divorce.

Experienced secondary-school students can move to larger institutions than the family, improvising scenes fraught with moral, social, or psychological issues in hospitals, political parties, industries, educational institutions, governmental agencies, legislative bodies, and so on. For example, students might role-play participants in a courtroom scene by writing out an unsolved crime, naming suspects, circumstances, victims, witnesses, motives, evidence at the scene, and so on. It is crucial that their case be conceived of in as thoroughly and fully detailed a manner as possible. Then they cast themselves in roles of defendant, defense attorney, plaintiff, prosecutor, judge, jury, and witnesses and improvise the entire adversary procedure of presenting cases and calling witnesses.

One high school teacher[8] reports a good response from her students who work in small groups to play a problem with these directions: "Decide together on a moral position or deeply held conviction that a person might hold. Then put a character who holds that position into a situation in which he is pressed to act counter to his belief."

One group of her students chose to act out the problem faced by a defense attorney who really believed that the end does not justify the means but argued the case of a radical who had murdered for a cause. In the improvised defense the girl acting as defense lawyer not only had to make the case for the man on trial, but also had to show how the attorney was struggling to explain why her stance in this case ran counter to her usual position on this matter.

Other students chose roles such as a student who believes "the clothes make the man" but finds himself falling in love with a sloppy girl, or a boy who believes a good grade-point average is very important but decides that making an *A* in a particular course is not worth it.[9]

Players do successive improvisations, changing factors, rotating roles, and discussing issues and solutions. This allows the problem to be examined and turned round to reveal new faces.

Minimal situations such as these lead into, or become a kind of, topic-centered discussion. Conversation about them occurs in incidental talk generated while setting up a minimal situation or while evaluating different versions of a scene. Or a situation may be one in which the characters are essentially just sitting around talking about some issue they have to make a decision about. The scene is dramatic, because the students are still taking a fictive role and the talk is a story action, but the improvisation takes a step closer to being a kind of spontaneous discussion. Examples would be a jury deliberating a verdict or a committee or a club deciding on whether to invite a certain type of person to be a member or not.

A "mock panel" might be set up; each participant would assume a role, and then the groups would discuss a topic from the points of view of the characters they have chosen. One of the mock panel members might be a famous historical person or his or her ghost, and the rest of the group could ask him questions. This type of discussion can be a stimulating application of what students know about the values, beliefs, and achievements of the person who is brought out of the past. What would Nat Turner say about the position of today's blacks? What would Thoreau say about our cities? Or Queen Victoria about the state of the British Empire? A variation of this interview is to have two people from different past eras improvise a conversation with each other. What would Jesus say to Martin Luther King? To prepare for a mock panel, students would need to "bone up" on their chosen person.

Thus we have shown that improvisation and discussion are the ends of a spectrum that stretches between them. Minimal situations can lead into discussions as well as drama. Mock panels will help induce awareness of how our ideas are rooted in

[8] Robin Henderyckx, Evanston Township High School, Evanston, Illinois.

[9] For more ideas see Sidney Simon, Leland Howe, and Howard Kirschenbaum, *Value Clarification: A Handbook of Practical Strategies for Teachers and Students,* Hart Publishers, New York, 1972.

our roles and character. The dynamics of drama and the dialectic of discussion are inextricably related. At any time you or the students can lift an embodied issue from the drama work and propose it as a topic for small groups to discuss, or vice versa. For example, an improvisation in which family members argue over behavior at home parties or how to share space or a car suggests several discussion topics—parental authority and teenage rights, the teenager's degree of maturity, and the pressure to follow social patterns.

The drama workshop

Like a writing workshop, a drama workshop is a working party in which members present their work to each other in turn and exchange suggestions for improvement. A valuable part of both the process of enacting scripts and improvising from minimal situations is the discussion that goes on as the group tries out various interpretations or evaluates the different renderings. Either you or watching students may make comments or suggestions when the action runs out or runs down. Watch closely what is going on. Be patient about letting students work things out, feeding in suggestions or descriptive reactions sensitively. Your chief role is to ask "What if . . . ?" questions about all the variables that they might change—setting, timing, casting, number of parts, kinds of relationships, tone, and so on. This is basically the same role you have when joining writing workshops.

You set the tenor for students' comments as you give personal responses as an onlooker: "The clerk seems very annoyed, but the customer doesn't seem to notice that." You might suggest things the actors may not have thought of: "Why don't you try it in another setting?" or "What would happen if the son asked his father *before* the mother entered the room?" Students make these same kinds of comments to each other following your lead. When the onlookers have themselves been working on an action they are now witnessing, or are about to replace the actors, these remarks can be very perceptive and pertinent, helpful both to the actors and to themselves.

The purpose of comments is not to criticize directly, but to reflect what the improvisation looks like from the outside and to widen the range of possibilities. One of the main values of improvisation is the *exploring of differences*—differences, for

example, between two-way and three-way relationships, in pace and rhythm, in language styles of different speakers, in the dynamics and balances of interaction, in settings and circumstances, in the order of acts, in behavior strategies. (All of these are aspects of both literature and real life.) If an improvisation seems lifeless and forced, the commentators need not make negative remarks about the acting. Taking their cue from the teacher, they suggest changes in the variables of the situation and in the casting. Sometimes, for example, if a scene is revolving repetitiously or keeps falling into pauses, it may help to suggest another ploy that A can use on B, or to propose that the two players change roles for a while. If playing alternatives is customary, then proposing changes will not be taken personally.

With experience students will begin to see that the more they can contribute to the expansion of each minimal situation, the more meaningful it becomes. Students should be encouraged to bring their personal experience into their improvisations because that material is precisely what makes a drama come alive and helps students learn to appreciate the relationship between an understanding of their own lives and an understanding of the world outside their experience. In small-group discussions after improvisations, students need an opportunity to talk about their feelings as well as their performance. From this they can abstract generalizations about what they were conveying and what that drama symbolized in their own lives. This discussion cannot be forced, of course, and for inexperienced or immature students it may not happen at all.

Drama workshops might be set up in a two-troupe arrangement whereby one group performs for the other, listens to their evaluation, and then trades places with the watchers. After this experience the groups might be ready to take turns playing for a larger audience such as the whole class, thereby gaining a wider response and feedback.[10]

Although most dramatic work can occur in self-directed working parties, as for other activities, regular whole-class warm-ups and occasional workshops for the entire class can be helpful, especially as students are getting used to improvising.

Drama periods can have a general structure that

[10] See the *English Through Interaction* films "Small-Group Improvisation," one at elementary level and one at secondary, for examples of one group reworking a minimal situation with some help from the teacher.

creates a sense of order and purpose but allows for a variety of current projects. For example, the entire group begins by doing a few warm-ups together and concentration activities, then goes into enactions and improvisations. Students often suggest pantomime ideas for everyone to try out simultaneously; you can feed in ideas that increase the range of body movements or that sometimes anticipate actions in a play or story the students are going to be reading.

Depending on what the current projects are, the next phase of the class period can consist of small-group work such as charades, improvising from a minimal situation, enacting an unscripted scene from a story, or rehearsing a scripted scene from a play. You pass from group to group offering occasional suggestions when a group seems to need more priming. This small-group work might last until the end of the period, but sometimes the whole class could be reassembled to watch some groups put on scenes or to coordinate the groups if they are working on parts of a whole. In some class periods the movement-to-sound warm-up might be extended into dance drama by clustering students for spontaneous interaction during the warm-ups and then letting these groups plan and act out the music with the usual rotation of roles. Pantomime warm-up could be part of the bigger action the groups are going to work on, or it could be the germ of an improvisational situation.[11]

The value of dramatic inventing

None of the activities presented in this chapter are merely "games for kiddies" or "enrichment." Rather, they are a serious, yet enjoyable, part of the business of classroom learning. Teachers should not feel that time spent on them is time diverted from the tasks of learning about language, literature, and composition or of teaching basic skills. Drama will definitely further such goals and frequently, by increasing motivation, will accelerate learning in other areas.

The purposes of drama at any age are to

1. promote *expression* of all kinds, movement

[11] For more on creative drama see one of the many good books on the subject such as Nellie McCaslin, *Creative Dramatics in the Classroom*, 2d ed., David McKay Co., Inc., New York, 1974.

and speech harmonizing and reinforcing each other.
2. limber body, mind, and tongue.
3. single out the verbal mode from the others and thus to activate speech in particular.
4. forge drama into both a learning instrument for other ends as well as an appropriate end in itself.
5. make the school experience with language fun and meaningful in youngsters' terms.
6. habituate students to working autonomously in small groups.
7. further peer socialization of a learning sort not usually possible outside of school.
8. gain intuitive understanding of style as voice, role, and stance, and of rhetoric as achieving effects on others.
9. develop in the more familiar mode of dramatic play those characteristics necessary for the less familiar process of discussing, such as attending, responding, interacting, and taking turns.
10. exercise and channel emotions.

We will explain how some of these purposes are fulfilled through drama and at the same time specify some other particular benefits of various dramatic activities.

ELABORATION OF STORIES AND IDEAS

Drama is especially useful in developing the capacity to elaborate overcondensed stories either of one's own or in literature. Most myths, legends, and folk tales that come to us secondhand are in summarized form, lacking much dialogue or specific details. The dullness of such summarized narratives is a big stumbling block in presenting these fine stories to children of a young enough age to be especially appreciative of them but not yet able to read the mature elaborations of them in the plays and epics of great authors. But they provide good "minimal situations," which children can then expand and bring alive through improvisation. Someone reads aloud the summary account, and a group takes as its minimal situation the few sentences that recount an episode. Expanding myths through improvisation repeats, in effect, what the great dramatists have done with them in writing. Dramatizing involves a slowing of pace, compared to narrative, a living through of an experience at life rate, at the lowest level of abstraction. Even historical material is put into the present, the here and now. Our senses are stirred directly.

As students expand digested actions through improvisation, they see the values and the possibilities of greater detailing, elaborating dialogue, gesture, and sensory data. Youngsters frequently overcondense in their writing, and improvising helps them learn to provide detail—to experiment with various forms of expatiation. Generally an important relationship in the process of writing is that of drama to narrative; drama elaborates narrative, and narrative summarizes drama. Novelists work within constantly varying degrees of résumé and cover a lot of story ground, moving back and forth in time and space, whereas playwrights present total action of only a few carefully selected scenes. By improvising dramas from narrative sketches, and, conversely, by writing narrative summaries of improvisations, pupils can grasp this abstractive relationship between these two orders of discourse.

At the same time it is important that students realize when it is appropriate to skip the detail and go for the summary, for the more abstract capsulizing of experience in order to categorize it and hold it in mind for further use or to use it as material for an essay. They need to see the value both of skipping detail and of deliberately presenting it. We know of nothing more useful in helping students write better stories than a clear understanding of which parts of a story should be elaborated and fully developed as scenes and which should be capsulized and summarized to provide the necessary information between scenes.

Children's skits or improvisations, like adult literature, illustrate some common human experience. They have a theme, and thus they provide a natural topic for small-group discussion when preshaped by preliminary discussion of the skits themselves. If small-group discussion and improvisation are coordinated, we feel sure a very powerful learning will result, because ideas can be dealt with several times in two modes, at two levels of abstraction. A topic is a distillation, in question or statement form, of particular instances of some theme, any one of which can be improvised, and discussion of improvisations distills themes into topics. In other words, by improvising the instances that come up in small-group discussion, the pupils can go from generality to example, and by discussing the material of improvisations in small groups, they can go from example to generality. (Material can come from literature, everyday life, social studies, and

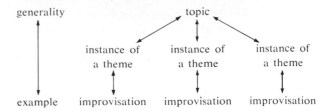

FIGURE 5.1 MOVEMENT BETWEEN ABSTRACTION LEVELS

so on.) This movement between abstraction levels is not only a vital issue in writing but also a major educational goal. See Figure 5.1.

NONVERBAL UNDERPINNING

Though movement to sound, pantomime and charades do not seem at first glance to relate directly to the development of speech, they in fact lay an important base for it. For children, speech is only one physical activity among others (as indeed it really is for all of us), and not usually a preferred one. As a specialized mode of communication and expression, it only gradually singles itself out from movement and gesture until, in print, it becomes totally separate. For children generally, speech *accompanies* other action and justifies itself only when it can do what other actions cannot. Movement to sound, charades, and pantomime permit the child both to develop his powers of nonverbal modes of expression and to run up against their limitations.

Body English helps students learn what words can do by doing without them. It is thus part of multimedia learning. In pantomimes and charades, one sometimes fairly bursts to speak those things difficult to convey by movement and gesture alone. Conversely, body English can say some things with greater brevity and power than words can. Also, sensory awareness and intuition are often heightened when talking ceases. Nonverbal expression remains throughout the student's school experience important as a supplement to speech, a base for speech, and an alternative to speech. What should be explored are the advantages and limitations of both. All students need ample opportunity to relate words and deeds and, when possible, to translate from one to the other.

In addition, physical action gives pupils a respite from paperwork while at the same time enhancing it. Most students—like the rest of us—are hard put to just sit and work with books and paper all day. Many of the problems that begin in the upper elementary and junior high years—destructive rebellion, alienation from school, dropping out, and delinquency—all can be alleviated if adolescents see school as a place where feeling and energy can be shaped and handled, instead of a place where these forces must be stifled. Many teachers are afraid that drama work will open a vent and create disorder, but nearly all people who try it find that it tends actually to lower tensions and help students behave better. Youngsters who tend to express most feeling and meaning through the body are allowed to remain on native ground while being drawn to explore the new territory of language.

SOCIAL GROWTH

Social growth is promoted because improvised drama captures the feelings as well as the mind; it demands high concentration, involvement, and response to others. Learners become more self-confident as they enthusiastically engage in natural dramatic activity. Through the active use of the imagination they identify with another person and thus view interpersonal relations or problems from a fresh perspective. By exercising and focusing their emotions they gain insight about their role in human interaction. Real feelings can be expressed in a situation made safe by the pretense "I am being someone else."

Role-playing provides an opportunity to learn through identification. It permits adopting and exercising voices and languages not usually one's own (including, for example, standard dialect if one speaks a nonstandard one). It also helps one understand from the *inside* what it is like to be, to truly identify with, someone else.

Dramatic activity not only mirrors the real world; it provides a wedge into it, letting the participants prelive the feel and texture of experience before they are thrust into the risk of the actual event. Even adults pretend or prelive experience in their imagination in order to get a hold on it. How many of us have rehearsed an important interview or "acted out" in front of a mirror an upcoming speech in order to prepare ourselves emotionally and intellectually for the challenge of the real event? Child's play and acting out provide important means of building social skill and self-confidence. Children need to repeatedly relive or prelive events that are fraught with mystery or tension—trips to the doctor, parental arguments, punishing behavior, or dangerous situations. In so doing they can begin to develop some of the skills needed to handle future experiences.

DISCUSSION

Significant and focused task talk is called for in putting together a creative drama or improvisation. As groups of students analyze a text or oral story, they need to decide its meaning, characterization, tone, style, and so on, long before they are sophisticated enough to use these words. The task of acting out simply demands this type of analysis, even if on a very crude level with young children. As students decide on an improvisation of a minimal situation, they need to play with variables and analyze the effects of each, arguing with supporting evidence for positions on issues posed by the task.

Discussion differs from drama in valuable ways that enable it to carry on where drama leaves off. It is more abstract and more verbal. Relatively, it immobilizes the body and detaches itself from things. The vocal mode is singled out. Emphasis is more on the content of speech than on speech as a behavior. Appeal is more to reason than to emotion. But none of these differences represents a clean break; in fact, discussion retains a dramatic underpinning that provides continuity from one to the other and should never be lost. Any experienced discussant acknowledges the big part that "group dynamics" plays in discussion, however intellectual the subject.

WRITING

Like small-group discussion, improvising is learning to write without going through the slow process of putting things on paper and waiting for delayed reactions. A student improvising gets fast, relevant feedback from partners, is constantly adjusting his language expression on the basis of its effects, and is drawing from his partners vocabulary, ideas, sentence structures, and so on. These he internalizes and thereby enlarges his own verbal repertory. Using the words of others as cues for one's own response is at the heart of both improvisation and discussion.

Dramatic work is not just a major means of pursuing oral fluency and expression but also a major way of improving reading and writing skills. Increasingly in the upper elementary, junior high, and secondary school years improvisation is taken to paper. Students can begin by recording an improvised dialogue and then transcribing it later, writing it up as a play script. The whole activity of pantomime can be extended by recording it in writing, comparing versions written by the performers and the audience. See page 159. Students can write scripts in the form of the improvisation they have been doing—scenes, dramatic monologues, soliloquies, or short plays—in comic, serious, melodramatic, or other modes. See Chapter 14, Actual and Invented Dialogue, for more on forms of drama.

In assuming a role in a drama, students practice shifting their point of view; this is a valuable experience for developing reading and writing skills. In trying to understand someone else's story or essay, for instance, a reader must mentally role-play the author, to try to see things as he would see them. In writing, the author has to take the point of view of the reader to see if what he has written makes sense and also to anticipate any questions or counter arguments that the reader might have.

COMPREHENSION AND THINKING

Whenever students take turns as actors or mimes and audience, feeding back responses, critiques, and interpretations to one another in discussion or written cross-commentary, they have a challenging opportunity to correct their own egocentricity. As they share responses, they compare interpretations. This can be a valuable way to treat inference— how we assemble cues into inferences and how it is that, witnessing the same action, we can infer different things. This uncovers the sort of hidden assumptions and subjective reactions that operate in our interpretation of real life. For more intensive work with inferences, you can deliberately plan for ambiguity in the skits so that, for example, some spectators will say that a pantomime is about a hunter stalking game and others will say it is about a detective tracking a criminal. A guessing game is an inference task.

No other activity—except game playing, perhaps—puts such constant pressure on the participants to think on their feet, make decisions, exercise independence, and respond to the unexpected in a flexible, creative way as dramatic invention does. Role-playing develops problem-solving skills, inductive and deductive reasoning, sorting and classifying, putting into sequence, and conceptualizing spatial relationships.

As the audience discusses a performance, the actors begin to see the effect of their behavior on others. Learning to act, learning to write, and nearly all other kinds of learning depend on just this: ascertaining the effects of one's efforts. Drama is life made conscious. That is why it can use physical, social, and intellectual forces so well to undergird and integrate the language curriculum.[12]

---

[12] We are much indebted to Rose Feinberg for particular teaching suggestions in this chapter. She appears with her class in the *English Through Interaction* film "Creative Dramatics."

See Guy Hendriks and Russel Mills, *The Centering Book*, Prentice-Hall, Inc., Englewood Cliffs, N.J., 1975. This book provides excellent exercises to help learners of all ages balance mind and body. It relates usefully to many recommendations in this text but especially to those in this and the following chapter.

Performing a text is rendering it for an audience. Players either hold the text and read from it or memorize it. Either way, they "stick to the script." In contrast to improvising, performing texts emphasizes fidelity to an author's material. Players rehearse. Including performing among the language practices amounts to laying a second reading curriculum over the first—and a rigorous one at that, for it automatically entails both silent reading and reading aloud, close textual analysis, and discussion of meaning and art. It both deepens and displays reading comprehension. Like small-group discussion, dramatic invention, and other oral activities, it deserves a solid and continual role in the language arts program at all ages.

Strictly speaking, of course, a script is material that is written specifically to be performed. In other words, a script is a planned oral presentation, written first and spoken later. It is a blueprint for others to follow. But since any piece of literature can be presented orally, any text can be considered a script. If it has a character voice or voices, as in a story, poem, or series of letters, it can be the script for a dramatic performance, even though it was not originally written for that purpose. Considering script then broadly, a large proportion of what students read, including each other's writing, is available for performance.

In addition to scripts written expressly for performance and other literature composed only to be read, there is a third source of scripts for classroom presentation—transcripts. Transcripts represent unplanned speech, spontaneous colloquy among different minds, spoken first and written down afterward—shaped not by some artful intention but by some communication need or public event. Because a transcript of a happening, no matter how formal or public, is not as complete as the event itself, it begs for re-creation. Whereas a script often provides clues to interpretation and stage directions, a transcript is more random in form and thus more difficult to interpret. See page 119.

A couple of activities from the other chapters lead well into performing. One is rehearsing a selection with the help of coaching from the teacher then reading it to a small group of the class (page 133). Another is dramatizing a story by borrowing the main events and improvising the details of dialogue and action (page 95). Young children tend to find the latter's mixture of fidelity and invention a more natural way to enact a story they have read than sticking to a script. Even when they perform texts, they tend to ad-lib some of it. And one way for players of any age to rehearse a scene is to improvise it from just one person's memory of the main action and gist of the dialogue. The more developed they become as actors, however, the more they understand the great amount of leeway any script must allow anyway for creative interpretation and technique even when one sticks to it. The improvisational activities of the previous chapter provide excellent background for the vocal expression of rehearsed reading, and the body-English activities stand players in good stead indeed both when staging the full action of a script realistically or when only pantomiming part of it suggestively.

A general continuity might take a student through these activities—reading to a group after getting coached, reading in unison, working up a reading with a partner for the class, participating in choral reading having voice parts, staging reading in one of the special techniques described later in this chapter, and memorizing and performing a play.

performing texts 6

Teacher role

Your role in helping students perform texts is *not* to direct the productions, but rather to feed into the small-group process pertinent alternatives as to how to proceed. Try to encourage independence by giving the students responsibility for carrying through their own selection of text, rehearsals, and final production. At the same time, of course, you need to set clear guidelines for group behavior and an overall sense of schedule and plan. You need to have a selection of materials available for those students who have real difficulty in finding their own and make yourself available to assist all of the students whenever they need you. Even when they don't perceive they need you, you note when groups seem to lose energy or reach an impasse, and you remind them of options they have, not deciding for them, but giving them a wider range of ways to proceed.

COACHING

During rehearsal you can suggest variables they can experiment with, such as:

1. Variations in volume, pitch, rate, and tone of voice to convey various qualities of emotion
2. The use of solo versus chorus for a voice part
3. The division of the lines among actors
4. The use of pantomime and physical action
5. Pauses in the flow of words to allow action to happen or to provide emphasis for words or actions
6. Physical placement and stance of actors and position of objects on stage
7. On-stage versus audience eye focus
8. The use of actual physical objects versus people playing the parts of objects
9. The use of representative "props" or portion of a costume
10. The use of chants, songs, light, dance, music, media, or physical objects
11. The division of roles among players

Rotating roles or playing at half or double speed will help students discover potentials they may not otherwise be aware of. Sometimes you can help recharge a scene by introducing a "What if . . . ?" question, such as "What if you were facing another direction when you said that?" If the reading seems "canned" or dull, sometimes improvising a scene

in the players' own words can engender spontaneity in the next reading of the script.

The practical importance of making oneself heard clearly and of projecting gives you a good opportunity to encourage distinct and forceful articulation of speech sounds. Omitting or weakening final consonants is a common trait of American speech. Point this out sometimes when you hear it, and demonstrate occasionally how to articulate vowels fully. Although it's not advisable to turn rehearsals into elocution lessons, still they are a natural occasion to practice "speech" in that sense. Sheer involvement in the emotions of a role will energize and clarify the voice. Pointers from you will also help; so will working with scripts that call for various dialects and listening to recordings by professional actors, to serve as models of effective euphonious articulation.

Act as a mirror to players to reflect to them what they sound and look like in rehearsal, the pace and pitch of their scene, and the mood or character relationship that comes across to you. That helps them to know if they are expressing what they intend. Set an example of mirroring and suggest that one of a cast do it for others rehearsing.

ARRANGING FOR AN AUDIENCE

An important audience for performers is the other members of a small group whose reactions to the oral presentation are solicited *by the performers* and taken into account in the next rehearsal. In this case, each of the members of the small group functions as a workshop participant working to help others develop skills of effective oral presentation. A workshop is also a good performing situation for players unready to act before outsiders. In a workshop spectators watch and comment just as they feed back in a writing workshop. All members are participants; there are no detached outsiders. Members react to other members' productions and work out common problems together. Each member gets an inside-outside view of both his work and the work of others. While learning an art or craft, he also becomes a sensitive, informed responder. Here, this means trying out tentative performances before a small group of classmates and giving empathetic feedback to other performers. The advantage of a workshop over sheer play is that one can learn from heeding feedback.

A small group of six can take turns acting out a script this way: If the script calls for a cast of three, three can watch and the other three perform and then take a turn at the same script while the first three actors watch. If the cast calls for two, four can watch while each pair takes a turn at the acting.

As students request opportunities to perform for a larger audience, you need to schedule whole-class sharing or audience sessions. These periods should not be too long, especially when the children are young. As students become accustomed to small-group process and to looking on the rest of the class as the recipients of their productions of all sorts—drama, writing, research, and so on—a relatively large proportion of class time will be spent in sharing. Your job is to balance the needs of the readers or actors with those of the audience.

Workshop process can be built into the activity directions for the performing practices to be described next. Each practice can be set forth on activity cards for self-directed work; however, you may want to lead an activity once or twice to introduce it to students.

Rehearsed reading

Reading aloud is the base from which performing a text is a natural extension. Working up a reading with one to three partners prepares well for bigger script rehearsals. A small group can render a text by simply reading in unison or by reading aloud one at a time. The goal may or may not be presentation to an audience. As a development of partner reading, playing with the text may alone sustain interest. Or the group may rehearse until they perfect a version to record.

Activity directions can make clear that players experiment with different voice volume, pitch, rate, pause, and tone. Encourage creative tinkering. For example, students can try out a tiny, soft voice, then a loud, bold; high, shrill; shaky, scared; stumbling, unsure; clowning, funny; or sad, sobbing voice. They can take turns reading in imagined situations such as at the bottom of an abandoned mine shaft or on a mountaintop where the voice echoes; they can try reading as if they were laughing, hiccupping, cuddling a sleepy baby, or standing on a lonely highway in the rain. They can assume roles that demand varying voices and read the passage again as it would be spoken by a king, a slave, a holy monk, a tough street-gang leader, or a lively entertainer. After the various readings the players can talk about how the meaning of the words themselves change with each reading.

Practice for rehearsed readings can include emphasizing different words in a sentence to illustrate how stress communicates meaning, as in:

- *I* like that painting. (You may not, but I do.)
- I *like* that painting. (It really pleases me.)
- I like *that* painting. (I am not crazy about the others.)
- I like that *painting*. (It's the thing I like among all the other kinds of objects.)

If you lead the whole class in some practice like this while doing choral reading, then small groups working without you can exploit the idea as part of working up any reading. Help them think of other contrastive ways of delivering the same words.[1]

The general procedure for rehearsed reading is to sift and discuss some reading selections, talk some about the main point and approach of the text chosen, then try reading parts to get a sense of who should take certain voices and how the piece should be generally treated, then cast and rehearse. Typically, this process interweaves silent reading (as members study the text a bit to size it up), trial oral readings (as they sound the text to listen for ideas about meaning and the best rendering), consulting the dictionary and other people for pronunciation and definition and other information, discussion of author's intention and characterization and so on (as they work out the content to be expressed), and textual analysis (as they dig for helpful particulars).

A student working alone may be directed to try out, and preferably record, several versions of a poem or other text. Then he can ask you and certain other students to listen to his versions and say how they differ and which is preferred for which reasons. Finally, the student can record or perform his synthesis of different versions. If a selection has several obvious or potential voice roles, this provides special challenge to the solo reader. If a small group chooses such a selection, however, it is better for neither you nor they to prejudge the number of voice parts when deciding how many

---

[1] For excellent exemplification of this practice, during a choral reading rehearsal led by teacher Charles Schiller, see the secondary-level *English Through Interaction* film "Choral Reading."

members the group shall contain. Let students discuss how many "voices," in one sense or another, that a text which is not a script contains. This is an extremely valuable learning that you don't want to short-circuit. If the group decides that a poem, say, would best be divided into three voice parts but the group contains four people, two can either double on one of the parts, often an interesting decision in itself, or one member can critique rehearsals. If short a person, the group can look for another member or decide to let one of them read more than one voice part.

A whole class may decide to combine their small-group efforts into a concert of readings that deal with a particular theme or event, interspersing individual and group readings.[2]

IN CHANTS AND SONGS

Chanting in unison with others is a very pleasant way to perform a rhythmical text. Young children especially delight in chanting together nursery rhymes, jump-rope jingles, and rhythmical games such as "Who Stole the Cookie from the Cookie Jar?" See page 255. As rhythmical texts are chanted, the children can keep the beat by clapping, snapping their fingers, stamping, or using simple rhythmical instruments. The pace can be speeded up or slowed down, the dynamics varied; a "conductor" of the chant might direct these variations.

When melody is added to chanting, we can have singing as a performance. Community singing is fun, and its value for language development should not be overlooked. For poor readers it provides another stimulus to sight-reading. For all students it builds confidence in expression. Follow the directions for choral reading given below. A small group can listen to a recording, learn the lyrics, and perform the song for the rest of the class; they can also teach the song to others. Some students may opt to accompany their songs with instrumental music. An interesting variation is "sing-say," a kind of delivery that emphasizes meaning but retains some of the melody. Encourage practice of this half-speaking, half-singing, for it produces interesting results and can help normal voicing become more euphonious.

[2] The *English Through Interaction* film "Readers Theater" shows a pair of secondary-school students working up a reading of a poem and connects this activity to Readers Theater, for which it is good preparation.

WITH PANTOMIME

One of the simplest procedures for young or inexperienced students is to read aloud while other members of a small group pantomime the action. A poem such as Mary Britton Miller's "Cat" is useful for this type of performing.

The black cat yawns,
Opens her jaws,
Stretches her legs,
And shows her claws.

Then she gets up
And stands on four
Long stiff legs
And yawns some more.

She shows her sharp teeth,
She stretches her lip,
Her slice of a tongue
Turns up at the tip.

Lifting herself
On her delicate toes,
She arches her back
As high as it goes.

She lets herself down
With particular care,
And pads away
With her tail in the air.[3]

For more mature students suggest sometimes that they slow the pantomime for greater clarity and that the reader adjust his pace to match. Instead of strictly pantomiming the action, players can express the mood of it with whole-body motions that are slow or fast, smooth or staccato, tiny or large, carefree or deliberate, delicate or powerful, and so on. At this point they have moved the motion close to dance, of course.

WITH OTHER ACCOMPANIMENTS

Dance and music are effective accompaniments to poems or other mood pieces. Selected or produced paintings or sculpture can focus a rehearsed reading. These or other scenes may be projected using

[3] Mary Britton Miller, "Cat," from *Menagerie,* Macmillan Co., New York, 1928. Used with permission of the author.

slides or movie films. Performers may decide to put a set of illustrations for a story or poem onto a long strip of paper and roll it around two broomsticks that have been inserted into holes near the open end of a cardboard box. The pictures can then be rolled in front of the audience as the story is read. See Figure 6.1. Drawings or paintings of characters and scenery can be backed with pieces of felt or flannel material and placed onto a board covered with felt to illustrate the various scenes of a story as another person reads it. At other times the best accompaniment may simply be swatches of colored material or projected colored light to reinforce the mood. The important thing is to see to it that the words have prominence and gain in significance because of the accompaniments chosen.

Every effort should be made to awaken students to the potential of synesthesia—the interpretation of one sense by another. This transmodality perception gives words a new power to evoke images and become symbols for wider experience. Without this perception, reading will remain for many children an experience isolated from all else they know. Rehearsed reading with multimedia accompaniments helps students extend the words back to the sensory experience the author is writing about. The power of the voice to evoke should remain central, but synesthesia can link this power to the power of other arts for a fuller experience.

Building on their experience with completely improvised puppet shows, students can move into scripted ones. One can read a script or narrative while the others perform the actions of the characters through manipulating puppets. This activity provides another opportunity for skillful interpretative oral reading. Both original scripts and adaptations from other narratives can be produced by students for puppet shows. More mature students may find putting on puppet shows for younger ones is a face-saving way to continue a mode of presentation they may otherwise consider too "babyish." See page 87 for more on puppets.

FOR A TAPE RECORDING

Any rehearsed reading or singing can be put onto tape and played later for an audience. This method avoids the problem of having the audience's presence inhibit the performance, and it has the added value of allowing the performers to listen to and assess the quality of their rendering, redoing it if they

FIGURE 6.1

are not satisfied. Practicing variant oral readings of a text with partners in preparation for making a tape recording provides a valuable opportunity to see what is implicit in a written text. Between tapings students can listen and discuss changes, thereby experiencing the potential and limitations of the written word. They may find it helpful to listen to a tape made by a teacher, other adult, or a classmate and compare it with theirs. Working toward the end of producing a tape provides a bracing stimulus to good reading; the tapes students produce can then be part of the classroom library for other students.

Recording a story, poem, or song might be the final stage in a progression that begins when a student listens to a selection that is read to him by the teacher or played on a tape and follows the text with his eyes, thus getting an idea through this model of how the piece might be interpreted orally, then reads it back and forth with a partner, practicing variant readings, then reads it silently alone, then reads it to a less-developed reader, and finally works it up as a reading to be taped and placed in the classroom for other students to listen to. This final recording might include sound effects.

USING RADIO AND TV SCRIPTS

Like audio recording, radio relies entirely on voice and other sound. This makes for an interesting medium, and much of the art of radio's golden era consisted of conveying everything without vision. Sound effects and narration play an important part, but the expressiveness of the voice must reign supreme. Scripting for radio requires special, skillful compensation for the lack of video. So as students work up readings, they may think about whether they will present them with or without visual presence. One way suits radio and audio-recording, the other TV and live performance. Encourage students to gear their rehearsals to the medium they have chosen.

If students are doing a radio script, they will have to focus on what the microphone picks up and not rely on gestures and actions that cannot be heard. Peers who are critiquing a rehearsal may do well to turn their backs on the performers in order to better focus on the auditory experience. Casting is best done with eyes closed. The performer frequently hears his own voice better if he talks to a wall and cups his hands behind his ears. The group may appoint a director who is responsible for the overall aural effect and timing. Pace is crucial because there are no visual clues, so understanding is often dependent on a slowing down. Anthologies of radio or TV scripts* are highly desirable classroom materials.

A TV performance, on the other hand, is geared toward both what the microphone picks up and what the camera sees. There are many more middle and close-up shots than long shots, so the actors' faces and voices are heightened. It is an intimate medium. Large-group actions or effusive stage gestures, which might be appropriate for staged performances, often lose their effectiveness on a TV screen. Video-taping equipment facilitates valuable experience in experimenting not only with voice and tone pacing, but also with accompanying physical action.

CHORAL READING

Sometimes called voice chorus, choral reading can be a very pleasurable and effective way for students to practice reading texts aloud. Often a large-group activity, it is social but unthreatening. It serves well to boost skill and confidence to the point of more individual performance. Besides strengthening students' decoding skills, it helps to develop their feeling for the artful flow of words, the intonations of voice, and the rhythms of language. Supported, and sometimes corrected, by the voices of the group, each individual can hide in the herd and let himself go. Better readers can carry along the less able ones, though it is also true that the latter can mumble uncertainly through, and that is why individual coaching should supplement the choral reading for these students. Nevertheless, shaky readers can be bold, make guesses when they are not sure, and suffer little risk of failure. The better readers will show them whether their guesses are right or not.

Choral reading at any age provides practice in sounding texts aloud. For students who are beginners in dramatic activities choral reading has the advantage of allowing individuals to participate wholeheartedly while testing out their talent under the cover of the group and without the fear of personal exposure. Dividing a chorus into voice parts prepares very well for individual reading of roles in play scripts.

For choral reading a common reading text is useful, but this can be written on newsprint or blackboard, or projected overhead. If the texts are written large and hung up around the classroom, they can provide occasions for informal small-group practice or individual rehearsal at other times in the day. Texts for choral reading should have strong rhythms and cadences and varied and interesting "phrasing" (in the musical sense). Poetry is excellent, and songs especially will help teach phrasing and rhythm, since the melody usually parcels out word phrases according to musical phrases. Texts that contain possibilities for different voice parts are useful for dividing a chorus into subgroups having different "roles." These voice parts might represent not just different characters but different moods, themes, places, or other elements that shift or repeat in a text. Deciding together how to assign text to subgroups can become a valuable part of preparing a choral reading and proves a very effective teacher of literature. Working with dittoed copies, a transparency projection, a chalkboard, or easel-stand poster enables the group to annotate the text with "stage directions" about how to read certain lines and who is to read them. Annotations can be written in by a leader as the group tries out and decides on various renderings.

Some leader is needed both during this arranging of the text and during practice. You or a student can conduct the group somewhat like an orchestral or singing conductor, working out certain hand and head signals that everyone learns. Depending on the literacy maturity of the students, the leader may need a pointer to synchronize voice with text. After some whole-class experience in choral reading, the activity may be pursued by subgroups of the class with the aid of only activity directions, if needed.[4] The conductor will be needed during performance as well as rehearsal, as for a musical concert.

On occasion you might proceed by dividing the class into groups, each of which works out its own rendering of the text. Then you bring the groups back together after each has worked up its own version. Let them perform for each other and compare versions toward the selection of a final rendering to do as a single large group.[5] This process should help prepare the students for later work in self-directed groups.

Large group or small, the steps for choral reading are these:

- Choose a selection and read it together or in pairs until everyone understands it.
- Then decide how to arrange the text for a choral reading. Although there are books that do this for you, the process of working out a good arrangement is a valuable one, so students should be encouraged to do their own arranging.
- Have each person read a line so you can decide if his voice is high, medium, or low. Group all the voices with the same quality together and use them for certain lines.
- Decide together which, if any, lines should be spoken by a solo voice, a subgroup, or the whole group and which lines would best be spoken by high, low, or medium voices.
- Read through the entire selection as arranged and make changes if needed to emphasize the important parts.
- Practice expressive fluency by making a list of the most important words and phrases and then reading them aloud in quick succession, one after another, changing voice and facial expression rapidly as the meaning changes.
- Read through the complete text again, using a different volume level for each different idea. Decide which volume and pitch level is best for each part to clarify the meaning. Try out various kinds of phrasing, intonation, and other vocal expression.

[4] The *English Through Interaction* film "Reading Activities" (elementary) shows a teacher leading a class in choral reading.
[5] This procedure and other useful practices can be seen in "Choral Reading" (secondary) in the *English Through Interaction* series.

- Experiment with pace. Decide which lines should be spoken more slowly, which more rapidly.
- Decide who is going to read the solo or duo parts; then rehearse; tape the rehearsals to hear which parts, if any, need more work. You may decide to add a guitar, piano, humming, or other accompaniment.
- Then share your voice chorus with an audience.

Special techniques for giving a rehearsed reading

STORY THEATER

Story Theater is a technique for dramatizing narratives. As the text of a story is read aloud or delivered from memory by actors representing the narrator and the characters, the action of the story is captured in movement and pantomime and often music as well. The style is poetically evocative. Actors fill out narration with their own action. Sometimes a character takes up the narration, speaking as a storyteller rather than a character. For example, a child might say, "And so he went carefully down into the well" as he pantomimes his hand-over-hand descent. Deciding how to divide up the text is part of the creative process of Story Theater, as it is also for Readers Theater and Chamber Theater, described later. Activity directions, for example, should array the options—to have one narrator throughout, or to have each character take his own narration in addition to his own dialogue, or to have a group play the narrator as a chorus while the characters do their lines and actions, or to have one group as narrator, one group reading dialogue, and another doing actions. If some players do only action, they need not hold scripts and are free to move, thus creating an interesting contrast in dynamics with the relatively immobilized readers, though readers may of course choose to memorize text and thus free themselves.[6]

Experimenting with who is to do what and who is to take the narration, and at what points, builds insights about how Story Theater productions can be effective. There is nothing to preclude a single player's doing more than one role, or more than one

[6] See the *English Through Interaction* elementary-level film "Story Theater."

player's doing a single role, including, of course, the role of the narrator; thus, any player should be encouraged to "accompany" any person who is acting out a given role. For example, while an individual reader or small chorus reads "And so she searched frantically for the mite," another small group could simultaneously perform that action. When the players in their assumed roles feel the need for dialogue, the narration might stop while they improvise it.

The framework for Story Theater needs enough structure so the story can go on but at the same time enough looseness so transformations can occur. For example, if the narrator says, "So they walked hand-in-hand into the deep forest," he must stop long enough for the actors to discover together if the ground is firm or muddy, if the weather is hot or cold, if the trees are close together or far apart and so on.

Actors work with only the simplest, most suggestive props, if any, and wear only the simplest costumes, if any. Ordinary objects may symbolize elements in the setting and can sometimes be used to represent more than one object. A ladder or a set of steps, for example, can be a window, a balcony, a mountain, or heaven—or all of these at different points in the story. If all the players are clad in leotards of a neutral color, one monocle, mustache, broom, head bandanna, glittery necklace, or handcuff can very effectively suggest a character and his stance in relation to the others.

Material

Paul Sills's production, *Story Theater,* is probably the best-known professional example of this technique. Audiences delighted in the way his company was able to lead them into the fantastic—into a world of dreams where the imagination was needed, where the audience experienced creation right along with the performers. John-Michael Tebelak's *Godspell* is another Broadway production that relies heavily on Story Theater techniques. Story Theater has special appeal for elementary children, who will enjoy both performing and witnessing it. It is an ideal technique for older students to use in performing for younger ones.

The material that best lends itself to Story Theater is simple narrative—stories from the oral tradition such as myths, legends, and folk tales or other strong stories that call for action, movement, or pantomime; the atmosphere comes from music, lighting, and dramatic animation. The goal is to sug-gest rather than explicate, to enhance the imaginative and poetic qualities of the tale, symbolizing its drama rather than stating or elaborating it.

Procedure

As usual, take an inexperienced class through once or twice yourself; then let subgroups of the class do it with their own director, following activity directions. Of course, you are always available to sit in and give reactions or remind them of alternatives. One way to introduce the Story Theater is to have the class choose a story they like that has enough physical action, dialogue, and narrative to exploit the technique well. Then break the class into groups and ask each to develop one scene from the story if the children are very young, or to develop the whole story. If each group does a scene, these can be strung together for a whole performance; if each does the whole story, these different renderings can be compared. A third possibility is for each group to do a different story and present it to the others. Whichever of these three you choose, you should move around among groups helping them discuss decisions about how to perform the text.

Warm-ups are important for any drama, but for Story Theater they are crucial. To set the mood for improvising and experimental, freewheeling rehearsals, lead theater games such as mirror exercises to help players tune themselves to one another, and to open up the space around them. Get them into a slow random walk (see page 90) and deliberately feed into that walk suggestions appropriate to the mood or action of the story they have chosen to perform. This provides an easy way in. You can call out objects that appear in the story and have the children get together in groups to form these objects— for example, a cow, a tall beanstalk, a golden goose. Encourage the players to touch each other and form the shape of the object with their combined bodies; this is a good way to help them learn to share space and stop competing with one another for leadership. It also helps them get over their tendency to pantomime a stereotyped vision of an object. For example, if three or four students have to combine themselves into a tree, they are less likely to stand in a traditional "tree" pose. They are more likely to become a different tree each time. If you ask them to be a tree swaying in the breeze, blown by a gale, budding with blossoms, or frozen in ice, you have more opportunities for breaking them into original and flowing shapes. The whole mood of "Anything is all right as long as you are concentrating on what the group is doing" should carry over into the development of the Story Theater production itself.

It is true that if groups choose different stories, they lose the advantage of a warm-up leading directly into each group's story. However, this is not a big problem because the important thing about the warm-ups is the mood they create—an atmosphere of cooperation, closeness, and willingness to give and take leadership from one another, which will hopefully carry over into their group interaction. Players need to sense when one player is to take the lead and the rest to support his improvisation, when the narration is to be the focus, when all are to pantomime as a group. Sensitivity to one another and to what is evolving is not easy to develop, but it should always be the goal.

Self-Directed Groups

When doing Story Theater as a self-directed group, players will probably find that they get on faster if one person is responsible for making final decisions when group members can't come to agreement, and will sit "out front" during rehearsals and tell the actors what comes across and how they otherwise look and sound. This job as director should be rotated from one production to another and perhaps even from one rehearsal to another. Make sure the director understands that his making decisions should not interfere with group discussion of role division, text division, use of pantomime, and so on but just streamline group action.

After selection of a story, encourage general discussion about what happened, what the characters are like, and what mood or theme needs to be brought out. Then as one person reads the text, everyone else can pantomime all the actions simultaneously (as for "Pantomime a Story" on page 91) just to get a feeling of the events and how they flow in the tale. For a second read-through, some members can volunteer to read or pantomime parts and others can take turns reading the narration. By a combination of discussion and trials, the group can cast and get into rehearsals. It is important to allow for improvisation during each reading and for continual adoption of new ideas into the rendition. This keeps rehearsals alive and performance fresh. Each rehearsal is discussed to see what changes need to be kept and what changes must still be sought next. This makes of rehearsal a perpetual kind of composition.

Definitions of Readers Theater vary somewhat. We are using the term to mean a group rendition of any kind of material in which two or more oral interpreters present a text, with or without the presence of a narrator, in such a manner as to establish the locus of the piece not on stage with the readers but rather off stage in the imagination of the audience. The performers of Readers Theater see the action as they read; they project that vision to the audience. Instead of acting out the play in a realistic manner, they suggest character by using voice, facial expressions, and gestures. Action is symbolized and implied; the imagination of the audience fills in the details, creating the theater in their minds. In this sense Readers Theater is closely allied to the performance of radio scripts, which also rely on vivid oral rendering and the imagination of the audience, the difference being that the readers' eyes, facial expressions, and gestures can be seen.

Staging is simple. Typically, stools for the actors to sit on are the only stage properties. Although some lighting and bits of costume can be used, they tend to be minimal. The same reader may assume different roles throughout the production, creating each new character with variation in the volume, pitch, rate, pause, and tone of voice. Also typically, the performers do not look at each other on stage but focus their gaze above the heads of the audience to a point at the back of the auditorium.

One of the reasons pantomime, Story Theater, and Readers Theater have gained greater and greater popularity with youngsters and teachers is that they leave so much to the imagination. Readers Theater has had its greatest success in secondary schools and colleges, rather than in professional arenas. Part of the reason for this may well be the fact that Readers Theater can be used so effectively to animate history, science, art, sociology, and literature curricula. Groups such as the Annual Mother Lode Readers Theatre Festival, founded in 1969 by Robert Crain, focus on group reading for the benefit of secondary-school students. The greatest benefit for the students, however, comes as they perform, not as they watch. Well-known professional Readers Theater productions are Dylan Thomas's radio script, *Under Milk Wood, a Play for Voices*; Jerome

[7] A good text is Joanna Hawkins Maclay, *Readers Theater, Toward a Grammar of Practice,* Random House, Inc., New York, 1971.

Kilty's adapted correspondence of George Bernard Shaw and Mrs. Patrick Campbell, *Dear Liar*; and Peter Weiss's *The Investigation*.

Material

Play scripts are the simplest Readers Theater material because the script is all there, and its presentation is clearly dramatic. All the students have to do with play scripts is cut them to suit the time limits. If the students decide to adapt dramatic poems, stories, or novels, they will do well to look for selections that contain the dramatic element that we expect in theater—compelling characters and situations or powerful language. As they rewrite the material for Readers Theater, they will probably decide to delete most of the ''he saids,'' and so on. A group may decide to use diaries, letters, biography, autobiography, memoir, or reflection as sources for bringing characters to life. Some of the most successful Readers Theater scripts, in fact, are collages of extremely diverse reading matter, including not only snatches of narration, lyrics, and songs but also nonliterary material such as ads, signs, notices, documents, memoranda, and news articles—any sort of material that may relate to the theme or subject matter of the script. Thus, like Martin Duberman's *In White America,* many Readers Theater scripts are documentaries of sorts, made up of many kinds of writing not originally intended to be part of a script.

So the Readers Theater scripts may, for students, be related rather directly to radio-scripting and to documentaries, with the very interesting possibility of developing and orchestrating an idea or a theme in a poetic way by selecting and ordering excerpts from many kinds of reading matter. In order to put a script of this sort together students will have to make many significant composition decisions. Whenever students combine materials from different sources, juxtapose them, and add transitions, they face problems common to most writing. Of course, students may prefer instead to write a wholly original script or to use the written work of their classmates as the source of a new script.

Procedure

Readers Theater can be introduced to any students who have mastered basic literacy. Experience with rehearsed reading and choral reading builds skills for this kind of oral interpretation. The group size for Readers Theater varies substantially depending on the nature of the material used and the experience of the students. Smaller groups, even as small as two, are usually better for beginners. Groups of four or five are sufficiently large to provide an interesting diversity of points of view and styles without being too large to manage. Occasionally, experienced students can prepare effective readings in groups as large as ten or twelve. Timing becomes especially important if students are putting together a script as well as rehearsing it. For certain students, script-making plus rehearsal may do well to evolve slowly over an extended period concurrently with other classroom activities. In this case about two weeks can be used for finding material and tying selections together. In making their own scripts, students need to read extensively enough to gather the necessary material and intensively enough to perceive the potential of the selections for Readers Theater. Then they need time for intermittent reading, interpreting, discussing, and rehearsing for presentation.[8]

During the first several days of the rehearsal period the students will work on interpreting the texts for themselves. As each person reads, it is best to let the words suggest images to play in his mind, to create, as it were, a visual presentation, a film in his head as he reads. Then he can begin to use his voice as if it were an accompaniment to the film. He can decide what the character he is assuming is like and read his lines as if he were that character. He can compare his rendering with that of others in his group, and based on these trials the group can decide who will read which lines. They can experiment with several students reading each part or with each person playing several roles. As they prepare to read aloud, they must naturally pay attention to specific features of the text, such as punctuation, pronunciation, and definition of words, as well as to deepening their own comprehension. Next come rehearsals; and as their rendition evolves, the students coach each other and continue to make decisions about role assignments, script revision, and staging.

The readers may decide to add subtle, stylized, underplayed body movements, not to render but to suggest an action. If this is done in slow motion, the impact is greater. The goal is simplicity and clarity,

---

[8] The *English Through Interaction* film ''Readers Theater'' (secondary) shows one group going through a cycle of collaging, rehearsing, and performing a script.

suggesting through minimal movement. For example, one group of students[9] staged a fight scene as part of a Readers Theater performance of John Lewis Carlino's collage for voices, *The Brick and the Rose,* a play about a boy who gets hooked on drugs and dies of an overdose of heroin. The players kept the fight scene in off-stage focus, which is explained in more detail below. The punches thrown were done in slow motion and aimed not at one another but in the same direction as the eye focus—toward the back wall. The boy who punched suggested a short strong punch to a midsection as if the other boy were in front of him. The boy receiving the blow, also facing the back wall, contracted his body slightly to receive it. The impact of these suggested movements was strong even though the readers held a book in one hand.

A student director may run rehearsals, as with rehearsed reading or Story Theater. He may consult with you, but all decisions are his, not yours. For texts in which there is a narrator, the group should discuss together the reaction of the narrator to the characters. As the group reads some of the narrator's lines aloud, they should be encouraged to discern the tone of his voice or his attitude toward the characters. If this changes, the reader who does the narration will have to show this. It helps if the group can decide on an attitude for the narrator to assume, such as: hard as nails, all involved, sympathetic, detached and cool, or unbelieving.

MATTERS FOR DISCUSSION, NO MATTER WHAT THE MATERIAL

1. The speakers—what they are like, how they are feeling, and how this can be shown; how each is to enter—by lifting his head from a nodding position, by turning from a back facing the audience to a front facing, by standing instead of sitting, by actually walking onstage, or what?
2. The setting—where and when events or speeches take place. To get at the mood of a piece, students should read aloud to each other passages that give the setting.
3. The action—noting the succession of events and their causes and making sure everyone sees how the story unfolds and why.
4. Aspects of style that the reader has to communicate—strong *images,* words that tell how things look, sound, taste, smell, and feel; the *rhythms* of the sentences, the long flowing lines, the short staccato stabs, and all the rhythms in between; and the *diction,* the author's particular choice of words.
5. The theme—the writer's central idea should be agreed upon; this one idea that seems to animate the whole work then becomes the readers' purpose.

As they rehearse, the student director can help the group determine which parts are best for off-stage, on-stage, or audience focus (see below); what volume is appropriate, and so on. Experiments with pacing and physical arrangement of readers can precede decisions, thus building an awareness of options and what is lost and gained by each. As usual, your role is to supply alternatives, when needed, and to ask "What if . . . ?" questions. Emphasize the fact that silence, which usually indicates a character thinking, is one of the strongest moments on stage.

As students near the time for performance, they might explore some of the subtler possibilities of Readers Theater, such as body placement and the varieties of focus just mentioned above. A common arrangement for Readers Theater is to have the characters sit in a line in front of the audience. Platforms may be used to add visual interest as well as to suggest different physical areas.

Usually readers have scripts in hand, although some groups prefer to memorize their lines. Obviously the less students need the script the more energy they can devote to concentrating on the images they are creating. By holding scripts in their hands, however, they are engaging in one of the conventions of Readers Theater. The script is a way to distance the audience and make it clear that they are not going to see the interaction presented. The people before them are without a doubt readers, not players; they will suggest action, but it is the audience's job to create the scenes in their own imagination. What they see in front of them are readers arranged in a formal sitting or standing arrangement.

When speaking, the readers may look somewhere over the heads of the audience at a spot on the back wall. It seems odd at first, but then it becomes clear. They are talking to one another even though they are not looking at one another. This is the "off-stage" focus, a unique technique of Readers Theater

[9] These students were working with Floren Harper at Staples High School in Stamford, Connecticut.

whereby it effects a more direct and personal relationship with an audience than is customary in a conventional play. It is more like a reader-book relation.

The readers pretend that there is a mirror along the back wall and that all of them are reflected there. See Figure 6.2. When reader number eight speaks to reader number two, he looks at number two's imagined reflection on the back wall. Their eye lines cross at about the middle of the room. If readers four and five were speaking, their eye lines would appear to be almost parallel. As the audience watches off-stage eye focus, they *imagine* the scene the actors are playing.

When students are rehearsing a piece to do in off-stage eye focus, let them rehearse several times looking at and talking to each other. It is easier for them to picture one another's reactions and expressions if they have practiced this way before performing with off-stage focus.

The other two options for Readers Theater are audience focus and on-stage focus. When the material clearly calls for a reader to speak directly to the audience, as does the narrator in a story, then the reader uses audience focus: he reads directly to members of the audience. If two readers want to move to the front of the stage when they have a scene together, they then use regular on-stage focus: they talk directly to one another, finish their scene, and move back to their places.[10]

CHAMBER THEATER

Another dramatic mode we highly recommend is Chamber Theater. It was originated by Robert S. Breen of Northwestern University and further developed by Carolyn Fitchett Bins.[11] It is a dramatic approach to narrative that fits this curriculum remarkably well.

Robert Breen defines it this way:

Chamber Theater is a technique for presenting narrative literature on the stage taking full

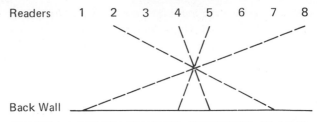

FIGURE 6.2 OFF-STAGE-FOCUS TECHNIQUE IN READERS THEATER

Source: From James Moffett *Interaction,* Level 3, Readers Theater, Houghton Mifflin, Boston, 1973.

advantages of all the theatrical devices available but at the same time preserving the narrative elements. What distinguishes Chamber Theater from Readers Theater is primarily the fact that the material for Chamber Theater does not include play scripts or other types of writing—only narrative, and that with less adaptation than that called for by Readers Theater. Also Chamber Theater is an actual staging rather than an interpretive reading, with the narrator performing as one of the characters or talking directly to the audience in a voice from the characters' world and inviting them to come in and see for themselves.[12]

Material

The narrative itself is the vehicle for presentation. Chamber Theater has the advantage of dramatizing the very element of fiction that poses a problem for some fiction readers—namely, the persona of the controlling intelligence or narrator and the dynamic relationship between him and the characters and the action.

Well-known Broadway productions that employ some Chamber Theater techniques are Edward Albee's *The Ballad of the Sad Café,* Thornton Wilder's *Our Town, War and Peace* directed by Erwin Piscator, and James Joyce's *A Portrait of the Artist as a Young Man* adapted by Frederick Ewen, Phoebe Brand, and John Randolph.

Procedure

A small group begins a Chamber Theater production by choosing a short scene from a narrative. A story with a good balance of action, dialogue, and narra-

[10] Floren Harper, Introduction, *Interaction* Level 3 booklet, *Readers Theater,* Houghton Mifflin Co., Boston, 1973, and "A Readers Theater in Your Classroom," *Connecticut English Journal,* Spring 1970, Vol. II, No. 2. We are also indebted to Floren Harper for other valuable help with this chapter.

[11] In the *English Through Interaction* secondary film "Chamber Theater," Carolyn Bins demonstrates with a class both the original Chamber Theater and her contributions to it.

[12] From a conversation with Robert Breen, February 1975.

tion works well. The material for Chamber Theater is usually fiction because of its literary value in clarifying point of view, but there is no reason why nonfiction such as autobiography could not be used. At any rate, the narrative is not rewritten as a play but interpreted dramatically as if already a script except for such minimal changes as removing "said Alberta."

In Chamber Theater the *narrator* plays a crucial role because the focus is on his relationship to the characters, one of whom may, in a first-person story, even be his former self, and the focus is also on his relationship with the audience. The chief ways of indicating these relationships are the narrator's physical position vis-à-vis the characters and the audience, and the division of lines in the text between narrator and characters. Working out passages for staging forces the students to look closely and critically at the fiction itself not only to determine what the narrator says but also to infer his tone or how he says it.

Dividing lines between narrator and character does not depend simply on separating narration from the characters' direct discourse, or even from their indirectly quoted speech and thoughts. Nor need the divisions of lines coincide with whole sentences. A narrator who is privy to a character's thoughts and feeling may share with him both narration and dialogue. A character may speak certain sentences or clauses of narration that describe his reminiscence, state of mind, or abstraction of a situation, just as he may take over from the narrator those portions of indirect discourse that paraphrase what he said or thought. During a character's inner debate, the narrator may utter one of the opposing positions to dramatize the conflict of selves. On the other hand, when the narrator is recounting events or summarizing a situation in the style of the character, the character does the speaking. When the ideas expressed in narration are also those that are going through the mind of a character, the narrator and characters may decide to read them in unison. To us, the interplaying allotment of lines is the most intriguing and original feature of Chamber Theater. It enhances narrative effects and throws relationships into relief.

The way the narrator shows his relationship through his physical position dramatizes the fact that he can move freely in time and space. He may stand behind a seated character with his hand on his shoulder and speak either directly to him or to the audience, he may poise aloofly on a raised platform or stair, he may face a character directly and speak to him, or he may move close or far away from characters or the audience. He may move in and out of scenes or remain central. Thus he is able to indicate stable relationships throughout a story and shifting relationships within a story. He may be omniscient, take a detached stance, speak in a lofty tone, become privy to a character's thoughts and feelings, comment satirically about him to the audience, become his former self for a while, alternate between objective reporting and identification, and so on.

The important thing in Chamber Theater as in most other student performance is to experiment. Players may decide that there is no "fourth wall" between the characters and the audience, so nothing is hidden from the audience. Instead of making entrances and exits, the actors may decide to remain in the background when they are not in character and move down to the main playing area when they are. They may pantomime the props instead of having actual objects or add actions implied by but not written into the scenes. They may have the narrator play also the part of a person in the scene who has a small part. Scripts may be read or memorized, and the production video-taped. Again, a student may direct.

Autobiographical Incidents

Much of this technique's effectiveness lies in what precedes and follows these readings. One of Carolyn Bins's contributions is in asking students, before they dramatize short stories, to tell and then enact actual autobiographical incidents from their own experience. If the teller's story is taped, this tape can serve as a script or reference for a Chamber Theater enactment. Students other than the teller may direct versions of the incident and may take the role of narrator without seeing each other's versions; then the student-author himself directs a version, playing himself as narrator while someone else plays him as participant. Interesting combinations are possible. The author's version allows the audience to perceive, visually, just how close the narrator is to the story he is telling. This stance will probably be different in versions that others direct or play narrator in, and these versions can be compared in discussion.

Talking about the dramatization of autobiographical incidents develops understandings on which discussion of Chamber Theater productions of short stories can be based. Comparing versions and evaluating performances provides a chance to see, hear, and feel point of view more powerfully than most students are able to do when reading silently; they examine not only human behavior but also the motivations that underlie it.

Chamber Theater technique is a brilliant way to translate flat print into tangible dimensions. Unlike adaptations that make fiction into something else (also a legitimate endeavor) it brings out what is peculiar to fiction.

SUMMARY OF THE THREE TECHNIQUES

Story Theater, Readers Theater, and Chamber Theater all consist of rehearsed reading; all divide text among actors in creative ways; all evoke rather than simulate realistically; and all assign actors to the narrator role. Whereas Story Theater and Chamber Theater stage narratives only, Readers Theater stages any material whatsoever. In Story Theater and Readers Theater, several actors may play one role or one actor may play several roles, but in Chamber Theater each actor takes one role as in realistic theater, because Chamber Theater's focus on the narrator's relation to the story and the characters requires consistency of role. Each features certain techniques—Story Theater, the interplay of voice and pantomime; Chamber Theater, the physical and vocal interplay of narrator and characters; and Readers Theater, the off-stage focus of action. Readers Theater is broader, and Story Theater and Chamber Theater are more specialized. Story Theater suits elementary school most, Chamber Theater suits high school most, and Readers Theater suits both very well.[13]

Enacting scripts

We will now consider acting out scripts, material that is written or adapted to be staged as a drama, unlike most of the material suitable for Story Theater, Readers Theater, and Chamber Theater. The big difference between Readers Theater and regular theater is that in the latter, on-stage focus is the

norm. Most playwrights work to maintain what is termed a *fourth wall* between the players and the audience. The relationship between the actors and audience is thus indirect—not direct. This is the convention of the play; the audience is watching the actors, who in turn pay no attention to the audience, at least until the curtain call.

Acting out memorized scripts is what most teachers think of first when they envision performing texts. This often evokes images of hours of rehearsal and the frantic tension of the final production of a play—complete with costumes, stage, lights, properties, and so on. If this is what text performances were as a regular routine, few teachers could justify them as a staple classroom process. Occasional performances of memorized scripts for a large audience are enjoyable and stimulating, of course, but regular rehearsed reading, text in hand, for an audience of one's classmates is by far the more valuable experience for the total language development of the student.

There is value for the student in acting out a story idea in an improvisation without a script, whether an audience is present or not. On the other hand, the value of acting out a memorized script inheres precisely in the fact of an audience. The whole purpose of a script is to hold actors to a presumably superior version of the action, a circumstance of little value to participants playing just for themselves, but important to beholders. For a rehearsed reading a director is optional, but for a play he or she is definitely necessary, to make decisions about staging, placement and movement of actors, and speaking of lines. Scripts can be acted out without being memorized, of course. In this case the action is somewhat inhibited by the scripts students hold, but the performers have the advantage of needing less time to get a play ready to share with their peers. Sight-reading of plays is shortest and simplest but worth least. It is all right as a way of becoming acquainted with an easy play, but advances in learning come from the work of rehearsals, which entail rereading, thinking, and discussing.

Play performing should begin much earlier than has been the norm heretofore. Primary-school children can read simple plays as soon as they can decode, and the fact that the material is dramatic provides a natural stimulus for perceptive oral interpretation. Children can first read the play silently or sight-read together, then take the parts of characters and read it as a play in a small group, and, finally, act it out as they read.

[13] There are excellent chapters on Choral Reading, Readers Theater, and Chamber Theater in this basic oral interpretation textbook: Wallace A. Bacon, *The Art of Interpretation,* Holt, Rinehart, & Winston, Inc., New York, 1972.

MATERIAL

For enacting, what is called for are scripts composed *for the purpose of performing.* Anthologies* of short plays (of one continuous scene, one act, or two or three scenes) with fewer than five characters are best for beginners, because they are going to work out direction and production as much as possible on their own. It is wise to put off very long or difficult plays until students have benefited from the dramatic experience that short plays and other kinds of acting such as creative dramatics make possible. We see no reason to rush Shakespeare, for example. Spending several weeks "studying" a play of his—deciphering it—is certainly not recommended. Better to wait until students can by some means perform his plays, at least as a rehearsed reading, because this will make them more comprehensible. The consulting of textual notes and analysis of text so tedious in silent reading come more easily as part of the practical and social process of working up a performance. A leisurely and thorough development in dramatic understanding will considerably increase student appreciation of Shakespeare when they do come to him, as well as give their language ability time to mature. See page 131, however, for *listening* to Shakespeare.

Adaptations of Other Texts

If materials other than scripts are used for enacting, they need to be rewritten as scripts and duplicated so that each member of the performing group has a copy. Rewriting stories or poems into drama scripts is, of course, a valuable composition task.

Most students enjoy performing plays, and this fact and the fact that there are far too few short published plays for classroom use make the writing of scripts to be performed by classmates a popular composition mode. Having the script author easily available for consultation with the players provides the actors with guidance beyond what is actually written. Student authors also get valuable feedback as the performers and directors face various script problems from which they can all learn: they cannot read the author's handwriting, or cannot tell how to read a line from the way he has punctuated it, or don't understand the timing of actions or what kind of person a character is, or don't know what the point is of a certain action or speech, or cannot figure out what the set really looks like, and so on.

Transcripts

Transcripts are a good source of texts for enacting that are seldom used. Although not composed or intended for performance, they look, in format, as if they were. Also, they are potentially dramatic and can be re-enacted into the dialogues or conversations that they were in the first place. If possible, recordings* of the original words should be available to compare with student-produced interpretations after, not before, the students perform them. Transcripts provide an opportunity for students to do role-playing without having to make up the words. A good feature of transcripts is that in most cases stage directions are not part of the text, so students have to fill in action and position according to their interpretation of what is going on. Transcripts* of interviews, trials, speeches, Congressional debates, informal dialogues, hearings—all can be used as scripts that constitute an interesting challenge for oral interpretation. Many successful plays comprise trial scenes. Students can edit a transcript into what they consider a performable version. Tone, characterization, motivation, and interplay all have to be inferred from the bare dialogue—a fine kind of practice in comprehension.

PROCEDURE

Selecting a script is a process not to be hurried; it provides a good motivation for wide reading to screen many plays. Not only texts but also professional recordings or student-produced tapes can be used for the selection process.

Reading in Role

After reading or listening to the play, the group members decide together who will read each part and meet together to read the script aloud. After they do this, they may, in some cases, decide this is not a script they want to perform, and they can look for another text. They can reread the play rotating roles and discussing the different renditions of each part. Sometimes they may choose to memorize a short script.

Rehearsals with Movement

After the students have rehearsed a script aloud several times, they are ready to add movement. The student director can block the movement by drawing a ground plan or floor plan and showing entrances, exits, placement of furniture, and levels and stairs that may be used. Then, scripts and pencils in hand, the cast can walk through the action in the playing space, following the director's plan. Either the author's stage directions or those of the director may be followed. Each actor can write his movements, or blocking, in the margin of his script to show which lines he moves on and where he goes. He should figure out why his character is making each of the moves he makes. It is often helpful to have the students improvise the scenes, putting them into their own words, and then going back to the lines as written. Gestures can be developed or elaborated during these improvisations. The actors should be encouraged to listen and respond to each other.

During rehearsals, the cast will discuss whatever problems they have in acting their parts. The director can lead this talk toward decisions or, when disagreement is strong, can make the decisions himself. Directors change from one playlet to the next, but the most capable students can be appointed at first. Students understand that whoever is director has the last word as regards *performance,* and that the script can be changed, but only through negotiation with the author. We suggest memorization be done as homework, but rehearsal time be allowed in class.

Halfway through rehearsals, lines should be memorized if they are ever going to be since depth of character occurs after this is accomplished. Scenes can be taped to help the actors evaluate what they are doing as they listen to the tape. They will then be able to hear if everyone's voice and articulation are sufficiently loud and clear. Again, rehearsal is a fine occasion to coach speech articulation and to encourage students to remind each other to strengthen final consonants and to enunciate both vowels and consonants more deliberately— without losing feeling and dramatic momentum.

The first full run-through of the play should be a nonstop performance. It is useful to video-tape this. The director can take notes to give the cast afterward. A double-time or fast rehearsal is good to help concentrate on picking up cues. This can be done while sitting down if each player tells his action as he says his lines: "Moving to chair. 'Whew!' She sits." The entrances and exits need to be polished. The director should make sure everyone can be seen and heard in every part of the audience area. An audience can be invited to see a run-through and make comments. Then comes a technical rehearsal for final adjustments by the technical crew, and finally a full dress rehearsal with costumes if the cast has decided to wear them.[14]

The value of performing texts

The processes involved in performing obviously *develop interpersonal skills.* Students get better at discussion as they practice it during selecting and rehearsing of texts. They also learn how to give and take constructive criticism. They have an opportunity to overcome shyness gradually and to develop poise before others. The pressure of putting together a performance emphasizes a common goal and puts a premium on working effectively together.

Like all oral performing, enacting texts *teaches* "speech" in the sense of articulation and elocution. In this curriculum such vocal traits as musicality, dynamics, enunciation, and expressiveness are considered factors of feeling and involvement that can develop best in speaking situations that release feeling and tie into real motives. Performing texts makes good articulation and expression a practical matter about which the student usually welcomes feedback and coaching.

In rereading, rehearsing, and performing a published script, one *comes to possess the language* in it. This means that students enrich their native vocabulary, phasing, sentence structure, and speech rhythms by incorporating those of creative writers beyond their immediate world. This is a much more powerful imprinting than occurs from merely reading a text once silently. And of course such new intake influences how a student speaks, writes, and reads in the future.

As audience for other students' performances, an individual becomes acquainted with more dramatic works than he would read alone. After a while he becomes a fairly sophisticated playgoer, ready for professional productions, and at the same time *becomes conversant with the dramatic literature* of his maturity level. This happens not just from the turnabout sharing of performances but also from the sifting and discussing of scripts that goes on as different groups try to select ones they want. This

[14] A good acting primer for high school students is Charles McGaw, *Acting Is Believing,* A Basic Method for Beginners, Rinehart & Co., Inc., New York, 1975.

collective knowledge is absorbed by individuals and also stimulates them to read.

As a performer, a student *deepens his reading comprehension.* At the same time he externalizes it, providing the teacher with a clue as to how well he understands what he has read. In order to interpret well, a student must read carefully and critically, taking on, if necessary, a new language style and tone and making it his own. The emphasis that dramatic treatment places on speaker, voice, and circumstance of utterance helps a student gain insight into all the literature he reads, whether aloud or silently. The careful reading that the performing process demands leads to insightful and authentic discussion about literature in order to solve problems of interpretation that are real and immediate.

Rehearsing a script—whether for a reading or acting performance—requires many close silent readings, makes the actor-reader think about the meaning and implications of what he is reading, necessitates attention to punctuation, allows the actor to truly work into the situation and role. In both rehearsing and directing scripts, one learns to fill out the text imaginatively—to inferentially relate dialogue, description, and narration just as one has to do (on one's own) in reading fiction, plays, and poetry. The actor also gains experience "hearing" a character speak and so is better able to distinguish an invented persona from the real-life author.

From the reader's point of view then, any text is a script. It must somehow be sounded out in the literal sense of simply decoding, as well, perhaps, as enacted in the sense of performing or in the sense of carrying out directions for action. Like a drama script, any text leaves much to be filled out by the reader from experience and imagination. This inference is generally what is meant by the term *reading comprehension.* Students used to seeing all texts as scripts will understand intuitively that they must role-play the writer and re-create his voice, his intonations as indicated by punctuation, his style or tone as indicated by word choice and sentence construction, and his ideas and intentions as indicated by overall organization and sequence and many other interplaying factors. Silent reading is playing out a text on the stage of the mind.

reading

The most useful thing to know about reading is the way in which it is unique. How does it resemble the other language arts and how does it differ from them? As a receptive form of communication, it differs, of course, from speaking and writing in being a comprehension activity. But how does it differ from listening, which is also a comprehension activity? Recall from Chapter 1, Basic Concepts, Table 1.2, The Two Levels of Verbal Coding (page 11), in which we distinguished verbalization from literacy. Verbalization translates thought into speech and constitutes the basic, oral level. Literacy translates speech into print and constitutes the derived, written level. Reading differs from listening by *including both verbalization and literacy at once.* When people read, they are decoding print into speech at the same time they are decoding speech into thought. Most of the tremendous confusion about teaching reading centers around this fact that *reading is made up of two very different activities going on simultaneously.* The confusion is reflected in the ambiguity of the term itself, which sometimes means literacy, or "beginning reading" ("decoding"), and sometimes verbalization or "reading comprehension." Probably nothing will help you more to teach reading than to clarify the relation between its two components.

What is unique about reading is not the intellectual part, the comprehending, which characterizes listening also, but the translating of print into speech, the literacy part. Conflict begins to arise, however, when someone says therefore that reading is only decoding print, because then someone else retorts with alarm that reading is no such shallow thing; it conveys meaning and therefore holds the key to humankind's highest thought. Both are right, of course. They are needlessly disagreeing about two different senses of the word. But it is critical for learning to note that the visual processing is what is unique about reading, whereas comprehension extends far beyond reading, not only to oral language but into nonverbal media.

One does not need to be able to read and write in order to comprehend and compose language, because both can be done orally, and often extremely well, by preliterate or illiterate people. So meaning is a larger, life-long matter and connected to literacy only because letters symbolize speech. Meanings are learned through one's total life experience and learned no more via "reading instruction" than any other way. With oral speech goes a stock of meanings. Reading teachers sometimes speak of "getting meaning from the page," and the expression is all right as a manner of speaking, but more accurately, people get meaning from the speech sounds that the printed words represent. Readers decode written symbols (by "word attack") into spoken symbols they already know (by "word recognition") to which meanings are already attached.

No one knows technically how sight and thought collaborate in reading. When two so closely functioning operations of the nervous system occur simultaneously, they tend to fuse in some way for greater efficiency. Thus a proficient reader probably comes to link printed words more directly to meaning than he did when he was first learning to read. He probably bypasses the intermediary of oral speech so far as to quit subvocalizing as he reads. In fact, it is most likely that instead of silently forming the words he reads, he is mentally hearing a speaker as he reads, for a good reader must be recapitulating from the word choice, phrasing, and punctuation a tone and an intonation by which the words would be vocalized if the writer were delivering them in person. In this book, when we speak of a reader re-creating the voice behind the page, we do not refer to subvocalization, which moves at the speed of speech articulation; we refer to imagination, which moves at the speed of thought. It is on the basis of this imagining that a silent reader may, at any time while reading, read aloud with natural and expressive vocalization.

In Part Three, Literacy—"The Basic Skills," we will deal at length with the literacy level of reading. In those chapters we describe how to teach decoding or word attack and word recognition by a combination of the phonics, sight-word, language-experience, and listening-while-reading approaches. This chapter focuses mainly on reading as comprehension. If you teach youngsters for whom beginning reading or remedial reading is a dominant issue, you may want to turn now to Part Three and read it or the lead chapter of it before continuing here.

We believe that separating somewhat in your mind the two very different aspects of reading will help bring about better coordination of word attack and comprehension in the learner's mind, paradoxical as that may seem. Once you distinguish each clearly as an activity inherently independent of the other, then you can see more clearly how students can learn to fuse them for effective reading. Youngsters should learn to decipher letters while also comprehending, because in practice, literacy and meaning should not be separated.

Our concern here for definition and clarity is no mere academic exercise. How educators conceive reading makes enormous difference not only in how schools go about teaching it but also in the balance of the whole curriculum.

The misconception of "reading skills"

There is a widely held misconception about the nature of the reading process. It is that reading comprehension is somehow distinct from general comprehension and thus can be concentrated on as a "reading skill." A long list of mental activities that any psychologist would consider general properties of thinking that occur in many different areas of human experience have somehow or other all been tucked under the skirts of reading. Recalling, comprehending, relating facts, making inferences, drawing conclusions, interpreting, and predicting outcomes are all mental operations that go on in the head of a nonliterate aborigine navigating his out-

rigger according to cues from weather, sea life, currents, and the positions of heavenly bodies. Not only do these kinds of thinking have no necessary connection with reading, but they have no necessary connection with language whatever.

It is understandable, in a way, that these skills have wound up as reading skills, because in reading, as in anything else, one is confronted with a set of phenomena that one has to make sense of, put together, comprehend. And it is true too that a reader has two simultaneous levels of phenomena to cope with—the letter symbols and the things or concepts referred to. But if he has learned to decode letters into voice, then he has no more to cope with than if someone were speaking to him. This is not to say that speaking and writing are the same. Writing is usually more pondered and more compact—more difficult in the sense of denser. But by the same token writing is more accurately worded, and the reader has the additional compensation that he can stop and study the words. A person who fails to understand a text either cannot decode letters, or else cannot understand the text for reasons that have nothing to do with printed words; he would not understand even if the text were read aloud to him. In other words, reading comprehension is merely comprehension.

According to the misconception, however, failing to comprehend a text is something more than just a literacy problem and yet still a reading problem. This is impossible if by *reading problem* one means a problem unique to reading. If a learner can sight-read aloud a text with normal intonation—the test of literacy—and still does not understand what he is sounding out, he has a thinking problem that is *reflected* in reading, but he has no problem *peculiar* to reading. The point is of the utmost importance, because whoever believes that incomprehension while reading constitutes a special learning case must then believe that "reading comprehension skills" exist and that these can be developed only through reading activities.

One result of this misconception is that many children spend a large amount of time plowing through various programs advertised to increase these so-called reading comprehension skills— "reading labs," "skill builders," "power builders," or "practice readers." Such programs consist mainly of sequenced reading passages about which students are asked comprehension questions. Scores often do rise on these built-in tests of reading comprehension because the activity itself is nothing but constant test-taking. The increased scores may have several meanings:

1. Increased scores may show that a student's *literacy* skills may actually be increasing, since any practice in comprehending texts exercises decoding at the same time.

2. Increased scores may mean that a student is learning to take this sort of test. Some youngsters quit reading the passages and simply go straight to the questions, referring to a passage if they need to. "You get used to the sort of question," as one explained. Even if the student cannot see the questions until after reading the passage, he knows as he reads that he will be questioned afterward in a particular way. This creates a very different frame of mind from ordinary reading. Also unrealistic is the short length of text and the short time span between reading and testing. For most real reading one has longer texts to remember for a longer time.

3. Increased scores may show merely normal growth in thinking and knowledge acquisition that would have occurred anyway without the exercises. This classic bugaboo of testing looms most at precisely the age when reading comprehension is tested most, which is when youngsters' mental growth is bounding along.

4. Increased scores may very well reflect other learning occurring elsewhere in the curriculum such as the growth of concepts and inference through social and environmental experience.

The only kind of control for such testing would be to put the same youngster through the same period of his life twice—once with and once without the treatment. Though a powerful reason to minimize any test scores, this lack of experimental control hurts comprehension testing far more than testing of factual material, because people have to acquire facts, whereas they are born with faculties for comprehending that will grow anyway. Finally, such constant comprehension quizzing can never show if youngsters will read if they don't have to, or will want to read. More likely, as many teachers learn the hard way, it will misrepresent reading and kill interest in it.

There is every reason to believe, in fact, that this read-and-test method does not and cannot significantly increase reading comprehension. We have just suggested that it may seem to work because it takes credit for intellectual growth occasioned by both normal maturation and learning experiences taking place elsewhere, in and out of school. Logically, too, one can expect a severe limit to how much reading comprehension can increase from silent reading alone, for silent reading is more the end than the means. Alone with a book, one comprehends it mostly according to what understanding one has *already* acquired, though of course any effort to comprehend on one reading occasion probably pays off somewhat on another. But what accounts for the understanding a reader is able to bring to bear on a book at any given moment are some experiences between readings—warm-ups and follow-ups that help him to grasp a text better when alone with it.

The only such factor in the "practice reader" method is the questioning after reading. We can concede that such questions might "get a student to think more about what he reads," but we think that if the same student were choosing his own reading selections to fit his interests and other language projects he was engaged in he would be thinking about what he had read anyway. The questioning, in other words, merely offsets the lack of intrinsic motivation. Certainly, as a reading follow-up it is of the weakest sort. What is needed for good comprehension are strong motivation before reading and strong intellectual stimulation afterward, neither of which this method affords. Many better ways exist, but—and here is the very painful rub—these other ways are not usually thought of as reading instruction or as testing reading comprehension skills.

The fundamental dilemma comes down to a contradiction in terms about *reading comprehension.* On the one hand, the misconception stakes out a vast domain of learning with the word *comprehension,* but with the word *reading* it implies a very narrow methodology for it. This creates an impossible double bind that accounts for much of the difficulty schools have now teaching reading. Reading becomes construed to include general intellectual activities like inferring. Vocabulary building and concept formation are placed in its domain, even though neither of these has any necessary connection with reading and can be effectively learned through talk. Subject-matter reading, as in science and social studies, is supposed to require additional "skills" that also fall under reading, when in fact what is difficult for the young reader are the vocabulary, the concepts, and the knowledge context, all of which can be learned without ever opening a book. There are educators who would have us recognize dozens of different reading skills; some even count a couple of hundred.

We question the whole concept of reading skills

beyond those of visual processing. We see nothing wrong in defining reading broadly to include comprehension, since it arises there as elsewhere, *so long as the means of practicing comprehension are correspondingly broadened.* This means that most of the activities recommended in Part Two, of this book, Basic Processes, and Part Four, Developmental Reading, Speaking, and Writing, teach reading comprehension. Just as comprehension itself extends well beyond reading, so must the methodology for teaching it.

Causes of incomprehension

First, some so-called comprehension problems are literacy problems incorrectly diagnosed. Many youngsters have in fact not learned very early to decode letters into voice and have limped along in reading, understanding some things but missing the individual meanings of some words and the total meaning of some word sequences because they are still having to devote too much attention to unlocking the letters. It is easy to confuse this case with the case of a student who decodes perfectly well but does not have some of the words in his vocabulary or has not grasped certain concepts yet, however they are worded, or has a general cognitive problem in putting facts together, or simply is not motivated to stick with the text. To the extent that a student has the first problem, the only *good* solution is the efficient literacy experience that he failed to receive before. To the extent that he has the other, the solutions lie in many activities besides reading—conversing, playing games of logic, doing dramatic work, writing, and simply getting more life experience. The test of literacy is to be able to read a text aloud with normal intonation. This does not mean that the reader understands the text. All literate adults frequently read texts they do not comprehend—even when they know all the words—because of inadequate knowledge of the subject matter, failure to grasp certain concepts, cognitive difficulty in relating statements, or failure of the *writer* to make himself clear.

POOR MOTIVATION

Given a sound literacy instruction, what causes reading problems? A major cause may simply be lack of motive. Some students have not yet become interested in language generally and in books in particular and do not see what they have to gain personally from either. This problem is clearly not going to be solved by practice reading and comprehension questions, but rather by receiving and producing language in social activities—listening to oral or recorded reading, singing, asking questions and discussing with peers, dictating stories, playing word games, and doing dramatic plays. Only widespread involvement in language can solve the problem of poor motivation, and that involvement, as most teachers realize, must occur first outside the realm of silent reading. Later, self-chosen books, as in individual reading programs, insure against loss of interest.

It is when motivation is an issue that two aspects of the uniqueness of reading come to the fore. The visual processing peculiar to reading makes it a *faster* medium and a *more solitary* medium than talk. The speed is generally an advantage. Most adults who read extensively find great frustration in other modes of receiving experience because they seem so slow. One has to receive video or audio transmission at life rate. Reading, on the other hand, can go at the pace of thought. Students should have ample opportunity for scanning and browsing in a great number of books so they can see the value of finding something they want in written form. Thus, they can learn for themselves the economical nature of the process of reading.

The solitude of reading will repel some youngsters as strongly as it draws others. Many low comprehension scores just reflect a dislike for immobilizing oneself with a book and giving up social exchange. For some youngsters being alone is virtually a punishment in itself; to be alone and *still* is too much. The whole of Chapter 6, Performing Texts, is about how to read socially and move around at the same time.

There is no doubt that the skill of reading is enormously valuable in our culture—more so, in fact, than many students learn about before they incur a reading problem. One job of schools is to array all the uses and pleasures of reading so that a learner can explore these to find reasons to make the effort to comprehend what is in books. Everyone has a different abstraction style, however, and to assert reading at the expense of these other modes of knowing mistreats the youngster who makes sense of the world largely in the nonverbal mode, by means of visual, rhythmical, or kinesthetic patterning, or the one who senses and intuits beyond language and thus is less verbal, or the one who can pick up information orally so economically that he has yet to find reading of value. Too often these types of youngsters (and these are merely illustrative types) are labeled as "learning disabled," "slow readers," or "verbally retarded." They are often issued bad report cards and may be lectured on the value of reading. Good education calls for figuring out a way to avoid downgrading the child's mode of learning and to extend his way of sensing and making sense of the world—first into conversing and, finally, as merely the top overlay on all other ways of knowing, into reading. We must recognize that for some learners this top overlay will never be as significant or useful to them as their other modes of knowing. Still, teachers can help such youngsters to add reading to their modes, to think of the written word as portable, permanent communication, easily accessible experience, and a source of entertainment—in short, a valuable extension of the world they already know. For far too many children the process of reading is a testing ground for their worth, a source of anxiety, an activity imbued with grave moral judgment. Nothing damages the motivation to read so much as its negative association with testing.

LACK OF EXPERIENCE

Another major cause of reading problems is experiential and, by definition, cannot be removed except in other activities. This does not mean to imply that some people have experience and others do not. It is simply that a book may refer to things with which a given reader has no acquaintance. These things may be physical objects, concepts, ideas, or a whole knowledge framework. Because the problem never ceases to exist, it goes far beyond "reading readiness." A layman reading about black holes in a journal of astronomy will probably have trouble comprehending. Aldous Huxley once said that our education is far too verbal, and that much of the literature presented to young people is meaningless to them because they have not yet had the emotional experiences that are prerequisite for understanding it. (Huxley was advocating more nonverbal education to the Friends of the San Francisco Public Library!)

Films and television can help enlarge experience and supply vocabulary. The practice of taking classes on field trips is well justified in this respect. Playing games with picture cards will also extend visual acquaintance with objects and living crea-

tures. See Chapter 13, Labels and Captions, for more suggestions for using pictures to expand vocabulary. Emotional experience and point of view can be enlarged by playing roles in dramatic work. The small-group process advocated in this book provides considerable social experience. Thus schools can, to some extent, acquaint youngsters with the things that words and sentences refer to, but reading comprehension will always stand in some ratio to what an individual has done, heard, seen, and felt in his personal life.

EGOCENTRICITY

Suppose a student is missing the point of the text because of subjectivity. Certain words or phrases have special power or private meaning for him; they trigger strong feelings or irrelevant associations that act as static to interfere with clear reception. These words or phrases arrest too much of his attention, causing him to ignore or slight other portions of the text, so that he gives a distorted reading, misconstruing statements or the relationships among statements. Once beyond beginning literacy any reader tends to fill in words and phrases subjectively, according to expectancy cues provided by salient letters, syntax, and the drift of the sense. But the problem reader may fail to see how his filling in does not square with meaning cues elsewhere in the text. Or he may be too undeveloped intellectually to infer unstated connections the author is implying. Comprehension questions reveal such failures to understand, but do nothing to help the reader know why he misinterpreted; they test but do not teach. The learner is wrong but does not know why, and will continue to misread.

Since egocentricity consists of being unaware that any other interpretation is possible, the learner needs other points of view on the text, which is exactly what he will get in a small-group discussion with peers. When he finds out that others his age read the same text differently, his egocentricity is challenged, and he may even be helped to perceive just how his subjective responses derailed him or made him obscure the significant with the insignificant. Such learning is much more powerful than being told by the teacher or the answer sheet that one was wrong, for in the latter case children tend to care only about being right, squaring with the authority, and often take a luck-of-the-draw attitude —"Oh well, next time I'll guess better." In drama work, on the other hand, students enacting a story or poem have to deal specifically with problems of egocentricity because differences in understanding crop up in the enactment and have to be straightened out.

Means to comprehension

The chief cause of incomprehension in learners for whom these preceding causes may not hold is a need of intellectual awakening and exercising. This covers a number of mental faculties that we will take up one at a time and indicate remedies for.

ATTENTION

The ability to attend closely to words of others and to follow their meaning sequences is developed through concentrated, interactive discussions among a small group of peers and through dramatic enactments and improvisations. The point here is that what each participant says himself depends on what his partners have just said. Unless he learns to attend, he has no basis for his own actions. This habit of interacting makes for active, responsive receivers and generates that attention to the words of others that is the indispensable basis of reading.

RECOLLECTION

Recalling depends on attention in the moment and on later efforts to retrieve the information acquired by attending. The writing process set forth in this book frequently consists of taking notes on ongoing events and basing later composition on these notes. The notes may be on the speech of others, when taking a turn as discussion recorder or when recording overheard conversation, or they may even be on reading texts themselves, as entailed in some advanced composition assignments. But most often, the notes are on other sounds and sights that the learner is registering. Frequently he tape-records and transcribes words. The general habit of deliberately storing and retrieving information—selectively noted—is thus established early and made integral to whatever experience is being registered.

As for recalling texts themselves, this occurs when enacting a piece of literature or when discussing, say, an expository selection. *In order to* act out a story or converse about a topic drawn from the reading, the groups have to recall together the actions or facts. And, of course, performing short

scripts requires actually memorizing the text (in which case the actor must try to comprehend it *in order to* perform it). Finally, a regular feature of topic-centered discussion is recalling what the group has said. Since recall is usually selective, it inevitably leads to the additional skill of summarizing.

CONCEPTION

Concept formation is directly fostered, outside the area of reading, by sorting activities, topic-centered small-group discussion, and card playing (see page 471). Whereas card games with special decks present the learner with standard concepts, which he learns by classifying instances of the concept, the framing and pursuing of topics in discussion crystallize, through group definition, some of the more slippery and ambiguous concepts that underlie words and that cause confusion in reading. Since, incidentally, card games are based on superclasses and subclasses, they also help the learner to recoghize *subordination,* which is another big issue in composition and comprehension. A guessing game like "Twenty Questions" develops a player's capacity to conceptualize larger categories for specific instances. Most concepts by far are learned by context from discussion, film viewing, and social interaction, before learned through reading itself.

INFERENCE

Let's turn now to the general and major faculty of putting two and two together, reading between the lines—otherwise known as *drawing inferences and conclusions.* From what an author says is true one is supposed to assume that certain other things not said are also true. Inference supplies everything from implied conjunctions of time and causality to the syllogistic reasoning that if statements A and B are true, then a reasonable conclusion would be C. In other words, anything that teaches relating and reasoning will foster this aspect of comprehension.

Many aspects of the program offered in this book will develop inference. Dramatization is helpful because it elaborates the text and thus brings out what is merely implied. Anything serving as a script —a story or poem or play—is bound to be incomplete. Even stage directions themselves do not by any means spell out everything. The actors must infer many of their positions, movements, expressions, and lines of dialogue, not to mention personality, feelings, and character relationships. Consider also the value of witnessing charades, pantomimes, and performed dramas, all of which require that the spectator put two and two together for himself. An important trait of drama, in fact, is that no guiding narrator or informant takes the spectator by the hand. And for the actor, the enacting of the text is one way of making explicit much of what is implicit. Students can practice deducing by playing board and card games of strategy and by working directly with verbal syllogisms, as on page 398.

Inferences can be shared in small-group discussion of reading; indeed this sharing and citing of evidence from the text to justify some inferences and not others is a major purpose of small-group discussion. But any good discussion, regardless of topic, furthers inference. A listener has to infer the implications of what any oral speaker says as much as he does those of what a writer puts in a book—perhaps even more because speech statements are less carefully worded and organized. All discussion teaches this aspect of comprehension. The effect of discussion on reading has not yet been measured, however, because continuous, regular, and well-trained discussion by peers in small groups has seldom if ever played a large role in the language arts curriculum. Our claim is that reading comprehension will benefit far more from discussion than from a program of practice reading with comprehension questions. This is so because discussion must deal continually with the speakers' understanding of each other's utterances.

The *reasons* for misunderstanding come out. Comprehension can be explored at its very roots. In the case of inference, for example, no matter what the subject is, the *process* of building and canceling statements inevitably calls attention to the implications in statements and the relationships among them. In fact, a large part of discussion consists, in effect, of testing the implications of statements. If the discussion, furthermore, is about a text the group has read, any disagreement not resolvable by pointing to a certain sentence is almost certainly to be about inference. As the group collectively makes clear the implications, each member not only can see what he missed but also can perhaps see exactly what he failed to relate. Generally, by participating in the group action of putting two and two together, the individual learns how to do it more accurately by himself.

The small-group cross-commentary in a writing workshop permits writer and reader to approach inference-making from both points of view at once and thus to see how it is a factor of rhetoric—that is, of compositional decisions that determine what the reader deduces and to which the reader must become attuned. Thus the student-reader says what he understood the student-writer to mean so that when one of them makes the wrong inferences they can pinpoint together exactly what makes and breaks reading comprehensions. See Chapter 8, Writing.

The central issue of all writing concerns how explicitly the writer should convey his ideas and how much he can assume that the reader will fill in. Judging this is no easy matter, for the writer has his own problems of egocentricity. Our point is that the learner should, from the outset, be let in on this issue as both receiver and producer. How much the writer has to lead his reader by relating and drawing inferences and how much the reader should be expected to do these things on his own are central to an English curriculum. Comprehension must be approached simultaneously from both reader's and writer's viewpoints, in order to understand how misreading occurs and to realize that reader and writer share responsibility for preventing it. Thus writing is one of the main keys to reading comprehension, especially if it includes commentary by the learners on each other's papers.

A pupil undergoing a reading skills program would be justified in feeling that the writer is always right, for whenever the pupil misunderstands, it is always *his* fault. By implication, when it is the pupil's turn to be writer, the reader can jolly well watch out for himself; any failure of communication is due to poor reading comprehension. The right-or-wrong multiple choice answers unintentionally teach the pupil that only a certain predictable set of implications and conclusions can be drawn from a reading text. (Notoriously, on standardized comprehension tests, brighter students often make mistakes because they see inferences other than the conventional ones the test-maker had in mind.)

If the learner is given plenty of opportunity, very early, to render his ideas on paper and to have them reacted to by his fellows, he can have the experience of being both understood and misunderstood in print. What did *he* leave out? What made *his* reader take a different direction from the one he was supposed to? The principle here is that when *reader and writer can talk together* they can reach a much profounder understanding of what the written word in fact is than when they deal only with printed texts. They get some insight into what both composition and comprehension hinge on—the incompleteness of a text and the fact that the writer must set cues and the reader look for them. When you become aware yourself of what you are putting in and leaving out, playing up and playing down, you understand that you must, when reading, fill out the text by relating items in it according to cues, the same cues that your own readers indicate you should put in your writing—such as main statements, paragraphing, transitions, emphasis, and subordination.

INTERPRETATION

Here we are into the complex mental operation of putting together inferences and structural cues, and of noting tone, focus, and emphasis. It involves sensitivity to word choice, patterns, symmetry, and form. In dramatic activities, students become attuned to tone and style by imitating characters and playing roles. The structural cues and patterns of word sequences encountered in silent reading can often be translated into visual, auditory, and spatial equivalents. An enormous amount of what students miss or misinterpret when reading can be attributed to a kind of childish passivity whereby printed words impose themselves with an authority that makes them seem either inevitable or arbitrary; the learner has no sense of the choices that have been made, whether these concern diction or sentence structure or overall organization. Through writing and discussion of writing he can become aware of how texts are created and therefore of the choices the author made. In order to interpret well, he must confront choice himself. The inadequacy of trying to teach interpretation through practice reading alone lies in the fact that a finished text provides no sense of alternatives. Without a background of alternatives there is no way to discriminate what the author did from what he might have done. This is why texts remain featureless to some students and hence difficult to interpret. The writing program presented in this book is based on compositional choices that range from selection and shaping of the raw subject matter to alternative ways of phrasing part of a sentence. As the learner works constantly on focus and emphasis in his own composing process, he becomes a more alert and perceptive interpreter of others' compositions.

Dramatizing and performing texts entail close interpretation in order to know what to render and how to render it. Players working up a performance must think about and discuss many aspects of the text, and this experience pays off handsomely during silent reading.

CRITICAL ASSESSMENT

As regards literary form and whole modes of discourse such as poetry, fiction, drama, essay, biography, reportage, research, and argumentation, this principle of learning to read by writing is pursued right to the very foundations of this program. Students produce all the modes of discourse that they receive. By learning these modes from the inside, so to speak, as practitioners, they have a clue as to how to read them. The writing assignments make possible a truly informed evaluation of reading texts, because particular composition-comprehension issues peculiar to each kind of discourse are examined closely under the dual writer-reader approach of the writing workshop, where criteria for judging are generated. (See Part Four, Developmental Reading, Speaking, and Writing, for suggested activities through which each of the nine modes of discourse can be experienced from the inside, as practitioner.) Again, dramatizing and performing naturally bring out features of form and the artfulness of the writer.

It should be clear at this point that reading cannot possibly be treated as a separate strand of a language curriculum. Because comprehension pervades all intellectual and verbal activities, it can be learned by many means. Hardly an activity in this book does not teach reading.

Whenever learners are using reading to get on with projects or games, or are entertaining themselves with written material such as stories, riddles, poems, jokes, or are finding out from printed sources things they are curious about or want to know, they are developing reading comprehension. Reading is a vehicle for general development.

To go off alone and curl up or pore over a book is a goal, not a means. For many youngsters, as we said, the solitary aspect of reading is in fact an obstacle to overcome. The best means will often be social—discussing, improvising, performing, playing games, working over each other's writing. Amid the anxiety about getting reading scores up, it will be hard for many teachers not to feel that such activities compete with "reading instruction" and must give way in priority to it. Shunting aside these other activities for these reasons may well be a fatal mistake. Skillful silent reading is dependent on wide experience, oral language facility, insight about human behavior and feelings, and mature thinking skills. The solitude of mature reading poses difficulties especially for people of little confidence, low self-esteem, or habits of dependence. In this way reading adds emotional factors to the perceptual and intellectual. Furthermore, a reader cannot query or otherwise influence a writer as a listener can a speaker. A book is nonnegotiable.

Some practices are not recommended. Besides sequences of read-and-test passages, we suggest not sequencing reading matter on any other than an individual basis and not organizing it around themes or units based on genre. Structuring a reading program around concepts of either form or content interferes with individualized reading, which should be initiated as soon as children can read at all and preserved through the years at all costs. Nothing you or anyone else can cook up by way of units or sequence will teach reading so well as guided individual choice in an interactive setting. The real learning will occur as individuals and small groups make up their own sequences and thematic or formal units. Setting up reading material and reading activities according to the nine kinds of discourse treated in Part Four will ensure coverage of all types of reading including literary forms. Your structuring best comes in the form of activity directions and organization of a classroom library. If you predigest form and content for your students, you will rob them of their education by short-circuiting their thinking.

The following activities aim to overcome the problem of how to understand language when the author is absent. In addition, all of Chapter 6, Performing Texts, and much of the chapters on discussing, dramatics, and writing contain activities directly teaching skills needed for reading.

Listening to texts

Long before they are able to decode or read aloud themselves children should hear good oral presentations of all kinds of literature that bring out the rhythm, music, imagery, and sound play of poetry and serve as a model of good speech articulation. Love of language is first fostered through the ear, not the eye, and from infancy onward children need to be fed good literature. Since young children or reluctant readers of any age are introduced to a very high proportion of their working vocabulary through oral rather than reading experience, listening to oral readings of literature is a very effective way to ease them into the vocabulary development that will make the reading process easier.

LIVE VOICE

You should read large quantities of stories and poems to students, sometimes assembled as a whole class, sometimes in small groups. Before children can read much themselves, this practice is, of course, a necessity if their appetite for literature is to be both nourished and satisfied. It also makes reading a common part of everyday life and shows many children of nonreading parents what books are all about and what pleasure and stimulus can be associated with them. It also puts you in a giving position. While receiving this gift, learners develop an urge to assume the teacher's power, to become able to do themselves what the teacher does. In this respect you become a model to emulate. Your continuing to read to children who have themselves learned how to read serves to show what good oral reading is like—how it re-creates a storyteller's voice, how it brings out moods and feelings and meanings, how it follows cues of punctuation and typography. Even for older learners you should periodically read, especially when the text contains a number of unfamiliar words or concepts, thus providing a good oral model.

If you do not feel confident about reading as well as your students deserve, you have several alternatives. One is to enlist aides. Call on parents, talented students, or other community people. A local amateur or professional acting group often has people who would be pleased to come in and read to youngsters of any age. For some time now such organizations as the Teachers and Writers Collaborative in New York City and the Poets in the School program have been arranging for local writers to read their own and other writers' work to students. Meeting a writer, learning something of his feelings about writing and literature, hearing him read, and discussing the world of words with him can exert a powerful effect on many youngsters, even cause a turning point in their attitude about books and language. A community reader of the students' ethnic or dialect group will ease identification with books.

For small children you may find a good local story-teller, a librarian or folklorist or talented parent, who knows both how to read and how to tell oral stories. This program's emphasis on student performing should pay off in good readers who can regale classmates or younger students. But teach yourself, too. Listen to good readers, live and recorded, and practice, perhaps listening to taped playback of yourself. You will learn a lot that you want your students to learn, about both literature and how to render it.

RECORDINGS

On page 57 of Chapter 3, Organization and Materials, we suggested setting up a listening library of recordings parallel to the classroom library of books. Two important reasons argue for supplementing live with recorded voice: (1) recordings can provide a far greater variety of dialects, styles, and voice types than, certainly, you alone, and probably more variety than you can muster even from a responsive community; and (2) recordings are available any moment students want them and hence reinforce individualization considerably.

One of the most effective ways to help students who want to learn standard dialect is to provide recordings that pose a model of standard English for those who do not hear a great deal of it. Parents of these children most often want their children at least to become familiar with the standard form, and listening to recordings is one way to do this without disparaging their native dialect, "correcting their grammar," or boring them with dull usage exercises. (See discussion of dialects on pages 19 and 179.) Standard-dialect speakers, on the other hand, should become familiar with other dialects—regional, ethnic, and national.

Not only is it pragmatically true that youngsters today will have to "speak each other's language" in order to get along well together, but dialectical variation constitutes an important part of the rich heritage of the English language. English educator Priscilla Tyler has pointed out there is not just one English literature but *nine*. A competent education in English and its literatures will include acquaintance with not only Irish, British, Scottish, Australian, black African, and West Indian or Caribbean variations, but also regional differences such as Appalachian, United States black urban, United States white Southern, Latino, Brooklynese, and New York

Jewish. These differences in how English is spoken will interest youngsters a great deal both for their own sake and for the sake of the richness they impart to our literature. Only recordings can bring this variety into the classroom, for most of the differences are *aural*. Sometimes a text written in non-standard dialect reflects nonstandard pronunciation by special, phonetic spelling. And some dialectical variations can be detected readily by differences in vocabulary or grammar. But without hearing a strange dialect a student cannot really grasp and appreciate it.

LISTENING-WHILE-READING

A perfect transition between being read to and reading for oneself is to listen to a reading of a text while following that text with the eyes. Recordings especially facilitate this practice in an individualized classroom and for older students (who may not want to be seen being read to). Listening-while-reading can teach both the decoding and comprehension aspects of reading. On page 201 of Part Three, Literacy—"The Basic Skills," we have set forth the practice that we call the lap method, as one of the main ways to learn to decode letters and punctuation. But it is very appropriate long after a student has become literate.

Listening to a text read well helps students learn to read aloud better; it helps them "hear the voice behind the page" when reading silently. They can hear all aspects of print brought skillfully to life —letters, typography, paragraphing, punctuation marks, and line settings of poetry. Pronunciations of words rarely heard in common speech are sounded while the listener is looking at the words, enabling him to read those words aloud when encountered and also encouraging him to use those words in conversation without fear of mispronouncing them. Modern technical texts can become accessible also despite unfamiliar terms, heavy loading of thought and information, and difficult sentence structures.

Hearing Shakespeare can almost obviate the need for textual notes, for professional actors not only can give pronunciations of old words and proper names but can make clear the meaning of words that have changed sense and unravel difficult syntax caused by older grammar and poetic compression. This is in addition to bringing out the drift of whole speeches, the characterization of speakers, and the dramatic interplay among characters.

Excellent discussion is often prompted by students' surprise that the voice they hear on a recording does not sound as they imagined it when reading silently.

Students can hear the tunes to songs so that they can sing them later on their own. All of the musicality and sound play of both song and poetry can be fully experienced only when heard; when heard while following the text, they demonstrate powerfully how much the reader must put into a text, how much a text is a script.

Hearing good models of everything from clear articulation to artistic interpretation will point the way for students' own renderings. Readers may outgrow literal "laps" (although that is debatable!), but they never outgrow their response to the lap method.

In fact, we offer it as a major solution to the classic problem of upper-elementary- and secondary-level students whose decoding ability does not equal their general comprehension. That is, they read no better than primary-school children, but their interests are much more mature. For years textbook writers have tried to cater to this very large segment of the school population by writing about drag-racing and drug addiction in Dick-and-Jane language. Approached this way, the problem is insoluble, because mature content couched in immature language creates a ludicrous effect and does not fool such students, who still feel the childishness and all too often do not respond well. We suggest solving the problem by making available to them recordings of texts that have content and language befitting their life experience.

Listening allows them to depend on another reader to sound out the text, yet at the same time teaches them to decode so that they can read independently. Students who cannot read anything but what is too immature drop out in large numbers between grades six and ten, or they linger in misery, accumulating life-long feelings of inadequacy and resentment. Making great efforts to give them plentiful—daily?—experience listening while following texts may well spare them either alternative. This is so important that we recommend you make way for it by dispensing with routines and giving it top priority. The solution may be unorthodox, but then orthodox approaches have not solved the problem.

Listening and reading may be combined in several other useful ways:

- Listen to a text first, then read the text.
- Read out loud along with the live or recorded voice, singly or as a small group. Or sing along.
- Try reading silently a challenging text, then resort to listening-while-following if the going gets too rough rather than giving up completely.
- Listen to some texts and read others silently when wishing to take in a lot of related material, like a collection of fables, but when reading all of them silently would tire.
- Read a text silently, then listen to the recording and compare inner rendering with the oral interpretation.
- Read a text silently, rehearse and record a reading of it, then play the class recording and compare.
- Listen to the class recording and use that version as an aid in rehearsing your own performance of a text.
- As a small group, read a text silently, discuss it together, then play the recording and discuss both text and recording, and find out if hearing it changed the ideas gained from reading and discussing it.

Reading aloud

There are two ways of reading aloud—sight-reading and rehearsed reading. By sight-reading we mean reading aloud a text one has not seen before. By rehearsed reading we mean working up a reading for others by practicing then presenting it. Reading aloud allows the learner to socialize reading both for enjoyment and for the benefits of feedback. It externalizes silent reading and thus gives the learner a chance to get help. With this help he can improve both his silent reading and his performing for others.

Some teachers may fear, understandably, that reading aloud encourages the budding reader to continue the habit of subvocalizing that he established when first making the transition from speech to print. Since subvocalizing keeps silent reading speed down to speaking speed and prolongs an inner activity no longer needed, it does seem desirable not to encourage it. But the solution, we feel, is not to eliminate reading aloud, which would exclude oral interpretation, for one thing, but is to increase time allowed in school for silent reading and to teach decoding so effectively that no need lingers to "sound out" while reading to oneself. See, furthermore, the recommendations for increasing reading speed beginning on page 222. A main aim of reading aloud, in fact, is to perfect decoding so that it becomes second nature and *frees* the learner to drop subvocalizing. The best course is to engender as much as possible both silent reading and reading aloud, for each is both an end in itself and a means to the other.

READING TO A COACH

How do you monitor and diagnose and coach a student's silent reading? A classic matter in the lower grades, this can remain an issue into high school for students who don't or won't read, or, in any case, score low. How do you know whether they cannot decode or have some other problem? To help a student to read, you must create occasions on which he sounds out the voice he is creating as he reads silently. Then you can coach him. See "Coaching and Diagnosis" on page 219 for suggestions on running these sessions and for our reasons for advising against the conventional "reading groups" of elementary school, which seem necessary only when students are all marching through a basal reader series and the teacher is tied down administering it. An individualized, self-directing classroom is designed, precisely, to create one-to-one occasions.

Listening to a student sight-read, then, should be done in a one-to-one session that is equally appropriate in elementary or secondary school but that can shift emphasis from literacy skills to comprehension and performing. It is a good occasion to discuss also a student's selection of reading material. The better a student masters the literacy test of sounding out a text and the more he becomes involved in group performances as described in Chapter 6, Performing Texts, the less he needs to sight-read for you. If he still needs coaching on decoding, ask him to read some portion as yet unread of a selection he is starting or working on. If you think the selection is not challenging enough to show what he can do, pick another for him to sight-read. But make sure that sessions include some reading aloud that allows the learner to feel his competence. A sight-reading passage can be repeated in a session until he reads it well enough to take some pride in his performance.

One way or another, it may be best for sessions to mix sight-reading with rehearsed reading. Encourage students to work up readings of selections or passages to do before a small group, or, if they wish, before the whole class. Direct them to use you as a rehearsal coach. They bring to you whatever they are working on and try it out on you so that when they perform it for classmates they can enjoy some success. For small children, the spirit of it can be, "Now *you* read to *me*." They may already have read the selection silently, or their reading it to you may be their first, a sight-reading.

The coaching part consists of letting the pupil know if he is reading too softly or indistinctly, failing to follow punctuation, or misunderstanding the sound value of certain spellings. If the reading is very halting, diagnose the problem: Is the student's decoding ability still poor in some respects, so that he has to puzzle out painstakingly? Is the text too difficult for him as regards either the amount of irregular spellings or the sophistication of content? Suppose he reads inexpressively. Merely saying that he does and adding a directive to "put more expression into it" is not very helpful, and may even lead to contrived vocalizing. It is better to ask the reader what he thinks is the feeling under the lines, or the mood of the story situation, then to ask him to "make me feel that" or to "bring it to life the way you do when you're dramatizing a story." Convey the idea that you want to be entertained just as much as he does. Of course, this "read-to-me" spirit can be easily destroyed if the coaching is delivered in a severe fashion. The diagnostic remarks and suggestions should be perceived by the child as truly helpful for his own purposes, one of which is to become a competent reader and another of which is to perform well for his classmates. Some aides may share this coaching role with you.[1]

READING TO CLASSMATES

Classmates not only can serve as audience, to furnish a motive for reading aloud, but also can coach each other to some extent.

Partner Reading

Partner reading is taking turns sight-reading aloud to each other in a group of two to four that has chosen to read a text together. Partners may have a copy each of the same text or may pass one book

[1] See the *English Through Interaction* elementary film "Reading Activities" for a good example of teacher coaching on a one-to-one basis, as well as for partner reading and student coaching.

around. The activity teaches more if all have a copy to follow while others read. The purpose is to allow weak or dependent readers to read while socializing and to pool their skills to read a text that any one of them alone might not have enough knowledge, courage, or motivation to get through. More sophisticated readers could choose to do this too, but more appropriate for them would be some kind of reading performance such as described in Chapter 6, Performing Texts.

Partners help each other with decoding, pronunciation, and comprehension problems while enjoying the social interaction. Activity directions explain that they should let each other know matter-of-factly when they think the reader has made a mistake. If they are not sure, they should ask or consult a dictionary. It's usually the case that if one mispronounces or asks what a word means or leaves a sentence hanging because he doesn't understand it well enough to read it properly, one of the others can fill in. If not, they still have more resources for formulating a question or otherwise getting help.

Often the group goes beyond mechanical help and gets into a good discussion of content following a side comment by one of the members. Sometimes they play with different styles or voices with which to read. Books of jokes, rhymes, riddles, limericks, or fables lend themselves to easy role-playing because they contain short dialogues and caricatures. Members may comment on each other's way of reading, from volume and clarity to tone and other expression. Their comments will become more helpful the more coaching they have got individually from you. Another possibility is to decide to read all together in unison, which is a good step toward choral reading (see page 110). All these variations and perhaps others can be suggested in activity directions for partner reading. Groups can form by choosing themselves or by your suggestion, but either way it seems most natural that members won't spread very much in ability, for the activity assumes more or less equal contributions, and if a member reads much better than the others he should choose or be steered to an activity such as the following.

Reading for an Audience

A student works up a reading to present to another individual, a small group, or the class. It is to prepare for this that he uses you as a coach. The idea is definitely to entertain and be entertained, so both reading and listening are well motivated. Part of your role may be to help the reader choose a selection and a length that will go over well after he has rehearsed on his own and with you. This is an activity that has to be voluntary, but once some students go around reading, the more timid may eventually be drawn to do so also, especially with a little encouragement from you and the reassurance of help as they rehearse. Experience doing unison reading for others, or taking part in choral reading, will also bolster courage.

A modest way for a student to begin is to read to just one other person—to you first, of course; then someone at home perhaps, or a younger child in a lower grade, or a classmate not as advanced. A student reading "below grade level" anyway can not only save face but gain self-esteem reading to someone even less developed than himself. (Make sure he's well enough prepared not to *fall* on his face!) Increasing the size of the audience generally requires more confidence, not to mention skill, since larger groups have more critics and are harder to please. Direct the listeners to make comments or corrections if they think these will be helpful to the reader, but remind them that a matter-of-fact tone will make it easier for them all when they are the reader. They can also talk about the content of the selection and go on, in fact, to do other things with it, if they like—dramatize, illustrate, look for other, similar selections.

Members can agree each to rehearse a selection for the others and present it in turn with the others on the same day or a sequence of days. The selections can be individually chosen or assigned by the group from some collection they are reading together or for some reason such as a project requiring that they all know the same selections. In addition to acquainting all members with all selections, round-robin readings have the extra advantage of sustaining student interest across a large number of texts.

Reading silently

Listening to others read, listening while following the text, sight-reading to a coach or with partners, rehearsing and reading aloud for an audience—all these reinforce each other and prepare for performance activities and for further, more independent, silent reading.

Teachers usually feel sheepish just letting students go off in a corner of the classroom and read, perhaps because during silent reading there is nothing you the teacher (or anyone else, for that matter) can do for the reader. That is the plain and most important truth about silent reading. The reader is on his own. Now, if the silent reading is to be followed by a comprehension test, the teacher may feel all right; after all, one will soon know what went on in that head during that silence, can weigh it and feel that it had a purpose. But to let a student read something he chose, to take no part in the act, never know what went on—well, for some teachers that's just too spooky.

The feeling is understandable—but unnecessary. For one thing, you can be sure that if you have done your part by stocking the room with plenty of good books of *all* sorts, helping the reader find what interests him most, coaching him if he needed it, setting up the many possible warm-up and follow-up activities for reading, and so on, something good will happen during that silent reading. So arrange with confidence for students to curl up and pore over a book alone on an individualized basis. While alone with it, the reader will increase his proficiency in visual processing, make well-motivated efforts to understand what someone else is saying, derive pleasure that will spur further reading, and broaden his understanding of experience and hence his comprehension of what he reads next. Some teachers declare some time as a "read-in," when everyone, including the teacher, just does some silent reading. Setting an example yourself helps.

Students should have frequent opportunity to vary their silent reading pace according to their goal. They need not only to peruse carefully for understanding and insight but also to scan rapidly to find specific information or get the main idea of a piece of writing. As small groups engage in projects or improvised drama, they often need information they don't have. Here is a very natural stimulus for students to explore classroom and library resources, using alphabetized sources of information and indexes, including the subject guide of the library card catalogue; they also see the usefulness of rapid scanning for information.

Most silent reading, in fact, will probably not be done in a vacuum but will be done as part of a group project or an individual activity for which activity directions stipulate follow-ups. Or, if cross-referenced as we recommend, books themselves may route readers to follow-ups. Reading will develop best when set in a web of other activities leading into and out of it, because these will make most sense of it. Interwoven activities carry silent reading along in their momentum. Many of these will be social activities that offset the solitude and create a balanced interplay of inner and outer life. But silent reading should not always be followed up. The sharing of what one has read is important, but so is solitary rumination. If students are always made to feel that reading in the classroom is preparation for something else, it is likely the "something else," even if it is a social activity, will be perceived as a test of some sort and the reading not be considered as a valued end itself—a way to pursue interests and entertain yourself.

Questions and other stimuli that invite a reader to reconsider what he read alone, draw it together more, and think further about it, can be positive and help him read more effectively the next time he picks up a book alone. But questions should not be the only stimuli and should be asked mainly by classmates. The stimuli should not be intended or felt as testing. Many activities will stimulate further thought about what one has read alone—discussing, illustrating, dramatizing, performing, translating to other media, imitating in one's own writing, parodying, carrying out as directions, and incorporating into other types of projects. All of these can be used also to evaluate reading. (See Chapter 21, Evaluating.) It would be hard to find a student who does not resent the inevitable quizzing, by the teacher or the printed questions, on what he has just read. He has enjoyed the story and now he must face the music, endure the commercial, pay the piper. Has anyone attempted to estimate the damaging effect of this on a youngster's will to read? In rat-and-pigeon psychology, this administering of a pain after a certain act would be called "negative reinforcement," when it is intended to discourage the act. How many *adults* would read if they had to face a battery of questions afterward? Indeed, how many adults *don't* read because they did have to?

Individualized reading

If the classroom library is diverse and extensive enough, or if students have access to a larger library, individuals can organize their reading around self-chosen subjects or a self-chosen genre of literature. The valuable process of browsing, scanning, and using tables of contents or indexes to find selections that are about the same subject or illustrate the same theme or are written in the same genre is usually confined to textbook editors or teachers, thereby robbing students of one of their most important learnings. Since in our culture no one can be sure which information will be of value in the student's later life, the most powerful capacity they can develop is the ability to find on their own the reading selections that they need or value.

As we envision it, individualized reading does not mean that every student is always reading a different book than everyone else is. It means that students choose their own reading matter and may do so with a partner or small group. They choose reading as they do other activities—in interaction with classmates, you, and environmental influences. We expect that individuals will want to read together in the sense of silently reading the same title, then coming together to follow up this silent reading experience with a group activity. Various activity directions suggested elsewhere in this book and this chapter provide for both group warm-up and group follow-up, so that often silent reading occurs in the middle of a sequence of interwoven activities. In short, individualizing means only that each student will put together from the beginning of his career his own reading program. Some selections he will read alone, but many he will share with others. A lot of his choices will, in fact, be group decisions, as with other language activities. The point is, though, that he chooses to throw in his lot with others to get the pleasure and practical benefits of partnership and group collaboration. Your role is to help students know each other's interests and who is doing what and to help them take advantage of these human resources.

GROUPING

A classic question repeatedly arises about whether students should be grouped for reading by ability (usually determined by comprehension-test scores, perhaps combined with teacher judgment). If reading is interwoven with other activities and put on an individualized basis, the question hardly makes sense any more. For one thing, it is not advisable to form semipermanent groups for reading only, since as we said, reading comprehension is just comprehension and can therefore be taught throughout the curriculum by means of a host of activities. Reading simply must have the warm-ups and follow-ups that the other language arts and other media provide. Second, if students are choosing their reading matter according to personal interests, as influenced by your counseling and by interaction with classmates, then the groups in which they read will be formed automatically on the basis not only of reading compatibility but of other compatibilities as well. Compatibility is a better principle than homogeneity, for group members do not have to be alike to get on well and profit from each other. To complement each other, in fact, may be more important, and you can make suggestions to them for group membership on the basis of what you know about them. But the old issue of grouping for reading tends to solve itself as students choose at once what they want to read, each other, and related activities.

Groups will form around a type of reading like mystery stories or memoirs, or around a subject such as horses or slavery, or around a theme such as getting lost or gaining self-control. Part Four, Developmental Reading, Speaking, and Writing, gives many examples of reading types. Groups will tend to make themselves homogeneous, in fact, as regards at least *interest*. Ability will probably range enough so members can learn from each other but not so much that they can't settle on the same title. And it is this particular choice of a selection that automatically controls membership of a group for compatibility. Better readers can tolerate weaker readers if the weaker ones do not force them to read something beneath them, as in fact happens necessarily when everyone in a class reads the same thing. When members come together after the silent reading of the selection, stronger can help weaker. The expectation of support from the stronger members encourages the weaker to take on a selection that would daunt them alone. Tolerance varies of course a great deal among youngsters, but the longer experience they have with small-group process, the more easily you will be able to help them achieve the balance of similarity and difference that they will learn from the most. Interweaving reading with other activities helps grouping more than you might imagine if you haven't experienced the effects of it, because individuals will choose each other for a group according to abilities in activities other than reading, such as a skill in drawing or a knowledge of machines, that will be useful to a project and make tolerating someone's weaker reading worth the effort.

EXCHANGING RECOMMENDATIONS

Solo reading can benefit from the diversity of classroom population. Students should have ways of exchanging tips on titles and perhaps the reading materials themselves if they own them or their family consents. An area of the chalkboard can be reserved to write titles one liked and wants to pass on. Work out a system for indicating how the title can be obtained. Another way to share suggestions for reading is to have each student who has finished a good book put a card with the title and author on one side and the reader's name on the other in a "book bank"—a box or envelope on the bulletin board. Other readers can look through it for ideas. Young children may draw pictures of each book on their cards; older students may write a brief statement telling why they recommend the book. Some students may prefer to record their recommendations on a tape for other readers to listen to. The important thing is that this activity be perceived as a sharing of good ideas, not a reporting on books.

Another way is for individuals to follow activity directions to meet as a group and bring with them a book or selection they want to recommend to others. Each displays and tells about his book and perhaps reads aloud a passage from it to sample the flavor of it. They invite questions. Often these help the speaker to think more about the selection. But it is important that these groups generally not have you present, because peer candidness and ease are what will make them work. Try to make the classroom a mental and physical central exchange for reading possibilities.

WHOLE-CLASS PROJECTS

Nothing in this curriculum prevents a whole class from pursuing a single broad subject or theme so long as within the framework there is opportunity for student choice of activities. Some projects that call for collaboration of subgroups can be worked out by the whole class, including satisfactory roles for subgroups and individuals.

If a whole class occasionally reads the same piece of literature, such as a novel or play, small-group process may still be employed. Each group can take a part of the text and work out a rehearsed reading of some sort, an improvisation, a dramatization, a panel discussion, or a translation into another media to share with the rest of the class. For instance, if most of the class members are reading Shakespeare's *Romeo and Juliet,* one group may read "Pyramus and Thisbe," another may read the script of *West Side Story,* and then all see the movie version and make comparisons. Let students generate themes. It often happens, for example, that one group gets hot on something and either draws the interest of classmates or calls upon classmates to help them enlarge their project. The original working party may want to find out more about a subject than their number permits and try to interest others in a division of labor so that different groups research different sources. Keep an eye out for such situations, and bring the possibility of the project before the whole class.

COMPILING ANTHOLOGIES

Using other books as models, a group puts together a collection of any type of writing that interests them —jokes, riddles, brain teasers, advertisements, photos of signs and other environmental writing, letters, poems, stories, and so on. Although ultimately this can become an individual activity—and personal poetry collections have great significance for many adolescents—it fits a group well because members can sift different sources and pool favorites and brainstorm ways of collecting and organizing.

Like dramatizing, performing, and other transforming of texts, anthologizing gets students to think a lot about what they have read and to share these ideas with classmates. They have to develop some criteria, implicit or explicit, on which to base their selection. How do they define the type they are trying to collect—proverbs, for example? Which riddles are better than others? (Both of these types, by the way, are often based on a metaphor.) What kind of letters? Or suppose the anthology is to cut across forms and center on a theme? What is the theme and how many ways can they find it written about? Or it could contain short stories about animals. Shall the stories be truth or fiction? Realism or fantasy? How do ghost stories and murder mysteries differ? Fantasy and science fiction?

Shall the order and juxtaposition of selections have any significance? What is the purpose of the anthology? Should that be explained in a preface? What about writing transition between selections? These questions of organization can be considered along with the physical matters of whether selections can be compiled by copying or by listing and citing sources. The motive is to pass to others what one likes.

Discussing reading

Discussion of a text students have read has traditionally been led by the teacher. As we noted in the last chapter, this is seldom a true discussion, and, besides, despite the intentions of both the teacher and the class, it is usually perceived to be a check on the student's reading. True discussions of texts are explorations and honest conversations.[2] These can begin with partners as soon as children read aloud. Without a teacher present, it is unlikely that they will perceive their discussion is a "test," and it is likely they will share naturally with one another confusions they may have had as they read. The student's spontaneous comments then are the basis of partner discussions. Asking a classmate for help in understanding some point in a text should become a natural habit in the classroom, not misbehavior, as it is sometimes considered. Comparing reactions and understandings with a partner often starts a good discussion because each can refer to the text to support his reading of it.

TALKING AFTER READING

In addition to activities like partner reading that invite discussion and to others that entail discussion —straightening out written game directions, rehearsing a script together, commenting on partners' writing, sifting information for a project— there should be activity directions for getting together after reading a selection just in order to discuss it. When a group of learners has finished reading a selection, they may come together to raise questions they have jotted down while reading. Like the partner discussions, these interchanges can help readers clarify their understanding of a text. The questions they pose may be confusions about things they know they did not grasp, something they want to know more about, or issues in

[2] For a good example, see the *English Through Interaction* film "Discussing Topics" (elementary).

the selection they want to talk about. They are directed to write these down and bring them to the group. Make clear that factual questions are not of the quiz-kid type but ones to which they really do not know the answer. They may share opinions or feelings about what they have read and compare their interpretations. This comparing is of vast importance, for it allows the reader to discover things he has misunderstood *without* knowing it. It also shows him that his reaction or interpretation may not be the only one justified by the text.

Older students who have each read the same text and have each written down a few questions on slips of paper may first spend a few minutes extracting subjects from the lists, noting overlaps and other connections among them before they begin their discussion. Several other procedures are possible, such as selecting only one issue from the slips, or taking several issues in order, or framing a single topic so as to include several points raised on the lists, or answering small factual questions first and then passing on to larger interpretive matters. Often, it will happen that the sorting itself will launch talk, and procedure will sometimes take care of itself. Basically, this process could be simply a specialized version of small-group discussion, for which reading selections supply the topics.

The topics must come from the students' curiosity, puzzlement, or interest. We believe that these discussions should essentially just extend reading responses into conversation. You could take part in some of these as recommended for training groups in Chapter 4, Talking and Listening, but take care that your presence doesn't cause some students to try to hide their incomprehension or, indeed, to show off for you their remarkable understanding. Students should feel that their candid questions and acknowledged confusion will not be used against them by adults or ridiculed by peers. You can help set a tone not only of collaborating on comprehension problems but also of just wanting to know how different people respond to the same text.

GRADUAL REVELATION OF A TEXT

A very effective way to provoke good discussion of a text is for the group to agree to stop reading the selection at one or more points and talk about what they think will happen next or how the piece will end. If you know the selection, you may suggest one or two stopping points, or the group may ask a student who has read it to do this. An option is for group members to write individually or collectively their version of the rest of the selection. They compare and discuss their individual versions, then finish the text and discuss again, or they discuss their ideas while writing a collective version and compare it with the text.

Very short selections like poems, jokes, riddles, limericks, and fables can be written out piecemeal or revealed piecemeal on a transparency projector so that halts are made at provocative junctures. Group members might take turns selecting and revealing a text. When something appears incomplete before us, we tend to anticipate the rest and to complete it ourselves, especially if we know something of the form it should have. The skill of the presenter is to pick the right stopping points. To make the activity clear and appealing, you might demonstrate it once to the class or an interested group. We will demonstrate here with a haiku.

The game is simple and enjoyable and makes students think about a great many things. In order to complete the poem, one uses all cues—the sense, the image or action, the syntax of the suspended sentence, the rhyme and meter, and basic rhetorical devices like symmetry and parallelism, contrast and reversal. One asks himself what, given the poem so far, would complete all these things and provide a fitting climax. And yet the presenter asks no question, analytical or critical, especially no question to which he knows the answer. He asks for a creative act, and that act *entails* a lot of intuitive analysis.

Suppose the haiku begins:

> *The falling leaves*

Without saying so to himself, a student looks for a predicate denoting any act appropriate for leaves, but the obvious one, *fall* is already in the participle. So he looks for another. Spin? Rattle? But what tense? If he is familiar with haiku, he will probably put the predicate in the present. But other things could follow here besides the predicate. An appositive? A relative clause? (He does not have to know their names in order to look for them.) The absence of a comma after *leaves* may cue him to the unlikelihood of either of these two. By now the group has volunteered a number of lines and made judgments about which would be best. The presenter reveals the next line:

> *The falling leaves*
> *fall and pile up; the rain*

It was *fall* after all! Perhaps our student perceives a connection between that repetition and the second predicate *pile up.* And again now he has before him a subject without a predicate. But he also has an image of autumn, a piling action, and a semicolon. Perhaps he is already getting a feeling of balance from the semicolon and the fact that the second clause is starting off just like the first. In thinking of an action for *rain,* he will consider the season and mood, the sentence pattern, and perhaps the likelihood of more repetition. A clever student may say "the rain rains" and then think of a rhyme word for *leaves:* "the rain rains and grieves." But he senses that the meter is too heavy (to many stresses) and adds a word to lighten it: "the rain rains down and grieves."

This thinking can go on out loud and benefit from other students' ideas. All the presenter has to do is ask which version they think completes the poem best; reasons are given for preferences, and new tries are made on the basis of these reasons. Whatever lines they arrive at, they have done some imaginative thinking and entered into the poem. They will appreciate the particular sense of climax and closure that the poet created, and understand better on their own what he was trying to do in the whole poem. It is surprise, half-divined, that delights.

> *The falling leaves*
> *fall and pile up; the rain*
> *beats on the rain.*[3]

The gathering perception may be of a very different pattern from this one, but always it is a multiple perception—of language, things, and feelings—for the words move with the movement of sensibility.

Transforming texts

To transform a text is to take the essence of what it expresses and transfer it to another form of writing or to another medium altogether. Drama-

[3] Reprinted by permission of Doubleday & Company, Inc. from *An Introduction to Haiku,* translated and edited by Harold G. Henderson, Garden City, N.Y., Doubleday Anchor, 1958, p. 125.

tizing and performing are transformations of text but are discussed in their respective chapters. Transformations make fine follow-ups to reading. They can motivate reading in the first place, then use reading to launch other worthwhile activities. They deepen comprehension by bringing students back to the text to rework it, often with partners, and secondarily, they permit you to evaluate comprehension because students' understanding of what they read is externalized.

STORYTELLING

Any tale that a learner has read can be shared with others by telling the events over again in his own way, paraphrasing. Imaginative and individual re-creation of the story, not fidelity to the written version, is what the best storytellers throughout history have always presented, and students should be encouraged to do no less. For most elementary-school children, hearing a story told makes them more, not less, likely to read the story later for themselves (just as seeing the movie makes adolescents want to read the book). Thus the process benefits both the teller and the listener.

TRANSPOSING TO OTHER GENRES

For students who find so-called creative writing a difficult process, who assert they "have no ideas" or "can't write," one process that seems simple enough is to transpose mode, to rewrite into another genre something they have read and liked. For example, a prose fable can be rewritten as a poem, an anecdote as a script, a story as a series of letters, a biography as an autobiography, a diary as a memoir, or a mystery story as a film script. This is a more challenging writing activity than it might first appear, for in changing a selection to another genre you are confronted with the limitations and possibilities of a different point of view, an altered scope, and a new ratio of scene to summary. The students who transpose mode in this way need not be told this; they will discover it as they work. What they learn in changing genre can be transferred to other writing tasks in which they will always be faced with such decisions as point of view, scope, and the relation of scene to summary—in short, with the potential and limits of any genre in which they choose to write. See the diagram on page 158 for other examples of transposition.

TRANSLATING TO OTHER MEDIA

Of course, rewriting prose or poetry as a script automatically shifts the medium from book to stage, radio, film, or television. Converting a short story to an audio script for radio or taping teaches a lot, for one has to render *everything* by sound alone. What does one do with author narration? With important visual features? What makes one writer's work easier than another's to transpose into sound alone?

Students with some training in music or dance might undertake to make a musical play of a story or to choreograph a story. Reading a brief text to the accompaniment of music or movement makes a modest beginning. This can be followed by conversion of a text to a musical script in which material is changed and some words chosen to set to music. Action might be stylized by means of dance vocabulary. Some whole texts might be pantomimed or danced.

Illustrating

Teachers have long known how much children enjoy drawing pictures to illustrate stories they have heard or read. Because nonverbal experience precedes verbal, very young readers find transferring words back into a more familiar nonverbal mode a very gratifying accomplishment. This valuable process should not be confined to the primary years, however. All through school students need ample opportunity to extend their experience of text by re-creating it in a nonverbal mode. Since true comprehension means capturing for yourself the quality of the author's sense of life, whenever this profound understanding comes, it effects a new synthesis of the elements within the reader. Often this new synthesis cannot be easily expressed verbally. Students should be encouraged to draw what they sense after a significant experience with literature. How much of some haiku can be caught by a drawing or photo? Which aspects *cannot* be illustrated? Suggest posting text and illustration and inviting opinions of classmates.

A single drawing may be used to represent a selection that a student wants to recommend to others, as he talks about the selection. Or he may make a diorama of a scene inside a box used as ministage. A series of drawings of key scenes, settings, or characters could be presented on an opaque projector while reading from or describing the selection. Other possibilities are to draw a series on a roll of paper and pull the roll through the frame formed by a box opening, project overhead a series drawn on continuous or separate transparencies, photograph a series of drawings and give a slide show by reading or talking while showing the slides, mount a series of captioned photos on a bulletin board, or make one into a book. Photos might be made of people pantomiming actions and of settings like those in a story, and this series could be presented as a slide show.

Filming

With the help of written directions or a local expert, some students could try doing a film version of a story or poem or play. A mime script is perfect for shooting without sound (Samuel Beckett's *Act Without Words,* for example), but more challenging is to do a script version of some other literary text, one still not requiring sound unless a sound camera is available. One student did a short one, for example, of e e cummings's "Balloon Man," aiming to evoke with the camera the vision and feelings of the poem. With sound, dialogue becomes possible and considerably opens up the range of adaptable material.

Even elementary-level students in some schools have made animated films by taking one frame at a time with a plunger attachment to a movie camera as felt, cloth, or paper cutouts of characters were inched about patiently into the story actions. Another way is to shoot frames of different cutouts of a character in successively different positions, which produces a more realistic effect of action. Dolls or clay figures and so on may be used.[4] See page 299.

IMITATING TEXTS

One of the best ways to appreciate the qualities of the literature you read is to write in that same mode. For example, a person who has tried his hand at writing a limerick or sonnet is likely to read them with greater delight and perception. Writing in any genre can enhance a learner's sensitivity to that form and thus provide a stimulus to reading it. See Part Four, Developmental Reading, Speaking,

[4] See Yvonne Anderson, *Making Your Own Animated Movies,* Little, Brown and Co. Boston, 1970.

and Writing, for specific suggestions for reading and writing activities for each of the nine kinds of discourse. There we have treated reading and writing together to emphasize that learners should write in the same forms they read.

One kind of imitating always popular with youngsters is parody. They can retell familiar nursery rhymes in ghetto dialect or make over old legends with modern caricatures. To make fun of or have fun with a style or content, you have to get to know it well. Older students might want to try parodying a particular author or work. "Story in Disguise" is a game of retelling a well-known story to see if classmates recognize it. Parodying and retelling can be either improvised or written.

Materials

Books are not the only reading matter. The shrewd teacher takes advantage of the many other forms of print and writing in addition to putting together the fullest possible classroom library.

TEACHERS' HANDBOOKS

In an elementary-school class you need to have handy a large, varied anthology from which you can pluck any kind of poetry or prose that seems right to read aloud or hand over to students. Two excellent omnibus volumes for this purpose are: *A Comparative Anthology of Children's Literature,* edited by Mary Ann Nelson (New York: Holt, Rinehart, & Winston, Inc., 1972) and *Anthology of Children's Literature,* edited by Edna Johnson, Evelyn R. Sickels, and Frances Clarke Sayers (Boston: Houghton Mifflin Company, revised edition, 1970). Nelson's *Anthology* is distinguished for its excerpts from books with protagonists from minority groups. The Johnson et al. *Anthology* has a longer and better collection of myths and legends. Both have good collections of folk tales. Johnson et al. organize these according to country of origin; Nelson, according to content.

Along with Northrop Frye and Bill Martin, we feel strongly that much of the first matter that is read to young children or that they read themselves should be poetry. The three Rs of poetry—rhyme, rhythm, and repetition—teach children a lot about individual words and patterns of words, and they do so in delightful and memorable ways.

A few favorite collections of poems for elementary-school children are:

Louis Bogan and William Jay Smith, compilers. *The Golden Journey, Poems for Young People.* Reilly & Lee Co., Chicago, 1965.

William Cole, ed. *A Book of Short, Short Poems.* Macmillan Publishing Co., Inc., New York, 1972.

Katherine Love, ed. *A Little Laughter.* Thomas Y. Crowell Co., New York, 1957.

Herbert Read. *This Way, Delight.* Pantheon Books, Inc., New York, 1956.

Carl Withers, ed. *A Rocket in My Pocket.* Holt, Rinehart & Winston, Inc., New York, 1948.

For older elementary or junior and senior high school students these collections are good for oral reading:

Stephen Dunning, compiler. *On the Gift of a Watermelon Pickle . . . and Other Modern Verse.* Scott, Foresman and Co., Glenview, Ill., 1966.

Richard Lewis, collector. *Out of the Earth I Sing: Poetry and Songs of Primitive Peoples of the World.* W. W. Norton & Co., Inc., New York, 1968.

Gwendolyn E. Reed, ed., *Lean Out the Window.* Atheneum Publishers, New York, 1965.

Geoffrey Summerfield, ed. *First Voices,* Books 1, 2, 3, and 4. Alfred A. Knopf, Random House, Singer School Division, New York, 1970.

Good collections of poems about city experience or by black writers are these:

Arnold Adoff, compiler. *I Am the Darker Brother: An Anthology of Modern Poems by Negro Americans.* Macmillan Publishing Co., New York, 1968.

Arna W. Bontemps, collector. *Golden Slippers, An Anthology of Modern Poems by Negro Americans.* Macmillan Publishing Co., New York, 1968.

A good bilingual collection for Latin Americans is:

Mario Benedetti, ed. *Unstill Life.* Harcourt, Brace & World, Inc., New York, 1969.

ENVIRONMENTAL WRITING

The classroom itself should be a display of reading matter—on bulletin boards, blackboards, and walls. For children who are still mastering decoding, tag-board labels beside each object provide another link between thing and word. Photographs or posters can have captions, individual storage bins have children's names, learning centers have labels and lists of directions posted. Bulletin boards should be repositories for student-produced writing for others to read.

The environment out of school that most youngsters live in is plastered with words already—street signs, advertisements, store signs, markings, and directions. These can be photographed or copied and displayed in the classroom to help make the tie between streets and books.

CLASSROOM LIBRARY

On page 56 we described a classroom library based on individualization rather than class sets. The chapters of Part Four, Developmental Reading, Speaking, and Writing, set forth all the kinds of reading matter that should be stocked in the classroom and that, indeed, are produced and read in our culture.

Principles of Selection

1. Materials should be chosen for the quality of their writing only, not for any pedagogical paraphernalia or thematic development. No literary terms or analytical structures need be part of the reading matter. Structural features of literature will be brought out through the other means we have been describing in this and related chapters—discussion, dramatization, performance, transformations, imitation, and so on—all of which very effectively develop literary interpretation and appreciation. Literature textbooks that are based on historical chronology, themes, and most literary critical principles are irrelevant not only to this program, but, in our estimation, to precollege education in general. Don't disdain because of its form *any* good reading matter that you inherit or that is purchased for you without your choice; you can't afford to. But when you do have a choice, we suggest that you follow this and the other principles.

2. Materials should represent as wide a range of types of reading as *any* students in the growth stage of your students might conceivably want to read if known to them—literary and nonliterary, utilitarian and scientific. Naturally, the exact types of reading material will differ somewhat at each of the four

main stages of development, but a classroom of any year should represent all nine kinds of discourse in some forms.

3. The range of difficulty should be *very* broad, fitting the reality of the classroom, not some fancied "typical" third or tenth grader. This not only allows for individual differences in reading skill but also facilitates the rereading of favorite selections or books, reading "below one's reading level" if a learner is tired of trying out an unfamiliar genre; or seeking challenges over the horizon.

4. The materials should represent a maximum variety of formats, from highly illustrated picture books or comic books to tightly printed adult-looking texts. The ideal is a tradebook rather than textbook look—diversity in type styles and sizes, styles of illustration, trim size, and general format. Graphics should vary a lot within one book sometimes and certainly across books, mixing color with black-and-white, drawing and painting with photos and collages and cutouts. The idea is not merely to appeal to everyone but to demonstrate graphic creativity and its relation to reading material. This is part of a multimedia curriculum, and older students do not outgrow art!

5. Try to get books that each contain only one kind of reading matter—riddles or reportage or first-person fiction—because such a physical breakdown facilitates tremendously a self-directing, individualized, small-group system of cross-referenced books, activity cards, and other interrelated materials. Readers can be helped to focus on the genre and define what it is by seeing several instances of it all in one book. The different genres will not need to be defined by the teacher or rote-learned by the students as information because those who read enough instances of a specific genre, such as limericks, will evolve their own definition of that literary form and refine it as they try their hand at producing their own limericks, looking back at the models when necessary.

6. Informational, social studies, and science books should be authentic, be up-to-date, and do justice to their subjects.

7. The preferences and reactions of the learners must play an important part in the selection of materials.

Five or six copies of any one title is enough. If the whole class decides for some reason to read a selection in common, this can be done a group at a time. For class singing or choral reading, copy the text on chalkboard, project it, or ditto it. (You or a leader may want to move a pointer, to synchronize.) Sometimes a group rehearsing a play script may need more than six copies if the cast is larger and all are on stage at once. But for these few occasions it is definitely not worth buying whole-cass sets of books, because if you do you will not be able to afford the variety of titles required by any individualized reading program that is not a sham and that is really working.

A student of any age who has not mastered decoding and is learning literacy as a beginning or remedial reader will probably benefit from if not actually need a few materials limited in vocabulary and designed to repeat basic sound-spelling correspondences in a varied but controlled way. For such books, see page 221.

There is a reference list on page 144 of the kinds of reading matter we recommend. Ideally each would constitute a separate book or so. The levels indicated are the four growth stages outlined on page 54. Actually, most kinds of writing hold good over a much longer growth range than one level, and many hold good for every age, but we suggest some shuffling and redesignating as students mature. Fiction, for example, breaks down at first more by content—animal stories, mystery, sports, adventure—and later more by form—fictional autobiography and fictional memoir, fictional diary, and so on. But science fiction remains such all the way through, and many elementary books feature form and content at once—riddles or fables, for example. As a general principle, reading types become more finely discriminated, like the following point-of-view breakdown of fiction and the breakdown of poems into at least some particular forms. Limericks, ballads, haiku, and sonnets deserve this sort of special focus, we believe, because they relate well to writing and exemplify some basic features of poetic form. Isolating other poetic forms could also be useful.

The breakdown of fiction by point of view in the secondary years certainly is no necessity. But it is the only breakdown by form that is basic and entails no preinterpretation by you or editors. It calls attention to fictional technique without a word being said, and it parallels the breakdown of nonfiction, which is significant, since fiction simulates documents. Autobiographies, memoirs, biographies, chronicles, letters, and diaries also correspond more or less to library divisions, another worthwhile consideration. In most cases the class will need several titles of each type.

Basic Processes

Level One

- rhymes
- poems
- songs
- game songs
- game directions
- jump rope jingles
- animal encyclopedia
- animal dictionary
- comics
- how-to-make directions
- signs
- animal stories
- nature stories
- modern stories
- folk and fairy tales
- scary tales
- riddles
- rebuses
- jokes
- tongue twisters
- captioned photos

Level Two

- adventure stories
- animal stories (true)
- animal stories (fiction)
- sports stories
- mystery stories
- fanciful stories
- science fiction
- true stories (autobiography, chronicle, etc.)
- information articles
- science encyclopedia
- game directions
- directions how to do and make
- charts and graphs
- maps
- signs
- humorous stories
- slang or dialect dictionary
- recipes
- jump-rope jingles
- tongue twisters
- jokes and puns
- insults
- riddles
- rebuses
- codes
- brain teasers
- proverbs
- fables
- folk tales
- legends
- myths
- plays (all media)
- comics
- captioned photos
- poems
- story poems
- limericks
- songs

Levels Three and Four

- diaries
- fictional diaries
- letters
- fictional letters
- autobiography
- fictional autobiography
- memoir
- fictional memoir
- biography
- fictional biography
- chronicle
- fictional chronicle
- adventure stories
- sports stories
- mystery stories
- science fiction
- humorous stories
- jokes
- limericks
- comics
- riddles
- brain teasers
- codes
- signs
- captioned photos
- charts and graphs
- maps
- advertisements
- slang or dialect dictionary
- information articles
- eyewitness reportage
- third-person reportage
- essays of reflection (informal)
- essays of generalization (formal)
- transcripts
- theater scripts (also mime and puppet)
- radio scripts
- film and TV scripts
- readers theater scripts
- dialogues and monologues (not written for performance)
- proverbs
- fables
- legends
- myths
- parables
- epigrams and sayings
- songs
- ballads
- narrative poetry
- lyric poetry
- haiku
- sonnets

For Level Four the main difference is an increase in the amount of research reported in reportage books, an increase in the number of more philosophical and theoretical essays, and the addition perhaps of a whole book of sonnets. For Level Four you could drop codes, limericks, comics, riddles, captioned photos, ads, and jokes, but the fact is that all of those can be very sophisticated. Unless very hard pressed, stock any reasonable possibilities when in doubt.

This progression, in fact, is really an accumulation, and dropping is hardly an issue. By adolescence, Level Three students should be offered all the types of reading matter; throughout secondary school, the changes occur in the maturity of form and content within these types rather than the introduction of new types except perhaps for rarer poetic forms, which can be encountered in mixed-poetry anthologies. Note that Level Three includes *both* content categories like adventure or sports and point-of-view categories like diary fiction and biographical fiction, so that students may search and learn either way. For fuller definition and detail about these types, consult appropriate chapters in Part Four, Developmental Reading, Speaking, and Writing.

Note that the types are not sequenced. For one thing, no one knows what a proper sequence might be for all students, and many kinds of reading matter are equally mature. Let students find their own level, but if you feel someone is merely afraid to advance, then suggest something more mature that you think the person would enjoy, or steer him into a group that would involve him in more mature reading. This is tricky; don't push too hard. If you are patient, most students will get bored reading easy stuff, perhaps under the influence of peers. That's one reason you want the class interactive. When material is not sequenced, no stigma attaches to reading easier books, and the weaker reader can build up self-esteem and, again, move on.

It is not necessary for you to have read all the books or other reading matter in the classroom. In fact, limiting learners to what you have read will only hold them back. Many ways exist in this curriculum for readers to check or to deepen their comprehension, to discuss a text with others, and to do a variety of things with what they have read, none of which require your actually having read a particular selection in order to help. It is obvious, however, that the more familiar you are with the reading material, the more able you will be to suggest what a youngster may read next. If an individual or a group is hot on animals, suggest ways they can track animals across fables, a science encyclopedia, animal fiction and true stories, poems, songs, and so on. You and they can make a whole impromptu curriculum out of animals that will help them see beautifully how the same subject is treated differently across different modes and genres.

Cross-Referencing

Cross-referencing books is extremely handy not only to point out interesting connections among books, but also to build in more self-directing structure to help students make decisions about what to do next. Cross-referencing consists of writing or printing into a book some optional routings, usually several choices, of where to go next: "See *Parables* or *Proverbs* next," or "Now try the activity card 'Voice Chorus'" or "Make a Slide Tape." Emblazon conspicuously and show students where cross-referencing is. Use your own system, of course, if the materials have not been made this way.

Cross-referencing can route students to another book that is related (fables to parables) or to another that is a step up in difficulty (comics to humorous stories) and to a couple of follow-up activities appropriate to that book (acting out a story for fables or performing a text for transcripts). If you route specifically very often—to one selection in a book—you will be programming; the possibilities are various enough without resorting to that. Students should understand that if they have a strong idea of where to turn next when finishing a book or selection, then they can skip the cross-referenced routing, but if not, they can try one or several of the options. A small team of teachers can best work out and build into their materials a cross-referencing system by pooling ideas and knowledge about the books they can get. Some continuity from teacher to teacher would help everyone. Several teachers might have their students share several classroom libraries organized the same way and perhaps cross-referenced from one room to another, for greater choice. Doing this work once will make daily life far easier.

Further Reading

It will be extremely helpful to have for each type of reading matter a list of some more titles of that same type available to the students, so that if they want to read more science fiction, say, than you have stocked in the classroom, they can consult this Further Reading list to know what other titles they might try to buy, borrow, or check out of another library. Ideally, a Further Reading list would appear at the end of each book*, but you and the students might make and post the lists in a notebook or on a wall. Such lists should contain periodicals and reference books also: if an adolescent reads a lot of factual material on nature, he should know about *Natural History* and the *Reader's Guide*.

SCHOOL AND COMMUNITY LIBRARIES

No classroom library, even if rather well heeled, is likely to suffice for a truly individualized curriculum. No school can afford to stock its classrooms with enough books if the reading program really takes fire. It is possible that the excessive control built into traditional reading and literature series is unwittingly designed to hold students back so that they don't read beyond the school's financial resources. Youngsters who really get the reading habit and who start asking many questions may very well exhaust the whole classroom library or at least those portions of it pertaining to their interests. They are ready to venture to a school or community library.

The teacher's role is to welcome this development and make the transition to the library as smooth and gratifying as possible. This is not done by elaborate and often defeating "library units" in which children are taught everything from the Dewey decimal system to the number of holdings in the library. Children do not need to learn how to become librarians; rather, they need to feel competent and comfortable as library users. A heavy load of information about how to do research—in the abstract—is seldom anything but a burden. A friendly librarian who takes seriously a young learner's question about, for example, where penguins keep their eggs warm, can show him how to use the index of the children's encyclopedias or browse through the books on animals and birds on the science shelves. If he still has trouble, the librarian can hand him Millicent Selsam's *Animals as Parents* and let him scan it for his answer. By meeting the learner where he is, the librarian gives him one successful experience in finding out what he wants to know; on this, he can build further research tasks. Later, when he's bursting with another unanswered question, he can be shown the subject guide to the card catalogue or the adult encyclopedias, but again not as an "introduction to the library" but as a way of expanding his power. He can be encouraged to share this newfound power with his friends.

ACTIVITY CARDS AND DIRECTIONS

A major type of reading material for both the beginning and intermediate reader is the list of directions for an activity. A list should be short, relatively simple, well-illustrated, if possible, and action-oriented. They provide reading matter of high interest, for they show students how to do things —how to play games, find out information, make things, or engage in group projects; how to carry on the reading processes described in this chapter; how to get started in small-group discussion, writing, or dramatic activities. In short, almost anything individuals or small groups can do can be listed on activity cards or wall charts for learners to unlock by reading.

Many youngsters who for some reason are not ready to read much in booklets may read a considerable amount from activity cards or other lists of directions just in order to know how to do the activities. The carrying out of directions is a natural check on reading comprehension. Since it is usually done in the company of partners, learners can check each other's reading. This reading material is by nature expository writing and therefore accustoms learners to comprehending this utilitarian type of discourse. It also provides a model for direction-writing by students.

Whenever as a teacher you find yourself giving directions to a group of learners most of whom have mastered decoding skills, you should ask if these could not better be listed and either posted or filed where students who need them could read them. Whenever learners prefer to ask you rather than read for themselves, you should resist the temptation to be "all-knowing" and deliberately withhold your expertise, thereby sending the learners back to the written material to find out what they need to know. If you set up a pattern of answering their questions, they become all the more dependent on you, and you will have a classroom of students waiting impatiently for you to help them. Individualized process will thus get hopelessly clogged.

With beginning readers, of course, you will often have to read directions with the youngsters at first, moving your finger over the words as they watch. Once they have heard and seen directions read to them, and once they have some knowledge of the activity itself, they will have some excellent aids to help them reread the directions for themselves later in the activity or on another occasion:

1. Since most of the activities call for partners or groups, learners can pool their knowledge and their deductive powers to figure out the words.
2. Illustrations help them remember the important actions.
3. Many of the same words recur frequently in all sets of directions.
4. Often the activity itself makes clear what certain words *have* to be and hence gives high payoffs to deduction.

OTHER STUDENTS' WRITING

Students following the curriculum in this book will pour forth an abundance of writing. They will be reading each other's productions constantly. This reading material has several advantages over printed texts: It is naturally controlled for maturity of content and expression, vocabulary, and sentence structure, and it is of interest because it is peer-written. It allows learners to talk to the authors and thus recognize the tentative nature of any writing. They can begin to discriminate textual features by seeing the texts change and thus become aware of these features in a book. In other words, the locally written texts of classmates not only provide additional reading material having a special social interest, but also bring reading down from the remote perfection of the printed page into the everyday realm.

Sometimes student writings will be in unfinished form as groups or individuals meet to exchange first drafts for reactions and commentary. Sometimes student productions will be printed and distributed for voluntary reading or projected before the class. Some of the writing will end in booklet form, thus joining the commercially published materials in the classroom library. The student-produced books are a kind of homemade version of the library because students write the kinds of matter that they read, that is, all the kinds of discourse arrayed in Part Four, Developmental Reading, Speaking, and Writing. Surely, this variety of student writing constitutes a formidable reading program. Youngsters will read generously in each mode of writing because doing so is entailed in group process. Student-produced material will not replace the vitally needed, rich input from the maturer culture with its greater resources of language and experience, but it will virtually double each pupil's reading practice. It builds a bridge from his local world to that cultural legacy he meets in published books.

Remedial reading

Prevention is always the best remedy. Individualized, motivated, small-group processes should prevent reading problems. If an older student still cannot decode, as determined by listening to him try to sight-read, then he needs some of the practices recommended in Part Three, Literacy—"The Basic Skills." Literacy is learned by essentially the same methods, whatever the age of the learner. Part Three is directed as much toward remediation as toward initial experience in decoding.

For whatever motivational, emotional, or perceptual reasons, many students get thrown into "remedial reading" who in fact are literate. Despite constant complaints and test indications that many secondary-school students can't read, the fact is that very few really cannot decode basic spellings. Usually, they are able to sight-read well enough to be called literate. But they *don't* or *won't* read or just don't understand. In this case the whole human being must be developed. These students need to find out for themselves that books and writing hold power and pleasure. Those who hide or minimize their literacy do so, usually, so that nothing unpleasant will be asked of them. They need occasions to pursue reading and writing with peers for their own purposes and without fear of losing self-esteem. Those who decode words but do not read sentences may be unable to sustain an activity like reading because they need other people too much or lose focus too easily. Their difficulties are general learning problems of motivation, conceptual development, and emotional health that must be remedied by a variety of means that are treated throughout this book—ample opportunities for social reading, oral speech and dramatic expression, involvement in *making* books, and other activities entailing meaningful reception and production of language. The important thing is to give the remedial reader as many opportunities for choice and self-discovery as the other students have.

We recommend that poor readers not be segregated into separate classes. The special "remedial class" often seems a necessity when all students are doing the same thing at the same time; if some stumble and fall by the wayside, it seems reasonable to pull them out. But part of the snowballing effect of reading failure stems from this segregation and its consequent effect on self-esteem. Abler children, moreover, should be tapped to help the less able.

Special decoding remediation can be given within the context of a regular self-contained classroom or a team-teaching situation. Self-directing phonics materials such as those described in Part Three, can be made available either in your classroom itself, if you have enough problem readers to justify the expense, nearby in another classroom, or in a school "reading center" or "reading lab." All that is required is a way for such students to get to these decoding materials on an individualized basis.

Doing remedial decoding, in other words, simply

becomes one other individual activity that some students do that others don't. No stigma is attached. And the same individualization frees you to work one-to-one sometimes with remedial cases. Some will need adult attention. Aides can help, and if the school has a reading specialist, that person can either circulate among different classes tutoring or have students come to a reading center during regular class time for both self-directed and tutorial work. If you have a good grasp of Part Three, however, you can teach remedial reading yourself.

Conventionally, poor readers whose problems go beyond decoding difficulties—if indeed the distinction is drawn—are made to undergo the sort of dull, mechanical course that actually requires the *most* motivation, confidence, and maturity to get through. It is they especially who plow through the phonics workbooks and the programmed test-read passages, doing little bits in little steps. This low-level technical approach has been tried for a long time and found wanting. A broader, more humane approach will be of most help.[5]

[5] The *English Through Interaction* films "A Pupil-Centered Classroom" and "A Student-Centered Classroom" contain a number of reading activities.

writing 8

Like *reading, writing* means two things at once. A person writing a letter or a poem, for example, is thinking out something and writing it down at the same time. He is doing two things that could be done separately. He might compose his letter or poem on a tape recorder one day and transcribe it from the tape another day. Or the two actions can even be performed by two different people. Balzac is said to have dictated his novels to a secretary, and John Milton, who was blind, is said to have dictated *Paradise Lost* to his daughters.

Just as comprehension is independent of reading, composition is independent of writing. We acknowledge this when we speak of oral composition and oral literature. The problems of composition are problems of selecting and ordering words and are essentially the same for the speaker as for the writer. Rendering one's own speech into graphic symbols, on the other hand, is mere transcription, taking dictation from oneself. Spelling and punctuation belong to transcription, not to composition. It is understandable that transcribing and composing should become confused, since a person writing does both at once. And, of course, the fact of writing does influence composition and cause written speech to differ from vocal speech: writing down thoughts permits revision and relieves the memory load. (In an oral culture, one revises by remembering and retelling.) But transcribing and composing are quite distinct activities and entail very different learning problems. Composition represents the verbalization level of coding, and transcription represents the literacy level.

This ambiguity about writing causes confusion in teaching equal to that caused in the teaching of reading. Grammar, for example, is thrown in with spelling and punctuation as "writing mechanics," whereas grammar has nothing to do with those transcription skills. Spelling and punctuation occur only in writing; grammar belongs to oral speech. It is a part of verbalizing, of the oral composing that goes on as a person puts his thoughts into speech. If grammar is to change or improve, it must do so through further composing experience, and this can take place either orally or while writing.

The more serious confusion concerns the general composition act of putting thought into speech. It is easy to fall into the mistaken notion that composition can be practiced only while writing. This compares to the fallacy that comprehension can be practiced only by reading. People talking are composing; they are putting ideas into words and sentences. Furthermore, even when just thinking, alone, people are composing to the extent that they are verbalizing their thought. A written composition is some edited version of a person's inner speech. Someone writing a composition is transcribing his own inner speech, and inner speech develops in a very large measure from outer speech. A writer is both author and secretary. If you can help your students to regard their inner speech as something they can transcribe any time to paper, they will take a giant step toward becoming fluent writers.

Talking to others and talking to oneself teach writing, because they are composing acts. So, above the literacy level writing can be taught, like reading, through activities other than itself that are oral, social, and intellectual. This opens the way for teaching composition by a rich variety of means. What you should do is arrange for those talking and thinking activities that will develop oral composition so that when students do transcribe their inner speech, they write something interesting and effective. Anything that can be said can be written, and if someone cannot say something (at least to himself) he will not be able to write it either.

Writing as transcription is treated in Part Three, Literacy—"The Basic Skills," under literacy in general. Basic spelling is learned by the same four main approaches as basic decoding—phonics, sight-word, language-experience, and listening-while-reading— the last two of which teach punctuation also. If your students are just learning to read and write or still haven't learned basic spelling, punctuation, and handwriting, you may want to turn now to Part Three and return to this chapter later. If your students have acquired basic literacy but still have some spelling and punctuation problems, you may want to look first just at the second half of Chapter 11, Decoding and Encoding Separated, where transcription skills alone are dealt with.

A section starting on page 235 deals with punctuation alone. The encoding goal of literacy is for students to be able to write down (spell and punctuate) anything they can say or understand if said to them. Small children, even preschoolers sometimes, can achieve this relative goal—the sooner the better, so that children can discover early the delights of writing and build confidence—but individual differences must be respected. Some children will take longer than others to develop the motivation or the necessary psychomotor coordination. Offer and encourage literacy constantly but don't try to force it.

All experience producing and receiving language teaches and refines control of grammar. See page 19 for more explanation and Appendix A for specific activities.

The chapters on discussing, dramatic activities, and performing treat composition, because they recommend practices in oral composition or in rehearsal of texts. The quality of inner speech is improved both through vocalizing one's own spontaneous thoughts during impromptu exchanges and through vocalizing the thought and language of authors during performed readings. The chapters of Part Four, Developmental Reading, Speaking, and Writing, deal with composition of each of the nine kinds of discourse, so they array the variety of specific writing students may do, from captions and riddles to short stories and original research. This chapter here takes up staple writing processes common to more than one kind of discourse.

Before children learn to write, they can dictate their stories to literate helpers. The point of this is to enable them to spin out a story fluently without having to worry about the mechanical problems of writing and without having to limit themselves unduly in length. Seeing their words rendered on paper helps establish a tie between vocal speech and writing. See page 204 for this procedure.

People need strong reasons for making that extra step to write down what they can think and say. So activity directions should make clear why ideas should be written down and what is to be done with the writing afterwards. Writing should not end in the dead-letter office of a teacher's desk. See pages 419–421 for suggestions on how to evaluate writing without spoiling it. Sometimes students very much want your personal involvement in their writing, which an individualized management allows well for by affording one-to-one sessions, but routinely taking up and "marking papers" eliminates a more authentic audience and limits writing to what you can process. Students cannot write enough if you alone have to process it. Arrange for them to use each other as audience, proofreader, and coach. The following recommendations aim to give writing a real purpose, to exploit cross-teaching among students, and to make the most effective use of your expertise.

Sharing written products

The basic purpose of writing is to replace speech. There are many good reasons for writing rather than merely speaking something, and activity directions should make these evident. Aside from intrinsic pleasure that many youngsters feel during the writing itself, the student writer usually has to have some communication goal that for practical reasons demands writing. The composition is to be distributed and therefore must be copied, or performed from a script, posted up where it can be read at any time, carried out as precise directions for how to do or make something, incorporated into further activities for which it is needed as a preliminary, preserved as a basis for discussion, and so on.

Compiling books seems to have a very deep and widespread appeal for most students. Exhibiting or reviewing their own written products gives them great satisfaction. When a youngster has a reason for writing—to share experiences in a way that is akin to the oral expression he is familiar with—he wants to compose and later perhaps also to revise what he has done. Therefore, as much use as possible should always be made of student writing.

Broadcasting and preserving makes the abstraction of writing gratifyingly physical and social.

Thus students should write a large part of the literature for the classroom. Too many youngsters think of themselves only as "consumers" and not as users of language. As creator one is more appreciative and discerning about the creations of others. Moreover, when students write, they read more, they become more involved in language, and they get caught up in cycles of giving and taking words that gather momentum and accelerate progress in both reading and writing.

Any of the ways to perform texts that are described in Chapter 6, Performing Texts, are appropriate for sharing student writing.

Not only bulletin boards, but also the backs of cupboards, bookcases, desks, walls, and even display boards hung from the ceiling can be used as places to show student writing. Directions for games or activities can be written by students and stored where other youngsters can use them.

DUPLICATING MATERIALS

Often students prefer that every one of their peers has his own copy of what they have written, or they want to distribute copies beyond the classroom. There are several ways to accomplish this. The simplest but the most expensive method of duplicating is Xeroxing. Carbon paper is something even young children can use fairly well, and it is cheap and useful when only a few copies (probably no more than three) are called for. When youngsters are a little older, and especially when they can type, they can make spirit masters and run off copies on a ditto machine. This method of duplicating is probably the easiest for mass distribution of up to three hundred copies. However, corrections must be made on the spirit master with a razor blade or other sharp tool. The results of the ditto process are in the familiar light blue or purple ink that will fade with time. If students have access to a Thermofax machine, they can make a spirit master from any page of print or writing that has a carbon base or from high-contrast photographs and then run them off on a ditto machine.

Mimeographing is a little more expensive than the ditto process, and cutting a stencil with a stylus or typewriter is a little harder than making a spirit master, but this method can produce more than five hundred copies; print or writing appears in black and will not fade. Corrections may be made with correction fluid.

MAKING BOOKLETS

This process can begin as soon as children can collect a set of their pictures together, paste them on paper, and staple them together between a front and back cover. One of the regular options in any student-centered classroom should always be the production of books. Beginning readers can make their own alphabet and number books and books about subjects of interest using photographs cut from magazines or their own illustrations with captions if they can find a helper to dictate to. Older children can put together longer books—coloring books for younger children; anthologies of favorite songs, poems, riddles, jokes, brain teasers, and so on; collections of individual compositions that members of a writing group wrote in workshop fashion, such as fables, memoirs, fiction stories, or haiku. Books can be accordian-folded in the Japanese tradition or rolled into a scroll, as well as conventionally bound.

Students can bind their own books in soft or hard cover. Soft covers can be made of construction paper or tagboard and fastened together with staples. If a two-inch piece of cloth adhesive tape, such as that sold in rolls in most art or stationery stores, is pressed over the bound edge, the staples can be neatly hidden. Books can also be held together by paper-holding rivets or punched with holes and fastened with brads or sewn together with yarn or string.

A more complicated process, but one that most teachers have found well worth the effort because of the beauty and durability of the final book, is to sew the pages together and then attach them to a cloth cover. If the pages are folded over in the middle, make holes along the fold using an awl, or a hammer and nail, as in Figure 8.1 (page 152).

If the pages are separate, stack them together evenly and iron on a white binding strip (sold at art stores) just the way the cloth adhesive tape is pressed over the bound edge of a stapled book. Then draw a guideline on the binding strip about a half inch from the edge. Along this line make an odd number of holes one-fourth inch apart with an awl or nail. Then, starting with the middle hole, leave enough thread for later tying, and stitch up to the

FIGURE 8.1

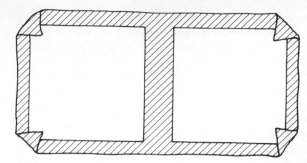

FIGURE 8.3

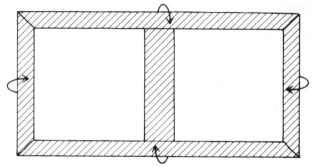

FIGURE 8.4

top, back down to the middle, down to the other end, and back up to the middle, tying the thread that is left over to the piece that was left hanging at the beginning. The thread should follow a path like the example in Figure 8.2.

Next, make a hard cover, taking two pieces of cardboard cut slightly larger than the page size and setting them side-by-side on a piece of strong material such as canvas, sailcloth, or heavy cotton duck; the pattern side should be down. For an average-size book the two pieces of cardboard need to be about three-fourths of an inch apart. Using a white casein glue such as Elmer's or a sheet of solid glue called drymount, glue the cardboard to the cloth. Drymount, available at art stores, becomes sticky when heated, so either an ordinary electric iron or a special drymount press is needed. Next, fold the corners over the cardboard pieces and glue them down (see Figure 8.3). Then fold the edges over and glue them (see Figure 8.4). Next, glue this cover to the end papers or the blank top and bottom pages

of the manuscript. An easier process for younger children is to do the front and back covers separately, gluing an end sheet over the inside of each. The easiest book cover of all is made of Contact paper, which comes preglued.

Probably the most spectacular book cover is made of marbleized paper glued to cardboard. To make this, fill with water a shallow pan wide enough to accommodate the paper you are decorating. Then mix one-fourth teaspoon of oil-base paint with a teaspoon of turpentine. Drop a few drops of the thinned paint on the water, swish around a bit, and then carefully lower one end of the paper onto the water. Carefully pick up this wet end and let the rest of the paper touch the water lightly, but do not submerge it. Only one side of the paper gets wet as you roll it over the surface of the water. Let it dry for a few minutes; then put it between two pieces of clean paper and under a weight to dry flat. Marbleized paper can be used for endpapers as well as for the covers of books.[1]

tie here →

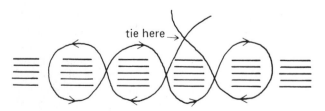

FIGURE 8.2

[1] For more suggestions see a book students can follow: Harvey Weiss, *How to Make Your Own Books,* Thomas Y. Crowell Co., New York, 1974.

Before a book is ready for binding, a draft can be shared with other classes as part of the preparation for final writing. For example, if the book includes specific directions for activities, youngsters in another class can read the draft and report back how well they are able to follow the directions. This feedback can then be heeded in the preparation of the final version of the book. When bound, the books students produce can be part of the class or school library with appropriate Dewey decimal numbers and cards in the card catalogue, or taken home to share with their families. The repeated process of writing, sharing, revising, and rewriting provides students with a graphic demonstration that the real test of writing is the sense it makes to others. Student-produced books build pride in the writing process.

Teachers who have made a speciality of book-binding report that it provides astonishing motivation for some youngsters to write. Physically making books inspires them to want to write something to go inside, to create the mental book.

Collective writing

When the learner is new to the writing process, he composes orally while a recorder writes down his words. Then some peer group processes can help him to write a composition for which colleagues act as coaches. Though sequence is generally from collective to individual, many primary-school children can write alone with great gusto and fine results, and less mature writers of any age will need to do a large proportion of their writing as collaboration. More mature students may periodically return to collective writing for new and challenging composition or because a task demands that group thinking be incorporated. Writing workshops can grow to be very sophisticated indeed and hence always form an important adjunct to solo writing. All the way through school, talking about a composition or trying it out on a friend helps a writer think out what he has to say. Some of this writing talk should be with you and some with peers. Your influence on individuals and small groups will indirectly affect all. They need to know you value their writing.

Collective writing occurs when youngsters work together in a small group to produce a single piece of writing. It is an appropriate process from the early years of schooling right up through secondary school. Students decide together what they want to write and how they want to go about it generally.

Then they work out what they want to say sentence by sentence as one of the group writes it down and makes contributions also. They can take turns scribing; it is good practice in the transcriptive part of writing. Typically, someone proposes a sentence and others accept it or amend it. Sometimes members may have to stop and work out underlying problems of selection and organization before they can resume dictating. At the end, the scribe reads back the composition and everyone listens for places needing revision. A good practice is for members to check out punctuation by having one read the composition as others read, listen, and say which marks to put in.

In general, collective writing might be used for the following purposes:

- To provide a context for students to pool their perceptions, feelings, and ideas in working on a common writing task
- To achieve writing that is both broader and deeper through the varied interaction possible in group work
- To provide the means for students to get varied and immediate feedback to their expressions of ideas and feelings
- To help students learn how to develop those group-process skills necessary for productive group work
- To free the teacher to concentrate attention on specific important problems as they arise
- To provide an opportunity for students to learn how to write collectively so that individual members of the group gain the skill and confidence to practice further alone.[2]

An excellent beginning for students unaccustomed to small-group process is to work with only one partner. Because mere pairing also reduces the ideas and help that each can receive, it is good to increase group size to three, four, or five as soon as the individuals can handle that degree of co-operation.

Short, concrete writing, like directions for a simple game or a script for a short skit, may also help launch beginners. Tape-recording may also help. Members can first discuss a version of the composition without scribing, then play it back noting down

[2] See the two separate *English Through Interaction* films for elementary and secondary levels called "Small-Group Writing" and two secondary-level films, "The Writing Workshop" and "A Student-Centered Classroom."

ideas or phrasing they want to keep, then dictate to a scribe, or tape and transcribe afterward. This may be useful not only for beginners but for any group facing a long or complex composition. Many individuals may find it easier to compose on tape and later transcribe and edit, perhaps with a partner. See page 245.

Activity directions should state the main steps, and you can find out if students need help. Some groups may be weak or inexperienced enough so that you will want to sit in until they get going well, but keep them from depending on you to run the group. It will work well as a self-directed activity only if they become responsible for it themselves. Don't contribute to the composition; just suggest alternatives for how to proceed if they get stuck, or for how to organize and state their ideas if doing so doesn't seem to short-circuit their own thinking.

Teachers who have tried collective writing attest that it has proved to be a tremendous source of motivation for the students they teach. The students' growing enthusiasm for communicating their feelings and ideas and their increasing capacity to find ways of communicating effectively make small-group writing a rewarding task.

The writing workshop

A writing workshop is simply any small group of students writing individual compositions of the same sort who exchange or read aloud their papers in order to try out their compositions and make suggestions to each other for improvement. It grows naturally out of small-group collective writing.

The writing workshop functions after the preparatory work and the writing of a first draft are over. The preparation time might involve reading some samples of related writing from literature, doing some warm-up activities, holding a discussion, and so on. Then comes the actual writing, revising, and rewriting. The time for this will be short at first, but by the time students are in secondary school they may be able to spend from five to eight days in this process. Motivation to revise depends directly on what is to be done with the writing afterward.

The ideal size of a writing workshop is three to five, three especially for beginners. But the length of the kind of writing and other factors of a given activity have to be considered also, since frequently a writing workshop is embedded within a project having several phases. Small size minimizes or eliminates the shy reluctance that many teachers have found keeps some students from wanting to show their writing to anyone but the teacher.

Some writing workshops may form just to do a single writing project together and then disperse as members choose next to do different things. But some groups may stay together as a writing workshop for several weeks or months in order to get the benefits of longer acquaintance with each other's writing traits. This develops a strong trust in each other's judgments about their writing.

PURPOSE

The primary purpose of a writing workshop is to provide an immediate audience for a student's writing, an audience whose comments can help the writer sharpen and enrich his own expression. It is based on the assumption that most writing problems involve failure to allow for the reader in one way or another and that peer readers can furnish each other useful feedback and suggestions. (See pages 32–33.) As members of a group gain practice in reading each other's writing, they become increasingly able to give and accept constructive criticism. Experience in a writing workshop builds a student's capacity to evaluate his own writing and to work on his own inadequacies and difficulties without heavy external prodding. The writing-workshop group helps him to appreciate a range of possible alternatives and to arrive at the best conclusions. Ultimately, the writer's decisions about his writing are his own, but they are based upon practical feedback from a real audience.

The first writing activities that are brought to writing workshop for discussion and revision should be brief, so that the group gains practice in the discussion of writing without having to spend a large amount of time reading lengthy papers.[3] Members respond spontaneously to each other's writing and also make suggestions for changes, including but not dwelling on corrections of spelling and punctuation. Marginal notations of a proofreading sort are made, but most other comments and suggestions

---

[3] See beginning tenth-grade groups discuss short selections in the secondary-level *English Through Interaction* film, "The Writing Workshop," which shows advanced groups also.

are exchanged orally. These groups have dictionaries available to help them resolve uncertainties about spellings, and the teacher is available for general help. What comes out in these sessions will reflect other learning experience, such as reading in literature, dramatic work, and punctuation practice, to name only a few. Trying to write the same kind of composition at the same time allows members to pool perceptions of the problems.

Many aspects of written language usage are merely automatic speech put on paper. Many ways of formulating and wording ideas are habits that can be improved by more extensive oral practice. Since writing permits revision and reflection on what one has said, the writing workshop focuses on this. It is not that revision doesn't occur constantly in conversation also, but that in writing, *longer* sequences of organization of language can be revised. So a special value in practicing writing itself is to work on revising longer continuities. Writing also pins down exact wording and phrasing so we can look at it and reconsider word choice and word order. Invite students to rewrite each other's sentences sometimes where phrasing is important, with the understanding that the original writer may accept or reject a proposed rewording. If the proposed changes are written in pencil in the margins of each other's first drafts, the original writer can decide whether or not to incorporate them in his final version.

TEACHER ROLE

Your paramount mission is harder and more fun than assigning grades or marking papers; it is to make group process so effective that pupils can teach each other. You help students learn how to do something that is very difficult—how to give and receive relevant, tactful, and insightful feedback. Your perception and expertise about writing are fed in at the time the group is struggling to improve a draft and making comments to each other about their papers. If they have made marginal notations on each other's papers, you look at these and note any problems that are common to more than one student. From time to time you can select sample papers and project them as a basis for a class discussion focusing on the issues involved and ways to revise the writing, if you think enough class members need such discussion at the same time. In most cases, raising issues in the workshops better befits an individualized approach.

The students should not be writing for you, the teacher. One reason some students see so little point in writing is that what they write has no social context except the thin thread that ties it to grades and to the presumably all-knowing and all-judging teacher—their only reader. Students should think of the workshop as basically self-directed but expect you to check by or sit in often, either on your own initiative or at their request.

Note for yourself which writing problems they are not picking up on, then tell them what you have noted—what they seem helpful about and what not. Ask them how they think a certain problem of order, for example, could be improved in their direction-giving. This should not result in mere prescription from either you or them, because most writing problems are relative to many matters of content and form, and learners must develop good judgment about them. Often the comments of inexperienced students will at first be naive, unhelpful, vague, and subjective. But being able to diagnose composition problems helpfully is precisely what they are out to learn. They won't begin with that skill. They will learn to diagnose and revise as they try out ways of saying things, get honest but sympathetic response from an immediate audience trying to write the same thing as they, trouble-shoot together, and try rewording or reorganizing each other's efforts. This tone of working together for mutual benefit is something you can help establish when you sit in.

Your main job is to ask each group the right questions about their reaction to each other's writing until they begin to see which kinds of changes would improve what bothers them. In a way, this is a kind of translating job between the initially vague subjective reactions one may have to a piece of writing —"It's monotonous"—to those specific aspects of the text that account for the response—long run-on sentences with *and* having no subordination. If you ask the group why they think it seems monotonous, someone will probably think of the run-on sentences, especially if you ask someone to read aloud a passage while you all listen. Then ask how they would revise the sentences to eliminate the monotony. Someone will suggest cutting up the sentences into shorter ones, dropping the *and*s. That may be as far as some undeveloped children will be ready to go at that moment. A more mature group, or that same group in a few weeks, may be able to go on and remark that they have merely traded monotonous sentences for choppy baby sentences but that the piece is still flat somehow. Ask them if they see another way to put the ideas together that loses nothing but is not flat. When ready, they will suggest combining, in effect, the kernel sentences so as to produce more complex ones with subordinated clauses. In other words, what is lacking is really subordination or other conjunctive relating besides *and*. This lack is the flatness.

But the original problem was not likely due so much to any ignorance of subordinate clauses, since these would have been encountered in conversation and reading, as to some "flatness" of thought in composing. If the group resists being pushed beyond a certain point, it may be that they are not yet mature enough to perceive the reader's need for ranking and other explicit relating of ideas. In that case you have to wait and let them grow a little more. On the other hand, one or two of them may be ready and can formulate the problem in some terms that will help the writer perceive that need. Or it may be that the writer can understand the reader's need for more explicit relating with conjunctions of time, place, and logic but just hasn't the verbal habit of using them. In his case, the words won't come out on paper until his oral fluency expands to include subordination in his sentences. The talk going on in a writing workshop becomes an important part of the oral experience that will make subordination and other sentence-embedding easy and natural for him, but it must assume much other oral practice in other language activities.

In a writing workshop, attention is on the actual learning issues, not on one's status with the teacher and on peer rivalry. Errors are exploited, not avoided. Writing is learning, not being tested on a sink-or-swim basis, as is all too often the case when a student discovers—too late—after he has handed in a composition, all the things that are wrong with it. Final products benefit from learning and leave a feeling of achievement, instead of revealing ignorance and leaving a sour taste. But it is you, the teacher, who has shown the learners how to do this for each other. Out of your spirit you create the climate of collaborative learning and helpful responding. Out of your understanding of language and composition, you focus the issues implicit in the assignments and set up model ways of commenting and proposing. But your reaction is as a real audience—an adult and cultivated one, to be sure, for that is what you are—but also as a first-person individual. As the students get older, you should be able to assert your own ideas and attitudes more

frankly, without fear of damaging student confidence and initiative. If students are accustomed to thinking independently and to working for their own reasons, not yours, you can play your personal point of view more freely in discussion and make critical judgments of their work, as a master among apprentices.

VALUE

The chief obstacle to cross-teaching, we have found, is the past conditioning of both teachers and pupils. There are no intrinsic reasons for this group process to fail. Any misleading of one pupil by another is tremendously outweighed by the increased writing practice, the constant and varied feedback, which no teacher could otherwise provide. And small groups tend to set misleading individuals straight. Our experiments showed, we believe, that even elementary-school children instinctively can spot some writing problems on their own; we have noticed that they are especially good at catching poor punctuational segmenting, run-on sentences with *and*, unnecessary repetition, obscure phrasing, and failures to allow for the reader's viewpoint.

There are also some important side effects that are generated by a writing workshop. The small-group atmosphere seems to encourage some students to be far less inhibited in expressing themselves than they would be before a larger group. And, because the students are writing for each other, their papers become much more interesting.

While the writer focuses on ways to improve what he has done, he has a chance to work on problems of comprehension. He alternates his role as writer and reader. As members of the group struggle together to find the best word for the exact rendering of an image or idea, they are led to confront an age-old problem in the diction of poetry—harmony versus surprise. As they try to find out what the writer means, they test the validity of a main generalization in an essay. In this constant movement back and forth from the revision of particular words to the testing of main ideas, both writers and readers develop deeper insights into effective communication and learn to appreciate the many devices used by writers to project a particular point of view, tone, or effect.[4]

[4] Writing workshop can also be seen, at elementary level, in the *English Through Interaction* film "Small Group Writing" and, at secondary level, in "A Student-Centered Classroom."

Writing stimuli

Students who claim they have nothing to say or can't think of anything to write about are assuming only a couple of stereotyped kinds of theme topics. They have not been licensed to open up for writing the huge reservoirs of experience they have stored within or can tap at any moment from their stream of consciousness. When people compose, they specialize their inner speech by focusing their attention on some part of their sensations, memories, feelings, or reflections. Imagination is some kind of interplay among these. Writing stimuli elicit verbal response that can be shaped for some purpose. Students must understand that good writing subjects lie everywhere at hand. Activity directions should show how to get at all of this material.

Part of the great importance of interweaving the language arts is that this generates marvelous stimuli and motivation for writing. Performing calls forth scripting. Discussion naturally extends itself to paper as students pursue ideas that social exchange has involved them in. Many kinds of writing begin with improvisation as a preliminary or even a first draft. Part Four, Developmental Reading, Speaking, and Writing, suggests many specific stimuli, according to the kind of discourse. Below are some general sorts. Often they come from the other arts, for some of the best language stimuli are nonverbal.

PICTURES

Assemble a large collection of thought-provoking photographs cut from magazines and perhaps mounted or laminated. Let each student choose one that he would like to write about. "Say what you think is happening in your picture. Make up a story from (or about) what you see." In a box put together a set of photographs of the same persons doing different things in evocative settings* and have the children arrange and rearrange them as a stimulus for stories. See pages 272–273, 300. File folders might each have a photo full of action pasted on one side and (for small children) a few words to be used in writing a story about the photo on the other. Also, students can cut out a series of pictures, put them in sequence, and make up a story to go with the arrangement. If cameras are available, students can take their own photographs and write captions or stories to go with them.

Good paintings, drawings, or pieces of sculpture often have a dramatic quality that provokes compo-

sition in words. An increasing number of very fine films to elicit creative writing are available for rental or purchase. Also, paint blots similar to Rorschach ink blots can lead to free-association composition. And pictures produced by the students themselves are a constant invitation to verbalization.

CONSUMABLE READ-AND-WRITE BOOKLETS*

Some students may be helped by consumable booklets that contain some words and pictures as prompters. By completing sentences, adding sentences, and drawing in pictures, the student co-authors the booklet. The focus of the booklets should be the child himself. He can begin to define himself and his environment on paper, as an act of self-discovery. Since he can keep each book, share it at school, and take it home, it will stimulate oral reading and talking as well as writing.

Read-and-write booklets aim at youngsters not yet ready to face blank paper and take off from story starters on activity cards. They may not know how to spell enough words to write whole sentences. Or they may spell fairly well but still want the feeling of a lot of guidance, of being told what to do. Or they may not value loose sheets of paper and may be able to take their writing seriously only when it becomes part of a book. For all such children read-and-write booklets give specific points of departure and often vocabulary, sentence structures, and spellings as well.

The trick of these books is to give the child the feeling that he is being told what to do, since he still asks for this, while actually leaving options open as much as possible. Several short booklets can create a sequence that progresses toward more open choice. In his book the learner can

1. trace words in dotted letters to learn the words and start "writing" the book.
2. fill midsentence blanks with obvious key words that have already been used and about which the context leaves no doubt.
3. fill sentence blanks with a word or phrase from a multiple-choice array *or* from an inner array of his own. (Any choice is right.)
4. fill unfinished sentences with his own choice of single words, phrases, or clauses.
5. write an indefinite number of sentences in a large space left for his written response to a very open-ended invitation to tell something.

In addition to calling for writing, the booklets can evoke drawings.

Such booklets can be appropriate up through seventh and eighth grades if open-ended enough and if some students still need this kind of security in order to write. The pages may be virtually blank, but the prompting and the appearance of external structure and benediction seem psychologically important to students who would choose them.

MUSIC

Recorded or live music can trigger a response in movement or language; it evokes mood. Students can be told simply, "Write what this music makes you feel or think of."

Songs too are a good stimulus for writing. They merge the melodies and rhythms of words with those of music and steep the children in the heady elixirs that are the primitive fountainhead of all expression. Music can free up bodily response, stimulate pantomime, and brew poetry. The notes and beats of music fasten down quite precisely the number of syllables in a line, the pattern of stressed and unstressed syllables that make up a metrical pattern, and hence the larger patterns such as those of stanzas, because singing words puts syllables in one-to-one correspondence with notes, which act as a kind of rack upon which language can be stretched and very pleasurably measured. Since all limericks have a uniform metrical pattern, they may be sung to the same tune. See page 263. Not only does a definite metrical structure afford youngsters a frame to flesh out with their own material, it often actually triggers the material. Words fit a tune, but a tune can draw forth words, also. Musical phrasing inspires verbal phrasing.

Many poems, then, may be written as new words for old tunes. Children sensitized by hearing and moving to music can clap and beat out the metrical form of familiar poems and fill these forms with their own feelings and stories.

For the most part, music has not been well used in the teaching of language arts. It is usually true that when one medium is joined with another, as language with music, both are enhanced and hold greater interest for students.

LITERARY FORMS

Youngsters often need transpersonal forms into which they can project feeling without knowing that they are doing so. The material of folk literature furnishes one kind of public medium. The technical forms of poetry and song offer another. Any conventionalized story, including the familiar Wild West tale or ballad or sea chantey, provides a vessel for holding powerful personal feeling and yet distances it in a communal pattern. Let students hear good live or recorded readings of literature in the form; then direct them to do their own rehearsed readings. Finally, they write a tale, poem, song, or chantey like the one they have heard.

Imaginative writing wells up from a source constantly enriched by an inflow. A teacher who wants his students to write should let them take in an enormous amount of folk literature and poetry from books and records. Not only do they absorb images and ideas that they can recombine in their own expression, but as they internalize the rhymes, rhythms, and other formal patterns, they are absorbing in a peculiarly effective way the vocabulary, locutions, and language structures bound to these patterns by association.

Not just folk literature, song, poem, and chantey can be imitated, however. Any genre the youngster chooses to read can be a stimulus for writing in that mode. Reading a short story in letters will often inspire a student for the first time to write fiction. Not just literature but *any* kind of writing—recipes, rebuses, brain teasers, codes, directions, advertisements, limericks, and so on—can provide a model for writing. See also page 261 for writing parody.

CHANGING MEDIUM OR MODE

A composing task that may seem less demanding to an inexperienced writer than producing out of his own head but that imposes almost all of the major problems any writer faces is to change a text from one mode of communication or type of discourse to another. Following are some of the possibilities, with arrows to indicate that they will work backward as well as forward:

a script ⟷ a story
an informative article ⟷ a transcript of an interview
a TV show ⟷ a script
a movie ⟷ a story
a pantomime ⟷ a story
a pantomime ⟷ a play with dialogue
a story ⟷ a shadow play
a radio play ⟷ a story
a story ⟷ slides with narration

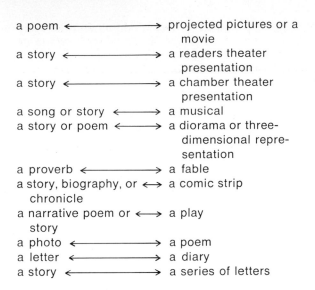

a poem	⟷ projected pictures or a movie
a story	⟷ a readers theater presentation
a story	⟷ a chamber theater presentation
a song or story	⟷ a musical
a story or poem	⟷ a diorama or three-dimensional representation
a proverb	⟷ a fable
a story, biography, or chronicle	⟷ a comic strip
a narrative poem or story	⟷ a play
a photo	⟷ a poem
a letter	⟷ a diary
a story	⟷ a series of letters

This transforming of a given work, discussed also on page 139, supplements the alternative of imitating a form.

RECAPITULATING IMPROVISATIONS AND PANTOMIMES

A small group does a pantomime or an improvisation before some classmates, who write an account of the skit as soon as it is over. Recapitulation is a different kind of writing than sensory recording (outlined on page 164) because by the time a story or presentation is over, one knows considerably more and interprets differently than he does in the middle of registering the events. A recapitulation reads much more like a summarized, connected narration. The important things are sifted out from less significant details, the behavior of the actors is understood in terms of the outcome, premature inferences are corrected, and the series of events is economically coded as a totality. Learning about such abstractive differences is one purpose of the process. But the main goal is experience in writing narrative.

Improvisations

The big question writers must decide in recapitulating improvisations is the purpose of their account. The degree of narrative summary or dramatic elaboration is determined by the uses to which the writing is to be put. If the goal is to produce a play script for another group to use in a performance,

then, of course, the recapitulation needs to be as full and detailed a reproduction of the original dialogue and action as possible. On the other hand, if the goal is to tell someone succinctly what the skit was about, a laconic summary might be appropriate. The important thing is that students know how to do both and to be able to revise in either direction when the situation calls for it.

The directions may tell the students first to write recapitulations without any prior guidance. The teacher can then project samples that illustrate varying degrees of elaboration, or a small group can compare its own papers. The advantages of each type of recapitulation may be discussed. The next time around, each writer is told to write his account for a specific purpose. A group has, in addition to the actors, three spectators who do not know what the actors will do. One will write a very short synopsis, to serve as a minimal situation for another group to improvise from; the second will write a longer narrative account, merely sampling the dialogue, to go into a class newspaper as a news item; the third will write a version that will as nearly as possible enable another group to use it as a script in putting on the skit for themselves.

Eventually all pupils might do all three kinds of recapitulation as well as be the actors. All these pieces of writing will have a function that will actually be carried out. In the groups, the students will read and suggest changes to the authors before the papers are handed over for improvising, printing, and acting out. These changes can include the adding of more detail and verbatim dialogue to the version that is to be used as the script. In effect, what pupils do is write synopses, narrative, and plays, but without inventing the story, which is what the actors have done. At the same time, the whole cycle of acting, writing, and talking is turned over in another way.

Pantomimes

The greater ambiguity of pantomimes makes them better than improvisations as a trigger to the process of comparing differences in inference and interpretation. Individual recapitulations of pantomimes may differ not only in accounts of the action but also in the ascribing of motives to the characters and the determination of the circumstances one should assume as background for the action.

After watching a pantomime, the onlookers write their recapitulations. The actors themselves may write their account of what they did as well. Then they all meet and read aloud and discuss their versions. What are the differences? Which account do they agree on most? Which title pulls together their overall interpretation the most effectively? The action may also come under scrutiny. Which particular gestures and movements led to very different inferences by spectators? Since the narratives are sure to vary in length and therefore in the ratio of detail to summary, some of the discussion can be about such variations. Then the actors can share their versions of what they were doing and compare these with those of the onlookers.

Some pantomimes, of course, will not be ambiguous, and certainly the players should not *try* to confuse the audience. Their intention should be to communicate. But some stories will inevitably lend themselves to double or multiple interpretation, and acting without the benefit of introduction, narration, or dialogue means renouncing the explicitness of language. Players can thus learn how much language can prevent ambiguity and in what ways body English must compensate for the loss of words.

Writing recapitulations in small groups is a particularly intimate and intensive way of sharing and reacting (using an audience of three people). The pantomimists get a full and explicit response to their efforts and a clue as to how to make their pantomime less ambiguous, and the process produces something—the stories. The writers know that the same will be done for them when they put on a pantomime. Ensuing discussion can, in addition to clarifying the exact effects on the audience, help the writers revise their papers for further use. That is, if the pantomime communicated well, as shown by a high consensus of the spectators, then the group collaborates in putting together a publishable version that draws on all the papers. If their versions are different, then each spectator's story can be separately revised and distributed. The writers might even be encouraged to carry the story further from its source by inventing along the lines of their original divergence. In this case, recapitulating a pantomime becomes one more point of departure for original story-making.

Sensory writing

Sensory stimulation is such an important source of composition material that it deserves special consideration. Also, we can illustrate with it many kinds of processes and perceptions that apply to all writing. Sensory stimuli underlie some of the writing types described in Part Four, Developmental Reading, Speaking, and Writing, especially in Chapter 16, True Stories; Chapter 18, Information; and Chapter 19, Ideas. We will dwell at length here on the process of sensory writing itself so you can apply to other writing how to work material from the ground up, put it through classroom interaction, and revise it into finished products. We hope too that our analysis of writing samples will help you to get a feeling for what youngsters may produce and what you may make of what they produce.

We begin with sensory recording, which is the writing down of ongoing events. The recorder writes down what he perceives as he is perceiving it. It is a way for schools to help youngsters become good observers, to pay close and conscious attention to the exchange between them and the environment at any given moment. Sensations are inner coding of outer things. To verbalize them is to transform sensory experience into understandings. By helping learners sense more you may help them to say more. And sensory recording resembles comprehension also, for in reading both books and reality one must make inferences, and the best interpretation is the one that allows for the most cues.

People look *for* and listen *for,* however. Looking and listening for their own sake are rare and sophisticated. Though an infant's attention is diffuse, we all begin very early to tune in and out, to select according to our desires and fears. To say that children have a great curiosity and live in close touch with nature is not to say that their observation is pure and even. We do not always understand their selectors, but they have them—psychic focal points around which they are organizing the world to map it for delights and dangers. So behind sensory abstraction lies a big motivational issue. Adults' efforts to train children to observe objectively are somewhat at odds with the learner's reasons for looking and listening, which relate to private concerns. We should honor his more primal motivation by selecting observing situations likely to engage his interest while at the same time directing him to focus where he might not have of his own accord, so that he may achieve some autonomy from his drives and observe more objectively what lies around him.

Because sensory recording, when done as an isolated activity, begs the question of motivation, it needs to be embedded in another activity for which interest is assured. To observe objectively and to write down observations for their own sake ask too much of most youngsters. What you need to do is find situations calling for observation. Even very young children will observe closely and talk and write about animals that are kept in the classroom, cared for, lived with, and experimented with. The familiar, pleasurable, and well-motivated activity can provide the context that will in turn motivate a new, different, and more advanced activity, in this case observing and writing. (See Chapter 16, True Stories, and Chapter 18, Information.)

ONE SENSE AT A TIME

One way to begin is by recording one sense at a time instead of all at once. Isolating each sense creates a small focus, to train attention, and also simplifies choices of what to record.

Sound

Prewriting practice focusing on sound can begin in simple relaxation periods: "Rest, close your eyes and listen. Relax completely and hear as many sounds as you can." After a few minutes: "How many *far away* sounds can you hear? Afterward ask students to list orally and compare the sound they heard. "Are there any unusual sounds? Familiar sounds?" Such a three-to-five-minute session could occur a number of times outdoors and in other places around the school as well as in the classroom. Since school sounds will be limited, tapes would increase the range considerably. Also, when the children do not know the sources of the sound, an interesting game can be made of identifying the site where the tape was made and the actions producing the sounds.

The isolated sense of hearing differs from sight in two ways that are obvious and yet not often considered. One is that for a sound to be produced, something must happen, whereas what one sees may be action but it may equally well be static, a still life. Hence sound falls into a sequence of happenings, and a record of them automatically becomes a story of sorts. Second, since hearing alone gives us very limited information, we are forced to *infer* more than we do when looking. Seeing informs us more fully than hearing and therefore requires less inference.

These two differences help to define the recording of sound: it is action-centered, and it involves some guessing. Both are qualities youngsters like. But, further, it can emphasize chronology and inter-

pretation. For the latter, tapes are obviously better, since students taken on location to record receive a lot of visual information about the setting and possible actions even though their eyes may be on their papers during the listening period. Another advantage of taping is that setting and actions can be chosen for their particular interest to youngsters. It is important, however, not to jam the tapes with sounds but rather to capture a series of distinct sounds that enables the listeners to distinguish each sound and that gives them time to write.

After the stage of listening without writing, students are ready to write down sounds. Place the class in the sound locale or play a tape to them. A homemade tape might present a short and simple sequence such as someone going out a door, whistling for a dog, placing a bowl down, and patting the dog while it eats; or a set of unrelated sounds such as the crinkling up of aluminum foil, paper clips dropping into a tin can, and popcorn popping. Tell them they are going to find out if they all heard the same story. Distribute overhead-projector transparencies and grease pencils or note pads and pencils to the students. Tell them that this time they are going to try to capture what they hear by writing it down in a short form. They do not have to use whole sentences and keep repeating "I hear...." They are going to "take notes," an expression that will be used a lot and that relates to their work as recorders for small groups. To save time, they may write single words and short phrases. This process of note-taking is an important prewriting skill that students need to develop. Tell them not to worry about getting down *everything* but to capture as much as they can. Also tell them not to worry about spelling but to make good guesses. This is a way of writing a story, and they can compare stories and do other things with them. Recording should probably have an upper limit of ten minutes unless the students are of high school age.

Next, discuss the order of recorded sounds. This can be done with the whole class immediately after they have recorded them or have returned to the classroom. (After about two whole-class sessions, they can carry on this discussion in small groups.) Project one of the transparencies or copy one of the student's lists onto the chalkboard and say that they are going to put together a sound story from their notes. "Probably no one person could note all the sounds by himself, and some of you may have heard things the others did not hear. So we will fill out the recording together." Read aloud the sounds on the transparency, then ask, "What other sounds did *you* hear?" As these additions are enumerated, write them on the transparency or chalkboard. "But *where* do they go—before and after which other sounds?" This leads not only to establishing chronological order but also to distinguishing it from simultaneity (sounds occurring together) and from repetition (recurring sounds). Discussing these temporal matters naturally entails using corresponding verb tenses and aspects—perfect, progressive, and repetitive ("It keeps on . . . ."). Help the class to set the record straight, writing the sound events in order of occurrence, placing simultaneous sounds side by side, and inserting repeated sounds at points where the students agree that they occurred. They can compare their inferences as they decide together such things as: What made that noise? What action took place? What did the noise sound like?

A second issue for discussion concerns the form of notation. Whether this should be brought up on another occasion is perhaps something for you to decide in light of your students' maturity and readiness. At any rate, looking at the transparency being projected, remark that some words tell the thing making the sound (*bell*, *airplane*), other words tell the action (*scraping*), and still others describe the sound (*click*). Sometimes a phrase may combine these (*bells ring, foot scraping, click of metal*). Point to the words that exemplify these different ways of recording, and note that this recorder used all of one kind, or mixed them, or used more of one than the other. Project another student's transparency or copy another student's list on the chalkboard and ask the class which ways of noting *that* person used. Then direct them to look at their own recording and notice what they did. Finally ask them which kinds of words do which things best. What do you want to know—the object involved, the action causing the sound, or what the sound is like?

The point is, of course, that recording, or note-taking, forces us to sacrifice some information for other information; things have to be left out. Also, the basic parts of speech are focused on in this way without being formalized—nouns, verb forms, and sometimes adjectives (*loud banging*). Students can discuss the practical matter of which kinds of words have which advantages for recording which kinds of information. This would be a good time to talk about how they might write up their notes—into a letter, a poem, a piece of reportage, and so on.

A fine opportunity exists here to increase and refine vocabulary. While comparing varient wordings,

students can discuss whether "bell" or "buzzer" is the best word for the sound source, whether the bell "rang" or "tinkled." Some recorders will have included adverbs such as "faintly" or "suddenly," and these can be shared and thereby provide a model for other pupils. Sometimes only one student may know the correct name for something heard ("air conditioner"), but that name is then made available to the whole class. You too supply vocabulary, of course.

After a session or so that you lead with the whole class, students are ready to work in small groups with tapes as their only sound source. The groups do essentially what the whole class has done before except that now they have the general mission of guessing where the tape was made and what was going on there. Whereas the school sound recording relied only on the socializing motive of comparing, now a guessing-game motivation is added. One person in each group is appointed as leader. He is to read his list of sounds, ask his colleagues what else they hear, and write additions onto his paper. Again they discuss when the sounds occurred in relation to each other. Since they did not see the objects and actions producing the sounds, which in most cases could have been made in different ways, the effort to determine which sounds in a record are the same or different will naturally cause the students to discuss differences in how they named the sounds. They may discuss which names are best and which assume more than they know (words for sounds assume least; words for action causing them, more; and words for objects, most). If one student challenges another's item "wheel turning," he is questioning not just the other's wording but the amount of inference he made. But all he says is "How do you know it was a wheel?" Is that the same sound as someone else's item "clicking"? To answer that, they have to check where the two items came in the sound sequence.

In other words, merely comparing their recordings carefully ensures discussion of several important relations of words to things. Students have to collect everybody's sounds, put them in order, and find out what different words they used for the same sounds.

When the class is reunited, the leaders are asked to report what their groups decided was the locale and action of the tape. The climax of the game element in these sessions comes when the teacher tells them what is happening on the tape. (Clearly, some skill is needed to tape a sound sequence that is neither too easy nor too difficult to guess.) Students who have had some experience with this can make their own tapes in various places around the school or community and ask their classmates to guess where the tape was made.

Touch

Recording tactile sensations also operates on essentially a game motivation. Place in paper bags or envelopes three to six tactually interesting objects —such as velveteen material, popcorn, a damp sponge, a peeled grape, sandpaper, a rough stone, a bead, or a safety pin—that are recognizable when *seen* by students, and give one bag to each group. A person reaches in and feels one of the objects, without seeing or revealing it, and says aloud what he feels—the shape, texture, consistency, and so on—but without *naming* it even if he thinks he can identify it. The rest of the group write down what he says as well as they can keep up with him. It should be explained that each person may miss some things the "feeler" says, but that the group as a whole will probably be able to piece his words together later. Tell the class, "Just write down key words." These monologues are usually brief.

Afterward, the group drafts a composite account of what the feeler said, the tactile description of the object, which can be revised as a riddle and in rhyme if the group prefers. This will be read before the class later to see if others can identify the object from the description of it. After all the members of the class know what the objects are, they may be able to change the descriptive words to more precise terms, such as *rough* to *gritty,* or *smooth* to *concave.* Then these descriptions will be put together as a riddle book and exchanged with other classes. To compose the description for the book, a group uses a collective writing method.

Activity directions should make one specific suggestion: if the description repeats "It is" and "It has," these sentences can be combined by using series with commas: "It is square, fuzzy, and thicker in the middle." Say that shortening in this way will make it possible to read a lot of riddles before the class and will save space in the books. This practice exemplifies how the combining of kernel sentences into more complex sentences can be built organically into an activity instead of set up as an isolated exercise.

Students can learn several things from this activity besides verbalizing their sense of touch, which of course is learning one way to describe. As record-ers, they are taking dictation. As drafters of something to be read to the class and to be passed to other classes, they are composing and editing. As guessers themselves of what each object is, they can learn, by the absence of names, how names simplify identification, and, conversely, how much can be said about a thing that does not appear in the name. Difficulty in guessing an object relates to the low sensory level of tactile information; ease in guessing relates to how *telling* the particular details are, whether the details mentioned are characteristic of many objects or of only a few, and whether these details combine to evoke the whole of the object. These issues can be discussed as the practical matter of which kinds of riddles are hard and which are easy.

Smells or Tastes

The same general procedure can be followed for guessing games dependent on olfactory or gustatory senses. Small jars with screw tops containing substances such as peanut butter, a cheese with a strong odor, pine needles, moist earth, a rose, or fish might each be opened in turn and smelled by one blindfolded member of a group and described to the rest of his group without naming what he thinks it is. The rest of the group write down what he says, and then together they write up a composite olfactory description of the object. They need to decide which is the best order for the descriptive details, which things, if any, should be omitted because they are either redundant or misleading, and what could be added or changed. This description can be presented to the class as a riddle or compiled into a riddle book.

A set of foods such as fresh fruits and vegetables like diced onion, carrot, turnip, lemon, apples; condiments like salt and cinnamon; or staples like flour, cornmeal, or sugar can be put into closed jars and tasted one at a time in the same manner as the smelling game. Or pupils may describe the taste of their favorite food without naming it, and the others may guess what it is. In either the smelling or tasting, we have another experience in verbalizing the nonverbal.

People naturally resort to comparisons to express what they touch, hear, smell, and taste. For something new or unknown they ask, "What is it *like?*" So trying to verbalize sensations causes youngsters to use similes and metaphors, which otherwise do not spontaneously crop up much in their speech.

Students mature enough to record on their own out of school can engage in multisensory recording as described in the following outline. Activity directions to the student appear with roman numerals. These are followed by indications of issues that can be raised in subsequent discussion. The discussion suggestions are addressed to you so you can think about the issues inherent in the activities, but it is better to write such discussion suggestions into the activity directions to students than to lead discussion yourself. The activities should be chosen by small groups to ensure good motivation, and you might sit in with a group to help them focus on these issues, but unless you have never worked before with the whole class on sensory writing you would do better not to impair the individualization for the sake of being able to lead whole-class discussion.

I. Record sensations at a locale away from school. Choose any place away from school that you would like. Go to that place with paper and pencil, and for fifteen minutes write down what you hear, see, and smell there. Think of what you write as notes for yourself later. These notes will be used to write something, to be decided later, that will be dittoed. Bring your notes to class. Don't worry about spelling or correct sentences; write in whatever way allows you to capture on paper what you observe in that time. You may also include your thoughts and feelings about what you observe. You may also want to say what things look, sound, or smell *like*.

• Two worthwhile issues can be raised and dealt with in the discussion of these first papers:

A. The difference between and relation between sensations and nonsensations, physical facts on the one hand and inferences, personal reactions, similes, and so on, on the other hand. Both should be valued, but it is important for the learner to be able to spot what he has mixed of himself with the environment. *Observation* thus takes on its double sense of sensory data and personal reaction. With a sample paper before students, ask what things in the paper might have been recorded by *any* observer and what things show traces of the particular person doing the recording. The use of "loaded" words and comparisons could be brought out as well as just obvious personal statements. Also, com-

pare two papers for the relative amount of sensory data versus personal reaction; ideally, this would lead to the discovery that, given the time limit, a gain in one is a loss in the other. Then have them underline words or sentences that they feel convey nonsensations. As a check for them, let them exchange papers and have a neighbor underline words or sentences that they feel convey nonsensations.

A good way to motivate this process might be to suggest that the class make reportage booklets containing two sections called "Interesting Places" and "Mood Scenes." Then they will need to focus as editors on decisions about how to classify and arrange pieces for publication. They will need to look at a set of notes and ask, "Given this set of notes, should the author play up his personal reactions, or should he stick more to straight reporting? Which does he have more of in his notes—reaction or observations?"

B. The *form* of the notes: word lists, telegraphic phrases, and whole sentences; amount of paragraphing and punctuating. Since these are notes to oneself, they should not be judged for correctness or intelligibility to others but only for their value as notes. Discuss the gains and losses of different forms of note-taking. Ditto or project two papers of contrasting form. What do you lose when you use just word lists? broken phrases? whole sentences? They should get some sense of which words are dispensable, which words or phrases capture a lot quickly, which suffer a loss of detail, and what the advantages and disadvantages are of longer phrases and whole sentences. (In general, lists cover a lot of items but lose the detail of *each* item, whereas full sentences modify, qualify, and elaborate single items, but don't cover as *many* items.)

Students should be encouraged to develop a notation style that works well for them—that enables them to go for coverage or go for detail, to strike whatever balance they want. This should help with the next two activities.

The purpose of the *second* activity could be introduced by an analogy: "Just as a photographer takes many shots to get the one he likes, let's try more than one collection of notes before we decide which is the best to reshape into our article for the literary magazine."

II. Record sensations at a new locale or time.   Do as you did in activity I, but this time change either the time or the place. If you went to an indoor place before, go somewhere outdoors now. If you went to an active place, go now to a still place. If there were no people where you went before, go where there will be people. Or you may return to the same place you went before, but go at a very different time of day, or when the weather is very different. Remember that you are to take notes of what you observe, see, hear, and smell and of what thoughts and feelings you may have about what you observe. If you have found a better way of taking notes since last time, use the new way.

• Discussion of these papers might center on two new issues, besides perhaps picking up the two earlier points if the students seem to want to pursue them.

A. Again with a sample before the class, ask if they can tell the time, place, and circumstances of the recording. How much can they tell of the mood of the observer and what he felt about the scene? Is there a main mood, impression, keynote, attitude, and so on? Does one sense dominate—sound, sight, or smell?

B. Try now to lead into the selection process of the observer. Get students to imagine what things were *left out*. Ask the writer of the paper to recall what things he did *not* put down. Ask everyone to look at his paper and compare it with his memory of the scene. First ask the authors of the sample papers and then the others how they came to include some things and reject other things. If they say they put down the "most interesting" or "most important" things, ask how they decided some things were more interesting or more important. This more or less unconscious selection process is at the heart of composing: some awareness of it should help later with activity IV.

Unique difficulties of recording are rooted in the fact that the observer may have no prior personal relation to what he witnesses; he confronts raw material that he must encode for the first time. These difficulties are qualified, of course, by the fact that any observer brings to bear on what he witnesses his memories of similar things or perhaps of the same things, so that the "raw material" becomes immediately associated with past experience and hence assimilated into the inner life. It is this association that makes certain things more "interesting" to an observer than others are. Thus, the degree to which you can figure out how to engage the inner life of pupils and help them draw on personal asso-

ciations is going to effect an increase in their involvement in the project.

III. Record sensations with some other pupils. Do as you did in activities I and II, but before you leave class plan with two or three other students to go somewhere at the same time. Decide together where to meet and when. After you meet, place yourselves at different points at that place (not too close together) and then begin to take your notes on what you see, hear, and smell. Again, include whatever thoughts and feelings you may have about what you observe.

• Read aloud all the papers of one group that had a common locale. Discuss what things all noted, what things only one or two noted, differences in physical vantage points, differences in inference and personal reaction or mood.

To prepare for rewriting, use this set of papers to confront the question: "What would you have to do to this paper [the sample before them] in order to make it understandable and interesting to other people?" See first what things they think of to mention without prompting. You may have to guide them a bit toward things they do not mention. Have them look at their own papers, ask the same question, and write some responses on the papers. Some possibilities are:

1. Clarifying some of the wording or references
2. Dwelling more on some things and less on others
3. Cutting out some things and adding others
4. Giving more or fewer personal reactions
5. Rewriting to avoid repetition of the same words or monotony of sentence structures (finding different words and constructions).

These discussions of activities I to III should make possible some successful collaborating in the small groups on activity IV.

IV. Compose one of the foregoing papers. Help each other to select and rewrite one of your papers. Take notes from activities I, II, and III to your group, and exchange all three papers for the three papers of someone else in the group. Read these three and decide which one could best be rewritten into an interesting composition for the class to read.

Write on that paper some comments. Say why you

think it has the best possibilities, and make suggestions about how it could be rewritten. Would you like to know more about some things; put some things later and move others nearer to the beginning? What suggestions would you make about changing the words and changing the way some sentences are written? If you see spelling mistakes, correct them. Try to be as helpful as you can; remember that the other person is doing the same thing for you, and that his comments will make it easier for you to decide what to rewrite and how to rewrite.

When you and your partner have finished reading each other's three papers and writing comments on them, you may talk about the comments. Then exchange with another and do the same thing again until you have been all the way around the group.

Next, look over the comments made on your papers and talk over with the other members of the group any questions you may have about what they said. You do not *have* to follow their suggestions, but knowing what they think should help you decide which paper to rewrite and how to go about doing it. *Rewrite* means not only improving sentences but also making large changes—adding new things, cutting out old ones, and moving other things around.

Now rewrite, in whatever you think will be the most interesting way, what you observed at one of your three places. All of the finished papers will be dittoed later for the whole class.

• Discussion of the finished papers should feature a comparison with the original papers from which they were rewritten. Ditto or project an activity-IV paper along with its predecessor and ask the class what changes the writer made, how he got from one stage to the next, and what purposes they assume he had for making such changes. For discussion pick two or three pairs that show different *degrees* of revision or different *bases* of revision.

Revision

Asking students to rewrite only one out of three recordings allows them to choose the material of greatest interest to them and to their audience and spares them from being stuck with a dull set of notes, in most cases. The very process of selecting the best set—through discussion, written comments by other pupils, and the author's own comparison of recordings—accomplishes a lot of the composing that one normally expects from written revision alone. Any act of composition begins with a selection and focus of material, from which different writing issues ensue. This is a fact both teachers and pupils need to grasp securely. The novice writer can grasp it by having to make decisions about his raw material.

The activity direction for writing up their notes into a composition for others would hold well for a revision of any first draft not written as notes. But revising notes establishes the revision process in a situation that provides an especially strong reason to rewrite—to put notes in a form that other people can understand. The principle underlying revision is that incorporating commentary should be justified by actual needs: it will provide final material for publication, and the amount of revision suggested will really require another writing. The first rewrite should be in pencil, so that if the paper stands well as is, except for minor alterations, these can be made by erasing and writing in. If much copying is involved, consider whether the amount of revision warrants another draft. Revision should be for a real purpose and not just to provide "clean copy," which, for that matter, the dittoed publication will provide (for folders, bulletin boards, parents, and so on). Learners have too much honest writing to do to be made to spend time copying. When the commentary from peers is helpful, the motivation is strong to make changes willingly. Putting together a publication, furthermore, motivates students to pursue their composing process until they have achieved a version they like. Once the concept of rewriting is extended well beyond just a notion of tidying up, then a further draft becomes more like an initial composition, and a fresh impetus to write arises again.

While remaining concrete and germane to the publication goal of the project, the issues raised in the process of revising can range among many important semantic, stylistic, rhetorical, and linguistic matters. A project such as this one can help establish the writing workshop as the means of getting into these issues through practical collaboration. For example, comparing recordings made in the same time and place can direct attention to alternative wordings for the same thing: "Which is better, considering mood and purpose, the word *flower* or *blossom*?"

The conjoining and embedding of short sentences to form fewer, more complex sentences come up for scrutiny as a matter of avoiding monotonous repetition. In sensory recording, the order of the words follows closely the order of events and results in short declarative sentences that repeat the same words and begin with *now, then,* and *next.* A student who revises merely by expanding kernel phrases ("coat falling") into kernel sentences ("I see a coat falling," or "the coat fell") ends up with a lot of repeated "*I*'s" or "coats" and a string of data predicated in a string of separate sentences. Comparing a telegraphic recording and a rewriting of it in full sentences leads to discussion of sentence elements and sentence expansions.

Although the heart of the matter is learning to build complex sentences by combining simple ones —a major linguistic development in the elementary and junior high years—it can be broached as a practical matter of style. Some will suggest joining sentences with conjunctions like *after, while,* and *during.* This leads to subordination, and here you must make sure that students' suggestions allow for proper emphasis as well as for style. If, for "The pole is breaking. He slid down the pole," someone proposes "While he was sliding down, the pole broke," suggest that maybe the author meant, "After the pole broke, he slid down," or "Because the pole was breaking, he slid down." The author is then consulted, as should happen often in these discussions. Comparison of alternative sentence structures is extremely valuable.

Another common problem in the rewriting of sensory recordings is the mixing of tenses. Many students get hung up between the present viewpoint of the recording and the past viewpoint of the revision and reflect this in a wavering of predicates between the two. This creates a fine opportunity to make students conscious of predicates as point-of-view indicators. See page 449.

Again, sensory recording offers rich possibilities for development of vocabulary. Some discussion should center on how things are named and include specific suggestions from partners and you to the writer about other words he might use.

Working with such raw material makes a good issue of titles. Setting up a working title, perhaps to be changed in the final draft, helps the writer think about the totality of his subject and about what he intends to do with it. All directions for compositions and drafts thereof should constantly remind students to entitle their pieces. Recordings themselves are obviously excepted, but as a lead into collaborative revision, you might ask a group to propose titles for a sensory recording that would do justice to it. If the recording has a natural unity or coherence,

proposing titles can bring it out; or if the recording is miscellaneous, the titles can suggest ways of reshaping that would build a unity from selected elements in it.

A titled composition can be tested out by blanking the title, asking others to title it, then letting them compare their suggestions with the author's original. This brings out discrepancies between intention and effect, such as misleading emphasis—which members can discuss—or reveals matching of intention with effect.

SAMPLES OF WRITING BASED ON SENSORY RECORDING

Our experience has been that sensory recording does evoke elaboration and detail. For example, two members of a class of slower-intermediate children not inclined to write voluminously on any occasion wrote the following sensory recordings. The first, an unrevised notation, captures the drama of a birth:

Meow, meow, shh, Nick is having kitties. Thump, thump, shh, Nick is having kitties. Ohhh, I know, scratch, scratch, Nick is having kitties. Oho, what do you know, she had three kitties.[5]

MY BACK YARD

It sure sounds funny how the wind goes through the trees. The smell of flowers blooming. The red pail laying in the grass. Our rope swaying across the air as if it was going somewhere. The wheel barrel like a ox pulls leaves. Trees are having buds. It's a beautiful night. The fence bending back in the wind. Our shed standing still there. I can hear the rabbits eating. I can hear the toad communicait. I can see our dog. I heared a bark from the yard. Our swing is trying to keep its balance.

Here is an enviable bit of imaginative perception. What we appreciate in this boy's notes is the rendering of the wind—the rope swaying, the fence bending, the swing set trying to keep its balance—all in contrast to "our shed standing still there." The kind

[5] This and the following elementary-school writing samples came from Franklin Elementary School, Lexington, Massachusetts.

of finely noted evocative details that teachers fall all over themselves trying to get students to put into their writing are here—the red pail lying in the grass, the wheelbarrow pulling leaves like an ox (comparisons are rare in children's speech and writing)—and yet we don't feel that the boy was striving for poetic effect or trotting out his prettiest adjectives to "do a description." He was really experiencing the moment and translating it into words.

Here is a fairly typical sample of a straightforward recording and revision of a landscape:

See	*Hear*	*Smell*
trees swaying	birds peep tweet	rich soil
grass	faint noises	fresh air
little bugs	from cars	
big gray rocks	bees buzzing	
branches shaking	dog collor shake	
a field of yellow	dog bark	
twigs braking	plane	
a tree house	leaves rustling	
birds over head	twigs fall to ground	

Listing by senses is a notation form adopted by a number of children and sometimes suggested by a teacher. It avoids "I hear" and "I see" but automatically eliminates thoughts and feelings, unless, as one teacher told her pupils to do, they add a column for these. Students who use the column form once or twice should then try other forms. For one thing, it encourages the minimizing of linguistic structures, reducing them to nouns coupled with an adjective or a present participle. The more dispensable parts of speech, such as articles and auxiliaries, are virtually eliminated; adverbs, prepositions, and conjunctions are rare. Consequently, a lot of details and relationships are lost. As one should expect, the sound column consists of action, the smell column of things, and the sight column of both. Here is the revision (activity IV):

I can see the little bugs fly through the air and great big gray rocks sit in the same place all the time. I can hear a dog collor shake when he walks. Just smell the fresh air. The rich soil. Thoses birds tweeting and bees buzzing. The trees swaying and the bright green grass. The whole field with a yellow blanket covering it. The tree house way up high. I hear leaves rustling when the wind blows the wind knocks twigs off of trees and I hear the twigs fall to the ground faint noises from cars and a plane overhead.

It is worth noticing how phrases were joined and expanded into sentences, or expanded merely into longer fragments that do not quite become sentences because the obvious predicates were unnecessary and because there was too little action to warrant other predicates. Writing up from kernel words offers a chance to work on what a sentence is and can do.

Now compare this revision with those by two other girls who were recording at the same time and same place as the first girl:

The sound of little birds singing fills the clean fresh air. A field of green and yellow is at one of me. Silence fills the air exsept for the pretty birds singing and a few cars going on their way. There goes an airplane roering through the sky. It is quiet and peaceful now. The sun gleams as we write.

We walk into the woods. The birds are chirping loudly. A car is going by very fast. Up above me is a tree house. The air smells fresh. Look at all those bright yellow dandelions. I wonder what Terry and Kathy are thinking. There goes a bird. Here comes two dogs. They must be repairing a road somewhere. There goes an airplane. It feels dark and creepy in here.

Only a few items were noted by all three children—the birds, the airplane, the fresh air, the car, and the yellow field. Only one identified the yellow covering as dandelions. Only two mentioned the tree house. Several things were mentioned by just one child—the bugs, the rich soil, the gray rocks, the sun, the bees, the twigs, the wind, the sound of road-repairing. Sensory recording should not become a contest to see who can cram in the most details, but, without *invidious* comparisons, children can see what items their companions caught that they missed or deliberately left out. Discussion may show that some of these discrepancies are due to differences in physical vantage points. Part of discussion can consist of inferring the time, locale, and weather as implied by the details (such implications are characteristics of haiku poetry). The mood established at the end of the second and third papers is very different—one of sunny peacefulness, the other "dark and creepy." (Is one observer in the field, the other in the woods?)

The three versions above are essentially miscellaneous enumerations, the hardest kind of material to shape into a unity. Mood is perhaps the best possibility. Real moments of being are made of just such miscellanies, but one should not expect children to be able to compose more than a mood from such a scene. All three revisions are of the simplest sort. Little more than verbal expansion has taken place; tense and point of view remain in the present; selection and arrangement are slight, probably because the children could see nothing central to focus on, as they might have, had there been more action or had they added more thoughts and feelings. Suggesting that they write their notes into a poem or make up a story to take place in the setting might inspire more interesting and purposeful writing.

From what looked like rather unpromising notes, a boy very consciously composed a mood piece:

ON OUR SUN PORCH

Hear: Birds singing
Airplane
Trees rustling
People talking
grinding of sand under
   peoples shoes
cars
doors slaming
looks like: everything
   looks gloomy
Houses
birds
people
cars
neighbor swings and
   play area
air plane
trees waving
I feel like I am lonley
   and cold everything
   smells like pine sap

As the day wore on the clouds had grown dark and thicker. All the children were in their houses and the only person in sight was the mailman as he slowly walked his route.

The birds that had been singing earlier had stopped and all was quiet.

Now there came a rustle in the leaves. Slowly it grew louder and finally it fell into a steady rythm.

The twitering in the trees gradually ceased as the birds settled down in their nests from the night and rain.

Besides shifting the tense and creating sentences, this boy deliberately omitted all details that did not suit his purpose.

Think of a title for the following piece, a revised recording by a girl:

Cars zooming down the highway looking like little toy cars going down a little toy road. Light taps of rain coming down on everyones windows. Splashes going up then down with children watching them gayly.

Once I heard one child say "What would it be like to be a rain drop?"

His brother Tom he asked "What would it be like to be one of those stiff people?" pointing to a tree.

Thoughts just filled my head with answers but they had gone away.

The first half establishes a setting with several images; the second half relates an incident that either happened in that setting or was recalled to the child by it. The piece seems split, but the halves are joined by raindrops. In proposing and discussing titles for it, other pupils would have to determine what kind of notion would contain it, how sharp or vague the title would have to be. They might ask the author if the second half were a memory or an observation, and he could clear up the ambiguity of "Once I heard one child say. . . ." if indeed they think it should be cleared up (for the whole piece reads like an impressionistic reverie and reminds one a bit of some of Dylan Thomas's evocations of childhood). The author's own title was "The Highway," which might have been an unconscious metaphorising of the composition itself—the inner trip that begins in one place and ends somewhere very different—or may well have been simply a reference to an initial image from which he carelessly strayed later. But in discussing his title, his classmates are helping him know what he wrote and at the same time tackling the whole business of coherence.

The following writing sample is by a twelfth-grade boy at Dorchester High School in urban Boston. Students in this class typify a kind of older school population that poses a problem for the teacher of writing. Though not the weakest students in their grades, most of them will not go to college and many are from families of little education and low socioeconomic status. They are not involved in schoolwork generally and have done little writing except for some impersonal exercises. Given their alienation and the late stage of their schooling—about to terminate for good—what writing assignments can engage them and help them learn something in the time remaining? Allowing for the effects that the teachers' sensitivity and compassion undoubtedly had,[6] still the invitation to put fresh experience into words seemed to bring some of these students back to life. Never having climbed very high on the abstraction ladder, unmotivated to write about books and remote topics, they like to observe, live close to concrete things, and can find some pleasure in verbalizing these things. Once interested, they can consider the conceptual and technical matters of shaping their material through revision. Unlike younger children, they seldom take notes in list form but record, rather, in whole sentences or full phrases. And they record more selectively, so that the subject takes on more shape from the beginning.

Here I am sitting on a bundle of papers in front of St. Ambrose Church. Just waiting for the children's mass to start. All around me I can see and hear the children. Some of them are arguing with their older sister about going into church alone. And others are asking me if there is any sunday school as if I should know.

In the sky and on the roofs I see several sea gulls there is one gull now who dives at us early in the morning. They have a funny way of flying, when they glide they do it with their wings bent. An old lady just bought a paper she looks like the type who checks the paper to be sure its all there. A cab driver just drove up and asked me if thise St. Peter's he must be blind if he can-

---

[6] The teachers were Grace Whittaker and Carol Shea.

not see the sign. Around me I can smell the fragrance of the grass also of the papers.

The original sentences were not greatly different from those appearing above, but some changes were made in word choice and sentence construction. Some details were cut, added, or shifted into a different order. This amount of revising was made without benefit of cross-commentary or of a newspaper framework but was aided by class discussion of samples.

The paper above shows the interest that so often inheres in a *place,* if it is well observed, even though the events are miscellaneous and the composition not very focused. A place has its own primitive kind of unity, the organic interrelationships of its sounds and sights. But the observer composes the scene by his very selection and by infusing his reactions. Composing pure description from randomness—making good writing out of anything at all—is a sophisticated skill.

At the risk of pulling sensory recording a bit out of the many contexts it may have, we have tried to present it as a base of operations. Options in activity directions should point out the kinds of writing that may be drawn from this sensory store—reportage, poems of description and feeling, settings for stories and plays, reflective essay prompted by some scene or moment. Along with memories, dealt with in Chapter 16, True Stories, sensing is a great source of what a writer has to write about. But it is rawer material than memories and hence poses more primitive problems of composing, throwing into relief that selecting and subordinating process that is the heart of all composing.

PART THREE

literacy—
"the basic skills"

the basics of teaching

"the basic skills"

Reading and writing entail far more than what we will deal with in this section. As we said in Chapter 7, Reading, and Chapter 8, Writing, each skill fuses the literacy and verbalization levels of coding. Someone reading is translating print to speech at the same time he is translating speech to thought. He is decoding in a double sense, necessarily. Similarly, someone writing is encoding in the double sense of translating his thoughts into language at the same time he is translating this language into letters and punctuation.

It is chiefly for meaning, of course, that people decode and encode at either level. This goal of meaning should never be lost, and that is why most of the rest of this book deals with it, that is, with how thought is put into and taken out of language. We believe that learning to decode and encode speech differs so much from learning to decode and encode thought that for a while we should focus on literacy separately. The aim of doing so, however, is only to ensure that meaning will be most effectively conveyed by written language.

What teachers commonly call the basic skills are the skills of transcribing speech into writing and of decoding writing into speech. The transcription skills are handwriting, spelling, and punctuating. The decoding skills include word recognition and word attack. Word recognition is recognizing a spoken word in print. Word attack is figuring how to sound a word from its spelling. These concepts overlap, of course, since both activities benefit from other common cues, and any orally known word successfully "attacked" can be recognized, but one difference is that word recognition may occur from memorizing the overall look of a word, whereas word attack occurs from specifically matching off certain spellings in the word with certain speech sounds. The concept of literacy decoding must also include knowing the typographical conventions of direction, spacing, paragraphing, and punctuation. See pages 25 and 246 for the objectives and breakdown of literacy.

Taken together, decoding and transcription skills comprise the old two Rs, or literacy. In the chapters of this section, we will treat them as opposites, *up to a point.* Decoding is *sounding out* spelling and punctuation. Encoding is *spelling out* and punctuating sounds. Paired association between any two sets works both ways, and each way teaches the other.

These "basic skills" are basic for literacy only, not for general discourse. All they do is bring about a shift from the prior, oral-aural medium to the new, visual medium. The *true* basic skills are speaking and listening.

This is not to minimize, however, the obvious difficulties that many children have learning to decode and transcribe. The point is that these difficulties can be greatly reduced by treating the two activities as nothing more than what they are—the matching of an auditory symbol system with a visual symbol system—and by treating meaning as nothing less than what it is—the matching of thought with speech. Meaning goes with the oral language, and as soon as a reader recognizes in the printed symbols the spoken words he already knows, he will get the meaning, or at least whatever meaning the oral words have for him.

The practical question is how best to get from a medium to which meanings are already attached to a new medium so that henceforth the same meanings may be conveyed in either medium. For blind learners this means associating oral speech with a tactile medium such as Braille. For deaf learners this means matching off hand signs or pictures with written words —that is, one visual medium with another visual medium. A handicapped person who has not already learned a tactile or visual symbol system will have to associate meanings directly with written words, dispensing with any intermediate sense. This is equivalent to a child's learning to speak, since he is symbolizing experience at the first level of verbal coding.

If people learned to associate meaning directly with *visual* symbols, as chimpanzees are now being taught to do (they have no vocal apparatus), then print could convey meaning independently of speech. Eventually, by association with oral language, print too takes on for people the meanings that speech conveys, but however much speech may fade into the background *after* a learner has become a proficient reader and writer, the literacy *beginner* will have to use oral language as a bridge to meaning. This is what we mean by matching print to speech at the same time as matching speech to thought. We cannot accept, as some educators seem to, the notion that the beginner can bypass oral language and translate print directly into thought, because people are not taught while babies to encode meaning into written words. We can believe, however, as we indicate on page 122, that a *proficient* reader and writer comes to associate meaning directly with printed words and can thus read far faster silently than he could if continuing to subvocalize. But in this chapter and the next we are concerned with how the learner *reaches* proficiency. By the time the oral intermediary is relegated to such an unconscious or automatic status that it ceases to be an issue, the learner has already learned to attack and spell words. For people of normal vision and hearing in this country, the main job of literacy is to match English sounds with English spellings, English vocal intonation with punctuation.

The reason that we have chosen in this book to treat literacy somewhat separately from comprehension and composition, even though we insist on the primacy of meaning, is to clarify the independence of each level *so that we can understand better what is going on when they interact.* This is strictly a strategy for our exposition, not a teaching strategy for use with youngsters. What prompts us to it is the great amount of confusion and conflict in the profession that seems to have stemmed from the ambiguous double coding involved in reading and writing.

Whereas thought can be matched with speech in a great and creative variety of verbalization, speech can be matched with print only according to fairly fixed conventions of spelling, punctuation, and other typography. These conventions comprise truly new information; one is not born knowing them. And matching sounds to spelling, intonation to punctuation, is mere perceptual pairing. In some way these have to be *taught*. Comprehension and composition, on the other hand, are deep operations of mind and spirit. People are born comprehending and composing, because these are part of our biologically given abstracting apparatus by which we *make meaning.*

If composition and comprehension are not conceived separately by teachers, then youngsters will not be allowed to practice them separately, which is the only way they will be practiced enough—orally as well as with books and paper. Separating them from literacy does them no harm, because they cannot, by their nature, lose meaning. The problem is that the opposite is not true. A media shift like literacy has no inherent meaning and relates to meaning only because it translates print into a medium to which meanings are already attached, oral language. Some people can sound out a foreign language from knowledge of its sound-spelling correspondences and still understand nothing of what they are pronouncing. So learning to attack and spell words *can* be divorced from meaning. The big issues of methods are: *Should* it be? Does it *have* to be? Our answer is no, except for a minimum of phonetic analysis done in conjunction with other methods.

Now, let's put the two levels of coding back together. They do interact during reading and writing. A reader needs only part of a printed word, or only some of a printed word string to guess the rest. Given so much of a sentence construction, only certain other sentence elements can follow. Given the accumulated meaning so far, a reader predicts what certain other words are and what certain phrases say. He uses the ongoing grammatical and meaning cues afforded by some words to attack the remaining words. For further description of this important part of the reading process see page 222, and see both it and page 139 for examples. Since grammar and meaning are already embodied in speech, a reader can use this *oral* knowledge to figure out for himself the *visual* and thus set up a circular process of using word attack to gain enough recognition of some words to use them in turn to recognize others he doesn't or can't attack with his knowledge of the sound-spellings. (The grammatical knowledge does not need to be taught; it was learned orally before he entered school.) The upshot is that some priming of the literacy pump should be all that is needed to set learners to teaching themselves to read. The idea is to convey to them, one way or another, enough of the conventions of spelling so that they can deduce generalizations about the rest on their own.

The way in which literacy and verbalization interact during writing parallels what happens during reading but is also different. Having to "spell out" one's thought in a double sense causes the writer to deliberate more about word and sentence construction. The act of writing down word strings no doubt influences how he verbalizes his thought and may even influence what he thinks too. Transcribing one's inner speech acts backward on the inner speech itself, setting up a circular process comparable, in reading, to interpreting some visual words on the basis of oral knowledge. Transcribing slows down inner speech or, more properly perhaps, makes it circle and mark time and, most likely, revise itself. Once a writer begins to encode a train of thought into words at the same time he is encoding the words into letters and punctuation, he puts himself in the middle of a verbal stream that at any given moment is partly visible and partly still invisible. He can see what he has already said, and this influences what he will say next, because the record serves as a kind of feedback to inform him whether he is saying what he means to say in the way he means to. So in addition to slowing thought, transcribing encourages self-editing by aiding memory.

Because the goal of literacy is to convey meaning by print as well as by voice, and because comprehension and composition not only take place at the same time as word attack and spelling but also interact with them, the most sensible learning practices will teach word attack and spelling in as close a relation to comprehension and composition as possible. This is in keeping with our principle of context governing text and of authentic discourse being the ultimate context because there resides meaning. All this is critical for motivation, which we have said must be especially strong to impel a youngster to acquire a *second* language medium. Meaning sweeps along the technical details.

Preparation for literacy

Unless impaired, children have all the development they need for literacy by age eight or nine at the latest, and some children learn to decode and to transcribe before they come to school, even as early sometimes as three or four years old. It is certainly true that many people may not have the motivation, opportunity, or the courage to read and write until much later, or never, but the teenager or adult who becomes literate has to learn the same things in the same basic ways as the smallest tyke.

The preschool or primary-school child who learns to read and write is more limited than a literate teenager or adult, of course, in what he can comprehend and compose with his literacy skills, but this disparity is not in literacy development. It is in general mental growth, to which verbalization is tied. So the child will get lost among word concepts too hard for him and sentence relations too complex for him. This is why we stated the two literacy goals relative to what a learner can understand orally. If a child wants to learn to read and write, he can do so at any time after some minimal sensorimotor development. He can also do so in a short time, depending largely on the strength of his motivation. Some young children have learned to read and write in three or four weeks, which shows that literacy acquisition does not inherently have to grow slowly, however long it may drag on for many other children. Greater intelligence may speed up literacy acquisition, as it does most other sorts of mental learning, but literacy does not require much intelligence nor does it have to wait on intellectual development. To the extent that more complex sentences have to await more intricate thought, some punctuation usages that attend those sentence structures will crop up only later, when functional. But staging literacy over several years, as in protracted phonics sequences, cannot be warranted.

The opportunity to learn to read and write should be offered children at every age from three on. The key word here is *offered.* No child should be forced to try to become literate, whether ready or not, just because he has arrived at a certain chronological age. Encouraged, yes; surrounded with literacy materials and books, occasions to get involved, people who can help him seize the occasions, yes. But schools cause real tragedy in many lives by forcing certain unready first graders to try to read and write, because many such children experience only failure in school from then on and drop out later. Not only do they not get an education but they may harbor all their lives feelings of resentment and inferiority.

The chief reason for this forcing, despite the better judgment of many teachers, is that any first- or second-grade teacher whose children do not all show certain reading scores by the end of the year may risk criticism or even job security. Many parents as well as administrators pressure teachers very strongly to get their child reading in kindergarten or first grade, and some minority parents suspect discrimination if a teacher does not force their child. Much practical evidence indicates that some children could learn with greater speed and ease if they simply waited a year or two, but such a policy would have to be understood by both parent and administrator, so that the one would know that in the long run his child would read better than if he had started in the first grade, and the other would know that the teacher had not failed with the child but had simply not forced him.

It is important to emphasize that you do not have to decide if a child is ready but merely have to refrain from forcing or blaming him, at the same time giving him every opportunity to learn literacy. Then if he really cannot get it going, everyone involved should assume that in time he will. It is true that other schoolwork presupposes after a year that a child can read, but a child offered every opportunity is not going to read yet anyway, however forced, and he can get information he needs for other schoolwork from live or recorded voice and from pictorial media, pending his readiness for literacy.

What we are recommending here is not, of course, indifference or casualness but an expectation that individuals will vary in their timing, so that if some don't take to literacy the first time around, no one panics or thinks that either child or teacher has failed. It could be that sometimes teachers may not be doing their job well, but if you individualize literacy, as we propose, not many children will be able to resist it; and far fewer pupils, in fact, will fail to learn to read and write than has been true with forced standardization.

AUDITORY AND VISUAL DISCRIMINATION

One kind of readiness required is specific—auditory and visual discrimination—to identify and distinguish different sounds and different letter shapes. Many activities and materials described in this book can bring along sensorimotor development, and some are often included in commercial literacy programs. What best develops auditory discrimination is hearing meaningfully distinguished sounds, and for this human speech itself can't be bettered, but musical tones and any other arrays of significant sounds that interest the child will help.

The real secret is to enrich the environment so that children can be constantly manipulating inter-

esting objects and comparing them for their shapes and sounds, among other features. Comparison is the key, and this occurs best when children can experience a lot, be active, and have access to a large variety of things to handle and play with. It seems to be true that sharpening one part of the sensorimotor apparatus sharpens the rest. The nervous system is interconnected and grows as a whole. So refinement of touch or muscle action of any sort, for example, will probably help handwriting, as any auditory and visual experience will help reading. In fact, development of either muscles or senses seems to develop the other, because of the close coordination that using either requires.

EMOTIONAL AND EXPERIENTIAL READINESS

The other kind of readiness relates to more general maturation that is prerequisite for learning any informational sequence. Literacy learning has to be embedded in a framework of motivation, emotional maturity, and general experience with people and things. To gain this kind of readiness children need to be talked with, read to, and taken places. They need direct experience with some of the physical and social things that books talk about. They need to handle books, turn the pages, and look at pictures. They need to find out what writing and reading have to offer—discover the pleasure and information in books, become aware of environmental writing such as signs. Older youngsters can understand how literacy may be necessary for getting a job and generally getting around, but small children unable to see that far ahead into the utilitarian possibilities must feel pleasure awaiting them in print, find out that locked in the letters are wonderful stories and funny games and things they want to know.

It is terribly hard for one teacher alone to give a roomful of children all they need for getting ready to read and write. You can read to them, try to get them to talk, give them objects to play with, let them look through picture books, and take them on visits. But you can go much further by mixing well-developed children with the underdeveloped, so that the one can help the other, and by including dramatic play and peer talk in the activities. Those children who have not been talked with should talk with children who are used to conversing. They should have a chance to play with more experienced children of their own age, and to pick up from the latter some of their knowledge of the world. If you are alone, you cannot possibly provide enough of these experiences for each child. You can, however, set up social games among small groups and lead the class in interactive activities. What has not been sufficiently exploited in reading readiness is peer interaction. In a heterogeneous class, more advanced children can begin the literacy program before less-experienced or less-motivated children and help bring them along. Besides talking with them, the more advanced children can read to them, interest them in books, and even impart some of their knowledge about letter formation and spatial orientation in books. In short, since the timing of literacy instruction depends on individual development, and since some children will consequently be starting it before others, an additional and powerful force—pupil cross-teaching—can be brought to bear on the critical problem of reading readiness.

The phonetic analysis to be learned

What literacy students have to learn implicitly and what you have to know explicitly are the set of English sounds and how they are spelled in various word structures. Phonetic analysis shows the comparative frequencies with which the different English sounds and letters occur in words, the characteristic ways sounds are blended and letters combined, and hence the spelling patterns or generalizations that, along with exceptions to them, can be inferred. The section that follows presents the most general phonetic facts of English for teaching literacy by any method.

However it comes about, phonetic analysis of words has to occur, whether it is learned alone intuitively or explicitly taught. English comprises several hundred thousand words generated by the combining power of only forty-odd sounds. You have to know how the twenty-six letters of the alphabet may be combined to make the forty-odd sounds when up to three letters may make one sound, when some letters may be mute in some circumstances, and when many sounds may be rendered by several spellings.

THE SOUNDS OF ENGLISH

In linguistics the basic sounds of a language are called *phonemes,* and their written equivalents *graphemes.* Linguists usually count forty to forty-

five phonemes in English, depending mainly on whether they consider some sounds as phonemes in their own right or only as combinations of other phonemes. It is the phonemes that the learner must match off with their various spellings. We will array them twice—first by some categories familiar to teachers and useful for spelling (see Table 9.1), then by categories of sound production adapted from linguistics (see Table 9.2). We have indicated by brackets in Table 9.1 which sounds we do not consider distinct phonemes but which you will often find included in literacy programs because English assigns separate spellings to them. These bracketed sounds cause disputes among linguists and teachers about how many phonemes English has. In Table 9.2, we have not included the bracketed sounds, because it aims at auditory discrimination. Phoneme spellings are underlined in sample words.

Not counting the bracketed sounds, this gives us

TABLE 9.1 PHONEME CATEGORIES AND SPELLINGS

Vowels			
Short:	BIG,	BAG,	BOG,
	BEG,	BUG,	BOOK
Long:	PILE,	PAIL,	POLE,
	PEEL,	PULE,	POOL
Diphthongs:	FOIL,	FOUL	
r-controlled:	FUR,	[FOR],	
	[FAR],	[FAIR],	
	[FEAR].		
Other:	PAUL,	[AGO] (schwa)	

Consonants			
Alphabet:	BELL,	DELL,	FELL,
	GULL,	HULL,	JELL,
	KICK,	LICK,	MILL,
	NEST,	PEST,	REST,
	SELL,	TELL,	VEST,
	WEST,	YEAST,	ZEST,
		AZURE	
Digraphs:	CHIN,	SHIN,	THIN,
	THEN,	[WHEN],	SING

sixteen vowel phonemes and twenty-four consonant phonemes, the same as in the Unifon alphabet shown on page 183. We consider that the four bracketed *r*-controlled vowels are just blends of some of the other vowels with *r* and that *wh* stands for no more than the blend of the sounds /w/[1] and /h/. Schwa, we deem, is the same sound as short *u*. The *concept* of schwa, however, is very useful, for it refers to any vowel spelling pronounced *uh* because it is in an unstressed syllable (ad–*mi*–ra–*tion*). Given the very large number of unstressed vowels in words of more than one syllable, schwa occurs at least as often in such words as all the other vowel sounds put together.

We sense a conflict between a list of pure phonemes and a list of basic sounds for spelling and reading purposes. English spelling, for example, acknowledges only two diphthongs, as above, but all the long vowels are diphthongized somewhat. The double-letter spelling of long vowels in many words testifies to their present or past diphthongal nature, but the spellings of *pail* and *coal* do not help us sound their modern pronunciation as do *foil* and *foul*. For their part, the digraphs do not cover all the consonant sounds uncovered by the alphabet: the sound in *azure* and *casual* has neither a digraph nor its own letter to represent it. Though useful to indicate, precisely, the aberrations of English sound-spellings, Table 9.1 needs to be supplemented by an array that sticks to the minimal forty phonemes and that categorizes them by how they are physically articulated (Tables 9.2 and 9.3).

Vowels

All vowels are voiced, that is, sounded by narrowing the top of the windpipe where the vocal chords are located so that expelled air makes the chords vibrate. Varying this hum produces the different vowels. What causes variation is shifting of the tongue and lips to make the mouth into a sounding chamber of different size and shape. Table 9.2 scales English vowels according to this physical articulation. Sound the sample words in order, and describe for yourself how you formed them.

Strictly speaking, Table 9.2 completes the listing of unique vowels, the others being combinations:

r-controlled: F<u>U</u>R (*uh* + *r*)
Diphthongs: F<u>OU</u>L, F<u>OI</u>L, K<u>I</u>TE and C<u>U</u>TE

[1] Slashes indicate the sound, not the letter.

TABLE 9.2 VOWELS SCALED BY PHYSICAL ARTICULATION

1. P<u>EA</u>T		11. P<u>U</u>LL
2. P<u>I</u>T		10. P<u>OO</u>L
3. P<u>A</u>TE		9. P<u>O</u>LE
4. P<u>E</u>T		8. P<u>AU</u>L
5. P<u>A</u>T	7. P<u>O</u>T	
6. P<u>U</u>TT		
(schwa)		

Long *i* and long *u* are spelled by two symbols each in the International Phonetic Alphabet, because they are made up of two vowels each that are ordinarily pronounced separately. Judge for yourself whether long *i* blends 7 and 2 in Table 9.2 and long *u* blends 1 and 10. It is true, as we said, that the other long vowels diphthongize also, but *e, a,* and *o* all start with a unique sound, even if they do slide into another vowel afterward (which we can ignore). It is well worth noting that these five vowel sounds also split in this way for spelling: long *a, e,* and *o* may be spelled with digraphs (*ai, ea, oa*) but long *i* and *u* never are spelled with digraphs in native English words.

Don't get frustrated if you have difficulty distinguishing which of two adjacent vowels in the scale is higher or lower. Linguists disagree about the placement of certain sounds. Some would change our scale in Table 9.2. But in trying to work out in these relative terms the articulation of the vowels, you will understand why some of your students have trouble with auditory discrimination and how you might help them. Vowels are generally harder to tell apart than consonants, precisely because they are sounded only by varying the vocal hum. At any rate, they are harder to decode and spell, and this greater difficulty seems related to articulation in two ways. One is that their acoustic instability has led to pronunciation changes not well reflected in the spelling, and the other is that some people confuse their sounds, and hence their spellings.

In English, vowels create nearly all the difficulties of reading and writing. Most consonants have a one-to-one correspondence with letters. A *c* may sound like a *k* or *s*, an *s* like a *z*, and a *g* like a *j*, but these create few problems compared to vowels. Consonants are most troublesome when they are silent attendants of vowels (*fought,* for example), so that in learning vowel spellings a student usually masters these accompanying silent consonants.

Consonants

Consonants may or may not be sounded in conjunction with vocal chord vibration (voiced). To make consonants, people have to do more than voice. We blow or pop or squeeze the air before or after the voicing. Again, sound these yourself. The sixteen consonants in Table 9.3 are the only pure consonants, and, significantly, they come in pairs. They are made only by stopping or frictionizing the air in the oral cavity.

The fricatives may be perceived as less clear-cut and hence may be less stable than the stops. They differ from stops also in the other sounds they can combine with. At any rate, fricatives cause more spelling problems.

Semiconsonants

The remaining phonemes are not pure consonants and, though usually classified as consonants, will be most usefully thought of as a special group having some kinship with both vowels and consonants. With the exception of /h/, they are all voiced and all play special roles in spelling that make it worthwhile to understand their peculiarities.

First, let's dispense with /h/, which in a sense is *neither* vowel nor consonant. It is not voiced, like a vowel, nor is it made, like a consonant, by exploding or hissing air in the oral cavity. We form an /h/ simply by blowing air through the top of the windpipe while constricting the windpipe slightly but not enough to vibrate the vocal chords. By its nature /h/ must only precede vowels in a syllable. Though anomolous, /h/ is not a cause of special spelling patterns.

NASALS

RA<u>M</u>—Lip to lip, diverting air column from mouth to nose

RA<u>N</u>—Tip of tongue to ridge behind teeth, diverting air from mouth to nose

RA<u>NG</u>—Back of tongue to soft palate, diverting air from mouth to nose

The position for /m/ is the same as for /b/, the position for /n/ the same as for /d/, and that of /ng/ the same as for /k/. Try these and compare. To make nasals we merely *place* the oral parts together. We stop but do not pop the air, and we stop the air only for the mouth, since it continues to flow, but flows out the nose. The main effect is to make the nose the resonator, instead of the mouth. This converts an oral hum into a nasal hum. In this way these semiconsonants may alter the sounds of vow-

TABLE 9.3 STOPS AND FRICATIVES

		Voiced	*Unvoiced*	
S T A O I P R		<u>B</u>EST	<u>P</u>EST	Lip to lip
		<u>D</u>ELL	<u>T</u>ELL	Tongue tip to ridge behind teeth (apex)
		<u>G</u>LASS	<u>C</u>LASS	Back of tongue to soft palate
STOPS AIR *AND* MAKES FRICTION		<u>J</u>EST	<u>CH</u>EST	Front of tongue to front of palate
M F A R K I E C T I O N		A<u>Z</u>URE	<u>S</u>URE	Tongue near and parallel to palate
		<u>Z</u>IP	<u>S</u>IP	Tip of tongue near ridge behind teeth
		<u>TH</u>IS	<u>TH</u>ISTLE	Tip of tongue to back of teeth
		<u>V</u>AST	<u>F</u>AST	Lower lip to lower teeth

els preceding them (*sing, rank*). Like the other semi-consonants, they are more just a *position* than a sound in their own right.

For the sake of a handy name, we will call the remaining four sounds vowel glides.

VOWEL GLIDES

LO<u>Y</u>AL—Middle of the tongue to palate as for long *e*

TO<u>W</u>EL—Lips rounded as for long *oo*

CO<u>R</u>AL, CO<u>R</u>D—Back of tongue arched toward soft palate

FI<u>L</u>IAL—Tip of tongue to ridge behind teeth

All four of these sounds—/y/, /w/, /r/, and /l/—are really just muscular positions that make sound only by the articulation involved in shifting from one vowel position to another.

The sound of /y/ is really the transition between long *e* and whatever vowel follows it. It's part of a diphthong, in other words, with at most an emphatic push of the tongue toward the palate in passing. The sound of /w/ is really *oo* plus a following vowel, with a little extra snap to the lips. Even at the beginning of words, both are vocalic. *Yet* is pronounced *ee-et*. Try to distinguish *funniest* from *funniyest*. The French spelling of *west* shows all this clearly (*ouest*). Pronounce it rapidly as *oo-est,* and you have *west*. This is why /y/ and /w/ can be used in alternative spellings of *ou* and *oi* (*cow* and *boy*).

All of these semiconsonants *influence preceding vowels*. As a result, they crop up consistently in special spelling patterns and downright irregularities. Besides the nasal-controlled and *r*-controlled patterns, there are many variants such as *all, awl, haul* in which the spelling of the same sound differs according to a following consonant. Remarkably often that following consonant is a semiconsonant. The reason, we believe, goes back to their articulation. As mediators or influencers of sounds rather than sounds themselves, they merge with vowels and other consonants in ways that create more spelling difficulties than stops or even fricatives.

Variation in Pronunciation

The pronunciation of English varies so much from one region or dialect to another, not to mention from one English-speaking country to another, that any sound list can be considered only a rough approximation of how a given speech community will sound out English spellings. Allow constantly not only for simple options like *toona* or *tyoona* for *tuna,* regional variations like *pahk* for *park* and *yelluh* for *yellow,* but for less obvious variations within each separate vowel sound. (Note, incidentally, how often these variations involve, as in these examples, the very diphthongizing of vowels and vocalization of consonants that we have just examined.) Called *allophones,* these variations within a phoneme are detectable but not divergent enough to warrant being counted as separate phonemes. For literacy purposes, several allophones have to be considered equal, because spellings cover just the phonemes, not the variant allophones within each.

Dialectical Variation

Some variations characterize a whole speech community and may depart so far from the more or less standard pronunciation of, say, television announcers and dictionaries as to conflict sometimes with a literacy program based on standard pronunciation. The matter has been hotly debated because many such speech communities are also ethnic minorities. In some urban black dialects, for example, the *th* of *brother* is pronounced like a *v* (*bruvver*) and the *th* of *path* like *f* (*paff*). Some consonants are not pronounced, and some vowels may diverge so far from standard pronunciation as to become another phoneme. What happens to a speaker of a nonstandard dialect when he tries to learn to read and write in a literacy program that matches off English spellings with standard English pronunciation?

Researchers have tried to answer this by comparing literacy results in nonstandard speakers taught in some cases by standard pronunciation and in other cases by their own pronunciation. The research is inconclusive, and so far no one has shown either by experimental research or by classroom experience that speaking a nonstandard dialect poses a problem at all for learning to attack and spell words. Many minority children have certainly encountered difficulties with basic skills, but other aspects of cultural gap between school and community seem to account for this, plus the general ineffectuality of traditional literacy teaching, especially with students not being taught to read and write at home. Speakers of nonstandard pronunciation—whether urban black or middle-class Southern white or immigrant—seem to make an automatic internal adjustment for dialectical differences in pronunciation as well as in grammar and vocabulary. They hear (and understand) standard English on national television, radio, and movies, if nowhere else, and infer for themselves an equivalence between how they hear a word there and how they say it themselves.

To make sure, however, that the nonstandard speaker is not placed at a disadvantage, you can use materials that include the dialectical sounding and spelling of such students. The problem is somewhat political in that a minority speech community may split into those who want their nonstandard dialect preserved to assert their identity and those who want it replaced with standard so their children can get jobs more easily. Both goals can be served. Words and sentences can be sounded for learners in both standard and nonstandard dialect, to help them reinforce their perception that certain sounds are equivalent for spelling purposes. And reading material can include selections written in dialect and spelled to render the dialectical pronunciation.

Since most reading matter is written in standard English, a nonstandard speaker should have opportunities to hear it while seeing it, in addition to conversing with standard speakers. The idea is to supplement—but *not* supplant—his native dialect. The only truly serious problem with dialectical variation anyway most likely stems from a teacher's prejudice against speech different from his own. It is not annexing a second dialect but feeling shamed that damages.

SOUNDING AND SPELLING PATTERNS

So far we have considered English sounds as isolated phonemes, but of course they do not function in isolation. Someone who says *bruvver* does not also say *ven* for *then*. Whether he replaces *th* with *v* depends on the position the phoneme occupies in the word. Whether *oi* is spelled *oy* depends on whether it falls in the middle or at the end of a word. More often than not, how a single phoneme is spelled, or how a single letter is sounded, depends on patterns—on how it is combined with its neighbors.

Alternation Pattern of Sounds and Stresses

Physical articulation generally causes vowel and consonant sounds to alternate with each other. Several consonant sounds can be blended into one cluster sound, but that cluster needs a vowel sound to voice it (*splash*). (*Consonant* means sounded with, and *vowel* means voiced). The minimum for a syllable is a sounded vowel. As many as four consonant sounds can be blended if a word ends with *s* as a suffix (*bursts*). Theoretically, one could sound endless strings of vowels, since they may be sounded independently of consonants, but in English no more than two vowels are sounded successively without a consonant between. The diphthongs *oi* and *ou* are really blends of two vowel sounds, and we sound two vowels consecutively in a word like *inebriate,* but sustained voicing without muscular articulation feels physically awkward enough, at least to speakers of English, that we limit vowel strings to two and prefer generally to place consonants between vowels as glides.

So the most basic pattern in English is an alternation of vowel sounds with consonant sounds—*CVCVCVC.* This compares significantly to the general alternation in English of stressed with unstressed syllables, as in the word *áltĕrńatĭon* itself. *C-V-C-V-C* is a *general* pulse, like the main English poetic meter and, like this meter, it may also occasionally break its own pattern by skipping or reversing beats. Compare, for example, a reversed foot in poetry that juxtaposes two stresses (tŏ /cŏntrŏl/ týrańts), with a word like *ignite* that places back to back a syllable ending with a consonant phoneme and a syllable beginning with a consonant phoneme. English vocalization alternates vowel phonemes with consonant phonemes or blends, and stressed with unstressed syllables, exceptions not departing far or often from this basic rhythm.

Lack of Alternation in English Spelling

The alternation of vowel and consonant sounds is not represented by an exactly corresponding alternation of vowel and consonant *letters.* And therein lie some major difficulties of English literacy.

Unsounded Letters

For one thing, some vowel and consonant phonemes may be spelled in English by a digraph, which is two letters standing jointly for one sound, like the *ch* of *chess* or the *oa* of *coast. Catch* even has a trigraph, and a word like *bought* has not only a digraph—*ou* —but two other unsounded letters as well—*gh.* In most cases, the pronunciation has changed over the centuries but not the spelling, so that instead of being spelled the way they sound, many English words are spelled the way they *were* sounded. But some unsounded letters simply serve another function than standing for sounds, as Carol Chomsky has pointed out. The *g* in *sign,* for example, was probably never sounded but serves to indicate that *sign* belongs to the word family of *signal, signify,* and *signature,* in all of which the *g* is sounded.

Whatever their origin, unsounded letters are a serious bugaboo of English literacy. They obscure the basic alternation of vowel and consonant sounds and make words *look* more difficult than they *sound.* Let's take *sheath* for an example. Letting capital *C* and *V* stand for consonant and vowel sounds, and small *c* and *v* for consonant and vowel letters, *sheath* is sounded *CVC,* for example (ʃ i ð in the International Phonetic Alphabet) but spelled *ccvvcc* in the conventional English alphabet. Because of the many unsounded letters, then, English written words tend to contain more letters than the spoken words contain phonemes. This greater visual complexity causes the novice reader to believe he has more to sound out than in fact he has and causes the novice writer to oversimplify his spelling.

Blending Consecutive Consonants or Vowels

Another factor obscures the fundamental pattern of alternating vowel and consonant sounds and makes difficult the matching of sounds with letters. Speech articulation tends to merge phonemes, whereas spelling breaks speech back down into the phonemes. Two or three consonants blended in a cluster feel like a single sound to the vocalizer. Hence *slip* feels hardly different to pronounce than *ship,* though *slip* begins with two consonant phonemes (*CCVC*) and *ship* with only one (*CVC*). Even a word such as *splash* feels closer to containing three sounds than the five it actually comprises. Vocalization, in other words, synthesizes sounds together, whereas writing analyzes sounds and singles them out one by one. This may be true even of some vowel blends, *roil* being perceived as *CVC* though spelled *cvvc,* because all English vowels diphthongize somewhat anyway, at least in America, drawling being only an extreme case of the national practice of making one vowel sound like two.

Once again, the effect is that written words contain more letters than spoken words do sounds. Although it is true that in this case the effect is subjective rather than actual fact, nevertheless this subjective experience must be allowed for in literacy instruction. If the learner feels, in matching a spoken word with its spelling, that he has more symbols than sounds, when this is not so, he may become boggled in reading or omit letters in spelling, *as if* the words contained fewer phonemes than letters.

English spelling does not alternate vowel and consonant letters to correspond with real or felt vocal alternation, because English written words either contain more letters than sounds or are perceived to contain more letters than sounds.

To summarize, English tends to alternate vowel sounds with single consonant sounds or blended consonant sounds. This general sound pattern underlies spelling patterns, but spelling patterns are more complicated because letters may not be sounded, or may be sounded one way in one word structure and another way in another, and because spelling separates sounds that muscles merge. The most important thing for literacy students to learn is when a letter is unsounded and when it is sounded one way rather than another. *When* means in which combinations of letters, in which word position, and in which word structure.

The Problem of Ambiguity

If every English sound had its own symbol and only one symbol, teachers would not have to be concerned about sound-spelling patterns, because no matter where a sound occurred in a word it would always be spelled by its own symbol. The English alphabet would then be like the International Phonetic Alphabet (IPA), which has special symbols for the sounds *sh* and *th* of *sheath* (ʃ, ð) instead of piecing together symbols by pairing letters (making digraphs). The IPA also has separate symbols for the long and short vowel sounds instead of making the same letters do double duty for both. But English symbols are makeshift and create tremendous ambiguity. The spelling *ou* stands for one sound in *rough* and another in *slouch. C* can stand for the same sound as *s* or as *k* (*lance* and *cat*).

Interpreting by Context of Pattern

What removes ambiguity is context. The immediate context of a letter that one must interpret is the rest of the word in which it appears. Interpreting a *g,* for example, requires noting which position in a word it occupies, which other letters neighbor it, and which arrangement of letters structures the whole word. A *g* is always sounded at the beginning of a word if followed by a vowel (*get*) but is silent if followed by *n* (*gnash*). Like *c,* it is most often hard before *a, o,* and *u* (*ingot*) and soft before *i* and *e* (*angel*). After *n* as a final sound, *g* is silent but causes the *n* to become more nasal (*sang*). These are examples of removing ambiguity by noting the position of a letter and its neighboring letters.

A writer trying to spell *gnash* or *through* does not even know from the sound of the word that *g* figures into the spelling at all, so if he spells what he hears, he writes *nash* and *throo*, both phonetically correct but conventionally wrong. The sound of *n* may be spelled *gn* or *kn* at the beginning of a word but never in the middle, where it will usually be spelled either by a single *n* or, if after a short vowel and before certain unstressed endings like *y*, by *nn*.

The structure of the whole word may also be needed to interpret a letter. For example, though silent before *n* at the beginning of a word, *g* is not silent before *n* in the middle of a word (*ignore*) because such words will have more than one syllable, and each of the two consonants will be sounded with its own vowel independently of the other. So syllabification is an important factor in interpreting letters. A six-letter word could contain either one syllable (*splash*), two syllables (*indict*), or three (*hiatus*). Each quantity of syllables marks a different word structure.

Syllabification also affects stress. Words of more than one syllable usually contain at least one unstressed syllable. This means that they contain one or more vowels that in most cases will be pronounced alike (the schwa sound of *uh*) no matter how pronounced when stressed. The fact that most unstressed vowel sounds may then be spelled by any one of the five vowel letters creates even more ambiguity than that caused already by sounds outnumbering symbols. Until he knows where the stresses fall, a reader does not know how to pronounce the vowel letters; and until he sees the word, a writer doesn't know to which of the five letters to assign a schwa sound.

Alternative spellings create most of the difficulty of English literacy, but, of course, given the lack of adequate symbols, this is not all irrational. The mute *e* of *knife* serves to signal that the preceding vowel is pronounced long, and the extra *n* in *funny* signals that the preceding vowel is pronounced short.

Having to sound out spellings and spell out sounds according to juxtaposition and word structure amounts to this: that in English it is not just letters that stand for sounds but relations among letters that stand for sounds. That is, sounds are symbolized not merely by the *identity* of the letters but by their *position* in combination with certain others in different word structures. This is how English contrives to represent forty-odd sounds with twenty-six letters. It is this basic relativity about which sounds go with which symbols that makes grasping patterns so critical.

Isomorphic Alphabets

Some educators have advocated special symbols, like the Initial Training Alphabet, that remove ambiguity by assigning to each sound its own symbol. The problems with this are: (1) a special alphabet eventually has to be matched off in turn with conventional English spellings; (2) until the transition is made, learners can read only specially printed material; and (3) they have to learn to draw (and later forget) the special symbols or else hold off on writing.

Nevertheless, the need for an isomorphic alphabet (one symbol to one sound) is so great both in and out of education that teachers may well find themselves trying hard to make such an alphabet work. The inventors of Unifon (see Figure 9.1) claim that only twelve days are required for learners to make the transition to the conventional alphabet and hence very little specially printed reading matter is needed.

Consider that Italian and Turkish have 27 symbols for 27 sounds whereas English has 379 letters and letter combinations spelling a minimum of 40 sounds. It takes an American child two years longer to read than a continental European child. Children of other language communities often learn to read with little instruction in a few months.[2]

As it is, American schools are nearly foundering on the rocks of basic skills. It's hardly an exaggeration to say that the added difficulty caused by English spelling may make the difference between whether public schools survive or become obsolete, for if they continue to bog down at the lowest level of learning, they will be of little use to youth in our stage of civilization. Consider too the pressure of computerization and the increasing need for electronic transcription of voice and electronic sounding

---

[2] Alan R. Burns, "Learning to Read: The Potential of an Isomorphic Alphabet," *Elementary English*, September 1973. The information contained in this article is helpful in considering the case for starting literacy learners this way.

UNIFON – THE NEW SINGLE-SOUND ALPHABET

A Δ Λ B S Ø D
AT / ATE / ALL / BOW / CELL SAY / CHAIR / DIP

E Ŧ Ǝ F G H I
HEN / HE / HER / FAST / GOAT / HAT / BIT

Ⱶ J K L M Ꞁ
BITE / JAW / KISS / LOW / MUSIC / NO / KING

O Ω Ꙩ Ꙍ Ƌ P R
LOT / OLD / LOOK / OUT / BOY / PIPE / RUN

Ꞩ T Ⱦ Ʉ U Ц
SURE / TABLE / THIRST / THERE / UP / DUE / YOU

V W Ʒ Y Z
VEST / WIG / AZURE / YES / ZEBRA

These symbols fall into the following pattern:

18 consonants are the same as in conventional English with S and J carrying all the soft sounds.

S IT SIT   JENTUL GENTLE

6 new consonant symbols: Ꞁ KING,

Ɛ CHAIR, Ⱦ THERE, ⊥ THIRST,

Ʒ AZURE, and Ꞩ carrying only the *sh* sound as in SURE.

The greatest help of all is the reinforcing of the vowel pattern by extending it from 5 characters to 16, thus covering all the 16 vowel sounds of English.

A BAT   U BUT   Ω OLD   Ꙩ LOOK
E BET   Δ ATE   U DUE   Ц CUTE
I BIT   Ŧ HE   Λ ALL   Ꙍ OUT
O HOT   Ⱶ BITE Ǝ HER   Ƌ BOY

Thus we have 24 consonant symbols with 24 consonant and digraph sounds; 16 vowel symbols with 16 vowel and diphthong sounds.

FIGURE 9.1 THE UNIFON ALPHABET

Source: Permission obtained from the Unifon Alphabet Foundation, 169 Westwood, Park Forest, Illinois 60466 to which the reader can address himself for further information.

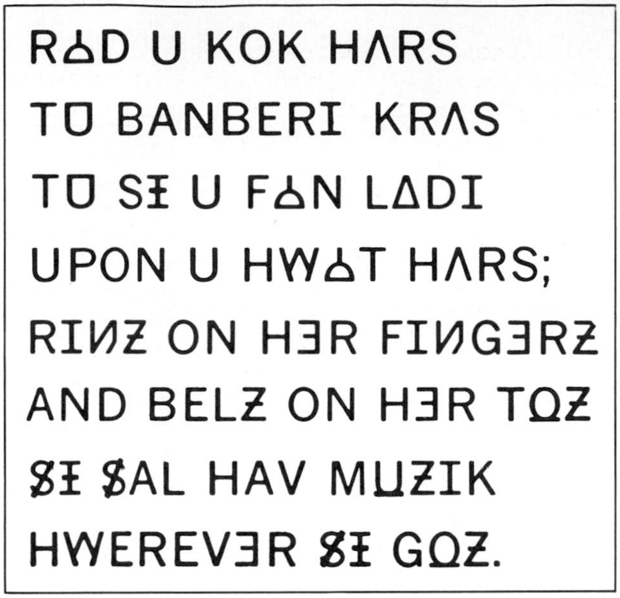

RⱵD U KOK HΛRS
TU BANBERI KRΛS
TU SŦ U FⱵN LΔDI
UPON U HWⱵT HΛRS;
RIꞁƷ ON HƎR FIꞁGƎRƷ
AND BELƷ ON HƎR TΩƷ
ꞨŦ ꞨAL HAV MUZIK
HWEREVƎR ꞨŦ GΩZ.

FIGURE 9.2 "RIDE A COCK HORSE TO BRANBURY CROSS" PRINTED IN UNIFON ALPHABET

Source: Permission obtained from the Unifon Alphabet Foundation.

of stored texts. It may be only a matter of time before the trouble and expense of the changeover become overbalanced by the advantages of electronics for storing and communicating words and for simplifying the literacy job of schools so they can get on to higher learning. Furthermore, English has been a second language in many countries for some time, and this trend seems likely to make a world language of it on a second-language basis. Some or all of these trends may well end in the adoption of an isomorphic alphabet for English.

Until such time, *patterns* of letters will remain of major importance in attacking and spelling words, because, lacking one symbol for each sound, the literacy learner will have to reckon with letter relations—not mere letters—as symbols of sounds. This becomes a key factor in deciding literacy methods. If context removes abiguity, then methods providing maximum context should be superior.

The four main approaches to literacy

All methods of "beginning reading" (literacy!) come under four approaches, differing mainly in the size of the *language* unit used as the *learning* unit.

LANGUAGE UNIT	APPROACH	DESCRIPTION
Particle of Word	phonics	Hearing a single sound while looking at the letter or spelling representing it (matching phonemes with graphemes)
Word	sight-word	Hearing a whole spoken word while seeing the whole written word, or saying a word and watching someone else write it down
Sentence Continuity	language experience	Dictating a discourse and watching someone else write down the words and punctuate the sentences
Sentence Continuity	lap method	Following a text with the eyes while hearing the text read aloud

So the main approaches differ, first of all, in dealing with successively larger language units—word particle, word, and sentence or sentence continuity—in which audio and video are synchronized. Sentence continuities make whole discourses, so the language-experience and lap methods are very natural in the sense that people engage in them outside of school (when they dictate or listen to someone read aloud). They are not, in other words, just teaching methods. Sight-word is less natural and more of a school method, but, still, some single words are whole discourses (labels and signs), and some sentences in speech consist of only one word. At any rate, as methods these three require little explanation.

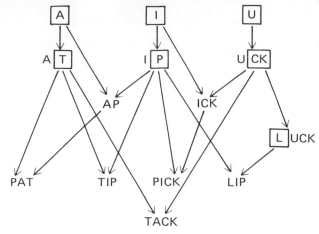

FIGURE 9.3 SYNTHETIC PHONICS

We will have to explain phonics a bit, however, since most practices based on word particles are far from natural or familiar language activities.

EXPLAINING PHONICS

All phonics programs are either synthetic or analytic. In synthetic phonics, word particles are built into words. The learner is presented each phoneme paired with its grapheme, one at a time; then these sound-spellings are combined to make whole words. This is a dual process of matching a sound with the letter or digraph that spells it, then of blending the sound-spellings into words. In Figure 9.3, each square represents the matching of a sound with its letter or digraph. The arrows represent the blending of these sound-spellings to form syllables and then words. Vowel phonemes are introduced first so that the consonant phonemes introduced afterwards will not have to be falsely sounded with an unwritten schwa. A learner should now be able to decode *tuck* on sight.

In analytic phonics the learner breaks down words into their component sounds and spellings by conceptually isolating the components. He sees and hears arrays of words in which the beginnings, middles, or ends of words are held constant to identify a certain phoneme then varied to contrast that phoneme with others. In Figure 9.4, the squares again represent the points at which a phoneme gets matched with its grapheme. Note that this time, however, the matching occurs at the end, after a kind of *unblending*. Again, a learner should now be able to decode *tuck* on sight. This systematic pres-

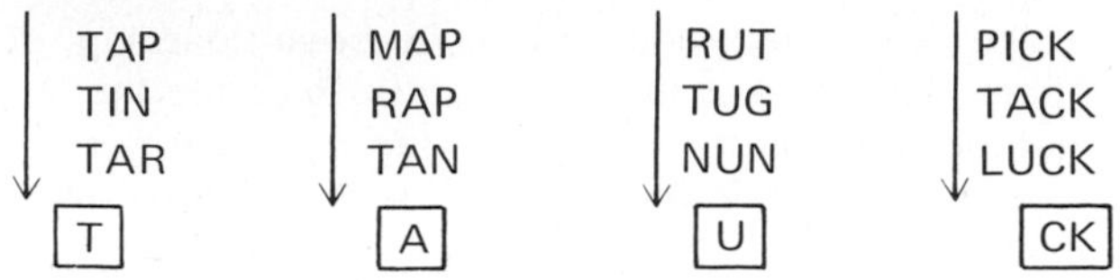

```
  TAP        MAP        RUT        PICK
  TIN        RAP        TUG        TACK
  TAR        TAN        NUN        LUCK
   │          │          │          │
   ▼          ▼          ▼          ▼
  ┌─┐        ┌─┐        ┌─┐        ┌──┐
  │T│        │A│        │U│        │CK│
  └─┘        └─┘        └─┘        └──┘
```

FIGURE 9.4 ANALYTIC PHONICS

entation of similarity and difference in phonemes isolates them in sight and thought while actually leaving words whole in print. Thus analytic phonics bridges between word-particle and whole-word approaches, but clearly the emphasis is on the phonetic components, not on the meaning, of words.

COMPARING METHODS

The old controversy over which method is best comes down to how large the matching units are. But, of course, when the size of the unit varies from nonsense particles like *ta* and *ip* to complete sentences in context, like "A hand clutched his arm" as part of a story, then indeed the unit may make considerable psychological difference for learning. Secondarily, the methods differ also in emphasis on reception versus production of language. Both factors merit high priority.

Successively larger language units have increasingly fuller meaning the closer they are to being a whole discourse. But the larger the language unit that is the learning unit, the less exact is the matching of oral and written speech. A child, for example, who has memorized each page in a story, from hearing it read over and over at bedtime, so that he knows when to turn the page, has synchronized oral speech with written speech in such gross blocks that we don't feel he is reading. The criterion in this case seems to be that he could not read those same words if they were recombined to form another text.

A similar argument seems reasonable at the middle level, the level of the word. A word has some meaning—whichever concept defines it—and is a much more precise unit than a page or sentence. But critics from the phonics school of thought would say that someone who has memorized a word by its overall look or shape still does not read if he cannot recognize or sound out another word that recombines those same letters. Critics from the "meaning" school of thought, on the other hand, might say that someone dealing with only isolated words finds so little meaning in what he is doing that he either drops reading altogether or fails to join written words into intelligible sequences.

Don't look for research to give the nod to one method over another. First, truly scientific research in the classroom is not possible, because too many critical variables simply cannot be adequately controlled. For years educators took seriously the verdict of some research comparing method A with method B, or one publisher's program with another, only to find that other research later failed to corroborate the first or contradicted it. One notorious trend is for reading results to reverse or shift significantly for the same children if followed for as long as three years. Long-range results are, after all, what we want, and they are particularly changeable and difficult to interpret, factors being even harder to control the longer the time span covered. Every publisher of literacy materials claims its research shows its materials work better, but such research cannot be trusted and always conflicts with both the research of other companies and independent research.

Jeanne Chall's finding[3] that methods emphasizing phonics teach literacy more effectively than those omitting or de-emphasizing phonics in favor of "reading for meaning" may be very misleading. It does not mean that phonics is better than the whole-word and the sentence methods. Hearing/seeing whole words and sentences can hardly be really omitted, whether called methods or not. Only the word-particle method may be left out. So programs omitting or de-emphasizing phonics are simply not exploiting all possible means, and hence are running more risks than programs including phonics along with other approaches. Furthermore, neither the language-experience nor reading-while-listening methods have been developed fully enough in enough schools, because of management problems, to make the full power of these known in any comparison.

What independent research does show over and over again is that reading achievement correlates more with parental and cultural influences than with anything schools do. The Coordinated Reading Studies, run during the 1960s by the United States Office of Education, aimed especially to compare one reading method with another, but found that achievement varied more within one method than between methods and concluded that some larger factor such as school atmosphere was determining reading growth,

[3] Jeanne Chall, *Learning to Read: The Great Debate*, McGraw-Hill Book Co., New York, 1967.

not methodology. The famous Coleman Report on school achievement sponsored in the late 1960s by the Department of Health, Education and Welfare indicated that the social class of students correlated more highly with all academic achievement than did any school variables. In the 1970s both the National Assessment of Educational Progress and the International Association for the Evaluation of Educational Achievement concluded that home and community play a more important role than school in reading achievement. Most likely, the old findings (or assumptions) that reading achievement correlates with IQ and with knowing the alphabet early merely reflect social class, since middle-class children usually learn at home the kinds of knowing and talking that IQ tests aim at, as well as the alphabet.

The consistent inability to identify a method or program that works better than others should make us think long and hard about several old assumptions. First, one offshoot of the fiscal accountability movement is a trend toward "learner verification," which requires schools or educational manufacturers to prove how well a method or program works. The long experience of classroom research dooms this trend to failure.

Second, for years many educators have assumed that because most schoolchildren learned to read and write, schools were doing the job and that the mainstay of literacy—the basal-reader approach—was working well enough. This approach preteaches most words in a given story lesson by the sight-word approach, allowing the learner to "read" the whole sentences of the lesson, and shunts the phonics or word-particle approach into a back-up presentation often drawn out over the primary years. Vocabulary is doled out slowly, and students are usually divided into three graded groups, with everyone within a group reading the same text at about the same rate.

The finding that home plays a larger role than school in reading achievement suggests that the basal approach has been given credit for learning that occurred, when it occurred, principally at home. The acid test is to teach literacy to poor urban children, and schools fail this test so often as to imply strongly that the traditional reading approach incarnated in basal readers did the job only for kids who were learning at home in addition. This reasoning seems borne out by the fact that as the middle-class nightly story time has given way to television, many children of well-educated parents have also begun to have the literacy problems formerly associated only with the poor.

The way most children have been learning at home is by what in this book we have called the lap method; they sit on someone's lap and hear a story read to them while following the text with their eyes. This look-listen method has not been dignified by being called a method and hence has not until very recently been the object of research. So investigation of reading methods has overlooked what may have been all along the major determinant of reading achievement for middle-class children. Similarly, before the recent work of Charles Read and Carol Chomsky, another home activity of great importance was not included in literacy research. This activity consists of a child writing down words he knows orally according to his knowledge of the alphabet, inventing the spellings. Some preschool children, who do this for play, learn to read more easily afterwards.

These examples of critical omissions make the more general point, which Caleb Gattegno has made well, that reading research has been so narrowly conceived that even if the variables of it were controllable, it could prove only the relative advantages among whatever practices had won a berth in schools at the time, not how, in an absolute sense, people might learn to read and write as readily as they learn to speak. On the other hand, research in learning psychology may be helpful, and investigating what good and bad readers do or don't do can be useful, as is Kenneth Goodman's work on reading miscues. (For more on Goodman see page 220; for more on Read and Chomsky see pages 233 and 235.)

Developing Criteria

Guidelines for how to teach literacy cannot come from research, but they can come from long-standing experience in and out of the classroom—if we think about it in enough perspective. The gist of the experience is that all four approaches can help some students sometimes in some aspects of literacy. The perspective comes from the criterion that basic skills must remain related to meaning and from the perception that the bigger the learning unit the more meaning an activity has for the learner, the more cues he will be able to exploit, and the more motivated he will be to do the activity.

Accumulated experience in both school and home indicates that some people have learned to read and write very well with no phonics instruction at all and yet others have failed without phonics, *at least under customary school conditions.* Only sentence units can deal with punctuation. Phonics and language-experience are strong for spelling and writing. Sight-word and lap method are strong for word recognition and reading. Phonics leans toward the auditory; sight-word toward the visual. And so on.

Critique of Phonics

A good way to work up criteria for comparing methods is to critique the one approach that is entirely a means, not an end in itself. Phonics is also the approach enjoying most support in the newer materials today—partly, we suspect, because its particle nature lends itself so well to programming and specific objectives.

Potential Drawbacks

Isolating letters creates a conflict with the alphabet. Alphabetical names use the long-vowel sounds, which may cause confusion for a while since a single vowel letter embedded in a word more often sounds short than long. Alphabetical consonants are all sounded with some convenient but phonically arbitrary vowel—*eff, bee, ess, tee,* and so on—and the names of some consonants—*h, w, y*—don't resemble the sounds they spell in words. You can offset these confusions by not teaching the alphabet until after the initial presentation of sound-spellings has become too firmly fixed in the learner's mind for him to be confused. However, children often learn the alphabet at home. In any case, conflict between the alphabetical names of letters and their actual spelling-sounds does not seem very serious and may, in fact, create confusion, when it does, in other methods as well as in phonics.

Problem of Isolated Consonants Because several consonants cannot be sounded at all without adding a vowel sound, presenting consonants in isolation should be avoided in favor of presenting consonants sounded with a vowel presented visually at the same time—*em, am, im, om,* for example. Difficulty comes when a consonant is presented in *visual* isolation and yet, being a consonant, has to be sounded with a vowel that can't be seen. Sounding it with the neutral vowel sound of schwa does not, of course, solve the problem, since that gives learners the impression that *k* and *m* are *kuh* and *muh* and leads to the criticism that phonics causes children to blend *c-a-t* into *kuh-a-tuh.* This certainly need not happen.

Fine Fixation A common criticism of phonics generally that applies more pertinently to synthetic phonics is that it produces "word calling." This negative term means that a decoder is sounding out each word or syllable so laboriously that he can't understand the sentences that the words make up. It is very true that some students may read badly because they are fixated in too small a focus, and the most likely school culprit would be synthetic phonics. It is also true that a child who reads smoothly and meaningfully because he has memorized all the words in advance, as in a common basal-reader approach, is not confronting the issue. The real test of whether he can read without word calling is whether he can read new words aloud with natural intonation as a whole, intelligible sentence. A child who has to puzzle out each word so slowly that he loses the continuity of sense and intonation simply has not learned to attack words well enough. As all proponents of a phonics approach emphasize, the point of the teaching is to make decoding second nature, fast and automatic. If a child is having too much trouble recognizing words in print, he cannot activate other cues.

And yet it is true that the fine focus that allows synthetic phonics to pinpoint the matching of spoken with written phonemes may also reinforce the tendency of some learners to fixate on too small a field. Too much phonics may well *create* such a fixation, even in a youngster otherwise having no such tendency. Combined with the meaninglessness of word particles, which undermines motivation, this small focus could prevent some learners from processing sentence continuities in reading and hence actually impede literacy even if the learner is motivated. That is, narrow fixation may shut out valuable cues of whole-word structures and is certain to shut out cues of sense and syntax, which operate only across word strings. And nothing can be done with punctuation within this field, either as reader or writer. Although we cannot agree with the view that phonics and sight-word should be banished from the curriculum at this time, we do agree that excessive focusing on word particles and whole-word analysis has been and remains a grave fault of much literacy instruction.

Critics of phonics have sometimes made the point that the irregularity of English spelling makes the teaching of phonics questionable. Certainly the greater irregularity of English makes phonics less effective than for some other languages, but to challenge phonics seriously on this score is extreme.

Even when part of a word is irregular the rest is often perfectly phonetic. Of English words 49 percent are phonetic; of the phonemes, 84 percent. In reading, this means that knowledge of sound-letter correspondences provides powerful cues for beginnings, middles, and endings of irregular words so that contextual and other cues can operate more effectively in recognizing the whole word. In writing, it means that even when a child misspells a word, he will misspell within a relatively small range of phonetic possibilities (for example, *-ir, -ur, -er, -ear*) so that his task of memorizing which spelling is actually correct is greatly reduced. Finally, the low generalizability of English sound-spelling correspondences works against all approaches, not just against phonics, unless one proposes total memorization, as with Chinese, as a serious alternative.

Not a Goal   The chief disadvantage of phonics is simply that it is not a language arts goal in itself. It is only a means to reading and writing, whereas sight-word, language experience, and lap methods all correspond to the actual target activities of reading and writing. This is one reason why it is important not to call the matching of sounds with spellings "objectives." See page 405. The more nearly an activity resembles a real objective, the less justifying it needs. The burden of proof rests on the advocate of phonics. From accumulated professional experience, however, we know that some children seem merely to memorize words one by one and soon come to a dead end because they cannot figure out or spell words they haven't seen before. But as we said regarding research findings, one doesn't know what to make of such experience. It may just show a lack of the right alternatives.

Assets

The very uncertainty argues for including phonics in some measure. So far as we know now, some form of it seems to be needed as insurance. Although many children have learned to read and write very well with no phonics, it has not yet been shown that all can. The lap method has only barely begun to be used in schools, not having previously been regarded as a method. The language-experience approach has had strong advocates and successful practitioners for some time, but these have been a minority of literacy teachers. Both methods, furthermore, require far more time than the teacher alone can give to each individual and hence have never proved their real worth. We hope that suggestions in the next chapter will so support these two methods that soon educators will have a fair chance to know if they can teach literacy, or at least reading, to any child without the aid of phonics. It is truly time to find out. Until then, schools that do not offer some form of phonics risk discriminating against some learners who may need it. This is what we mean by phonics for insurance. But this argument has to be advanced only for an eclectic individualized program in which the alternative methods are fully developed and learners who are generalizing sound-spelling relations well for themselves would not have to take phonics.

Nonstandard Dialect   Synthetic phonics bids fair to help especially those learners whose dialectical pronunciation is not standard, as explained on page 179. Dropping final consonants, for example, or substituting one phoneme for another in certain word slots can occur only with whole words. Starting with phonemes and then blending them helps a great deal to clarify standard sounds and their spellings. Unbound word particles cannot be dropped or supplanted, and when blended to make words they are more likely to resist dialectical tendencies to drop or supplant than when presented already bound into word structure.

Disability   Clinical evidence from teachers working with learners having a tendency to reverse letters or to have more than normal difficulty segmenting and discriminating sounds seems to indicate rather strongly that synthetic phonics helps overcome these and perhaps other literacy-learning handicaps that educators call variously by such terms as *dyslexia* or *reading disability*. The fine focus and the word building of synthetic phonics call special attention to the differences that letter shape and letter order make.

Spelling   The case for phonics is much stronger from the productive than from the receptive viewpoint. Word attack and spelling are different as well as similar. Spelling is harder. Whereas a reader can take advantage of grammatical and meaning cues to fill in words and fill out sentences, and therefore does not have to attack each letter or word directly according to sheer appearance, the writer must summon everything from within—sound, sense, and sight. He must know the sound-spelling correspondences much more explicitly and more precisely. Spelling sounds requires more analysis and more consciousness, it seems fair to say. The reader has external givens by which to infer from known to unknown. With a little visual knowledge he can activate a lot of oral knowledge to apply back to the visual. He can operate more intuitively perhaps. At any rate, his job is more to synthesize, to pull all evidence together into a whole. The speller faces a task more characterized by analysis. He not only has to parcel his thought out over parts of speech; he must segment the speech flow into its finest particles—phonemes—and write them down in the finest graphic units—letters—and he must sequence these particles in a precise order that accommodates not only the sequence of phonemes but the subsequences of letters that symbolize them. One can argue reasonably, then, that spelling is very much like the basic activity of synthetic phonics: one blends phonemes into words graphically while hearing them being orally blended (in the mind, in the case of the speller.)

Spelling consists also of reproducing already memorized words as visual wholes. In critiquing phonics we have in a measure been critiquing sight-word also.

All things considered, then, sight-word and phonics may be well justified for spelling even if they are not for reading. The fine focus good for spelling may secondarily help word attack inasmuch as a good speller is usually a good reader in the sense of sounding out a text well. But the fine focus could have negative side effects. All this calls for balance.

We believe you will teach basic skills most successfully by finding a way to mix these four approaches that allows for fine *and* large focuses, for sending *and* receiving. Presenting the synchronized sounds and sights of English, at all three levels of language, in both directions, *has* to work—given good general conditions, such as positive atmosphere and personal readiness, necessary for *any* learning—because this synchronized two-way association at all language levels is the very definition of literacy.

an integrated literacy program

10 literacy program

L iteracy methods relate closely to literacy materials. Books alone are very ineffectual in teaching beginning reading and writing for the simple reason that books are one medium only, the visual, whereas literacy learning requires both auditory and visual at once. Books presuppose that either the teacher or the learner supplies the vocal sounds. If the teacher does, he cannot individualize the management of literacy learning. In order for the learner to supply the vocal sounds, he must already know their spellings. Wise judgment in teaching beginning reading and writing to large numbers of youngsters depends on weighing well the bimedia supplements to books.

Book programs for literacy have chronically failed for lack of *plentiful, synchronized audio*. Basal readers, for example, have consistently failed to individualize because the teacher has to supply the live audio and hence has to present sound-spellings en masse (either to the whole class or to the classic three "reading groups" one at a time). And basal readers and workbooks have consistently assumed that learners would supply their own vocal sounds, which means that most of the sound-spelling correspondences are not so much taught there as *reviewed* there. If parents do not supply audiovisual synchronization at home with the lap method, the big question is how *do* youngsters actually learn which speech sounds go with which letters in which word structures?

This chapter deals directly with that question, and in doing so it necessarily must focus on audiovisual materials of some sort. The human voice certainly ranks high among the audio materials. Our strategy is to determine when live voice is better and when recorded voice from a machine is better; when the live voice should be the teacher's, aide's or another student's, and when the learner's; when the recorded voice should issue from a recorder or phonoviewer and when from a film soundtrack. We hope that treating literacy methodology as interplay of material and human resources will prove most practical.

Joining these considerations with those from the last chapter, we will describe literacy activities from now on under two main headings—look/listen and look/talk. The first combines the lap method with sight-word and a certain amount of phonics. So look/listen integrates activities with sentences, single words, and word particles for which someone other than the learner supplies the audio. There is no separate phonics program. Phonics is woven in and out of activities having larger focuses. Look/talk combines the language-experience approach with some sight-word. Look/listen and look/talk balance word attack and spelling, since for the one the learner receives the language of others, and for the other he dictates his own.

Look/listen and look/talk create a step between oral and written language practices. In both cases someone else who is literate acts as intermediary between the learner's oral knowledge and the new visual medium. The other person (real or recorded) sounds out the text or spells out the learner's speech for him until he can do these things for himself. Being read to and dictating are temporary substitutes for reading and writing. By means of them the learner matches off speech with print within himself. Next, he reads to himself and dictates to himself. Finally, as we said, he even dispenses for the most part with his own internal oral intermediary. This progression from oral speech to inner speech to nonspeech seems to us a paramount truth of literacy learning that we have tried to build into our recommendations. The Balinese dancers teach their youngsters by holding them from behind and moving so that the youngsters' bodies move with theirs until a time when the adult steps back and the learner continues moving on his own from within. This internalization from the social to the personal seems a natural, effective way to learn to read and write as well. This approach can be implemented by having some literate person translate for the learner between voice and print while the learner participates.

Look/listen and look/talk will feature whole discourse but, to prime it, will employ some single words and, to a lesser extent, some word particles. The smaller focus will not last long at any one time and will constantly alternate with larger focuses. As with actual vision, frequent shift of focus precludes permanent fixation and fosters flexibility. The new knowledge called literacy is, after all, visual and small; the reader must be forever heeding both letters and sentences, and the writer must always be building his sentences letter by letter. Furthermore, the whole literacy program offered in this part of the book is to be integrated on a day-to-day basis with the activities recommended elsewhere in the book.

Our recommended program comprises three main activities:

- Seeing and hearing a special audiovisual presentation of intermixed phonemes, single words, and sentences
- Following a printed text with the eyes while hearing it read
- Dictating while watching the words being written down

These should be considered a basic spelling program as well as a basic decoding program. They suit any age and so deal with beginning or "remedial" reading and writing. The learner engages in all three at once. Individualizing consists of varying the ratio among the three to get different emphases for different learners and of eliminating activity 1 for those learners who already know the phoneme spellings or are readily generalizing them on their own as a result of doing activities 2 and 3. We suggest that literacy students do some of each virtually every day in mixture with the other language arts activities suggested in this book.

We will describe each in the order above for purely expository purposes—again, all three go on at once—mainly to show how practice with smaller focuses can feed into visual processing of larger fields.

An audiovisual presentation

The idea is to present to the learner over a period of weeks or months a sequence of about three dozen brief sound shows lasting only one to three minutes each that reveal how the phonemes are spelled, the letters formed, and the intonation punctuated. Spatial and other typographical conventions can also be established this way, but how much literacy information can be conveyed depends on the media the teacher has available. Format should also permit individualizing so that students can view the shows in small groups or alone, seeing only the units they need, as often as they need. The presentation may be fitted to:

- A series of placards, slides, or transparencies with live voice
- A slide-tape with recorded voice
- A synchronized phono-viewer of some sort using either school-made or manufactured visuals and recordings
- Sound films of animation

The first three above can employ only still images in series and differ in some important respects from moving pictures. First, we will illustrate a couple of the short sound shows with still images only.

STILL IMAGES WITH SOUND

The samples in Figure 10.1 (page 192) are somewhat simplified; more material might be added to each session, and some changes from one visual to the next might be phased over several interim visuals in order to approximate animation. The first sample exemplifies an early session, about the seventh or eighth, following the previous presentation of three short vowels, three consonants, and the articles *the* and *a* (containing schwa). The letter formation at the beginning would obviously be clearer in animation. All but the first three frames are sounded out on the audio as they are shown.

A number of typical things need to be brought out here. A new phoneme has been introduced—stroked on visually, then sounded (but only with a vowel, because it is a consonant), then sounded with other vowels to clarify its constancy across different combinations, then used in the first and last positions of different words, and finally submerged in the word flow of whole sentences. At the same time, the

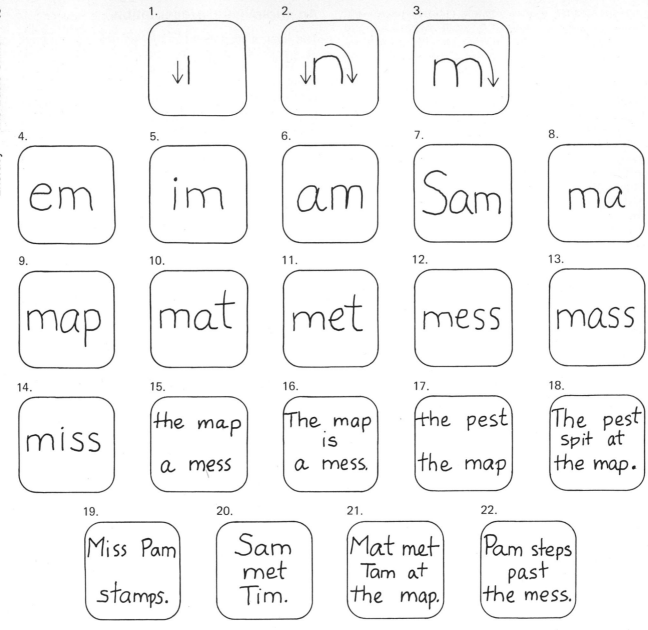

FIGURE 10.1 EARLY SESSION IN SEQUENCE OF STILL IMAGES WITH SOUND

previously presented phonemes are rehearsed and contrasted by means of the new phoneme (*em, im, am,* and *mess, mass, miss*). The focus moves fast from single phoneme to syllable to word and phrase to sentence (and will move eventually to sentence continuities). The session includes periods and capitalization for sentences and capitalization for people's names. The intonation on the audio makes clear what are isolated words and phrases and what are sentences.

The sounding out can also be used to make the isolated sentences funny or otherwise interesting. Controlled vocabulary can generate outlandish images and situations, in no more than a sentence or two, that have great appeal for youngsters (à la Dr. Seuss). Adopting character voices can make such a sequence very entertaining, and the whole session should have a light touch.

The learner will not absorb everything on one viewing; rerunning is expected and encouraged and adds to the importance of individualizing, since some will want or need to rerun more than others. Keep in mind that, however spread out, the total running time of this entire series of sound shows is only about an hour and a half.

With a repertory of only a few sound-spellings, the learner is reading whole sentences. He can stamp or write his own words and sentences with this repertory. Other follow-up activities are described later in this chapter. He can read along with the audio during reruns, or he can turn the sound off and give the audio himself. It is of the utmost importance to remember, however, that the learner is not limited to what he learns from these controlled presentations. On the same days he has these sessions—lasting only a few minutes even with reruns—he is dictating his own discourse to a transcriber and following a book while hearing it read, both of which will give him practice with normal discourse.

Our second sample (Figure 10.2, page 194) occurs about two-thirds of the way through the sequence. It features different spellings of long o (o, oe, oa, ow), a major spelling generalization, and continuities of sentences.

Short and long o sounds are directly contrasted. The spelling generalization about a final mute e changing a vowel from short to long is conveyed by transforming one word into another and by doing so several times with different instances. This may help a learner start to perceive this pattern in other texts or perhaps to corroborate and cinch an intuitive inference he has already been making about it. Some variant spellings of final /z/ are also given (goes, rose, grows).

Sound shows at this stage can bring out the need to use the structure of the whole word in order to sound out or spell out certain phonemes. How long vowels are spelled depends on their position in the word and on neighboring phonemes. It is for this reason that focus on the isolated phoneme cannot remain useful for long. The skill of making such

sound shows is to spell out the same phoneme in different letters and to sound out the same spelling in different phonemes in such ways that the learner picks up the patterns. But it is critical to realize that total and systematic coverage of all patterns is not needed. This presentation is not the only means for learning sound-spellings, after all, and is meant mainly to support the language-experience and lap methods until those alone will suffice. Some students simply will not need to finish the sequence; once having grasped the *idea* of the system, and armed with some phonetic knowledge, they will figure out the rest.

Making or Choosing Materials

Whereas the first sample show relied on the technique of replacing, adding, subtracting, and reversing letters while holding the rest of a word constant, the second sample show employs the technique of arraying words that exemplify the same pattern (*no, go, so* or *road, coach, toast, board*). Be sure the materials you make or choose employ these two techniques to bring out patterns. Listing or massing words of like pattern helps the learner to infer this pattern from some instances. Transforming one word into another shows the differences that a change of sound or a change of spelling makes for the other. Change a spelling, hear the difference:

$$flash \rightarrow clash \rightarrow clack \rightarrow click$$

or

$$top \rightarrow pot \qquad pets \rightarrow pest$$

(Deliberate reversal heads off or corrects unconscious reversal by making reversing a focused issue.) Change a sound; see the difference:

$$\begin{bmatrix} soot \\ foot \\ look \\ cook \\ took \end{bmatrix} \longrightarrow \begin{bmatrix} sight \\ fight \\ light \end{bmatrix} \longrightarrow \begin{bmatrix} sought \\ fought \end{bmatrix} \longrightarrow \begin{bmatrix} caught \\ taught \end{bmatrix}$$

Some smaller pattern, but one often encountered, may come out if you keep changing the vowel phoneme in a certain position: What emerges here is that gh is silent following some vowels and before t in some monosyllabic English words and, secondarily, that either au or ou may spell the aw sound before such a gh. However consciously or uncon-

1. rob

2. robe

3. rod

4. rode

5. Not that note!

6. no go so

7. goes

8. goes toes toe hoe

9. cot

10. coat

11. coal

12. soap

13. road coach toast board

14. row

15. show throw

16. Did Moe blow his nose?

17. I hope not!

18. The crow might fly in and bite his nose.

19. Hollow the hole. Follow the goal.

20. A rose grows in the snow on the road.

21. Will Hope go get the rose.

22. No! Hope is so slow!

23. The rose froze.

24. Suppose Moe goes and rows the boat.

25. Suppose Flo grows up like a goat.

FIGURE 10.2 LATER SESSION IN SEQUENCE OF STILL IMAGES WITH SOUND

sciously acquired, it is these patterns that the learner must put into operation if he is to read or write. Grasping them is the very essence of learning the "basic skills."

Transforming words can also demonstrate such regularities in spelling changes as occur when a verb is shifted from one tense to another:

hop → hopped → hopping
hope → hoped → hoping

This transformation relates in turn to:

hop → hope   rat → rate   mill → mile

From the examples above we can see that combining phonemes or letters in various ways can do a lot more than merely show how to blend them. For one thing, even some matching cannot be done clearly until a given spelling is situated in a whole word. Compare *law* and *awash*. And the *augh* or *ough* spelling occurs before final *t,* never before, say, final *l,* when the sound is spelled *aw* or *au* (*crawl* and *Paul*) or final *ll,* when it is spelled *a* (*fall, tall*) or final *st,* when it is spelled *o* (*cost, lost*).

Second, since blending frequently produces a whole word, it really engages the learner also in the sight-word method of learning literacy. Synthesizing particles into words builds word recognition directly on particle recognition and hence teaches word attack. Transforming one word into another pursues word recognition down into the perceptual problem of identifying particles when embedded in different word contexts and when therefore blended with different phonemes or letters. Finally, the examples show how patterns of blending constitute the very phonetic rules that are the ultimate aim of literacy teaching.

Sequencing Phonemes

We propose the sequence of phoneme spellings listed on pages 477–478 in Appendix B. One could certainly find good reasons for making changes in it, but it should serve at least as a practical base from which to vary. Each number represents a separate session.

Although one sequence for all is generally avoided in this curriculum, the conventions of print are public fact and have some principles of ordering that apply to people generally. Still, a sequence may be used individually by starting it, stopping it, and breaking into it at different places—and by following it or not.

The order of presentation is most sensibly determined by these three factors:

- The frequency with which the sounds occur in English
- The comparative difficulty of spelling the sounds
- The value of juxtaposing certain sounds for contrast (as *ss* and *zz*)

Short vowels are easier to spell, being rendered generally by a single letter and by their own letter.

Distinguishing the sound of one from another is harder, however, than for the long vowels. The answer to this, we feel, is that an audiovisual presentation can ease this very problem by deliberately contrasting them through juxtaposition. Some teachers argue also that long vowels should come first because they are pronounced like their alphabetic names, which children often learn before starting a literacy program. This reason, however, is not as compelling as the need to go from simple to complex spellings. Long vowels are commonly spelled by more than one letter. They and other sounds spelled by digraphs can be fed in, along with diphthongs, after sounds spelled by single letters. So making up a sequence means harmonizing these various factors in some practical way that enables learners to go from easy to difficult, absorb at a reasonable rate, and be able to combine sound-spellings into recognizable words as soon as they possibly can.

Color-Coding

It is a good idea to color-code spellings according to sounds, so that a sound is always represented by the same color regardless of how it is spelled. Thus the short *e* in *bed* and the *ea* in *bread* would be colored alike but differently from the long *e* in *recede* and the *ea* in *bead,* which would share another color. But keep down the number of colors and the complexity of color combinations. If not used sparingly, color-coding risks boggling the mind. It is probably better not to color-code consonants, because they do not change sound value nearly as much as vowels, and by not color-coding them, you will not have to resort to very fine shades in order to have enough colors for the vowel sounds. The main thing for consonants is that they be distinguished as a class from vowels, so color them all black or all brown or some other color not used for any of the vowel sounds. Color *y* and *w* as vowels when sounded as vowels or when locked into letter combinations spelling vowels (*cry, boy, down*). If you will go back now to our two samples and imagine some of the instances color-coded, you will get some idea of the value of color in bringing out likeness and contrast and thereby strengthening the learning impact of both transformations and arrays.

Recording in Dialect

Making your own tapes has the advantage that you or someone else in the community can record the audio in the dialect(s) of the learners. Interestingly, dialectical variation in pronunciation can hardly arise with isolated phonemes, because these variations depend on the relation of a phoneme to the rest of the word in which it is embedded. In presenting *b,* for example, by means of a syllable like *ab,* there is no reason to pronounce it *ap* or *af* even if these are dialectical variants in some word structures of the students at hand, since it is not situated within a word structure. If you are presenting the digraph *th* you want every learner to know that it stands for the two sounds of THin and THen that exist in standard English. But a dialectic recording can allow an urban black learner to hear "bruvver" when he sees the word *brother.* So presentations intermingling phonemes with words also intermingle, in effect, standard and nonstandard pronunciation, which is one good way to help a learner to attach his home speech to standard spellings. (In using the lap method he will also hear "brother" pronounced in standard dialect, and this too will help him equate the two pronunciations for spelling purposes.)

Media Matters

If you use your live voice as the audio, this either ties you up with one group at a time or forces you to abandon individualization and march the whole class together through the sequence. It's essential to avoid either of these bad alternatives. Unless you have an aide free all the time to sound out a unit presentation whenever a working party wants to take on one, you will do well to use recorded audio.

Whether you make or buy the visuals and recordings, we suggest you consider these matters:

- The visuals need to be locked into sequence within each show so that students can't derange them.
- Each visual has to be synchronized so that when it becomes visible, the audio for it comes on automatically.
- Each show or session has to be independently set up or separately packaged so that students can get out one from anywhere in the sequence without having to run through the whole sequence to get to the session they want. The short length of a session may not suit some machines made for units of longer playing time.
- It is far better if the apparatus permits students to replay a show very easily so that they will not be discouraged from this important part of the activity.

- If the learners are small children, you'll need either equipment they can operate themselves or at least some that a helper can quickly get them into.

Bought or homemade, all materials requiring a machine pose the problem that, except in the unlikely case of multiple machines, only one party at a time has access to the materials. But it's better to tie up a machine than a teacher, because a free teacher can supervise individualized activities and thus enable different parties to do different things while one of them is using the machine. To the extent that requiring a machine limits access to materials, it becomes especially important that the materials teach as much as possible during the time a party has access to them. This consideration may turn out to be your deciding factor in reviewing options.

MOVING PICTURES WITH SOUND

One important part of deliberations is to contrast the value of successive still images with that of moving pictures. For bisensory learning such as literacy, you simply have to think through the pros and cons of alternative media.

Advantages

There are many advantages of film—enough to make it the best medium for presenting sound-spellings. Movies animate letters and punctuation marks. Three good features distinguish it from still-image gear.

1. While holding a visual field of several words or sentences, it can indicate by flashing or panning which of them are being sounded. This synchronizes within a sentence or within a continuity of sentences, whereas phono-viewers cannot hold larger units of language on the video while signaling which parts are being sounded at each moment.

2. During silences between sounding, the viewer can actually see taking place the adding, replacing, reversing, and deleting of elements while everything else in the visual field remains the same (Figure 10.3[1]). This makes quite clear exactly which visual

[1] In the figures in this chapter illustrating animation, a few frames must stand for many such interim frames, as the dots between frames will signify.

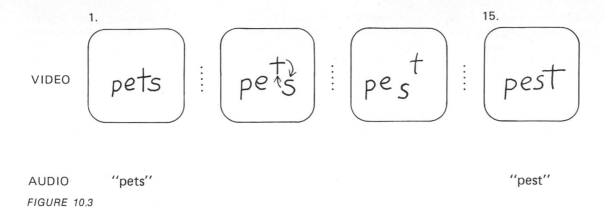

FIGURE 10.3

symbols remain the same and which differ from one speech sounding to the next. It also rivets attention to the one thing that changes and to how it changes. This gets at the essence of literacy, which is that a change in either sound or sight makes a difference in the other, and that you have to know which changes make which differences. By contrast, still images replace each other totally, so that the viewer has to compare mentally the present image with his memory of the one before and determine for himself which changed element in the video is responsible for the change he hears now in the sound (Figure 10.4). Even a single-word image like *pets* may be hard to compare quickly with its successor *pest* if you're just getting used to letter shapes and to which go with which sounds. The transformation will probably be more effective if the viewer can see the *pe-* hold fast while watching *s* and *t* animate on the screen into each other's former place. This advantage holds true for *all* transformation—of changes in whole words, punctuation, and capitalization as well,

although a simple transformation such as our example can be approximated by a rapid succession of still images.

3. Animation is more engaging than a succession of still images. If you are to invest much money in machinery in order to embody several methods and aspects of literacy in the materials you run through it, you certainly want the medium as attractive as possible.

More specifically, animation can do the following:

1. Show blending of words into larger units by flashing each word as it is sounded or by panning it up or across frame
2. Stroke on a letter or punctuation mark in the manner a learner should draw it, to teach handwriting
3. Make a letter grow bigger or smaller to establish its shape across size differences or to focus on capitalization

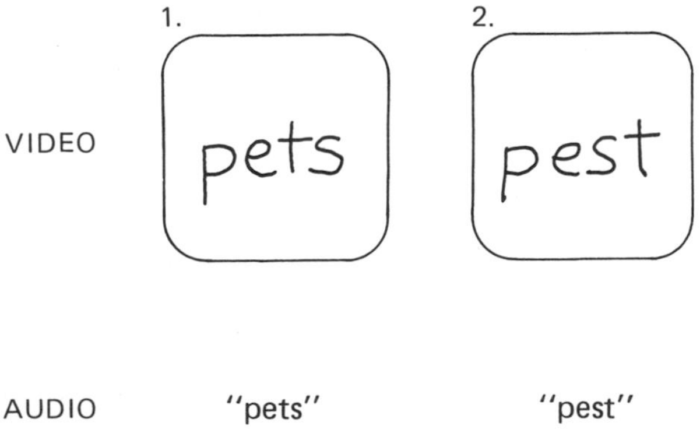

VIDEO

FIGURE 10.4

4. Teach top-to-bottom and left-to-right movements by adding letters or words one at a time vertically and horizontally on a held field

5. Hold the same words but change the punctuation, to match off punctuation marks with their vocal intonations (Figure 10.5)

6. Show a single letter doubling itself or a double letter becoming single, to identify congruent shapes and to contrast the sound values of single versus double vowels (Figure 10.6)

7. Interchange rapidly two letters having the same sound value in a given type of word (*sent* and *cent*), to show equivalence

8. Compare unfinished and finished sentences, to show what a sentence is (Figure 10.7)

9. Make a letter change itself into another letter, to strengthen visual discrimination and bring out differences in letter shapes (Figure 10.8)

10. Clarify and emphasize important spelling and punctuation "rules" (Figure 10.9)

Figure 10.9 shows also, by the way, how color-coding can be much better exploited when joined with animation. Note the color change also in the punctuation transformation in Figure 10.10, page 200. Perhaps both of these examples give some idea of how moving pictures not only can get across "rules" better but also have power to make sense of them. Making a one-sentence series out of three kernel sentences is a grammatical transformation that speakers punctuate orally by intonation and that commas render in writing.

Animation, in other words, can demonstrate beautifully the transformations of letter shapes, word spellings, punctuation, and capitalization that literacy students need to learn. Animation is by nature a transformer.[2] Furthermore, it establishes a model for

[2] For the original and extensive development of this idea see the book to which the authors of this book are indebted: Caleb Gattegno, *Towards a Visual Culture,* Educational Solutions, 80 Fifth Ave., New York, N.Y. 10011.

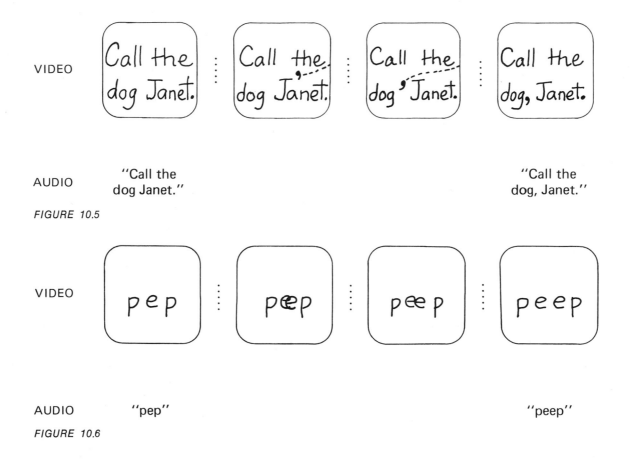

FIGURE 10.5

FIGURE 10.6

VIDEO

| He will. | : | he will | : | he will | : | He will stand. |

AUDIO   "He will."   "he will. . ."   "He will stand."

VIDEO

| he will stand | : | he will stand | : | He will stand up. |

AUDIO   "he will stand. . ."   "He will stand up."

FIGURE 10.7

FIGURE 10.8

VIDEO

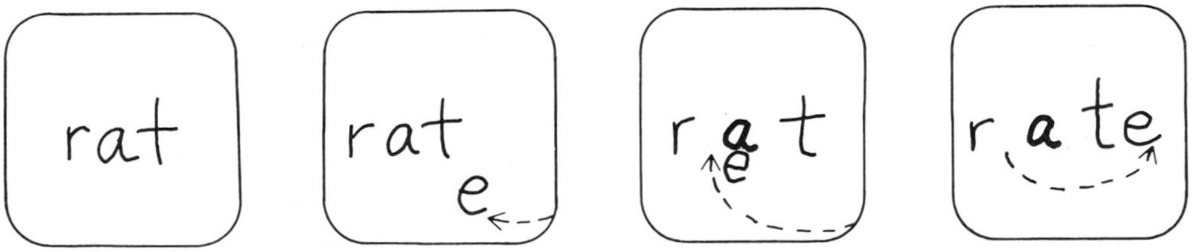

| rat | | rat e | | r a t e | | r a te |

(Note: Color of *a* changes.)

AUDIO   "rat"   "rate"

FIGURE 10.9

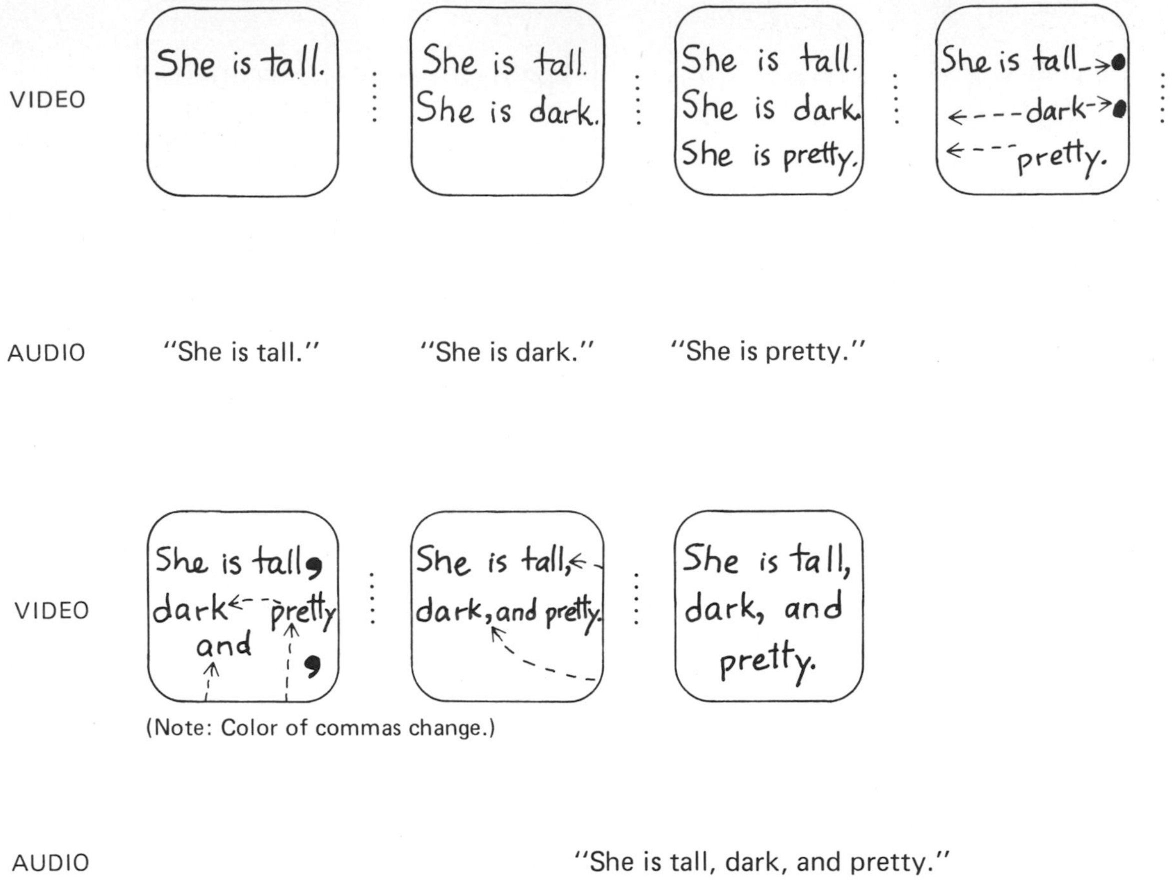

VIDEO
She is tall.
She is tall.
She is dark.
She is tall.
She is dark.
She is pretty.
She is tall
dark
pretty.
AUDIO
"She is tall."
"She is dark."
"She is pretty."
VIDEO
She is tall,
dark pretty
and
She is tall,
dark, and pretty.
She is tall,
dark, and
pretty.
(Note: Color of commas change.)
AUDIO
"She is tall, dark, and pretty."

FIGURE 10.10

the learner to follow in shifting his role from viewer/listener to active manipulator of the written language.

Format

Students who have already been exposed once to some phonics but need "remedial" work may be able to absorb ten to fifteen minutes of such animation on an occasion, but generally and initially, each session should be limited to one to three minutes' running time. So although one alternative is short reels, the better format is sound-movie loops, which are available as cartridges that can be inserted into a projector as cassette tapes are into a player. The combination of being a loop and a cartridge makes individualization and self-direction feasible. One can only hope, however, that cheaper devices for viewing short sound films will be marketed soon, perhaps modeled on simpler "toy" machines. Several companies now offer sound film-loop projectors, usually in super-8. The best solution may soon appear in the form of adapters for television sets permitting film cartridges to be viewed through sets schools already have, though color may be a problem for a while.

As of this writing (1976) only two sets of animated literacy films have come on the market, but you should look around for others and compare. One is "Pop Up," eighteen one-minute lessons on super-8 sound cassettes or sixteen-millimeter reel, part of Caleb Gattegno's *Words in Color* program (Educational Solutions, Inc., New York). The other is "Sound Out," thirty-four lessons of two to three

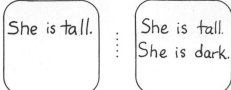

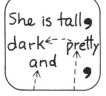

minutes each on super-8 sound cassettes, co-authored by Bobby Seifert and James Moffett as part of the Literacy Kit of *Interaction*.[3] The line of reasoning about literacy methods and resources developed in this book recapitulates the thinking that led to the development of "Sound Out."

People have of course learned to read and write for a long time without animated movies or any other modern audiovisual gear, but we recommend them strongly for success in teaching literacy in a system of mass democratic education and in a culture where such machinery already has a grip on children that schools can help to make positive. Also, from a purely logical point of view, bimedia machinery is the most effective kind of material for literacy, and movies may not cost any more, or much more, than gear for showing still images with sound. But if you cannot afford either, make cards and use community aides for live audio.

Audiovisual machinery and multimedia games can be expensive, and costly school spending should never be merely rationalized, but, in the total picture of literacy teaching, some special expense for sound-spelling presentation may truly save money in the long run. Consider that for many children this initial matching and blending sets up well or badly the whole course of decoding and spelling for the future. Along this line, consider too the enormous expense of teaching decoding, spelling, and punctuation year after year when it does not take the first time around. Not only are "remedial reading" classes very expensive, since they usually rely on special teachers and special materials, but much of the regular budgets for reading, language arts, and English are spent for what, in all honesty, can only be called remedial work also, since the chief learning issue for many youngsters for many years remains to learn how to master basic reading and writing. Prevention is not only better generally than remediation but also a good deal cheaper.

Arrange for your students to include viewing time in with their other literacy and language activities. Counsel according to individual diagnosis. Chapter 11, Decoding and Encoding Separated, suggests a way to diagnose literacy needs. When feasible, you may help two to five learners come together to view a lesson if they need the same sound-spellings at about the same time. Since each lesson lasts only a

few minutes, even if rerun once or twice, learners should be able to get plentiful access to the machine without having to group themselves too grossly.

The lap method

Unlike phonics, the lap method is simple to do and relatively cheap. The problem is not explaining how to go about it but convincing teachers that it really works for many youngsters and might work for all under the right conditions, even without other methods. The research conclusion about home learning, reported on pages 185–186, may support this contention. In addition, the same accumulated professional experience that tells us some children seem to need phonics instruction also tells us that many children learn in school to read splendidly—figuring out new words all the time—with no phonics instruction at all. They do this apparently by generalizing for themselves the phonetic rules—which letters in a word match which sounds in the word—as they earlier generalized for themselves the basic grammatical rules. Human beings are born with such analytic-synthetic ability, so to see it operating on printed words, as on other arrays presented to them, should occasion no surprise. If an infant did not analyze speech sounds and match them off with meanings, he would not start to speak. It may well be that if many learners seem to need others to help them analyze words and generalize the sound-spelling regularities, that may only be because schools have never afforded students the huge amounts of ore it takes for that kind of smelting.

So it may very well be true—and we suspect it is —that given words enough and time, virtually any person *might* learn to read by the lap method alone, if in the beginning he followed with his eyes a moving finger that allowed him to synchronize the audio and the video, voice and print. One question might be whether a public institution can ever flood each child with the copious flow of love and words it takes to induce such spontaneous phonics learning. By arranging properly, it can indeed. The teacher's lap is not the only one, nor his the only literate voice. For younger children there are the real laps of aides, including older children, and for both older and younger learners there is the figurative lap of the phonograph or tape recorder. And of course the

---

[3] Changes in format may occur for these two film series, so check with their developers.

audiovisual presentation we have just been describing teaches by the lap method to the extent that it shows and sounds whole sentences. Even to the extent it does not, still it may give many youngsters just the boost they need to start generalizing for themselves by the lap method.

HOW IT WORKS

What happens when a person follows a text while hearing it read is that he matches off speech with print very grossly at first and then more and more finely. Gradually he analyzes the big blocks of print, discriminates among the different words, and narrows his synchronizing focus down more and more —from a whole page or paragraph to a sentence, then to a phrase or word, then eventually to each of the forty-odd phonemes of English. We know this must happen because children have learned by this and nothing else.

Let's take the classic case of the middle-class child at story time. The book is a child's book, and each page bears only one or two sentences, sometimes only a word or so, usually illustrated. The effect is of a series of captioned pictures. Hearing the story over and over, held on the lap so he can face the video and get the audio right at his ear, he virtually memorizes the text so he can tell the reader when to turn the page and whether he left something out. He knows what is on each page and so has synchronized at this gross level. Many things help him to match off oral words with written words—the typographical isolation of some words on the page, the repetition of words that he can at once see and hear, the prominence of some words printed large or naturally set off by front and end positions in the sentence. Often he asks to have pointed out a printed word standing for something he is especially interested in. Or the person reading may habitually move his fingers by the words as he reads them. Some words are used to label or caption or title things in the book and so stand out also.

Once a few words can be recognized roughly, they serve as bench marks to keep the child synchronized. Then the process snowballs very fast: the more words he can cue from, the more specifically the young reader can synchronize the other words and begin to crack the whole code. He finally notes, for example, that the same sound occurs every time he sees *which, what,* or *where* and infers that *wh* stands for that sound. So even with no sound-letter

instruction at all, a person could learn to read and spell entirely from the lap method—but only, in most cases, after many, many hours of hearing and seeing the same or similar words recur.

The very lack of self-consciousness and of instructional situation that has caused this method to be omitted from the official repertory of reading methods accounts partly for its great success. The learner becomes rapt and self-forgetful and relaxed. Within this deep absorption, the mind unconsciously works over the data and begins to infer the sound-spellings and "rules." To use the lap method in a school situation means arranging for this same pleasurable absorption, protected from pressure or conscious striving. Don't be fooled by the apparent easiness; children do most of their deepest learning in just this undeliberate way. And don't be fooled by the apparently huge gap between looking at and listening to one lump of a whole story and getting down to matching off a vowel sound with its spellings. Much other matter that children learn is at first globally perceived and has to be refined down.

One obvious drawback to the lap method is that the learner may be looking at one word while hearing another. So precise synchronization is the crux of the problem. Second, it requires very large amounts of look/listen experience with texts, and this experience must to some extent be individualized. The following suggestions aim to solve these problems as well as to continue offering alternatives among material and human resources.

LIVE VOICE

The base for this method is simply reading aloud to students. Once accustomed to hearing stories read, and motivated by the pleasure to want to hear more, they will find it natural to start looking at the text and will usually want to take over eventually and read for themselves.

Teacher Reading

One way to show and read texts to students is to read aloud to a whole class from an opaque or overhead projection or a chalkboard while using something like a flashlight arrow-indicator to synchronize. If a controlled-reader machine is handy, use it to read from, but it is not worth buying for this purpose. Read for natural flow and sense without letting use of the indicator slow down too much or break up your rhythm, intonation, and expression, and don't use a controlled reader if it prevents this.

Once again, tying yourself down by supplying the audio represents the least desirable practice, because you have to ignore individual variation and serve out the same text for all students. But with no money and no help and very few books, you could still further literacy in the class by choosing texts cleverly, developing your reading expression, and generally making the practice as absorbing as possible. Remember, lots of it. Some every day could build up powerful reading and spelling skill, especially if concurrent with other literacy and language activities. For beginners, choose texts that have the kind of incremental repetition children like, because repetition helps them recognize and cue off certain words. The rhyming and typographical form of poems are good for this too.

Older students who are weak readers or "non-readers" will enjoy these sessions if the texts are interesting and mature enough for them, as they can be since all that students have to do is follow. Dependent students of any age can go ahead and be dependent but at the same time begin to gain the means of independence in a very unthreatening way. Older children who have apparently failed to read usually recognize some words and so are at the point where the snowballing could start any day. They can follow known words well enough to be pretty sure of looking at the unknown words at the same time you are sounding them. The lap method is limited to no age and may prove especially useful for older students who are supposed to read but don't. It enables them to tie into texts mature enough for them in content but too difficult to decode alone. Just be sure to avoid any feeling of childishness about the situation.

Students Reading

To the extent that members of a class do vary in literacy background or understanding it will be possible to use some to read to others. Even in first grade some children have had enough lap method at home to be able to read fairly well either by the time they enter school or soon afterward. In succeeding years the spread in literacy ability broadens so that it should be increasingly easy to find adept readers to give the lap method to their peers (and without the curse of it seeming babyish). Besides

freeing you to individualize, student readers add the appeal of peer interaction.

Arrange for a strong reader to read aloud to one or two others still learning. Let them choose a text and settle in somewhere comfortable in such a way that the listener(s) can easily see the text. If it doesn't interfere with their delivery the readers might move a finger along the text to synchronize listeners who need it. If you feel your readers are a bit shaky themselves, have them rehearse their texts with each other to work out kinks. If you can't muster enough good readers from within the class, arrange for older students to come into your class periodically to read in this way. Small children love to have the attention of older children on them and usually respond well to this big-sister or big-brother relationship. Since this kind of pairing has other uses that we will mention later, you could make standing arrangements with other teachers about pooling your students together. Volunteers are best.

Aides Reading

The lap method is a major and staple way in which parents, student teachers, or other community helpers can contribute substantially without either teacher or aide having to prepare. All that is required is that the person be competent in literacy himself. Although a special time might be set aside for aides to come in and read, an individualized classroom can avail itself of aides at any time, which is more effective and convenient all the way around. Just explain to aides the importance of students seeing and hearing the text simultaneously and how this will help them to learn to read and write.

RECORDED VOICE

Recordings enable students to look/listen independently of other people. This makes individualization possible when live readers are not numerous enough. Recordings also save face for students old enough to have learned to read, but still unable to, who feel ashamed being read to by another person. Once again, people power may be cheaper but is not always easy or desirable. Best of all would be to have both people and machines available. Some youngsters will prefer one to the other, and sometimes one or the other will fail you. See page 57 for making recordings and page 131 for more on this method.

The language-experience approach

We shift now from look/listen to look/talk. The language-experience approach might be described as the writing counterpart to the lap method in reading. The learner dictates something he has to say to a literate person who writes down the words verbatim so that the learner can see how his oral words look written down. If he watches his scribe write, and if he or the scribe reads back his own words as they follow the writing together, this can be an effective way for the speaker to learn sound-spelling correspondences, especially since the personal content makes for very high interest and close attention. Like the lap method, only in reverse, this provides the learner with a literate person who can mediate between the learner's oral knowledge and the strangeness of written language so that he can learn to translate between media himself. The scribe might write the words with light pencil and then let the speaker trace over the words with a porous pen or crayon.

Like any large-unit approach, language experience requires a vast volume of instances of words before most learners can generalize well the sound-spelling correspondences. The words are not phonetically controlled, and the larger the unit, the harder it is to break it down into components. But this volume is not impossible in school if parents, older students, and other aides are utilized.

With one teacher to service twenty-five to thirty-five kids in the traditional classroom, it is a tribute to the effectiveness of the approach that it has worked as well as it has. Dictation can become a much more powerful force in literacy if every learner has the opportunity to dictate something almost daily. Like the lap method, language experience is simple and cheap and anyone who can read and write himself can implement the method. The use of aides is critical here, in fact, because, unlike phonics and the lap method, the language-experience approach allows no choice between human and mechanical means. Until such time as machines are developed to type out words when someone speaks into them, we will have to rely on people to take dictation. Use parents, student teachers, community volunteers, students from upper grades, and more advanced students. The same arrangements made to engage readers from outside could be made to engage scribes, and many outsiders might be willing to do some of both on the same occasion. One easy way to arrange for this is to exchange halves of the class with a classroom of older youngsters and pair off older with younger pupils.[4]

Watching one's words being written down is a powerful learning method, but, as with the lap method, this power has seldom been felt in schools because classroom management doesn't usually permit each individual who needs it to dictate enough for it to take full effect. The large quantity is necessary, again, with a whole-sentence approach, because the student is doing the phonetic analysis on his own, unblending words into particles and generalizing intuitively the sound-spelling correspondences. It is easier, however, for the learner to synchronize spoken with written phonemes than in the lap method, because a scribe writes more slowly than a reader delivers. And some dictating is of single words only, which also helps to focus on more specific units of language. Finally, the learner can remember many of the words because they are his own.

Aside from offering learners opportunities to generalize spelling, the language-experience approach helps them very much to memorize the overall look of words. It parlays sight-word into a continuous, meaningful process. The spontaneous words are uncontrolled for phonetic regularity, of course, so at any given moment the speaker is seeing how separate, uncontrolled, and perhaps highly irregular words are spelled. That's the short-range effect occurring within the long-range effect of generalization.

USING SINGLE WORDS

An extremely valuable literacy practice is to write down for students words that they ask for. Personal, highly charged with feeling, phonetically random, these words complement beautifully the impersonal, phonetically controlled words that come up in the teacher-prepared presentation. Each has something going for it. The chief advantage of talk/look lies in the student's involvement with words *he* proposes. This extra interest ensures heightened attention to the overall look of each word, for whole-word memorization. So arrange for you and aides or other students to habitually write out on request whatever words a learner wants. Don't worry about spelling difficulty and rarity. The point is that the learner has some cherished or fascinating word that he wants to possess visually as he already does orally and

[4] See the *English Through Interaction* elementary-level film "A Pupil-Centered Classroom."

emotionally. Give it to him. Make a lot out of the process of collecting words, remind the students constantly that they can do this, and keep connecting their growing stock of word cards with activities that call for them. See Sylvia Ashton-Warner's book *Teacher* for her fine development of this method with Maori children.[5]

Word-Card Collections

Give each student a little drawstring bag or box or ring that opens. Give him also some tagboard or other paper of fairly heavy stock and direct him to cut out some blank word cards. Whenever he asks for a word, write it in pencil on one of his blank word cards and tell him to trace over the pencil lines with crayon or Magic Marker of his color choice. Or, depending on how advanced the student is, you might spell out the word orally as he draws or stamps the letters on the card. In either case, have him say the word while looking at the spelling. The learner keeps the cards in his bag or box, or if he has a ring, punches holes in the cards and strings them on the ring. Emphasize possession: these are *his* words. Sometimes the words have another, immediate use such as a label to identify some object the student keeps in the classroom or at home or some item in a display he has made.

This collection has many uses. Classmates can compare, trade, copy, and borrow words. They can use them to make playing cards by drawing or pasting on larger cards pictures of things that the words refer to. They can make sentences with them on a flat surface, fashion poems with them, and compose other kinds of writing. In trying to make sentences they will discover that they lack dull but necessary words like simple verbs, prepositions, and conjunctions, for which they now have a need and can also ask. Partners can turn word cards face down and take turns picking them up one at a time and reading them as the other tries to spell them back. They can spread them face down on the floor then try to guess from memory where each is, saying the word first before turning a card over. They can alphabetize their cards, following the order of a simple dictionary if they need to, then copy off the words in order onto pages of a blank booklet. Add illustrations and they have their own dictionary. Partners collaborating on one dictionary will pool their word

cards and learn new words. Various uses for these words are scattered throughout Part Four, Developmental Reading, Speaking, and Writing, and students can increase their stock of words by copying favorite words from signs, games, books, and so on, once the words have been identified for them.

Charts, Captions, Maps

Youngsters often want to know how to write words as part of a project they are doing. A number of such activities are described in Chapter 13, Labels and Captions. Encourage them to label the parts of some drawing they have made and to ask either you, a classmate, or an aide for the spellings. Often they want to label something they have made or caption a story picture they have drawn. Launch them into keeping charts of the growth of a plant or the behavior of their pet or the weather and other activities described in Chapter 16, True Stories, and Chapter 18, Information. These can be done by small groups too. Charts often call for single-word entries and repeat some words so that learners recognize them. Launch map-drawing also, another type of graphics that requires labeling of parts and captions. Proper names and titles offer an opportunity to teach capitalization also. In this regard, students can start keeping name and address books of friends and classmates. They dictate these, collect them on slips or cards, alphabetize and make booklets out of them. Accustom students to reading all such words to classmates soon after you write them down.

USING WHOLE SENTENCES

The basic procedure, which can be posted or set forth on an activity card for the use of both aides and students, goes like this, put as directions to the learner:

1. Sit down beside your helper so that you can watch him write.
2. Tell your helper the title of your story. Watch him write it down. Tell your own name next.
3. Now tell him your story. Watch him write it down.
4. Read your story out loud with your helper. Help him put in any punctuation marks that will make your story sound the way you want it to read.
5. Then read your story to a friend while he looks on.

[5] Sylvia Ashton Warner, *Teacher*, Simon & Schuster, Inc., New York, 1963.

Explain to aides or other scribes that since the normal intonation of speaking often gets broken up by dictating, they should ask for repetitions to check on how to punctuate the speech flow. Step number 4 should help too. If uncertain, the scribe should say the words a couple of ways, ask the speaker which is right, then perhaps explain the difference the alternatives make in punctuating. Explain also, to student scribes, that if they are unsure of spelling or punctuation to check with you. It's important for student scribes not to mislead the learner, but it's also important to make checking matter-of-fact so that the scribe doesn't lose face in front of his charge.

The content of a dictation can of course be anything. Younger children usually apply "story" to practically anything they have to say. The material can be a recent incident, a made-up tale, a description of a pet or parent, a certain routine, a favorite object or person or activity, or directions for how to make something or play a game. Sometimes members of small groups will tell something they did together or dictate collectively some routine entry in a log they are keeping about a class pet or experiment. For groups it may be better to write large on an easel pad so all can see well. Such large sheets are good for posting. A pair or trio can make up a play together by improvising the dialogue several times until they get a version they like. Then they sit down on either side of a scribe and dictate their lines, watching as he writes and prompting each other if they need to.

LOOK/TALK FOR ALL AGES

Like reading aloud to students, taking dictation from them is so associated with primary school that you have to be careful to keep older students from feeling childish and humiliated. Look/talk is a major literacy method, and many older students need all the literacy strategies available. It shouldn't be limited to the early years simply because that is where it is first used. Some older students, in fact, are so gun-shy of books and paper after failing to read and write for many years that look/talk may be by far the most appropriate method for them. The problem here is that we can't let them save face, as with the lap method, by plugging into a machine. Pairing the older nonreader off with a literate peer may solve the problem for some. Others may prefer you as scribe because they feel more embarrassed dictating to a peer than being seen by peers dictating

to an adult. (After all, you two might be conferring.)

Since collective writing is one staple procedure in this curriculum, occurring with literate as well as illiterate students, it can provide cover. Counsel students behind in literacy to participate frequently in such writing groups. Suggest in conference alone with them that they contribute a lot by dictating things to say and that they make a point of watching the scribe write down their words. Point out that by doing this they can learn to write for themselves. Say you think dictating to others would help them learn; then ask how they would like to go about it. Another possibility is for such students to talk into a tape recorder then watch as someone else transcribes the tape. This adds a degree of indirection that may suffice to forestall embarrassment for some. It is, at any rate, an option you can give older students. Taping has another advantage, incidentally, that might make it useful for younger children too: being able to talk at normal speed, without waiting on the scribe, keeps intonation natural and hence makes transcribing punctuation easier.

The amount of space we have devoted to each method by no means indicates the amount of weight you should give to them. The lap method and language-experience approach, dealing as they do with natural discourse, are simply much easier to describe than the sound-spelling presentation and require far less by way of materials outside of regular school supplies. For the most part, let all students try all things; then, on the basis of observing results, students' own testimony, and other evaluation, begin to counsel different students to go somewhat different ways so that some get more of one method than another.

Games for active practice

The preceding activities initiate learners into the correspondences between speech and print. The following activities allow the learner to rehearse this new knowledge and to continue to shift his role from receiver to manipulator of it. Obviously, the best way to practice literacy is to read and write real discourse; the purpose of the games here is only to expedite students to this point. Since the games focus on building or recognizing isolated words, they constitute a substantial spelling program, which is their first justification. Secondarily, they will reinforce word attack and teach letter shapes. Again, it is difficult to know how much word games may be actually needed for decoding, but we believe that entertaining, interesting, and creative word games at the outset of literacy will obviate the need later for a long, dull series of "spellers" or other systematic spelling program. Further, it seems very likely that while launching spelling well these games will, in fact, reinforce decoding without bad side effects. The old phonics exercises so strongly and justly criticized by many educators not only were allotted far too much time and importance, they were also dull and pointless because they occurred neither in a game situation nor in a communication context. They were also required for all children, regardless of need. Honest individualization makes it possible to keep many possibilities open and determine to your own satisfaction which justify themselves and, if so, for whom and for how long.

The activities that follow depend on the learner or a partner to sound the audio. If *look/listen* was an apt term for some of the initial learning activities, *look/say* might fit these well. Game materials provide the video, and game rules provide the audio by generating interaction among players. Sometimes fellow players provide the words to be sounded, sometimes chance does this, and sometimes the learner himself. Students sound out words and hence must already have some phonics knowledge—collectively at least—of the particular spellings. But while one player of a game may only be practicing a sound-spelling or word he already knows, another player in that game may be learning from him that sound-spelling or word for the first time. Similarly, given a certain game, players will alternate between presenting spellings to each other and sounding out spellings presented to them by their partners.

Practice games must be numerous and must overlap, for three reasons. One is simply that variety allows learners who tire of one game to continue to practice the same learning in a fresh game. Also, relationships learned in several different materials or media become more sharply generalized. Finally, since learners will be following different routes through these materials, they must have more than one opportunity to encounter a certain sound-spelling or spelling pattern. Counsel students individually to do one or another activity according to how much they seem to need, for example, reinforcement of basic sound-spelling generalizations,

whole-word memorization, word-making for spelling, or refinement of phonetic spelling to fit actual conventional spelling.

LETTERS AND STAMPS

Basic is a set of cutout letters, rubber-letter stamps, and/or letter cards. Cut out felt letters for kids to stick on a felt-covered board, or cut letters out of masonite, wood, sandpaper, and so on. Or buy letters made of some moldable substance such as plastic. Ideally, the letters and stamps should be of the same style and size so that they can be matched. Letter shapes should include upper and lower case and manuscript and cursive. If you follow the letter style on page 477 for the audiovisual presentation, do so for these too. Their size should be large enough to see and handle easily but small enough to permit making sentence continuities in some manageable space—one to two inches high. It would be good but not essential to have punctuation marks and even the numerals one to nine also in cutout or stamp form. Sandpaper letters increase the tactile experience. You may either cut them out of sandpaper or write the letters on tagboard squares in mucilage with the rubber tip of the bottle, then sprinkle sand on. When you or the children make cutout letters, you might cut vowels, regular consonants, and influential semiconsonants (*w, y, m, n, l,* and *r*) from material of three different colors so that students begin to discriminate among these three groups. Get a stamp pad or two, and if you have the money, buy several pads in different colors. If neither cutouts nor letters are possible, then print letters on squares of tagboard with Magic Markers.

Other useful materials are stencils that can be brushed over to print letters, letter cooky cutters for making clay letters to fire (if the school has a kiln) or for making dough letters to bake, or magnetized metal letters over which a sheet and iron filings may be placed.

Making Letters

You might help some of your students to make, each for himself, a set of either letter cards or cutout letters. Cutting out letters teaches the shapes kinesthetically. Students will have many uses for them. Let each youngster copy carefully or stamp a model array of the alphabet and cut these apart so that he has a permanent letter set to keep in a little drawstring bag or box or can to make words with. Beginners might make two or three letters at a time as they learn them with the phonemes they spell from the audiovisual presentation. Like their own word cards, these accumulate as a personal collection. You should give students the English letter frequency, so that they can make words or short sentences that require more than one copy of certain letters. They will need around one hundred capital letters and one hundred lower-case letters in ratio to each other according to this frequency.[6] Personal, homemade copies of punctuation marks (on cards) and of numerals would be useful too. Just making their own set of letters causes a lot of learning even before youngsters begin to put them to use. They may learn the names of the letters while learning to identify and form them. Although alphabetic names conflict often with the sounds of the letters as used in words, it is difficult to talk about spelling or handwriting if you cannot refer to the letters.

Uses

Youngsters like manipulating objects and stamping. Think of the cutouts as "feelies," as tactile means by which learners can "grasp" letter shapes in conjunction with seeing them. Laying out letters makes conscious issues out of backward, upside-down, or reversed letters and creates occasions for learners to correct each other. And youngsters love to stamp. Both letters and stamps allow them to write words and sentences, in effect, before they can form letters. But they should be encouraged to practice drawing letters at the same time, using the letters and stamps as models.

With these materials students may do many kinds of solo and partner literacy activities:

- Stack one solid letter on another of identical shape, for visual discrimination
- Stamp a letter; then place on top of the stamped image its solid-letter counterpart, for visual discrimination
- Draw a silhouette around the stamped image, for handwriting

[6] 11-A; 2-B; 2-C; 3-D; 10-E; 2-F; 4-G; 3-H; 9-I; 1-J; 2-K; 6-L; 2-M; 5-N; 9-O; 2-P; 1-Q; 7-R; 4-S; 5-T; 3-U; 1-V; 2-W; 1-X; 2-Y; 1-Z.

- Match lower case with upper case, to distinguish capital letters
- Match a manuscript letter with its cursive counterpart, to learn cursive
- Combine letters to spell a word, and sound it to themselves
- Combine letters to copy some printed matter, for letter recognition and blending
- Combine letters to make a word for partners to sound out
- Combine letters to spell out a sentence or story

In addition, solid letters can be used to play tic-tac-toe and Scrabble-type games, and stamps can be used to make labels, word cards, and other materials for other activities. Working with partners enhances the fun of these activities and acts as a spelling check.

TIC-TAC-TOE*

An easy way to get into word-making games is to play the familiar game of tic-tac-toe with letters instead of X's and O's. Players take turns, each adding a new letter to ones already played, to make a word first. The game by nature restricts choice, which is good for beginners, and is further restricted by whatever subset of sound-spellings the players have so far learned. Since such players may also just be learning to form letters, they might play by stamping or by placing solid letters into the squares.

SCRABBLE-TYPE GAMES *

A good kind of game to follow up tic-tac-toe, or to alternate with it for variety, is played like the popular Scrabble. Rules and format may vary somewhat, but this type essentially just extends the idea of tic-tac-toe by increasing the number of squares and permitting players to build words over a larger area. This increases options and makes the game more sophisticated than tic-tac-toe, but again, if players use only the subset of letters they know, the game adjusts automatically to fit players. They can use either the letters they have made so far for themselves or select out a subset from the full class set of stamps or letters. Or they may draw or trace a matrix and write in letters.

Games of the tic-tac-toe and Scrabble sort may be played repeatedly, since increasing one's set of sound-spellings makes playing them always somewhat different. Besides stimulating experimentation with sound-spellings, the game gives students a good reason to get used to looking in the dictionary or querying others and broadens their vocabulary. Be prepared for much querying about which spellings are words and which spellings are correct.

"TAP AND SAY" *

In another kind of word-making game, players point to letters with a limb of their body instead of moving the letters themselves. The game consists of one player successively pointing to or tapping several letters to spell a word for other players to guess. The letters may be stamped randomly on a piece of paper or pasteboard, written on a chalkboard or spread over an area of the floor if in solid form. The letters remain in random order as players indicate them one after another (Figure 10.11). A variation of of the game, called "Phonics Hopscotch," may be played with large drawn or cut-out letters on the floor by hopping from one to another or by tapping one at a time with a foot.[7]

Setting Up

The collection of letters to be played with can be limited to whatever subset of the alphabet a party has so far learned sounds for. Players pick out those letters or stamps that they now know and make the random display with them. As players learn the sounds of other letters, they can expand this subset and thus periodically revive interest in the game. You or an activity card can direct them to set up some letters as pairs—digraphs like *oa* or *ch,* the diphthongs *oi* and *ou,* or consonant blends like *st* or *nd.* This facilitation makes it easier to grasp how more than one letter sometimes spells only one sound, but it is appropriate only for beginners.

Value

This variant blending game adds an important asset to letter-moving games: it forces players to use faculties other than vision to put and hold spellings

together. The selecting and ordering of letters is done by muscle movements, as in letter-moving games, but since the letters are only tapped, not

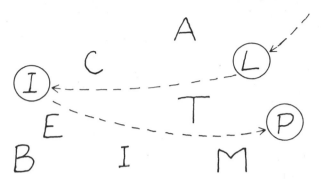

FIGURE 10.11 TAPPING OUT LIP

moved, the path of movement is all that remains, so the resultant spelling or word has to be held in the "mind's eye." Spelling *lip* this way is a different kinesthetic and mental experience for the player tapping out the word and requires that fellow players also actively visualize the word for themselves. Variety of physical and mental experiencing enlivens and strengthens learning.[8]

DICE GAMES *

"Games of chance" are very useful, because they ensure that learners will have to try to sound out letter combinations neither they nor their partners may have made themselves—a good decoding practice and test. The dice bear letters on their faces and are shaken and rolled to see what letter combinations they will offer. Allowing for some repetition of letters on the faces, the number of letters on the dice is a good four times the number ever cast. Since letter order is not given, players try to make words by sounding out different combinations. Scoring can encourage longer words that use all or most of the letters thrown. Partners pool their phonics knowledge to sound out spellings and can check accuracy of spelling. Players try to make up words they already know by shifting the thrown letters into

---

[7] "Phonics Hopscotch" was invented by Juanita Ingle and her first-grade pupils, who may be seen playing it in the *English Through Interaction* film "A Pupil-Centered Classroom."

[8] "Tap and Say" and "Word Turning," described further on, were developed by Caleb Gattegno for his *Words in Color* program (Educational Solutions, Inc., New York), where they are called respectively "visual dictation" and "transformation games."

different combinations. This is excellent for spelling and heading off any tendency toward reversal of letters.

Graduated games can be created by progressively increasing the number of cubes rolled at once and by stipulating particular cubes bearing certain letters. If cubes are color-coded and bear either vowels only or consonants only, then game directions can say, "Take two red and two blue cubes. . . ." and hence automatically exercise players in building words of, say, the *fate* and *feat* patterns. So game directions based on number and color of cubes can establish a progression of games emphasizing different word structures as well as paralleling the sound-spelling sequence (page 477) being presented via look/listen materials. Consonant digraphs can probably be better learned if printed on the cubes as such—*ch* or *wh* on one face. To keep score, players write or stamp down the words they make. Games can be played solo but are more fun in small groups, and partners can check each other. Players can also play collaboratively instead of competitively if they keep only a group tally.

A store-type game such as Spill and Spell is made for adults as well as children and has only one set of cubes and directions. For players not already literate but trying to become literate by means of the game itself, you need to buy or make a set of dice and directions especially to enable literacy *learners* to blend words from an expanding set of letters and a sequenced order of spelling patterns.

LETTER-MOVING DEVICES

You and the students can make with fairly common materials some game devices that allow players to pull or rotate a letter at a time through a little window set among some fixed letters. The effect is a kind of do-it-yourself animation that enables a player to make words by changing letters within a frame of fixed letters. Once more, the set of letters need be only those the student has learned so far, allowing him to play early in his literacy program. The number of letter places can be adjusted to focus on different word structures and spelling patterns.

Pull-through Devices

With cardboard or construction paper, for example, you might make a device like that shown in Figure 10.12.

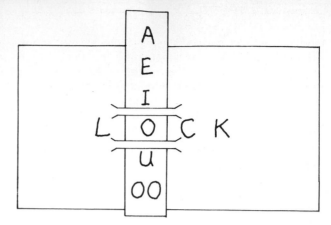

FIGURE 10.12

You might then think of a game name like "Unlock" or "Lucky Lock" to print on the sheet. Game rules should be short and sweet and universal for all such devices so that kids can get right into them and be told orally in a moment how to play, either solo—"See how many real words you can unlock. Keep count"; or with a partner—"Take turns locking a word in the window for your partner to unlock." Directions might also tell players to copy the words they get by stamping, printing, or spelling them out with solid letters. Partners may also keep score noncompetitively by seeing how big a score they can run up together.

But you need many such devices, based on different phonemes and spelling patterns. Try to make games interlock phonetically. Imagine, for example, that you set up the game "Cook the Boot" (Figure 10.13) to follow the game shown in Figure 10.12. The double *o* that did not work in the first game will work here.

The game in Figure 10.14 builds in certain initial and final consonant blends, and gives a choice of long or short vowels. This allows for the fact that either may occur in this word structure.

Flat-Wheel Devices

Pull-through devices are only one kind of contrivance that you or students can make. For variety, use devices of the type illustrated in Figure 10.15 (page 212).

Each circular band of letters is printed around the circumference of a disk, and the disks are stacked concentrically and pinned together in the

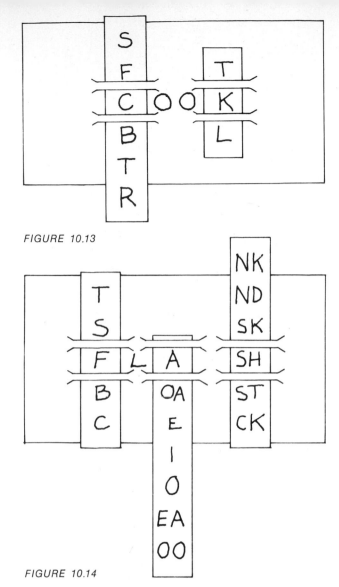

FIGURE 10.13

FIGURE 10.14

machines such as letter blocks, skewered on a rod, that rotate to line up letters.

211

An All-Purpose Device

If you carry the concept of such letter-combining devices to its logical end, you arrive at an all-purpose device of, say, five letter spaces that would permit a player to put any letter of the alphabet in any position to form any word containing up to five letters. To exploit all of these possibilities, it must be possible for players (1) to blank out some positions sometimes in order to make shorter words, (2) to have a better chance of getting some letters on a band than others, and (3) to set letters in some positions before starting play so that some word structure is given within which players can manipulate the other letter places.

For permanent, all-purpose devices some kind of three-dimensional machine is necessary. For one thing, since half of the advantage of moving letters is to get chance combinations to try to sound out, the device must enable letters to move freely, out of the player's control, once set in motion. Strips, disks, and other two-dimensional contrivances don't ordinarily accommodate this. Finally a straight strip is too long when imprinted with enough adequately sized letters, and disks limit severely how many letters can move through the windows near the center.

An ideal solution for all these problems is to fix each band to the edge of a wheel, so that letters face out like seats on a ferris wheel, and to rig a ratcheted movement so that the letters rotate around and fix one at a time in the window. Imagine a row of either three or five parallel ferris wheels rotating on the same axle independently of each other so that any seat on one can line up with any combination of seats on the others. Or, to add the row of windows and the ratcheting, imagine a slot machine with letters appearing in each place instead of fruit. Any wheel of our device can be set or spun by hand one at a time. This line of thought and some practical experience led up to the development by some *Interaction* co-authors of the three-wheel and five-wheel "Word Spinners" (Figure 10.16, page 213), which we single out here because of their unique format as of this writing.

Making Devices

Even if you buy or make all-purpose devices, you might also have activity cards that direct students

center with a brad that permits players to rotate the disks one at a time by thumb or finger. A windowed strip running from brad to top edge frames the word formed. The device illustrated in Figure 10.15 focuses on the long-vowel pattern *cvvc*. Since only a handful of consonants can come at the end of such words, the smaller disk can contain enough letters for that position in the word. This aspect of the wheel form, in fact, helps make this point.

Imagine other devices in other forms, including three-dimensional constructions. Look around in stores selling educational toys. Besides various sorts of letter-combining wheels, you will find simple

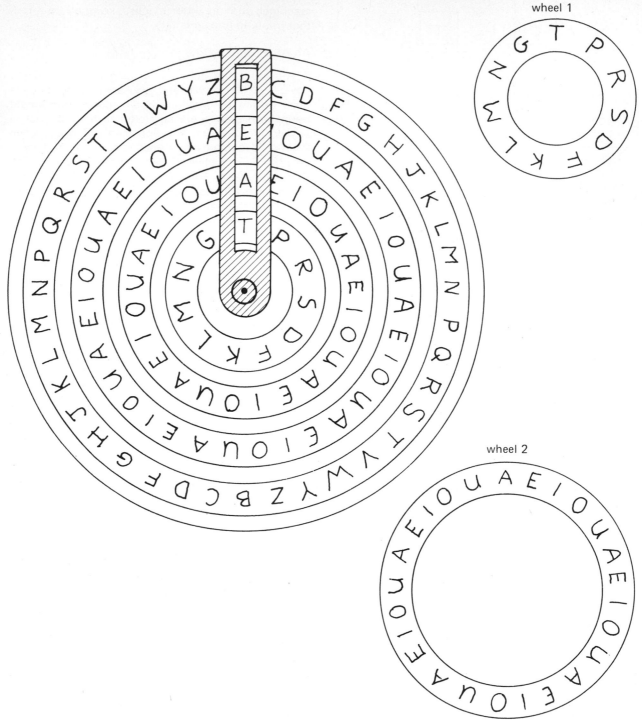

wheel 1

wheel 2

Wheels 3 and 4 are made in the same way.

FIGURE 10.15 FLAT-WHEEL DEVICE

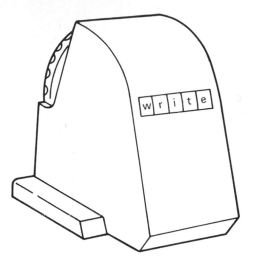

FIGURE 10.16 FIVE-WHEEL INTERACTION *WORD SPINNER*

they don't yield words, or to add another band of initial consonants to get seven-letter words like FREI*GH*T and BROU*GH*T or to blank some positions sometimes to get words like EI*GH*T and OU*GH*T or NEI*GH* or SI*GH*.

Special Value of Letter-Moving Devices

Making and playing with these devices entails first-rate learning of sound-spellings and can be done at any level of maturity by varying the difficulty. The learner gets insight about the spellings of English sounds that stick well because he has experimented. He is, in effect, systematically trying out various possible combinations in a scientific way and drawing conclusions from his research. By changing some letters while keeping others constant, he can see how the same spelling spells different sounds in different contexts (*flour, touch*) and how the sound value of a single letter changes with changes in neighboring letters it is combined with (*moose* and *mouse*). We urge you to look over again now the sample devices on preceding pages and to make them or similar ones and experiment with them. The very arrangement of a device can set up a word structure or spelling pattern.

And yet, this experimentation is really fun because the learner is controlling or making the device; he manipulates physical objects; the unknown outcomes create suspense; the recognition of familiar sounds in unfamiliar spellings is a pleasure; and the activities permit socializing. Devices can be made in funny and ingenious ways that become interesting in themselves, especially if the form of the word relates to the form of the device. Two windows spaced apart can be eyes; a strip of letters can be a tongue pulled through a mouth, etc.

Be sure, however, to remind students to check out spellings with other people or some printed matter, because they will sometimes make a letter combination that could logically spell an actual word but that doesn't happen to be that word's conventional spelling (*acks* for *ax*). In fact, understanding this problem of phonetic but wrong alternative spellings is one of the main things a beginner has to learn about English phonetics. Spelling phonetically but incorrectly is one stage, and a very important one, in literacy growth. But because these devices raise the very issue of phonetic versus conventional spelling, they create occasions to move on from the one to the other. This does mean a lot of checking,

to make the strip, disk, or other sorts of games. This serves two purposes. One is to cover some spelling patterns of more than five letters. Second, a very interesting and original way for students to "keep a spelling notebook" is to take a pattern they have learned or discovered and set it down in the form of a moving-letter game. Suppose, for example, that a learner has inferred for himself or been shown that *gh* is spelled but not pronounced after a vowel sound in a lot of words ending with *t*. He makes a game to express what he knows already, to find out how far his "rules" go, and to help other students learn. His device (Figure 10.17, page 214) will yield such five-letter words as NI*GH*T and SI*GH*T as well as six-letter words like KNI*GH*T or TAU*GH*T.

He makes a disk type because strips would be too long for bands 1 and 2, because *ght* can be fixed at the center, and because the third position requires only vowels. He could eliminate some letters from the first two bands but only by assuming his knowledge of the possible words is complete. Since part of the point of the game is to test and revise his "rule" and to set up a game from which classmates can draw conclusions, he does not select but puts the whole alphabet on band 2, once at least, and all the consonants at least once on band 1. Now by trying out all the combinations, checking for real-word spellings, and perhaps making some lists or cards of the real words produced, he and classmates can explore the pattern. They may decide to eliminate some letters in some positions because

FIGURE 10.17 STUDENT-MADE DEVICE FOR EXPLORING A PARTICULAR PATTERN

but for younger children you can set up the devices so that most letter combinations will make actual words and will make correctly spelled words. Older children can pool their knowledge and explore with a conscious game objective of discovering which letter combinations are unpronounceable, which are pronounceable but not English words, which are phonetic but incorrect spellings of English words, and which are correct English spellings. The learning value accrues by no means to spelling only. Whenever partner or chance presents a word, the learner faces a word-attack situation. This is why both chance and choice, spinning and setting, are ideal. Chance features word attack, and choice features spelling. In lieu of spinning, however, partners can serve by setting letters for each other.

"WORD TURNING"

How do you change a *dog* into *a cat*? By replacing one sound-spelling at a time:

$$dog \rightarrow dot \rightarrow cot \rightarrow cat$$

"Word Turning" is turning one word into another by adding, deleting, reversing, and replacing sound-spellings. These are the same four transformations that students can watch in animated phonics films, where they will get both the idea and inspiration for "Word Turning." In full-blown form the game requires a beginning and an ending word, and the player(s) must transform the first into the last by successively performing any of these operations on it. Each step must result in a real word, as in the example above. As a solo game, the point is simply to find out how to get from one word to the other and so is like a kind of puzzle. As a partner game, the point may be to get from one word to the other in the fewest steps or to otherwise compare different solutions, since usually more than one series of transformations will turn one word into another. Or if only one way exists, players may time how long it takes them to get the second word. One version of the game is to see who can make the longest string of words when all players start with a common word. Finally, players may work out transformation chains then give each other the first and last words to see if their partners can figure out the steps in between.

Setting Up Directions

The basic rule is that players change one word into another by changing one *sound* at a time. In the example above it makes no difference whether the rule directs players to change letters or sounds, but when players start working with words having more letters than sounds, it becomes important for them to understand that changing a sound means making whatever letter changes are necessary to spell the new sound. Consider these two changes:

$$maid \rightarrow mood \qquad or \qquad tin \rightarrow chin$$

The first change entails replacing one digraph by another, and the second change entails replacing a single letter by a digraph. The rule *could* be to change letters, but that can create much confusion, and besides, letter-moving devices cover the possibilities of changing letters.

The implications of the basic rule will increase gradually as a player's subset increases through look/listen activities. Double consonants and consonant digraphs make an easy transition into the extra-letter spellings of the long vowels. A player can be well acquainted with the idea of the game and see the fun of it before getting involved in the implications of the game rule about changing sounds, not letters.

To understand the questions that the rule may raise, and the implications of it that students can grasp, consider the following game task of transforming *loot* into *sick*.

$$loot \rightarrow look \rightarrow like \rightarrow lick \rightarrow sick$$

Is this legitimate? players may wonder. First of all, in replacing the *t* sound by the *k* sound, we have secondarily changed also the sound value of *oo*. It is good for players to notice that *oo* has a different sound before *t* than *k*. Second, in replacing the sound of *oo* in *look* by the long *i* of *like*, we have had to add a final mute *e*. But this too adheres strictly to the game rule about changing sounds, because if you put a long vowel into this slot in this kind of word structure, you have to add the mute *e*. Next, changing long *i* to short *i* (*like → lick*) makes us drop the *e* again in favor of final -*ck*, and this transformation is a variation of the *bit → bite* transformation that applies generally to short and long vowels. Encourage players to discuss together whether certain transformations are legitimate. They will then have to thrash out the *spelling* rule because of the implications of the *game* rule.

Another way to make the game easier at first is to introduce the four transformations one at a time. You can make or buy a sequence of six to eight activity cards* that takes up one operation per card and that then puts all four into play at once.

Players should always say aloud the starting word and each subsequent word they change the first into. This helps a solitary player keep focused on sound changes and helps partners to check each other.

Materials

Directions can suggest several options for materials. Although beginners may play directly on activity cards by tracing and printing, once they have learned the operations and the game and done the card samples, they either stamp or write on paper, write on a chalkboard, move solid or cutout letters or letter blocks, or change settings on letter-moving devices. The advantage of writing or stamping lies in seeing the whole sequence of steps when finished and in having a record. This is desirable because players sometimes compare different steps to the same end or score by counting the number of steps.

But some players, especially beginners, who will make only two or three simple changes, may prefer to stamp or to manipulate other materials. For remedial work with older students, paper or chalkboard is all you may need if you can explain directions to some and let them teach others. See "Stepwords" on page 252.

ANAGRAMS

This popular old game consists of making one or more new words out of the letters of a given word. Beginners can play with words like *tan* and get *ant* and find out that *nat* sounds right but *gnat* actually spells the word. A word of four letters dealing with long vowels might be *meat* (*team, mate*). Such short words allow players to try out all possible letter combinations. While one player manipulates the letters, the other can look up words in a dictionary, if mature enough, and both can try to sound words.

Beginners can start with the familiar game of finding little "kangaroo" words in big ones, like *every, very,* and *day* in *everyday.* Later they can rearrange letters as well and thus find in a word like *valentine* such words as *lean, in, it, live, eat.*

More experienced players can rearrange words of more than four letters, such as:

> plates—staple—pastel—petals—pleats
> kitchen—thicken

or phrases such as:

> breakfast—fast baker
> constraint—cannot stir

Collections of these can be put onto wall charts or into riddle books.

CARD GAMES *

Clumping together *which, while,* and *what,* or *aid, mate,* and *say* is like making books of hearts and jacks. Put into the form of card games, the traditional phonics activity of matching words having the same sound can become a very entertaining and very effective activity. In the form of workbooks or worksheets, often accompanying lessons in basal readers, this word matching usually seems boring and pointless to youngsters, because there the activity is neither authentic discourse nor a game. The problem has been the methodological fault, again, of trying to do in book form what by nature cries for a medium of manipulable parts. Cards bearing words or pictures are perfect because they make the activity a real game, permit physical grouping of words, make possible cross-teaching among partners, and may be used over and over again, unlike consumable workbooks.

Cards may have just a word each on them or have a word on one side and on the other side a picture of the object that the word denotes. Decks might specialize in short or long vowels, easy or hard consonants. Decks you buy can serve as models for students to make more. Common games like rummy and concentration are good and can be supplemented by other pairing or book-making games. Pictures permit a simple solo or partner game of matching purely by sounds, without looking at the printed words, then of matching words to pictures by saying one and looking at the other. Making and playing card games can become an important and creative activity as youngsters take their own word cards and pictures, sort them by sound, organize them into decks, and exchange and play them. It may help older literacy students fasten down sound-spellings, and it relates to other language games in the form of card decks. See Appendix A, page 471.

Card decks may also be used to play on game boards* where a token is moved toward some goal. With or without card decks, game boards may take many forms, but the main idea is that some matching of sound-spellings causes tokens to be advanced.

Personal word card collections as mentioned on page 205 are good for games. Phonetically uncontrolled, often irregular, favored by the learner, these cards foster a fine kind of whole-word memorization. Chapter 13, Labels and Captions, suggests other sources for this collection.

A good solo game is simply to place the cards face down, turn them over one at a time, and try to sound them, placing aside those one cannot sound or is unsure of. The learner can get help with the ones he missed, then run through again some time and compare his scores for both occasions. This is a good guessing game (of *educated* guessing, which is half of reading). Playing with a partner gives students the advantage of checking each other and of playing with each other's cards. Checking is important for making sure that a player says the right word. Another student's cards furnish both new words for initial learning and known words for review.

Another good look/say activity for either individuals or partners is to turn over and say word cards that have pictures on one side. This is good, of course, only for words that can be depicted, though an individual might draw and recognize his own version of more abstract things such as *love*. The pictures act as a check when an individual is playing alone, since he has only to turn a card over to know if he has sounded out a word correctly. A partner can look at the picture on one side as a player tries to say the printed word on the other side. The one who is checking is also initially learning a word if he did not know it before, since he can be shown the printed word after his partner reads it.

BINGO *

A caller reads aloud words from a call card. Players each have a card bearing, say, twenty-five word squares. Whenever a word is called that he sees on his card, a player covers it up with a chip or scrap. The first player to cover all word squares in one row or all word squares on his card yells "Bingo!" and wins. Different degrees of difficulty are easy to arrange, so that the game can be played equally well by very young or maturer learners. Bingo affords good practice in word recognition for both caller and player, and game directions can build in a checking system.

Typically, a player will know some words on a card and not others, so some he will recognize from memory of the whole word and some he will have to attack for the first time. He is greatly aided by the process of elimination, because there are only so many words in front of him, dwindling all the time, that might be the word he hears called, and among those, only certain ones contain one or more of the sounds in the word called. This situation stimulates deduction from purely phonetic clues, since there are no pictures or other meaning clues. Sets of playing cards with call card can be bought or made in an order of difficulty based on the phoneme sequence suggested on page 477.

Summary

INITIAL LEARNING

METHOD	MATERIALS (Other than standard supplies)
Audiovisual presentation of phonemes, words, and sentences combined	Cards, slides, or transparencies with live or recorded voice—make or purchase
	Or
	Phonovisual machines, preferably for sound movies
Lap Method	Texts and recordings of the texts—make *and* purchase
Language Experience	None

GAME PRACTICE

ACTIVITY	MATERIALS (Other than standard supplies)
Making words by handling letters	Cut-out letters and letter cards—make Letter stamps—purchase Solid letters—make or purchase
Tic-tac-toe	None
Scrabble-type games	None
"Tap and Say"	None
Dice games	Set of special dice with rules—make or purchase
Making words by shifting letters on a device	Pull-through and rotary devices—make and perhaps purchase some as models

ACTIVITY	MATERIALS	ACTIVITY	MATERIALS
Making words by shifting letters on a device	All-purpose, three-dimensional machine—purchase	Playing board games	Game boards with game rules—make *and* purchase, or make only
"Word Turning"	None	Playing bingo	Game boards, call cards, and game rules—make *and* purchase, or make only
Playing anagrams	None		
Playing cards	Card decks of controlled words with game rules—make *and* purchase, or make only		

W hat we have been describing in the last two chapters is a combined word-attack and spelling program. Be sure to read those chapters before reading this one, which pursues literacy into the differentiation of decoding and encoding in order to deal with what is unique to each.

Decoding

Chapter 7, Reading, lays out the various activities by means of which learners practice reading and become more proficient at it. Developmental reading is dealt with throughout the chapters of Part Four, Developmental Reading, Speaking, and Writing, where, in effect, "reading in the content areas" is covered. Certain specialized graphics such as maps, charts, graphs, tables, and codes become issues there. Here we will still emphasize cracking the code, the regular code. But of course any time someone cracks the code he is involved in comprehension, and his comprehending helps him further crack the code.

COACHING AND DIAGNOSIS

On page 133 of Chapter 7, we described a general coaching session for tutoring reading. Part of such a session may consist of diagnosing a student's decoding from listening to him sight-read. How a reader sounds out a text reveals many things. It may well be the best means of perceiving what is going on in a learner's head as he reads alone. On the basis of these perceptions you can give pointers and counsel accurately about which methods and materials will help him most. Hearing a student sight-read is very important at any age if diagnosis is still needed at all.

There is a tradition in elementary school, however, of dividing a class into three or so "reading groups" of different levels within which each student reads aloud while the other members sit idle with the same book in their hands. This is very inefficient and actually only an unrealized effort at individualization. The old reading groups assume that all students are reading the same thing at the same time, and the division into groups aims to make some allowance, in rate at least, for individual differences. But it can't, of course, so trying to coach and diagnose in groups is not likely to succeed. A major reason for instituting self-direction is to free you to tutor. While other students are doing various other language and literacy activities, you can listen to readers one at a time, just a few a day perhaps, and coach and diagnose them on the basis of what you hear and observe while they read aloud to you alone.

You don't need a separate time and place for coaching and diagnosing. It can be just one of many things you do as you move among your students or as they come to you. You might simply ask someone who is reading silently to read some of his text aloud to you. Or you might tell the class you want everyone to bring something to read to you two or three times a week. Not all children will need coaching and diagnosis, but they may all want to read to you, especially if the sessions feel positive. If the child reads laboriously, he doesn't suffer the embarrassment of his peers waiting him out and getting restive or contemptuous, and you don't have to worry about group management and trying to quell those who are getting bored. You're not now trying to do tutorial in a group. Make the sessions positive by being as helpful as

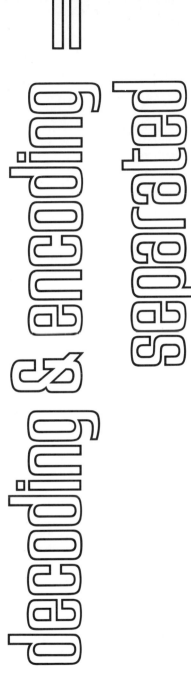

decoding & encoding separated

possible. Let them see you as a supporter who makes it possible for them to get competent and to feel good about themselves. Sometimes they might read to you a text they want to read to classmates or to younger children or their parents; let them use you for rehearsal.

The teacher who looms as only negative judge is one who simply doesn't know how to be specifically helpful. So concentrate on noticing the *kinds* of mistakes a reader makes (diagnosing) and on showing him how to overcome them. This is the serious, learning part of the sessions, but the *tone* of them can be warm and playful, and by all means make the student aware of his strengths. When students are working on different sorts of reading matter, you can sincerely be a lot more interested in listening than when all are reading the same thing and you have heard it year after year. A bonus to these tutoring sessions, which need not last sometimes more than three to five minutes, is that you are evaluating as you teach and will feel more directly in touch with the decoding progress of individual students.

Analysis of Oral Reading

To be most helpful in coaching and diagnosing, try to become as expert as possible in interpreting your students' *misreadings,* in doing what Kenneth Goodman and his colleagues have called "miscue analysis." Though done as research, their work parallels what a good reading teacher should do. Look at *Miscue Analysis,* a collection of reports and articles edited by Goodman.[1] One point the authors make is that *all* readers miscue somewhat and reshape the text in their own way as they try to make sense of it. Miscuing should not be regarded as bad but rather as *indicative.*

The following sample from the miscue research will give an idea of their process of noting and interpreting oral reading.

Here is a sentence from one story used in our research, and the miscues one pupil produced in reading it:

© But I remember ~~that~~ the cameras, moving close to the crib and Mr. Barnaby bending over ~~and~~ saying soothing things, to Andrew—but not too loudly.

[1] Kenneth Goodman, ed., *Miscue Analysis,* National Council of Teachers of English, Urbana, Ill., 1973.

The reader omits a word and some word parts, inserts a word, substitutes other words, goes back at times to correct himself, and comes out with a meaningful sentence. We must be concerned with more than his superficial behavior. We must infer from it the process he has used and his competence with that process. He inserted "that" but corrected when he realized the pattern he had created was not acceptable syntax. He omitted "and" but did not correct because it was not a necessary element.

We start in miscue analysis with observed behavior, but we do not stop there. We are able, through analysis of the miscues, to see the process at work.[2]

Researchers audio-tape the reading and make notations on a work sheet that is a copy of the text.

Our recommendations are a free adaptation of miscue analysis, the main difference being that Goodman and company do not analyze as such a student's interpretation of spellings. Since you want above all in these sessions to listen in on how a student reads when he reads silently, it is better not to interrupt or correct him but just to attend closely and tape if you can. Your eyes have to be following the text as he reads, of course. You want to pick up on recurring characteristics. You may have to think about his reading before talking with him about it, or you may play the tape over later. You can coach at the end of the session or later on. Unlike when you are coaching for a rehearsal, you are not now interested in improving delivery and effect. You are looking for deeper and general reading traits. After you have distilled for yourself what some of these are and what they imply about a student's instructional needs, then you can convey to him in some practical form what you think you perceived.

As the student reads aloud a reasonably challenging text, note the following:

- Which elements of the text he ignores—certain phonemes, whole words or phrases, or punctuation
- Whether he replaces pronunciations, words, and grammar with dialectical variations of these, that is, whether many of his miscues are really a fairly systematic translation, common for many children, between their dialect and standard dialect

[2] Goodman, p. 5.

- Which spellings he sounds out incorrectly, not because of dialectical variation but because of inadequate understanding of sound-spellings and spelling patterns
- Which combinations of sound-spellings trip him up—consonant blends, vowel-consonant combinations, polysyllabic words
- Whether he follows punctuation and capitalization and, if not, which kinds he ignores or misreads
- Which kinds of mistakes he corrects himself and whether they are important to the meaning or not
- Whether he reverses sounds and words or otherwise rearranges elements
- Which substitutions seem to constitute "reading into the text" subjective expectancies, preoccupations, stereotypes, and so on
- Which sounds, words, or punctuation he inserts into the text
- Whether his phrasing and intonation fit sense as well as syntax and punctuation
- Whether he sounds involved or "calls" words mechanically

Remember that you are not just score-keeping; you want to spot *patterns* of misreading that will apply to other readings. Why do you think the student is reversing or rearranging elements or inserting or substituting things? Does he aim for meaning or settle for doping out each phoneme as it comes up? Do his phonics errors show ignorance of certain spellings or spelling patterns? Does his intonation fail to allow for sentence stops or not indicate commas and dashes? How close are the intonational contours to how he would speak the same sentences if they were his own? What do his self-corrections show? Most of all, of the three main kinds of cues —phonetic, grammatical, and semantic—which do you think he is following most? Least?

You need to know whether the student's reading can be improved by strengthening visual or oral cues. Since good reading occurs when oral and visual are closely interacting, as when the reader takes cues from some key letter clusters to get some meaning and with this drift of the sentence sense, unlocks in turn other letters, you want to know where the weak and strong points are in this rapid oscillation of attention. Without sight-reading analysis it is hard to know whether problems lie in weak phonetic interpretation of letters and punctuation, in failure to predict upcoming sentence elements and ideas from ongoing ones, or in some poor coordination of all incoming cues. Consider other cues too, such as typographical layout, headings, illustrations, captions, paragraphing, and so on. Advise students to orient from overall organization downward to detail. It is heeding and relating *all* cues that makes the best reading. Some students may not crack the visual code well enough to gain access to the sentence structure and meaning, which are locked, after all, in their oral knowledge. They need enough more fine focusing to benefit from those language cues. For them you might counsel certain games rehearsing sound-spellings. Some, on the other hand, may be so hung up on visual detail that they cannot process larger units. They may in fact have had far too much phonics already and should drop it for pure lap method so that they will learn to use visual knowledge only to get to the oral knowledge, not as some end in itself or as a nearsighted, painstaking scrutiny that loses all purpose. So analysis of sight reading can show you how to counsel a student about which of the activities described in the last chapter he needs to emphasize.

If your course in teaching methods does not offer some experience listening for and interpreting misreading, ask for it. If on the job, tape some sessions and ask other teachers to listen both to the reading and to your later coaching. Discuss what each of you thinks certain misreadings show and what they indicate you should say to the student. See pages 417–419 and following in Chapter 21, Evaluating, for diagnosis by games and other means.

SPECIAL BOOKS FOR BEGINNING DECODING*

As a transition into the reading of regular books it is very helpful to make or buy some special books having a controlled vocabulary.

One kind of book simply transfers to pages the sound-spellings, words, sentences, and sentence sequences taken directly from whatever audiovisual presentation was used (described in the last chapter), with some words perhaps recombined to make a slightly different text. Phonetically controlled words are hard to make the *usual* sort of stories from, but they can be put together into some short entertaining sequences that because of the very limitations in vocabulary force the author into the sort of zaniness children love. Many of the words can be spoken by cartoon characters in comic-book fashion as well as spread over signs and other things in the background of the scenes and used to caption as well. These booklets can be vastly more interesting than standard primers and still be not only phonetically controlled but limited in places to single words, phrases, and sentences without violating either grammar or reading pleasure. Several of these very short books might cover in series the sequence of sound-spellings so that beginners could have some fitting books to read without waiting until the whole sound-spelling presentation is over. But after these booklets there should be no more phonetic controlling and no more sequencing of reading material except individually.

Chapter 12, Word Play, and Chapter 13, Labels and Captions, suggest kinds of reading matter that are easy because short and simple but that are not phonetically controlled. Some, like tongue twisters, do naturally focus on sound-spellings, however.

INCREASING READING EFFICIENCY

Let's shift now beyond the beginner stage. The overwhelming majority of adults are held to the speed at which they learned to read, even though their early reading habits are no longer functional for them. This is an absurd state of affairs, especially in an era of information explosion that requires adults to assimilate huge amounts of print. And it is this state of affairs that has prompted so many professional people and university students to seek out commercial courses that will do for them what schools never did. The problem of reading efficiency is one that schools must deal with. This does not mean that people *should* read fast but rather that they should be *able* to read fast when they want. The principle of flexibility—reading different texts in different ways for different purposes—is a principle now well established among many reading experts, but it will remain a hollow conviction if schoolchildren are stuck with their original habits and thus have no real options.

Visual Processing of Words

The proficient reader does not give equal attention to all words or to all parts of words. He does not need to. There are many cues of word structure, syntax, and sense that make it unnecessary to process every letter, word and phrase in the same way. In a very real sense, we do not see everything in a text even when we "read" every word of it. For example, proofreading for typographical errors is very difficult because we unconsciously "fill in" the obvious—the letters we know are there because of how the rest of the word is spelled, articles and prepositions we know are there because nothing else could occupy certain slots in the sentence. This means that if errors exist in these obvious positions, we will miss them. Familiarity with the text makes proofreading even more difficult, because we fill in even more. For another example, the Cloze procedure of deleting some letters and words from a text does not prevent readers from getting all the meaning of the text—provided that deletions are of *redundant* items, that is, of items that are dispensable because their information is conveyed equally well by other cues. If more important items are deleted, however, the text will become ambiguous or cryptic. Compare:

_ole_ant
tol_ra_t

Surely the letters deleted in the first were more essential, while those in the second were more redundant. Compare also:

I _____ have found it _____ to believe.
I would _____ found it difficult _____ believe.

But redundance is relative to the knowledge and experience of the reader:

Give _____ this _____ our _____ bread.
Marx's theory of historical _____ derives from _____'s concept of thesis and _____.

Scanning and guessing, in short, are integral to proficient reading. Swiftly, automatically, we attend to critical cues and infer what is in between. As we are reading along, we constantly corroborate inferences by matching them against our ongoing interpretation. Occasionally, when something doesn't seem to fit, we "regress"; we flick our eyes back to a word or phrase and discover, for example, that what we took to be *importing* was actually *imparting*. It is useless to object that this is mere skimming or sloppy reading; it is what every proficient reader does, including those whose comprehension is best. See pages 138–139 for an extended example of following syntactic and semantic cues.

Differences Between Visual and Auditory Processing

Actually, not all of this perceptual scanning and mental processing is unique to reading. When we listen to someone speak we attend in the same selective fashion and have no more need to "hear" every syllable, in order to understand everything said, than we need to "see" every syllable when reading. Both seeing and hearing partake of the same general data-processing system. But there are differences too. One is that reading involves eye movements. Another is that reading concerns arrangement in space, whereas speech concerns movement in time. We can assimilate spatial information faster than temporal information—read faster than listen. These two differences are related: *how* fast we can assimilate visual information depends on how we have learned or not learned to move our eyes during reading. But that depends in turn on the fusion of sight with thought that we spoke of earlier.

Eye Movements

A number of oculomotor studies have determined that reading consists of a series of fixations that last about a quarter of a second each, regardless of the reader's speed. About 94 percent of reading time passes in fixation. The rest is spent moving the eye from one fixation to the next. Time is lost, of course, in sweeping back to the left margin and in regressing. Since nothing can be seen during movement, only during fixations does true reading occur. Comparison of the eye movements of fast and normal readers shows that the fast reader fixates less often and regresses less often. The number of fixations, however, depends on how much area the eyes take in at each fixation and on what spatial pattern they create in moving over the page. It seems that the very fast reader moves his eyes in irregular fashion, which probably means that he fixates on critical textual points that he has learned to scan for, wherever these may occur on the page. Since we are told that four words represent the maximum area spanned in one fixation, very fast readers who comprehend well could not possibly be catching every word. By good scanning, they must be getting the maximum benefit of redundancy. To this add the fact that the most rapid readers move their eyes vertically down the page, swinging to left and right in a smaller arc than do normal readers. They do not waste time sweeping from right margin back to left, like a typewriter, then moving all the way out to the right again. Their vertical movement undoubtedly also enlarges the span of each fixation into a circle so that they catch words above and below the line of type fixated on.

How do habits of eye movement come about, and should they be changed? This is where the second difference between reading and speech must be considered—the difference between visual and auditory processing, spatial arrangement and temporal order. When first learning to read, children have to relate print to speech in order to recognize letter combinations in a book as familiar vocal words. Moving at first from one word to the next, they sound out words in succession just as one utters them in speech. Thus they learn the horizontal, left-to-right convention of reading and thereby learn at the same time the habits of eye movement that characterize the normal adult reader. This initial learning intensifies the habit of vocalizing while reading, and this habit, too, persists into adulthood, in the form of subvocalization. Thus the reading speed of normally proficient readers remains bound to the slow temporal order in which words are successively spoken. The advantage afforded by visual processing—the more rapid assimilation made possible by spatially presented information—is mostly wasted. Excessive phonics drills no doubt make this plight far worse than it need be.

Both practical experience with fast readers and such considerations as we have just surveyed have led some reading experts to conclude that normally proficient adults read much more slowly than necessary and that good school education should include the breaking of habits learned in beginning reading —namely, subvocalization and regular, horizontal eye movement. If these reading experts are right, as we believe they are, then a valuable kind of instruction has been much neglected. Educators have been justifiably wary, however, about believing the claims of speed-reading methods. The issue is whether one trades a gain in speed for a loss in comprehension.

The "Speed Reading" Controversy

"The claim that most of us can increase our reading speed dramatically without loss of comprehension remains unsupported." [3] This conclusion of Richard Graf states the prevailing view of independent researchers. For the viewpoint of the most experienced proponent, Evelyn Wood, see "Should You

[3] Richard Graf, "Speed Reading: Remember the Tortoise," *Psychology Today*, 7, no. 7 (December 1973), 112–113.

Teach Speed Reading?".[4] But for greater persuasion read, in advertisements for the Evelyn Wood Reading Dynamics Institute, the testimonials of famous leaders who swear by the results. We have the word of experimental researchers against the word of people who have experienced and paid for the course. A couple of factors may explain this discrepancy, aside from the many tricky difficulties of measuring reading comprehension, which we will not get into. A key word in the quotation above is "dramatically." Usually, both the commercial courses and the researchers trying to judge their claims shoot for too large an increase in speed. It seems quite reasonable, in view of visual processing as we have just examined it, that more modest but very worthwhile gains would be quite realistic to expect without loss of comprehension. Second, Graf reported that a small minority in his study did make big gains without losing comprehension and speculated that these gainers may be brighter. So speed and comprehension are not inherently incompatible, at least not for some people.

It is not necessary to take sides in the controversy as the combatants have set it up. We know logically that visual processing *has* to be faster than auditory, we know that many people read faster than others without loss of comprehension, and we know that some of these faster readers say they increased efficiency by practicing certain techniques. If it is possible for people to read silently much faster than they can read aloud, then it makes sense to offer students a chance to learn to do this. Part of the deadlock over speed reading in schools is caused by the usual assumption that all kids would have to undertake it, whereas the more reasonable assumption is that only certain students would have enough motivation and enough of whatever else the gainers had in Graf's study to be successful. And even those for whom the techniques are right have to find their own time.

There is some reason to believe that fast readers go into a somewhat altered state of consciousness characterized by unusually strong focus, absorption, and self-surrender. Adepts may not be necessarily brighter but may command especially good coordination between the brain hemisphere that processes serially and analytically, associated with verbal learning, and the brain hemisphere that processes spatially and synthetically, associated with nonverbal learning. Thus the latter, ironically, would permit more rapid grasping of the ideas and images behind the collective words, in a happy marriage of the sequential and the simultaneous. Readiness for special practice in reading efficiency, then, probably goes beyond decoding proficiency to include strong motivation and concentration as well. The reader should no longer need to match print with voice, to subvocalize, but should be able to drop voice as an intermediary between print and ideas. He must practice until new habits are established, and he must go into a state in which linear detail can interplay closely with global perception and intuition.

We recommend that after the primary years you let students know of the possibility of increasing reading efficiency and make available directions for going about it (and that during the primary years you don't overfixate children on a fine focus!). The process is self-screening. Only students who want to and can will choose and stick with it. But you need to think of which students you might counsel to consider it, and if the process isn't supported well enough by you or by partners it may fall through unnecessarily. You might relay or adapt the following directions, preferably via activity cards or poster.

DIRECTIONS FOR READING FASTER [5]

The eye is quicker than the tongue. If you want to read faster, you want to quit reading at the rate you can *say* what's on the page and start reading at the rate you can *see* what's on the page. In the beginning, we all read to ourselves as if we were reading aloud, but if you have now become a fairly good reader, you can break old habits and make new ones—if you will practice enough.

You can practice alone, but the best way is to form a group with two or three others who want to read faster. Agree to meet at regular times and to practice a certain amount of time in between. You can help each other stick to the practice, talk over the techniques, and test each other on what you have just read.

It has been found that good readers read in "big chunks." They "take in" IDEAS, instead of reading "word for word."

[4] Christopher T. Cory, "Should You Teach Speed Reading?: A Talk With Evelyn Wood," *Learning,* 2, no. 7 (March 1974), 31–34.

[5] Adapted from *Interaction* activity cards "Reading Faster I" and "Reading Faster II."

Of course, you have to read at different speeds for different types of materials. Easy reading should go faster. Hard reading takes more time.

There are some habits that slow down your reading and keep you from reading for IDEAS.

Do you point to words with your finger? If so, this will slow you up.

Do you move your head from side to side when you read? If so, this will slow you up. Move your eyes instead.

Do your lips move as you read silently? Can you feel your throat moving when you read silently? If so, you are reading each word to yourself as though you were reading out loud.

Put your fingers on your lips or on your throat to try to stop them from moving. Again, only the *eyes* should move.

If you have been doing any of the above things, you have to practice until you get better reading habits in their place.

Read each of the sentences below. Which way do you like to read the best?

It is probably the way you have been reading.

1. You / might / have / developed / certain / reading / habits / when / you / were / young / and / did / not / know / what / you / were / doing / when / you / were / reading. /
2. You might / have developed / certain reading / habits / when you / were young / and did not / know / what you / were doing. /
3. You might have developed / certain reading habits / when you were young / and did not know / what you were doing / when you were reading. /

PRACTICE UNTIL YOU READ LIKE NUMBER 3.

If you are not reading like number 3, practice making *bigger* eye jumps and *fewer* eye jumps, as in number 3. Keep your head and tongue still, and flick your eyes in as long jumps as you can make and still grasp what you're reading.

It may help at first to get a book of your own, put in slash marks on some pages, as in number 3, and practice with those pages. Move your eyes from one slash group to the next. Then practice without slashes.

Always have someone test you on what you have read by asking questions on the book. There is no use reading fast if you do not understand what you read. The questions should be both fact questions and thinking questions.

Now, PRACTICE, PRACTICE, PRACTICE.

When you can read in the manner of number 3, advance to the next stage.

Time Yourself

How fast are you reading now? Choose a story or an article that a partner thinks will be easy for you to read. Using a watch with a second hand, time how long it takes you to read the piece you chose. Divide the number of words by the number of minutes it took you to read them. The result is your reading speed in words per minute. You can use this score to measure progress. BUT THERE IS NO USE INCREASING YOUR SPEED IF YOU DO NOT UNDERSTAND WHAT YOU HAVE READ.

Comprehension

Now have one of your partners ask questions about what you have read. He can look at the book and ask some factual questions and some thinking questions. If you get seven out of ten questions correct, okay. If you get fewer than seven correct, choose an easier story or article and begin again.

Now look at the [example below]. Key words or word clusters have been made to stand out. This shows how a fast reader might move his eyes so as not to waste time "reading" each word. He is reading *ideas*. His eyes travel rapidly down the page picking out *new information* and passing over more lightly what may be half-guessed from what the writer has already said. The fast reader gives first attention to words that tell him the most and uses other words to back up and fill in his understanding. The [following] bold and dim words illustrate this difference in attention.

Much work has been **done** to try to **find** out

whether parent **birds recognize** their own **eggs.** The **results vary** with the kind of bird. In a **series of tests** with **herring gulls,** it was shown that the **gulls could not distinguish** their own **eggs** from **other gull eggs.** If they were **presented** with brightly painted **wooden eggs,** the **gulls accepted** them as well as their **own.** Using the **wooden eggs, experiments** were **done to find** out whether **the size, the shape, or the color made** them acceptable to the gulls. The **important factor** was found to be the **round shape. The gulls always selected round models** in **preference** to **rectangular-shaped ones. Color** did **not matter** too much, except that **red** was **less attractive** than other colors. Also a **larger-sized egg stimulated** the gulls much **more** than a **small-sized one.**

Some birds will sit on anything if it is in the right place. **Even stones** and light **bulbs are accepted by** them. Yet there are certain birds, like the **Atlantic murres,** that **can distinguish** their own **eggs** from their neighbors'. These birds **lay** their **eggs** very **close together** on **rocky ledges. Eggs** of **three** different **birds sitting** near each other **were exchanged.** When the birds returned, **each rolled** its own **egg** back to its **original place.**

From Millicent E. Selsam, "Eggs," in *Animals as Parents,* William Morrow & Co., New York, 1965.

The best way to read faster is to break the habit of following each line one at a time from one margin to the other, like a typewriter, and to start sweeping your eyes down the page with only enough side-to-side movement to let you take in everything [see Figure 11.1].

Move your hand across and down the pages [as in Figure 11.2] as a guide and pacer for your eyes.

Now get a book and go through it page after page this way VERY FAST—faster than you can understand—until you have the knack of it. Practice this way on several occasions, still reading too fast, but gradually slow the pace down. Level off at the speed where you can just barely understand what you are reading. Practice at that speed.

Keep your speed always at a level that stretches you. Have others in your group question you on what you've read. Time yourself now and then to measure progress.

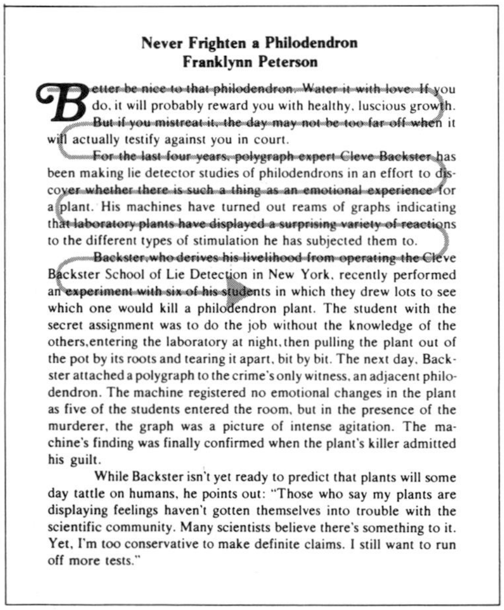

Never Frighten a Philodendron
Franklynn Peterson

Better be nice to that philodendron. Water it with love. If you do, it will probably reward you with healthy, luscious growth. But if you mistreat it, the day may not be too far off when it will actually testify against you in court.

For the last four years, polygraph expert Cleve Backster has been making lie detector studies of philodendrons in an effort to discover whether there is such a thing as an emotional experience for a plant. His machines have turned out reams of graphs indicating that laboratory plants have displayed a surprising variety of reactions to the different types of stimulation he has subjected them to.

Backster, who derives his livelihood from operating the Cleve Backster School of Lie Detection in New York, recently performed an experiment with six of his students in which they drew lots to see which one would kill a philodendron plant. The student with the secret assignment was to do the job without the knowledge of the others, entering the laboratory at night, then pulling the plant out of the pot by its roots and tearing it apart, bit by bit. The next day, Backster attached a polygraph to the crime's only witness, an adjacent philodendron. The machine registered no emotional changes in the plant as five of the students entered the room, but in the presence of the murderer, the graph was a picture of intense agitation. The machine's finding was finally confirmed when the plant's killer admitted his guilt.

While Backster isn't yet ready to predict that plants will some day tattle on humans, he points out: "Those who say my plants are displaying feelings haven't gotten themselves into trouble with the scientific community. Many scientists believe there's something to it. Yet, I'm too conservative to make definite claims. I still want to run off more tests."

FIGURE 11.1

Source: Adapted from *Interaction* activity cards "Reading Faster I" and "Reading Faster II."

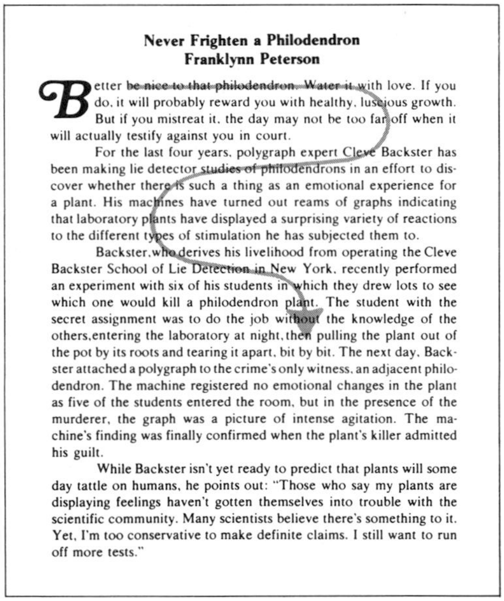

Never Frighten a Philodendron
Franklynn Peterson

Better be nice to that philodendron. Water it with love. If you do, it will probably reward you with healthy, luscious growth. But if you mistreat it, the day may not be too far off when it will actually testify against you in court.

For the last four years, polygraph expert Cleve Backster has been making lie detector studies of philodendrons in an effort to discover whether there is such a thing as an emotional experience for a plant. His machines have turned out reams of graphs indicating that laboratory plants have displayed a surprising variety of reactions to the different types of stimulation he has subjected them to.

Backster, who derives his livelihood from operating the Cleve Backster School of Lie Detection in New York, recently performed an experiment with six of his students in which they drew lots to see which one would kill a philodendron plant. The student with the secret assignment was to do the job without the knowledge of the others, entering the laboratory at night, then pulling the plant out of the pot by its roots and tearing it apart, bit by bit. The next day, Backster attached a polygraph to the crime's only witness, an adjacent philodendron. The machine registered no emotional changes in the plant as five of the students entered the room, but in the presence of the murderer, the graph was a picture of intense agitation. The machine's finding was finally confirmed when the plant's killer admitted his guilt.

While Backster isn't yet ready to predict that plants will some day tattle on humans, he points out: "Those who say my plants are displaying feelings haven't gotten themselves into trouble with the scientific community. Many scientists believe there's something to it. Yet, I'm too conservative to make definite claims. I still want to run off more tests."

FIGURE 11.2

Source: Adapted from *Interaction* activity cards "Reading Faster I" and "Reading Faster II."

Try more and more to use this method in your regular reading, at least when you can do it without feeling you're losing anything. Use this method only when it seems right—but use it.

Encoding

Encoding at the literacy level consists of handwriting, spelling, and punctuation—the transcribing skills. These are learned up to a point by means of the same practices and materials as for decoding, but here we need to add to those and to take the encoding point of view. We will deal first with activities unique to each of these skills, then with some activities that teach all three at once.

HANDWRITING

Children are generally taught first to print "manuscript" and then to do the flowing writing called "cursive." Like other aspects of literacy, the means of teaching handwriting vary according to whether you lead a class through it as a whole or individualize. It is reasonable to teach how to draw letters in the course of presenting the basic sound-spellings so that the drawing of the letters will be associated with the spelling and sounding of them. So in choosing the medium of presenting phonemes —cards, phonovisual machines, movies—you are to some extent choosing the means of presenting letters. Animation can be especially effective in showing letter formation and the relations among different letter shapes. The bulk of learning to write, however, consists of (1) discriminating and identifying the shapes by sight and touch, and (2) forming the shapes by muscular movement. Because vision and muscles have to be coordinated, this learning is often called sensorimotor, and all activities that develop perception and muscle control and coordination of the two will prepare for handwriting. In this way even games and crafts may further literacy.

Identifying Letters

It is very helpful to have three-dimensional letters* that children can manipulate, two-dimensional letters that they match and trace around, and perhaps also some rubber stamps* for practicing visual identification in an entertaining way. Two-dimensional letters can be made by tracing and cutting out of sturdy stock. On page 207 and following we recommend such materials and mention matching games to identify letter shapes.

These games can be played alone, or one player can select a letter from one set for his partner to match with a letter in the other set. Let children who know (or aides) teach the names of the letters to the others by naming the first letters of words in an alphabet book (see page 269) so that they will be learned in order and can also be sounded in the word they spell in the book.

Forming Letters

A good learning order is to *draw first some circular, rectilinear, and curving shapes* used in forming letters, then to *trace letters,* then to *copy letters* by looking back and forth. Another order is from *capital* manuscript letters to *small* manuscript letters, then from *manuscript* to *cursive.*

Activity Cards

Handwriting activities can be conveniently individualized on activity cards numbered sequentially. The learner traces shapes and letters with his finger; then, clipping tracing paper on top of the card, traces and draws the shapes and letters with crayon or pencil. Make or buy a set of cards bearing shapes, small and big printed letters, and cursive letters*. It will take around forty card sides to present shapes and letters and to provide adjacent space for copying. Allow for practice in connecting different cursive combinations. Printed parallel lines with a lighter parallel line between them helps distinguish small from capital letters. Tell the pupils to place their tracings in a folder so you can have a record of their progress. Cards should have a place calling for a student's name. Show and explain the cards to the whole class, provide a simple chart to allow them to break into the middle and find their right place, and make directions simple and pat, perhaps with the aid of pictograms to indicate drawing, tracing, and copying. One set of cards is enough for a class, since individuals will be using different cards at the same time or doing other activities.

Traditionally, the teacher draws the letters in front of the whole class and pupils imitate his strokes on paper at their desks, but this is poor procedure, because some children may already know how to draw at least some of the letters, some will need to go slower than others, and often the teacher's body position is confusing as he both draws on the board and talks to the class. It is far more efficient to use activity cards. Not only do they provide for tracing but a learner can simply skip letters he can form already, and he can do only as much with each new letter as he needs. Children can begin cursive any time they are ready, and the advanced will help teach the others. But don't push cursive. Consumable booklets are available in which children trace and copy as with activity cards, but these imply that each child should do all the pages, and booklets cost a lot more than cards and tracing paper, especially over a long period of time.

Manipulables

For variety children can also do the following:

- Trace around solid or cutout letters with pencil, if the letters are large enough, then color in the letters.
- Stamp out letters, then trace around the stamped silhouette with crayon or Magic Marker.
- Cut out traced letters (if cut in felt, they will stick to a felt board).

Other Media

Pleasure and multisensory learning will be increased by arranging for children to practice forming letters in finger paint, wet sand, and clay. Besides the models provided on the activity cards, you should have a large array of printed and cursive letters posted so that they can be seen from those places in the classroom where children would be forming letters with various materials. The chalkboard itself is fun for many children; let them use it a lot to practice on. Get colored chalk, and in one corner of the board paint three parallel lines to guide those who need them.

Above all, get children to write through the many means suggested in Chapter 8, Writing, and in Part Four, Developmental Reading, Speaking, and Writing. The recommendations here only help with the technical aspects. The real growth of handwriting comes through composition. Don't nag about handwriting. It will become more accurate as children try to read each other's work and as they practice constantly in real writing.

SPELLING

The two preceding chapters have been about spelling, for learning the basic correspondences between sounds and letters is learning to spell. Here we will simply narrow down to the uniqueness of spelling, treated alone for a moment.

A good half-dozen ways exist to improve spelling, beyond the literacy base already described:

- Prolific writing practice
- Prolific reading
- Self-diagnosis
- Proofreading
- Spelling games
- Special books

Spelling Through Writing

Because they are so broad, it is hard to convey how it is that plentiful and continuous experience in reading and writing teaches spelling very powerfully without special effort. It seems too easy. But by plaguing students too much with isolated small skills, schools prevent them from logging the quantity of reading and writing it takes to show how the big things automatically teach the little.

The main thing is for the writer to plunge ahead with what he has to say and make educated guesses on spelling without fear of penalties for errors. Spelling improves with constant trying, but kids who write a lot and with pleasure will make many mistakes for the simple reason that they dare to try to spell any word they can say. But if they are made to feel that spelling errors are shameful, they will not attempt enough writing to practice as much as they need. Whether composing or transcribing, the continual groping to put words onto paper causes students eventually to find out how those words are spelled —to generalize, to memorize, to ask others, to consult the dictionary, and so on. The conditions for success are that they care about what they are saying and that they not feel penalized for misspelling what they are trying to say. The value of dictionaries is slight if students have few occasions to write their own sentences, or if papers go nowhere but to the teacher's desk. But if they care, they will look up the first letter or so, the easiest to spell, then guess two or three alternatives for the next letter until they find the right one, then look nearby to find the word. You want to so involve youngsters in pushing from speech to print that *they* take the initiative to spell out what they have to say.

Spelling Through Reading

The visual memory of words seen repeatedly in reading helps to standardize student spelling perhaps more than anything else besides basic literacy training itself. Plentiful reading not only provides the quantity needed from which to generalize the regularities of spelling and to notice minor patterns but it also provides many occasions to visualize *irregular* words and eventually to memorize them. When most people are unsure how to spell a word, they write it down and look at it, to compare the sight of it now with the sight of it on other occasions and so to see if it "looks right." Locking the overall look of a word into visual memory seems to have a role in successful spelling comparable to the great role of auditory discrimination in word attack. Reading while also *listening* to the text fastens words in memory doubly well, because hearing a good vocal rendering of words reinforces the sight of them, especially if the oral reading is vivid and hence *memorable.* Clearly, the language-experience approach and the lap method can set up very powerful spelling momentum. Solo writing and reading can carry these to fruition.

Self-Diagnosis

The most effective single thing you can do to help a student improve his spelling is to show him how to diagnose and correct his own spelling errors. This process is equivalent to tutoring in decoding, and you might sometimes combine both in a private session or at any rate use what you learn from your analysis of a student's sight-reading to diagnose his spelling problems. Keep in mind, however, that you want to turn over to him the diagnosis. Show him how to classify his errors so as to reduce them to a few *kinds,* each of which has its own corrective action.

The procedure is to circle or list some of a student's errors as you are going through his writing folder and classify them according to categories given below. Self-diagnosis can be done by learners of any age, at their own level of development, and is far superior to formal spelling programs that take every learner on a tour of every kind of mistake.

Besides being boring and time-consuming, speller series are extremely inefficient, because their shotgun approach does not aim at just what each student needs. Such an approach is just an institutional symptom. Any given student makes only certain errors. He should not waste time surveying the whole field but should zero in on his own particular difficulties. It has often been argued that the study-test approach with word lists teaches spelling effectively if boringly. For one thing, many educators challenge this claim that it is effective. Also, if the amount of time spent studying and taking tests on word lists were spent reading and writing while getting pertinent and timely tips from the teacher on individual difficulties, it would be seen that word lists do not compare favorably for spelling efficacy and, in addition, take time away from reaching the true goals of reading and writing.

Self-diagnosis furthers these main goals and takes little time for each student. You need only go over spelling errors once in a while and not at all for some students. The more successful you are at transferring the diagnosis to students, the less time anyone will spend. The sight-word learning involved in memorizing word lists can obviously take place from seeing words over and over while reading silently, from reading while listening, from watching others write down one's dictation, and from writing down words for which the spelling is given by the dictionary or other people. These are more interesting and memorable ways of doing the visualization that is supposed to be the strong point of memorizing miscellaneous words.

Classifying Mistakes

Let's take some errors from an actual piece of student writing:

ferther	stoping	srill
fawsett	cloged	kichtion
turpintine		

"Ferther," "fawsett," and "turpintine" are all logical errors based in fact on this student's understanding of sound-letter correspondences. For example, *er* and *ur* are both possible spellings for the sound; to be wrong with "ferther" and right with "turpintine" is a matter that can be corrected simply by memorizing the troublesome parts of the words, for nothing else can tell him which alternate spelling to use when the sound is in that position. The same is true regarding the *aw* and the *s* in "faw-sett," which are alternates in English for *au* and *c,* given the position. Unstressed *in* and *en* ("turpin-tine") are also logical alternates.

But doubling the consonant after a short vowel and before the verb ("stoping" and "cloged") is a regularity of English spelling that if grasped can spare the student from making such errors. For this no memorization is needed, only a generalization.

"Srill" seems to belong to a third category of er-ror, faulty pronunciation, since the student seems to write pretty phonetically. You should ask him to pro-nounce the word, in order to check this hunch; then you would pronounce the word so as to bring out *sh.* "Kichtion" could be a phonetic spelling—*kich* plus the *tion* of *nation*—but might involve some mispro-nunciation too, so you should hear the student say it.

Sampling typical misspellings gives us three main categories of errors, to which we will add a fourth, the reversal of letters.

Some misspellers have a tendency to reverse let-ters or otherwise juggle them out of order. This kind of crossing of wires may not betray an ignorance of phonetic knowledge either, being usually a neural condition, but it may interfere with such knowledge or make it hard to acquire. Most likely, you will never know for certain why a child who reverses does so. (Finding out whether a child also reverses numerals, however, might shed light on his problem.) Whatever the cause, your method of helping will be the same —to counsel the student to work with materials that especially focus on letter order. Multisensory se-quencing helps uncross the wires and to reinforce correct visual memory. See the following section on "Counseling."

Counseling

Each learner grasps or fails to grasp different as-pects of spelling. Help each know what he knows and what he doesn't know. Encourage youngsters to call on all sources of help but also to learn to diag-nose their own kinds of mistakes.

If a student misspells unphonetically, you will need to clump together for him those of his mis-spellings that are alike, so that he can grasp the phonetic "rule" he is ignoring. For example, sup-pose in looking over a youngster's writing folder, or in observing him play spelling games, you notice that he doesn't seem to know that adding a mute *e* usually makes the preceding vowel long (*mad—made*) or that the *k* sound in the final stressed posi-tion is spelled with a *ck* (*kick*). A little thought can reduce a discouraging quantity of misspellings to a very few manageable remedies. Point out the words he misspelled for the same reason and suggest a certain letter-moving device to make or to play with that will teach the rule or make it memorable. Show him how to clump together himself those errors that are of the same type in the sense that they could all be corrected from knowing the same phonetic generalization.

If he misspells *phonetically,* however ("bleek" for "bleak"), he is at least misspelling logically by well-educated guesses. You should tell him just that (so he will distinguish and take credit for a superior form of error) and add that all he can do to improve in such cases is to memorize the one phonetic variant—"bleak"—that happens to be correct. That is, he is right by the system but wrong by conven-tion. The value of the system, however, even with a highly irregular language like English, is that it re-duces possible spellings from virtual infinity to a couple or a handful of real possibilities, one of which is right. It is better, for example, to memorize one out of two to four possibilities for a word than one out of chaos. Phonetic knowledge narrows down the field that the mind must select from and, in the process, allows logic to aid memory. It may help some youngsters to convey this notion to them.

A learner may *seem* to misspell some words un-phonetically, not necessarily because he does not know the relevant phonetic facts but because he does not *pronounce* those words conventionally, at least not in conformity to standard pronunciation upon which correspondences are based. Demon-strate the standard pronunciation and explain that the spelling conforms to it: for example, "pen" rather than "pin," "hold" rather than "holt." When someone writes "correck," for example, ask him to pronounce the word and check whether his spelling *is* right, at least according to how *he* says it. Then tell him the word is spelled "correct" because many people say it this way (pronouncing the *t* clearly). The same for "he go," which is usually not a mis-spelling or a grammatical mistake but an accurate transcription of the writer's pronunciation of a dia-lect in which some *s*'s are not sounded. The learner has to know when his pronunciation is causing him to mispell, whether from being nonstandard or from being merely confused. Younger children especially just may not have the sound of a word straightened out yet. In either case, sound the word according to how it is spelled and connect the spelling to that pronunciation, but do not make the learner feel wrong for pronouncing the word as he was taught at home. All he needs is some help in making that mental adjustment between his dialect and the standard one. You will no doubt have to help establish this equivalence in particular cases—allowing for possible deviations in your own pronunciation!

Generally, when learning a spelling regularity seems to be indicated, counsel students to look at a certain part of the audiovisual presentation, play with certain word games from the last chapter, make or work with a certain letter-moving device. Sometimes you might state a generalization or strategy if you think a student can benefit from it.

Since vowels cause most misspellings, it may be helpful to have in mind a general strategy for attacking them. The short vowels are spelled with remarkable consistency. A student does not have to understand the term *short vowel* so long as he at least associates those sounds together as a group.

If you hear a short vowel, spell it with its own letter alone, but note these small patterns of exception:

built	death	double	flood	gyp
guilt	breath	couple	blood	crypt
build	health	rough		rhythm
guild	wealth	tough		hieroglyph

When short vowels depart from this rule, it is because of the influence of certain neighboring consonants. By noticing the consonants between which these spellings lie, students can learn these small but important patterns of exception and also learn to look for others. Short vowel sounds virtually never occur at the ends of English words, and position does not affect short-vowel spelling very much.

To determine the spelling of a vowel other than short, you have to notice, first, what comes after the vowel—another syllable, a consonant, or nothing; then second, in some cases, which *consonant comes after; then third, possibly,* which *consonant comes before.* (basis, mail, way) (medium, relief, spree)

This is a key strategy. Since *position* of letters symbolizes sound as much as do the letters themselves, students need somehow to become aware that vowel sounding and hence spelling are determined by what follows them and, sometimes, secondarily within that framework, what precedes them.

Some words don't follow even any minor spelling patterns (*women, colonel, people*), at least regard-

ing some key sound, and there is nothing for it but to memorize them as single words. It helps students to know that such words exist and that sheer memorization is all that can correct misspelling of such words.

By summarizing and placing in an order of elimination, overall strategy can be stated like this:

1. Compare pronunciation with standard to detect differences.
2. Practice sequencing letters if needed.
3. Learn what the phonetic system can help with.
4. Memorize what it cannot help with.

That is, becoming aware first of dialectical differences or personal disarrangment provides a framework within which a student can zero in on spelling difficulties that all people face in common—generalizing the phonetic regularities and ascertaining which spellings are systematic and which have to be memorized.

Further suggestions to the teacher for counseling on spelling are implied in the following directions to the student, which we offer both as guidelines you may find useful in tutoring and as an example of how diagnosis and correction may be placed in the hands of the learner.

Self-Correcting Spelling

Below are directions to the student for going about self-correction with a partner or so.[6] Adapt these directions to the understanding of your own students, and help them find appropriate partners. Use page 210 and following to guide students in using and making letter-moving devices. Encourage them to brainstorm together for words of the same pattern and then to try out their pattern on a device. If they associate their word lists with these games, students will be better motivated to write error lists and think up supplemental words for them.

The best way to learn to spell is to read a lot. Most people seem to go by the *look* of a word when they are trying to spell it. So give your eye memory lots of chances to see how words look. Seeing the same spellings over and over again will fix them in the mind.

Writing a lot helps very much also, because when you write you practice spelling. Never be

---

[6] These directions are adapted from the *Interaction* activity cards "Do-It-Yourself Spelling."

afraid of *mis*spelling. Always try and make a good guess. This card will give you some ideas about how to make "educated guesses."

English spelling makes more sense than you might think at first, and there is a lot you can do to stop making mistakes. Some of it you might do alone, but the best thing is to get together with a partner who also wants to get better at spelling.

There are only a few reasons for spelling errors. Find out why *you* misspell. Everybody knows you should spell a word the way it sounds. But you can do that and still make an error. Following are some things that might go wrong and what you can do about them.

1. You may misspell a word because the correct spelling fits one way of saying the word but you say it another.

Suppose you say and spell "whup," whereas the correct spelling and pronunciation is "whip." Some people don't sound out *t*'s, for example, and so don't spell them; they write "wanning" for "wanting." Many people don't sound out the endings for words and so don't spell those either; they write "he go" for "he goes" or "three boy" for "three boys."

Ask other people, including your teacher, to say a word. Listen to find out if they say it differently than you do. Which fits the spelling better? No way is wrong, but some ways are harder to spell. Listen to different ways that people say words on the recordings in the listening library.

2. You may misspell a word even though you write down the correct letters if you write them down out of order.

That is, you may juggle or reverse a couple of letters ("retrop" for "report," "snigle" for "single," or "feats" for "feast"). Compare your spelling with the right spelling to see if you do this. Try to say the word the way you spelled it. Ask your partner and perhaps others to try to say it as you spelled it too.

If you often write the right letters in the wrong order, you might be able to master the right order by doing crossword puzzles and by playing other games where you can put letters in order or move them around. Play "Tap and Say," tic-tac-toe, Scrabble-type games, and games with solid or cutout letters and rubber stamps, letter-dice, and letter-moving devices.

3. You may misspell a word even though you spell it the way it sounds, because in English many sounds can be spelled more than one way.

Most spelling errors are of this kind. For example, there are three ways to spell the *n* sound at the beginning of a word—"nash," "knash," or "gnash." Only the last one ("gnash") is correct if you're talking about someone who's grinding his teeth. If you know what the three ways are, at least you can make a good guess then check it later.

And if you look for *pattern*s in spelling you can often see clues about *which* spelling is correct. (One pattern holds for "furry," "silly," "petty," and so on.)

Here is another useful way to figure out which spelling of a sound is correct.

Suppose you are trying to decide if the spelling is:

adiration	aderation
adoration	
aduration	adaration

Think of that word in another form—"adore."

Which of the following words is correctly spelled—"decluration," "admeration," "inspiration"? Think of these words in another form.

When the vowels (*a, e, i, o, u*) don't get stressed in a word—like the *i* in PRES-i-dent—they all tend to sound alike. Read aloud, for example, some of the following words and ask your partner to try to spell them *without looking at this list*. Then trade off for the rest of the list:

president	comparable
democratic	composition
precedent	history

janitor	illustrate	consolation
manager	industry	abolition
major	immigrate	competent

Now find in the following list another form for each word you just read.

preside	compare	comparison
democracy	compose	composer
precede	historical	historian

janitorial	illustrative	console
managerial	industrial	abolish
majority	migrate	compete

These other forms of the word *stress* the vowel and *bring out* its sound so that you can *hear* how to spell it.

Which spelling would you choose for each of these words?

critisize	gradual	nashun
criticize	grajual	nation
	gradjual	

rashul	ritechus	medicine
racial	reitchus	medisine
ratial	righteous	
	righcheous	
	richeous	

Check your choices against these forms of the words:

critical   grade   native   race   right   medical

So learning families of related words can help. Suppose, for another example, that you write "sine" for "sign." You didn't hear the *g*, so you didn't spell it. But if you know related words like "signal" or "signature," where you can hear the *g*, that helps you to remember it in "sign." Sometimes when English words aren't spelled as they sound, it's because the spelling is used to show family relationship instead of sound.[7]

Can you use that trick with these words— "muscle," "bomb," "soften," "condemn"?

Which letters are silent? If you can't think of related words in which these letters are *not* silent, ask other people or look in the dictionary.

[7] This point has been well developed by Carol Chomsky in an article from which we have drawn some of the words used as examples: Carol Chomsky, "Reading, Writing and Phonology," *Harvard Educational Review,* 40 (May 1970), 287–309.

In fact, ask or look any time you think a word might have another form or might belong to a word family. In the dictionary *declare* and *declaration* are placed close together. If you find one and look around nearby, you can see the other.

Sometimes the spelling depends on the meaning—*meet* or *meat, sole* or *soul.*

Many jokes and puns are based on words that sound alike but are spelled differently (homophones): "The little pig thought his father was a boar." [See page 251.] People sometimes confuse correctly spelled words that don't sound exactly the same but sound close, like *affect* and *effect.* Notice if some of your mistakes are mix-ups like this. If so, use the meaning to help you remember the spelling.

Many words are made by combining a root word with common forms that are stuck onto the front or end of a word.

These are called prefixes and suffixes. We can use these words themselves for examples: *pre* is a common combining form meaning "before," and *suf* another meaning "after." The root word is *fix,* or "fasten." *Prefix* has one *f* and *suffix* has two because both *suf* and *fix* already have an *f.* Or take the word *misspell* itself—one of the words most frequently misspelled! People wonder if it should have one or two *s*'s. Don't wonder. It has one for the prefix *mis* (meaning "wrong") and another *s* for the root word *spell.* So—two *s*'s: *misspell.*

Try to notice these front and end forms and how they are spelled. Then when you spell the many words made with them, you'll avoid a lot of errors.

Spellings fall into patterns that you can see if you look at lists of similar words. These patterns can help you remember some spellings. Get familiar with spelling patterns as you read and write. Knowing one part of the spelling of a word will often help you remember or figure out which spelling is right for another part.

Useful things to do with a partner:

• You and your partner look through your writing folders and other written work for misspelled words. Help each other collect these in a spelling notebook for each of you.

- You can write your trouble words down in useful groups. Reserve a few pages for each kind of spelling error or spelling pattern. Think of as many words together as you can that follow the pattern of one of your words when correctly spelled. You can use these lists to play letter-moving games with.
- Trade trouble words with each other when your partner's words would be useful to include in your notebook. Can you guess which reserved page your partner is putting a word on? Do you agree? Ask others for help when you can't agree which problem or pattern a word should go under.
- Make up funny sentences by putting as many trouble words in a sentence as you can. Have your partner read these aloud to you as you write them down.
- Ask your partner to read your misspelled words aloud so you can write them into your notebook. Try to spell them the right way from memory or by using some clues. Check if you're right. Turn about with your partner.
- Take some of your words listed by pattern or kind of mistake and ask your teacher to help you make a letter-moving device for it [page 210] or to find and use one someone else has made. You can turn your word lists into games that are fun to play and that will also help you to spell better.

Finally, some words just have to be memorized. Again, this is where lots of reading will help you.

Proofreading

Some investigators of spelling errors have reported that at least half of student mistakes are with words they know how to spell. Most experienced teachers have probably come to realize that they could waste a lot of time correcting errors on student papers only to have them say that those were just "careless mistakes." Slips of eye and hand do account for a very large part of what teachers too often assume are errors of ignorance. The point is that processes of proofreading should go on among students, who can point out errors to each other in the writing groups when they exchange papers. Proofreading in groups teaches each individual to proofread alone. Peers often know a word is wrong even if

they don't know how to spell it, and even if they occasionally give each other wrong spellings. In the long run everyone still comes out well ahead because group proofreading pools the spelling knowledge of different individuals at the same time that it calls to a writer's attention his careless mistakes with words he really knows. You should not be a proofreader. Direct students to do this as a routine part of writing workshops, and encourage them to look up words none of the group knows how to spell. What makes proofreading really work is the antipation of doing something interesting with the writing after it has been improved.

Special Games and Books

A number of well-known spelling games may help some youngsters focus precisely on letters and letter order in an entertaining way. "Hangman" (known by other names also) is the prototype of the spelling game based on guessing letter by letter a word that one player has in mind. The idea of such games is usually to guess all the letters, writing them down, before a certain limit runs out. In "Ghost" players try to keep adding letters to an ongoing spelling without being the one who brings some word to an end. A good game for segmenting and sequencing letters into words calls for massing many letters into a block then trying to find as many words as possible in the block by reading letters in various directions. Spelling bees are all right for spellers of the same level, but it would be better for students to write their spellings instead of spelling orally, as is the custom, because spelling aims at writing, after all, and visual memory is what counts most.

Crossword Puzzles

Printing in the letters of the words in a crossword puzzle, a letter per box, enforces spelling precision and gets at any tendency to reverse or juggle letters. Checking takes place automatically, for if each box is not correctly filled, efforts to put other letters in later will reveal the error. Weak spellers can work together and pool their spelling capacity. Looking up the spelling of words in the dictionary becomes natural as an adjunct of the sport. Crossword puzzles represent a fine combination of attractiveness and effectiveness.

Encourage students to look for crossword puzzles in magazines and newspapers and to bring them to class; but since many of these may be too hard, especially for elementary children, you may need to buy some consumable booklets of puzzles made for school use*. See also pages 251–253.

Making Dictionaries

Another activity valuable and pleasurable for spelling precision is making one's own specialized dictionary for a certain lingo or subject-matter vocabulary (described fully on page 377). It motivates students to find out exactly how the words they want to include are spelled and to become involved in the more technical ways that dictionaries treat the sounds and spellings of words. They learn, for example, the way standard dictionaries indicate how a word is pronounced, stressed, syllabified, and changed before certain endings. At its greatest depth, making dictionaries engages students with etymology and hence the historical determinants of spellings.

General

Although further maturation will not, as we said of literacy generally, advance spelling *capacity* beyond the primary years, there are some important reasons why spelling has to improve slowly after literacy has been accomplished. If English had an isomorphic alphabet, as soon as a child became literate he could spell any word at all. But an English-speaking learner will only gradually learn irregular and alternative spellings, that is, *conventionalize* his spelling, because grasping the basic system isn't enough when the system is so imperfect. A lot of small generalizations and a lot of ungeneralizeable spellings place a heavy burden on memory and offset the learner's main asset—his logical ability to summarize data.

Time and experience are in favor of the learner, however, because the more words he encounters, and the more differences in words he encounters, the more grist he has for his classifying mill, the more he can generalize patterns and memorize the ungeneralizeable, and the more he can categorize his errors as we have suggested. The fact is that sheer volume of language experience—oral and written—is the best teacher of spelling. This is not a debonair view. The human brain is made to produce just such generalizations as the spelling rules, but the data of English is so confusing that teachers must be patient about the final conventionalizing of student spelling while at the same time making possible the massive experience in hearing, saying, seeing, and writing words that refines spelling until the irregularities and alternatives have been memorized. Teachers do not usually value enough the logical (phonetic) sort of misspellings. A student who writes "fawset" for "faucet" has accomplished the major, thoughtful part; now all he can do is memorize which alternative spelling happens to be right in this case. Seeing the word more will do the trick, so let him read a lot. Auditory and visual perception, the generalization of patterns, the memorization of irregularities—all will be learned from total language saturation.

The research of Charles Read [8] has shown that preschool children will invent, for fun only, their own spellings of their speech from nothing but the alphabet and knowing nothing about how adults use digraphs and position to symbolize phonemes. Their invented spelling is logical and consistent enough that one can codify rules from samples of it, as Read did. These children later adopt standard spelling with no difficulty and may even have an edge on other children. At any rate, they not only learn to read more easily than most children but seem to teach themselves. They are used to working out a system on their own and then modifying that system to fit the conventions of the rest of the world.

So encourage phonetic rendering as the great base of spelling and count on massive reading and writing experience to conventionalize spelling away from phonetic writing when phonetic writing differs from convention. Only within the frame of phonetic regularity can all the adjustment be made. The belief that a formal, explicit spelling course is needed stems from the failure of schools to enable learners to get this massive experience, and the more that such programs take time away from reading and writing, the more they fulfill their own prophecy that spelling requires special, continual instruction! Allow learners to see and use the data of English spelling and they will master it with no more direct instruction, beyond the literacy program itself, than the sorts we have described here.

PUNCTUATION

Punctuation is like spelling in that it translates speech to print. Learning punctuation also involves perceptual pairing and applies equally to reading

---

[8] Reported in Carol Chomsky, "Write First, Read Later," *Childhood Education* 47, no. 6 (March 1971), 296–299. See also Charles Read's monograph "Children's Categorization of Speech Sounds in English," *Research Report* 17, (1975), National Council of Teachers of English.

and writing. As with sound-letter relations, the task is to match some graphic symbols with some voice qualities—in this case, some things like commas and periods with some other things like pitch and pause. It helps to think of two kinds of punctuation, oral and written. Preschool children and illiterate adults can talk all day and have no punctuation problems, because the voice indicates the segments of speech in meaningful ways. The issue of writing punctuation is how to transcribe certain significant voice qualities such as stress, pitch, and juncture (the interaction of which we will call somewhat inaccurately but conveniently "intonation"). The issue of reading punctuation is how to translate commas and periods back into voice qualities.

Learning Punctuation by Vocal Intonation

Punctuation is not part of grammar. It may reflect grammar, but only because intonation does. Above all, good punctuation is a set of signals showing the reader how to read the flow of words as the speaker would say them. It should be presented to learners in this way, not as rules. The auditory principles that underlie the rules are simpler to understand, more profound, and more accurate. All the rules do is overgeneralize the relations among sense, syntax, and sound. "Separate clauses by commas" merely echoes the fact that a partial drop in intonation, together perhaps with a pause, *usually* separates them. The rule is inaccurate because it is rigid. Educated writers often do not separate clauses with a comma if the clauses are short and if no ambiguity results. What the rule describes is not always true of what we do, and what the rule prescribes is not always indicative of what we should do. What we should do is punctuate with pencil as we do with voice. And that is a simpler principle to follow.

Moreover, to understand the old rules you have to understand first a whole body of grammatical terminology like *restrictive clause* or *appositive,* and even if one understands all this, it isn't sufficient because grammar alone does not determine punctuation. The factors of meaning and rhetoric also come into play. Much punctuation renders tone and emphasis.

The simplest way to accommodate all the real facts of punctuating that fuse together in verbal expression is to heed and imitate the vocal intonation whereby we intuitively render grammar, sense, and rhetoric all at once. Most punctuation can be heard, certainly the basic kinds. Indeed, if most punctuation could not be heard, print would not be very effective or expressive. Print tries to reproduce the voice with various devices, such as paragraphing, capitalization, italics, and punctuation marks. Only whole sentences reveal intonation (and sometimes even a larger context is needed). This is why, of the four main literacy approaches, only the language-experience approach and the lap method can teach punctuation.

The chief hurdle to punctuating well is not being aware of what one hears. Children hear and produce intonation with ease—in fact, with such ease that they are almost totally unconscious of what they are hearing and producing. The features of intonation are especially important cues to meaning when one's vocabulary is limited. Even when he does not understand the words, the child can tell from vocal cues much of an adult's meaning and intention. It is fair to say that children are at least as responsive to intonation as adults, probably more so. But in order to punctuate with periods and commas as they punctuate orally, youngsters will have to raise their intuition to the level of awareness.

Let's put it all this way. Except for questions and exclamations, which are obvious, a drop of the intonation contour almost unfailingly calls for a punctuation mark. The issue is which one—comma, dash, semicolon, colon, or period? Even if he chooses unwisely, a learner who puts *some* mark of punctuation there has fulfilled the first principle of punctuation—to segment the flow of speech. Whether a comma or a period is called for depends on the length of pause and on whether the intonation drops merely to a lower point, somewhat suspended, or all the way to the bottom for a distinct closure. (Read this last sentence aloud.) A true comma splice would occur only when a full drop was mistaken for a half drop; a period after a sentence fragment would occur when a half drop was mistaken for a full.

It is true that some of the more sophisticated usages governed by logic are not necessarily audible. One cannot always hear, for example, when two sentences are joined by a semicolon or colon and when they are separated by a period. And one would be hard put sometimes to distinguish by ear alone a colon from a semicolon or a comma from a dash, or a series of commas from a series of semicolons. Even here, however, rules do not help, for in such cases a writer usually has an option as to which mark to use.

Another kind of logical punctuation that may or may not be audible is internal punctuation of individual words—apostrophes and hyphens. There is no way to hear the apostrophe of possession and contraction. It must be explained through instances and demonstrated through transformations. Hyphenation, however, can almost always be heard, because pitch is sustained through a compound word. Compare: "He entered the second grade" and "He entered the second-grade classroom." Or compare: "He counted three, toed sloths" with "He counted three-toed sloths."

Sequencing

In the name of "scope and sequence" too much has been made of order in learning to punctuate. Comma usages have been parceled out over many years of schooling, whereas any learner allowed to read and write as much as he should will encounter or need to use many different kinds of punctuation fairly early and all at once. Let a student's reading and writing capacity automatically program the punctuation. The sentence structures he can handle in these activities will determine how many comma usages he needs to know. Overcontrolled reading material tends to hold back punctuation, because of the avoidance of "difficult" sentence structures. Individualizing is the only way to be sure of not holding someone back.

It is helpful, however, for you to recognize three rough stages of punctuating, related to sentence structure:

1. Full stops—periods, question marks, exclamation marks. These all do the basic segmenting of the speech flow into sentences. They may as well all be learned at once, because they can all be used with no other punctuation in the same simple sentences. Included here are capitals for sentence beginnings and names, hyphens for compound words, and apostrophes for contractions and possessives.
2. Internal punctuation—commas and dashes. This includes series, relative clauses, appositives, direct address, and all other comma usage that segments or sets off parts within a sentence. Dashes are just emphatic commas, indicated vocally by heavier stress and/or longer pause.
3. Semicolons and colons—the connectors between sentences, that is, between independent clauses that *could* be separate sentences. These are the logical, hard-to-hear punctuation marks.

The marks for dialogue—quotation marks, suspension points, dashes for interruption, italics for stress—can be learned any time and depend on when the learner has first contact with quoted speech.

This rough breakdown is enough to help you gauge general sophistication and to judge sequencing in materials you might make or buy. Obviously, comma usages are many and sometimes subtle, optional, and inaudible, but it is better not to worry about ranging these in order. Instead, help students develop the perception about sound, sense, and syntax in various usages as they see them in reading or need them in writing. The following practices are meant to accomplish this.

Presenting Punctuation

Because it requires whole sentences, punctuation is particularly hard to isolate. How can students first find out what the marks are and how they are used? The traditional way, which we reject, is to program usages as rules to be memorized in grammatical terms. The presentation that really works is reading. Children first become acquainted with the shapes and usages of punctuation marks from seeing them repeatedly in the same sorts of situations in texts. Often, in fact, the rules contradict or omit some of these situations. At any rate, you cannot present punctuation marks separately, one at a time, as you can phonemes, and since whole sentences are necessary anyway to indicate when the marks are used, you may as well just work the learning of punctuation into the reading and writing practice, where, in addition, it can be connected with voice.

Listening While Reading

We have here, then, a strong argument for much experience with the lap method of reading while listening and for the language-experience approach, both of which show and sound punctuation at once. Following the text while listening to a good reader sound the intonation allows the learner to associate periods, capitals, question marks, and exclamation marks with the stopping and starting of sentences, and he can hear the differences among declarative, interrogative, and exclamatory intonations. He can hear and see simultaneously the pause-and-half-drops of commas and dashes, the change of personal voice indicated by quotation marks, and so on.

Recordings are a great help. Just listening to them a lot while following the texts will help students of all ages link voice with punctuation. This is one of those kinds of learning that sounds almost too simple but still provides impressive results if done often enough. Professional reading brings out memorably the purposes of punctuation.

Dictating While Watching

Watching a scribe write down one's dictation is one fine way to become aware that speech emits more than word sounds and that these extra things—the intonation—have to be symbolized on paper just as much as the word sounds. See page 204.

Transformations and Contrasts

On page 200 we give an example of a series transformation done in film animation. Please look back at that. For another example:

> "We caught a glimpse of Oswald Pickering, who is the hero of the Underground."
> "We caught a glimpse of Oswald Pickering, the hero of the Underground."

This shows clearly that an appositive is an abridgment of a relative clause, or that any appositive could be expanded into a relative clause. But the grammatical terms are not at all needed in presenting this to students and will only make it harder for them to get the chief point, which is that the two constructions share a kinship in sentence function —to give incidental information that is indicated by their being set off both in speech and in print. Such a transformation brings sense to bear on sound to reinforce and make more explicit the intuition behind oral punctuation. Incidental information or thought—whether set off as it is here between two dashes, or whether put between parentheses, or whether cast as a relative clause or appositive—is among the easiest cases of punctuation to hear. Transformation may be the only really good way to deal directly with contractions (*can not → can't, we would → we'd, it is → it's*).

On page 199 we give an example of contrasts between finished and unfinished sentences, and on page 197 an example of the same word string punctuated as two different sentences. Transformation is only a more particular kind of contrasting, and contrasts are probably the most effective way to raise oral punctuation to awareness and associate it with appropriate written marks. Film animation is certainly the most effective medium for contrast, since the viewer can hear a sentence vocalized one way, then watch it change before his eyes and hear it vocalized the second way.[9] But you and your students can transform and contrast also. Follow the same principle with intonation as with other speech sounds: change something in the print and show how that changes the speech, or change something in the speech and show how that changes the print. (See punctuation games, page 243.) If you make or choose the materials to use in some kind of audio-visual presentation of the sound-spellings, include punctuation in those visuals that show whole sentences, and perhaps make some special visuals for punctuation.

Teacher Examples and Explanation

As a supplement to other means we will describe, you might do a standup presentation, once or twice only, if you have many students that you feel will learn from a bit of lecture-demonstration.

Contrasting In the first place, explain that when we talk, our voices rise and fall, pause and go on, lean hard on some words and lightly on others. Illustrate: "He likes candy," and "He likes candy?" Which is the question? How can they tell? Then say, " 'At night I sleep.' That is a sentence. My voice rounds it off and you can tell it is finished. This is a sentence too: 'Get your clothes.' And so is this: 'What did you eat?' Now, suppose I say, 'At night I sleep—' Is that finished? Why not? The whole sentence is 'At night I sleep in my bed.' " Go on to pair off "Get your clothes—" with "Get your clothes off the bed," and "When did you eat—?" with "When did you eat the pie?" Make up other finished and unfinished sentences and ask them which is which. Then they can make up some pairs.

Relate speech to print by saying, "But there is no voice in a book. How are we going to know how to read the words the way the person would say them? When we write, how can we let our reader know where our sentences begin and end?" This is the

---

[9] The *Interaction* "Sound Out" films show and sound punctuation throughout but focus exclusively on it in the last two cassettes.

place to illustrate the use of periods, capitals, and question marks. Later, commas are introduced the same way.

Contrasts can get across many kinds of punctuation. For example, write an ambiguous sentence—"They saw many-colored butterflies"—and ask someone to read it aloud. Can it be read another way? How would you show the difference to a reader? Ask them for examples of other compound words, remarking that two words that are compounded in one sentence may not be in another. After they are sensitized to the audible difference, make a statement to the effect that just as your voice joins the two words in speech, so the hyphen joins them in print. Some capitalized words can also be distinguished by ear: "I live in the white house," and "I live in the White House."

Defining a Sentence Defining a sentence as a complete thought is futile; not only children but linguists and philosophers as well do not understand what a complete thought is. It could be a word, a phrase, a sentence, a paragraph, or an entire book. The only way a sentence can be defined is by vocal segmentation, the sense of closure conveyed by a complete intonation contour (which of course expresses the intuition of syntactic completion). Children know a sentence when they hear one, and this operational definition is what teachers should utilize. Often a student mistakenly puts a period and capital in the middle of a sentence even though he would read the sentence correctly. This results, I believe, from being confused by directions about how to punctuate. But the more common mistake is the failure to segment the word flow at all, a failure that frequently persists—needlessly—into junior and senior high school, causing dreary hours of proofreading by a long chain of teachers. The problem is not that difficult. That it persists is testimony to the inadequacy of the rules approach and the complete-thought definition.

Meanings of the Symbols Compare the different punctuation marks to rest symbols in music, and describe them as a progression of increasingly larger breaks—comma, dash, semicolon, colon, and period—while remarking that the length of pause alone may not be enough of a clue to which of any two marks is called for, and that, furthermore, emphasis and meaning make a difference too. A dash is a kind of comma—but more emphatic. Like an arithmetical plus sign, a semicolon merely adds one sentence to another; this summing indicates closeness between their actions or meanings. A colon is like an equal mark: the sentences on either side of it restate each other. These last three sentences illustrate the usages they talk about. If illustrated, the practical purpose of using semicolons for a long series and commas for subseries contained within it is easy to grasp and remember. In fact, presenting sets of instances of each of these kinds of punctuation will do more good than lengthy explanations. If you state generalities about the instances, state them logically, not grammatically. If you give out a summary sheet, limit it to illustrating inaudible cases . . . and to one page. We have done all these things in this paragraph, but for students you need more instances, of your own making or finding.

Such an account of written punctuation will probably cover all but the most abstruse of possibilities and will prove serviceable throughout the later years, even for options. Many teachers don't want to bring personal option into the picture, because it would seem to present punctuation as a subjective matter of "anything goes." But a virtue of the intonational approach is that the voice is a remarkably objective guide, indicating personal options in a public medium. That is, one does not punctuate as one pleases; one punctuates as one speaks. Most personal options can be heard. When they cannot, the few logical principles stated above will supplement vocal discriminations.

Don't try to cover and explain very much. You can count confidently on the following procedures to teach both right practice and right understanding of the many punctuation usages and principles that you can't cover in a presentation.

Punctuating Unpunctuated Texts

The main procedure that we recommend for teaching punctuation simply narrows listening while reading toward a focus on the relation of intonation to punctualization and toward a more active student role. The procedure is for students to read an unpunctuated text on a consumable sheet while listening to a reading of it, to put in the capitals and punctuation marks, compare and discuss their choices afterwards with partners, and then compare their punctuation with the original text. This is a relatively natural and remarkably effective way to learn both to read and to write punctuation that is based on vocal intonation plus logical understanding, that requires no grammatical analysis, and that students find pleasurable and interesting because of the figuring and suspense as well as the content of the texts, if well chosen.

*Prepared Texts and Recordings**

Coordinate this with your preparation for the lap method itself. You can spin off your punctuation programs from whatever materials you make or buy for general reading-while-listening. You need (1) short selections or excerpted passages from books you have for the reading program, printed without punctuation on consumable sheets; (2) recordings of these selections, preferably excerpted also and spliced back-to-back on cassettes that are set aside for punctuation practice only and on which selections can be found easily; and (3) directions posted or set down on activity cards.

Texts Choose selections according to both the inherent interest they hold for your students and to the sorts of punctuation marks and usages included. Be sure to include a great range of both punctuation difficulty and general reading difficulty, of different discourse, in prose and poetry, and of stylistic variety. If the sheets are loose, number them in an order of difficulty, or buy or make booklets or pads fastened in order. Include title and author of the passage, for practice in capitalizing these, and leave a place at the top for the student to write his name. At the bottom cite the book and page number of the original passage. Each student's sheets can be kept in or next to his writing folder and used for evaluation and diagnosis.

Recordings You could, of course, read aloud passages live to the class or subgroups of it while they punctuate, but again, this ties you up too much and works against individualization. It may be a good way to introduce the process, however. Better to record, have someone else record, or buy recordings along with the texts. See page 57 for criteria for recordings.

The hard part for punctuation is making or finding recordings that balance well the sometimes conflicting needs for expressiveness, on the one hand, and slow pace, on the other. You want the reader to make his rendition intrinsically interesting as a reading and yet not take so much liberty that he replaces the author's with his own punctuation. To some extent, however, any reader not a robot will, and this itself will teach students something about oral and written punctuation. Oral readers have to breathe, for one thing, something that an author doesn't take into account, and as actors they often want to time the words according to their feeling for pace and suspense. So readers will sometimes pause where there is no punctuation. The imposition of interpreter's on author's punctuation need not be so much a problem as an occasion for additional learning.

Try to reduce the time and frustration of searching for these relatively short passages by numbering them to correspond to the sheets and by sequencing them on tapes containing nothing else, if you can.

Directions Orally, or on a poster, activity card, pad, or booklet, give some directions to the students more or less like the following:

- Choose a partner who is ready to do the same punctuation page that you are.
- Write your name in the space for it and find the recording selection numbered the same as your page.
- Find the place on the recording where that page is read.
- Listen to the tape and fill in with a pencil the punctuation the way you hear the voice put it in. (Wherever you hear the reader punctuate with his voice, write in periods, commas, and other marks. Go by pauses, rises, falls, and other voice expression.) Replay any part any time and fill in any marks you didn't have time for at first. Draw lines through letters that should be capitals and make capitals later.
- Play through the whole selection. Write in capital letters above the printed letter and check over the rest. Make any changes you want.
- Talk with your partner about the marks each of you put in. If you differ about something, read that part aloud to each other the way that fits how you punctuated it. Now play the recording and listen to how the reader reads it. If you still differ, discuss why you think you do. If your partner really convinces you that he is right, change your punctuation.
- Go to the book, and open to the page listed at the bottom of your sheet. Compare your punctuation with the author's. If yours is different from that in the book, circle your mark(s) and talk with your partner and perhaps your teacher about why yours might be different. You may

want to listen to the recording again to hear if the reader's voicing follows the punctuation in the book. If you don't think it does, do you see a reason why the reader might have chosen not to follow the punctuation? If others in the class have done the same page, you might find out what they did.

• Tear out the sheet and place it in your folder.

The parentheses in the fourth instruction indicate an optional or additional wording that might be used only for older students. The fourth directive is the critical one, and you have to adjust it to understandings your students have, or you and they have together, about the relation of intonation to punctuation. Include along with directions, if needed, some labeled pictures of the punctuation marks so that students can pick up the names of the marks to use in talking about them.

Teaching, Not Testing   Be very sure not to let students think of this as a test. Although you can use their accumulated sheets to help you evaluate their writing skills, the main point is not to test but to teach. If they get the wrong idea, they may simply copy from the book in the first place and never do the learning part, the listening and discussing and thinking.

For one thing, it is possible to differ with the book in some cases and still have punctuated reasonably. Some authors choose to omit some commas that are unnecessary to the extent that some sentences have to be read as though there were a comma in a certain place whether the comma is written in there or not. And occasionally the author or the performing reader will be more wrong than the student just because authors are not always objective or consistent nor performing readers completely submissive to authors. But considering the hundreds of punctuation marks a student may be dealing with in frequently practicing this procedure, the number of such dubious cases will be unimportant except to teach him some further realities of reading and writing. Furthermore, students may actually be learning new punctuation usages for the first time—awarely, at least—and can justly say that they shouldn't be expected to "get right" those usages.

If students feel you are using these sheets as tests and that you don't like a lot of disagreements with the texts, they will become unduly frustrated and self-critical when they do not agree with the author. Tell them to *expect* disagreements sometimes with

partners and authors and readers but to keep listening and talking until they are satisfied that they know where differences lie. The more sophisticated the texts and the students, of course, the more will disagreement be an issue.

The opportunity to discuss discrepancies in punctuation is critical. When students disagree among themselves or with the book, they find out in a direct way which kinds of punctuation are *not* audible or not easy to hear and what their function is. Eventually students can learn to distinguish optional from indispensable punctuation by seeing similarities in the kinds of punctuation they most often disagree about. Even when this approach fails to resolve a question, it will do so in revealing ways that will also teach about punctuation. If, for example, one student joins two independent clauses with a semicolon while a partner does so with a colon—and both are hearing the same pause in the same spoken sentence—then subsequent discussion may well lead the students to consider the logical difference between the two marks. Likewise, the factor of style (tradition or innovation) in punctuation may be discovered. And the students will observe that actors take liberties that they would take themselves if trying to render a certain text well. This realization ties in beautifully, in fact, with their own efforts to work up, and perhaps tape, rehearsed readings.

To give you a more realistic idea of the whole process with its possibilities, we reproduce below two sample passages—one for elementary level, one for secondary—each in unpunctuated, uncapitalized and punctuated, capitalized versions, the latter corresponding to the author's versions. We suggest you try to punctuate the first one in your mind. That is, read it out loud, imagining some punctuation. You will not have a given voice for it, so your job is much harder than the students', for the second passage at any rate. Note the kinds of punctuation usages and issues raised by each passage. Our circling indicates punctuation about which there is less consensus and which therefore may be harder to hear or more optional or more freely interpreted by the performing reader.

UNPUNCTUATED AND UNCAPITALIZED VERSION

Cassette 3   Name _____

25. Taken from: the witch (an eskimo tale)

   ronald melzack

while yarayato and topkin were playing with all the beautiful toys in the house they saw an old woman who was sitting on the floor suddenly the woman got up and closed the entrance of the house with a large stone yarayato looked into a small room behind them and saw all the children that had disappeared from their village they were tied together

yarayato knew at once that the woman was a witch she had placed the toys near the village in order to lead children into her house

yarayato said to the witch now that were in your house i suppose you are going to eat us youd better make sure that your door is closed tight so that we cant escape

Folk Tales 1, pages 79–81

PUNCTUATED AND CAPITALIZED VERSION

Cassette 3   *Name* _____

25. Taken from: The Witch (An Eskimo Tale)

Ronald Melzack

While Yarayato and Topkin were playing with all the beautiful toys in the house, they saw an old woman who was sitting on the floor. Suddenly the woman got up and closed the entrance of the house with a large stone. Yarayato looked into a small room behind them and saw all the children that had disappeared from their village. They were tied together.

Yarayato knew at once that the woman was a witch. She had placed the toys near the village in order to lead children into her house.

Yarayato said to the witch, "Now that we're in your house, I suppose you are going to eat us. You'd better make sure that your door is closed tight, so that we can't escape."

Folk Tales 1, pages 79–81

Appropriately enough for elementary youngsters, this selection gives plenty of practice recognizing the beginnings and ends of sentences. If a child has never thought about distinguishing the voice of an author from the voice of personages in his story, the quotation marks will be new punctuation marks and usage for him, but for others this passage will only reinforce these marks. The passage limits internal punctuation to a few types—a very audible comma after a long introductory clause, the inaudible contractions (which checking against the book will make unaware students notice), and the one optional mark, the circled comma. An author or a reader who wants to emphasize purpose ("in order that we can't escape") may place a comma here, and that emphasis is what makes it optional, since the meaning would be clear without it. Such options can easily be made audible, however, and will be found even in very early reading material unless it has been utterly sterilized to avoid all the contamination of life outside schools. A certain amount of them at this stage will make minds flexible and thoughtful and able to deal with the more numerous and more subtle uncertainties of the next example.

UNPUNCTUATED AND UNCAPITALIZED VERSION

Cassette 1   *Name* _____

1. Taken from: crazy willie and the choco bars

katherine prescott

when i was six after the second war to end all wars my father bought a little gray house in pulchra washington for twelve dollars and moved us in temporarily for the next five years every winter the house grew grayer and grayer every summer the grass on the roof grew taller and taller until by fall it could have kept a couple of goats alive every winter great udders of rain water formed under the wallpaper on the ceiling and every summer the udders shrank back into withered brown cloud shapes nothing so grand as fiery horse drawn chariots but more like lopsided snowmen toppling over

Fictional Autobiography 1, page 53

PUNCTUATED AND CAPITALIZED VERSION

Cassette 1   *Name* _____

1. Taken from: Crazy Willie and the Choco Bars

Katherine Prescott

When I was six, after the second War to End All Wars, my father bought a little gray house in Pulchra, Washington, for twelve dollars and moved us in temporarily for the next five years. Every winter the house grew grayer and grayer; every summer the grass on the roof grew taller and taller, until by fall it could have kept a couple of goats alive. Every winter great udders of rain water formed under the wallpaper on the ceiling and every summer the udders shrank back into withered brown cloud shapes

—nothing so grand as fiery, horse-drawn chariots, but more like lopsided snowmen toppling over.

Fictional Autobiography 1, page 53

Like so many passages where the writing itself is interesting anyway, this excerpt intrigues both students and teachers trying to punctuate it. The recording used in field-testing and teacher workshops was an excellent rendering by a professional actress. That she conveyed punctuation well was shown by the fact that, however they disagreed about how to punctuate many of the circled places, most people felt punctuation was indicated there and got the sense of it; what they weren't sure of was just which means the author had chosen to express it. For example, nearly everyone caught the special way "War to End All Wars" was read—like a title—but used quotation marks instead of capitals, a reasonable alternative. Some were not sure whether to put a comma or semicolon after "grayer and grayer," which the actress read with a clearly more-to-follow intonation. Some hesitated between putting a dash or comma after "cloud shapes" and underlining "nothing," which the actress had stressed in order to bring out the emphasis of the dash. The comma after the name of a state is virtually impossible to hear, being mostly a visual convention, but it can be learned from this passage. The comma before "until" is an option for emphasis, like the one in the preceding sample. If the reader follows the author, it can usually be heard.

What both students and adults found with this selection, and will find again and again, is that they seldom disagree over some punctuation—the largest part—and that if they replay and discuss the places lacking much consensus, they either find reasonable alternatives, or they zero in on just which punctuation cannot be heard, or they become involved in writing and performing technique. We predicted those few places in this selection where people would not punctuate the same. In comparing and discussing, students too will learn what is impersonal and what is personal.

This passage contains a lot of punctuation lessons, including bread-and-butter stuff like "fiery, horse-drawn chariots" and about a dozen other usages covered by standard rules. It makes no difference whether a student is just learning some of this for the first time when he checks with a partner or the book, or whether most of it is reinforcement, except that he should be spared from feeling inept by letting him practice with a number of other passages before coming upon this one. This is why some rough common-sense order of easy to difficult is advisable.

Impromptu Texts and Live Voice

As a supplement and variant for prepared texts and recordings, set up the following activity, which allows students to choose the text and to interpret the punctuation by their own reading. Directions to students go something like this:

- Write a brief story, or copy out some part of a book that you like, leaving out all punctuation marks and capital letters.
- Exchange unpunctuated papers. Read the original text to your partner as the punctuation tells you to. Reread parts or all if asked. Take turns.
- Each of you put in the right punctuation and capitals for your partner's story when it's your turn.
- Check your punctuation against the book or your partner's original story. Talk over differences. Ask your partner to read it again if you want. Ask other class members or the teacher to talk about your differences too.

Punctuation Games

These games too show youngsters the value of punctuation by removing it. The main point is funny ambiguity. Try saying these in different ways and punctuating them accordingly:

- what is this thing called love
- may I call you George
- what do you think I'll shave you for nothing and buy you a drink

But the point can be just to think up sentences that can be said more than one way and to see how many ways one can think of punctuating one string of words.

"Get the Point"

One player writes on chalkboard or paper an unpunctuated, uncapitalized sentence that he knows two or more ways of punctuating. He writes these ways down beforehand to show later. His partner reads the word string aloud and puts in punctuation marks and capitals that will fit the way he said it. If the first player accepts this version, the second player erases it and tries another until he has exhausted his ideas for how to read the word string. Then the first player shows him the sentences he wrote down beforehand, and they compare to see if one thought of any punctuation the other did not.

The same idea can be spread around a class as a kind of ongoing sport by means of activity directions that tell students to make up, or to take from books, magazines, and newspapers, word strings that can mean different things when punctuated differently, then to ditto or post these unpunctuated so that everyone in the class can try his hand at discovering the possibilities. After a while the author or collector posts the sentences he has in mind. This is one of those verbal games that can become a fad and do a lot to raise language awareness. Try to keep a few rotating on the bulletin board.

Composing and Transcribing Dialogue

One reason this program emphasizes scripts and transcripts is that punctuating conversation tends to bring up a greater quantity and variety of punctuation problems than regular prose or poetry. Conversation has more front and end sentence tags, more stressed words, more interruptions, and more unfinished sentences. It also helps many kids really understand the value of punctuation as a guide for *recapturing* speech—this being the very particular aim of scripts and transcripts. Finally, dialogue helps kids distinguish sentence fragments. If in answer to the question "When are you going?" someone says "In the morning," the latter is a true sentence as defined by intonational closure, the only honest and reliable definition. But if someone writes "He planned to go. In the morning," but reads that aloud in one intonational contour, he has committed a sentence fragment.

Making scripts can take the form of solo composition, group composition, or transcribing an improvisation (see page 278). Whatever the source, students writing a script become more aware than usual of writing as the rendering of voice on paper and become more sensitive to punctuation. The words are coming from characters who are supposed to be actually speaking, and a script-maker is trying to capture the personality and emotions of the characters in what they say and by how they say it. This is a perfect situation for relating intonation to punctuation. You or an activity card may have to give them, in fact, a few extra pointers that they won't have learned from nondramatic punctuation:

- "That's what *you* think!" (Italicizing shows emphasis.)
- "I'll be happy to do it (if I can't find a way to get out of it)." (Parentheses can show a different or lowered voice.)
- "Sometimes when I see that room I wonder . . . I wonder if maybe he did live there." (Three dots—suspension points—can show that the speaker paused, hesitated.)
- "Well, if that's the way you feel about it . . ." (Suspension points can show the sentence trailed off and was left unfinished.)
- "Put up your sword or I'll—" (A dash shows the sentence was broken off sharply or interrupted.)

Reading Aloud

Performing of texts is, of course, a corollary to the above. Students-as-actors will have to heed punctuation especially closely for cues about how to deliver lines. Nothing is so likely to make punctuation seem important and functional as this experience. Actors are *grateful* for punctuation and far more expert at reading it than most educated adults. All of the many kinds of rehearsed reading in Chapter 6, Performing Texts, will work wonders for learning punctuation.

You can listen for punctuation during the coaching sessions when students read alone to you. Diagnose which marks or which marks in certain situations a student ignores or misinterprets:

- Basic segmenting of the language flow into sentences
- Segmenting of parts within sentences
- The setting off of clauses, phrases, and tag words from the main body of the sentence
- Inaudible marks that are purely conventional or logical
- Optional punctuation, sometimes inaudible
- Hyphens and contractions and capitals

Tell students, when coaching, to read the way the punctuation tells them to. Keep depicting it as signals to guide the reader, to help him re-create the silent voice behind the words. Tell the students what you perceive about their understanding of punctuation from the way they read it. If they don't believe it's important, counsel them to play "Get the Point." Steer them to particular unpunctuated punctuation sheets that contain the kinds of problems they personally are having. It is during coaching sessions for both reading and writing that you can match off students with the right punctuation practice, if they need any, and the right partners for it. Transcribing their own speech might be the best avenue for some —their improvisations, if they lean that way, or just their solo writing on the tape recorder.

When students are writing in groups, tell the scribes to read aloud to their groups what they have written and tell the others to say where the periods and capitals go. Before passing on a group composition, they should test sentences in this way. Individuals writing alone should pair off, read their papers to each other, and check each other's punctuation. The writer understands that he is to read so that his listener can follow most easily; the listener says where he thinks the marks go. Of course, children just learning to read often read aloud haltingly, without being able to create the intonation contours they would if speaking the same words in conversation. But a pupil reading his own writing does not have to decode the words one by one.

TRANSCRIBING

Taking down live or recorded speech gives students excellent practice in all encoding skills at once— handwriting, spelling, and punctuation. The following activities help to teach transcribing skills:

1. Taking dictation from classmates or younger children
2. Watching someone else take down what one dictates and then reading it together later (See page 204.)
3. Acting as scribe for a group
4. Writing down from memory such oral material as songs, jokes, recipes, and so on
5. Writing a lot, which is taking dictation from one's own head
6. Proofreading each other's spelling and punctuation, checking with other people and the dictionary when not sure of spellings, testing punctuation by reading aloud whole sentences
7. Taping something and then transcribing it afterward (See page 298.)
8. Taking down live speech

We have spoken about most of these in other places. Here are just a few more ideas about some of them.

Transcribing is writing without composing—just putting given sentences down on paper. Who gives the sentences? In one case the oral culture one lives in supplies the ready-made words—the jokes, riddles, songs, scary tales, sayings, recipes, jump-rope jingles, limericks, nursery rhymes, and other folk material passed on by word of mouth. These can be written down and made into booklets by groups or individuals. All the student has to do is transcribe what he remembers. Composition is not a factor, and he can concentrate on transcribing skills for a well-motivated reason.

Dictation from Classmates

Activity directions tell partners to take turns dictating to each other something they have written or some interesting passage from a book. They should choose something funny or exciting or absorbing— either a complete selection of short length or an intriguing excerpt. Riddles and jokes and anecdotes with a punch line are all good. But a big part of the motivation of taking dictation is to see later how close one came to writing the passage down the way it was in the book. Partners can help each other check out the spelling and punctuation. If one of them wrote the selection, they can compare the composition with the transcription and go over any differences. Did the author punctuate his composition the way he read it to his partner?

Transcribing from a Tape

Many students should do a lot of this. For many it will be an important way of composing too. Those lacking confidence to put thoughts directly onto paper should be encouraged to talk into a recorder, then to transcribe this later, making changes in wording and ideas at the same time, if they want. Separating composing from transcribing just may make a lot of sense to youngsters in an oral-electronic age to whom writing often seems strange. Once they have said what they have to say the easy way—orally—then spelling it out, especially with a partner to help, may not seem too daunting. Directions have to make clear, however, what the purpose is, what they can do with the transcript—ditto it, post it, give it to others to act out or to carry out, and so on. Partners are important, because such

Literacy—"The Basic Skills"

TABLE 11.1 CONVERSION TABLE OF LITERACY SKILLS, MATERIALS, AND ACTIVITIES
All reading and writing develop literacy skills; this lists only what aims particularly at literacy.

Materials, Activities / Skills	Identify different vocal sounds (auditory discrimination)	Identify different letter shapes and punctuation marks (visual discrimination)	Draw letters and punctuation marks (muscular coordination)	Observe the spatial conventions	Match each sound with its spellings (phonics)	Match punctuation to Intonation	Combine sound-spellings to read and write whole word (word attack, spelling)	Combine words and punctuation to sound out sentences with normal intonation and to write down sentences with correct spelling and punctuation
AUDIOVISUAL SHOW	X	X		X	X	X	X	X
GAME MATERIALS								
Card decks	X				X		X	
Game boards	X				X		X	
Bingo					X		X	
Dice		X			X		X	
Scrabble-type		X			X		X	
Letter-moving devices		X			X		X	
Stamps and letters		X		X	X		X	
Word cards					X		X	
Crossword puzzles				X	X		X	
OTHER GAMES								
Tic-tac-toe		X	X	X	X		X	
"Tap and Say"		X			X		X	
"Word Turning"		X		X	X		X	
Anagrams		X			X		X	
"Get the Point"						X		
Spelling Games					X		X	
BOOKS								
First readers				X	X	X		X
Dictionary-making					X		X	

Materials, Activities	Skills	Identify different vocal sounds (auditory discrimination)	Identify different letter shapes and punctuation marks (visual discrimination)	Draw letters and punctuation marks (muscular coordination)	Observe the spatial conventions	Match each sound with its spellings (phonics)	Match punctuation to Intonation	Combine sound-spellings to read and write whole word (word attack, spelling)	Combine words and punctuation to sound out sentences with normal intonation and to write down sentences with correct spelling and punctuation
OTHER ACTIVITIES									
Reading while listening		X			X	X	X		X
Dictating while watching					X	X	X		X
Reading to teacher		X				X	X		X
Transcribing tape				X		X	X		X
Punctuating unpunctuated texts			X				X		
Spelling self-diagnosis						X		X	
Performing texts							X		X
Taking live dictation				X		X	X		X
Matching letters			X						
Forming letters				X	X				

kids need support often, not to mention some pooling of literacy knowledge. Also, transcribing from a recorder requires running the tape back and forth a lot while one writes, and four ears are often better than two for making out those hard-to-hear places.

The tape may be of someone else's voice. A student may have done an interview with someone and now wants a transcript of it. Or a group may have done an improvisation and now wants to turn it into a script. Encourage transcribers to ask you or classmates to listen to passages they aren't sure how to spell or punctuate. They have to decide too how much they want strict fidelity and how much they want to edit out "uh's," changes of mind, and so on.

Taking down Live Speech

It is very hard to take down speech as fast as most people talk. Passages cannot be rerun as they can when recorded on tape. Inexperienced transcribers can work out as a group some shorthand for common words and assign a transcriber to each speaker when there are more than one, as for a panel or skit. The group should brainstorm ways of taking notes and recapitulating what was said. This is useful for situations where they can't have a recorder, and once experienced, they can take down chance conversations overheard, a source of interesting dialogue for relaying directly or for using in their writing.

To teach transcribing is *not* to ride herd on mechanics. This is partly why we distinguish transcription from composition. When writing, youngsters should feel uninhibited by concern for spelling and punctuation, drawing spontaneously on what they have learned about these things in other contexts. They should be encouraged to write any words, use any sentence structures, that come into their heads. We strongly urge you not to take up, correct, and grade papers. See page 421 for alternatives in evaluating.

A teacher who marks up a paper for mechanics almost inevitably establishes a value scale for students upon which transcriptive errors rank higher than content and composition. Only the future will tell us how much student writing has been made inferior by penalizing spelling and punctuation mistakes. Like the girl who said she used the word "bar" instead of "trapeze" in a story because she was unsure how to spell the latter and didn't want to be marked down for it, most students adopt the error-avoiding strategy of using only words they are sure they can spell and sentence constructions they know they can punctuate. In the long run, avoiding risks can't possibly reduce error. Student strategy should consist of making educated guesses and of checking with the teacher, other pupils, or the dictionary. What educates the guessing are your diagnosis and coaching and the many other literacy practices we have been describing in this chapter and the preceding one.[10]

[10] These three chapters have benefited considerably from our experience creating the *Interaction Literacy Kit* with coauthors Yetine Bradley, Robin Caro, Juanita Ingle, Bobbie Seifert, and Irving Wasserman, all of whom taught us much.

developmental reading, speaking, & writing

12 word play

In the chapters that follow are further suggestions for carrying on the basic processes presented in Part Two—talking and listening, dramatic inventing, performing texts, reading, and writing—in each of the nine kinds of discourse. Although the chapters take up the modes somewhat in the order of difficulty, this is not to imply that any one form is ever "outgrown." Because of small-group process and student choice of sequence, on any given day several kinds of discourse will probably be going on at the same time, except for occasional whole-class activities and regular audience sessions. You do not teach directly the unique characteristics of or distinctions between the different kinds of discourse; rather, students try the full gamut, discovering for themselves the potential, appropriateness, and limits of each. The assumption underlying all of these suggestions is that students will talk and listen and write in the same forms that they read. In a general sense, reading selections are models for composition; an appreciation for and understanding of them increase as students try their hand at making up their own.

Word play is the category of discourse that includes tongue twisters, puns, word puzzles and games, pictographs and cryptograms, brain teasers, concrete and typographical poetry, lighthearted verses and songs. Poems that are more vehicles of thought or significant feeling than verbal contrivance will be considered in other chapters. The emphasis in word play is more on gaming than on communicating, although meaning is never lost, of course. Sound and rhythm are played up, thus bringing out the kinship with music and dance. Word play is sporting with the medium as medium. This focuses on rhyme, alliteration, assonance, meter, stanzaic form, and phrasing in the musical sense; it plays on sense and imagery to create the humor and nonsense of unusual connections.

This is a good medium for learning technical aspects of the language, such as phonics, spelling, homonyms, and syllabic stress, because these aspects are treated as fun. Students can play with small units—words or phrases—in contexts that give them meaning, twisting them in ways that surprise and delight. Much authentic language development can thus occur in these smaller units without extracting them from a context.

Because it aims at language creativity, word play encompasses the highest skills of poetry, which exploit the full resources of language—sense, musicality, and movement—to spring the mind and spirit. The poet is a profound player with language.

The word as thing

TONGUE TWISTERS

Words have sounds, rhythms, spellings, and visual shapes—all qualities that can be played with, turned around, responded to. Books of tongue twisters* provide alluring reading matter. Partners and small groups can read them aloud, first slowly and then faster and faster. Children can make recordings and compare them, do choral readings, hold contests, and make up new tongue twisters to share. They are delightful verbal playthings.

Tongue twisters provide phonics reinforcement through repetition of consonants, consonant blends, vowel sounds, and digraphs. They also exercise physical articulation and auditory and visual discrimination, stringing together words that are *nearly* alike. The game is to catch the *differences* between:

- Same sound, different spelling—"which witch," "tooted the flute"
- Same spelling, different sound—"placed plain plums on plaid plastic"
- Same letter, different combinations—"freshly fried flying fish"
- Same ending, different beginning—"the Smith youth's tooth was underneath"
- Same beginning, different ending—"Tom threw Tim three thumbtacks"
- Similar spelling, one consonant substitution—"sheik's sixth sheep's sick"

PUNS AND CONUNDRUMS

The peculiarities of English spelling are a source of a great many of children's favorite jokes. For many older students Ogden Nash's puns and zany slant rhymes provide a handy model for their own composition. Collections of riddles and puns not only provide popular texts but also call for close and careful reading to discriminate between similar spellings. Puns—like much of the greatest literature in our culture—are deliberately ambiguous. See page 442 for a discussion of appreciation of ambiguity as a sign of growth.

Homographs

Homographs and homophones provide a rich source for jokes. *Homographs* are words that are spelled alike but differ in origin and meaning. They may either be pronounced alike like *butter* (the food) and *butter* (one who butts), or be pronounced differently like *wind* (breeze) and *wind* (coil up). For example:

How can you make a slow boy fast?
Don't let him eat.

Do you know how to drive a baby buggy?
Tickle its feet.

Homophones

A great many of children's riddles are based on *homophones*—words that sound alike but differ in

meaning, origin, and sometimes spelling, like *bear* and *bare*. Here are a couple of riddles based on homophones:

What is a cartoon?
Music to drive by.

How is an army officer like corn?
Both are colonels. (kernels)

Or a joke:

Two fishermen came to a lake and read the sign posted there: "DON'T FISH HERE." One of them said "Yes"; the other one said "No." Then they began to fish.

Or a poem:

I saw a pair of peers
Sitting on a pair of piers
Paring a pair of pears.

Conundrums

These are more elaborate verbal riddles that pun more than once in the answer. For example:

What is the difference between a cat and a sentence?
A cat has claws at the end of its paws, and a sentence has a pause at the end of its clause.

What is the difference between a person late for a train and a schoolteacher?
One misses trains and the other trains misses.

Made-Up Words

Puns can be the basis for new words that play on the sound and meaning of combined words. In brainstorming sessions students can think up new words our language needs, such as *zappy* for a feeling that is part surprise (*zap*) and part *happy*.

SPELLING PUZZLES

I Sentence You

Partners or members of a small group take turns giving each other a word. The other person has to make a sentence using in order each of the letters in the word as the first letter of each word in his sentence. Thus, if a player says "cat," the other player must quickly come up with a sentence like "Charles always teases." Players can time each other. Teenagers will have longer words and a shorter time to answer than young children. When elementary-school youngsters are just beginning, they may not need to time each other at all because they may give up after a short time anyway.

Forbidden Letter

Everyone in a group agrees on a letter of the alphabet that will be forbidden. Then a questioner is chosen who does not need to omit the forbidden letter. He may ask any question he likes, and the person answering it must be sure to use words that do not contain the forbidden letter. For example, if the forbidden letter is *k*, and the questioner asks, "What do you think of this weather?" a player cannot say "It's O.K." or "I like it," but he can say "It's all right." If a player uses the forbidden letter, he is out of the game. Each player in turn answers a question, always omitting the forbidden letter in his answer.

Spelling Riddles

To make these up, youngsters decide which letters or combinations either must be avoided or must be always included. For example, if they decide that the the letter *i* is to be shunned, then they can make up a riddle like this: "My aunt has eyes, but she cannot see everything. She can see a dollar, but she cannot see a nickel or a dime; a boy, but not a girl; men and women, but not children."

If they decide that any word the fictitious person likes must have a double letter in it, then they have a riddle like this: "Mrs. Wiggles likes coffee but not tea, kettles but not pots, kittens but not cats, and puppies but not dogs." The person who answers the riddle must figure out the spelling principle involved.

Stepwords

These are pairs of words of equal length that can be changed from one to another by changing one letter at a time in such a way that a new word is formed each time. For example, you can change *salt* to *bite* this way: *salt → sale → bale → bile → bite*; or *black* to *white* thus: *black → slack → stack → stalk → stale → shale → whale → while → white.*   Students

can make these up and pose them as riddles and hold contests to see who can move the fastest from, say, *dry* to *wet*, *heat* to *cold*, *east* to *west*, *poor* to *rich*, or *sick* to *well*. See also "Word Turning" on page 215.

Palindromes

A *palindrome* is a word that can be read forward or backward, such as *tot*. Guessing games can be made up of definitions of palindromes, such as:

What is a baby's garment?	bib
What is a legal document?	deed
What is midday?	noon
What is a joke?	gag
What is flat or even?	level
What are arias?	solos
What were Adam's first words to Eve?	Madam I'm Adam

Some words yield a new word when read backward, such as:

tea—eat
straw—warts
ten—net

These can be made into riddles, such as: "What word will reverse a *piece* to get a *snare*?" (*part—trap*)

Beheadings

Some words when "decapitated" become other words. Thus *glove* becomes *love*. Many words can be beheaded more than once such as *braid* to yield *raid* and *aid*. Riddles can be devised giving definitions of these words in a series, for example:

dish—tardy—consumed (plate, late, ate)
cost—cereal—hard water (price, rice, ice)
put—intertwine—foremost (place, lace, ace)
stored—lugged—was indebted—married (stowed, towed, owed, wed)
defraud—warmth—devour—preposition (cheat, heat, eat, at)

Cappings

This game is like "Beheadings" except that a letter is added to, rather than omitted from, the front of a word to form another one. The word gets a cap at the front. Thus, members of a small group think up as many riddles as they can that are like these:

Cap a word that is a garden tool with a *b* and get a device that stops cars and trains. (rake—brake)
Cap a word that is aged with an *s* to get paid for money. (old—sold)

Here are others:

ox—box	able—table	nap—snap
ought—sought	ounce—bounce	hop—shop
ale—tale	led—sled	hen—then

Dizzy Words

A popular puzzle that children can begin to make up as soon as they have mastered basic literacy is a square in which their partners can find and circle words written either forward, backward, or diagonally. Here is what a "Dizzy Word" square looks like before and after the words are circled:

 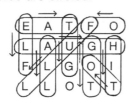

Beginners can start with words that can just be read forward; they can progress to backwards and diagonal readings.

More mature students might construct word squares that have words that can be read both from left to right and from top to bottom. Here are two such common squares:

```
    T  E  A          R  E  A  D
    E  A  T          E  L  S  E
    A  T  E          A  S  I  A
                     D  E  A  R
```

Puzzles can be devised that give only the definitions; thus for the two squares above, the puzzles would be:

Nine letters: beverage, consume, consumed
Sixteen letters: peruse, instead, a continent, darling

Crossword Puzzles

This popular word play in which words are arranged in crisscross patterns and definitional clues are given should be a regular option for students. Correct spelling is crucial to success with it as noted on page 234, and new words are added to the player's working vocabulary as he guesses the words called for by the clue and tries to fit them into his blank puzzle.

Beginners can construct and exchange simple crossword puzzles like this one:

B	E	A	A	N	A
T	M	T	T	T	D

The player fills in the blanks with a word (in this puzzle he is told it is a man's name) that when written across completes six three-letter words reading from top to bottom. In this case the word is *Alfred*.

Commercial Games

A great many commercial games like Probe, Anagrams, and Scrabble, like the puzzles listed here, not only impose close attention to spelling, but also provide a challenge to come up with new words. Using heavy cardboard, students can make their own playing pieces with letters of the alphabet painted on one side and design their own Scrabble-type boards.

VOCABULARY GAMES

As with spelling games, commercial dictionary games provide a fine opportunity for students to learn new words. The popular Password is another game based on word definitions. Old favorites like "Ghost"* and "Hangman"* stimulate both vocabulary and spelling growth.

Streamlined Ghost

Members of a small group take turns making up word pairs or compound words; the last word of the first pair must become the first word of the next pair. Thus a group might string along this sequence: *lunch box—box spring—springtime—time lock—lock up—upstairs;* or this one: *red hot—hot dog—dog collar—collar button—button hook.* Anyone who gets stuck must start a new pair and take the first letter of the word *ghost* against him. When he misses five times, he is a streamlined ghost and nobody may talk to him.

Dictionary Sentences

Each person will need a pencil, paper, and a dictionary. He opens the dictionary to any page and finds a noun and a verb. He then adds as many other words as he can find on that one page to form a sentence that makes sense. The only other words he may add are articles and prepositions. Thus, youngsters might come up with such sentences as these (see page 377 for more dictionary games):

> Peaceful peacocks pay peachy pawnbrokers.
> Entirely enthusiastic entrants entrap enthralling entrails.

Categories

Based on the commercial game Facts in Five, this stimulates vocabulary growth and accustoms youngsters to thinking in categories. First, each player draws a grid with five spaces across the top and down as in the diagram in Figure 12.1. They take turns suggesting one of the five different categories of items such as clothing, book titles, or countries, and list these along the left-hand side of the chart.

Then they select any five-letter name or word in which none of the letters is repeated. In Figure 12.1 the word *chant* was chosen. The object of the game is to think of words within the chosen categories that begin with the same letter at the top of the grid. A time limit is set, and the person who has filled in the most words at the end of that time is the winner. If students use dictionaries, they have a good way to discover new words.

I'm Thinking of a Word

This game and the next are rhyming games. This one is played by partners:

> A: I am thinking of a word that rhymes with *bear*.
> B: Is it a fruit?
> A: No, it is not a pear.
> B: Is it a female horse?
> A: No, it is not a mare.
> B: Is it unusual?
> A: No, it is not rare.
> B: Is it something you do with clothes?
> A: Yes, it is *wear*.

Stinky Pinky

The leader thinks of words that make a rhymed phrase, such as: "fat cat," "soggy doggy," "effective directive," or "Afghanistan banana stand." He tells

	C	H	A	N	T
Actors	Christie	Hoffman	Andrews	Newman	Taylor
Food	cabbage	hominy	artichoke	nuts	turkey
Presidents	Coolidge	Harding	Adams	Nixon	Tyler
Authors	Camus	Hersey	Alcott	Nin	Thoreau
States	Colorado	Hawaii	Alaska	Nebraska	Tennessee

FIGURE 12.1 PLAYING "CATEGORIES"

the group how many syllables are in his words by saying that he is thinking of a "stink pink," "stinky pinky," "stinkety pinkety," or a "stinketeroo pinketeroo," but he does not tell them what the words are. Instead he gives a definition. For the phrases above he would say: "obese feline," "wet pup," "fruitful command," or "Asian fruit market." The partner or group members then try to guess the rhymed phrase.

RESPONDING TO WORDS

When young children play with words, they fall quite naturally into acting them out. They can even take turns "acting out" something as minimal as a letter of the alphabet for their peers to guess. For example, they might sit in a straight-back chair and pant as a way to dramatize the letter *h*, crawl through the grass like a snake for an *s*, or be a clock ticking for a *t*.

Before children can read anything, they can act out characteristic actions of animals, using a book of pictures* as a stimulus, and their classmates can guess what animal they are pretending to be.

Sound Effects

Here is one for very young children.

The teacher chooses a story with a lot of repetition. (A folk tale is especially appropriate.) He hands out a card to each child on which is written an action or a sound that appears in the story, especially if it is a repeated sound. For example, if the story is "The Three Little Pigs," words like *build*, *huff and puff*, or *knocks on the door* could be on the cards. As the teacher reads the story, he stops when one of the words or phrases on the cards is needed. Then all those children who have the appropriate card do what their card says.

Chants and Cheers

Any rhythmical words can be accompanied by clapping, movement, or dance. Tongue twisters, short verses such as nursery rhymes, limericks, or jump-rope jingles, school cheers and chants, and rhythmical games all lend themselves to this.

Names of the youngsters can be chanted and clapped to emphasize their rhythm (JEN-ni-fer BROWN, for example). Several names can be juxtaposed in such a way that the metrical pattern is pleasing. For example, "CIN-dy, Pa-TRI-cia, CHRIS-to-pher, DON" can be chanted several times just

to experience the rhythm. Any words can be put together in this way, of course. Proverbs, place names, short verses, school cheers, and song lyrics are all easy to chant and lend themselves to accompaniment—marching, hopping, stamping, or making other motions in unison.

Pictographs and cryptograms

REBUSES

A *rebus* is pictographs or letters arranged to suggest a word or syllable. The figures may simply be letters of the alphabet that are cited by name rather than used to present the sound they represent. Thus this rebus:

YYURYYUBICURYY 4 me

reads:

Too wise you are, too wise you be, I see you are too wise for me.

Position may also indicate meaning as in:

stand	take	2	takings
I	you	throw	my

which reads:

I understand you undertake to overthrow my undertakings.

Young writers can put messages or stories into rebuses, using such figures as a drawing of a bee for *be*, DK for *decay*, BUT for *beauty* and other pictographs, in addition to letters and numbers, wherever they find a syllable or word for which these can be substituted. A reluctant writer might find putting together a rebus story for a younger child an effective stimulus. Collections of rebuses* can be part of the classroom library to provide beginning readers with easy-to-decode material. They also make for phonics fun. See Figure 12.2 on page 256.

PICTURE LANGUAGE

Telling stories in a series of pictures is a fairly simple process, but creating an alphabet of pictures or hieroglyphs, like the Chinese alphabet, which stylizes ideas in pictographs, presents a much more challenging task and moves into the complexity of

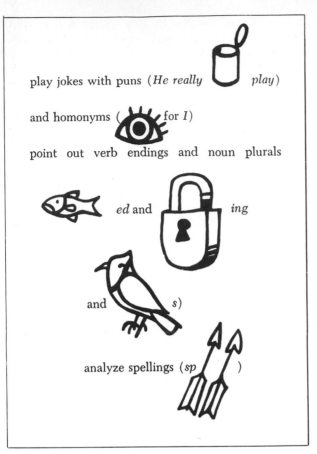

play jokes with puns (*He really* play)

and homonyms (for *I*)

point out verb endings and noun plurals

ed and *ing*

and *s*)

analyze spellings (*sp*)

FIGURE 12.2 REBUS MESSAGE

Source: From James Moffett *Interaction* Teacher's Guide, Level 1, Houghton Mifflin Company, Boston, 1973, pp. 88–89.

devising a code. Models of pictographs such as "Indian Winter Counts"[1] can stimulate the development of picture language. Not only stories but also ideas or essays can be represented in pictographs, whereby different pictures represent separate categories or abstractions. Graphic presentation is never outgrown; the maturity level of the students will determine the degree of sophistication of their representations.

WORD PICTURES

When the word is looked at as an object, its shape and arrangement of letters can be played with to suggest visually what the word means.

[1] See *Interaction* Level 3 booklet Chronicle 1 for this example.

Letterheads

Personal initials or names can be presented pictorially and used for personalized stationery or stylized signatures, symbolizing interests or values, as in Figure 12.3. Letterheads for famous real or imaginary persons can also be designed. Making up a monogram, a family crest, or an individual coat of arms is another way to visually depict interests and values and build positive self-concepts.

Concrete Poetry

Older students might try their hand at concrete poetry, which unlike traditional poetry, which appeals to both the eye and ear, appeals only to the eye. It is a graphic presentation; the meaning depends on the way the words are placed on the page. For example, in the poem in Figure 12.4, both the intertwining of the letters and the serpent connotation of the *S* say visually what a conventional printing of the word does not.[2]

Typographical Poetry

Like concrete poetry, typographical poetry depends for its meaning on the arrangement of the words and letters on the page. Unlike concrete poetry, it

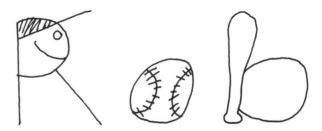

FIGURE 12.3 LETTERHEAD

FIGURE 12.4 CONCRETE POETRY

[2] Pedro Xisto, "She" in *Anthology of Concretism*, ed. Eugene Wildman, The Swallow Press, Inc., Chicago, 1969, p. 120. Used with permission of the publisher.

FIGURE 12.5 STUDENT TYPOGRAPHICAL POETRY   **257**

Word Play

SOME HOUSES HAVE PEOPLE,
SOME HOUSES HAVE Birds,
SOME HOUSES HAVE ELEPHANTS,
BUT MY House HAS WordS

uses conventional capital and small letters rather than altered or distorted versions of the letters. Examples of the kind of typographical poems sixth graders can do are shown in Figure 12.5.

More mature students can use typewriters to experiment with typographical poetry in which complete words within other words are set apart and played on as in this poem by e e cummings:

> *tw*
>
> *o o*
>
> *ld*
>
> *o*
>
> *nce upo*
>
> *n*
>
> *a(*
>
> *n*
>
> *o mo*
>
> *re*
>
> *)time*
>
> *me*
>
> *n*
>
> *sit(l*
>
> *oo*
>
> *k)dre*
>
> *am* [3]

CIPHERS AND CODES

Collections of ciphers and codes*, which appeal to youngsters' love of secrecy and private language, stimulate very careful reading and provide a model for devising a way to send private messages. Young children have had more recent experience than most adults at code-cracking, for as infants they heard spoken language as a foreign tongue and as illiterates they found the written word a perfect cipher in which unfamiliar symbols encoded familiar sounds.

Ciphers substitute secret symbols for individual letters or rearrange letters in a predetermined way. In order to use ciphers, one must substitute the secret symbols for individual letters, literally spelling out a message correctly letter by letter in the right order. Some ciphers such as *igpay atinLay* (pig

[3] Untitled poem, copyright 1949 by e e cummings. Reprinted from his volume, *Complete Poems 1913–1962*, by permission of Harcourt Brace Jovanovich, Inc., New York, and courtesy of MacGibbon & Kee Ltd., London.

Latin) may be spoken as well as written. A side benefit in working with ciphers is that one has to analyze the language, thereby learning such facts about English as the relative frequency of different letters and spelling patterns.

Codes, on the other hand, are alternative languages with symbols for whole words or ideas, not individual letters. Codes, which include pictographs, cattle brands, and food-dating systems, give youngsters an alternative to regular language and hence a way of detaching themselves from the native tongue, so deeply embedded in our life from childhood as to be difficult to objectify otherwise. Like mathematics and foreign language, codes enable us to objectify the native language, conceptualizing syntax and parts of speech in a new way. Students become aware of the arbitrariness of any language and the possibility of creating new languages that may serve them better for certain purposes. Students reading ciphers and codes are introduced to a means of communication that has been in use since Biblical times.

One easy way for students to construct a cipher is to substitute numbers for letters or letters for numbers. For example, the letter *m* could be *1*; *n*, *2*; *o*, *3*; and so on, with the numbers continuing at the beginning of the alphabet after *z* is designated *14*: thus *a* is *15*, *b* is *16*, and so on. Another simple method is to substitute letters of the alphabet that are two or more letters ahead of each letter. For example, if the letter three steps ahead were substituted for each letter, the message, "Meet me at 10:00," would look like this:

Phhw ph dw 43:33.

Transposition or scrambling is another method of cipher-writing that a child can figure out and enjoy using. Here is a cryptogram or message written in a scrambled cipher:

TNTX HIHO ESEB KIML EYAI

To unscramble it you write each of the four-letter "words" in a vertical column like this:

> T H E K E
>
> N I S I Y
>
> T H E M A
>
> X O B L I

The first line is read left to right; the second, right to left; the third, left to right; and the last backward, so the message is: "The key is in the mailbox."

Scrambled ciphers may be made more complicated by rearranging the regular order of the vertical columns, putting them in some other predetermined order such as with the even vertical columns together first, and then the odd ones. Thus the square above is changed from:

```
1   2   3   4   5

T   H   E   K   E

N   I   S   I   Y

T   H   E   M   A

X   O   B   L   I
```

to:

```
2   4   1   3   5

H   K   T   E   E

I   I   N   S   Y

H   M   T   E   A

O   L   X   B   I
```

Dummy letters can be added at regular predetermined intervals to further throw the reader off. Let students experiment widely in developing their own codes. The possibilities are endless.

Telegram writing

Although not usually considered word play because of its informational function, you can introduce writing telegrams as a kind of game, staging contests to see who can get a particular message into the fewest words. This challenge is never outgrown, although the process can begin in the primary grades. At first you might ask the children to write a message limited to fifteen, twenty, or twenty-five words, depending both on their ability and on the complexity of the story situation surrounding the message. Here's a way you might get young children started:

• You want a friend of yours to stay overnight with you. You send him a telegram inviting him and tell-ing him what he should bring with him. You have to tell him all the information he will need, but you also want to keep down the cost of the telegram. Each word costs a dime.

This activity sets up a requirement that a minimum of words should convey a maximum of meaning, which is a valuable pressure for any writer. Children will practice arithmetic as they weigh the cost against the adequacy of the information conveyed and will start thinking in terms of which words are worth a dime.

This activity results in fragments rather than whole sentences. Like taking notes of sensory experiences or interviews, writing telegrams is a process in which word economy is the crucial issue. Unlike note-taking, however, telegrams are addressed to another person, rather than to oneself, and thus they must communicate, albeit briefly. As youngsters see which words are essential, they have valuable experience in separating content words from function words that merely show relationships within sentences. See pages 444–446.

If alternate telegram versions of the same message are compared, the youngsters can see how a number of their peers dealt with the problem of information versus economy, and can discuss loss of intelligibility, adequacy of information, and unnecessary words. In so doing, they can learn the risks as well as the advantages of stripping down language. By trying to adapt their writing to fragments, they can see for themselves the advantages of writing in whole sentences.

Older students can pretend to be in emergency situations of all sorts and write telegram messages of fifteen or fewer words or write on papers no more than two inches square to be sent by carrier pigeon. Telegram writing can also be in cipher or code.

Brain teasers

Like tongue twisters, riddles, insults, and jokes, brain teasers are embodied in the oral folk culture among children, who enjoy stumping one another. Collections of brain teasers* beg to be shared with a partner, so they make good texts for developing oral reading skills.[4] Brain teasers can be collected from classmates or new ones made up and shared

[4] For teenagers, see also books such as: May Swenson, *Poems to Solve,* Charles Scribner's Sons, New York, 1966.

via tape, transparencies, booklets, and so on. Less verbal children can put together picture riddles by using just parts of familiar objects, the way Tana Hoban did in *Look Again!*[5] As with collections of riddles, students need to figure out a way to keep the answer or punch line hidden until the reader has a chance to puzzle it out for himself. For example, if youngsters make riddle books, have them put each answer on a different page than the riddle.

Brain teasers are logical problems and develop thinking especially, as they exercise memory and concentration. Puzzles of all sorts are a kind of equation in which a student works his way from the unknown side to the familiar side, as in solving math problems by balancing the sides. They provide mental workouts—verbal, mathematical, spatial, pictorial—which are fun and intriguing. If students cannot get an answer, they still enjoy *seeing* it and sharing their puzzlement with classmates.

More kinds of humor

INSULTS

One of the ever-present trials of a teacher is taunting, teasing, and fighting among students. Any way that this urge to put one another down can be converted into playful sparring is all to the good. The key is *playful*, and to use words as substitutes for deeds and wit for war is to move a long way toward a maturity that far transcends language. If a book of insults* is present in the classroom, it has the effect of objectifying name-calling so it tends to lose its personal sting. Because insults are plucked from their tense interpersonal context, the best ones can then become not those that hurt the most but rather those that are wittier and more entertaining.

Many animals swell up, "display," bark, or substitute other harmless behavior for fighting in potentially hostile confrontations. In a similar attempt to defuse or forestall conflict, people will shout, brandish fists and weapons, beat their chests, boast, jeer, "jaw" at one another, and insult, as facing armies do in Homeric and other epics. Such behavior becomes ritualized or stylized into a kind of

game, as it has in the black tradition of "dozens," or "signifying," which is a contest to top each other in witty or outrageous insults. An art form frequently arises out of just such a serious function.

Once students have established insults as a game and art form, they can create within it, making up insults of their own and trying to top each other. They can write down ones they have heard and post them or collect them into books. Like jump-rope jingles, game rhymes, limericks, jokes, riddles, tall tales, tongue twisters, and ghost stories, insults are a part of an oral culture waiting to become high-interest reading matter that is then exchanged and fed back into the oral culture. Thinking up good insults frequently produces comparisons, as does making up riddles and proverbs.

Epithets are popular among elementary children. These are words, phrases, sentences, or short verses that describe some quality or attribute that the speaker considers characteristic of a person. They are typically insulting in the "Roses are red, violets are blue . . ." tradition of autograph books. Here's an epithet:

> *Ho Hum Harry,*
> *Lovesick and too young to marry.*

If you feel your class is not ready to sling insults about and still stay friendly, you can have them write verbal characterizations of famous people and see if the rest of the group can guess who is the subject of each epithet.

JOKES

Fun and humor often involve word play. Because jokes are usually based on mind jumps, they provoke deduction. Many are in riddle form and tease out thought in the same way that brain teasers do. A great many focus on misunderstandings of word usage, such as those in the familiar teacher-pupil dialogues, thereby developing vocabulary in a playful way:

Teacher: Make up a sentence using the word *notwithstanding.*
Pupil: His trousers were worn thin at the seat, but not with standing.

Other jokes arise from the ambiguity of misplaced modifiers, such as in the remark the mother made on Thanksgiving: "You know, we ate an awful lot, even

---

[5] Tana Hoban, *Look Again!*, Macmillan Publishing Co., Inc., New York, 1971. This is a book with holes in the page, and provides a model that is easy for children to imitate.

the children." Students can watch for and collect ambiguities in want ads or signs such as:

Boy wanted to deliver pizzas, about 16 yrs. old.
Buy your candles here. Do not go elsewhere to be cheated.
You get a good deal at this store.

Dialogue gags are good for partner reading and for preparation for taking part in script performing or voice chorus reading of poems. Verbal-visual jokes wherein the word denotes one thing and its illustration depicts another that is pronounced in the same way is a visual pun, providing an entrée into homophones.

Writing cartoons affords an opportunity to co-ordinate words and graphics and leads into the dialogue joke of comics. Writing anecdotal jokes leads into the composition of longer invented stories. As youngsters write down orally familiar jokes, they learn to use the script format for pure dialogue and to use quotation marks for dialogue embedded in narrative. Collections of jokes and cartoons* are alluring for weak or timid readers because the entertainment is high, the text short and easy, and the illustrations typically profuse.

PARODIES

Parody is exaggerated imitation to make fun of someone or something. Improvised impersonations of TV advertisers, entertainers, teachers, and other figures are part of the oral culture of schoolchildren. From this base youngsters can be led into the writing of parody—deliberate exaggeration of a certain event, character, or writing style. Good written parody of style is a sophisticated art, one that calls for isolating the manner of writing from the content and deliberately making fun of it. When youngsters put a written text into another, inappropriate or unconventional form, the result is often parody. Models of parody to read and imitate can be found in newspaper columns like those of Art Buchwald, magazines such as *Mad,* and joke books.

Satire is like parody except that the target is broader—poking fun at whole institutions or societies. Cartoons and comics are often satirical; to enjoy and imitate these is to move toward an appreciation of classic satires such as *Alice in Wonderland* or *Gulliver's Travels* as commentaries on society.

Short poems

Even the most cerebral or lyrical of poetry has its playful elements, its deliberate contrivance to make us wonder at its form. Because words have sounds, shapes, rhythms, and ambiguous meanings, they can be juxtaposed in ways that not only tease thought but also create something new—to be looked at, toyed with, and responded to on its own terms.

NURSERY RHYMES

Collections of these rhythmical and dramatic short verses should be part of every young child's reading material. They stimulate imagination, kinesthetic response, and imitation. Through nursery rhymes children are introduced to alliteration, assonance, repetition, beat and meter, and rhyme.

The oral folk tradition—nursery rhymes, counting-off rhymes, marching verses, jump-rope jingles, chants for waiting, square-dance calls, and so on—features action accompanied by verse. Children like to repeat words like "higglety pigglety," "to market, to market," and "clickety clack" over and over for the sheer pleasure of their sound. Beat and meter are best learned by physical action, and once children can beat out patterns and stresses, they can read them aloud better. Kinesthetic experience leads to conceptualization and then to imitation. As youngsters synchronize movement to phrasing and syllables to beats, they internalize physical rhythms into language rhythms; this process stands a good chance of making reading easier. Because oral literature has arisen as part of social interplay, collections of street verse such as jump-rope jingles* in the classroom help break down barriers between outdoor games and school books.

Mature students can make up new nursery rhymes based on the rhythmical patterns of traditional verses, using rhyming dictionaries or thesauruses. Some will be satirical; most will be humorous. Writers can retell traditional rhymes in deliberately untraditional language—scholarly, elevated, slang, and so on—to create humorous parodies.

FOUND POEMS

Word play is often merely novel juxtaposition. Students can cut out phrases or other excerpts from ads, magazines, or catalogues and glue them together in word collages, poems, or posters. Sometimes a complete statement becomes a poem just by being isolated or shifted to another context.

COMPARISONS

At the heart of poetry-making is metaphor—highlighting likeness, quality, and nuance through comparison. Reading and making up comparisons build poetry appreciation.

Metaphor Game

Here is a game for teenagers to accustom them to metaphor-making. One person goes out of the room, and the class decides on a famous person whom "It" is to be, a person known to everyone in the group. Then "It" returns and asks questions, each question calling for a metaphorical answer. For example, if the famous person is Harpo Marx, the questioning might go like this:

> It: If I were an animal, what would I be?
> Class Member: Giraffe
> It: If I were a brand name, what would I be?
> C. M.: Honor (for harmonica brand name)
> It: If I were a shoe, what would I be?
> C. M.: A hush puppy
> It: If I were a food, what would it be?
> C. M.: Coconut
> It: If I were a place, where would it be?
> C. M.: The Grand Hotel
> It: If I were a historical figure, who would I be?
> C. M.: Helen Keller

The game continues until "It" either guesses who he is or gives up.

Comparison Poems

Collections of short poems* that feature comparison provide evocative reading matter and a stimulus for group or individual composition. Students who are recording sensory experience (see page 160) often find themselves resorting to simile and metaphor. In their effort to freeze a moment in time they not only sketch in words that they sense, but they find ways to compare it to other experience. This comparison may be simile: "The binocular owl, fastened to a limb

like a lantern all night long";[6] or metaphor: "Morning is a new sheet of paper for you to write on."[7] A single original line that picks out something and compares it so it is experienced in a fresh way may be more profoundly poetic than the most elaborate of versifying.

The best way to appreciate comparisons and feel comfortable using them is to become steeped in the figures of poetry. Instead of belaboring the difference between similes and metaphors, you would do better to present many poems based on a central comparison and let the class try writing similar poems. In "The Country Bedroom," for example, Francis Cornford begins, "My room's a square and candle-lighted boat," and continues the comparison for the rest of the poem's eight lines.[8] When a student sets up a single comparison as the frame of his poem, he *magnifies* the analogizing process that underlies both the conventional figures of speech embedded in language and the novel metaphors of creative thought.

It is true that younger students do not often make original verbal comparisons, but a technical approach does not help. As for comprehending other people's comparisons, we do not think that students have trouble except when the terms or allusions of the comparisons are unfamiliar to them. So-called literal-mindedness does exist, but we believe it is due either to unfamiliarity with the figurative use of language or to an emotional defense against ambiguity. (See page 442.) In any case, teaching comparison as a *concept*, explaining it, serves nothing except to make analogy seem falsely esoteric. Actually, nothing is more common and automatic than analogizing, since all of concept formation and generalizing depends on perceiving likeness in discriminably different things. It is the uncommon and verbally explicit comparison that teachers are after. One learns metaphor out of the need to metaphorize, to make the unknown known, as in the sensory writing described on page 163 or to make the familiar unfamiliar, as in "The Country Bedroom."

Mature students with much experience with comparison may be ready to experiment with metaphy-

---

[6] Quotation from "The Woods at Night" by May Swenson is used by permission of the author, reprinted from *To Mix with Time,* copyright © 1963 by May Swenson and Charles Scribner's Sons, New York.

[7] Quotation from "Metaphor," copyright © 1964 by Eve Merriam, from *It Doesn't Always Have to Rhyme.* Used by permission of Atheneum Publishers, New York.

[8] Francis Cornford, "The Country Bedroom," in *Cavalcade of Poems,* ed. George Bennett and Paul Molloy, Scholastic Book Services, New York, 1965.

sical conceits—a form of word play in which one not only extends a metaphor but makes an unusual, even far-fetched comparison. Through profundity and absurdity, results bend the mind and are often funny, as John Donne well knew back in the seventeenth century. See his poem "The Flea." *

See also pages 6 and 440.

DIAMANTES AND LIMERICKS

These may be less "poetic," in the sense of striking deep at feelings or putting experience into lasting and noteworthy artistic form, but they are nonetheless valid as word play.

Diamantes are like cinquains (see p. 391) in that they have five lines; they are in a form that is easy for even very young children to follow. Here is one form of diamante:

First line: Your name
Second line: Two words describing you
Third line: Three words telling what you can do
Fourth line: Four words telling how you feel
Fifth line: Your name again or your nickname

Here's another:

First line: One word naming a thing
Second line: Two words describing it
Third line: Three words expressing action
Fourth line: Four words expressing a feeling
Fifth line: Another word for the title

An alternative for this last pattern is to have the fourth line contain two descriptive words as the second line does. Following that pattern a junior high student wrote:

Bird
Small, feathery,
Flies, soars, lands
Ugly, crushed
Squished [9]

Here's another variation on this pattern:

First line: One word naming a color

[9] A student in a class taught by Peter Downing at Pawtucket Junior High, Lowell, Massachusetts.

Second line: Two words telling how you like that color
Third line: Three words telling what the color looks like
Fourth line: What the color does for people who see it
Fifth line: A metaphor of the color such as what sound is like it

Iris M. Tiedt originated seven-line poems in a form shaped like a diamond that look like this and move from a subject in the first line to its opposite in the last line:

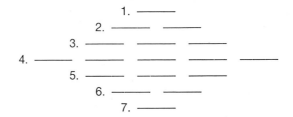

1. One word—subject noun
2. Two words—adjectives
3. Three words—participles
4. Four words—nouns related to the subject
5. Three words—participles
6. Two words—adjectives
7. One word—noun, opposite of the subject

A group of students can agree on a beginning and ending word and then each can make up his own diamante and compare it with the others. Here is one written by a twelve-year-old boy:

Snakes
Long, sly,
Slithering, hating, killing
Scales, tails, teeth, nails
Eating, resting, sleeping
Furry, playful
Kittens.

Any words that are opposites can be the starting and ending words for seven-line diamantes: *land—sea, day—night, hate—love, summer—winter, child—adult,* and so on.

Limericks are highly regular, strongly rhythmical and rhymed verses*, popular with many students.

Some limericks are nursery rhymes, as "Hickory Dickory Dock," some are tongue twisters, and others play on puns. The absurdities created by trying to make the matter fit the rhyme are part of the humor of limericks. As youngsters become saturated with this form, they will want to perform and compose their own verses.

Unlike the more complex forms, the form of limericks need not be described or analyzed. As students become familiar through reading and listening to limericks with the rigorous constraints of their rhyme, meter, and number of lines, they will begin not to take liberties with the form but rather to use their wit to invent imaginative proper names, wild action, and hilarious images to fit the model.[10] Limericks are actually a kind of joke; they or other forms of light verse might become a kind of classroom fad that will be of great value in developing word choice, sentence structure, fanciful invention, stylistics, and verse techniques.

Limericks have a two-part thought form, subtler than their meter and rhyme patterns but related to them. In this respect they are like haiku. See page 379. Students might work in pairs, one composing the first two lines of a limerick and the other finishing it. As students work with this form they sooner or later discover its thought form. This teaches some the use of the semicolon as nothing else ever would. It also gives students a legitimate one- or two-sentence unit within which to work closely on word choice and sentence structure without wrenching a unit from some context. Limericks can be sung to a tune such as the example in Figure 12.6.

OCCASIONAL VERSE

Any teacher who can evoke from students what has been termed *occasional verse,* composed for a specific event in a social group—birthday, holiday, special achievement, and so on—is fostering a communal form in a venerable tradition that dates back to the time of Pope and Dryden. Encourage students to versify as an appropriate way to mark a significant event. Lighthearted rhyming is word play at its best. Some of the French forms with their regular rhyme, meter, and repetition patterns—triolet, rondel, rondeau, villanelle, and ballade—might be appealing mediums.

[10] See the *English Through Interaction* secondary-level film, "The Writing Workshop."

There Was an Old Man with a Beard

FIGURE 12.6 LIMERICK

Source: From *Interaction,* Level 1, Songs, p. 43.

Triolets

The *triolet* is an eight-line poem that uses two rhymes, abaaabab. Lines one, four, and seven are identical, as are lines two and eight. It is almost impossible to repeat so much in such a short poem without seeming playful; for example:

A TRIOLET

A triolet fits on a postal card.
  The triolet's for me.
Ballades spin on for many a yard
(A triolet fits on a postal card!)
To France With Love From Indolent Bard—
  Hail, Gallic brevity!
A triolet fits on a postal card.
  The triolet's for me.[11]

[11] Howard Cushman wrote this to a friend traveling in France; it is from an unpublished manuscript: Howard Cushman, "Poems For All Occasions," July 1973, p. 6. Used by permission of Jeannette Cushman.

Rondels

A *rondel* usually has fourteen lines and two rhymes; the first two lines are exactly repeated as lines seven and eight and again as lines thirteen and fourteen. Here's one by Austin Dobson:

> Too hard it is to sing
>   In these untuneful times,
> When only coin can ring,
>   And no one cares for rhymes.
>   Alas for him who climbs
> To Aganippe's Spring:
> Too hard it is to sing
>   In these untuneful times.
>
> His kindred clip his wing,
>   His feet the critic limes;
> If fame her laurel bring,
>   Old age his forehead rimes:
> Too hard it is to sing
>   In these untuneful times.[12]

Rondeaus

A *rondeau* is typically fifteen lines with only two rhymes. The first word or opening phrase of the first line is repeated as a refrain as the ninth and fifteenth lines. Here is one with a play on words at the end:

RUSS TO KATE

> "Love—Russ to Kate" the legend ran;
> And that is how the thing began.
>   Not half a dozen words, but four,
>   That morning in the flower store . . .
> Or was it with the book or fan?
> And who will say it was your plan
> To terminate the long, sweet span
>   Of bachelorhood, what time you swore
>   Love, Russ, to Kate?
>
> But such the frailty of man,
> Fate sends him sprawling if it can . . .
>   The denouement? Ah, that's a bore!
>   You'll write—or try a teaching chore—
> To eat—and let from Feb. to Jan.
>   Love rusticate.[13]

[12] Austin Dobson, *The Complete Poetical Works of Austin Dobson*, Oxford University Press, New York, 1923.

[13] Cushman, p. 1. Originally published in a house organ of the Buffalo Athletic Club, 1926. Used by permission of Jeannette Cushman.

Villanelles

Like the rondel and rondeau, the *villanelle* has only two rhymes and typically nineteen lines, but some villanelles are longer or shorter. The first line is repeated as the ninth and fifteenth, and both the first and third lines are in the final four lines. Villanelles are always divided into tercets, or three-line stanzas of interlocking rhyme: aba, aba, aba, aba, aba, abab. The final four lines are a quatrain. One of the best known poems in this form is Dylan Thomas's "Do Not Go Gentle into That Good Night," which, unlike most villanelles, has a serious subject. This poetic form lends itself well to light verse.

Ballades

A *ballade* consists of three eight-line stanzas rhyming ababbcbc, and a four-line envoi, which is a conclusion or dedicatory stanza. The last line of the first stanza is used as the last line of the other two stanzas and of the envoi. For example:

BALLADE OF WINTER TEDIUM

> *This time each year I get out of sorts*
>   *With the joys of my fellow man at play,*
> *Pursuing their so-called winter sports*
>   *In a spiritless, sweaty sort of way.*
>   *"Are hockey and basketball here to stay?"*
> *I wail in a manner bereft of reason.*
>   *"How long must we wait a happier day?"*
> *"How many weeks to the baseball season?"*
>
> *I've put up with football at far resorts:*
>   *Rose Bowl, Cotton Bowl; Blue and Gray.*
> *For soccer players in frozen shorts*
>   *I've shouted a feeble hip-hooray.*
>   *But one thing now I'm impelled to say,*
> *Though voicing it be akin to treason.*
>   *We've suffered enough! Let us be gay!*
> *How many weeks to the baseball season?*
>
> *Let squash and racquets on snooty courts*
>   *In properly social strife hold sway.*
> *Bowling or billiards? Excuse these snorts!*
>   *Who could consider such stuff au fait?*
>   *"Ah well," say I, "and lackaday.*
> *Enough of these games when the weather's freezin'!*
>   *"I sing of Spring with a too-ra-lay!*
> *"How many weeks to the baseball season?"*

Coach, watch that runner on third, he may
  Try stealing home if they've got the squeeze on!
This is the crucial year, Olé!
  How many weeks to the baseball season? [14]

Cyrano delivers a classic ballade as he duels in the first act of *Cyrano de Bergerac* by Edmond Rostand.

Chain Verse

Like terza rima, where stanzas of three lines each rhyme aba, bcb, cdc, and ded, any repetition of a rhyme, word, phrase, line, or group of lines to tie up a section of a poem with the succeeding section constitutes chain verse. Students can take turns making up four lines of rhyming verse in a abab pattern. The last line of the first person's ditty has to become the first line of the next person's. Granted, this kind of word play is not for everyone, but if you have compulsive versifiers in your classroom, capitalize on it. They can do more to interest the rest of the class in verse forms than all the best books on prosody.

Pantoums

Like chain verse, this Malayan form is written in stanzas that interlock through repetition; the second and fourth lines of each four-line stanza become the first and third of the succeeding stanza. In the last stanza, the second and fourth lines are the third and first of the first stanza, so the opening and closing lines of the pantoum are identical. Here's part of one written by Brander Matthews:

EN ROUTE

Here we are riding the rail,
  Gliding from out of the station;
Man though I am, I am pale,
  Certain of heat and vexation.

Gliding from out of the station,
  Out from the city we thrust;
Certain of heat and vexation,
  Sure to be covered with dust.

. . . .

[14] Cushman, p. 14. Used by permission of Jeannette Cushman and the *Philadelphia Bulletin.*

Ears are on edge at the rattle,
  Man though I am, I am pale,
Sounds like the noise of a battle,
  Here we are riding the rail. [15]

COUPLET COMPLETION

Another way to play with verse forms is to take the first line of a famous poem or couplet and write a second line that is in the same meter, that rhymes, and that continues or deliberately contrasts with the thought of the first line. The result will be a couplet with potential for humor. For example, if you start with Robert Frost's line, here is what you might get:

Whose woods these are I think I know, [16]
His putter's in the bag below.

As students put together verses, they fall into an interest in the technicalities of poetry. Rhyming dictionaries and other books that spell out various stanzaic and rhyme-scheme options will be of interest. Versifiers need to know how many feet are in each line and what the regular beat of a poem is. To scan poetry before they have enough experience with it to be curious about its form has turned many students away from a mode of expression that is more to be played with than studied.

Songs

Poems and songs are closely allied, for to sing is to internalize metrical patterns as well as tunes. See page 158. Making up new words to a familiar tune is a good way to ease into verse composition because the notes and beats of the music fasten down precisely the metrical scheme of poetic form—the number of syllables and the ones that are stressed. Pauses, staccatos, the steep intervals between notes, lengths of phrasing—all elicit words and word clusters as well, perhaps, as images and ideas of actions. Such cues set up free thought associations, which determine the chain of ideas.

[15] Originally published by The Century Company and quoted in *The Complete Rhyming Dictionary and Poet's Craft Book,* edited by Clement Wood, Halcyon House, New York, 1936.

[16] From *The Poetry of Robert Frost* edited by Edward Connery Lathem. Copyright 1923, © 1969 by Holt, Rinehart and Winston. Copyright 1951 by Robert Frost. Reprinted by permission of Holt, Rinehart and Winston, Publishers, the Estate of Robert Frost, and Jonathan Cape Ltd.

A small group can make up new words for a familiar tune and write them on a transparency, which can then be projected while the group reads or sings it and others follow the written words. Then the whole class sings the new lyrics.

Like occasional verse, songs can be composed to mark important events and holidays. The performance of this original material then is part of the celebration. Making up new words for a tune provides a lure to parody. If students deliberately choose words that do not fit the mood of the tune, they have a satire in song like the lively-tuned disaster ditties that Tom Lehrer sings. In some cases it is fun to keep many of the words of the original song or to make puns on them as in "O beautiful for spacemen skies" instead of "O beautiful for spacious skies."

Song lyrics printed either in booklets* or on the covers of record albums provide high-interest reading matter in any classroom. Recordings can be used for learning the tunes, for sing-along sessions, and as models for composition and performance. Song lyrics like those of the Gilbert and Sullivan operettas are verbal patter; others like "Van Lingle Mungo," * a catalogue of names, are a sort of language game.

Composing tunes for poems is another activity appropriate as a way of extending the effect of language. Encourage this and song-writing—lyrics and tunes—as much as possible. It is an excellent way for many students to write and appreciate verse and perhaps the deeper qualities of poetry as well. Many American teenagers live in a musically sophisticated subculture, and this can be tapped for language development. Anything from school pep tunes to long ballads in the folk tradition can be composed and contributed to the peer culture. A sound collage might be put together the way Simon and Garfunkel recorded "Silent Night" with a newscast in the background. Little by little the song grows fainter until it is finally overwhelmed by news reports of various violent events. Any theme can thus be presented with reading—either individual or choral—and singing or instrumental music simultaneously, letting each part alternate in dominance, much as in a jazz combo. Students can relate poetry and music to scripts and drama by collaborating to write a musical.

Word play is fun, but we include it as a significant part of this curriculum because at its best it is also a creative response to experience. When words are the playthings, language power cannot help but increase.

labels & captions

13

Despite the philosophy of some English teachers, a great deal of communication in words occurs in units smaller than a sentence. Labels and captions are good examples. A *label* designates a name for a thing, usually in a single word or a naming phrase. A *caption* is a statement about something, explaining or commenting on it. It is either a sentence fragment, a whole sentence, or a paragraph.

What makes it possible for language to communicate in these small units of words or word clusters is the fact that a nonverbal context—an object, a place, or a picture—conveys the rest of the message. For example, a label on a can says in effect: "This can contains ————," so that the label need be only the one word that names the contents. Likewise, a caption for a picture provides an extension of but not a substitute for the picture. The double-media communication of graphics-with-words is an important kind of experience, comparable to interpreting a spoken "text" in the context of voice, gesture, and situation. This kind of discourse is by its nature multimedia and links words to their environment in a way that is an extension of "reading in context." When children engage in show-and-tell or adults in a talk-demonstration or a long monologue about an object, as suggested in Chapter 4, Talking and Listening, their explaining is an oral equivalent of written labels and captions, using words in the context of the thing to which they are a supplement. Education often neglects labeling and captioning because they occur so much outside of books and are not pure prose continuity; yet they comprise a great deal of what we read and write—packaging, charts, graphs, maps, headlines, titles, and marquees. It is important to recognize the pervasiveness of this interdependence between words and things in our culture; this kind of communication is at times very sophisticated.

Labels and captions are easy in one sense and difficult in another. They are easy in that nonverbal clues to their meaning can be read in connection with them. However, they pose a difficulty in that they may present a boiled-down version of a fuller experience. This process of extraction affords an opportunity to understand the ambiguity that results from the elimination of function words (prepositions, conjunctions, and so on) and inflections (word endings). Labels and captions are not always used to extract and clarify, however; they may be used to deliberately distort or satirize as in joke signs that mislabel or the popular books of baby or animal faces with captions that are purposely absurd or inappropriately sophisticated. Much of cartoon art is dependent on just this kind of deliberate irony.

Labels

Any object, picture, chart, graph, or map may be labeled. In the process of labeling, diction becomes more precise and phrasing more apt. Like telegrams, labels need to be both effective and brief. If youngsters are still mastering literacy, they will have a good reason to letter legibly and spell correctly if they make tagboard labels for objects in the environment—their own coat hook or cubbyhole, doors, windows, shelves for specific items, containers for supplies, the clock, piano, a class mailbox, objects in a playhouse or store, pieces of pretend money, or whatever. A classroom plastered with labels is an environment to be "read," a place to practice sight-reading. Outdoors, trees, plants, and playground equipment can be labeled, and children can go searching for identifying words on buildings, on manhole covers, in concrete sidewalks, or on gravestones.

BULLETIN BOARDS AND DISPLAYS

Any array of art or written products calls for apt labeling. Selecting, arranging, and labeling these is a challenging exercise in itself, one from which learners of all ages can benefit. Certainly decisions concerning what goes on the bulletin board or into a classroom display should be made by the learners more than the teacher.

Three-dimensional displays of models can be assembled in a classroom museum and clarified with labels. Encourage students to bring in unusually old or interesting curiosities from home. They can affix written information about their history, origin, use, and so on—that is, caption, as well as label.

An interesting exercise in not only labeling but also perceiving is to pick up objects at random, bring them into the classroom, then look at them as if they were found by a group of archaeologists who arrived at this place and found only these things but no people to explain them. How might the archaeologists label each one? What function might they guess each to have? What might they project from these objects about the culture they represent?

PICTURE CARDS

Not only objects but pictures too can be labeled. Children can make their own sight-word cards with pictures on one side and words on the other to use with a partner for sight-reading practice. Another way to make card decks is to put the picture and its label on the same side of the card. A deck like this can be used by partners who take turns drawing a card and acting out what the picture and label are for the other person to guess. Older youngsters can use these labeled card decks* for various rummy-type games. Beginners will probably use single words as labels. As they get older, they can be encouraged to use more precise terms and more elaborated phrases, leading into captioning. See "Captions" on page 271.

PICTURE BOOKLETS

Animal books with a picture and name of a different animal on each page can be put together by very young children. After they have had some experience in book-making, their pictures can be captioned instead of labeled, presenting information about each animal as a kind of miniencyclopedia. A bulletin-board display or book of pictures of class members with their names underneath can help beginners learn to read each other's names.

Making alphabet, number, color, shape, or coloring books can give beginners another opportunity for writing labels for their drawings. Each page can have a separate letter of the alphabet (a capital and a small letter), a number, or a color with its illustrative picture. In a shape book the pages themselves can be in one shape (square, circle, triangle, and so on), and each of the pages can show one of the things that can be drawn using that shape and its name. For example, in a "Triangle Book," one page might have a picture of a tree that is made of overlapping triangles, as in Figure 13.1. Other pages could have other items made from triangles. Younger children may color in outline drawings of items in a coloring booklet that also contains a label for each item (which they might trace).

CHARTS

A chart is really just a step beyond a drawing. Charting is a good way for less verbal children to move from pictures to words. All it takes is adding labels or captions to their drawings. Later they display what they know about a subject in drawings, diagrams, or photographs that break the subject down more into its parts and functions. Since charts almost never stand alone but need words to explain them, they provide excellent experience in reading and writing labels and captions and in coordinating words with graphics. As youngsters try to put information onto charts, they discover the

FIGURE 13.1 TRIANGLE BOOK

usefulness of this kind of diagramming and the value of visual presentation as well as labeling to get across a lot of information in a little space and few words. They can use charts to depict the relation of parts to the whole, as in a diagram of an airplane, or to array items similar in some respects and different in others, as in a comparative set of pictures of reptiles. As children mature, they can put their information into more stylized and finally abstract graphic representations.

Chronology can be shown on a chart as a time line labeling the important events at the appropriate spots on the line. A youngster's first time line might be one of his own lifetime or of the most recent year of his life. Later he can take a longer sweep of history. Relationships can be shown on a chart like a family tree, which is a chart that presents information by branches and position rather than function words.

Playing with rummy-type picture card decks* in which families of objects are pictured and labeled may prove a good way to become familiar with the elements of a chart. The cards are like a chart in modules that can be considered separately and then combined with each other, often in more than one way. Children might be interested in making a chart showing all the cards in either a conventional card deck or a special deck with information about animals, plants, fish, authors, or whatever. Charting the deck poses a kind of logical and informational puzzle.

GRAPHS

Labeling should not be thought of as an activity appropriate only for young children. The process is important throughout schooling whenever graphic representation of raw data is called for. See Chapter 18, Information. A graph is more abstract than a chart; it is a visual conceptualizing of information, a matrix type of data presentation using coordinates. Generally graphs represent quantities laid against some measurement grid. Like charts, they need succinct labels to help the reader know what is being abstracted on the graph. Making their own graphs helps students develop more efficiently the sophisticated skill of graph reading.

Elementary school youngsters can begin by making simple daily temperature graphs or total attendance tallies in the form of a bar or line graph. Graphing can, of course, complement regular math work by translating arithmetical figures into drawings and these drawings, in turn, into words. Children thereby make mathematical statements or sentences in a form that in some respects is more familiar than arithmetical notations. See Figure 13.2.

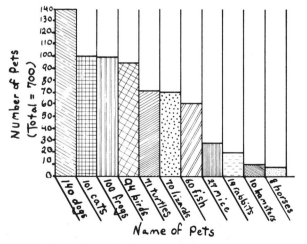

FIGURE 13.2 SAMPLE STUDENT GRAPHS

Source: From James Moffett *Interaction,* Level 2, Charts and Graphs, Houghton Mifflin Company, Boston, 1973.

Every classroom needs to have collections of different types of charts and graphs that students can read and use as models for their own charting and graphing. A booklet of nothing but charts and graphs* is unusual and valuable because students may compare and define for themselves what charts and graphs are and what different things may be done with them—what the possibilities are. Charts and graphs are easy in the sense that they are pictorial and nonverbal, but they are also difficult, because the relations they depict—between quantities or parts and wholes or members of a class—are logical relations that are in themselves rather abstract. Thus charts and graphs are a concrete way of depicting abstractions, with words playing a mediating role.

MAPS

Maps and a globe need to be available to create an awareness of this special medium. If possible, a booklet of nothing but maps* should be on hand to show what different kinds of maps have in common and to sharpen observation by displaying differences from page to page. They are a worthy kind of reading matter within themselves. Students need to become experienced with both reading and making maps as an alternative or supplementary way of saying something. They need to discover what it is that maps can say best and what can be said better in prose. They can see for themselves how verbal labels and captions function to explain and exploit maps. Technical aspects of maps such as keys and projections may be focused on and imitated.

Maps feature not only proper names and other labels but coding as well. Thus they will have some of the same appeal as rebuses and codes, described in the previous chapter. We have found that maps hold an inherent fascination for youngsters, who should be allowed to play out their love affair with them. Maps need not be "taught" so much as pored over and puzzled at until they yield their meaning. Because there is no order, the reader has to move around and back and forth until the pieces come together and until he becomes curious enough about the symbols to find the key. Learners like the code-and-puzzle aspect, but to avoid frustration they may ask questions or get a partner. Of critical importance is the opportunity for students to steep themselves in the medium without the fearful anticipation of tests or the negative association of writing a report afterwards.

For beginners, obtain literary maps from well-known storybooks such as *Winnie-the-Pooh*'s woods or *The Hobbit*'s Middle Earth. Later, students need not only road and street maps and maps of states and countries but also maps showing distribution of rainfall, resources, wildlife, and so on; older maps showing some changes both in mapping and in knowledge of the world; spatial maps such as star charts; and photographic maps made by means of such recent technological innovations as x-ray, high-altitude, and thermal photography, which depict facts in ways we cannot see unaided.

All sorts of physical and psychological material may be put onto a map; mapping is basically a symbolizing of experience. Children can begin by making simple floor plans of their room, home, or school, or maps of their neighborhood, labeling the streets, buildings, and other features. They can make treasure maps for others to follow. Older students can map inner feelings, thoughts, or interests as well as outer reality, labeling different areas of the head, for example. The fact is that once interested in maps, even less-developed students will see the many interesting possibilities of the medium for both fun and fact.

Captions

Captions do more than name; they explain and develop a definition. Thus they lead into dictionary definitions and encyclopedia entries of the illustrated sort. Like labels, captions are always attached to things or pictures. One of the values of captioning and of comparing the ways different persons caption the same thing or picture is to check on egocentricity. Students become increasingly aware of how differently various people see and say things.

THINGS

Captions, like labels, can be found all over the environment. Museum displays, cornerstones, historical markers, instructions on new clothes, and some old gravestones feature captions—facts, statements, or explanations that clarify or add to what they are attached to. Classroom exhibits and displays of objects also can be captioned. Various work areas in a classroom call for captions that show students where to store things or how to proceed.

PICTURES

Students' Drawings or Photographs

Because young children usually find art media a more appealing and easier vehicle for expression than words, they need ample opportunity for drawing and painting. Children's pictures usually encapsulate a story or have the makings of one within them, and so they lend themselves well to captioning. Writing captions can be facilitated by having available a stock of homemade caption strips of the right size to be Scotch-taped to the bottom of the art paper. After a group of children finish painting or drawing, each child can get a strip and write on it what his picture is about. Then the children assemble in small groups to look at each other's pictures and to read the captions, taking turns holding up their pictures and talking about them. As each picture is held up, the caption is folded back and the rest of the group guesses what the picture is about. Then the artist reads his caption and answers any questions the other children may have about it.[1] Many captions will need further explaining because not everything is in the picture and because things the caption refers to may not be evident to the other children. The point of this discussion is to provide an opportunity for children to elaborate orally what the caption summarizes in writing. As children increase in their writing skills, they will be able to add to their caption strips at the end of a discussion an expansion of their original caption. Later they may decide to write a story based on their picture, telling what action precedes and what follows the picture and answering in a narrative some of the questions their classmates asked. This story with the picture attached can be read to the class or displayed.

Captions for drawings can be exchanged, and children can draw new pictures for those captions. Then these can be compared with the drawings done by the first children. Comparing and contrasting these focuses on what words imply and how they can be interpreted. Another way to do this is to have each child caption his own drawing on a

separate paper and then exchange drawings but not the captions. Then each child captions another child's picture, and that caption can be compared with the one the artist did.

Youngsters' drawings on card decks or in picture booklets as described on page 269 can have captions instead of labels, thereby expanding the use of language through a process that is already familiar. What they are compiling are minidictionaries or miniencyclopedias with *visual* definitions.

Not only drawings or paintings but also photographs brought from home or taken by the youngsters can be captioned in books such as "A Typical Day in Our Class," "Our Trip to the Beach," or "My Family." A class book can be assembled, devoting a page or two to each member of the class with his photograph or sketches of him in various characteristic acts or poses, each appropriately captioned, of course.

For students who are fascinated with the process of taking pictures, collecting and captioning these for a bulletin-board display or a booklet leads into language development. Captioned photographs focusing on a single subject, such as beautiful places, sports events, animals at the zoo, or strange sights around the school, provide high-interest classroom reading matter.

Cutout Drawings and Photographs

Found pictures—photographs, drawings, cartoons, advertisements (most of which are little more than illustrations with captions), and so on—cut out and put into scrapbooks are a provocative stimulus for discussion and a trigger for captioning. These student-compiled scrapbooks also provide high-interest reading material for classmates. For those who are weak in reading skills, captioned pictures appeal because the words are few, and many of them are defined in the pictures.

Students can discuss how to caption collections of photographs that show action or invite alternate interpretations. This process leads to an awareness of differing interpretations and a refinement of perceptions. As groups discuss the aptness of alternate captions in order to select the best for display, they need to provide their peers with visual evidence for their choices.

Young children can use collections of photographs mounted on cardboard * in the same way they use their own drawings as a starting point for

[1] See this activity in the *English Through Interaction* elementary-level film "Do and Talk."

captioning, putting their captions on tagboard strips and then exchanging these with classmates who try to match each person's captions with the appropriate photographs. Or, each student might write a caption for a photograph and then hold up the picture to see if the other members of the group can guess what his caption is. Another thing to do is to have each child in turn hold up his captioned picture before the group, but not show his own caption, while the other members write on a slip of paper a caption for what they see in the picture. The child who is sharing his picture then gathers the slips and reads them aloud; the fitness of each caption is discussed. Afterwards he reads his own caption, and his colleagues compare it with theirs.

Collages

Thematic statements may be expressed in collages of pictures and words pasted onto large pieces of paper. Students need not limit themselves to found pictures; they can use their own snapshots and drawings as well. If students choose a subject they feel strongly about, and if they experiment with the composition possibilities of this medium—juxtaposition, spacing, arrangement, overlapping, or cropping of pictures—the result can be an effective statement in picture and word. If students cut out and glue words, phrases, or sentences into a collage, the result might be a kind of concrete poem. In addition to making collages of things that interest them, students might be asked to find pictures or words that center on themes such as who they would like to be in five or twenty years, their real self versus their ideal self, a pressing social issue, or a mood created by a piece of literature, music, or art.

NEWSPAPER HEADLINES AND MAGAZINE HEADINGS

A newspaper headline or title for an article is a special type of caption, which tends to attract attention to a text as well as perhaps to summarize it. Writing headlines and titles is a good experience for students of any age. Focusing on what would get someone to want to read something is an experience in imagining the reader's condition; this is important for any type of communication. Often an evocative photograph with its own caption serves as a way of arresting attention and leading into a written text.

Gradually youngsters move from pictures with captions to a series of pictures that tells a story, comic-strip fashion, to stories in which the words do most of the telling. Finally, the word-picture ratio is reversed until the text is primary and the drawing, secondary. Of course, all the artwork of students should not be appropriated for writing purposes, but one of the goals in writing captions is to build toward the power to communicate in words alone. See pages 276 and 300 for more suggestions on how to move from captioned pictures to invented dialogues and stories.

Captions of particularly evocative pictures may run to several sentences and hence may be a way for some students to begin to write informative articles without being daunted by blank paper. Also, if the pictures are ones they have cut out or taken themselves, the subject matter is likely to be personally interesting enough to insure good motivation for writing informative statements. The first step is an entry in a miniencyclopedia; then they go on to an informative article illustrated with pictures.

WIT

More mature students find in captioning an opportunity for wit, puns, irony, alliteration, and jokes. Captions not only have an epigrammatic quality but also force the writer to think about what the words may say that the picture has not already said. This leads into matters of verbal style that no picture is capable of and also into more abstract sorts of past background or general circumstances that cannot be visually conveyed. In other words, as mature students work with caption-writing, they become aware of the value of words and their interpretative role as they compare captions they have each done for the same picture. When words say what *cannot* be seen, they supply information or interpretation; when they say what indeed *can* be seen, the result is often amusing, especially if the style or tone of the language is deliberately inappropriate.

Editorial cartoons are usually drawings with captions and are more sophisticated than comic strips, which are a series of drawings with the dialogue in balloons. Cartoons depend on wit or incongruity for their humor; they may teach, satirize, or insult. Caricature and other exaggeration in the drawing are juxtaposed with a succinct, often understated caption. Because the allusions may be subtle or unfamiliar, cartoon reading and producing make difficult demands, appropriate for mature students. Projecting cartoons with an opaque projector and reading and discussing the captions together can help less sophisticated students understand them.

Reading and writing labels and captions not only provides significant learning from kindergarten to college but also gives beginning or weak writers an easy place to start to build the skills that they need for other kinds of communication presented in the rest of the chapters of this part of the book.

In this chapter we are combining two of the discourse goals—actual dialogue and invented dialogue. By dialogue we mean all kinds of conversation and discussion between or among two or more people. If the persons are spontaneously interacting as their own selves, this is an actual dialogue. When this talk is written down, it is a transcript. If on the other hand, the speakers are role-playing, they are improvising or engaging in an invented dialogue. When this imagined conversation is written, it is either in the form of a script or a dialogue written as a narrative or a comic strip.

Reading a script or transcript is easier for a less-developed language student than other types of discourse because the language of such texts resembles ordinary talk. At the same time, if the scripting is artful or if the transcript reflects a model of heightened language, it can provide an example of expressive and eloquent discourse that can make clear by contrast the looseness, imprecision, and dullness of much common conversation.

More than any other types of discourse, actual and invented dialogues emphasize the interrogative mode and are often informal in style or tone. They can provide models for alert and involved give-and-take. Nowhere is this more evident than in the special kind of question-and-answer dialogue so familiar in comedy duo routines. Most students enjoy reading and performing these. Another kind of question-and-answer dialogue is the interview, a very important kind of actual dialogue in this curriculum. See page 366.

Actual or invented dialogues are types of discourse that lend themselves most easily to acting out, although any other texts can be performed also. See Chapter 6, Performing Texts. Interpreting and writing scripts involve understanding stage directions, as described on page 361. In this chapter, as we suggest types of dialogue, we assume students will talk, improvise, witness, write, read, and perform them.

Actual dialogue

Actual dialogue is such a common, natural, and pleasurable experience, we often discount its value, especially as a classroom activity. As noted in Part One, Basic Concepts, conversing, in fact, provides the most pervasive and significant of all processes in the development of language facility. Actual dialogue includes all oral exchange, such as ordinary socializing, task talk, brainstorming, topic or panel discussion, monologues, interviews, trials, hearings, and debates—any talk in which speakers are not pretending to be other than themselves. Most significantly, it is a *two-way* transaction—a spontaneous give-and-take among speakers. Actual dialogue is a broad, fundamental goal because it embraces the whole oral base of language and the basic skills of spelling, punctuating, and paragraphing entailed in transcribing speech. Chapter 4, Talking and Listening, and Chapter 11, Decoding and Encoding, present ways to promote actual dialogue at the verbalization level and to transcribe it. So here we shall consider only the actual dialogue that is written—transcripts.

TRANSCRIBING SPEECH

Transcribing and reading transcripts are very important activities seldom before ensured a place in the curriculum. They provide a good opportunity for students to see the relationship between written material and its oral counterpart.

Writing down actual dialogue provides one of the easiest transitions from the familiar world of oral interchange to writing. One way to write a transcript is to tape a conversation and later listen to the tape and write it down, replaying the tape if necessary. Another way is to take notes as you listen and then write up the transcript from these notes. Either way, students develop transcribing and editing skills. See "Transcribing," on page 245.

Classroom conversations, telephone chats, overheard dialogues in public places, interviews, TV talk shows, or public events such as court trials or the deliberations of legislative bodies can be taped and transcribed. This transcript can in turn be used as a script for a performance, re-creating the fullness of the event itself.

READING AND PERFORMING TRANSCRIPTS

There are as many types of transcripts to read and interpret as there are kinds of dialogue, ranging from snatches of random conversation to tightly planned lectures. Books of transcripts* that include such task-oriented dialogue as the exchanges between the astronauts and ground control, or such public events as trials, hearings, interviews, debates of public officials, and deliberations of legislative bodies are invaluable in acquainting students with the range of this type of text.

Transcripts are among the most important sources of documents in this century for the creation of more abstracted materials such as biography and history. Reading and performing these transcripts of public processes (see page 119) may teach far more than anything else in school might about how our government and civic bodies function. Relevant information and moral issues are presented in a way that students find more familiar than essays may be. See page 114 for the process of making Readers Theater scripts, for which transcripts may furnish excellent material, as in Peter Weiss's *The Investigation*.

Invented dialogue

Under this heading we shall consider primarily the reading and writing of invented dialogue, mostly in the form of scripts. Dialogue in narrative form will be covered in the next chapter. See Chapter 5, Dramatic Inventing, for a full treatment of the ways that fictive dialogue can be produced orally. One type of invented dialogue we are not including in this chapter is dialogue of ideas, which is like dramatic dialogue only in the situation of its utterance: it moves away from emotion (which is at the heart of dramatic art) to intellectual discourse, and thus is more akin to essay than dialogue. See Chapter 19, Ideas.

MEDIA ALTERNATIVES

Any invented dialogue can be presented in a number of ways, each of which has a different potential and set of limitations. If the fictive conversation is a script that depends largely on intonation and verbal interaction rather than visual image and scene, it lends itself well to a TV or radio show. If part of the drama of the script is in an unusual appearance of a character or setting, a TV or puppet show or play or video tape (see p. 291) might be more appropriate. For a lighthearted or humorous script or one with fantastic characters, an animated film might be best. If the script calls for several very different settings or fast-paced action, a film might serve well. See page 298. The important thing is that students be aware of their options and select a medium that best suits their own purposes. To assure that students become aware of various alternatives, have on hand for students to look at and imitate collections of scripts for various media.* See page 292.

Radio and TV Scripts

When youngsters first begin to invent radio and TV scripts, they can improvise a dialogue, tape it, and revise it if they choose. Deciding who they are to be and in what place with what problem is usually all that is necessary. The tape can be transcribed for another group to perform. Each episode can end with a cliffhanger to ensure that the audience will tune in to the next show. An announcer, commercials, music, and sound effects—all can be added. The script can be rehearsed and taped for an audience. Any script can be expanded into a series in the radio and TV tradition. See page 109 for ideas about performance.

Comic Strips

One of the best ways to ease children into writing invented dialogue is to have them use the comic-strip medium, a form that is a familiar and popular one for most youngsters. Begin by remaking comic strips; tell youngsters to do this:

- First, cut out different comic strips from newspapers and cut off the words. Then glue these pictures onto strips of paper, exchange them with other students, write new dialogues, and put balloons around them. Add words for sounds such as screeching tires or write explanations, such as "The next morning . . . ," as needed. If you prefer, you can put your dialogues onto a tape instead.
- Next time try cutting out characters from different comic strips and putting them together in the same story.
- Try using a cartoon instead of a comic strip and write what the characters are saying to each other in script form below the picture.
- Next time start with the dialogue. Either copy a dialogue from a comic strip or write up one of your own and have a friend draw a set of pictures to go with it.

"Comics-to-Fill" booklets*, containing pictures with empty balloons to fill with dialogue, provide an attractive lure for interpreting what is implied in movement and facial expressions and for generating appropriate dialogue. Students can be plunged into worlds peopled or operated differently from ours, thereby creating fantasy or science fiction. As a result of their efforts to find suitable dialogue to match the old-fashioned dress of characters in the squares following a time-machine episode in a "Comics-to-Fill" booklet*, one group of seventh graders in Evanston, Illinois, got interested in the *eth* endings of verbs used in the seventeenth century.

As youngsters compare their different dialogues, they move into issues of interpretation or aptness. They may decide to contrast spoken words with gestures or facial expressions by, say, having a character who looks scared try to sound courageous.

Students can read their filled-in comics to classmates or to younger children, allowing the listeners to see the pictures as they read aloud. Or dialogue in pictures can be used as scenarios for acting out radio shows by assigning the depicted action to a sound-effects person and to a narrator, and the dialogue to other actors. Students can be directed on an activity card to go on to make their own comic books by drawing panels as well as writing the dialogue, using these same characters or others of their own invention.

Comics and cartoons provide an appropriate medium for riddle or joke writing. For example, in jokes such as "What did one hose say to the other hose? You're a little squirt," the question can be depicted in a picture and the answer in a balloon above the big hose's head. Dialogue jokes in comic strips can be rewritten as script in joke books.

Filling in comics makes students aware of dialogue by isolating it. Seeing how narrative can be carried by dialogue is good preparation for writing regular scripts, converting poems into choral-reading scripts, and even punctuating and voicing dialogue embedded in fiction. Like films, comics put the narrative into pictures. Balloons become what in narrative are the quotation marks or script format.

POINTS OF DEPARTURE

Photographs

Pictures of people or animals can stimulate dialogue writing. If two pictures of individuals are picked at random—cut from magazines, found in books, or chosen from a set of photo cards*—youngsters can discuss what kind of persons they think these people are and then invent a conversation between the two of them. They may want to improvise a whole scene taking the parts of the two characters depicted. Another way to do this is to start with a picture showing several people and improvise a conversation among them. If students like the resulting dialogue, they may decide to perform it for the class.

A variation is to have each member of a small group start a cartoon sequence by cutting out a face or figure and pasting it at the left end of a long strip of paper, approximately five by twenty-two inches. Then each student passes his strip of paper to the person on his right, who in turn makes up something for the character to say and writes it in a cartoon balloon. He then adds a new character and the third student writes a response to the first character, and so on.

For more mature students, photographs may be a stimulus for monologue writing. A large group might mix up a set of cutout photographs of individuals, and take turns selecting one. Then each person looks carefully at the picture, noting the age, clothing, posture, hands, look in the eyes, setting, and the activity the person depicted is engaged in. Then each person writes out what the person in the picture is thinking or saying to himself. The photographs are set out in a line, the monologues exchanged and read, and each group member takes a turn guessing which monologue belongs to which face, omitting the one he wrote himself, of course.

Pantomimes

Students can watch a pantomime by other students and write out an appropriate dialogue to go with it. Then they can read this script as the pantomime is performed again. Or they can improvise an oral dialogue as they watch the pantomime being performed.

Memories or Shared Experiences

Real events can spark script-writing. Recalled dialogue can be re-created or reshaped and expanded into a script. Personal experience is always a good source for any writing because the feelings are real. See page 328 for ways to tap memories.

Minimal Situations

Just as improvisations can take off from minimal situations (see page 96), so can written scripts. The only difference is that a script is done by one person instead of a group and on paper instead of with voice. Suggestions for characters and situations can be written on activity cards or made up by the students. Each member of a small group might write for fifteen to twenty minutes taking off from the same minimal situation and compare his script with the others at the end of that time. In this case it is best to keep to one single, continuous scene unrolling in one place. Since drama by definition is re-creating events at life rate, the playing time of the script would be the same as the time the action would take in real life. Putting the matter this way helps keep the scene truly dramatic and emphasizes the fact that a script is a blueprint for enactment.

Improvising

Improvising is another effective point of departure for dialogue writing. Beginners can tape improvised conversations and transcribe them as scripts, or improvisations that are going well can be deliberately interrupted and taken to paper. Collections of scripts* in the classroom serve as models for the punctuation and form of scripts, thereby eliminating the need to "teach" script writing.

One way to organize an improvisation-to-script-writing process is to divide a group into performers and transcribers. As the performers act out the improvisations, the transcribers write down in note form what is said. Each transcriber concentrates on just one performer. After the improvisation is over, the two groups get together and write out the play. At this point they can revise and sharpen it. Here it is important that both groups agree not only on *what* was said but also *how* it was said. They will need to decide which punctuation marks and spacing best reflect the intonation and stress. For example, they might write:

> Carol: Good evening!
> Carol: *Good* evening?
> or
> Carol (sadly): Good evening.

Finished scripts of improvisations can be rehearsed and performed or exchanged with other groups to be performed by them.

Taking off from Literature

Fables, folk tales, myths, legends, Bible stories and other synoptic narratives can be fleshed out into scripts. In one ninth grade, drama and script-writing were used in a study of myths. The students took the characterizations and plot summaries from Edith Hamilton's *Mythology* and expanded them into group-written scripts, which they then rehearsed and performed. They used the texts only as sources, which meant that individuals read them in whatever way they thought best (including skip-reading) to glean what they needed to know for their drama. What actually happened was that in order to make up the dialogue and compose the scenes, the groups had to straighten out the action and interpret the characters by discussing them and by referring to the text for evidence. This class got very involved in the dramatizations. Another class in the same school read and studied the myths as texts. After reading a number of the myths, this class began to groan and lose interest. At the end of the year, the two classes took the same factual test on the myths. The class that had enacted them remembered them as well as the one that had studied them with the teacher. Students, moreover, who had been known to read with poor comprehension seemed definitely to understand and remember the material they had dramatized much better than they usually remembered texts they read and studied.[1]

You can draw a minimal situation from a scene in a story, play, or novel that the students have read. This would be an off-stage scene referred to by the characters or the narrator but not directly presented. For example, we are told that one character informed another of something important. How did he say it, and how did the other react when he heard the news? Or, what do you suppose Cinderella's sisters said to themselves as they went home from the ball?

A SCRIPT-WRITING SEQUENCE

In general, it is best to begin with simple plays having only a few characters and move to longer and more complex ones with more characters. Begin with short duologues and keep the dramas short as long as students still lapse into narrative. After they have written some complete scenes, they may find it possible to sustain dramatic and interior monologues.

As a blueprint for moment-to-moment action, many scripts represent a far greater detailing of story than any narrative, which is always some narrator's *summary* of such things as dialogue and movement. In other words, as a direct simulation of action, plays represent the least abstracted, most detailed rendering of a story possible. Students who have had experience scripting tend, when writing regular narrative, to have a better sense of how much detail is required and when to include or exclude it.

Because they are so used to narrative, inexperienced students tend to write a play as a plotted story that jumps a great deal in time and space. The result is a series of very brief snatches of scenes arranged to plant the seed of a plot, show the main action, and reveal the aftermath. In such efforts one can see too much concern for a final twist or smash ending. Misuse of stage directions is one of the symptoms—narrating a short story, often with telltale lapses into the past tense. Stage directions should contain only what can be seen and heard, except for an occasional indication about how to stage and act the scene. Explanations of background circumstances, recounting of offstage action, and descriptions of thoughts and feelings do not belong; they merely show that the student is still thinking of narrative, not drama.

Veteran improvisers are not nearly so likely to confuse dramatic writing with narrative. In any case, don't warn the students about these problems in advance, for more learning will take place if they write scripts spontaneously and find out about the problems for themselves when others try to enact their script or discuss it after a trial reading. What helps to head off the narrative tendency, if there is one, is to make initial playwriting a direct extension of improvisation and to make the directions clear—a single, uninterrupted scene playable in, say, five minutes, with stage directions that read like a sensory recording, and containing no more than two or three characters. This last stipulation keeps the dynamics manageable and makes dramatic focusing easier. See page 286 for ways to help mature students move to writing dramatic monologues with no stage directions at all.[2]

Short Duologue

A duologue is a drama consisting of just two interweaving voices and often having no stage directions. Here is a duologue composed by one of a group of urban summer school students (mostly black, who had just finished the seventh or eighth grade) who had been taken on a school-sponsored trip to the beach the day before. Their memory of that experience was their point of departure for scriptwriting.[3]

---

1. Put him in the pot and cook him.
2. O.K. You can have it.
1. That nasty creature.
2. What do you mean, nasty? I got my toe missing because of that.

---

[1] This bit of research with the test, which was initiated for his own purposes by Joseph Hanson, then head of the English department at Weeks Junior High School in Newton, Massachusetts, was not controlled in a very scientific way but was of the practical sort teachers often conduct in order to make choices among different methods. If only for your own satisfaction, we suggest you replicate this experiment.

[2] See the elementary- and secondary-level *English Through Interaction* films, "Small-Group Writing" for group writing of short plays.
[3] Their teacher was Kenneth McElheny, working in the Harvard-Boston Summer School with Teresa Hamrock of the Lewis Junior High School, located in the Roxbury section of Boston, Massachusetts.

1. I don't care if it bit your head. Get it out of here.
2. O.K. But the next time I'll be back with a shark.
1. You do and I'll get a whale.

Another student could only eke out the following:

---

1. Want a crab?
2. Eeeek!

These duologues are brief, a fact that is partly explained by the students being unaccustomed to writing much. However, they do have the element of drama. By dispensing with stage directions, they have thrown the burden of action onto the dialogue, which is where it belongs in a drama. Whereas some middle-class children writing under the constraint of duologue for the first time often have to rig it in an artificial way, lower-class youngsters seem to have a knack for letting the speech capture the situation, perhaps because their language is more oriented to action and setting. Working with a title was the point of departure for this inner-city boy about to enter the ninth grade.

AN UNDERSTANDING

JOE: Me, I'm going to the movies with Bob. O.K.?

MOTHER: No, it isn't O.K.

JOE: Why not?

MOTHER: Because you said you'd clean the garage today.

JOE: I can do it some other time. Please?

MOTHER: You're doing it today and that's all there is to it.

JOE: Oh! Come on, Ma, I promise I'll do it tomorrow.

MOTHER: Joe, you heard me.

JOE: Oh, all right you ch——

MOTHER: What did you say?

JOE: Nothing, Ma, nothing. Ma can I go after I'm done?

MOTHER: Yes, Joe when you're finished you can go. And Joe,

JOE: Yes, Ma.

MOTHER: There's a quarter. Buy yourself a Coke.

JOE: Oh. Thanks Ma! [4]

Three-Way Dialogue

The next step might be a conversation among three people. Following a statement of a minimal situation, a boy in a summer school program that had introduced improvisations wrote this:

Situation—You want to go to the ballgame but you don't want to take your little brother.

Scene—Saturday afternoon warm and beautiful day for baseball.

JACK: Mom, I'm going to the ballgame.

MOM: Alright (*overheard by little brother*)

JOE: Can I go with you Jack, please

JACK: No!!!

MOM: *Who* the hell is doing that Hollering

JOE: Jack is. He won't take me to the ballgame.

JACK: Man, he's always going with me. I didn't go with him when he went to Brocton.

MOM: I know but you know how he likes the Yankees.

JACK: I don't give a da——— darn who he likes.

MOM: I dare you to swear and I'll whip your ass so bad you won't go to the ballgame at all.

JACK: Alright I'll take him give me his money

MOM: Go get my pocketbook (*Joe goes to get it*)

JOE: Mom I can't find it

MOM: Oh shit I left it in the back seat of the car and your father took the car.

JACK: Dats tooo bad (*he says to Joe like a baby and giggles*)

JOE: (*crying*) Ma you're stupid

MOM: (*with belt in her hand whips Joe*) How dare you you bastard.

JACK: So long Mom I be back after the game. [5]

The language here is a real reflection of environment, we think, not an attempt to scandalize. If the

[4] Supplied by Graham Ward, director of English at the Brooks Academy Summer School in North Andover, Massachusetts, a program for inner-city students.

[5] The author was about to enter seventh grade in the Milton Academy Summer School for inner-city students under the leadership of the director of English, Richard Herrmann.

teacher can avoid feeling unsettled, permitting this realism will yield a very worthy payoff for both writing and emotional expression. The shift in dynamics, incidentally, that accompanies a shift from two-person to three-person interaction warrants some attention in workshop discussion, since it throws light on both literature and life. At some point in this stage of dramatic writing some duets and trios could be juxtaposed and compared either in workshop discussion or in class performances.

A Complete Short Play

The following playlet is a fairly typical effort by a middle-class seventh grader to develop a continuous action into a climax and to handle a fairly large cast of characters. The reader will find the scene rather hard to follow, first of all, because the child had never learned earlier to punctuate by ear. Dialogue writing makes very clear the inadequacy of teaching punctuation by rules and teacher correction, even when done in first-rate schools with able children. Also, the child was not quite ready to control an action as ambitious as this one. He had not had enough prior experience handling fewer characters and a single, simple scene. Allowing for these deficits in experience, the attempt to shape dialogue and action into a purposeful composition was rather good.

THE MYSTERIOUSE DOORKNOB

Cast

Jin Jones—the father
Mary Jones—the mother
Sue Johns—There twelve year old daugh-

ter whos set on being a private detective
Jack—her eleven year old brother
Patty—her ten year old sister

Setting

The Living Room

MARY: Jin are you sure you put the cat out

JIM: Yes dear I'm sure

MARY: The nights so dark do you think Sue can take care of Jack and Patty

JIM: Yes dear I'm sure besides we won't be gone long and its not a school night there all around the same age anyhow.

MARY: If you say so now lets say good by to the children Sue Jack Patty were leaving now if any thing happens we will be at the nunber (*shows peace of Paper*) you can all stay up till we get home

JIM: Yes and heres the key lock the door when we leave and don't let any one in. Good by (*they leave*

SUE: Okay first well watch hony west then the smothers brothers then the man from UNCLE

JACK: It always has to be your way oh comon lets watch something else there just showing repeats

PATTY: Ya oh comon

SUE: Theres nothing good on oh so I guess well have to watch. . .

PATTY: Well lets see whats on (*Jack goes to turn it out all of the sudden the lights go out*)

JACK: We blew a fuse all go try to fix it.

SUE: No!

JACK: What do you mean by no its just in the closet

SUE: (*in a whisper*) Someone might be in there

PATTY: Oh Sue you're cracked Jack heres the flash light

JACK: (*All of the sudden closet door twists*) Help! (*It stops*)

PATTY: I'm scared

SUE: Go get my privet eye soutcase Patty comeon Jack give her the flash light and let's hide behind this chair

PATTY: No! not me there may be more people around

SUE: She's right

JACK: Shut up there may be someone listening to us (*all of the sudan Mother and father burst into the room*

MARY: I told you Jin I'm sure I saw the lights go off when we pulled out oh children are you all right!

PATTY: Ya Mom

JIN: Sue why didn't you lock the door or call us (*closet door knob moves again*

JACK: Dad theres someone in the closet!

JIM: What!

MARY: Oh no my poor baby! (*father gets stick opens door looks in attaches to wires together light goes on, shuts door*)

JIM: Mary you naged me hard to come home because the cat was in the closet

MARY: You said you put the cat out!

JIM: So I did

And they all start to lagh

Although there were better plays written by the author's classmates (most of whom are more literate, we hasten to add) we have chosen this one to reproduce because one of us was present when it was performed and discussed. The comments from the other students were as follows: They appreciated the way in which the father's negligence, the main-spring of the action, was planted in the opening exchange and returned to at the end but felt that several problems combined to spoil the main effect. The play depended a lot, they said, on the audience's seeing and hearing things to which the players were supposed to react—the sound of the cat, the doorknob turning, the lights and TV going on and off—but which the production did not allow enough for (and which, indeed, would to some extent have required better facilities). As a result, both the title and some of the actions seemed pointless. The fact that the audience did not laugh at the end, as they were supposed to, was attributed to some of these failures of effects as well as to some confusion in the writing. The actors said that a number of the lines had had to be changed during rehearsals because they left character and action unclear. To this comment the audience added that the behavior of the characters was inconsistent enough to confuse them about which children were supposed to be fearful and which were not. For his part, the author said he would have directed a couple of things rather differently. A very positive suggestion from the class was to build up the scary atmosphere more—with stormier weather, horror show on TV, and the telling of ghost stories. Perhaps this discussion illustrates the kinds of learning that can take place in a workshop atmosphere.[6] See pages 100 and 154.

The eighth- and ninth-grade dialogues written in that same middle-class school were of high quality, partly because of the emphasis we placed on drawing dramatic material from familiar experience.

When the students did write scenes about far-fetched or fantastic characters and actions, they almost always fell into cliché—borrowed stories from books, movies, and television. With rare exceptions, the shaping of realistic material showed more creative imagination than the so-called making up of situations. But, again, mere injunction or admonition is not the best educational strategy; if some children need to ignore the emphasis on realism, it may be better to let them learn from peer reaction whether their far-fetched inventions are worthwhile or not. The problems may simply mean that their imagination was not allowed to develop earlier.

In practically all the dialogues that were written in these grades, even in the casual, slice-of-life conversations, one saw efforts to compose the scene in various meaningful ways—to define a relationship among characters, to contrast personalities, to comment satirically, to differentiate styles of speech, to set up conflicts, to bring out social and moral issues. One teacher said this process produced the best writing of the year; students wrote at great length and enjoyed doing so.[7]

A Play of More Than One Scene

Experienced students might try one-act plays containing two to four short scenes that distinctly develop a dramatic idea. The activity card directions need not stipulate multiple scenes; they merely need call for a complete play performable in, say, twenty or thirty minutes. The number of scenes and characters is left to the author.

Here is a sample play by a ninth-grade girl that illustrates what high school students might go on to do with playwriting. Her introduction and her abstract designation of the characters show the representative value she intended the characters and actions to have. Like professionals, amateurs often make general statements through their dramas.

[6] The workshop teacher was Elizabeth Cawein, Weeks Junior High School, Newton, Massachusetts.

[7] The teacher was Eugenia Nicholas, Weeks Junior High School, Newton, Massachusetts.

BUT MOM . . .

Author's introduction

Names have been omitted except where necessary (as in the dialogue) because I feel the scenes are too typical to pin down to one family.

Scene I

(*It is a typical study. The walls are dark wood. There is an overhead lamp lighting up the room. A middle-aged lady, dressed in a black sweater and pants, is sitting at the desk. She has a cigarette in her hand. She is tapping absentmindedly on the ashtray. A young girl of about fifteen can be heard reading a paper she is holding. As she finishes, she looks up.*)

DAUGHTER: Well? Any comments?

MOTHER: Very good for a first draft.

DAUGHTER: Mother, I read you the first draft two days ago.

MOTHER: Oh, (*absently*) did you?

DAUGHTER: Yes, and you told me to rewrite the part about the type of love between parents and children. Do you have any final corrections?

(*There is a pause. The mother doesn't seem to be concentrating on what is being said to her. The daughter is waiting for a reply.*)

DAUGHTER: Well—? (*She puts the paper on the table*)

MOTHER: I'm thinking. (*Then she seems to be talking aloud to herself*) I better call and change my hair appointment to nine o'clock.

DAUGHTER: Mother!

MOTHER: Hmmm?

DAUGHTER: You're not listening.

MOTHER: What? (*Pause*) I'm sorry dear, I wasn't listening.

Scene II

(*The table in the kitchen is small and has been crowded into a small nook. The area has been painted another color. The purpose behind this was to make it look like a separate breakfast room.*)

(*The daughter is sitting at the table reading. The mother summons her while entering the room.*)

MOTHER: Why can't you *once* have the table set before your father gets home?

DAUGHTER: But Mom, we're going out for dinner.

MOTHER: Never mind the excuses. Why don't you go upstairs and start getting ready, dear. The Shermans will be by for us at seven and we don't want to keep them waiting.

DAUGHTER: But Mom, it's three-thirty.

MOTHER: I know, but sometimes it takes you a long time to get ready. Besides, I want you to look nice for them. You want to make a good impression on them, don't you?

DAUGHTER: Mother. I am not concerned with looking nice for *them*—I am not out to impress people. I want to look nice for myself.

MOTHER: O.K. How about for your father and me? We like to see you look nice.

DAUGHTER: Hmm.

MOTHER: If not for us, do it for your brother. He's dating their daughter. You don't want them to think he comes from a family of slobs.

DAUGHTER: How come he doesn't have to go tonight?

MOTHER: You're making it sound like a chore to go out with us. You know, if you want to stay home tonight you can. We aren't twisting your arm. It costs a lot of money to take you out and there are plenty of other things we could be doing with it instead.

DAUGHTER: You still didn't say why Alan got out of it.

MOTHER: Alan "got out of it" because he had already made a date for tonight and it wouldn't be polite to break it.

DAUGHTER: But Mom, he's going out with Rene Sherman!

MOTHER: (*What her daughter has said finally dawns on her*) You know, you have a point there.

FATHER: (*As he enters he pats his daughter on the head*) Yes, I always said she was a sharp kid.

DAUGHTER: Oh, Dad.

FATHER: How about playing a little tennis?

MOTHER: Mel, I thought she should be getting ready to go out.

FATHER: But Ruth, it's three-thirty!

Scene III

(*Father and daughter enter the house wtih their tennis rackets. The clock on the wall shows that it is close to six-thirty.*)

MOTHER: Did you have a good game?

DAUGHTER: Yes, and boy am I exhausted.

MOTHER: Mel, you shouldn't have let her work herself up like that. She just got over being sick.

FATHER: But Ruth, she was better two weeks ago.

MOTHER: I heard her blow her nose yesterday.

FATHER: I'm sure tired. We had to stop at the gas station on the way home because the tire was flat and I did't have a spare.

DAUGHTER: Come on—let's get ready. The Shermans will be here in less than a half-hour
(*Daughter and father start up the stairs together, but Mother suddenly calls out to them*)

MOTHER: Wait a minute dear. Could you stay down here a minute and help me roll a ball of yarn?

DAUGHTER: Now?

MOTHER: Well, I want it for tonight.

DAUGHTER: But Mom, we're going out to dance. You can't knit at the table.

FATHER: Maybe she wants to tell some interesting yarns.

MOTHER: All right (*she continues in a rejected tone*) go upstairs and get ready. It's OK. I'll do it myself and if I don't finish then I won't finish. So I won't knit tonight.
(*She is obviously waiting for a response, but she gets none, she goes on to add:*)

MOTHER: If it was a sweater for you, I'm sure you'd be able to find the time.

FATHER: Why don't we get dressed first, and if we have any time, *then* roll the yarn.

MOTHER: You know there won't be time after we get dressed. You've got to do it now.

FATHER: But Ruth, it really isn't shorter if you roll yarn first and then get dressed, or . . . Oh, never mind. It's no use.

Scene IV

(*The door bell rings. The mother, dressed in a simple black cocktail dress can be seen in the hall running towards the stairs. She sees her reflection with the pink wall paper in the mirror and stops*)

MOTHER: Somebody else get it please—I'm a mess. It must be the Shermans. (*She starts back to her room*)

DAUGHTER: Joyous raptures.

MOTHER: (*from her room*) Make sure you know who it is before you open the door! (*The daughter takes one last glance in the mirror, straightens her hair and gallops down the stairs. She pulls the curtain to the side to see who is outside. Forcing a big smile, she sighs and opens the door. Suddenly without warning she is bombarded by six-year-old twin boys dressed in suits. One has a cowlick and both have devilish grins. Then in walks a little girl, obviously a little older than them and feeling more dignified.*)

DAUGHTER: Won't you come in? Mom and Dad will be right down. (*The Shermans enter. You can tell by their faces all the fun they had getting the children ready and over there.*)

GUEST: I hope we're not too early.

MOTHER: (*Coming down the stairs putting her last*

few hairs into place mumbles to herself) three and a half minutes.

GUEST: What's that?

MOTHER: *(Blushing slightly)* I said Mel will be down in a half a minute. Let me take your coats and we'll go inside for a drink. *(The telephone rings. The daughter runs into the study and answers it.)*

DAUGHTER: Hello? *(pause)* John? *(Pause—sarcastically)* No, you don't have the wrong number, you just have the wrong person. *(She hangs up)* *(The guest's voice can be heard as they approach the study)*

GUEST: Oh, Tommy brought his crayons with him. *(They are now in the room)* Is it all right if he draws on that paper until we're ready to leave? *(He is pointing to the paper that the daughter had read to her mother that afternoon.)*

MOTHER: Of course, it's only a first draft of Amy's and she doesn't mind. Do you, dear?

DAUGHTER: But Mom . . .[8]

For one thing, this play raises the important technical issue of scene-breaking: how many scenes, and which ones, are required to dramatize successfully a given piece of material? Does *But Mom . . .* need four scenes, and what is their effect?

Learning About Technique

Somewhere in the learning cycle through which such a play passes, this issue of technique should be raised. The sooner in the cycle the better, perhaps, but not necessarily always. The whole cycle can include a drama workshop reading and discussion of the first draft (duplicating enough copies for acting scripts would certainly facilitate this), or silent reading of the first draft in a writing workshop, followed by written commentary and discussion (exchanging manuscripts in a small group); a rehearsed reading or performance before the class; and preparation for publication by a group of editors who consult with the author and incorporate the reactions of audience and actors.

Overfragmenting a play into small scenes may represent a lingering confusion of narrative with drama, an immoderate eagerness to score an ideological point through plot manipulation, or simply an unskillful, uneconomical constructing of the material. Scene shifts mean time pauses and perhaps new locales. Are these justified? They also introduce problems about how to indicate in the dialogue facts that cannot be seen—the new time and place, their significance, and what has occurred in the interim. Putting such information in the mouths of the characters can come off as well-motivated and integral action or as obviously phony talk for the audience's benefit. Pacing is also involved in scene shifts. Is

each scene as long or as short as it ought to be for what it tries to do? The speed of both the individual scene and the succession of scenes has to be considered here—the rate at which an audience assimilates certain actions and the cumulative effect of short and long scenes.

These dramaturgical matters, which are exactly those that the professional faces, can be raised by students in their own ways at various points in the cycle, but if necessary you may raise them. Do this while sitting in on a writing group or acting group, sometimes at the end of a class reading, if a certain problem seems to be widespread but unrecognized. Often one thoughtful question is enough: "What would happen if we dropped this scene?" (To let the students test whether it is justified or not.) "What if Charles dramatized a meeting in the shop instead of having the girl just refer to it?" (To open up other compositional possibilities.) Pace can be focused on by your personal reaction: "I felt that scene went by too fast (or dragged in the middle). Did anyone else feel that?" Most of all, try to spot the technical implications buried in *student* commentary and to make them emerge so that students will then spot them for each other.

Learning to Describe

If one glances back through *But Mom . . .*, looking only at the stage directions, he will become aware of how much description the play contains. A virtue of playwriting is the opportunity it affords to practice the accurate and significant rendering of appearances—the look of a room, the look on someone's face. Far from being an exercise, play description is purposeful and functional—an indication of what the prop people should do and a relevant adjunct to the action. The writer has to think about real spatial relations, on the one hand, and about significant

---

[8] This student was in the class of Joseph Hanson, head of the English department at Weeks Junior High School, Newton, Massachusetts.

selection of details, on the other. Production of a play will often put description to the test of clarity. Moreover, since stage directions also include an account of the action, the writer must coordinate description and narration in ways characteristic of other writing as well.

Dramatic Monologue

Monologues are like dramatic duologues and dialogues in the situation of their utterance, but they are more like "ideas" in their content. See page 454. Thus, while still emphasizing personality and behavior, as in dramatic dialogue, monologue also continues to move students toward idea and essay writing. Monologue calls for isolating and sustaining an individual voice, thereby taking the fundamental posture of the writer, who is a monologuist. Sometimes monologues can be performed by having different players assume different moods or attitudes of the same character, thereby heightening the distinctions between them. This process is similar to splitting the lines in chamber theater or choral reading. See Chapter 6, Performing Texts.

Dramatic monologue is a sustained solo voice talking to at least one other person; interior monologue is an inner, private voice. Improvising is a good starting point for either. Most dramatic monologues, at least in real life, are sustained solos occuring in the midst of dialogue; only in literature are they sometimes excerpted as self-sufficient speeches. Therefore, a good starting point is to introduce monologue into small-group work as part of a duologue in which one character dominates and the other is reduced to incidental reacting: a parent gives a lecture during an argument with a child; one character tries to "bring around" another who is sulking; or a salesman gives his pitch. Next, players think of situations in which, for the entire scene, one of the two people does all of the talking and the other reacts silently or merely mumbles an occasional reply or is cut off whenever he opens his mouth.

A somewhat different point of departure is the more formal situation of an individual addressing a group. Examples are a coach giving a pep talk at half time, a treasurer explaining to the board why an organization is short of money, a television announcer giving news or weather or a commercial, a young person giving an excuse to an adult, or a boss giving directions to his workers. Several other students silently play the listeners, and students take turns being the monologuist.

Improvising prepares for writing a dramatic monologue, which is simply improvising on paper, using the same kinds of minimal situations as starting points. At first a situation might be stipulated in a cartoon to link the process to dialogue-writing from comic strips.

The first time or two that students write dramatic monologues, direct them to set up the monologue in script form and stipulate a playing time of two to five minutes. Later they can be directed to strip the writing down to voice only; the accompanying action, the time and place, and the identity of the listeners all have to be reflected or implied in what the speaker says. The monologue is written as a straight piece of prose, without opening and closing quotation marks. It may recount an incident and thus constitute a kind of short story told by a participant.

A Sample Student Monologue

To show how much a sophisticated ninth grader can do with this form, here is a long dramatic monologue one girl wrote. She indicated the listener's responses with spaces.

Hello dear, I'm Mrs. Fox. I live upstairs in 302. I thought I'd come to welcome you to the neighborhood. May I come in? Have you been married long?

You just got married? Isn't that sweet! Maybe that explains it.

Why I haven't heard much talking down here since you moved in. In the evenings, that is. You probably don't know very many people around here. During the day you seem to have plenty of workmen here, but in the evenings—no one.

You'd better watch out for them—the workmen—I could tell you stories about brides getting involved and . . . what's that?

Oh, you read *Women's Life* magazine too? Well, I was just telling you for your own good.

You must really be lonely every night here home alone with your husband, just being married and all. Do you or your husband play chess? You must come to dinner one evening next week. Harry and I would love to have you. He'd just adore playing chess with—

Oh yes, thank you. —with Richard, and you and I could sit and chat.

Really, Neither of you plays chess? That's a shame. I'm sure Harry would simply love to teach Robert—

I'm sorry—to teach Richard to play chess. It would break up a dull evening for you both.

I'd like to tell you a little bit about the neighbors. Some of them are busy bodies who always go around minding everyone else's business. Like Helen—She lives down the hall in 210. Just the other day, Midge (310) was listening in the heater duct and heard Helen telling someone about Charlene getting married to some millionaire New Yorker and then trying to poison him for his money. Imagine. Well, I'll tell you something and this is a fact. I know, because I heard from May, and she was told by Leslie, who said she had a very reliable source. You see, Charlene didn't rea . . .

Of course I'll excuse you. Your dinner comes first. I'll just sit and wait until you've finished preparing it and then we can talk until Ronald, or is that Raymond—whatever—gets home.

Don't worry. I wasn't thinking of offering assistance. You see, ordinarily I would because I just had my nails done because Harry and I are—

Yes, don't they, though. You're a dear—because Harry and I are having a dinner party tonight for some very influential people in a golf club because Harry wants to join. Personally, I don't see how anyone would want to waste his time hitting a little ball around with a stick. It's beyond me. Well, as they say, you have to make some adjustments in every marriage. You'll find that out, dear.

Getting back to dinner—I would ask you to come, but you know how it is. I have so many things to do before they come. I should be home right now, putting—

I wouldn't think of leaving you here alone for the rest of the afternoon.

I have to put out cigarettes and tell Joanne—that's our maid—(rather stubborn but irreplaceable) to put some almonds in the string beans. You simply must try it sometime when you and Ralph have company. Excuse me a moment . . . yes? Joanne? Oh good Lord, a half an hour earlier? Yes. Thank you . . . That was Joanne yelling down the heater duct. I hope you don't mind. It's so

much more convenient—Lilian and I used to use it all the time (she used to live here). A darling girl. She dyed her hair, though. We used to have tea together three times a week. She did wonders with this place. She had a knack for decorating. It's done very simply now, but I'm sure once you get settled you'll have the place fixed up: a new rug, some new drapes, another chair. Maybe you could use an interior decorator. They're expensive, but they could do wonders with a place like this. I know of a good one—oh, what's her name? Well I could get her number for you if—

Oh you don't think you'll be calling in a decorator? When you decide to start, do let me know. It will be such fun to go around from store to store helping you pick out things. I did that with Lilian. There's the telephone.

Certainly.

He wants you to go pick him up at the train station? You have to leave now? Of course, you probably haven't had time to pick out another car yet. Harry does business with a gentleman whose brother sells Lincolns. I'm sure he could get you a fair price.

Yes, of course, Well, it's been nice having this conversation with you. perhaps we can continue it another day. I'm glad I came down. I think it's good for neighbors to get to know each other.[9]

Self-exposure of the speaker is one of the things best accomplished by this form, and this girl, like many other students, exploits the advantage fully. The resulting satire is often exaggerated but not inappropriately so for the age; it is heavy to a degree one would expect from young adolescents and Sinclair Lewis. The cards are stacked, but within the exaggeration there lie many subtleties of language and behavior—all shown, not described. So much of the art of plays and fiction consists of making the characters reveal themselves without author commentary. Students who have tried this art recognize it when they see it and read literature with better comprehension.

Consider, for another example of literary technique, the matter of understatement. At the same time that dramatic monologue overplays the speaker, it underplays the listener. The scene above was actually a conversation, but it is made to appear as

[9] Weeks Junior High School, Newton, Massachusetts.

a monologue by merely reflecting instead of quoting the words of the young wife. A novelist constantly makes decisions about whom to quote, when to quote, and whom to quote when. As much as anything, what accounts for the success of the famous opening scene in *Pride and Prejudice* is that Jane Austen quotes Mrs. Bennett directly and throws the brief replies of Mr. Bennett into indirect discourse, thereby putting the grossness of the one on display and investing the other with a sly and winning irony somewhat like that of the bride in the scene above. It frequently happens that the reader of a dramatic monologue identifies with the listener, not with the speaker.

Understatement and the speaker's self-betrayal are artful creations by the writer. Instead of setting out to teach these literary techniques as concepts— and spoiling good literature by presenting it as examples of the concepts—the teacher does better to let the students *practice* the techniques. Then they will see what an author is doing *while* they are reading instead of needing to have it pointed out to them afterward.

Dramatic Monologue as a Poem

Mature students may be encouraged to write the dramatic monologue as a poem. To do so involves them in the important matter, so often encountered in both lyric and dramatic poetry, of harmonizing the natural diction and rhythm of speech with the artifices of poetic language—the greater richness of diction, inversions of word order, metrical and rhythmic patterns, and breaking of lines. Why would a writer depart from daily speech? What does he gain? Why do so many dramatists not concern themselves about realistic language? If they write dramatic speech in poetry, students will know. Furthermore, associating dramatic monologue with poetry will accustom students to listening for a character voice when they read *any* poetry, for even if he is not creating a character as such, but speaking in his own voice, the writer of a poem selects a tone, stance, and style that is not always the same for every poem; he creates a speaking personality out of some part of himself.

Interior Monologue

An *interior monologue* is what a character situated in a given time and circumstance is perceiving and thinking. Although it is merely a simulation of trains of thought that go on in us all the time, as a school writing project, it can look very different from anything the students are familiar with. The most effective point of departure for interior monologue is a minimal situation for improvising in which one character speaks his thoughts aloud as he engages in some action. There may or may not be other people in the scene; if there are, they pantomime. Students who have created dialogues and dramatic monologues will find shifting the monologue inward to be a fairly simple and very understandable variation.

An activity card might feature a photograph and ask students to imagine what a person pictured there is thinking. Or students may be told: "Make up a character whose way of thinking and speaking you feel confident you can imitate; imagine him somewhere doing something; then write down in his own words what he is thinking and feeling during this situation." With concurrent drama work, and with a previous program such as we have been recommending, students should have little difficulty with this.

Directions for writing an interior monologue are essentially the same as for an improvisation. Length is specified in terms of speaking time. At first the monologue should be written as a script with stage directions, and then, on subsequent occasions, as a direct presentation of voice alone. The former corresponds to soliloquy in the theater, and the latter to a kind of fiction or poetry. Soliloquy is an internal monologue spoken aloud for the audience, not the other characters, to hear.

The script form may be an easier way to make the transition to paper. To the extent, however, that the character's thoughts are reflecting what is going on around him, stage directions may be unnecessarily repetitious. On the other hand, a contrast may be intended between the thoughts and the surrounding action. The direct presentation of the inner voice alone takes more art, since no other source of information supplements the voice, and the resulting indirection is often more enjoyable for the reader, who must re-create more from inference. The difference between writing an acting script and writing a version to be read is itself valuable to learn about. Theatrical soliloquy and the fictional technique of interior monologue can also be related in this way, which would be a considerable help in reading literature.

Sample Student Interior Monologues

Below is a brief, simple interior monologue written

by an inner-city boy during the summer before he entered ninth grade:

JUSTICE?

Why'd she have to pick on me? I didn't have my hand up. She could have picked on any other kid in the class. I don't know the answer, and she knows it. Why doesn't she pick on some other kid instead of staring at me? The whole class is looking at me; waiting for my answer. If I'm bright, so what, big deal; there'll just be another time. What could the answer be? Good, she's looking around the room; maybe she'll pick on someone else. Then I'll be the one that can laugh and make fun of him. I'll be able to stare at him; make him nervous. No? She's looking back at me and I still don't know the answer. Don't look at me, you idiot, pick on someone else. Wish there never was school or teachers. Good, she's looking around the class again, so maybe she'll pick on someone else. She always picks on me; pick on someone else! I wish the bell would ring—oh no! She saw me looking at the clock! Now she's mad. The bell!!! Saved!! No! She won't let the class go; she's keeping us after. She can't! At last, I'm free! [10]

One virtue of this kind of writing, as this paper demonstrates, is that the movement of language is fitted to the movement of mind, a virtue that goes far beyond dramatic writing. It is what makes even an abstract essay seem to live and breathe, to put us in the writer's mind. There is a special kind of self-expressive value too: under the pretense of putting words in the mouth of an invented character, a student can write many real personal thoughts that he might be embarrassed to offer frankly as his own. Consider also the detailing of thought and feeling in this paper compared to the less effective, generalized *statement* of feeling a student would produce in a paper the same length written in response to "My Most _____ Moment." Because drama is a moment-to-moment thing, assignments based on it will inevitably produce detail.

As a chronicling of thoughts, an interior monologue is a kind of story, but the content of the thoughts may range over many things that do not belong to the moment. The monologue may utter not only present sensations but also memories of the

[10] Brooks Academy Summer School, North Andover, Massachusetts.

past, speculations about the future, and general reflections of all sorts. Thus it may contain bits of narrative and personal essay. The chronology of the present provides an easy and meaningful way to talk about and relate many things that teachers often try to get at by more logically arranged assignments. The able ninth-grade girl writing below is doing essentially what the boy just quoted did, and has even made up the same situation, but her powers of elaboration are greater. Her title expresses some of what we have been trying to say.

MINUTES OF MEDITATION*

The class is always ready to go at the end of the period, no questions are raised. I just sit here, like a fool, always wanting to inquire about something, but never daring to do so. Well today I must force myself, or I'll flunk tomorrows test. Only five minutes of the class left. Let's see, how should I phrase the question? This is really silly, I have been in school seven years, and every year it is the same thing, I don't dare ask the teacher a thing. Luckily in the past someone else has asked my question, but there were times when someone didn't, and I forfeited. Let's face it one shouldn't be afraid of a teacher anymore, he has superiority, but not so much, that he would punish you for asking a simple question.

Four minutes, ohh my stomach is jumping with butterflies, it's as if I was going to perform on stage, which I wouldn't do in a million years. I guess I'm just one of those people who can't face another person. I must stand up for my opinions and what I want. It may take me a few minutes (like now) of meditation, before I will do something. I'm sure all people have gone through what I'm going through, they just cover up for it. I certainly admire these people. I remember a time last year when someone told me "Gee, I'm scared!" and I answered "Why should you be scared? just try to relax, and forget the people in the audience" (she was in a play). There I was giving her advice, and I sit here a year later, trying to convince myself to relax.

Three minutes, the time passes so quickly, I wish the minutes would be hours. These kids around me, always jutting their hands into the air. So brave, no that's ridiculas, they are just not timid like me, I'm sure I'll learn how to speak up, I better! or else I don't know what I will do. In High School I probably will have to contribute (as I should now) in order to get the full benefit of what's being learned, and I better start right now, marks close soon. I remember on my last report card, the teacher's comment was "—should contribute more' the same comment for years. My marks are good, but they would improve if I contributed more. I have all these ideas in my head which are just right, or answers, I could have kicked myself for not saying.

Two minutes, ohh my hand is getting shaky, my stomach suddenly hurts, maybe I'm hungry, which is highly possible being fourth period, but it is really nervousness. I better look interested in the class (I'm trying) I don't want my teacher to think I'm idle. (Boy would he be surprised to hear what goes on in my head, he'd probably think a whole dictionary is pouring out its words, like salt). Now I'm beginning to bite my nails, a stupid habit, I should start eating carrots, maybe that will stop the biting, I have read it does. I'll ask my mother to buy a package today, and I'll eat them at home whenever my hands become idle, for instance when I watch television. When my hands are idle, or when I'm nervous, they seem to creep up to my mouth.

One minute, I should begin to rehearse what I'm going to say. Ah, "Mr. — I would like to ask you a question" no! that's much to formal. There must be a better approach, "Ah, excuse me, about the —, is it blah, blah, blah, etc.?" That's better, but I bet I won't use any planned approach, I'll just say what comes natural. That's actually the simplest way. The kids are beginning to pack up, a signal for teachers to give out the homework assignment, sure enough, oh what a bother, all the books away, and one must drag out a notebook, usually at the bottom of the pile. Let's see, now I'm getting tense, this isn't as if I was going to be executed, it's a normal everyday thing (to me it isn't though!) Oh what should I say, my stomach is doing somersaults.

There's the dismissel bell, everyone jumps up, luckily lunch is next, so maybe noone will be around when my turn comes, and yet I'd feel better if there was at least one of my friends with me. No, I have to go through it by myself. I'll just take a deep breath and ask the "deadly" (but important) question. Well . . . here goes! [11]

As the paragraphing indicates, this monologue is basically ordered by time, and yet a personal organization of ideas is laid over against mere chronology. There is a coherent subject—the girl's timorous indecision—and it is developed. This subject, incidentally, is essentially that of T. S. Eliot's "The Love Song of J. Alfred Prufrock," which is also a kind of interior monologue. When this girl reads Eliot's

[11] Weeks Junior High School, Newton, Massachusetts.

poem later she will enter into it with much greater ease than she would have without this experience.

Inventing Soliloquies for Literary Characters

The students do not always present themselves in thin disguise. Often they try to become another person, to extend themselves by imagination into an invented state of mind. One fifth-grade girl considered to be of average cognitive skills wrote:

I better not let that Cinderella try on that slipper, it just might fit her. My daughters have to fit the slipper, they just have to! If they don't my life will be just ruined, just ruined. (Knock-knock) Oh I better let him in. It will be sure to fit me or one of my daughters. Darn it didn't fit one of my daughters. Oh No! he wants Cinderella to try it on' It FIT! Oh No! I'm ruined, Oh dear! I'm simply ruined! The End [12]

The dramatic possibilities of this are spendid. It can be acted out as a soliloquy, the silent roles being done in pantomime.

Making up the thoughts of a character in literature is one way of entering into and fully comprehending both the character and the work in which he appears. One ninth-grade teacher asked her class to imagine an interior monologue for Achilles as he is sulking in his tent listening to the sounds of battle.[13] These were written straight off during fifteen minutes in class. One boy wrote:

My friends and enemies alike die, out there on the battle field in honor. While I swift footed Achilies sit here and sulk by the quick sailing ships. My strong principles or the battle field. I can find no honor now.

If I go into battle my principle will be broken. I will do a great injustice to myself. Yet if the gods keep me here the Greeks, fellow warriors, will call me a traitor or a coward. There is no honor in that.

I must go out to the battle field. How can a man be so cruel as to leave his companions to fight until death! My friends Odysseus and Ajax out there fighting trojans while I sit here and have pitty on my self.

[12] Estabrook Elementary School, Lexington, Massachusetts.
[13] The teacher was Lucy Woodward at Weeks Junior High School, Newton, Massachusetts.

Pitty why should I have pitty. Has not Agamennon ronged me. Did he not take Brisius my fair prize, did he not shame me infront of my men and was it not because of his greed that I am sitting here. Yes! Let the Greeks say where is the coward Achilles. And they will open their eyes and see there own greedy King Agamemnon has drove Achilies away; taking his prize, insulting him and relieving him of all honor.

I Achelies am doing right to sit here. And I will do it until I am given back my honor and my prizes.

In order to be Achilles for fifteen minutes one must draw on what one has read and put it together meaningfully. Such papers not only can *show* reading comprehension for the teacher's benefit, but can *increase* reading comprehension. This is the general benefit of the dramatic approach, which causes the student to actively work over and complete in his mind what an author has presented to him.

Alter Egos

Another kind of improvisation for mature students that lends itself to both dramatic and interior monologue is improvising dialogue with a double cast. Immediately after one performer talks, his alter ego, or other self, carries on a monologue of his unspoken thoughts. Then the other performer responds to what the first participant said (not to what he thought), and then his alter ego monologues his thoughts.

Playing two selves is an extension of this alter-ego technique. One person imagines that there are two selves within him—like Dr. Jekyll and Mr. Hyde—and with a friend he improvises a conversation between these two selves. For example, a student might improvise or write a discussion between his hopeful and his cynical self. The degree to which the student stays close to his real feelings and beliefs is the degree to which this kind of writing is going to be vital, of course. We all carry on interior dialogues, sometimes quite unconsciously, in order to sort out and make decisions about things. Thus, this technique of improvising interior monologues is a good one for focusing on inner conflicts and problems. As these inner dialogues are discussed with peers, similarities and differences between the two selves can be highlighted.

See Chapter 6, Performing Texts, for a full treatment of this process. Any student script can be given a trial reading in a small group, enacted either as a play or puppet show, and duplicated or put into little anthologies that can be read along with professional one-act plays. In small groups students read each other's scripts aloud, taking parts and assigning a reader to the stage directions; they discuss the playability of the script for potential enactment and edit it for duplicating. Some scripts are memorized, rehearsed, and performed.

Student scripts provide a much-needed type of classroom literature, for there are far too few good plays for children. These playlets are very convenient for enacting since they are short and constitute a basic education in dramatic literature that will transfer to professional plays. Before being duplicated, all the scenes can be put to some kind of dramatic test so that everything from punctuation to characterization can be revised. The printing furnishes multiple copies for enactment by other classes, as well as copies for silent reading.

The most compelling motive for creating a script is to have it performed; thus it is very important that time and space be arranged to make possible the sharing of student plays, radio plays, films, video tapes, and so on. Performance usually leads to further revision or rehearsal. Performance may be as a rehearsed reading.

The matching of language to character is one of the more valuable issues that come up whenever students prepare to perform one another's scripts. For example, if they are going over interior monologues together, they might ask: Does the style sound "thought" or does it sound "spoken" aloud to someone else? As they juxtapose dramatic and interior monologues, they are helped to discriminate between inner and outer voices. Does the style seem appropriate to the character and to the situation and state he is in? (Is he agitated or reflective, for example?) Does the language flow with the movement of thought and feeling, or does it seem to be organized by some logic external to the character? (This distinction helps to define "formal" writing.)

As students react to each others' scripts, they test their quality by the most relevant touchstone: is this a good script for performance? They inevitably set up the criterion of realism or credibility. As students read aloud a classmate's script, he has a chance to tell them if they are presenting what he had in mind. If not, the fault may either be in their reading or in his writing of the script.

Once perfected, a script, including directions for production, can be shared with other students who might perform it for the class. The results of their performance can be compared with the intent of the author. The repeated process of writing, sharing, revising, and sharing again provides a constant demonstration that the real test of good writing is the sense it makes to others.

READING

For the most part, mere silent reading of plays should be deferred until after creative dramatics and enactment have made it possible for students to bring a play script to life in their minds without missing or misunderstanding what is going on. Critical questions and comprehension questions imposed by the teacher cannot overcome the handicap of failing to interpret *as one reads*. And silent play-reading is difficult: plays are by nature incomplete texts and require a lot of inference and imagination on the part of the reader. We recommend that until fairly advanced in dramatic understanding students read plays silently only as preparation for rehearsed reading or memorized enactment.

Collections of short plays* can be used for reference when children want to know how to set up and punctuate their own scripts, and they can be used along with student-produced plays as material for performing. Fan Kissen has compiled several anthologies of short plays children enjoy. Older elementary youngsters might find plays to perform in such collections as William Birner's *Twenty Plays for Young People* (Anchorage Press, Anchorage, Ky., 1967), Rowena Bennett's *Creative Plays and Programs for Holiday* (Plays, Inc., Boston, 1966), Gertrude Kerman's *Plays and Creative Ways with Children* (Harvey House, Hudson, N.Y., 1961), or *Plays, The Drama Magazine for Young People,* edited by A. S. Burack.

By junior high, short scripts* from adult literature, including radio and TV scripts as well as plays, are popular for small-group oral reading and performance. Two good collections are Christian Moe's and Darwin Reed Payne's *Six New Plays for Children* (Southern Illinois University Press, Carbondale, 1971) and Lilla Heston's *Man in the Dramatic Mode* (McDougal, Littell, Evanston, Ill., 1970). For some good monologue, duologue, and triologue plays, see

Reading & Staging the Play, An Anthology by J. Gassner and E. J. Little (Holt, Rinehart and Winston, Inc., New York, 1967).

As a teenager looks for the duologues or triangles with which he is familiar in his own playwriting, he finds it easier to relate to the goings-on in Shakespeare or Ibsen. Students can read plays aloud as a small group, improvise or act out scenes for the class, and work out with arrows or other graphic symbols a representation of the character interactions. There is something structural about both human emotions and human interactions. That is, you can replace the content of a feeling or the content of an exchange with another and something will still remain the same—something like the pitch, vibration, or intensity of the feeling (whether it is love or hate, fear or elation) and, in interaction, something like the pattern of energy, the lines of force. We ride the momentum of a particular dynamic until another dynamic cuts across it. Once one is tuned into varieties of pitch and pace and lines of force, one is on to drama, because it is the intensities and vectors of energy that carry a play, and this affects the participants and the observers more than what the drama is about.

Dialogue Poems and Stories

Not just play scripts but any pieces of literature that have a character voice and a dramatic treatment can be read and performed as dialogue. Dialogue poems and stories provide a model for student writing, and treating this material dramatically helps students pick out speaker, voice, and circumstances of utterance and helps them discriminate between invented persons and real-life authors.

If students have collections of dialogues* that cut across conventional lines of reading-matter classification to bring together disparate pieces of literature—be they scripts, stories, or poems—that have in common only the performance potential of created voices, students can see the array of options they have for writing dialogue. This is especially true if they can hear some of these performed as readings.

For many students the juxtaposition of scripts with poetry or certain types of short stories with subjective narrators makes the latter accessible for the first time. The voicing of a poem may be clearly a dialogue as shown by speaker indications, stanzaic assignments, or the breaking of lines or stanzas. On the other hand, voicing need not necessarily be according to different characters. It might be according to different voices of the same character or according to different moods or attitudes of the poet, as in a monologue.

Students need to see both prose and poetry as options in writing dialogues; this way they can become aware of the way characterization, tone, and other effects are sometimes more vividly rendered in poetry. They can also see that it is possible to tell an entire short story in little more than dialogue.

Some short stories that are virtually all dialogue are "Petrified Man" by Eudora Welty, "Zone of Quiet" by Ring Lardner, and "How Do You Like It Here?" by John O'Hara. Stories containing no thoughts or commentary, only description and narration, come close to being scenarios. When students discuss one of these, for a rehearsed reading, they need to discuss whether there will be a loss in transfer, and, if they think so, to appoint one person as narrator. He can read only those parts of the narrator's lines that are not really the equivalent of stage directions. See also "Chamber Theater" on page 111.

Students can begin their reading of dialogue poems and stories with duologues such as old ballads like "Get Up and Bar the Door," a light exchange like William Butler Yeats's "For Anne Gregory," or Dorothy Parker's short story "Telephone Conversation." Since dialogue poems and stories usually contain little physical action and have no stage directions, the encumbrance of the script is not a great handicap, and they lend themselves conveniently to a rehearsed reading or enactment.

Value of Discussion Preceding Performance

Small-group discussion to determine how to perform a duologue or dialogue is an opportunity for significant learning. For example, some of the best discussions of poetry students can have may concern whether Henry Reed's poem "Naming of Parts" is uttered by one or two characters. Our understanding of it is that the first two-thirds of each stanza is spoken aloud by the army instructor to his trainees, and that the last one-third of each is the inner voice of a trainee ironically echoing the instructor while at the same time drifting away to more appealing things than rifle parts. In one class, some students made a good case for both voices issuing from the instructor—one being official and the other private. Though the shifts in speaking style do not support their case very well, the alternating of interior and dramatic monologue by the same character is some-

times used, as in Dorothy Parker's short story "The Waltz," to convey just such a discrepancy between what one really feels and how one has to behave outwardly. The story could be acted with three people—a woman dancing with a man while her other self curses his clumsiness.

When one person utters himself in two different voices, two roles are called for, so that both interpretations of the Reed poem produce essentially the same dramatic result. All the students agreed that the stanzas split into two voices, even though the voices are unmarked in any way by typography, because tone, language, and attitude all shift. But the last stanza breaks the pattern and causes disagreement about whether it is all interior monologue or a fusion of both voices. Discussion of the stanza is required in order to decide which actor will read it. It happens that both Henry Reed and Dylan Thomas have recorded the poem, in very different ways. After dramatizing the poem themselves, students listened very intently to hear how these poets indicated the shifts of voice they had discussed (and also to find support for their interpretation). A companion poem by Reed, "Judging Distances," consists also of two alternating voices, but in this case both are clearly uttered aloud by different people—instructor and trainee again—though still unsignaled by quotation marks or spacing.

Dramatic Monologue

As with dialogue, students read poems, short stories, and plays cast in this form as they write them. Recordings of dramatic monologues are particularly helpful.

Comedy Monologues

Recordings of dramatic monologues by comedians such as Lily Tomlin, George Carlin, and Lenny Bruce afford a good introduction to the reading of monologue literature and have a strong appeal for students. Whenever a character assumes a role toward another character listening in a definite time and place, he is engaging in dramatic monologue.

Plays

Most plays have at least one good monologue, and certainly the theater can provide the literary equivalent for what students are writing. In fact, from Greek drama on, the developed solo speech has been a standard feature of drama. It is used to relate the past, reveal the thought and feeling of a character, build and sustain an argument, and so on. It is an elemental dramatic unit that, along with soliloquy, duologue, and dialogue, makes up the playwright's compositional repertory. In selecting scenes to enact, students should include monologue scenes. And of course the students should enact some of their own.

Whatever the source to which you turn for literary dramatic monologues don't confuse students with other kinds of monologues; the speech must occur in a definite time and place and be heard by another character. These constitute what is meant by *dramatic*. Once the concept of dramatic monologue has been thoroughly established, however, then other monologues having a character speaker but an unspecified setting and audience may be introduced. Dramatic monologues should be performed, and for a while any silent reading that is done should be in preparation for presentation. Because different students will be presenting different selections for the class, everyone will become acquainted with a number of monologues. For monologues extracted from plays or for poems, several successive readings or actings of the same text could be compared in discussion.

Dramatic monologue provides a fine occasion for learning to react. Stress the fact that the silent partner, in responding, stays with every line as much as if he were speaking. Partners reverse roles so that they play both sides of the duo. The other pair in their group watches them, comments, and takes its turn both ways. In this manner, both the understanding and expression of the lines gradually evolve. In passing, the teacher can ask and answer questions that will help this development.

Poems

Poetry is rich in dramatic and interior monologue. Both of these shade off into other kinds of poems having a disembodied, unsituated speaker who is more the author himself than an invented persona. Students who have role-played the speaker in dramatic poems can more readily pick up the tone, style, attitude, and posture of a poet speaking distinctly in his own voice. Much of the reason for acting out poems with characters is to become attuned to what is often called today the "speaking voice" in a text. When you read with an ear to performance, you try to take on the tone, style attitude, and posture of this speaking voice. Pre- and postperformance discussions correct "misreading," in all senses

of the word. Then, when reading disembodied voices, students can interpret them accurately alone.

Memorization When a poem is not very long, it is best to memorize it as a script for performance. Memorizing poetry is an old-fashioned practice that has now fallen into disrepute because it was so often unmotivated and arbitrary. The only justification (besides being able to pass a test on the lines) was that the lines were famous, and every well-bred person should know them. In the worst light, the purpose was only a kind of name-dropping, but the fact is that memorizing has another, very profound value. As poet Richard Wilbur put the matter in a poetry course in which he required memorization, one takes the poem to heart, makes it a part of oneself, absorbs the sounds and rhythms and images, warms to the language, becomes enthralled by the incantation. Every professional actor has had the experience in learning a role of discovering more and more beauty and meaning in his lines, if they were good, and of eventually falling in love with them. A couple of such experiences can permanently influence a young person's feeling about poetry and language power. When memorization is for performance, the negative aspects of the old-fashioned practice are eliminated. The student has a real purpose and motive. He does not simply rattle off lines in rote fashion; he interprets and expresses them. Connections between words and actions, furthermore, create cues that make memorizing easier.

Example of "My Last Duchess" * Present duologue and monologue poems in mixture, so that groups have to determine the voicing (but only after they have improvised and written monologues). Nonspeaking roles are always pantomimed. Robert Browning's interior and exterior monologues represent the most dramatic: speaker, listener, and time and place of utterance are all specifically indicated. Let's take an exterior monologue, Browning's "My Last Duchess," a chestnut that even very bright high school students have seldom understood when it is simply read aloud and discussed in class. After silent reading, the group straightens out together the facts of the action, the meanings of lines, and the characterizations. (In general, editions of poems should be used that give glosses on difficult words and allusions; in addition, a big dictionary and one or two other reference books, for mythological and biblical allusions, should be available to consult in the classroom.) An actor delivers the lines of the duke, drawing aside the alcove curtain, gesturing to the portrait, and so on, while another plays the emissary, reacting in revulsion to what he hears until finally he starts prematurely down the stairs, an action that prompts the duke to utter a line that few students seem to understand outside a dramatic context, "Nay, we'll go together down, sir" (*together* being stressed, of course). Later, some of Browning's longer dramatic monologues, such as "Andrea del Sarto" and "Fra Lippo Lippi," might be assigned for silent reading.

Short Stories

"Haircut" and "Zone of Quiet" by Ring Lardner, "The Apostate" by George Milburn, "Straight Pool" * and "Salute a Thoroughbred" by John O'Hara, "The Lady's Maid" by Katherine Mansfield, and "Travel Is So Broadening" by Sinclair Lewis are short stories written as pure dramatic monologue, that is, having a specific audience and setting and often containing ongoing action. Such stories shade into others like "Why I Live at the P.O." * by Eudora Welty, in which a relatively disembodied character addresses the world at large in an amateurish way, almost certainly giving a naïve, unreliable, or prejudiced version of the events.

Kinds of Literary Monologuists

Some character monologues are uttered by types—John Suckling's "A Ballad upon a Wedding" * (country bumpkin), Thomas Hardy's "The Man He Killed" * (Wessex commoner), and Rudyard Kipling's "Sestina of the Troop Royal" (professional soldier). All three of these are in dialect. If a poem does not indicate the exact setting or the particular listener, students should imagine a fitting place and audience —and also the motive for the monologue. Thomas Wolfe's short story, "Only the Dead Know Brooklyn," * would go well with these poems. Other monologuists are well-known personages from history and mythology. Christ utters "The Carpenter's Son" * by A. E. Housman; Simon of Zilotes, "The Ballad of the Goodly Fere" * by Ezra Pound; and one of the three wise men, "The Journey of the Magi" * by T. S. Eliot. Because they are centered on Christ, these three poems are interesting to take up together. Thus, as with the love-argument poems, the selection by technique coincides sometimes with a similarity of content. Alfred Tennyson's "Ulysses" * is especially interesting because a student can make a good case

for its being either exterior or interior monologue. Is Ulysses addressing his retinue in actuality or in his mind?

Like many a monologue poem in which the poet addresses his mistress, John Donne's "The Flea" * is a love argument but an especially dramatic one because each stanza is a reaction to something the beloved does while he is talking. "Why So Pale and Wan" by John Suckling is also a monologue prompted by ongoing action. Many love poems spoken by the lover to his beloved do not indicate ongoing action and have only a vague setting but nevertheless are spoken *now* to a particular audience of one. John Donne's "Break of Day" * and "The Good Morrow" have this sense of immediacy, and Matthew Arnold's "Dover Beach" has, for all the lover's meditation, a strong setting and feeling for the present ("The sea is calm tonight. . . ." "Let us be true to one another . . ."). Consider also Andrew Marvell's "To His Coy Mistress." *

Interior Monologue

Reading interior monologue, like reading other kinds of dramatic writing, will advance students' literary understanding and appreciation at the same time as it develops their power of written expression. Although interior monologue may seem at first glance to be a minor literary form, not worthy of much time, it would be a great mistake to think so. It cuts across genres, being found in plays, fiction, and poems—found in two senses.

First, some whole plays, short stories, poems, and even a few novels are cast as sustained interior monologues. As both readers and writers, students should pursue the whole matter of artifice and realism in the authors' efforts to render thought and feeling more accurately in a language that one does not hear spoken. Sound, rhythm, imagery, incantation, students can discover, may express the inner life better than the banal everyday speech that they have used for the sake of realism. Many poems are either straight dramatic and interior monologues or modifications of them in which the setting of the listener is less specific but the speaker is clearly a created character talking in his own idiom to someone else or to himself. By just this kind of distancing, these monologues graduate into the public voices of detached first-person and third-person narrators.

Second, like dialogue and dramatic monologue,

interior monologues are commonly *embedded* in poetry and fiction, as well as in plays, making up, in fact, a goodly portion of many short stories and novels. An excellent commercial dramatization of *Alice in Wonderland* [14] put all of Alice's thoughts as written by Lewis Carroll into the first person, prerecorded them, and played them through a speaker system at appropriate moments when the actress was not speaking; this ingenious separation of inner from outer speech makes one realize how much of the original book consists of Alice's thoughts. Keeping track of and interpreting different speakers may not be so difficult on stage, but in a novel speakers change with a minimum of signaling.

Interior monologue poems include Amy Lowell's "Patterns," * and Robert Browning's "The Laboratory," both with women speakers, and, with a man, Browning's "Soliloquy of a Spanish Cloister." * Short stories such as "Late at Night" by Katherine Mansfield and "But the One on the Right" by Dorothy Parker also have female speakers. "The Laboratory" and the Parker story require nonspeaking males for the drama. Either sex, of course, could perform most of the more meditative interior monologues such as John Keats's "Ode to a Nightingale." * The writing and reading of reflections (see page 388) can coincide with interior monologues, which can shade off into philosophical poetry by disembodied authors. Eugene O'Neill's *The Emperor Jones* would probably be accessible at this point. After an opening duologue, it becomes soliloquy, addressed to dumb phantoms that actually appear to the audience. If done by the whole class as a rehearsed reading, the role of Emperor Jones could be rotated while other students pantomime the figures from his past, the "little formless fears," and so on. T. S. Eliot's "Gerontion" and "The Love Song of J. Alfred Prufrock" * are possible poems for very mature students.

Monologues and the Understanding of Literature

A surprisingly large number of poems may be successfully treated as some kind of monologue or dialogue and hence can benefit from dramatization. Reflective poems sometimes take the form of duologue as well as interior monologue. See page 387.

The fact that dramatizing poems takes longer than reading them silently can be offset by letting differ-

ent groups perform different poems before each other. Thus, instead of all students reading all the poems, each student should act out some and be spectator to others. Actors can explain to the audience allusions and other things they have learned. Two or three versions of each poem can be presented to the whole class. During one of these the audience can follow the text. Then everyone compares versions in discussion. Presenting classmates a script they don't know adds more purpose to performance.

Most fiction contains characters' accounts of events inserted into the author's narrative. Whole chapters of *The Brothers Karamazov,* for example, are narrated by one character to another. And authors constantly quote directly as well as paraphrase the thoughts of characters. A lot of work with dialogues and monologues not only helps students stay alert to shifts of voice but also helps them *size up what is said in the light of who is saying it.* Dramatic experience ties words to speakers and situations, and thereby grounds style, thought, rhetoric, and language to the realities that produce them. When reinforced by students' own writing, this experience will transfer itself to those remoter speakers who author books and to the anonymous voices of advertising and propaganda.

Many plays contain both exterior and interior monologues, which are often set pieces like the sergeant's report at the beginning of *Macbeth,* or the disguised Orestes' account of his own death, or the great soliloquies from both Elizabethan and Greek tragedy. Many of the latter are reflective poems situated in a drama.

Since class reading and performing of long plays requires assigning different portions to different groups or individuals, such plays may as well be divided into duologues, dramatic monologues, soliloquies, and group colloquies when doing so does not break dramatic momentum. In older theater it is the entering and leaving of characters, in fact, that defines most of the scenes anyway. Greek tragedy, for example, lends itself very well to this division: the succession of episodes and interludes usually consists of rather clearly separated duologue confrontations, dramatic monologues, soliloquies, choral odes, and group dialogues. The acting groups deal with these excerpts in the manner described for complete short scripts—poems, one-scene plays, and short stories. Finally, let's not forget that student writing itself will supply many short scripts of interior monologue.

[14] By the Children's Theater of the Charles Street Playhouse, Boston, Massachusetts.

T his discourse goal includes all invented narratives in either prose or poetry. These stories recount a series of imaginary events, usually in the past tense, although they may be written in the present or future. If they are written wholly in dialogue, we consider them scripts, dialogue poems, or comic strips and treat them in the previous chapter, Invented Dialogue. Invented stories comprise many types of writing and most of the world's great literature—folk tales, fables, parables, myths, legends, epics, ballads, modern story poems, short stories, novels, science fiction, detective and mystery fiction, and so on. It is an important goal both for experiencing the various kinds of literature others have created and for exercising one's own creative imagination.

As in the previous chapter, we shall concentrate here on written composition and reading, but this is not to de-emphasize the oral activities, which are covered elsewhere. See Chapter 4, Talking and Listening; Chapter 5, Dramatic Inventing; and Chapter 6, Performing Texts, particularly. As with other types of discourse, all invented stories can be made up, dictated, improvised, talked about, heard, read, written, and performed.

By calling this and the previous goal "invented," we do not mean to imply that these are the only types of discourse that exercise the imagination. All good writing is imaginative, even when the point of departure is as factual as sensations (see page 160) and memories (see page 328).

In this chapter we shall confine our discussion to the kind of writing that is *intended* to be fiction—an invented story, not a true account. But this does not mean that fiction is not rooted in the real world, for all verbalization is reality-based, in one sense or another. There is no such thing as "pure imagination"; even the most far-fetched of fantasy inventions are indirect recombinings of experiences, either from real life or from books, television, films, and so on. If we call the source of inventions imagination, that is only to say that their derivation from reality is too indirect and unconscious to know. Lying like the truth, to use Daniel Defoe's phrase, must not be deemed frivolous merely because its importance is personal and playful rather than utilitarian.

Media alternatives

Like other types of discourse, invented stories can be received from or put into a variety of different media. An increasing proportion of entertainment in our culture comes to us through nonprint media, and this fact has to be faced by any teacher of literature. Films and TV shows particularly have preempted the role of casual, simple fiction in the lives of most Americans. But films will often stimulate interest in the books on which they are based. A good movie, like the classic "Wizard of Oz," if shown often enough on TV, can make even a rather dully written book continue to appeal to each new generation of children. Whenever we ask students to invent stories, we should tie the process to at least as many options of media as they have experienced already so they can produce a taped story, story in pictures, film or animation, booklet, literary magazine, puppet show, or performance.[1]

[1] For practical how-to information on using media, see Betty Jane Wagner and E. Arthur Stunard, *Making and Using Inexpensive Classroom Media,* Learning Handbook, 530 University Ave., Palo Alto, California, 1976.

Developmental Reading, Speaking, and Writing

Long before children can write stories easily, they can make them up. They compose stories to tell each other or put onto a cassette tape and share later. The advantage of the taping process is to facilitate revision. All a youngster need do when he's dissatisfied with a part of what he has said is to rewind the tape and rerecord his revised version. This method of composition is an appealing one for weak writers of all ages. Taped narratives can be presented as radio stories. If the youngsters are literate, or have help from someone who is, they can make transcriptions of the tape later. See pages 244–245.

One way to facilitate oral composition in a kindergarten or primary grade is to set up a quiet story booth where a child who wants to compose may go to find a tape recorder and an empty tape. He tells his story onto the tape, puts his name on it and "mails" it in a class mailbox. Then a day or two later he gets his story back, all written up and delivered by an aide or older child who has transcribed it. Someone then reads his story with him, and he illustrates it if he likes. This process is not quite as valuable as a language-experience approach to the mastery of reading (see page 204) because the child doesn't watch as his words are transcribed, but it has the advantage of stimulating oral composition and simplifying a process by eliminating the need for the author and transcriber to get together at the same time.

ILLUSTRATING

Even before children can read, they can tell a story onto a tape, draw pictures to illustrate each scene, and then project the pictures through an opaque projector or fasten them all together and show them one by one as they tell the story (described on page 109). Another way to share a picture story is to draw with a porous-tipped pen onto transparencies and show them on an overhead projector while playing a tape or telling a story. One version of a comic story (see page 276) is to put a series of drawings into frames and write narrative underneath each picture.

An invented story can be presented as a slide show. The author decides which scenes to illustrate, and has classmates pantomime the key actions of the story—dressed in costume if the author chooses —while he takes pictures of them. He adds any pictures of settings he may need, and then he arranges these and shows them to the class while he either tells the story or plays a tape of his narration. Mature students might decide to tell a story using more than one projector, synchronizing the pictures to create a montage effect. They would need to write up a clear set of cues for the students who are to change the slides.

FILMING

Stories can be put into film scripts, as was noted in the last chapter. Although youngsters can go out and simply shoot a film, they are likely to get a much better product and waste less film if they write a film script first. For this kind of narrative they need a great deal *more* description than they would for a straight story or play. Just as in drama they need to think of scenes, in a film they need to think of sequences. A series of shots linked together tells a story, as in this series: four people playing cards; a close-up of a wink across the table; a long shot of all the players at the table; a slow panning of all their faces; a zoom-in to a close-up of a card passed under the table, and so on. In a film script these separate shots are described as specifically as possible—the more mature the students, the more detail, of course—with notations on camera angles and position (long, medium, or close-up shots, zoom in or out, panning, and so on). Notations on sound effects or words for any dialogue, narration, or description (voice-over) need to be added. Instructions for shooting any titles or opening credits have to be on the script as well.

Obviously, putting together a film script cuts across various kinds of discourse. Not only invented narrative, but invented dialogue, description, information, directions, and label and caption writing— all may come into play.

Although films pose different technical problems, they throw up some of the same composition challenges that face the writer of narrative. In both cases what the viewer or reader is permitted to know and when he finds it out are critical. To thoroughly assimilate the hard fact that most good film makers, like most good writers, discard a high proportion of the footage they shoot might help amateurs develop the necessary stomach for the revising and editing process that success in both media demands.

Sound film projectors are expensive. A much less expensive way to put film and sound together is to use 8 or Super 8 millimeter film equipment with a tape recorder. The synchronization will not be exact, but for voice-over narration or commentary, sound effects, or music, a tape is quite effective. Students will need a stopwatch to time the film sequences and the tape.

Making animated films of their invented stories is a process that fascinates students of all ages. See page 141. Young children may not need to write anything before they start shooting. As they get more experienced, they may find it helps to make notes to themselves. Sometimes a set of sound effects is more effective than a narration in words. Sound can be recorded on a tape most efficiently by doing it at the same time as the picture is shown. The projector will have to be in another room and projected through a glass window onto a screen in the room where the sound is being recorded if the noise of the projector is not to distort the sound track.

VIDEO TAPING

If your school has video-taping equipment, show the youngsters how to use it. It has a compelling fascination for most students, who can learn to use cameras and other equipment in a comparatively short time. Video scripts pose the same composition problems as films, but the medium is less flexible because you cannot edit after the picture is recorded, unless you have special and expensive editing equipment. This is a valuable problem, of course, because it imposes the need for a tighter script to work from. Other advantages of video tape are that picture and sound can be recorded simultaneously so you can effectively use dialogue, and that shooting can take place indoors without special lighting.

WRITING

See Chapter 8, Writing, for a full discussion of ways students can share their written compositions by making books and duplicating stories.

Points of departure

The secret of getting students to write inventions lies not in any one or two sorts of stimulants (many kinds will work well), but in the teacher's ability to capitalize on provocative forms and current subjects, and to point out to children the writing possibilities in their improvisations and in their previous writings. This takes flexibility and alertness. It means that the kernels of story ideas are lying about every-

where and that once children are licensed to convert a sensory description to a short story by imagining an action in that setting, or to start making up something from the random meanings of rhyme words, or to transpose a "minimal situation" into a narrative, they will solve for themselves the problem of getting an idea. For small groups the teacher should be a storehouse of ideas—for transforming one piece of writing into another, for transposing an action, for converting body English to written English.

The only essential requirement is that youngsters be involved in the writing; otherwise all snappy ideas will fail. They have the feelings; all they need are materials and forms, some stuff they can shape and project their feeling into and some structures of language and literature that fix feelings "out there," impersonally before them. But the students have to be awash in good literature, imaginative writing that has art and wit and bite. They have to hear it, see it, read it, take off from it. A true commitment to letting youngsters write will solve more problems than volumes of advice.

We believe "creative writing" is a staple of learning, not Friday afternoon fun or the luxury of lucky "advantaged" children who are mastering the "basics" on schedule. The testimony is ample from many hard-working teachers in the inner city that their students can learn basics only after they have become persuaded that the world of letters has something in it for them. The greatest formalization of instruction and the least self-expression have traditionally occurred in the urban schools, where youngsters can learn the least from formalization and most need self-expression. The basics for children are feelings and motives. A ghetto child needs more so-called creative writing, not less of it. Once persuaded of the personal value for him of writing, he will attack its technical aspects.

Although there are many good ways to get the process of inventing stories going, probably the least effective way is simply to assign themes. Research studies such as that of Dr. Donald Graves, who found that the output of writing of the seven-year-olds he studied was in *inverse* proportion to the number of writing assignments they had, show that merely making students write is not enough.[2] Some-

[2] Donald H. Graves, *Children's Writing: Research Directions and Hypotheses Based upon an Examination of the Writing Processes of Seven-Year-Old Children,* University Microfilms, a Xerox company, Ann Arbor, Mich., 1973.

how a climate must be created wherein written products are called forth. Writing fictions seems to require a context, a stimulating situation of one sort or another—caption writing, cartoons, lyrics for songs, involved discussion, reading around a subject, dramatic activity, immersion in a particularly literary form, and so on.

Of course, if directions—to "make up a story" or "write a poem"—work well for some students, then give them just that. As one eager eighth grader put it, "I want to write a novel. Is it okay if I work on it in English class?" Since the goal is self-initiated writing, any student who is already at the goal needs only encouragement and interested readers. It is for the other students that we suggest these stimulants, some of which also have value in themselves, such as learning what forms are available and how different subjects may be treated.

As you coach and counsel small groups and help them focus on significant compositional issues, don't lose sight of the fact that their small-group discussions are for appreciation and exhibition as much as for critical commentary. Expect the group members to respond naturally to a paper; then play from these responses by a few impromptu questions and observations of your own until the students relate their responses to specific features of the paper that elicited those responses.

IMPROVISATION

As noted on page 103, improvisation can be taken to paper, recapitulating its verbal output into a story. Children do not even have to master literacy to be able to record their improvisations in writing. In one kindergarten class the children worked in groups of three to plan a balloon voyage. Each small group painted onto large sheets of brown wrapping paper a huge balloon and hung it with the others on the class bulletin board. A day was set aside for "going up in their balloons"; they made plans and improvised their preparations—cooking and packing in anticipation of the launching. When the day came, they all gathered in their groups and took off in their gondolas, hanging on to imaginary balloon ropes and awed into silence. Then they chatted together about their adventures in their gondolas. After a few minutes they landed. Each went to an adult or older child who was there in the room and told him about his adventures, which were written down and later typed up and compiled in an "Up in a Balloon" book. A typical account was:

We saw:
a bluebird
Trees—tops of trees and apples
Another balloon with people in it.
A kite, pink and gold and red, and we saw the sunny sky and moon out in the daytime.
A storm came by and it rained, and the balloon got wet and we got soaking too. The balloon almost got struck by lightning. And then we saw another balloon with a radio playing a beautiful song. We saw people on the ground, our Moms and Dads, and flowers.
We saw some construction, and somebody almost fell in the hole. Some people were stuck in a tree and we helped get them out and put them in our balloon. Then we listened to records.
We saw an "S" balloon, gold and pink and yellow, all beautiful.
We landed in Hawaii. There's swimming. It's sunny. We had Hawaiian juice. It looks like pretty flowers. There was a lot of juice. We drank the whole can. We were so hot. We had been up there for three hours. We sat on beautiful Hawaiian pillows.[3]

Although this group of five-year-olds was obviously not yet ready to handle the tense in a sustained story, there were distinct narrative elements in their account. Sense impressions—imagined ones—were part of their improvised trip; these lent concrete detail to their inventions.

PHOTOGRAPHS

A set of photo cards* or collections of photographs students have cut from magazines and newspapers can spark invented stories in the same way they do invented dialogue. See page 277. When a student works with photographs, he arranges a logical sequence of events by physically ordering the photos before he starts writing. He might begin by writing captions for each photograph (see page 157); it is but a short step from that to a full-blown narrative account. Beginners can tell or tape rather than write their stories. See page 273.

[3] Alice Beck was the teacher of this class at the Hubbard Woods School, Winnetka, Illinois.

A photograph or series of pictures can be studied by a small group, and then each person can go off and write a story telling exactly what is going on in the picture(s), what happened before, what could happen next, and what each of the characters is like. Then the group can come together to compare their stories.

More experienced students can take a single photograph and write a series of short accounts of what is happening, each from a different point of view. For example, if the photograph is of an emotion-charged human interaction, they could write it up in the following ways:

1. In a very brief account, giving the facts as concretely and objectively as possible—the writer's stance is that of a reporter looking on from the outside
2. From the point of view of a participant, selecting personal details most important to him
3. From the point of view of a spectator with a sense of humor[4]

STORIES IN THE ROUND

In Chapter 8, Writing, we made a case for group composition (page 153), whereby the sheer pleasure of socializing can be transferred to the composition process. Beginners can turn a group of photo cards* or photographs face down and take turns drawing one. The person who draws the first picture starts a story based on that picture. The next person picks another photo and has to continue the story and at the same time use the information in his picture. This continues until the last person turns over a picture; it is his task to use that photo to finish the story. Another thing to do is to deal five out to each person and have each one make up a story for the rest of the group, using all five pictures.

Youngsters can take turns telling stories; one person starts and when he stops, he points to another person who must take it up from there and continue at that precise point, even if it's in the middle of a sentence.[5] Beginners can do this in pairs; later a small group can take turns, taping as they go, if they like.

[4] For other ideas, see Hart Day Leavitt and David A. Sohn, *Stop, Look and Write,* New York, Bantam Books, 1972.
[5] The *English Through Interaction* film "A Student-Centered Classroom" shows tenth graders doing this.

Another more difficult way to do this is to have each person contribute only a phrase, so the first three participants might say:

> "Once upon a time . . ."
> "there was a mean old witch . . ."
> "who was invisible . . ."

The third person adds a phrase that would logically follow, such as "and who lived in the attic above John's garage"; then it's the next person's turn.

The next step is to time each person's contribution. Here's one way:

- Appoint a timekeeper, ideally one with a stopwatch or a clock with a second hand. Then the person to the right of the timekeeper starts telling a story.
- At the end of a minute, the timekeeper says "Stop" and the person sitting to the right of whoever began takes up the story where the first person left off. The second person too only has one minute.
- Then the timekeeper calls "Stop" again and the next person goes on with the story.
- Continue until the story is over.

Next time take turns writing a group story:

- When the timekeeper says "Go," each of you start a different story. At the end of three minutes, when the timekeeper calls "Stop," pass your paper to the right.
- The timekeeper waits until each person has read what is on the paper that has been passed to him. When the timekeeper again says "Go," each of you write an installment to the beginning you have just read, not to the one you wrote.
- Continue to write for three-minute intervals and then pass on until each story has returned to the person who started it. That person then finishes his story—using, of course, the material the others have added.
- Then read the final stories aloud.

If you want some funny and disconnected stories, have each person write his episode and turn down the paper. The next person doesn't read what the other person wrote but just continues a story.

Mature writers might want to collaborate as a small group on the writing of a novel. First, they need to agree on the characters and some basic sketch of a plot. Then they can divide up chapters and—either as individuals or in pairs—write up a separate chapter. When they come back together, they can read their chapters in order, smooth out transitions, revise parts that don't fit the whole, and so on.

STORY STARTERS

One time-honored way of priming the writing pump is to give youngsters a starting sentence or phrase —a place to begin. It might be a setting, such as a doctor's office, a thick forest, an abandoned mine shaft, a TV studio, the gondola of a hot-air balloon, a submarine, an old covered bridge at night, a decrepit, leaning fishing shack, or a seat in a roller coaster. Then imagine somebody in that place. Is it a man, woman, child, animal? What is he, she, or it doing?

Another way is to start the action:

- One evening I was walking toward the edge of the lake in a swirling snowstorm. I was all alone; I couldn't see very far ahead. All of a sudden I heard a sound.
- The castle, which had stood solidly beside the sea for a thousand years, was the only mark on the horizon. I was paddling my small boat toward it when . . .
- It all began when Mom announced firmly, "From now on things are going to be different around here."
- Until that Saturday no one would have ever said Jerry was particularly clever, or even very helpful, for that matter.
- "There's no trace of her up here either—not even a suicide note," Jim yelled hoarsely.
- Linda just stood there paralyzed; her chest was just one huge pounding heart.
- She hadn't ever really wanted to go along with the idea; but here she was.
- "Come 'ere, you guys and see this," Hank called excitedly. Little did we dream he'd . . .
- I woke up to the sound of men shouting. At first I'd forgotten where I was.
- With a thunderous crash, a huge boulder sealed the hole they had just crawled through.

Story starters like these can be made up by students and each one placed on a separate index card and kept on hand. Beginning writers need less elaborate beginnings. They might respond well to such simple starters as:

- There were two little kittens who . . .
- She looked down and there she saw a tiny baby.
- Over the hill came a big . . .
- Mary heard a loud noise.

After a little experience small groups can decide together on a problem that a character might face that would make a good story. Then each member goes off alone and thinks up a solution to the problem, either writing notes to himself, taping a story, or writing one. When the members get back together, they share their stories, deciding then whether to write them up as separate tales or to combine them all into one group story.

A recording might provide a good start. Listen to just a snatch of any part of a recorded story, and then write out the rest. Compare this composition with the recording.

Here is what one boy in a low-ability class of fifth and sixth graders wrote from an unfinished story starter that ended with "a big red . . ." The capitals and punctuation did not have the benefit of group proofreading.

All of a sudden there it was, a big red sign that said Ghost Realty. Just then a man walked in. He said that he was looking for a haunted house. The man in the chair said that there was one house on a iland about a half mile from Long Iland. The owner died about a week a go and the man (buyer) said, "I will take it." *Wait*. In order that you may buy the house you will have to spend the night in the house." "Ok, I will spend the night in the house." "Ok, than it is settled." "Fine, then you will take me out in a rowboat tonight." "Good."

Out in a rowboat that night he rowed him up to the iland and when the man let him of he rowed back as fast as he could. He looked back and then went up the stairs and went in side. He looked all around then he saw a stair case. He went up it then he herd a voice. It said, "if the log rolls over we will all be dround," and then he ran in a room as fast as he could and there siting in a washbowl sat three ants on a mach stick saying, "if the log rolls over we will all be drowned." [6]

---

[6] Our thanks to Rose Arnone, Cochituate Elementary School, Wayland, Massachusetts.

STORY ELEMENTS

The three elements of character, setting, and plot can be a starting point.

- Each of you write on one side of a slip of paper the name of an interesting character. On the other side put the word "Who."
- On a second slip of paper write the name of a good place for a story to take place and put the word "Where" on the back of that slip.
- Then on a third slip write a description of what a character is doing or a problem he might face, putting the word "What" on the back of the slip.
- Put each of the "Who" slips in a pile face-down and shuffle them. Do the same with the "Where" and "What" slips.
- Then each of you draw one slip from each of the piles and make up a story or poem using that character, place, and problem. You may add characters, places, or events.
- Share these stories and revise and write up the best ones.

Another variation of this activity is to divide up the characters into kinds, such as "timid" or "wise," and the plots into "obstacles" and "ways to overcome obstacles." In addition, another category could be added—"Things," or objects that must be used in the story somewhere, such as a stethoscope, a magic stone, a broken shield, a gold ring, a highchair, vanishing powder, or lightning.

For young writers you might put onto word cards emotionally evocative words such as *ghost, robot, monster, lonely, magic, spy, jet,* or *puppy;* or pairs of words such as *snapped off, gobbled up, haggard witch,* or *ran away.* Then they can draw from one to six or so of these word cards as stimuli for a story. As with other composition, oral precedes written. First graders might use their sight-word cards as starters for taped stories. Activity card directions should remind students that stories may be written as poems. See page 316.

One fifth-grade teacher asked her pupils to think up several interesting words, then to choose one to write a poem, story, or script about. One word was *mysterious:*

MYSTERIOUS

There's a mysterious house on our street
It's where Oak and Flag Street meet.

People say they hear noises when it's dark.
And the creaking of gates, when chirps the lark.

It's very old you know.
It's where all the weeds on Oak St. grow,
I went there once to see what it's like.
And I almost fell off of my bike.

For, there from the back window,
There came a giant frog.
He didn't look like any I'd seen in the bog.
He was really quite frightening.
He held a sword, and threw it like lightning.

Well that sword just missed me,
And I ran home fast.
And my bad dreams stopped only
The night before last.

My advice to anyone
Whom it may concern
Is stay away from there
For if you don't, say a prayer.

Another word was *fish:*

THE FISH STORY

The ocean was a silver cup
With a deep scalloped rim;
And all the fish I took up
Were big enough to swim;
And had speckled tails.
There were not any in between
The rest, I guess, were whales.[7]

Two students can each write a story and then pick out fifteen or so important words or pairs of words from their stories and list them. Then they exchange lists and, without looking at each other's stories, each writes a new one using each of the words on his partner's list. Afterward they can compare the second stories with the originals.

[7] The teacher was Rose Feinberg, then at Happy Hollow Elementary School, Wayland, Massachusetts.

Just as an object can be a stimulus for an informational monologue or improvisation (see pages 73 and 86), so it can be a start for a story. Youngsters can put together into paper bags objects that might be used together in a story—a feather, a toy drum, and a sharp rock; or a paper clip, an old pulley, and a needle. Then they exchange bags with each other, and each person tells or writes a story using all of the objects in his bag. The story either can be about characters who have used those objects in some way or other, or can explain how all of the objects were used or came to be together.

Youngsters can bring white elephants from home wrapped as packages but not tell each other what they have brought. Then they can take turns opening them and holding them up for the rest of the class to see. Anyone who wants that object has to make up a story about why he would need that particular item. The idea is to come up with the funniest and most exaggerated tall tales possible. The one with the best story gets to take home the object.

Doors opening and closing, people walking or running, vendors shouting their wares, jet engines revving up, cars starting and stopping, fire sirens wailing, dogs barking—all can not only enhance a story but also get it started in the first place (see page 161). Students can collect fifteen or twenty different sounds on a tape recorder and then tell or write a story to go with them. As the author tells or reads his story, he or a friend can turn the tape recorder on and off at the appropriate times to enhance the story. By using a second tape recorder, students can rerecord the sounds along with the narration or reorder the sounds.

Teenagers have found a sound track a good starting point for film-making. What they do is collect sounds first and then make up a shooting script telling a story that uses those sounds, reordered to fit the story. Then they set up scenes, post a shooting schedule, and appoint editors to write down what each of the shots is and to time them. Appropriate backgrounds are set up, costumes decided upon, then the scenes are rehearsed and, finally, shot. Synchronizing the sound track and the film usually calls for editing of both.

SENSORY RECORDING

Using sensory recording as described in Chapter 8, Writing, is another way to start an invented narrative. Here's what one boy wrote based on these sensory notes:

---

1. I can hear my friend slurping on a watermelon.
2. I can smell the freshly cut grass.
3. I can see and hear my nextdoor neighbor squirting his hose on his new grass.
4. I can see and hear my friend laughing.
5. I can hear in the distance, cars going along rt. 2.
6. I can hear the wind blow against the trees.
7. I can hear one of our neighbors hammering away at his house.
8. I can hear my friends yelling down the road.

OLD FARMER BROWN

Once upon a time, there was a farmer, his name was Old Farmer Brown. One sunny day he planted a seed. He did not know what kind of a seed it was. Farmer Brown had other jobs to do besides planting seeds. He had to cut and water the lawn, and he had to fix the steps that broke in half the year before. After a few months, he went back to see how his mysterious seed was growing. All of a sudden he started laughing. He found that his seed had turned into a plant that looked like a green football. He decided to see what it tasted like. It was watery and tasted somewhat like a melon. "I know what I'll call it!," exclaimed Farmer Brown, "I'll call it a WATERMELON!" After that, Farmer Brown went running down the road telling everyone about his discovery.[8]

Apparently this boy amalgamated his slurping friend and his busy neighbors into the single figure of Farmer Brown. Besides taking for his central object the watermelon that opened his recording, he employed also the cutting and watering of grass and the seasonal setting. Although he probably borrowed from other stories the name of Farmer Brown and the theme, he has created a fresh story of his own.

Any experience—nonverbal or verbal—can be taped for stories or poems. So can observations in nature study, discussion of social studies material, reading of nonfiction, and many other subjects dealt with in class. Playing by ear, you seize a moment

[8] From Franklin Elementary School, Lexington, Massachusetts.

of high enthusiasm for some content, take the spin-off from that activity, and turn it toward writing: "Why not write a story about such an animal (somebody in such a situation, something taking place in such a region)."

MEMORIES OF LITERATURE [9]

Retelling remembered literature is not strictly inventive, but it will prime invention. Students re-create in their own words an especially memorable scene or moment from a book, play, or movie without looking back at the original text. Emphasis is on choosing a scene that stands out later because of the strong feeling it aroused in the reader or viewer. The key is vivid involvement, and the source may be any that the student knows. He begins by putting himself back into the scene, becoming part of it, perhaps taking the role of a character in it, making it happen again.

The purpose, of course, is not to recapitulate accurately the original; in fact, the teachers who developed and tried out the assignments were casting about for a stimulus for imaginative writing because they found that their children could not easily make up a story from scratch. These fifth- and sixth-grade pupils liked the activity very much and wrote better stories than they had in other attempts. Besides endorsing this process for its own obvious value, we see helpful connections between it and other activities in this program.

The samples reproduced here bear subtitles that name the main feeling of the re-created scene. In some cases, the teachers who were trying this assignment had the class designate a theme in advance—some emotion or quality that might give the pupils more to go on when selecting their scenes. In other cases, the pupils chose a theme for their scenes after they had written them. We are inclined to think that such focusing is unnecessary and, when the theme is preselected, possibly obstructive. But you might do well to run the same sort of mixed trials and judge for yourself.

A fifth-grade girl of superior ability re-created this moment from the well-known film:

[9] For this idea we are indebted to Frank Lyman and Kayda Cushman, then at Estabrook Elementary School, Lexington, Massachusetts. They devised it and provided the samples printed here.

SOUND OF MUSIC

Friendship

Maria sits quietly and thoughtfully on a bench near a glassed-in room. Crunching through the leaves, Captain Von Trapp sits beside Maria, "I want to congratulate you and the Baronese," Maria said standing up.

"Can you marry someone when you like somebody else more?" questioned the Captain who was growing used to Maria.

"No, I guess not." replied Maria softly.

It is clear that this girl has chosen a personally meaningful bit of action involving someone she could identify with. This reads almost like a play script, with only movement and dialogue—no author commentary or character thoughts.

The playability of this type of writing is a happy effect of the emphasis on re-creating a *small span of action*. One of the chief difficulties with children's written stories is that, because they cannot write at great length, if they encompass the whole of even a moderately long action they are forced to over-summarize it in a dull way. By stressing a scene or moment and by directing the children to put themselves in that scene, you can effectively steer them away from synopsis toward detail.

In discussing their papers together the children will discover that some stories are not readily dramatizable, even though they cover a short duration. For example, this story by a sixth-grade girl of high ability:

WITCH OF BLACKBIRD POND

"Comfort"

She ran without reason or decorum, past the houses of her pupils, past the townhall, past the loiterers at the town pump. Without having chosen a destination in her mind, her feet had. They lead her beyond the outskirts of the town, into a Great Meadow. She took a path that led off into the meadow and flung herself down on the long, earth-smelling grass. Slowly, the meadow with its vastness began to fulfill its promise.

This girl does not employ the wholly external viewpoint of a movie or the wholly internal viewpoint of an interior monologue; using a common novelistic technique, she tells the story in the third person but from the viewpoint of a single character. Thus the load is on narration, description of scenery, and accounts of feeling in the author's words but as perceived by the character. This is hard to dramatize and therefore presents a special opportunity for learning. In sifting stories for those that can be fairly readily acted out, pupils will learn about various fictional techniques in a very pragmatic, intuitive way. If a story does not lend itself to acting out, they have to think about why this is so. Too much description? Too indirect a relaying of the character's inner life? Too much commentary by the author? Does such a story have to be read and only read? Could it be *adapted* in some way for dramatizing or for filming?

Generally we see this activity as an extension of memory writing (see page 328) into the realm of reading and fictive creation. The extension allows for secondhand experience and for imaginative rather than factual material. It is a repeatable activity because the content is always different. It engages pupils because this content is essentially personal feeling conveniently projected into a scene that the child makes his own. It is a kind of literary appreciation that makes good sense. To ask a pupil to write, in a book report, what he liked about a book will not get the same quality of response, for all a child can do in a book report is summarize the plot and make a couple of shallow generalities.

Types of literature

If youngsters are steeped long and fully in good literature of all sorts, the first stories they write may well be very obvious borrowings of content just as their play-acting is largely taking on the roles they see around them, but through this imitation they identify with storytellers and become like them.

Not only is this imitation desirable, but so is changing a piece of literature into another form. Thus each of the types of literature we shall distinguish below is not only a model but also a point of departure. As youngsters, say, read comic strips and summarize the pictures and action into a narrative, they are learning a lot about what a story is. Changing any nonnarrative into a story develops one's storytelling style. We shall now distinguish various types of invented narrative. We do not mean to imply, however, that this categorization is what is to

be taught directly. Instead, we advocate arraying all these kinds of literature in the classroom and letting students discover the differences between them as they work in small groups with various types. To approach literature definitionally is to short circuit youngsters' own thought. As they steep themselves in a form and share it with others, they come to their own understandings of it, which are far more solid than any verbal overlay that describes something they have yet to experience and internalize. The types we are presenting here then are "for you to know and the students to find out," but in their own way and in their own time, *not* by your telling them. One of the most fruitful discussions students can have about literature involves their efforts to distinguish for themselves between, for instance, legends and myths or between fables and parables. Any authority that attempts to do this for them deprives students of an important part of their learning. Defining forms should be a long-range experience involving reading, writing, and discussion without any outside intervention to force premature closure of issues. If a student asks what a parable is, for example, refer him to examples of it.

As you will see, we are not making the usual distinctions by length—short story, novella, or novel. All of fantasy or realistic fiction may be any of these; to students new to any genre, a shorter version may be an easier beginning.

POINTS OF VIEW IN RELATION TO TYPES

Invented narratives break down roughly into four types—folk literature, individually authored narrative poetry, fantasy, and realistic fiction. Another kind of breakdown cuts across these types—namely, point of view. The following discussion of types of literature and points of view can be diagrammed as shown in Table 15.1.

In the squares where there is no check, we mean to indicate that a form of literature is not traditionally written from that point of view. This is not to say that a student could not transpose, say, a folk tale into a series of letters. It simply means that in so doing, he is changing it from the form in which it originated in the oral tradition to a new one.

Third Person

When a narrator refers to all the characters as *he*'s or *she*'s, he is writing in the third person. The nar-

TABLE 15.1 FORMS OF LITERATURE AS
POINTS OF VIEW

	Folk Tales	Fables and Parables	Myths	Legends	Narrative Poetry	Fantasy	Realistic Fiction
Third Person							
Fictional Chronicle	√	√	√	√	√	√	√
Fictional Biography	√	√	√	√	√	√	√
First Person							
Fictional Memoir					√	√	√
Fictional Autobiography					√	√	√
Fictional Diaries					√	√	√
Fictional Letters					√	√	√

rator does not choose to identify himself in the story; when he does that, he is writing in the first person.

Fictional Chronicle*

Some third-person invented stories like Shirley Jackson's classic, "The Lottery," have no central character but focus on a group. These stories and novels, which we are calling fictional chronicles, tend to have purposes and themes rather different from those of fictional biography. Fictional chronicles are relatively impersonal and emphasize communal experience. A great many myths, legends, science fiction novels such as Ray Bradbury's *Martian Chronicles,* realistic novels such as Margot Benary-Isbert's *The Ark,* and fantasy like Sheila Burnford's *The Incredible Journey* are written from this point of view.

Students can make up chronicles by thinking of some group whose members all undergo some event more or less together, though perhaps each in his own way, like the characters in "disaster" stories of shipwrecks, earthquakes, fires, and so on, or in stories of expeditions and team sports.

Fictional Biography*

If third-person invented stories with one central protagonist are termed *fictional biographies*,* students can make the association between these and their nonfictional counterpart—biographies*. Alternating between reading fictional biographies and biographies will probably help many students sustain interest in both and appreciate some of the important differences between making up stories and telling true ones. Third-person narratives occur in all types of literature—folk, narrative poetry, fantasy, and realistic fiction. Some of these, like folk, sports, adventure, mystery, humor, and science fiction stories, focus more generally on action and plot. Regular nontopical fiction zeroes in on character, changes in the inner life, and the *qualities* of experience so the reader is engaged more with the sources of action in the inner life and, conversely, the impact of external events on the inner life. Narratives that focus explicitly on inner life tend to be in the category of realistic fiction.

First Person

Fictional Memoir

The narrator of a memoir identifies himself but does not focus on himself; his main subject is another or others he has known. Thus memoir often tends to be a privileged, firsthand view of a person or group but still seen from the outside. Memoir is the hinge between first- and third-person narrative—a kind of biography or chronicle but filtered through a narrator close enough to the people and events to be an onlooker, confidant, or perhaps occasional participant.

This me-talking-about-him point of view is used for various purposes by professional writers. Fictional memoir tends to lend itself to colorful and humorous personal styles of storytelling, which students may appreciate particularly when reading a story in conjunction with listening to a recording of it and when writing such stories themselves. Part of the great flexibility of fictional memoir is that it may be a kind of stylistic exercise for fun, creating a character voice, as in dramatic monologue, that is in itself interesting or funny. Read or listen to Damon Runyon's "Earthquake" * or James Thurber's "You Could Look It Up," * for example.

Another main part of its flexibility lies in the range of subjects that the narrator can tell about when he is not focused on himself. This permits the story-teller to adopt a character voice and vantage point while at the same time telling a story focused else-where. Students can discuss why a writer will choose to tell a story through the eyes of a charac-ter who is himself more observer than principal. Consider Edgar Allan Poe's "The Gold Bug," "The Murders in the Rue Morgue," and "The Fall of the House of Usher," precursors of the Sherlock Holmes stories told by Watson. Often the title indicates the focus on "other" rather than author: Sondra Spratt's "Hoods I Have Known" and O. Henry's "A Municipal Report," F. Scott Fitzgerald's *The Great Gatsby,* Joseph Conrad's *Lord Jim,* Willa Cather's *My An-tonia,* and Alain-Fournier's *The Wanderer (Le grand Meaulnes)*—all fine reading matter for high school and excellent instances of artfully exploiting the relationship between the first and the third persons.

One advantage of reading real and fictional mem-oir side by side is that students can see how the vantage point that is *necessary* to use in writing one's own memories may be adopted as a deliberate strategy in making up a story. The best approach to discussing point of view is in writing-workshop discussion of students' own efforts to tell a story. They should be encouraged to consider the fictional memoir whenever their subject would seem to ben-efit from a kind of mediation between subject and reader.

Especially interesting, by the way, are alter-ego stories, like Joseph Conrad's "The Secret Sharer" * and Jean Stafford's "Bad Characters," that have a dual focus on both narrator and protagonist and thus hover between autobiography and memoir. And as for dual focus, are John Knowles's *A Separate Peace* and Robert Penn Warren's *All the King's Men* autobiography or memoir? Ask students in advance of reading to decide which each is. The question will increase understanding.

Fictional Autobiography*

Just as made-up stories in the third person are des-ignated *fictional biography,* so their counterparts in the first person are termed *fictional autobiography.* Again the similarity of the terms calls attention to parallels in the storytelling technique of the fiction in a nonacademic way and permits students to see for themselves the many similarities between actual first-person documents and the type of fiction mod-eled on it.

The parallel may also suggest to students some alternative ways to write about their personal experi-ence, including the possibility of distancing and clarifying it by fictionalizing true events. Students who read fictional autobiography are often confused by and curious about the parallels they find between the fiction and the actual life of the author. Writing their own fictional autobiographies helps students understand from the inside how the pretense of writing fiction often serves to free a writer from in-hibitions he might feel if he were offering the experi-ence to others as the truth about himself. Through this process they gain insight as to why writers choose the fictional mode.

A happy circumstance of fictional and actual au-tobiography is that it usually features an older person telling about his experience as a younger person, often about problems of growing up. This makes it very easy for adolescents to identify with it. It also naturally provides a double perspective on this youthful experience—that of the narrator as a participant at the time of the event and as an author recalling those events after much intervening experi-ence. In a sense, this dual perspective affords young people what they do not yet have and therefore en-hances the appeal inherent already in material cen-tered on growing up.

Fictional autobiography can be written as a story of an incident like John Updike's "A & P" or as a retrospective about a phase in the narrator's youth like Frank O'Connor's "My Oedipus Complex," Joseph Conrad's "Youth," or Ivan Turgenev's "First Love." This point of view has been a standard tech-nique for the novel of growing up, of education-by-life, exemplified by Charlotte Bronte's *Jane Eyre.*

Professional writers of fiction sometimes use a first-person point of view to create an imperceptive narrator, a person telling the story who says more than he thinks he says, because he does *not* under-stand the experience he's telling about, at least not in the same way the reader does. This is an espe-cially useful fictional device, since it does deliber-ately what students, and indeed adults, often do unintentionally when telling about their personal experiences. Students, for example, who read Muriel Spark's "You Should Have Seen the Mess" * will have to come to grips with the distortion in that story, that is, the fact that the values of the girl tell-ing it are very different from those of many readers and hence make the readers feel that the story is biased, as indeed it is.

Encountering fiction told by an imperceptive nar-rator raises the possibility for students both to write such stories deliberately themselves *and* to perceive how their own and each other's personal accounts, true or fictional, may indeed seem biased in exactly the same way as "You Should Have Seen the Mess." Such deliberately biased stories are much like many dramatic monologues, which rely on the same technique of self-exposure. See page 293. Also, taking a very different tack, students may read letters to the editor and letters to advice columns and detect exactly the same sort of bias as in some fiction. In fact, writing deliberately biased material can become a very popular class sport among teenagers, along with detecting *unintended* bias and distortion in each other's writing. All of this helps overcome egocentricity.

When students of ours have written stories told by a naive, imperceptive, or unreliable narrator, they have done so as a result of reading such stories and of working with many sorts of first-person speakers. That is as it should be. Given a free fiction assignment, students will choose the technique often enough to provide samples for discussion. And discussion of this kind of writing is especially beneficial, precisely because of the discrepancy between the narrator's perspective and that of the reader and author. Interpreting of both real life and literature is involved. Consider in this dual way the following story, done by a prep-school senior.

REQUIEM FOR A SUAVER

Ernie Finster was packing his bag when I came into the room (Actually his name wasn't Ernie Finster, but his parents would give him hell if they ever knew that someone was writing about him and using the family name).

"Well, Ern, I just found out, if there is anything I can do, I'd be glad to——."

"Cool it, Roscoe, I think I can swing this one by myself." Old Ern always talked like that.

"Yeah, okay Ern. I just thought that there might be something I could do for you to sort of help pay you back for——."

"Yeah, well, man, now that you mention it, there is something that you could do for me. I've got a little package here for the dean. I wonder if you would mind slipping it under——."

"Hey, come on Ern, I can't do that. Ever since that time on the Howdy Doody show when you slipped me that package and then started yelling: "It's a bomb, it's a ——.""

"All right, all right, I get the message, can it. I just wanted to throw the suspicion off of me."

"Great. Right on to me. Super."

"All right, I said forget it. It was a poor idea anyway."

Ern put on his madras jacket and then took a quick look around the room to make sure that he had everything that he wanted. He stopped, gasped, ran over to his dresser and picked up a couple of dark blue capsules.

"Jesus Christ, I almost forgot my 4-X's."

He dropped the prophylactics in his jacket pocket, hauled the suitcase off the ground, and tramped out into the hall. Everyone who wasn't at the lacrosse game came out of his room to wish Ern good luck.

"See ya, Ern."

"Good luck, man."

"Take 'em easy."

"Swing gently, Ern boy."

"Etc."

Ern, of course, was not at a loss for an appropriate phrase. Climbing on top of his suitcase, he raised one madrased arm lyrically into the air.

"Albeit that I appear to be leaving you, for ever and ever, remark that the paths trod upon by the eternal suavers are few indeed. If not in Tel Aviv, then Madrid, or if not in Madrid, perhaps the Gold Coast. Just remember to keep your arms outstretched in widespread supplication to the gods, and who knows where or when they will bestow upon you the glory of my presence."

The applause and shouts of approval were deafening. Eager hands helped him down off the suitcase, clapped him on the back, and met with Ern's own in a last gesture of farewell.

After downing the two flights of stairs Ern and I left the dorm and headed for Front Street. The thought came into my mind that this was probably the last time that Ern would ever walk upon the old asphalt paths of dear Darby. It was a kind of sad thought, and I looked over at Ern to see if maybe he felt the same way that I did.

But of course, I should have known better. Old Ern was taking the whole thing in stride the way he always did. Nothing ever bothered old Ern. He was always the same, unchanging, stalwart picture of perpetual suavity. And it made me kind of laugh at my own, uncalled for, sentimentalism.

We got to where the bus was supposed to be, but of course, in good old Darby tradition, it wasn't. So Ern and I sat down on the curb and waited.

After about a minute, Ern pulled out a tube and lit up. I was about to protest when I remembered that the school rules didn't apply to him any more. This thought reminded me of the reason for Ern's getting kicked out, which, I soon remembered, I didn't know. I wanted to ask him about it, but was afraid he would think it was a pretty wet question. After all, what difference did it make, in the long run, as far as the history of human existence was concerned?

But I asked him anyway, and it didn't seem to bother him too much at all.

"You know that big gray cat of Doc Spauldings? Well, I was drifting along back from the gym and I saw that big daddy standing out on Doc's lawn, just staring at me, great big cool looking eyes, you know, just staring. And I thought, 'Jesus Christ,' would that motha look suave with a California lean; like a hot rod, you know. So I picked up the Doc's hedge clippers, which happened to be lying on the grass, and chopped off the cat's back legs, about half way up. It was really wild. You should have seen that daddy running around on his stumps. Christ, it nearly killed me. Anyway, the cat ran into the house bleeding like a motha, and about thirty seconds later, Spaulding's old lady comes bombing out screaming for the cops and the militia, and god knows what else. Christ, she never shut up. I turned around and started walking back to the dorm, but only got about a hundred yards before old Twinkie Parsons came running up from behind, grabbed me and dragged me back to the scene. Voila."

"Suave, Ern," I said, knowing it must be, "but why did you do something like that?" (Not that it was any more unusual than anything else that he did, but it seemed to be not quite in the same good taste in which he usually acted. In fact, it smacked of a different Ern altogether, and I was curious.)

"I had a pet rabbit once when I was seven, by the name of Flopsy. One day my mother told me to build a cage for him and put him outside because he was stinking up the house. I built one out of a cardboard box, and I guess that it wasn't very strong. Anyway, the first night he was out our neighbors' cat broke into the cage and tore him into little pieces. I sat there for five hours trying to put him back together."

If old Ern hadn't immediately burst out into his tremendous rolling laugh, I would have thought that he had slipped his trolley. I think that I laughed even harder than he did. Good old Ern, he's a million yuks.

The bus came around the corner and stopped in front of us. Ern stood up, slipped into his imported French shades, and mounted the bus. He paid the driver and then turned and nodded to me in a kind of final acknowledgment of our friendship. I raised my hand in sort of a half salute and smiled. Ern turned and walked down the aisle, stopping long enough to put his bag in the rack before slipping in beside some gorgeous college

broad. I saw her look up at him kind of surprised like, as if she knew exactly what he was after; and then I laughed, because, as the bus pulled away, I knew that it didn't really matter if she knew or not.

The narrator's worship of his suave hero falters only for a moment—after the cat story—but he recovers and reaffirms his faith in good ol' Ern, because he needs to. If, like the author of the story, he were to see Ern as a very sick boy, he would be lost; he would have to renounce the whole James Bond, schoolboy mystique that he believes he lives by. Though this invented narrator may very well be the author as he was a couple of years before, he is distinctly not the boy who wrote the story. From first sentence to last, the author has made sure that the reader will know one from the other.

The art by which a narrator betrays himself is the sophisticated art of Alan Sillitoe's "Loneliness of the Long Distance Runner," Henry James's *The Turn of the Screw,* Ernest Hemingway's "My Old Man," Fyodor Dostoyevsky's *Notes from the Underground,* and similar stories. Some students will try out subjective narration and fail in the first draft, thereby provoking one of the more interesting discussions of technique that students can engage in.

On the nonliterary side, suppose that other students who read "Requiem for a Suaver" worship the Erns of their world. They are unaware of the story's irony. This is precisely how personal values and private understanding of experience determine how one interprets what one reads, whether in fiction or nonfiction. No amount of literary knowledge can prevent someone from reading a subjective narration as an objective memoir or autobiography. Literature always breaks back ultimately into life. Seldom do more involved or fruitful discussions take place than those about amateur and professional stories narrated by teenagers whose perspective is transitional between stages of maturity. Try, for example, "My Sister's Marriage" by Cynthia Rich or "Why I Live at the P.O." * by Eudora Welty. Some students will be taken in; others will not.

Fictional Diary

Diaries and correspondences are day-by-day approaches to writing invented stories that limit the time span and thereby magnify ongoing detail and feeling. This is an advantage for inexperienced storytellers. As a literary technique, diary writing may not occur to young people until they see this form isolated in a separate book of fictional diaries*

Many nineteenth- and twentieth-century novels, not to mention *Robinson Crusoe* in the eighteenth century, either are or include diaries. To focus on examples of this form is to make accessible a mode of fiction that features the natural language of the speaker and hence may become a vehicle to display the style and language behavior of the diarist. In this way diaries may be thought of as monologues and, like them, may serve as an occasion for creating or performing language of a strongly stamped style. Because of this, they lend themselves to accounts of madmen, like Guy de Maupassant's "The Diary of a Madman" * or to science fiction such as Daniel Keyes's "Flowers for Algernon," * where there is an organic connection between form and content. In both, changes in the mental state of the diarist are reflected in changes in his style and language.

Students can pretend to be anyone else—another member of their family, a class member, a captain of a ship or space ship, a famous historical person, an animal, an inanimate object, and so on. The form lends itself to satiric, humorous, or fantasy treatment.

Fictional Letters

Like diaries, fictional correspondence offers students an opportunity to let a monologuist reveal himself. An exchange of letters, moreover, is a kind of dialogue at a distance, falling somewhere between a conversation and a monologue. It is an appealing mode of fiction, which is a bit more difficult than a diary, for the writer has to create two "letter voices," one for each character, and, as in an improvisation, carry on a story by implication. The reader needs to fill in the gaps between the letters. The feelings of the writer for the receiver can be either expressed openly or implied. Changes in attitude can reflect either what the recipient of a letter has read or what he has misread. Problems may be compounded if one of the writers composes phony letters as in Fyodor Dostoyevsky's "A Novel in Nine Letters." *

A good way to begin is to have students make up a single letter, such as a letter of apology, a complaint letter, a "Dear Abby" letter, or a request for something and compare their efforts or exchange letters and write fictional responses. See page 384 for more on this. A further step is to write a short one-way correspondence.

One point of departure for this fictional correspondence is to stipulate a relationship of two characters such as father and son, lawyer and client, private and general, customer and complaint department, a person with a problem and a newspaper advice columnist, a parent and school counselor, or two lovers. Another is to put together a story as a collection of letters from various people concerning a single problem or person, who need not necessarily be one of the correspondents.

Writing fictional letters can best be done in conjunction with reading epistolary fiction. Discussion of both professional and student stories can help readers become aware of what is going on between the correspondents and the motive for writing each letter. Discussion of the style of the letters may focus on such questions as: Do the two correspondents sound alike or could you tell them apart if you were read scattered excerpts? Are there differences in their vocabulary, the kinds of sentences they use, or the way they move from topic to topic? Can you say what each is like as a person?

The fact that the correspondence is colloquial writing may justify mistakes in spelling, punctuation, and other mechanics. Classmates should consider the possibility that mistakes are intentional in characterizing certain kinds of correspondents, but, on the other hand, students will often have occasion to remark that a well-to-do or well-educated person, as characterized in X's letters, would know better than to commit such and such a mistake, or would not use the kind of kiddish expression or slang that X has attributed to him.

Mark Harris's *Wake Up, Stupid* is a modern epistolary novel, Bel Kaufman's *Up the Down Staircase* mixes letters with memos and other documents. Short stories that would interest adolescents are "Jupiter Doke, Brigadier General" * by Ambrose Bierce, "Life at Happy Knoll" * by J. P. Marquand, and "Marjorie Daw" * by Thomas Bailey Aldrich. Once interested in the form, some students may well want to read some eighteenth-century epistolary novels like Samuel Richardson's *Clarissa,* Tobias Smollett's *Roderick Random* and *Humphrey Clinker,* and Fanny Burney's *Evelina.*

Both the *Interaction* program and the anthology *Points of View* by James Moffett and Kenneth R. Mc-Elheny[10] contain other short fiction for school use that is sorted according to the point-of-view categories just set forth in this chapter.

As a student's compositional repertory increases with his experience in all kinds of writing and in

[10] James Moffett and Kenneth R. McElheny, *Points of View,* a Mentor book, New American Library, New York, 1966.

different points of view, he has a wider choice of modes for his invented stories. As you counsel and coach students, encourage them to draw on all the various forms they have become acquainted with through reading and to try putting a given story idea into more than one type of literature (story, narrative poem, fable, science fiction, and so on) or point of view to see which works best. They can experiment. They can see what happens when the narrator does not identify himself and reveal channels of information, and they can compare that with what happens when he includes himself in the story and openly reveals his relationship to his subject matter.

It is through first-person discourse that one truly learns third-person, even though he has been familiar with the latter from his first nursery tales. For handling the material of actuality, furthermore, first-person is more appropriate for students. In inventing, however, they need to draw from the whole repertory of narrative techniques. (Many amateur stories are bad because the authors do not know what the possibilities are.) Both the method of Chamber Theater and the way this program develops third-person out of first-person should help them to write third-person fiction with good judgment (and not just automatically). There is no point in assigning exercises that stipulate third-person or that take up one technique after another. The main thing is that the whole curriculum should sensitize students to discriminations among narrative relationships so that choice, whether conscious or unconscious, becomes possible.

FOLK NARRATIVE

Folklore is that vast body of literature that has been preserved and transformed by generations of storytellers from those times when voice and memory alone were what bound together one generation's experience to the next. Folk literature was not originally authored by individuals, but professional writers have usually relayed it to us from the oral tradition. Folk tales, myths and legends, fables and parables, ballads and romances, epics and songs—all are folk narrative. They are the expressions of the culture out of which they swelled, now long gone. Students can imitate the old forms and perhaps invent their own new ones.

Folk tales were not created especially for children; they speak, rather, to the child in everyone.

They symbolize deep feeling and serious thought in fantastic figures and events, so children may find in them a fusion of the imagination and intellect.

Folk tales are old, oral, and international. They originated in oral form, have been retold over generations, and have been collected and written down, oftentimes in different versions. The basic distinction between tales, which originated for telling, and stories, which originated for reading, blurs considerably when tales have been literarily retold by skillful authors, as most classic material has, often in fine-quality picture-book format, or imitated by such masters or form as Hans Christian Andersen—in both cases retaining the original oral quality. Tales are usually harder for silent reading than "children's literature," written for children to read themselves. Thus tales should be heard before they are read. As children hear, tell, vary, and re-create tales, they are perpetuating the grand tradition of folk literature. In primary classrooms children become acquainted with tales by hearing an adult or older child or a recording. As they get to know and love a tale, they try reading it. Oral familiarity makes word recognition easier and aids decoding. Collections of folk tales* belong in elementary classes as a supplement to hearing the teacher and others tell them. Young children love repetition, and the tales are characteristically full of refrains.

Learning to tell tales, varying them according to individual emphasis, is a valuable experience. Tellings can be recorded to add to the cassette collection in the classroom. Many folklorists at universities are quite interested in variants of oral tales and would welcome recordings and transcriptions of children's tales, jump-rope jingles, street rhymes, and other oral literature.

Fable and Parable

Both fables and parables are highly pointed narratives in prose or poetry. They are short and direct, stripped down to nothing but what brings out the implicit statement or moral, and they do not linger over description or narrative detail or characterization or any other aspect of stories often enjoyed for its own sake. Thus they provide a model of lean concentration, of how to tell a story economically with a strong focus and subordinated detail in order to make a point, a model that contrasts with the longer rhythms of other forms of literature. Some folk tales have a parable aspect, but unlike parables and fables, they revel in exotic plots and detail for their own storytelling sake.

The difference between a fable and a parable is that a fable always has an explicitly stated moral at the end whereas a parable is a story that teaches but stops just short of stating its thought explicitly. In addition, a fable often has animal characters and inanimate objects that act like human beings whereas a parable typically has human characters.

By treating both fable and parable as specialized kinds of stories, you can make clear that not *all* stories are to be read for their moral or to interpret some symbol, an incorrect idea that many students now have. One reads different kinds of tales differently, according to whether they invite one to savor events for their own sake or to distill conclusions from them. Fables and parables encourage readers to infer a generality—either a truth or an imperative —and to interpret symbolically, but this way of reading comes as an appropriate response to the purpose of the writing—often signaled by its form—not as an indiscriminate reaction to all stories. Being pushed to find "hidden meanings" in or to state the underlying idea behind every piece of literature turns students off from reading and in fact subverts the main point of most stories, which is to entertain the senses and the imagination so that the mind is more inclined to entertain the ideas embodied in the story.

Fable

Fables* are short enough to make easy reading and to fit a natural writing length. These popular and readily available tales, part of a rich literature stemming from Aesop through La Fontaine and including the Bidpai fables and Jataka tales, are especially suitable for discussion, acting out, or imitation. The fable is a form we especially recommend.

Whereas few elementary-school children are capable of, or even interested in, sustaining generalizations throughout a whole discourse, they are quite able and motivated to make single generalities and to insert these into their stories and descriptions. Thus a fable acts as a natural bridge between narrative statement and idea statement. The moral itself must be an explicit assertion in the present tense, as a generalization is (see page 376); it is a statement of the idea that the narrative *embodies*. Fable contains two kinds of idea presentation—examples and generalities. For a youngster not ready to abandon his characteristic mode of narrative for abstract essay, the fable leads toward a transitional kind of narrative that prepares for generalization writing. Later activities can more fully develop this explicit intellectual transformation of *what happened* into *what happens,* or *when* into *whenever.* See Chapter 19, Ideas. What differentiates fable and parable from other narrative is just this cognitive shift from pure story (once-upon-a-time) toward the illustrative story (typical of many times).

Here are some of the activities that might be spurred by fables:

- Write a new fable.
- Write a new version or modernization, perhaps in a very different style, of a traditional fable.
- Read a fable without the moral; then write a moral and compare with the original. See page 75.
- Take a moral from a fable and write a new fable to precede it.
- Take proverbs or other generalizations and write fables to illustrate them. Test these by having a classmate read each fable and write a moral for it. If it is close to the author's generalization, the fable makes its point.
- Turn a parable into a fable by thinking of a moral that seems to fit it.
- Convert a fable into a poem.
- Find a fable that was not intended as such in a newspaper or magazine and write a moral for it.
- Collect fables into a class book, using both student-written and published fables.
- With a few other students, write several different fables for the same moral and post or print these together.
- Test a fable by taking off the moral and asking other people what moral they would give it.
- Discuss the truth of a moral. See page 383.

In addition to such activities, which exploit the fact that a fable consists uniquely of a story plus an explicit statement, many other activities involving animals may be inspired by fables. One of the successful ways Herbert Kohl helped Harlem children start writing was through reading and making fables.[11] Here is what one eleven-year-old black girl wrote for him:

[11] The following two pupil papers appear in Herbert Kohl, *Thirty-six Children,* New American Library, 1968. Reprinted with the permission of the publisher.

Once upon a time there was a pig and a cat. The cat kept saying old dirty pig who want to eat you. And the pig replied when I die I'll be made use of, but when you die you'll just rot. The cat always thought he was better than the pig. When the pig died he was used as food for the people to eat. When the cat died he was buried in old dirt.
Moral: Live dirty die clean.

Both the tale and the moral show real native wit. "Live dirty die clean" shows how moral writing can help children practice the rhetorical devices and pithiness of epigrammatic statement. An eleven-year-old black boy wrote this one:

Once a boy was standing on a huge metal flattening machine. The flattener was coming down slowly. Now this boy was a boy who love insects and bugs. The boy could have stopped the machine from coming down but there were two ladie bugs on the button and in order to push the button he would kill the two ladie bugs. The flattener was about a half inch over his head now he made a decision he would have to kill the ladie bugs he quickly pressed the button. The machine stoped he was saved and the ladie bugs were dead.
Moral: smash or be smashed.

The allegorical aspect of fable allows the boy to express impersonally the painful conflict, probably only too familiar to him, of having to hurt another to save yourself. In short, fable is an excellent form to put experience into and for making statements about that experience. Fables can be in poetry:

> There once was a man named Jon
> Who had no shoes to put on
> So he went to a wizard who turned a lizard
> Into some shoes for Jon.
> The shoes were small and he wanted them big
> So the wizard turned Jon into a fig
> Now the shoes are too big for him

The moral of the story is: Don't wait till the shoe fits, just wear it.[12]

[12] Written by a ten-year-old girl in a multiage classroom, Happy Hollow Elementary School, Wayland, Massachusetts.

Parable

The parable provides a good transition from fable to more complex and symbolic literature. Imagery, action, and imagination are there in all their allure, while at the same time the parable is clearly a vehicle for thinking and making statements about nature and man's experience as part of it. Some science fiction also shows this exuberant combination of rich, pleasurable fantasy with serious intellectual work.

A parable is like an example used to support a statement, but the statement itself is not quite made. The point has to be inferred. Making the point—stating the main idea or moral for themselves—is a good activity for students who have read a parable together. They can compare morals they write for it individually, or they might write other short stories that show the same thing they think the parable shows, thereby adding another instance or example to support the implied statement. Reading parables may help students to recognize themes in fiction.

Many of the activities suggested above for fables would work well with parables too.

Myth and Legend

Like other folk literature, myth and legend are told from a narrative point of view that is a very impersonal third person, because the experience they present is *communal*, not individual, and whoever is narrating is merely speaking for all. This fits well the child's unself-consciousness and undeveloped sense of separation. Myth and legend have a point of view and subject that are akin to those of science fiction.

Myth

Myth is the literature that declares a culture's core beliefs and values. This literature is an important key to understanding how a people explains itself and the world. It is because of this particular explanatory power that myth has a fascination for youngsters who are also in the process of explaining many forces, phenomena, and relationships in their experience.

The creative intelligence that flowered forth in myth resembles remarkably well what goes on in children's heads during their years of relatively concrete thinking. Like earlier people, they too put together from their experience with the natural world, their observations, and their imagination—without science or abstract thinking—a concept of the world that makes sense.

Myths are full of wonder in a double sense—full of imagined marvels and full of wonder about why the world is as it is. Like other folk literature, traditional myths cannot be "created" by students, who can but imitate and experiment with their form as they make up original creation stories and explanations for natural phenomena. Looking at certain natural events or photographs of them and imagining how men who lived before the age of science might respond to them are one way to start.

In the Kipling *Just-So Stories* model one eleven-year old wrote:

HOW THE TOAD GOT HIS WARTS

Dedicated to All Toads and Frogs

Long ago all toads did not have warts and they all admired themselves and looked at themselves all day in mirrors. They were lazy, which made the spiders not worry about being eaten by the toads . . . which made the spiders lazy. And that meant the flys were lazy because they had no spiders to worry about.

The world had too many spiders and flys. Months later . . . . a tadpole was born. Again months later the tadpole was a toad, but he had warts, and all the toads were mean to the toad . . . and the toad was very hungry so he ate most of the lazy spiders and flys.

Years later the strangest thing happened. The toad found he had powers. He could leap tall Oak trees at a single bound . . . . . . he could swim faster then a submarine . . . . . he could even croak "I WISH I WERE IN DIXIE."

In a puff of smoke all the toads had warts. Then in another puff of smoke the toad was a smooth frog! And one of the toads from long ago is in the school of National. Her name is Chess . . . . owned by yours truly, ME!

And that's how the toad got his warts.[13]

Students might try making up a myth to account for or make sense of such facts as that people are all different from one another and behave in unique ways or that such puzzling phenomena abound as electricity, radio signals, cancer cells—or love. Creation myths explaining how the world began are popular. A group project could be to make up a whole *mythology*—a series of related myths, in which the same characters, setting, and objects recur, as in Greek, Norse, or Hindu mythology. These can be pulled together as a booklet or performance.

Another tack for teenagers is to explore the myths of our own culture—its set of ideas, conventions, prejudices, values, traditions, world view. What unquestioned assumptions do we operate on? How are these reflected in our advertising? In what department stores sell? What do Americans do to impress each other at parties, and what does this tell us about ourselves and our values? Some of our myths are capsulated in slogans like "Blondes have more fun." These can be examined in relation to the whole cultural mythos; this process leads into reflection, as we shall show in Chapter 19, Ideas.

Legend

Whereas myth is primal religion and science, legend is idealized history; both are literature. Legend speaks to the need for heroes and heroines—powerful, even superhuman people with whom to identify, people who by their deeds show us how to transcend our condition. The reading motive embodies a wish to overcome the limitations of smallness and

[13] Our thanks to Wanda Lincoln, teacher of a multiage class at the Demonstration School of National College of Education, Evanston, Illinois.

inexperience and to feel omnipotent. Seeking heroes is also part of a search for positive models to imitate; this search leads readers to realistic fiction and true stories of sports and adventure, as we shall show below and in the next chapter. However, the fantastic elements of many legends make them kin also to fantasy and other folk literature. Legend is balanced between possible role models on the one hand and wish fulfillment on the other, corresponding exactly to its mixed origins in historical truth and popular romance. Collections of legends* can be read by younger children for the folk heroes and by teenagers for models for identification. Students of minority cultures need ample folk literature in their own tradition such as the bilingual legend *Un Nombre Chistoso* by Veronica Leal Gonzales, illustrated by Gloria Osuna.[14]

As in updating fables, creating legends in modern dress is a way to internalize legend-making. Students can take a traditional story and set the whole thing in the present, retelling it in modern language and style. Another way to start is to brainstorm first about what kind of hero our culture needs. Then students can create such a hero, deciding whether to give him outstanding human qualities, perhaps extending some actual personage, or to give him superhuman powers that no one they have heard of has. They can set that hero to work on one of the seemingly insoluble problems people face.

Ballad

Much of folk narrative was originally sung as ballad. Traditional folk ballads have the same appeal to the ear as tales. Because they belong to the oral tradition, what remains after generations have sung them by memory tends to be dramatic and starkly evocative, for transitional material and elaboration—if there ever was any—was forgotten by the generations of balladeers on whom we are dependent for the survival of this form of literature. A great many of the best ballads in the folk tradition have a special dramatic quality because they are told mostly through dialogue and have a sense of taking place now rather than being recounted from the past. Thus there is a strong link between this type of invented narrative and invented dialogue. Because so many folk collectors and singing groups have steeped themselves in and have imitated this traditional nar-

rative song form, you will find a ready audience for it among teenagers. And of course ballads should be performed and heard rather than read. Comparing different renditions can provide models for student interpretation of ballads.

Encourage students to renew old ballads by writing new verses to the story or by putting a new story to a ballad tune they know. Here is part of one done by a group of fourth and fifth graders who were inspired by the East Coast blackout of 1965. Fitted to the tune and meter of "Sweet Betsy from Pike," this ballad shows the stimulus of both a subject and a form.

BALLAD OF THE BLACKOUT

At half past five Tuesday, November the ninth,
The lights went out and it gave me a fright.
We lit all our candles.
'Twas a spoo-ooky sight,
When the lights went out o-on that Tuesday night!

(Chorus)
The people were all right when candles were light.
But electricity is a much better light.

"What happened?" said Sally.
I said, "I don't know."
"What happened?" said Willy
While tying a bow.
They pushed the wrong button and turned to reverse.
The main truck line shorted with one great big burst.

(Chorus)
The li-ghts went ou-out.
The hou-ouse got dark.
The moo-oon came ou-out.
The do-ogs did bark.
The babies cri-ied,
The pe-eople sighed.
And tha-at's what happened on Tu-uesday night.[15]

. . . .

Another approach is to take a tune from any other song, borrow a stanzaic pattern from a ballad, and then put together a new ballad based half on bor-

---

[14] Veronica Leal Gonzales, *Un Nombre Chistoso*, The Center for Open Learning and Teaching, Berkeley, California, 1974.

[15] Written by a group of fourth and fifth graders in the Franklin Elementary School, Lexington, Massachusetts.

rowed elements and half on the words or a story idea. More musically developed students should be encouraged to make up their own tunes or to collaborate with others to do words and music. Ballads that emphasize dialogue lend themselves to the assigning of roles in performing or singing.

Ballads* may be easily related to history and social studies, since many important events were cast into ballad form at the time they occurred in order to broadcast them or commemorate them.

NARRATIVE POETRY

In addition to ballads—narrative poems in the folk tradition—there is a large body of story poems that have known authors and thus are not a part of folk literature. These poems, unlike ballads, are often in first as well as third person. They pose models for student storytelling; fictional biography or chronicle, or autobiography or memoir—all can be cast as poetry. Collections of narrative poems* array options in stanzaic form, rhyme schemes, metric patterns. Suggest that students retell favorite folk tales, fables, legends, original stories, and so on as poems. Groups can divide up and each do a stanza in a collaborated poem. Like ballads, narrative poems lend themselves well to performance.

FANTASY

Fantasy, like folk literature, presents a world where magic abounds, where the logic of the everyday is turned on its head and things are not what they seem. In many children's libraries this fanciful literature is often given a label such as "Wonder Tales" and shelved near the Dewey decimal "398" section where folk tales sit. In other libraries fantasy is shelved in with realistic fiction, and there is no way for a child hungry for that world that never was to find it easily.

Many of the classics in children's literature—*Alice in Wonderland, Winnie-the-Pooh, Pinocchio, Mary Poppins, The Black Cauldron, The Children of Green Knowe, The Borrowers, The Hobbit*—are fantasy. Their counterparts in adult literature are novels such as the *Lord of the Rings* trilogy or *Watership Down* and the great allegorical works of Western literature like John Bunyan's *Pilgrim's Progress*.

Works of fantasy do exactly what creative thinkers do; they take apart the familiar world and reassemble it in startling ways that show relations and implications one does not usually think of. To follow fantasy is rather like floating up in an observation balloon. The novelty of that perspective lets us see things we were never aware of before.

Fictional Animal Stories

An ever-popular type of fantasy for children are animal stories told from the animal's point of view so that people are only dim figures at the edge of the action. Youngsters identify here with the *animals,* who, in many cases, have very human characteristics. The advantage of this point of view is that it gives children an opportunity to identify with creatures that are in some ways less confusing, more understandable, and more like them than real adults in their real world. In the Kipling tradition of closely observed detail, good animal fantasy builds stories on factual realism. Thus readers can use animal lives as symbols for their own emotions and at the same time acquire factual knowledge about animals. Classic animal fantasies for children include such books as *Charlotte's Web, Rabbit Hill, The Wind in the Willows,* and *The Tale of Peter Rabbit.*

Ghost Stories

These are part of the oral literature of children at camps and slumber parties. Collections of scary tales* play into another reading motive that most children have—the desire to feel awe, the pleasurable chill of mixed fear and marvel, and to feel wonder, that strange mixture of intellectual curiosity and amazement. Reading ghost stories can start youngsters telling, retelling, and writing down the oral literature that is always floating about among schoolchildren. Encourage them to retell from memory or write down any ghost stories they know. By including ghost stories under fantasy, we do not mean to rule out the possibility that there may be real ghosts, but simply to note that most literature treats them as fantasy.

Science Fiction

This type of fantasy, although appealing to the students' love of wonder and imagined worlds, is actually the most difficult of the categories of fiction. Despite its emphasis on plot and action, most science fiction sets up certain premises—physical laws or dimensions or perspectives—from which the action "follows," so that the plot is a kind of working out of the ramifications of the premises. In addition, science fiction usually carries a heavy baggage of true or possibly true information that is woven into, or causes, the events of the story.

This is not to say that science fiction should not be a regular option for upper-elementary and teenage students. It is becoming an increasingly popular kind of reading matter in our culture, one a great many students respond to. Some classes might want to subscribe to a science fiction magazine or book club.

Like myths and legends, fables and parables, science fiction is a way of thinking and making statements in story form, is charged with a sense of awe and mystery, and calls for an imagination that embraces the far-out. Science fiction incorporates humanity's knowledge of nature, reassembles this so as to explore the frontier between possibility and impossibility, and ultimately branches into the mystery of the universe, both as an object of actual curiosity and as a humbling and fearsome unknown. It has been called predictive myth.

Fantasy-writing can be stimulated in many ways. Creating make-believe stories, especially those featuring animals, is popular even with preschoolers. Such a simple project as drawing a monster picture can be a beginning for a fantasy story. Kenneth Koch found that asking children to tell as fantastic and preposterous a lie as they could think of produced some fine fantasies and poems.[16] Tall tales and exaggerated yarns can be swapped, taped, or written. Students might enjoy a tall-tale contest to see who can tell the most fantastic, the funniest, or the most ingenious tall tale. These tales can begin with stock beginnings such as:

> I dreamed I was a . . . and I . . .

or:

> One morning I woke up and I was . . . a candle
> an ice cube
> a ball-point pen
> an animal
> a dime
> a piece of
> driftwood
> invisible

Students can write these tales as first-person fan-

---

[16] Kenneth Koch, *Wishes, Lies, and Dreams*, Chelsea House, New York, 1970.

tasy—autobiographical accounts or series of diary entries.

Keeping records of dreams and daydreams is a good way to get material for fantasy. The vivid and bizarre images of dreams—most of which are forgotten—can be recalled if they are remembered immediately on waking and recorded in some way. Dreams are accompanied by feelings, often strong ones, which can be tapped for stories or insights about oneself. See Chapter 19, Ideas. Nightmares are an effective resource for horror stories.

REALISTIC FICTION

In this category of fiction are the stories and novels that are set in a world governed by the same laws of time and space and the same logic of cause and effect that we find in the customary world. Although they are fiction, for the happenings they present never took place in just this way, they could have happened. This is a popular category for both children and adults. Good fiction has a sense of reality, at least one fully rounded character for the reader to identify with, and an inventive plot. Here we are in the world of believable characters. Be they kings or antiheroes, they are people we can identify with, and indeed it is this identification that is a strong motive for reading realistic fiction.

We do not need to build a case for realistic fiction, as it is the major kind of literature in most reading programs and literature anthologies. If this literature is also recorded*, it provides a fine opportunity for arraying the varieties of dialect and accent. In many juvenile libraries special categories are set apart—animal (many of which are fantasy), humor, adventure, and mystery stories. Humorous stories* and joke books* are often shelved together. In junior high collections, sports, adventure, and detective novels are often set apart. Detection-deduction in the Agatha Christie and Sir Arthur Conan Doyle tradition has the same appeal as codes and brain teasers. See pages 258 and 259.

Writing realistic fiction can begin with either an interesting character or an idea for a plot. In small-group discussion students can create an imaginary person who feels as they do but has specific characteristics that they detail as precisely and fully as possible. Then each person goes off to write an adventure for that character, giving him a difficulty to face. Encourage students to tell what the character is feeling along with what he does and says. Teenage storytellers might do well to talk about which parts of a story should be full scenes with detail and snatches of dialogue and which could best be simply summarized plot. Work with drama should help writers particularize scenes in narratives.

Memories are another good beginning point. Let students search their past for a moment of self-awareness or self-knowledge, in the model of James Joyce's epiphany experience—when they suddenly discovered that they were capable of really hurting another person, that they were in love, that they could hate someone wildly and irrationally, that they knew they had done something really well, and so on. Then have them use this moment as the basis for a story. Start by jotting down all the things that led up to this self-awareness; then go over the list and select those events, details, and characters that seem most important and that seem to lead to the moment of awareness.

Sometimes a setting can be the beginning point of a story. Small-group remembering of a place or sensory recording can start the process. Then each person can take the real place he remembered and described for the group, put other objects into the setting and then a character or two, and see what happens to these people in that spot. The idea of orchestrating characters, deliberately playing off opposite personality types can be introduced to mature students.

These last four chapters of Part Four encompass discourse goals that process actual experiences, not invented ones. In this chapter and the next, Directions, the discourse will for the most part order real events chronologically to tell what happened or what steps you take in order to make or do something. By and large, the final two chapters, Information and Ideas, deal with generalizations as to *what happens.*

True stories are narratives of real events, experienced firsthand, observed, or learned through research. They comprise remembered experience in diary, journal, letters, and autobiography and observed or relayed events in log, eyewitness report, news story, memoir, case study, biography, chronicle, and history. Some true stories may be poems. True stories develop factual accuracy as students use language to communicate sensory experience (to describe what they are perceiving as they perceive it) and memory (to tap stored perceptions). It comprises both what is usually called *nonfiction* (meaning it is not invented and it has literary value) and much discourse that is ordinarily reserved in schools for social studies and science but that should be made available in language arts. Creating their own true stories ensures that students will deal with certain problems of abstracting and composing and will know thereby the nature of such information when they encounter it as readers. As with other types of discourse, youngsters can often read certain types of true stories several months or even years before they can compose them. Almost all of these types of narratives are never outgrown.

Students can receive and present true stories in the same range of media arrayed in the last chapter for invented stories on pages 297–299. A true story made into a film or radio or TV presentation results in a documentary. Slide shows are particularly suitable for true accounts such as those of pets or classroom trips, sports events, and other happenings. See page 73 for ideas on show-and-tell stories and page 117 for ways to stage stories of real events. Here we shall emphasize reading and writing narratives.

Writing about self

True stories may have as their subject the self, others, or things. The raw material in any case comes largely as nonverbal data, thereby providing a valuable opportunity for *languaging,* for shifting into words what as yet is a mixture of feeling, sensation, image, and thought. As one struggles to put personal experience into language, the experience itself becomes perceived, clarified, distanced, symbolized, ordered, understood, and even mastered in a new way. Not just personal experience is mastered, however; a key to creating a rich community with others is acquired.

CALENDAR

Procedure

Probably the easiest beginning point for a true story is a calendar, a day-by-day record of what one is either scheduled to do or has done. Very young children can make up one large class calendar on tagboard with large blocks for each day of one month. Then together they can make suggestions for you to write on the calendar for each day, making two kinds of entries—reminders of things that are scheduled for the immediate future and records of what happened in the immediate past. At the end of each day you meet with the children to pull together a listing of one or two major events of the day, recording them in note form on the calendar. At this point you can show by example how to write times and distinguish the halves of the day—*A.M.* or *P.M.*

The next step is to have each child keep his own calendar. He can either make up a monthly calendar on a large sheet of paper or tagboard and post it or cut up sheets of light-colored paper into squares about seven by nine inches, punch two holes along the nine-inch edge, and place enough of these leaves onto two notebook rings to equal the days of the oncoming month. With crayons or colored felt markers, the children write at the top of each leaf the month, day of week, and date. This repeated writing of the names for the days and months should ensure their learning to spell them.

The children are told what they will be doing with their calendars. A few minutes each day will be set aside especially for them to make entries. The children turn to the leaf for that day, look to see what they have written on it before, then write down on future leaves what they or their family are going to do. (Looking back prompts memories.) Then, on the leaf for the current day or the day before, they note things that they did then, or that happened then that they would like to remember later. Explain that many adults write notes to themselves on a calendar so that they will remember things they have planned to do; the notes usually say what, when, where, who, and perhaps other things. Then say that some people keep a diary of what they do and what happens around them so that they can look back later and recall what went on. This is like writing a real day-to-day story in pieces.

The children should understand that the calendars are theirs, that they will keep them at the end of the year, and that you will not look at them unless asked to. They write for themselves, in whatever way the words come, not being held to complete sentences or to dressing things up for the teacher. They may draw decorations and illustrations on the calendar. Remind them, however, that if they do not write clearly, they may not be able to read their entries later.

Purposes

Keeping calendars helps to develop an objective sense of time, which in turn facilitates kinds of thinking based on it. Planning, tying events together, continuity, cause and effect, cyclic regularity, and the consistency of the self all relate to the public concept of time. This is not to say that it should replace the child's subjective sense of living in a timeless moment, to which he has a right and which has an existential reality not to be supplanted. Being practical and official, calendars are an appropriate learning to associate with the *public* concept of time. (Children's spontaneous stories, on the other hand, should not be brought into this association by imposing chronology on them.)

Keeping calendars is writing practice of a real and well-motivated sort, a variant of sensory recording that can serve in turn as base for other writing such as letters. Also, calendar-keeping leads into the keeping of nature journals and logs and lays a foundation for personal diaries where records of inner perceptions as well as outer events are kept.

DIARY

A diary, like a calendar, is a day-by-day true story, based on the memory of very recent events, noted within a day or so of occurrence and kept for later use. What is unique about calendars, diaries, journals, and logs is their serial nature; the writer's point of view is at once beyond some events and yet still in the middle of others.

Procedure

In soft-cover notebooks students record for a few minutes nearly every day—in a time period that might be regularly set aside from other class activities. Some primary teachers find that this is a good way to "settle" a class at the beginning of a period. They put down the date and anything else they want, such as reminders, past events, thoughts, feelings, dreams, wishes, or ideas for poems or stories. Such a diary is also a kind of writer's notebook, not a strict record of events. For children who have kept calendars, such a notebook will not seem strange. They will be used to looking over their calendars and seeing how pieces might be summarized or "talked about" in an oral monologue, a letter, or an autobiographical story. Emphasize personal freedom. The student does not even have to write anything at all on some days. He does not have to show his notebook to anyone or use it for later writing unless he wants to. All you do is open all the possibilities.

Keep open the option of writing a letter instead of an entry. Then if a student feels on some days that he would rather write what he has to say to a friend or relative in a letter rather than write a diary entry, he has a good lead into this kind of personal writing.

Private diaries can be written by students of any age. They are frank miscellanies into which a student can pour any spur-of-the-moment thing he is prompted to write down—not just narrative incidents but reflections, imaginings, and so on. Sometimes, especially if some students say they have trouble thinking of something to say, suggest that they look around the room and write down any thoughts suggested by what they see. Encourage them to keep writing, filling up as much paper as they can, wandering to any subject, feeling, or idea. If the writing is dull, no one will object: practice is the goal. The idea of the process is to tap the constantly flowing stream of consciousness.

The diary remains private unless the student chooses to share it or put it in his writing folder. The important thing is to preserve the right to privacy so the diary is real and expressive for the student, an outlet for sensitive feelings that might not otherwise be written honestly for fear of exposure. For some students of low self-concept, however, the writing may not be taken seriously if it is not read by the teacher.

Using Diaries for Later Writing

Periodically, you can have students look over their diary entries and use them (1) as a trigger for an expanded account, thought, incident, or observation building on an entry, adding details from memory to develop a true story about something that happened in a short time interval; (2) as material for a digest or summary that reduces the diary to about one-third or one-fourth its length, trying to catch the essence of the scattered incidents or thoughts that seem related in some way and treating them together; or (3) as a source of material for a reflective poem or personal essay, as described on pages 392 and 395. You might word a summary activity this way:

> Write an account of the material in your diary. Feature both what seems important to

you and what you think will be of most interest to others. You are free to cut out and add material and to reorganize it. Don't use the dates; select and summarize so that you blend things into a continuous, whole piece.

Problem of Abstraction

We tried this activity in two classes taught by the same teacher.[1] The results varied from a very miscellaneous digest to interesting specializations. Some boys featured sports; several girls had the idea on their own of digesting a diary as a letter to a friend; one student did a recurring event in the present tense of generalization (a music lesson); some began with a paragraph of generalization, then deliberately settled on one event or period; one divided the material into school, social, and home life; and some organized by very rational categories. The poorer papers were the unselective ones—the meaningless inventories of days or the generalized miscellanies. Ninth graders in another school[2] turned out a similar variety. Among the better papers were a typical but specific account of Saturdays, done in the present tense of generalization, and a selection of four incidents showing a shift in perspective.

We see in all of these results a consistent problem of abstraction—how to compose a unity out of a miscellany, and, secondarily, how to reduce material without losing detail. Most of all, one has to select, but along with selecting there must occur some reorganizing and restating of what is retained. Weaker students without preparation flounder on these abstractive problems; stronger students solve them in ingenious ways. But how much does poor motivation play a part? If the diary is meager, a good summary is hard to write.

Social Interest

Students in one class were very positive about both the diary and the summary. They agreed at the outset that they wanted very much to read all of each other's summaries. Whereas another class would not hear of such a thing in the beginning, they too ended by asking the teacher to let them read aloud all of the summaries. Both classes did so. Their very strong interest in each other's lives is something we have often observed among students of all ages. It

---

[1] Lexington High School, Lexington, Massachusetts.
[2] Weeks Junior High School, Newton, Massachusetts.

gives them a great incentive to read what their classmates have written. They want to know each other better but do not feel free to show this interest very directly to other students they do not already know well. Somehow this important social motive should be tied in with this and other writing assignments.

Sample Diary Summaries

These three diary summaries illustrate some of the great variety of ways students go about abstracting their material and show both the problems and possibilities of this process.

Snapshot Technique

The first excerpt from a diary summary is by a girl who chose the snapshot technique. She selected entries rather than items from entries, probably rewrote them somewhat, and juxtaposed them for a slice-of-life effect, obviously trying to exploit rather than overcome the miscellaneousness of the material.

There I stood staring at the building which seemed so strange and different to me. Although I had been going there for two years, it still seemed as if this day wasn't real. As I stood in front of the school, I saw faces of many people, some of whom I had known before and others were completely strange to me. Suddenly, I found myself walking up the stairs trying to find my way around. Then there it was my room number. I looked at it for a few minutes quite reluctant to enter. The numbers kept reappearing in my mind. I knew I must go in, and suddenly I was sitting down in the classroom a bit bewildered and lost. As the hours past, I became accustomed to the teachers and my fellow classmates. There was much commotion that day. All the students were meeting new and happy faces, but there I stood trying to start a conversation which just wouldn't start. I finally got control of myself and got up enough courage to speak to a girl sitting next to me. The time seemed to pass quickly and when the bell rang for school closing I couldn't believe that it was over. I got my books and ran quickly out to catch the crowded bus. After some trampling over a tangle of feet, I made my way to the safety of a nearby seat.

What do you know? After much misgivings, I finally got to the dramtic school. I never thought that I would make it. There were about fifteen girls in the class and they all seemed friendly. Of course, there was always one stuffed shirt in the group. She thought that she could control the class. Then the teacher came in. She was a rather young looking woman. I looked at her suspiciously, in case she had thought that I was a good subject to deal with. It seemed as though I was here for at least a year, as the two hours seemed to drag on so slowly. Then it happened! I had to get up and pantomime a most ridiculous subject. Of course, I really didn't rebel in doing it; but it did seem kind of funny. Well, somehow the hours passed and with a sigh of relief I had gone through the first agony. From now on I won't be so self-conscious.

Today art class and this was quite a relief from dramatics. This time at least I could do some independent creative work. I won't be a great artist, but it won't hurt to try. My first picture didn't seem to look like anything very much, but with a few adjustments it might do as a "Rhembrandt." The class was rather small. There were about six kids in the class. The kids were all nice and they really could draw well. My teacher was very nice and helped me with my drawings. What a mess! I got paint all over my good blouse. Well, I'd better be more careful next time. Soon the class ended and it was time to leave. It was now dark out and there stood my mother's car. I ran quickly to get in because it had just started to rain.[3]

Though she has not tried to face some of the tougher difficulties of the assignment, still this girl has written rather good accounts of bits of her experience. If nothing else, the assignment has elicited several personal narratives that seem to be written with interest. Not much abstracting has taken place, but the cutting was worthwhile.

Categories-of-Experience Organization

The not very able boy who wrote the following has assimilated and organized his material to a much greater degree, but the material is more meager, whether because he overabstracted or because he simply did not keep a full diary, we don't know. His summary represents the categories-of-experience way of abstracting, which is effective here and also gives him a chance to talk about at least one important thing he has learned from his experience during the five weeks.

[3] Weeks Junior High School, Newton, Massachusetts.

MY SUMMARY TO MY DIARY

The past five or six weeks if you count February vacation have been truly progressive for me. There are many miscellaneous happenings which would not interest you so I will not write about these, but I will discuss the general things that have been important to me.

The first and most important thing in my life has been grades. I've been trying or partialy trying to boost my grades up and I have been succeeding in three subjects however the other two I do not want to mention because some of you are in those classes with me. My main incentive has been a trip to California during the next vacation. Not for very long but It will be enough. I will be going by myself and no one will be taging along telling me what to do which has been the tendency of my family in the five week span. My main obstacle for getting good grades is the dull routine, day after day. Go to school come home do home work go to sleep and go back to school the next day. It seems to me there must be a better way but I guess no one has found it yet.

The second thing on my list has been my music. I have been in about four concerts in these five weeks playing in the band and the orchestra and I have one coming up this weekend with the band. The jazz combo to which I belong has begun to move, develope and really sound like something. Enough with the music. If I went on you'd get bored.

I have been on the swim team and I have really found out what its like to work for something. I had before but not to this extent. The reason I hadn't before was because my parents are not the very strict type and ecinomically they havn't done too badly. But getting back to swimming, of course, I didn't make the first team but I did swim a couple of relays and I did swim in the I.V. meets. I found out what alot of boys are really like underneath because it comes out when he is tense and under the pressure of competition. I found that some kids who smoke and drink can really be good guys if they want to be and some kids who are maybe in A.P. and are real snob types can be real nice guys.

Also throughout my diary there are many places were it says I met someone today. I suppose this is a good sign. I don't know but I feel the more friends one has the better off someone is when he or she gets in trouble.

As a sort of conclusion I would like to say that Mrs. Lyon picked a great time for me to write a diary. I don't know about you but I've had a great time.[4]

---

[4] Lexington High School, Lexington, Massachusetts.

The lack of detail, whether the fault of the diary or of the summary, would probably have been prevented if some of his colleagues had read his diary before the stage of composition.

Thematic Abstraction

The excerpt from the boy's summary that follows represents one of the more sophisticated efforts to abstract meaningfully around themes, feelings, or ideas that, in retrospect, some of the incidents seemed to illustrate. One consequence is a mixture of generality and narrative, statement and example, which this boy carries much farther than the one who did the preceding paper: he has organized most of his summary around two stated themes, whereas the last diarist categorized his material by *areas* of experience (schoolwork, music, swimming) into which he inserted his general observation, for example, about boys under pressure. In both papers we can see the emergence of ideas and personal essay, which is one of the more promising turns that diary summaries can take. As an approach to essay, this assignment has the advantage of keeping generalizations in close relation to the actualities from which they were generated. This boy's generalizations are still very concrete and personal, but he is on the pathway to essay.

Somehow I always get myself into crazy situations by doing everything the hard way. This can be shown using the example of when the class had an assignment to catch flies for examination in Biology.

We were supposed to have the flies in the next day but that afternoon it was cool and cloudy. It wasn't a good day for flies because they like sunny days where they can sit on the concrete and sun themselves. Seeing that there were no flies to be netted on the concrete, I put some sugar water and raw meat outside in a jar for a few hours. That day turned out to a very bad one because I didn't even get any ants.

The next day I went to school without any flies. Nobody else had any either but there were a few bees brought in. It's frightening to look at bees through a magnifying glass which are sleeping off ether and can fly off at any minute. The next day we had to have flies or else.

We got out of school. I was getting my bicycle and I saw a nice big fresh mound of warm and smelly dog feces. I told one of my friends nearby. We didn't know if we would have an equal opportunity at home, so we went in and got some jars. We ended up with enough flies for the whole class and the Biology teacher was very happy with them, but this jubilance was neutralized when she picked up the jars and got dog feces all over her hands.

Another example of the way I go about everything the hard way is my method of getting notes for reports. Instead of going down three blocks to the local branch library, I go three miles on my bicycle to the main library because there are more magazines on world happenings there.

After I get home from school I only have one and a half hours for work because it takes half an hour to get to the library each way. Most of the time is wasted there because I spend most of my time looking for James Bond books, reading the electronics magazines, and looking at all the other things there.

I decided to spend a whole Saturday afternoon there so I didn't have to rush and could read more electronics magazines. I went with a friend on our bicycles. Halfway there I went through a shortcut which my friend didn't know much about but which I went all the time. He kept on going the long way and was going to meet me at our usual rendez-vous point.

Halfway through the shortcut in a desolated side-street my pedal suddenly fell off. For fifteen minutes I tried to screw it back on again.

I finally gave up and tried to ride my bicycle again. It was very difficult because you have to go at a good speed and the single pedal keeps on dropping down because it is off balance. I came to the rendez-vous point but my friend had already left so I went home to fix the pedal.

Halfway home I discovered I had a flat tire so I had to walk the rest of the way. It took two hours to fix the pedal and the flat tire, so in the end I had a half an hour to go to the branch library. Doing everything the hard way gets you no further than if you didn't.[5]

The events of a diary can be viewed either as once-upon-a-time particulars or as instances of typical or general things. An important purpose of diary summary is to give students a chance to view them as both and thus to move away from pure narrative. Probably most students will find writing a summary too difficult an abstractive feat until high school, but

[5] Weeks Junior High School, Newton, Massachusetts.

students of any age can keep diaries and use them as a source for true stories about particular personal experiences.

Purposes

As a daily habit, diary writing can become a period of meditation and self-collection. It is also a time to rehearse one's writing alone, just as young children learning to talk rehearse speech alone in their crib before falling off to sleep. It is relaxed practice. The students can make of it what they want—and what they make of it may continually change. But because they will write under the influence of present circumstances and in a particular state of mind, the entries will inevitably become in some sense a record.

To whom is a diary written? Many people who keep diaries on their own are writing to their future selves, or to an image of some ideal reader, or unconsciously to a real and meaningful figure in their life. The purpose may be practical, but it is often just self-expression and fantasy communication for its own sake. This does not mean that sometimes a student will not want someone else to see what he has written—to call the teacher over or show his diary to another student.

The main purpose of diary writing, like sensory recording, is to provide a wealth of fresh raw material for later composition aimed at an audience. The chief learning value in reshaping a diary into a true story for an audience is in solving the problem of how to abstract from an abundance of fairly miscellaneous but personal material that is already written down. It may well be a student's first experience in summarizing a document, in this case, one of his own. The whole process is a way of phasing writing —starting with spontaneous, private notation and leading to selective, public composition. There are also several other purposes—to help make writing habitual and natural; to give importance to everyday occurrences and feelings; to encourage the notation of specific things of the moment, and to create a record of long enough duration to provide earlier and later perspectives on the same events.

Parallel Reading

Reading diaries* provides a model that emphasizes the immediacy of point of view—in the middle of events—and the personal nature of communication that was not originally intended for publication.

Many students have real trouble at first in putting personal feelings onto paper. Adolescents have a special affinity with diaries, which emphasize identification and inner response to growth and to outer events that don't quite make sense. In their search for role models students who enjoy reading true-life stories of their heroes will take naturally to the reading of diaries, which are often shelved in libraries with biography and autobiography.

Another advantage of diaries such as "Feeling" * by Vaslav Nijinsky is to focus on one's self-perceptions and how they differ from or are confirmed by the perceptions of others—a common preoccupation of diarists. They provide a model for introspection. They also provide a rich source of information about other periods of history. For example, Queen Victoria's diary* gives a fresh vitality to a historical personage now a household word. Students should get to know the kinds of documents from which history is written.

JOURNAL

Another approach is writing not a private diary but a public journal to be read by others. We are defining a journal as more impersonal and public than a diary, which is written more about oneself and to oneself. Students of any age can write journals focusing on some external event; these can become an extended sort of eyewitness reportage of the progress of something they have a chance to observe often. A specialized journal focuses on one set of experiences relevant to a single activity, relationship, school subject, and so on. This focus decreases to a considerable degree the abstraction problem of summarizing.

Procedure

On an activity card you can suggest this set of steps for a small group:

- Pick an activity or changing situation that you are either participating in or observing. This could be learning to play a musical instrument or to master a sport, training a pet, or watching a process. It could be observing play rehearsals or a community project or practice sessions of a team. Decide on a time limit of from four to six weeks to complete your observations.

- Record in your journal frequent observations of the progress or development of whatever you have chosen to observe.
- Meet again as a group in a week and either read or summarize to each other what you have written in your journals. Talk about the material you are getting and begin to plan how you might use it later.
- Do this at the end of each week.
- When observing is over, talk over each other's journals and suggest ways to get each experience across best. Then write a summary of your journal and share your summaries with the class.

After some experience with specialized journals, students may be ready to summarize a long, miscellaneous journal.

Purposes

A great advantage of journal writing is that the writer can benefit from small-group suggestions about how to summarize. Thus casting the diary as a journal solves the dilemma of privacy—good for content but depriving the writer of help. Each of the types of day-by-day accounts can be used for a different purpose: diaries can provide an ongoing source of expressive and sensitive material that can be plucked out and written up independently, whereas journals can provide bodies of material covering a certain time span that can be summarized. The latter requires, we think, that the record be available for others to read at any time—during the entry-keeping, as a stimulant, and before summarizing, as an aid in composing. A wise policy might be for members of small groups to exchange and read each other's entries and give reactions while the journal is still in progress. Having a readership while they are keeping the journal creates real motivation and makes the entries richer. Then, when time for summarizing comes, students in the same group will be already familiar with each other's journals and in a much better position to make suggestions for composing. The journals themselves, then, would be considered pieces of writing for their own sake (which does not mean that they have to be written very formally), and would be sometimes printed and discussed along with the summaries of them.

Parallel Reading

Because journals* are firsthand concrete accounts of day-by-day events, they can be read by fairly unsophisticated elementary students. They provide a good way to make historical events come alive, dramatizing the problem of re-creating history by showing children how little we know about certain happenings. As they read journals like that of Captain Scott's last expedition*, they can re-create in an improvisation what it must have been like—something that is only sketched in the actual account. To read how Columbus himself reported what he found*, what slaves themselves said about slavery*, what Lewis and Clark* said it was like to encounter Indians, or how Davy Crockett recorded the last days at the Alamo* is to identify with the people who made history and thereby to have a key to understanding more generalized accounts.

As a model for the kind of specialized journal for an audience suggested above, students can read such accounts as "Surviving Outward Bound" * by Nancy Axelrad Comer.

LETTERS

As noted above, writing a personal miscellany as a letter instead of a diary can be a regular option. Children can use their calendars as reference as they write a letter to some real person (grandparents almost always make enthusiastic and grateful recipients) telling what they have been doing recently. Experiment with the length of time to be referred to —a few days up to a whole month. Suggest that children decide whom they want to write to and then read through their calendars and pick out events that they want to tell that person about and think he would like to hear. Then they write a newsy letter covering many things or dwelling on only a few.

Procedure

A stationery pad and envelopes might be kept in a "mail corner" along with a mailbox and stamps to buy, perhaps. You can be on call to help with mechanics if the child asks for help, but otherwise you need not intervene or "check out" a letter. You may need to post a chart with the form of a friendly letter and sample envelope. Older students can use collections of letters* as a model for form. If you

remind children that the mailman cannot deliver a letter unless he can read the name, street, and city, you provide a genuine motive for careful handwriting. Primary children enjoy walking with the teacher or aide to a mailbox near the school to post their letters. Of course, once introduced, writing letters need not depend on calendar keeping; the children may be asked occasionally if they would like to write a letter and then be given time for and help with it.

A letter grab bag might be set up in a classroom. Each student writes a letter to a "secret" recipient to which he signs a fictitious name. Then all the letters are put into a grab bag, and each person who wrote one draws out another one. He answers it, addressing the answer to the fictitious name who signed it. Or you can set up mystery pen pals between students in different classes. A student in your class writes to a student he doesn't know in another class. In the process of exchanging letters, the two correspondents try to find out as much as they can about each other but without revealing their identity. They can sign fake names but answer all questions honestly. Eventually, the teacher can arrange a meeting between them, of course. Pen pals in other countries intrigue some students and can be the start of lifelong friendships.

A more mature student may choose to write a letter to himself on a Monday morning telling himself what he thinks he will be doing through the week, a kind of diary in advance. Then he can open that letter on Friday and compare the Monday expectations with the Friday realizations. The next step might be to write a prediction letter for you to keep for a specified period of time—from two weeks up to a whole school year. Burying letters in a time capsule intrigues some students.

Instead of being true stories, some letters may be largely information or requests for it—or ideas as in expressions of greetings or sympathy. Any personal letter can be written in unconventional forms such as rebuses or codes and illustrated in a variety of ways. Keep open the possibility of a letter as a poem.

Purposes

Besides motivating the writing process, letters provide an outside audience and a need to shape a message for a particular receiver. The value of knowing how to write letters has long been recognized in school curriculums. Many good teachers have encouraged the writing of real letters for real purposes because it teaches far more than isolated exercises in form and style. We do not recommend assigning impersonal courtesy letters, stressing proper form and etiquette, for this tends to make of letter writing just the sort of onerous duty that makes so many adults hate to write letters, or worse yet, to go to guidebooks for models of how to write, say, a letter of condolence rather than to speak humanely to another person out of the confidence born of experience in sharing in writing honest feelings with one another. If letter writing is kept a matter of self-expression, more children, we are sure, will write them. Since the diaries students have been writing probably contain plans and practical reminders, it may often suggest the need to write a "business" letter to order something, ask about something, and so on. Instead of beating the students to the jump, and teaching a unit on business letters, it would be much better to have them ask you for advice as a real need for help arises. Your job is to set in motion activities that will call for real letters.

Parallel Reading

Both diaries and letters provide an opportunity to recognize the imperceptions of a narrator. Encourage students to read the sort of letters people write in to magazine and newspaper columns giving their accounts of how their husbands have abused them, how their daughters have shown ingratitude, and so on. Are the students persuaded by the accounts? If not, what betrays distortion? What do they think the truth is?

Both diaries and letters provide samples of the lower-order kinds of documents upon which biography and chronicle and ultimately history are based. Readers of this kind of material are in the position of researchers going to primary sources; they can see for themselves how much selecting or digesting a biographer or historian must do. They can, in fact, write some biographies or chronicles themselves using diaries and letters as their sources. This will be a natural extension of the process of using their own past diaries and letters as material for autobiographical incidents. See the following section.

Collections of letters*, including some in poetry as well as prose, are like diaries in that they offer readers a fresh view of history undigested by others, a view that retains the feel of the time and allows readers to draw their own conclusions. Letters such as those of Nicola Sacco* provide an internal view of the celebrated Sacco-Vanzetti case. Others, like Pliny's letter to Tacitus*, give a vivid true story of a historical event such as the destruction of Pompeii.

BOOK ABOUT ME

Most primary children enjoy putting together booklets about themselves. An appropriate first autobiography booklet may well be one dictated to an older child or aide who transcribes it for the child to illustrate. Tell each child he is going to be the author who writes the book and the illustrator who draws the pictures for it; the book is to be about himself. Ask the children for suggestions for the kinds of things that might go into such a book and list these on a large chart—such as "My Family," "My Bed," "My Toys," "My Birthday," "My Favorite Things to Do," "When I Was a Baby." Then each child puts his name on the cover and copies the first suggestion, say, "My Family," on the bottom of the first blank page of drawing paper. His "Book About Me" is begun. The chart of suggestions for each page of the book can be hung at a learning center where children can go to work on their booklets.

Consumable booklets* that focus on personal experience and relationships and have lots of space for drawings and evocative open-ended questions might be an effective stimulus for some children. As they mature, devices like "then . . . then" or "but then . . ." may be added to evoke longer written responses. Unfinished sentences are best when they leave the main clause to the child ("When I am sad I . . ."), thus inviting longer and more open completions that could run to more than one sentence.

Older youngsters can put together a slide-tape autobiography, taking pictures of people, places, and things that are an important part of their life—parents, friends, house, favorite possessions, and so on—and presenting them with a commentary.

MEMORY WRITING

Writing memories differs from composing diaries and letters in the time lapse between the experience and its recording. Writing a true story based on a diary entry is closely related to writing up an autobiographical incident from a spontaneous flow of memories. Summaries of diaries and journals such as those that cover a "phase" of one's life provide a fine link to the writing of autobiography and memoir. If the writer is featuring himself, he is writing autobiography; if he is featuring other people and things, he is writing memoir. Both benefit from experience in writing diaries and letters.

However, writing up a memory is quite different from abstracting from a diary, and in a real sense memory is easier, for it provides selection itself; only the personally meaningful material is remembered—and precisely because it is significant. Irrelevant detail is forgotten. One is already involved in the material, and so, at the moment of recall, it exists already in a selectively digested form for wording.

The composing of memories is in many ways similar to that of sensory writing, and much of what was said about the latter in Chapter 8, Writing, will apply here. Both are unspecialized and personal compared to writing about others, which we shall take up later in this chapter. Student response to writing memories has been very good at whatever age level we and other teachers have tried it; it should probably be a continuous activity throughout school. The main thing for the student is to learn how to tap memories for their fresh material and how to select and shape this material into compositions.

Generally, teachers who tried this process in early experiments with fourth and fifth graders reported that the youngsters liked writing memories very much and that getting them to stop was often difficult. The appeal, as with invented dialogue and stories, lies in the highly personal content, to which significant feelings are attached. Memories tie into these feelings. But, whereas the actualities of his past refer rather explicitly to experience the child is willing to acknowledge, his far-fetched stories allow him to refer obliquely and symbolically to feelings he cannot acknowledge. Both kinds of writing are important.

To inaugurate the process and build toward later self-direction, you might lead the whole class together at first.

Procedure for Beginners

I. Spontaneous Flow of Memories Look around the room at different things until something you see reminds you of something from your past—a place, person, or event. Write that down. Now what other memory does that person, place, or event remind you of? Once you get started, keep writing down your memories. Capture each one quickly. Don't worry about their being jumbled or jumping from one time to another. Write the memories in whatever

way captures them quickly; these are notes for yourself. Don't worry about spelling or correct sentences; just record as many memories as you have time for. Stop in about fifteen minutes. These notes will be used for a later activity. For right now, it is better to get a lot of memories than to go into detail about one of them.

To launch this first step, try the association process orally in small groups. Most teachers who have tried the process find it helps to demonstrate themselves. Look around the room, settle on an object, and tell the students something it reminds you of that happened once; then say what other memory that brings to mind, and so forth. You may then decide to ask a student or two to volunteer to do what you just did. Then have everyone write his flow of memories and again ask for two volunteers to read or project their papers.

Discuss the different ways used by students to note down memories on these sample papers and also ask the rest of the class to look at their own papers and say how they went about it. Again, the relative advantages of list, telegraphic, and full styles might be discussed, including the issue of coverage versus detail. Although the activity directions call for coverage, many students will add detail. Since they are registering their own memories, they can control the speed of the material better than when recording external events, as in sensory recording.

Focusing first on the sample papers and then on their own, get them to discuss the *sequences* of recollections: Why did memory A lead to memory B? What are the connections? What feeling, idea, or mood seems to go with certain of the memories? The class can speculate about the sample papers, then ask the authors for corroboration of what they have said.

You may decide that your class needs to summon memories orally and tape them before writing them down.

II. Expanding Single Memory Look over your list from step I and pick out a memory of some incident that interests you and that might interest other people, one that you would like to do more with. An "incident" would be something that happened on a particular day, unless you feel that what happened on two or three different occasions goes together as one memory. Now think about that memory and write down, as notes for yourself still, all the details you can recall that are connected with it. In other words, for about fifteen minutes, write down everything you can remember about your incident and about your thoughts and feelings at the time. Exchange your paper with others in your group and talk about any problems they have understanding it and how these can be solved.

Discussion of these papers should center on the narrowing-down process, the focusing. This is critical for helping the author to get the point of his selected recollection to emerge, and each writer can look at his own paper and apply the discussion to it. Sample papers might be dittoed or projected with step I so that comparisons can be made between steps I and II. Ask what things the writer selected *out* in doing step II. Then ask what new material he added. Once the selection of memory and its expansion in detail have been clearly established, ask the group why they think he chose that memory over the others. Then ask the author.

Now ask what more he might do to it for an audience. Does he still need more detail about some aspect of it? Does some of the detail seem unnecessary? Unnecessary for *what*? What seems to be the main point or feeling?

At this point break the class into small groups for collaboration. Have them continue the issues raised in discussion by reading and writing comments on each other's papers. They should have both papers with them and will probably need a good half hour for this discussion. If they decide their papers need a final writing incorporating the suggestions of the members of their group, this can be done in or out of school and shared or compiled into a class booklet.

Possible Problems

Starting a chain of memories presents no difficulties to youngsters, whatever their ability or intelligence. They seem to fall into Proustian procedure with ease. Two possible confusions can arise with some students, however, as experience has shown. One is to mistake mere thought associations for memory links, so that *flag* might lead to *patriotism* and to *soldiers,* and so on. The other mistake is to restrict oneself to memories associated with items in the room and thus to keep returning to the present setting in an alternation of sensations and memories.

It is true that the process begins, as sensory recording does, by looking at one's surroundings, but you can make clear that present sensation is only a springboard and that once in the past, one stays there unless the chain breaks, at which time he returns to the surroundings for a new point of departure. You can easily ward off these misunderstandings by clearly demonstrating a memory chain of your own, perhaps noting a few memories on the board. After a good demonstration no one is likely to misunderstand the process.

One practical matter is to keep the chain of memories in step I and the expanded memory of step II close enough together in time that children do not lose interest in following through. Step II may well be done at home the day step I is done in class. Organizing a folder in advance, with directions and blank pages stapled in, might help more careless children keep their papers together.

Sample Student Memories

Here are three final compositions that are good but not among the best in a class that was part of the initial trying-out of this curriculum. They are chosen rather for their representative subjects and treatment. The first two are by boys, the third by a girl— all from fourth- and fifth-grade classes.[6]

A long time ago I got a "Revell" weather forcasting kit. Since I was wearing my Sunday suit, I quickly changed into jeans and an old shirt just to find that there was no more glue.

After a five day wait, I rushehed upstairs to my room, got the "duco cement" the new glue and got to work on the oarnge, white, and clear, plastic pieces. I did all the easy parts first then came the hard part, the annemometer. But finally after about 2 weeks it was all finished. I was all through. Boy was I glad.

MY FIRST TURTLE

I remember the day that I caught my first turtle. It had been a fairly warm day and my sisters and Peter Flynn had decided to go to the swamp. We though we might catch a snake or some other animal. This time would be different.

[6] Franklin Elementary School, Lexington, Massachusetts.

I was wearing a black coat with some tall green boots. I can't recall what anyone else was wearing. It was a warm day, with a clear blue sky.

As we were walking by a murkey pond, I saw something that looked interesting. I was following my sister, and she steped over something that looked like a unripe pumpkin with yellow spots on it. I picked it up and all of a sudden feet and a head came out of it. Startled at this, I dropped it. But when I saw it was a turtle, I picked it up again. I told everyone else and they conguralated me on my good luck, and we continued our journey.

Several youngsters, influenced by discussion, chose to write their notes in a pyramidal form of note-taking (following) because it obviates writing "I remember" and "That reminds me of . . . ." So this memory chain began with spotting a flutaphone in the classroom:

FLUTAPHONE

boring music	practicing at home	
Miss Brown	practicing piano	having to take
		time for it
chorus	piano lessons	recitals
performances	getting up early	riding lessons
	for practices	

Actually, these capsule memories are noted in a dryly abstract way, none of them being an incident, and yet from these the student reconstructed a very specific underlying incident:

Piano lessons remind me of a recital I had this year.

The room was full of chairs, each occupied by either someone's mother or a student. I was to play fourth.

"Merry is now going to play an english folk song," my teacher announced. I stood up and walked up to the piano. I could hear and feel my heart pumping and wondered if the audience could. When I was done I heard a lot of applause.

"Now Merry is going to play a composed song, she composed it." My piano teacher announced, "The name is 'memories.' "

I played my short minor song and turned around to get up.

"Please play it again, its so short and I think the audience will enjoy it more."

So I did, got applause and left the piano seat happily.

Preadolescents are not inclined to state feelings as explicitly as this girl did; they either assume that such things are self-evident, or they are not introspective enough to identify and name them. A composed memory that others feel is pointless and uninteresting almost always fails to make clear the core experience that made the memory stand out in the first place. Discussion can be helpful in indicating that more explicitness, or perhaps just a more emphatic handling of facts, is needed. The core experience here was obviously pleasure, the flush of success and attention. It is rather hard to find a meaningless memory, and the meaning engenders the coherence. This children intuitively understand, but an egocentric failure to allow for the reader, among other things, can obscure the coherence.

Here are three more compositions from the same school that illustrate the other extreme of note-taking where many of the spontaneous streams of memory are more copious and colorful than the compositions derived from them. Such rich notes give one pause: How much should teaching push for the standard coherence that defines a composition? In elementary school do the losses sometimes outweigh the gains? When the notes are mere lists of words and phrases, these questions do not arise, but when we read the easily flowing memories and sentences of a paper like this girl's, we wonder if we shouldn't just let be.

As I look on top of a radiator I see a gallon jar with dirt on the bottom of it and with dirty water. That reminds me, once I was swimming in salt water and I was laying down but then I got up.

Suddenly I found me walking in freezing water. Suddenly I fell into a drop by the wind. Which reminds me of a green type of fly that stays near water, and when you are on sand It comes along and stings.

Once I was playing in some sand near water and one came along and landed on my arm.

I was so excited that I ran and jumped into the water and that scared him away.

That reminds me, once I was on a raft (floating) in the salt water and I was drifting into a drop with one of my friends, she pushed me off. Some one had to come and get me out.

Though scattered in time, her memories connect easily, forming a natural psychological continuity, and yet are kept distinct by the paragraphing. It is this spontaneous flow that the children like so much. For her step II she took the last memory:

Once I was on a plastic floatable raft. I was on the raft with my friend in the salt water. We were going with the curent going into a drop and there was no possible way to stop. My friend got excited and by mistake she pushed me off and the curent was so strong and my friends parant had to get in their boat and come get me out.

The gains of expanding were: more detail about the raft ("plastic," "floatable"), more explanation of the situation (there was no way to stop drifting, and her friend pushed her off "by mistake"), and more specification of who rescued her and how ("friends parant ... in their boat"). These are all good changes and additions, fulfilling the purpose of step II and showing the ability to "fill in" for the reader's benefit. But the sentences are hardly improved, the first one being choppy and overlapping as though she had suddenly become overformal. In doing a final revision, interestingly enough, she tightened up the sentences by herself; a partner broke the last run-on sentence into two. Though it is only stylistically different, we include it to show that important sentence development can occur without teacher intervention. The direction of these revisions that she did on her own is toward a mature economy of construction.

Once I was on a plastic floatable raft with my friend in the salt water. We were going with the curent, into a drop and there was no possible way to stop. My friend got excited and by mistake she pushed me off and the curent was to strong. My friend's parent had to get in their boat, and get me out.

These are typical of the gains and losses that the teacher needs to be alert to and to weigh when working with serial assignments. Compare the notes and composition below, done as a two-stage assignment by a boy:

I saw McGath a then I thought of my brother when it was his first birthday when he stuck his hand in the cake and took a big gob of cake out and ate it then it was SyClops the one eyed, 25 foot man then it was Voyage to the bottom of the Sea when down went inside the inside the whales tummy, the spider too, a snout comming out of a nose, JoHanna Katy disecting a frog disecting a crayfish, throw up (sick), spit, an old lady some messy (soming that comes out of your fannie.

If we are not mistaken, this is what critics mean by *visceral writing*. Among the good qualities required of language arts teachers a strong stomach is perhaps too seldom listed. This is a child writing in freedom and with relish. There is naturalistic realism and literary allusion side by side, strung together by private associations but in an obvious continuity. What the piece lacks is grammatical coherence and a more definite focus, both of which he achieves in the composition:

When it was my brothers first birthday he stuck his hand in the cake and pulled out a big gob of cake and shouved it in his mouth. He had a mouth covered with chocolate cake.

The sentences are good, he "sticks to the subject," and he has even expanded slightly. (He replaced "ate" by "shouved it in his mouth," and added the whole last sentence, which makes the point of the anecdote—his baby brother's comic appearance at the moment—a core experience that hardly needs belaboring.) As a succinct summary of a single incident, this is admirable. But what have we traded for it?

Actually the question is a bit false. It is possible to have our cake and the spiders and frogs too: instead of thinking of serial writing as stages toward "the real thing," called a composition, both teacher and pupils should probably conceive the related pieces as things in themselves, all equal in worth but for different reasons. The fact that one is base for another should not debase it. In fact, to distinguish, and to value accordingly, the variousness of writing is an important goal of the language arts. While discriminating between writing for himself and writing for others, between notes and a public composition, the child can also appreciate each for its own sake. This means that speaking of a staged assignment is using a misnomer, and that you would do better to consider each piece of writing as an end in itself and not merely as a means; what we really mean by staging or phasing writing is that one piece is used as stimulus for another, in the manner of chain reaction.

The following memory chain shows, we think, how pell-mell writing encourages children to spin out the longer, more complex sentence constructions that they will try out freely when talking but will not often risk in writing. We have italicized two especially exemplary passages:

I see a top of a house and it is white. It reminds me of going up to maine at My grandparents cottage. That reminds me of the time Gail, Robin and I and Nancy were in maine and hid in someones pyle of hay when they came bye. The White on the house also reminds me of the ski slopes when I first when on them. That reminds me of up in maine when we went to bonds. *We called to 17 year old tommy manahan who lives two houses away in maine a boy scout as he went bye. That reminds me of when My Family and I went to the end of the lake and saw the lake and the ocean be divided by a huge metal that was aquad shape and sliding down the slide that lead to the ocean.* That reminds me of when I first learned to water ski I fell and fell and then I Finally got up and made it First time around. That reminds me of when I caught my First Fish. It turned out to be a gold Fish. The remind me of when we went to canipe lake Park and I went on the biggest Roller coaster in New England. I also went on the house of seven gables and you see statues and *I saw a statue of a man having his head sawe in half* and going throw the huge barrels. That remind me of when I was four and went to boston with my mother. The reminds me of when I first learned to dive at Hayden day camp. That reminds me off the time Gail, Robin, and me went up the dirt road in maine and picked Blueberrys and rasberrys. That reminds me of the time I almost Drownded

watersking. That reminds me of the time gail and nancy and I went in Mrs. Pratts canal

---

The first italicized sentence contains three modifying phrases ("17 year old," "in maine," and "a boy scout," the last being an appositive), a relative clause ("who lives two houses away"), and a temporal clause ("as he went bye"). This represents the embedding of five potentially independent kernel sentences into the main kernel sentence, "We called to tommy manahan." Of course the sentence is badly ordered and is overloaded with information, but the girl has usefully exercised her developing sentence-building ability. In the next sentence she tries out a construction involving a verbal complement of the predicate—"saw the lake and the ocean be divided by a huge metal...." An adult's first impulse might be to use a participle here ("I saw the ocean being divided") but the girl is intuitively following a grammatical regularity, since she would say, using the active, "I saw something divide the ocean." In not using a participle, she has merely analogized from the active complement and thus written the passage "be divided." In the other italicized passage—"I saw a statue of a man having his head sawe in half"—she does use a participle in what is a subtly different grammatical situation, the case of a verbal form modifying a preceding noun rather than complementing a preceding predicate.

Such an accurate intuitive discrimination between constructions that one would expect a child to confuse makes one marvel at the powerful cognitive operations at work in language acquisition. Rarely if ever do teachers of any grade attempt to explain grammatical distinctions as fine as this. Such linguistic feats, which greatly surpass the expectations of any grammar teaching we have heard of, are persuasive evidence that the child's perceptions about what he hears and reads are the real teachers of grammar. But our point here is that he needs a lot of free writing practice in which to rehearse and recombine these constructions on paper without fear of correction. This girl's composition based on the notes above was a disappointment:

THE BOYSCOUT

One time a year ago in the summer. My Family went to maine. We go to maine every year. We live in our grandparents cottage. In Front of the cottage is a lake. We Have a motor boat, sailboat, rowboat and water skis. We go to bonds a store usally by boat but this time we went by car. My sisters Ellen and nancy went with me. Tommy manahan a 17 years old boy past and we said "Hey boyscout are you going to help a lady cross the street. When my mother came to the car she said that he told her what we said and we all started to laugh.

Again, we suspect that the choppy, overlapping "baby sentences" of the first half stem from an over-concern about writing correct sentences, which may very well have caused her to open with a sentence fragment. The backfiring strategy is to parcel out speech in short and therefore "safe" units. The result is less mature writing. The sentence in step I about the boy scout, which becomes expanded and framed here as an anecdote, has undergone an interesting transformation. No doubt realizing that her former construction was overloaded and unreadable, she took out the dependent clauses, simply dropped some information, shifted "17 year old" from the adjectival to the appositive position, and converted what had been the appositive before—"a boy scout" —into a quoted direct address. Certainly children should get a chance to flex their intelligence and ingenuity in linguistic ways by reworking their own sentence structures, but if fear of error plays a part, they will regress instead. This paper shows both aspects.

A few miscellaneous points on these two papers. First, another pupil gave considerable and helpful attention to this girl's problem with capitalization. Second, the original title of the piece was "The Hey," apt but neutral; either the girl herself or another youngster—we don't know which—changed the title to "The Boyscout," which has the same playful irony that inspired the incident itself. We can only urge, again, the strong emphasis on titling and revising titles as a way for children to help themselves make explicit their core experience and to compose a coherence around it. The girl here has more information than she needs to recount her anecdote, but, given her starting point, she has already focused considerably, and she will have plenty of other occasions to practice further.

Finally, examining papers from such activities as these, as we have examined these two, can give you many useful insights about how your students' minds work and how they come to do the types of things with language that they do. In this way you can conduct your own research—not essentially different from that of some linguists and psycholinguists—that can help you think about what you are doing and ought to be doing.

Procedure For More Experienced Writers

We recommend next a three-step process. The first two steps are those presented on pages 329 and 330. Here is the third:

III. Final Composed Memory Go to your group with your step I and step II papers. Exchange these with each other. After you have read a partner's, write comments on his step II paper that will help him to rewrite it as a finished composition. (You will all rewrite your step II's for your classmates to read.) Your comments can be about any of the things just discussed with the sample papers. Do you think the writer chose the best memory? What things about the memory do you think he should bring out most when he rewrites? What would you like to hear more about? Do you really know how he felt and what he thought at that time? Are there any things he should cut out? Are the words he uses the best ones? Could his sentences be reworked? Can you guess why the writer found this particular experience important and memorable?

Then exchange papers again until each of you has read each of the papers. Afterward, you may talk with the others about their comments on your step II.

Finally, rewrite your step II paper. Follow the suggestions the other students made, when you agree with them. Make all the big and small changes it takes to make your memory clear and interesting for the class. Share your memories or compile them into a class book.

You may choose to ditto or project all three papers of a couple of students, so that others can survey the entire process by which those authors got from first to last stage. Discuss the decisions and changes they made between steps I and II, and between steps II and III. In one case, you might show step III first, then II, then I—work backward from the finished product. When moving the other way—from I to II and III—ask the students to guess what choices the author is going to make between one stage and the next; then show the next paper. Get them to relate the writer's progressive decisions to their own judgment about the final version.

It would be good to have a number of step III's read aloud to give the class an idea of some of the different results of memory writing—different points and moods—and also to carry through the idea that the whole class was their audience.

In experiments, seventh-grade students who had done some sensory recording but had no prior experience with memory writing showed more willingness to revise and more ability to discuss compositional issues than elementary-school children. It is still important that the directions specify a precise *incident*. Some seventh graders tried to assimilate the project to conventional topics like a trip or summer vacation, which cover too much time and space for the length of writing they will do, resulting in a dull, overabstracted account, and causing the student to create a trivial organization based on a time span or place instead of on a mood or feeling.

Small-group cross-commentary by students is essential for motivating them to elaborate, for showing them the needs of the reader, and for helping them make compositional decisions. Sometimes these sessions may be preceded by teacher-led class discussion of sample papers, designed to clarify issues they all face.

Sample Student Memories

Here is a *three-stage series* done by a seventh-grade girl and typical of a number of able middle-class students:

MEMORIES

Spontaneous Flow of Memories

When I was little, I used to ride my tricycle all through the basement. Thought it was so much fun. When I was about six, there was a fire in our furnace. Two fire engines came. Everyone was running around throwing sand into the furnace. I took someone's hat, my dog, and pretended I was coming to save the day on my horse. They kicked me out! When I was at camp 3 years ago, we took a motor boat, went out to an island, and had an overnight. After we made supper we went fishing off the dock. I fell in the lake & had to be pulled out! I remember when I made a line pulley with my

house & the house next door, the girl & I sent messages during the night to each other. I remember the time up at Camp Union, on the last few nights, when we had a square dance. One of the teachers fell off a chair & hurt his legs. I remember the first time I ever came to visit Weeks. Rainy cold. The front door steps looked gigantic.

AN ISLAND ADVENTURE

Single Expanded Memory

It was a muggy night, during the summer 3 years ago. Up in Oakland, Maine. We were going to an island in the middle of a lake for an overnight. Motorboat was overloaded with people, food & sleeping bags. Front of the boat was high in the air. Waves from the boat were all white & foamy. Water was splashing through the air, causing it to be chilly for a few minutes. Many trees on the island. A few lashings between these trees. Long dock. Washing pots and pans in lake. A fish swam into one girl's pots. Screaming and running. Fishing—something tugged at my line and pulled me into the lake. All wet. Had to be pulled out!

Pitching tents—got conked on the head with some else's stake. The ground was very hard to sleep on. Heard loons crying. Sounded very weird. Two other girls crawled into my tent because we were all scared. It collapsed on all of us. We were too tired to put it up again so we left it down until the morning.

AN ISLAND OVERNIGHT

Final Composed Memory

It was a muggy night during the summer about three years ago, up in Maine. We were going by motorboat to an island in the middle of a lake for an overnight trip. The motorboat was overloaded with people, food and sleeping bags, and the front of it was high in the air. The waves from the boat were like soapsuds in a washing machine. Water was splashed through the air, causing it to be chilly for a few minutes.

There were many trees on the island and a few lashings between them. After supper we decided to go fishing off the long docks extending from the island. We dug up some worms & hooked and baited out poles. I stood on the edge of the dock waiting for a bite.

Suddenly I felt a small tug on my line. I got very excited and pulled slightly. This time I felt that my line was being pulled out of my hands. I though that I had caught a large fish and kept struggling. I pulled the rod back until the string was taught. The next thing I knew was that I was sitting in the lake. My line had gotten knotted with someone elses and we were both on different sides of dock so that we couldn't see each other. She thought that I was a fish when I pulled on the lines. I also thought that she was a fish when she pulled back. I was so embarrased! I had to be pulled out of the lake because the bank was too slippery to climb up.

That night when we pitched the tents, I got conked on the head with a stake & was knocked out. That was quite an experience!

So goes the expanding and focusing process when the three stages are meaningful, but sometimes during experiments with elementary-school youngsters a stage-II paper was too much like the final stage-III: the student had composed so well in the second stage that only minor revision was needed. The process can seem too rigid. The best solution is probably to let the small groups discuss which students should go a stage further and which not, and to give groups the editing function of preparing copy for printing. Thus when a composition is judged complete, a student stops, but his colleagues suggest final revisions to make in whatever manner is most

practical for printing—either writing in changes or doing a new draft.

If students are intimidated by any kind of writing, like those in the class from which the following paper came, you may have to modify considerably the process described here, at first anyway. The approach has to be very gentle—no criticism and revision for a while—and the memories should be stimulated by a kind of emotional focusing. The teacher elicited this brief but meaningful piece by placing around the room several blown-up photographs of provocative subjects and then asking the students to write down a memory that one of the pictures reminded them of. A black girl wrote this:

I remember when I was a little girl. I was singing a rain song. It was cold with the splashing of the rain in the puddles. The frogs were cracking the skies were black and all the duck were saying quack quack. I loved to walk in the rain it made me feel so clean inside. Although it was cold around me I was warm and safe.[7]

In this class, the students were encouraged to read their papers privately into a tape recorder and to play them back, and their papers were frequently printed up after help with spelling and punctuation. The purpose was to bolster confidence and certify their writing—emotional matters that, with these students, have to take priority for a while over the exploration of compositional alternatives.

As Director of English for the 1966 Upward Bound Program at Tougaloo College, near Jackson, Mississippi, Charles Thurow chose to use memory writing with the program's students (all blacks just out of the eleventh grade and chosen for their educational promise) as the first of several activities drawn from the program presented in this book. He wanted his students to have a chance to write about firsthand material in their own language without worrying about mechanics and right answers, to become involved with their own writing and that of others. Initially, they were unwilling to write at all and virtually unable to talk about writing. For them,

[7] Harvard-Boston Summer School located in the Roxbury section of Boston, Massachusetts; the class comprised children about to enter the eighth and ninth grades.

composition had always consisted of grammar and rules for mechanics.

Putting down spontaneous memories, expanding and revising some of them, seemed eventually to open them up and get them going. All the memory papers of his sixteen students were surprisingly full —considering that six of the sixteen could not produce at all for a long time. On each other's papers they wrote very helpful suggestions about rephrasing, adding and deleting information, clarifying passages.

The writing done by the Tougaloo students is a fair representation of what many other children who are strangers to writing might do when asked, at this late age, abruptly, to write something from their real experience. For this reason we reproduce one of the revised memories that we think makes interesting reading, but the majority of the other papers were as long and as literate as the one printed here, and all had at least some of the color and feeling and force of this.

Also, this sample represents one of three different directions in which the memories went. It tells an *autibiographical incident.* Other directions were toward memoir and recurring experience.

SAINT BILLY VISITS AT 9:00 P.M.

Several years ago when I was just a little girl my cousin Vernistine and I lived with my grandmother. I was about nine years old my cousin was twelve.

Mother told Vernis there was a man who collected all, all bad kids at night. Vernis replied, "I don't believe you"! Mother said slowly—alright, I'll see. Vernis disbelieved her. This Vernis had to see with her own eyes. Later mother said, since you don't believe me. write him a letter and put it outside some where.

Late one evening Vernis wrote the letter. Vernis ask, "Callie come go with me"? With out asking any questions I followed her to put the letter on the bank of the lake. After delivering the letters we came back to the house; however, Vernis cracked jokes with mother. There is no Saint Billy! Mother replyed yes there is— you will see tonight!

Saint Billy always knocks three times before coming into a house.

About nine o'clock we heard three loud knocks, and the front door open. Saint Billy walked into the room and said, "good evening". I looked back and there was an ugly, undescribable man standing in the door. I started screaming I cried for about one hour or more. Vernis was down on her knees calling on God.

Saint Billy ask, "Can one of you dance or sing?" We replyed, no Sir. He said frightening as he pull a sack from his pocket, I'll get one of you to night. I screamed louder and louder, "make him go away"!

My grandparents laugh until they cried.

Later Saint Billy gave up and went home or somewhere. I was so glad. I don't ever want to see him again.

Adolescents with whom we tried the three-stage memory writing differed from elementary-school children in that they were more willing to elaborate first for the sake of garnering more material in step II and less inclined toward an early closure. Whereas step II seems like a natural end to most elementary-school children, it can be viewed by older students as still preliminary note-taking.

Purposes

If you think about how much of writing in the later years, and of adult writing, draws on memory for its material (including later, the memory of what one reads), and if you acknowledge the universality of the compositional issues entailed in memory writing, then you see how central it is to this curriculum. Together, sensations and memories are the individual's storehouse, from which—however bizarrely imaginative or abstractly formulated—all his writing must necessarily proceed. Not all of people's recordings and reportings get written, but they occur inside anyway, and we further abstract these into the generalities according to which we see the world and according to which we take action.

When these processes are themselves the basis of activities, then writing becomes an external and explicit replica of what ordinarily happens inwardly and hiddenly. A pupil can thus gradually become aware of how he knows what he knows, and of how his experience shapes his thought. As for his fancies and fictions, they are merely a less direct mode of recombining and synthesizing these same raw materials. Asking a child to write down sensations and memories not only shows him that the real stuff of speaking and writing lies all around him and within him at any moment, but it validates this stuff; it says plainly that his individual experience is of great worth, something to turn to, not away from. See page

388 for a discussion of stream-of-consciousness writing, which aims at a free flow of sensations, memories, and reflections. When any free flow of writing is shared through the group process with others and compared with their expression, it is given the perspective of public reality.

The reason for a two- or three-step process is to avoid a student's drawing a blank or telling the gist of a memory so quickly that it is lifeless. Conventional assignments try to solve the problem of getting an idea by specifying topics such as "My Most Thrilling (Frightening, Surprising, and so on) Moment," or "The First Time I Learned a Sport." Like most writing problems in a one-stroke assignment, the problem of giving body and detail to an incident is not handled until the teacher's post-mortem commentary comes along, when the pupil is confronted with the should-haves and made to feel in the wrong. Also, we think blanket topics make for canned themes. Not only do they work poorly as a stimulant but, in categorizing students' experience for them in advance, they by-pass the most worthwhile compositional issues that learners should grapple with. Such assignments always stipulate the abstract classification of events and usually also the feeling or mood that is to provide coherence. All the student does is fill in the blanks with an event—which reduces writing issues to a rather low level. And here begins the long years of nagging about detail. Elaborating appears as an obsession of teachers rather than as an organic development, as a part of the process of coming up with something that communicates to one's classmates.

The underlying goal in spontaneous memory writing is to keep composition on a deeper, cognitive basis, since at heart it is the classifying and ordering of experience—information processing, if you like. By spreading the composing over stages we hope to lay bare for examination and influence the internal processes of writing that in conventional assignments remain more hidden and less tractable, if they are put into play at all. Selecting one incident would come as a meaningful narrowing down of the first, miscellaneous array. Expanding into detail would follow, before the final draft, as a filling in of what one had staked out, like pointing to a city on a map and then looking at the inserted plan of that city. Stage III would again be a bit of selective abstracting, this time around a "core experience" that discussion with partners would have helped to emerge. Thus the student would be working up inductively from a wealth of material instead of working downward deductively by trying to flesh out a given abstraction. Both sensory and memory writing are harder than topical assignments, because they pose greater difficulties for the writer's egocentricity and thus demand more objectification. This teaches more and requires some process for opening internal composition to external feedback. The point of any process is not to avoid problems; it is to engage with the right problems in the right way. Memory writing does this well and is an activity we can recommend with great confidence.

AUTOBIOGRAPHICAL PHASE

We distinguish here between *incident* and *phase*, defining the latter as a portion of autobiography that "covers" a long period of time and therefore includes summaries both of recurring events and of incidents occurring at different places. This distinction in time-space coverage implies differences in abstractive tasks for the writer.

Procedure

Here are the directions for this kind of writing:

> Tell what happened to you during a certain period of your life covering many months, perhaps even a year or so—some "phase."

Phase is emphasized; the portion is not miscellaneous, but focused. To distill a period of weeks, months, or years in one to two thousand words requires drastic editing of events. It is this editing process that teaches.

The two main issues that characterize this activity and that you might use as a guide for class discussion and small-group work are: What idea of "phase" does the writer use as his criterion for relevance in selecting and emphasizing? And what efforts does he make or fail to make to offset the abstractness of summary? Fragments of autobiography should not be résumés of fact with no concrete qualities of the original events and feelings. And yet, if the student narrates too much in detail, quotes too often, and stays entirely in moments of the past, he cannot come near telling what happened over a period of months. The crux of the assignment, then, lies in some balance between precise actualities— what people did, said, felt, and so on—and some all-encompassing theme—a notion of a trial gone through, a stage of growth experienced, a set of circumstances lived through, a relationship developed. This theme may or may not need to be directly stated, depending on how obvious it will be to the reader, which is not always an easy thing to guess in advance. However, it will need to be organized thematically rather than chronologically. As for vividness, this calls for shrewdness about when to pull in for a "close-up" of a certain scene and when to summarize in a few sentences the less important or repetitive events. Although necessarily abstract as a whole, a summary need not be abstract in its parts. A general statement about what occurred "in the meantime," or what occurred habitually over a long period, can be cast into concrete words and phrases, and specific references.

Sample

The following portion of autobiography was written by a boy who came to Phillips Exeter Academy for one year as a senior, having already graduated from a Greater Boston high school the year before. It is untitled because at that time one of us was having seniors write a long autobiography in installments, a practice we do not recommend because it allots too much time for one kind of writing. Since the educational background of this rather atypical Exonian is part of his subject, we will let his own words evoke it.

When I was in the fifth and sixth grades, my mother wanted me to become an altar boy. I disliked the idea before I even knew what it was all about, and when I knew, I disliked it even more. Every Saturday morning when everybody else was out skating, I had to go to church and try to learn how to answer the priest in Latin. There were about thirty boys in the class, whose mothers had also made them come to the lessons. They all claimed that they were never prepared for the lessons, but it was evident that their mothers had made them study the Latin during the week. My mother had tried also, but it just would not sink in, mainly because I did not want it to. I hoped that I could prove to both my mother and our priest that I was too dumb to learn how to serve mass. When I was called on in class, I would stand up and give a phrase I had heard somebody else give earlier in the lesson. The kids thought it was kind of funny giving the right answer to the wrong question. Sometimes if he called on me two or three times I would give the same answer. Once he got mad at me and asked me if I was trying to be funny. I denied it

and told him that it simply was the only response I knew. That afternoon he called my mother and told her that if I did not have my lessons prepared in the future and continued to disrupt the whole class, I would have to give up the idea of being an altar boy.

Every afternoon that week my mother had me come in and study that foolish Latin. In the evening she would make me recite what I was supposed to have learned. My brother by this time had learned more Latin than I had. He would just sit there and listen every evening. When I did not know the answer, he would give the responses to my mother. This would always bring on the old song and dance about why couldn't I do it if my little brother could. The answer was that I did not want to learn it, and he did. He enjoyed making a fool of me, so every night that he tried to humiliate me when I went over the lesson, I would beat him up. He would scream and run to my mother, and she in turn would beat me. It was a losing battle and I was always on the short end.

Eddie had shown such deftness for Latin that she thought that he too would make a fine altar boy. On Saturdays, my brother would know the Latin as well as any of the older boys in the group. He had slaved all week just to show his stupid brother up, and I knew it. All was not lost, however, because I too knew my Latin. The priest was amazed and thought that if I could learn the Latin, then surely his class was making fair progress. Actually what I did was to have a friend of mine in the class sit in front of me, and I pinned the Latin card to his back. When I was called to write, all I did was read it off his back. The reason I was able to get away with this was that the priest did not know the Latin either, and as I was writing the priest was looking at his missal to see if I was saying it correctly. I really made fine strides this way. Every week I knew the Latin. Everything was going fine until one morning I read the priest's response on the card instead of the altar boy's. Everybody started to laugh because they all knew what I was doing. What really finished it was my friend made the mistake of turning around to laugh at me. When he did, the priest saw the Latin card that was pinned to his back. He did not say much, he just came down and tore the card off the boy's back, and my friend told him that he did not know that it was on there. The one who had a lot of talking to do was Eddie. He made sure he got home to tell his version of the story first. My mother was really mad, and screamed at me for about ten minutes. She finally hit me on the nose because I started to hum and tap my foot while she was trying to give me what she called constructive criticism. So with a bloody nose, I took my brother's skates out into the back yard and pounded the blades against the fireplace until they were too dull to ever try to skate on. My father was not too mad that I had used a bit of outside help in my Latin assignments. In fact, I think he thought it was a little humorous but did not show it openly.

The following Saturday there was a final written test in Latin. I asked the priest if I could go into the next room because it was quieter. When I got in there I took out my father's missal that I had taken from his bureau, and copied down all those responses that I had to know. Then I turned to the back of the book and answered all the questions about the priest's vestments. I did not care about cheating, I just wanted to show up my brother. Well, I passed with flying colors and substantially outdid my brother. When my brother and I served our first mass, my brother would answer the priest so loud that anybody in the church could hear him. I just mumbled except when all we had to say was "Amen." I liked the funerals best of all because they were usually on school days. The funerals in our church were usually at nine or ten in the morning, so we would have the whole morning off. I had a friend from school who was also an altar boy and asked to serve on the same funerals so we could walk to school together. His mother had told him to stay away from me, but he did not mind getting into trouble either.

When the funeral was over, we would walk as slowly as we could the mile to school. We used to stop along the way to ride a donkey or chase sheep. When we got to school, if it was too early, we would sit in the woods until lunch time and then go in. I was an altar boy until I was in the eighth grade, when I was thrown out because of fighting in the church. We weren't really fighting. We were just rolling around on the altar when we were supposed to be practicing for a wedding.

Most of the time my parents are hard to get along with, but during that year they were unspeakable. My father kept me in almost every Friday and Saturday night for something I had done either at school or at home. I did not mind getting in trouble for something I had done that was really wrong, but some of the things I was kept in for made me fight my parents even more.

Friday night would find me reduced to watching television for not making my bed, being late for breakfast, or hitting my little sister. One of the worst was having to stay in for not untying my shoes before taking them off. My father would come into my room every night after I was in bed to check my shoes. Just for spite I used to take them off and untie them. I could not stand my parents during those years and neither could my

friends. They would not come into the house because I was always fighting with them.

I was playing varsity hockey that year, and my father even kept me out of some of the games. He would take my skates away for a week at a time for some really stupid reason. The only reason I was kept on the team was that the coach missed the same games I did. Our coach was Butch Songin and at that time he was playing quarterback for the Boston Patriots.

I tried to live in my own world. When I came home from skating I would go up to my room and only come down for meals. If I was watching television or sitting in the den and my father walked in I would get up and leave just to avoid an argument.

Things got progressively worse at home and at school. I was not doing much of anything. In February my father decided to bring me into Boston University to take a battery of tests given as a course of guidance. They told me I was there to see what courses in school would fit me best, but I knew I was there because my parents wanted to know if I could do the work I was supposed to be doing and if I could why wasn't I? The tests were the type in which you play with blocks, puzzles and ink spots. Also, someone would flash pictures in front of you and ask you what was the first thing that came into your mind. At the end of the thirty-hour testing period they came to the conclusion that I was quite bright but had difficulty in reading and spelling. My scores ranged from a perfect score in abstract reasoning to about twenty-five percent in reading and spelling. They also told my father to lay off me and in this way I would come along myself because I would not be fighting them. However, the next term he went back to his old suppression because I came home with two D's and two E's.

About this time I got sick of everyone, my teacher and my parents. The teachers were really wearing on me, and I thought that our priest was the most two-faced person I knew. During the football and hockey seasons everything was fine with him. But as soon as hockey was over he too started to climb on my back. I got very fresh and gave everyone a hard time, even teachers that were the type not to fool around with. One teacher used to talk about a certain element in the room that should be removed. So now I was an element: she even called me an element of refuse. One day when she was talking about this "certain element" I started to laugh. She got so red I thought she would explode. She started to cry and said until I left the room she would not come back in. I sat in the class all day while she sat out in the hall, where she had moved her desk. I was not going to leave, I would have stayed there for the rest of the year and the following if I had to. The next day her things were back in the room. She publicly proclaimed that either I left the school that year or she would. That summer she left.

The organic unity or theme is clear—the contest of wills between the author and the adults in his environment. This paper benefited from suggested revisions, but these concerned sentence ineptitudes—the residue of a language handicap—not the selection and shaping of material. He knew what he wanted to say. He had his own unerring touchstone that guided his choice of what was relevant and what was not. When the cunning with which he waged war against others was put in the service of writing something real, he showed more craft and wit than many students who had had far more practice. It is amazing how so-called writing problems clear up when students *care*. Again and again we have seen students write "over their heads" when an assignment invited them to use native intelligence on raw material they were greatly involved in.

Issues for the Writing Workshop

Organization

The sample above illustrates several additional issues that the assignment should engage students with. One is the transition from chronological organization to a thematic organization by ideas. Most accounts of a phase combine narrative with essay. That is, either the paper generally progresses chronologically but contains topical paragraphs in which time stands still while a general point is made, or the progression is a development of general points illustrated by bits of narrative taken out of chronological order. These organizations naturally occur because a portion of autobiography has the double goal of telling what happened while summarizing in a meaningful way. Before revising, students should try to decide, with a given paper, what presentation is best.

If you will look back over the sample above, you will notice that the level of abstraction varies considerably, according to whether the author is recounting a single incident that happened only once, summarizing recurrent or typical events, or describing a general situation. In a rough way the paper

moves from the time he began learning to be an altar boy until the summer the teacher left (the exact period of time covered being not very well indicated, as a matter of fact). The result is not a narrative in the sense of a series of events; it is an account of a worsening situation or relationship, illustrated by events and marked by events, but not fastened down to particularities in precise order. How he prepared his lessons, how his brother tried to show him up, what he did on funeral days, the way he and his family behaved toward each other, the spread of hostility toward other adults—these are situations or stages that he usually introduces by more abstract sentences of the sort that teachers have been fond of calling topic sentences but which are generated spontaneously by the very needs of the assignment. If a student adds a title to his autobiographical phase, he needs to abstract even further to the most all-encompassing word or phrase—a process that can point out irrelevant material, revealed by the very struggle to include it under the title.

Vantage Point

The second matter is time perspective. What enabled this boy to disengage a thematic unity from the welter of past facts was a certain emotional distance. From a remoter vantage point one can see patterns. Autobiography is characterized by binocular vision: the writer splits into I-now and I-then, which means that he looks at events from the remembered viewpoint of the past and from his present viewpoint. In the sample above, for example, though the boy says his parents *are* hard to live with, still it is obvious that he would have given a vastly different account of those earlier years if he had not changed considerably since then (as indeed he had). For one thing, an account written at the time could hardly have been so intentionally funny or so devoid of anger and self-justification. It is remarkably "objective."

When we say that *Great Expectations* is told from Pip's point of view, or *To Kill a Mockingbird* from Scout's, we mean, of course, that they are told from the points of view of two middle-aged narrators[8] who have framed their childhood perspective within their later perspective. Compare *Catcher in the Rye,* narrated a year after the events, with *A*

---

[8] A narrator is the persona telling the story, not the author of the book.

Separate Peace, narrated fifteen years later. How well a student succeeds in defining themes, then, will depend partly on how far he stands from the events in time. Discussions of papers should allow for time lapses and consequent perspectives. Personally, how one abstracts his past is critical, for the basic function of abstracting is to guide action. The very effort to write large-scope autobiography may help to induce a maturer perspective, as perhaps it did for the boy here.

When autobiography shifts from incident to phase, the writer risks exposing both himself and others, precisely because the assignment calls for some truths of one's life. The dilemma is this: it is the real material of their world that students want most to write about and can learn most from, but it is the same material that threatens both the writer and the people he writes about. The answer is, without being prissy about it, to screen what is printed in the class publications. This discretion can be a very good moral issue for students to discuss as editors, consulting the teacher and sometimes the parties involved. When possible, identities can be masked. And we should remember that more than one parent has risked exposure out of pride in what his child has achieved. Good policy sometimes might be to show the writing to parents first of all. In the case of some of our projects, furthermore, a school principal has explained to parents what sorts of writing would be going on and what benefits their children would derive from them. The dilemma should be put to parents also. This advisement helps considerably to stave off offense, which is frequently just a feeling of being left out.

Parallel Reading

Autobiographical writing is accompanied by the reading of actual autobiographical excerpts*, in prose and poetry. Do not analyze these as models; in the course of discussing both their writing and the reading, students will make their own connections. They will note the narrator's relationship to his subject and that the less he is the center of action, the more his point of view is external, and the more he becomes a filter for what he observes—the more his account is moving away from autobiography and toward memoir (see following section). Showing autobiography and memoir side by side helps call attention to an important difference in the focus of much reading and writing. As students write both, they begin to know from the inside, so to speak, the

decision an author makes regarding his point of view and the degree of abstraction, the latter determining whether he is treating an incident or a phase. They can interpret what they read partly by noting decisions of selection and emphasis.

A major motive for young people to read autobiography, and biography as well, is to search for role models and to identify with persons who have done what the reader would like to do. There are a great many fine autobiographies written by members of minority groups. Readers should have access to those of their own ethnic culture.

We suggest a triple juxtaposition in the curriculum —of student autobiography, fictional autobiography, and actual published autobiography. A valuable interaction of the three takes place, we believe, in the minds of students and gives considerable dimension as well to their discussion of each. They could read in common a fragment of true autobiography for discussion. Then let each student read a whole autobiography by some person who interests him—a book from the public library or a paperback that he can purchase if he wants to. Ask the students to bring these books to school; allow them some in-class time to begin reading them, some out-of-class time to continue, and encourage them to read on their own. This might be individual reading to *follow* their writing. Like diaries and letters, autobiographies are the stuff of history and can be read as source documents.

Writing about others

The types of true stories about the self we have just looked at have parallels in types of stories about others. As with other literature, certain pieces do not fall neatly into any one category. Some journals are as much about others as about the self, and first-person writing can turn out to be mostly memoir in which the focus is centered on another person rather than the self. Memoir is the bridge between author focus and other focus.

MEMOIR

Like autobiography, memoir is first-person narration. The directions differ, however, from autobiography in that the writer is asked to focus outside himself:

Tell an incident that you witnessed in the past in which you were involved only as an observer.

The word "incident" automatically focuses the composition somewhat and throws emphasis on action rather than on setting or mood. In order to specialize memoir even further, and to include nature observations in the writing program, we differentiate the directions into nonhuman and human subjects.

It is crucial that the teacher allow the students enough length to tell the incident well—two or three pages. A lot of very bad writing has been induced simply by limiting narrative to a paragraph or some other small wordage. Such limits force the student to overcondense and to state the facts in an abstractly lifeless way. Strictly demanding an arbitrarily high wordage, however, can cause padding. The ideal is an organic length determined by the writer's judgment *as developed by previous writing experience.* There is evidence from our experiments that students who have done sensory recording, memory writing, and dialogue writing learn to write fluently and fully, to detail and expand without just trying to pad.

Firsthand Nature Incident

The following sample illustrates nature narrative drawn from memory. One of us read more than one hundred memoirs written by junior high students, was hardly bored a single time, and was astonished by the fullness, the interest, and the generally high quality of the accounts, even when some of the authors obviously lacked verbal skill. We chose this sample almost at random and certainly did not screen for the best. Besides the unquestionable effectiveness of the teacher of these classes,[9] the successful results, extremely consistent for that generally able student body, seemed to be due to the subject. Recounting animal incidents, storms, and so on is an especially happy activity for students of the middle grades. This girl's paper is unrevised and uncorrected:

The breakers crashed the rocks and ran away with a hissing sound. The gray sand was dotted with birds' prints. It was a bleak November day at the beach dark save for the thin watery sunlight breaking through the clouds. The wind whistled through the waving dune grass and made whitecaps on the waves.

Suddenly the peaceful silence was broken by a flock

[9] Eugenia Nicholas of Weeks Junior High School, Newton, Massachusetts.

of hungry sea gulls flying over head, hunting food. There was a bag of garbage left on the beach by some careless picknicker, and the gulls, smelling this delicacy, were already landing around it. After a few minutes the scene had turned into a complete battle. Squaks, screeches and the swoosh of wings accompanied this "tug-of-war" combat which involved the survival of the fittest. Food was pulled between beaks, stepped on and sent flying into the rumbling ocean.

Two particular gulls, I noticed, were engaged in a life or death wing-to-wing combat. There was an old strong gull who looked like he'd been through many similar episodes like this, and a young brown-speckled gull. The young one had what looked like a moldy sanwich and was contentedly pecking at it, not bothering a soul. The old sly bird spied this jealously and made up his mind to get it. He opened his large beak and snapped at the diner's tail so hard that the younger jumped away from his dinner. The other seeing its' chance grabbed the morsel and flew to a nearby jetty. After recovering from its shock the brown-specked bird. In his anger he began to circle round the other greedy gull and finally swooped down hitting him hard. There, silhoueted against the gray sky the two birds fought, not a playful romp, but a fight which meant the loser would forfeit a rare meal, for their was little to eat these cold days. One may even be killed, because if there was a sea gulls manual, they were using every trick in the book. The sandwich lay barely touched next to the hysterical birds. All the other gulls had flown off satisfied or to seek out more food, but these gulls continued their ordeal. The younger was beginning to weaken and the other would jab at him fiercely when he paused. Blood was flecked on the older's white breast but he was not loosing strength. Finally, when the younger looked too weak to even eat the food, the other gave him one fierce push that sent him tumbling off the jetty, and landed, a crumpled heap in the water. The poor thing apparently had broken it's wing and now he was at the mercy of the angry sea. He bobbed a few times, gasping but finally disappeared in the inky ocean. The sly bird, happy with his victory snatched the sandwich in his beak and started to fly away. But, suddenly against the sky I saw his figure falling into the sea for he was too tired to carry the food and fly. The sea gull joined his enemy undersea.

Incident Focused on Another

The personal memory that follows was written by a black girl in eleventh grade, who had limited educational opportunity.[10] The protagonist is her brother; she is both confidant and eyewitness. However, since she was not present at all the events, she has to tell some of it as it was told to her. This kind of very involved but peripheral narrator is the "first person" of many published memoirs and of fiction such as *Life with Father*.

MEMORY OF MY BROTHER ACCIDENT

The most terrifying thing that ever happened to me was on December 24, 1962. My second brother was shot with a 16 ga. shotgun. At the time he was fourteen years old. This is the way it happen, My brother James and cousin (N. C. Mayers.) went hunting around 1 O'Clock that morning of the day he got shot. N. C. was behind James, N. C. had his gun loaded as they was walking alone James shouted look there is a squirrel at that instant N. C. pulled the trigger on his gun. The bullets hit my brothers left hand below his elbow. This James walked Alone for about ten minutes meanwhile N. C. had stopped and was staring in disbelief. James finally went to hold up his hand and said, Man look my hand has been shot and he only looked and said they're going to cut my hand of. This He walked on to my uncle's house and said Uncle Mob open the door I been shot. My uncle didn't believe him because he had been carrying on a lot of foolishness. After about five minutes of convincing my uncle he finally open the door and stared in horror at the blood and the condition of James hand. My uncle was tall, dark around 65 years old he lived in a three room house on his farm about twelve miles from civilzation. He told James to set down and gave him a sheet to put his hand in while he go down to the barn and hitch his mules to the wagon because he didn't have any other mean of transportation.

It took Uncle Mob about 15 Mins. to drive from his house to ours in a wagon. After Uncle Mob and James get to the house my parents was at work and had the car. All of us came out of the house and looked at James in horror but James was smiling then we all begin to cry and scream my oldest brother got on the horse and at no time at all he got my cousin to take James to the hospital. He took him to Brandon hospital but the doctors there said they had to cut his hand off but the university hospital in Jackson might could save it so they took him to the University. I cannot give a

[10] With thanks to Charles Thurow, director of English for the 1966 Upward Bound Program at Tougaloo College, near Jackson, Mississippi.

description of the hospital nor doctor because I wasn't there. By this time my Uncle had notified my parents and they was there. The doctor asked my mother permission to cut his hand of and she refused. He explained to her that wasn't but two leaders holding his hand together and the arm will never be anymore good anyway. My mother still refused so the doctors took him into surgery and sewed his leaders together and put his arm in a cast for six weeks. After the six week period they put his hand into a mending bandage for four more weeks after the four weeks period his they left his arm bear which didn't look so good but he still had it and after a short time he started using his left hand as good as his right hand. And now which is four years later my brother still thanks my mother for not signing the paper.

My Cousin N. C. went out of his head for about 2 days he didn't come home and didn't say anything to anyone because he thought we would blame him for what happen two years after the accident N. C. died of pneumonia and someone had stab him with an ice pick.

Phase of Someone Else

Just as autobiography can be either an incident or a phase, so can memoir. Again, the focus is on a longer time span than a single incident. The problems are similar to those of autobiography except that the writer is on the outside looking in. Not having been at the center of the experience, he must *infer* that experience from what he knows firsthand and from empathic understanding. Whereas the demon of autobiography is one's lack of distance, the chief difficulty in writing about others is too much distance. If the narrator was not at the center of events, and is not the person who underwent the main experience, then how does he know enough to give an account of them?

The answer to this depends partly on whether his subject is an individual or a group. So let's specialize memoir into biography (he) and chronicle (they). Thus the shift of focus from first to third person is followed by the subdivision into singular and plural. This way of casting activities is not merely logical; it stipulates the relation of the writer to his subject and hence the forms of information the writer has to work with.

Procedure

Here is how the directions were worded for eleventh-grade classes at Exeter:

Tell what happened to someone you know during a certain period of his life covering many months, perhaps even a year or so—some "phase." Refer to yourself if doing so enriches the account, but keep the focus on the other person.

The directions are structural, rather than substantive: what a student is to write about is defined by some relationships between him and his material, not by topics. How does the writer know his subject? He knows it through three channels of information—what he saw and heard himself, what the person told him, and what was generally known about the person in the community or circles in which both moved. As informant, then, the narrator may play three roles, which we call eyewitness, confidant, and chorus. These roles give him access, respectively, to particular events, to the inner life, and to general background. The kinds of information he can convey, the point of view he can take, and the emotional closeness he feels toward his subject depend very much on which roles his actual relationship to the person permitted him to play at the time of the events. If, for example, he was not a confidant of the person, he cannot tell what the person thought or felt except by inference, a situation that forces the writer to interpret or conjecture more than he would as confidant. The point is that certain qualities of the memoir are determined by circumstances that limit the writer's options and must therefore become compositional issues during writing and during cross-commentary.

Sample

One eleventh-grade Exeter boy wrote about a roommate of two years before who had been required to withdraw. The result is a kind of firsthand case study, as were many of the biographical memoirs done in response to this assignment. The author was, for Exeter, a fairly average student in English, performing in the C to B range. He was a thoughtful and sensitive person but not a very skillful writer. The paper is presented unrevised.

THE INEVITABLE

As is the case with certain types of students, the Phillips Exeter Academy was not the right school for Albert Lockhart. All of the blame should not be placed on the school. His parents, some of his friends, and I did much to cause his failure. People too often ask, "What was the matter with Al: you should know, you were his roommate?" I usually say he just didn't try, but I know that this wasn't actually the reason.

No one can deny that this school puts a lot of pressure on the student and at the same time allows him much more freedom than most prep schools offer. Some students do well under these conditions. Al Lockhart did not.

I liked Al from the first time we met. He was about my size and was interested in nearly the same things. I was conscious of the fact that he tried to impress upon me how much he already knew about the school and how it was run. I soon learned that he was from a large city in Connecticut and that he had attended a country day school for three years. This didn't bother me too much but when he kept kidding me about not ever having had algebra I got a little aggravated.

During the first few days of school we went everywhere together. Gradually we settled down into a daily routine and seemed to separate a little. In the fall he was running cross-country and I was playing golf so we didn't usually see much of each other during the afternoons. We soon found that we had made the same friends and we usually ate with the same group.

We had many petty arguments, but prep roommates always do. Al liked the window up whereas I wanted it down, he liked the record player turned up and I wanted it off. These were only minor differences which we could settle by a little yelling and swearing at each other. Compared to most of the preps who had roommates we got along very well. But there were also minor habits that aggravated us, little things that one doesn't notice until forced to live with somebody over a good length of time. Al seemed to always go out of his way to show his dislike for certain people. There were boys in the dorm whom neither of us cared for, but Al always tried to let it be known to everyone. He would never eat at the same table with certain people or go into another room if there was somebody already there whom he didn't like. At first I didn't mind this but finally it became very annoying to have him constantly finding fault with everybody.

There were certain subjects on which Al was pretty touchy and I must admit I didn't ever go out of my way to prevent any of these arguments. He was always quick to jump to the defense of the country day school which he had attended before Exeter. Someone would complain about how much harder it was than their previous school. This defense became harder and harder for him as his grades continued to drop. I used to kid him about not going to church when he was at home.

This served no purpose except to convince him that church was a waste of time.

I didn't know Al's parents especially well. From what I had seen of his mother she seemed very nervous and talked continuously while in a group. Without question she was the dominant figure of the family. His father always reminded me of the typical football fan who never missed a game and lived only to serve the dear old alma mater. He was quite friendly, drank a lot, was willing to lay down his life for Yale, and followed his wife's orders without question. I'll never forget the time Al and his mother argued over whom he should take to a formal dance at their club. Al wanted to take some girl he knew from a town nearby but his mother wanted him to take another girl, a friend of the family. After yelling at each other for several minutes his mother held up her hand and said, "Now, Al, I know what's best and I don't want to hear another word on the subject." Then she walked out leaving Al nearly in tears.—Another time over Thanksgiving Al and I were at a party with two girls. After the party Al's father and uncle picked us up. Both of them were nearly drunk and his uncle could barely keep the car on the road. Al's girlfriend, who had been in a wreck less than two months before, became very upset and told his uncle she would rather walk if he wouldn't slow down. When we finally got back to Al's house he was in tears and so angry that he swore at his mother for nearly five minutes before going to his room. What upset me so was the way his mother took no blame for having let them come after us.

Needless to say, many of Al's problems stemmed from his parents but the school itself did much for his determent. Besides being insecure I have always felt that Al had an inferiority complex. Probably both were caused by the same things. Al didn't complain a lot but he did make many excuses for his shortcomings. He did well in his first year of cross-country and was expected to make the varsity the following year.

When grades came out for the first time, Al failed history and got several D's. He was very upset for a little while, and just sat at his desk staring at the wall. I was beginning to get worried about him but when he began to swear and slam books down I knew he was all right. I thought he would settle down the next term, and he did for a little while, but then the free afternoons the preps have became too much of a temptation. Al and Rick Cannon, the boy who lived across the hall from us, became very good friends. Rick was a very congenial guy, was quick witted, and was liked by most of the students. His one fault was that he couldn't settle down to work. I don't believe he completely finished any assignment after the fall term. Like Al, Rick had

the habit of making excuses for everything that went wrong. Al and Rick would usually spend the afternoon wandering around town or watching the winter sport's teams practice.

Sometime towards the latter part of the term when things were really beginning to go bad Al started going around with Win Nickerson. Win represented the group in the school called "Negos." He spent most of his time at *Van's* smoking with the rest of this group and complaining about everything in general. Al had failed to make the first group in the prep sports program and this had been a letdown. His grades were very low and his attitude towards the school was rebellious.

I have always thought one of the main factors causing Al's failure was his inability to admit his own shortcomings to himself. This is why this was a bad choice of schools for him. The competition here forces a boy to know just where he stands in relation to everyone else. When he first came he was anxious to show everyone what he knew and how much he could do, just like everyone else tried. But what he couldn't accept was himself as he really was. We all have high ideals of what we think we are and at some time in our life these are shattered and we are forced to see ourselves as we really are. Al could not admit defeat or accept the fact that he was not as good as he had thought. Instead of admitting certain weaknesses and trying to improve he merely invented ways and excuses to hide his weaknesses and pretend they weren't there. He was finally forced to realize that he was only deceiving himself and then he gave up completely.

When Al became friends with Win Nickerson his career at Exeter slid rapidly. This was only a bold attempt to withdraw from the school, its pressure, and everything he was fighting. Rick Cannon had his faults but one thing he could not be accused was being a "nego." He had a strong sense of school spirit and he disliked Win Nickerson and that group very strongly. As always, Exeter forced Al to choose between the groups he wanted to be associated with and unfortunately he chose Win.

Everyone asked what happened to Al; what caused the change from his prep year? To me there was no change. Anyone who knew him well could see what Exeter had in store for him, but instead of helping him I let things be. I'm not sure I could have prevented what happened, maybe only prolonged it, but I still failed to do my part, as did everyone else.

Double Organization Again we see a general chronological tracing of stages in a progression, but the narrative organization is overridden by thematic organization even more than in the altar boy's biography. Although some paragraphs are enchained by time, most are topically related, because the author wants to score certain abstract points.

For one thing, he is seeking causes: what can explain Al's decline and dismissal? The nature of the school, family background, the boy's personality, the influence of friends he made—these are possible causes, all mentioned in the beginning and taken up one at a time later. Thus the paper is partly organized in the way many analytical and explanatory essays are—by causal factors.

Second, he wants to bring out something typical or representative in his roommate's plight. More than one previously successful, well-prepared student, accustomed to excelling in his hometown, has gone away to a selective school or college and found he was only a little fish in a big pond who had to reassess himself in the stiffer competition. Many an enthusiastic prep has turned sour, sought escape, and started to wash out. But most recover, or at least avoid dismissal. How did Al differ from these and from the author himself? It is the representative aspect of Al's story that makes it a kind of case. In fact, this writer's interpretive account of his roommate's career resembles somewhat, even in a number of the points made, some actual cases that a faculty committee, which included one of us, once wrote as part of a special study of Exeter.

Issues for the Writing Workshop

The revisions this paper needs represent rather well the writing problems that workshop and cross-commentary would deal with. One concerns the channels of information. We might expect that a roommate on good terms with Al would have served as a confidant and therefore been able to relay to the reader more about what Al thought and felt during this phase of his life. But Al's inner experience is virtually absent. In such a case, the writer's colleagues should ask him about the omission. Could he include more of what Al confided to him? If Al never talked about his thoughts and feelings, shouldn't the reader be told this? Did the fact that Al kept problems to himself explain why the author was unable to help him (since the author wonders if he should blame himself)?

As for organization, it is clear that the author has some difficulty fusing the narrative and conceptual continuity, the very difficulty the teacher would expect students to run into. The paragraph beginning "Needless to say" is snarled within itself and does not lead well into the following paragraph, because the author got onto causes in describing the parents and then could find no connected way to resume chronology. Should he discuss causes along the way, only at the end, or in both places? Should one alternate narrative and general commentary from sentence to sentence, paragraph to paragraph, or section to section? Also, some important chronological information was lost in the shuffle between narrative and ideas. We should know, for example, just when the boy was expelled. Almost any student besides the author can point out omissions or ambiguities.

Let the group propose solutions to these problems with each paper in turn. Your part is to help the students see, for example, that the particular form of organizational confusion mentioned above is inherent in the assignment and lies behind their variously expressed misgivings about such and such a paper.

Group Focus

This type of memoir is suitable for mature students with considerable experience with other types of memory writing. Here are the directions:

> Write a narrative about a developing trend or situation that took place in a group or community that you know about.

This shifts the subject from the third person singular to the third person plural and thus broadens it from an individual to a group experience. This shift automatically makes the subject more general, since the author must see something common in the behavior or activities of a number of individuals. In other words, he is concerned only with some action that shows one aspect of a number of people; they are trying to raise funds for schools, ostracizing some other people, vandalizing for entertainment. *Chronicle* is defined as group narrative. It is still memoir, however, because the narrator is the observer. Counterparts of this activity are case studies about groups or autobiographies in which one's experiences are part of a group's activities. A "group" could be anything from a large block of townspeople to a clique within the school. The classification of behavior that underlies a student's story may be a very simple one based on physical action, but he is very likely to classify also the motives or traits behind this action. This amount of generalizing is a natural concomitant of the assignment and will often provide the point of the account or be a conclusion of it.

The eleventh-grade boy who wrote the following group memoir was having a hard time not only in English but in other subjects as well. He was a good athlete and a hard-working student, but his academic background was weak by Exeter standards, and he was intellectually undeveloped when he arrived the year before.

EVEN WITHIN THE LINES

My neighborhood is a typical middle class Negro neighborhood. The homeowners try to make sure it looks as nice and neat as possible. All the homes are worth between $18,000 and $25,000. Most of the homeowners are well educated, most of them being school teachers. By 1957 our block was completely filled except for three lots. One was next to our house. It was quite narrow, so narrow that it looked as if it might be part of our lawn. Across from it were two lots owned by old Mrs. Hathcock, who planned to will them to her two sons.

In the summer of 1957 the lot next to our house was bought by Mr. Gray and he announced plans to build on it. Although several people were skeptical about his plans, no one refused to sign the petition he had to present before he could get city water and start laying the foundation for his house. The house went up very quickly, and the time taken to build it was an indication of its value. It had been made mostly of used lumber taken from demolished homes and it was much too large for the lot. It was wooden and white, which made it unique in the neighborhood. All the other homes were made of dark brick and are set far back on their lots. Mr. Gray's white wooden house stood about five yards from the sidewalk and was worth about $8,000 or $9,000. It was completely out of place in the neighborhood. When our neighbors realized what was being built, they raised a great uproar. But it was too late to do anything about the situation. They would just have to wait and see what Mr. Gray made of his property.

Everything went fine that first year, although the house was out of place, no one could complain about the way My Gray kept it looking. It was as neat looking and well kept as any of the other homes, if not more so. By the first part of 1959 it began to show a little wear. That winter Mr. Gray caught pneumonia and was hospitalized for several months. By the time he was able to resume taking care of his house, it was in very bad shape; the wind had been very tough and had taken off part of his roof and a great deal of his siding and the old wood used in the house had become infested with termites. The more the house deteriorated the more restless his neighbors became. They were not interested in his problem. They were only concerned with the value of their property, which was decreasing along with the deterioration of Mr. Grays' property.

By the late fall Mr. Gray was desperate. He had done the best he could to keep the property value up but he had neither the funds nor the health to do it successfully. He had a new problem. It seemed that the petition he had had passed when he had first built his house had been registered in the wrong office and he had to obtain a new one. He needed to have at least twenty-five names on the petition; he was only able to get six. He was beaten when his neighbor on the other side, Mr. Wilson, offered to buy his property for a low price. He had no choice—he had to take it.

Just before winter hit, Mr. Wilson had the house torn down and the foundation filled. Now again our block is a straight row of dark brick houses and there are three vacant lots on it.

It's interesting to know that man's inhumanity to man doesn't cease, even within color lines.

The four middle paragraphs all start with time expressions, indicating the narrative order, but each paragraph contains statements about the growing alarm and antipathy of Mr. Gray's neighbors. The first paragraph starts in the present tense of generalization, then shifts to the past tense for the transition into narrative. The last paragraph returns to the present tense of generalization but asserts a more abstract statement, philosophical rather than expository. The author created this structure by treating the needs of the subject, not by following teacher advice or corrections, though his experience with previous narrative assignments surely helped him a great deal to see what he should do.

The only indication of the first person is "our," but the account could only be told by a local inhabitant, a member of what we've called a "chorus." The subject is more impersonal because it is plural. The author has no "confidant" information; the inner experience is the collective reaction of the whole neighborhood to an intruder. Had he known Mr. Gray well, however, and known his mind, the story might have been very different—a biographical fragment. So the paper is chronicle because of the point of view the writer *had* to take: he knew only what everyone in the community knew; he was only a member of a chorus (though a dissident member).

This memoir is clearly one long example of the broad generalization stated in the last sentence. When a student writes any sort of firsthand narrative, most often he spontaneously presents his story as an instance of some truth applying beyond the material at hand. This is why memoirs become cases almost automatically—if they cover a long enough period of time, such as a phase.

Parallel Reading

In addition to memoir fiction, students can read within the very large body of actual memoir*. The motive for reading memoir is less to identify with the narrator, who may indeed be relatively unimportant, than to find out about what some other individual or group was like. Many memoirists, for example, are read because they associated with an important individual or took part in some noteworthy activity. They are valuable as informants privileged to play confidant, eyewitness, or group-membership roles. Thus focus may be close to that of biography or chronicle, and interest in a given memoir depends on prior interest in a given subject. One wants to know more about the life of some scientist or entertainer or about political affairs or archaeological digs, so one chooses a memoir by a person who worked with or lived with the personage or participated in the political affairs or digs. Memoir presents information in an attractive way—via narrative and personal channels. Whatever topic or activity a student is interested in, he will almost surely find some memoir featuring it. Reading each other's memoirs may help considerably to value and to pursue this kind of material.

EYEWITNESS REPORTAGE

Reportage is consciously sought out, whereas autobiography and memoir tap an unplanned residue of experience recalled at a time when the author has decided to write it down. Eyewitness reportage is a narrative account written from notes made at a locale the writer has chosen to go to for the purpose of gathering material. Thus it is not unlike the sensory recording described in Chapter 8, Writing, in that the intent is to go, observe, and record; what gets recorded are the here-and-now events as they happen. Students who have done sensory recording will find this on-the-spot note-taking familiar.

An eyewitness report is limited to what can be learned by observing at a certain time. This kind of fact-finding breaks down mainly into visiting a locale or interviewing a person or perhaps doing both at once. Like memory writing the report of this kind of observation results in an eyewitness narrative, but the compositional problems are different. Memories are already digested and classified, but, at the time of writing, one's choice of material is limited. Planned observation, on the other hand, produces an overabundance of unselected detail to be shaped, but the reporter can seek out his material. The writer of memory has fewer options, for both the whole and the details; the writer of reportage has choices to make about when and where to observe, which sensations to record at the scene, and how to digest the notes later.

TV documentaries are the visual counterpart of eyewitness reportage. If video equipment is available, a situation or activity in the school can be video-taped, showing what went on and interviewing persons on the scene. Students can take movie or still cameras into the community and capture significant action to be presented later with an appropriate commentary by an anchorman, describing where the cameraman is and what is going on.

Whenever a student goes out looking for material, he may experience moments he wants to convert to poetry. Writing poems of observation alongside longer prose accounts keeps the writing honed—not only for rendering particulars but for charging them with meaning. See page 379.

The following poem was written by a boy who did not usually do skillful or inspired work. His prose was limp and characterless. These were the three best sentences he wrote all year:

EIGHT BALL

He breaks the two to the side pocket right,
With kalaidescope colors runs the three through the
  seven,
Then banks the one true on the green.
With sweat-laden fingers he powders the cue
And calls the eight left corner down.
The white knight charges, ramming
The black towards the awaiting
Abyss and
In.[11]

---

[11] A tenth grader at Phillips Exeter Academy.

Youngsters who have done some sensory note-taking will be able to set up a newspaper and act as reporters covering scenes. The process of deciding on the format, regular features, and who does what will lead the class into a highly focused examination of the layout and organization of actual newspapers. As they peruse these, they may decide they want such items as editorials, news stories, feature stories, a sports page, a joke and puzzle column, an astrology chart, ads, photos, reviews of books, movies, or plays, weather reports, a fashion column, a "Dear Abby" advice column, cartoons and comics, or a crossword puzzle, thereby calling forth many kinds of discourse other than true stories. No matter how simple or elaborate their newspaper operation, they will need to appoint editors to think up reportorial assignments, proofreaders to go over the stories as they come in, a layout committee, and a duplicating and collating team.

What the youngsters decide to do for eyewitness reports will probably include more things than those we would ordinarily call news, that is, everyday actions at locales that have meaning to the students as well as new events and seasonal changes. You might suggest that, like city editors, the students should keep a lookout for both coming events and for places or scenes that have standard human interest.

Each student goes to his locale and takes down what he sees and senses, as fully as he can but selectively. The earlier experimenting with different ways of recording should help him strike a balance between general coverage and the detailing of selected things. Back in the groups these papers are exchanged, read, and discussed with the particular aim of helping each other produce the best possible journalistic copy. Your direction of this process occurs at the small-group discussion point unless you decide to project certain papers for the whole class to discuss.

Workshop Issues

In the small groups, where the students are acting as newspaper editors readying copy for publication, several compositional issues are almost certain to arise from the nature of sensory reportage. One is tense—whether to convert a present-tense recording to past-tense narrative or leave it as it is for the sense of immediacy. But a decision about tense may depend on other related issues, the main one of which is general unity or purpose.

Although the eyewitness reporter chooses the spot, he has little control over what he will see and hear there; he is working with more random elements than when recalling material. (But deciding on what scenes to cover will show how much the choice of locale is itself a compositional act.) Coherence or meaning will depend very much on *how* he sees. The point of the reportage can be any number of things about the character of the locale, the behavior that goes on there, the atmosphere, and so on.

In addition to tense and coherence, there is the need to decide how important to make the observer. First person is neither good nor bad. In making suggestions to each other for revision, the students will have to consider how much the reporter is to include himself in the report. When is it good strategy to give a strong personal touch? Should he stay out entirely, play lightly in and out, or color all that he sees with his own reactions.

If students find a lead to a coming local event— a parade, a store opening, a strike, a construction operation, a political rally—they may have a focus for some good eyewitness reportage. Writers who have developed the knack of composing randomness into a short sketch might take on these feature stories while students who need more focus report more conventional news. This latter group may be helped by the reporter's adage that a good story covers five *W*'s and an *H*—*W*hat happened, *W*hy it happened, *W*here it happened, *W*ho was involved, *W*hen it happened, and *H*ow it happened.

Parallel Reading

Students should, of course, read newspapers, not only as models of style and treatment, but also as sources of ideas for feature stories.

Collections of eyewitness reports* in the classroom can include transcripts of sportscasts or other blow-by-blow accounts of action; miscellaneous accounts characterizing a place rather than reporting news; travel logs; single short eyewitness incidents; and first-person accounts by professional reporters that show their eyewitnessing before it gets written up into impersonal third-person newspaper stories. Gerald Durrell's *The Overloaded Ark* or Charles Darwin's *Voyage of the Beagle* contain eyewitness reportage of both man and nature. Any first-person, firsthand reportage in which the narrator plays essentially an observer role is apt, whether fictional or actual, for reading the two side by side helps clarify their differences and similarities.

A great many poems, like many of Robert Frost's, comprise personal observation of a scene or brief action—some about nature, some about people. Reading some of these may inspire some students to write eyewitness accounts as poems, especially if you make clear that poems represent simply another mode in which to write about what one witnesses.

Comparing Reportage

A good way for students of any age to point up egocentricity is to stage an event in the classroom—a pantomime or short skit or surprise happening such as two men in white coats coming in and roughly commandeering one of the students out of the room. Then have everyone who witnessed the event write an account as if he were being interrogated on a witness stand at a courtroom trial, recording the basic facts as he perceived them. Each account can be read and discrepancies discussed.

A way for a pair of children to get at this comparison is to start by thinking together of something that happened at school—a movie, an experiment, an assembly, a ball game. Then they make up some questions such as: What happened? When? Who was there? What did they say? What did it look like? They ask six or more people each of these questions and write down or tape-record their answers, later comparing responses and talking about the different things different people remembered.

One student can tell about something he saw happen recently, taping it as he goes, if possible, while the rest of the small group act as reporters by writing down everything they can as the speaker tells the story. Then the speaker can repeat his story or play the tape of it while the writers check their notes with the speaker's words. They exchange papers and discuss the different versions, seeing who took the most detailed and correct notes. These notes can then be written up as true stories and again compared.

LOG

Comparable to day-by-day accounts like calendars and journals are logs. These focus not on the narrator, however, but on external events. A log can be written like a calendar on a wall chart or in a book with blank blocks or pages for each day's entries.

Students can keep logs of anything that changes —weather, growing plants or animals, attendance, stores of classroom supplies, passers in the hall, cars on the street, phone calls in the office, scores at sports events, phases of the moon. Observations are made at intervals, and descriptions are recorded as dated entries in the log. These logs can be used to make wall charts or graphs, summaries of recurring events, or generalizations in the form of informative articles. See Chapter 19, Ideas, for more on this type of expository writing. Primary-grade children can begin their logs as drawings with captions; older students can keep a higher proportion of their record in words.

Discoveries that come when growing animals are closely watched in the classroom not only delight learners but provide a rich opportunity for careful observation and accurate reporting. For example, bird, hen, or reptile eggs, a newborn mammal, larvae, or tadpoles can be brought for youngsters to care for and note their food, ideal environment, including temperature, and other requirements. The children can set up a routine for taking care of the animals. Since waiting for an egg to hatch or an animal to reach a new stage may leave little to observe at times, it is best to have more than one thing growing at once. Observation need not be daily if little is happening. With planning—and luck—you can have the children record special events like births, moltings, and metamorphoses. And they can observe at times of particular events, such as the feeding of ladybugs to leopard frogs. Nature study should not be just cute—it can include preying and mating. The cycles and relationships in nature will teach the most and provide the most interesting material for recording. The child is rare, if he exists, who is not entranced by watching a caterpillar become a butterfly.

An alternative to growth as a project structure is the complex workings of social insects. It is possible to buy "ant farms" that have a transparent wall for observing.[12] At the end of each week or so, youngsters can list the most interesting things from their logs. More mature students might summarize logs into a more abstract sort of reportage in which *recurring* events and observations are generalized. This makes an excellent lead-in for expository writing.

---

[12] An excellent resource for teachers is the *New UNESCO Source Book for Science Teaching*, United Nations Educational, Scientific, and Cultural Organization, Paris, 1973.

The most appropriate parallel reading texts for young children are the logs their classmates have kept. High school students might enjoy one of the fine nature observations such as Henry David Thoreau's "Journal" * or Karl von Frisch's "The Language of Bees," * both of which move from recording to reflection and generalization.

THE CASE

A case study is a true story that is an extension of eyewitness reportage, combining a write-up of "what I see" with "what others say" and a summary of "what I saw and was told on several occasions." Data is gathered through a *series* of visits or interviews. (See Chapter 18, Information, for a discussion of interviewing.) To this process might be added "what others have *written,*" the use of documents. The combination of several purposeful visits and recourse to documents justifies the use of the term *research,* a process that involves a synthesis of different firsthand accounts, or secondhand information, or both. (See page 370.) Unlike most research, however, a case study is usually written as a narrative, not an essay. The general procedure for a case is to keep a specialized journal of visits and to summarize it later. The use of documents might be to frame the research with past background or general context. The research breaks down into two sorts, the first of which is a kind of case writing.

The best ideas for subjects will no doubt come from the students themselves, once the main task and its purpose are clear. These can be best evoked by a question: "What would you like to know more about that you can become more informed of through either visiting or experimenting?" Let students use personal interests and knowledge from other courses as a springboard. They can keep a journal on any sequence of events that they know will start and end during a certain length of time (days, weeks, or months) and be accessible to them for periodic observation—rehearsal for a play or concert, preseason practice of an athletic squad, the stages of a construction job, the growth of something in nature, the ups and downs of another person, like a dropout, whose situation may be especially worth tracing, or a person who is in the process of becoming or has become some kind of celebrity. Where appropriate, photos, tape-recordings, or interviews can be part of some visits.

Purposes

Cases constitute an important kind of writing that is practiced extensively in our society. One can draw examples from the professions. A social worker periodically visits a family on relief and writes a report, based on notes, of the family's changing conditions. A psychotherapist writes up notes of interviews with a patient and produces a psychiatric case study. A naturalist observes the behavior of ducks or fish and describes the patterns that emerge. And schools of law and business have for some time relied on case reading as a way of plunging their students into actual situations such as they will encounter professionally. "Getting down to cases" is looking at real instances that have representational value for demonstrating typical issues. An account of the course of a lawsuit, a commercial negotiation, a piece of legislation, or a labor-management dispute serves as a window on certain sorts of practical problems that the account embodies. When used for discussion and exercise in decision-making, the case is often presented incompletely, the conclusion being withheld until the trainees have had a chance to resolve the problem themselves.

One of our articles of faith—founded, we believe, on some real truths—is that older adolescents are capable of doing on a smaller scale what adult practitioners of a career do. The point of role-playing the professional is not only to learn how to be a lawyer, foreign-service officer, scientist, or businessman but to be able to understand and *care* about what those people are doing. More basically, the purpose is to understand how it is we know what we think we know. Even if his future job will be too humble to require case-writing, a student should learn from direct experience how the information of his world is created. In fact, the principle justification of any writing program is not so much to prepare students for careers as it is to develop their thought and understanding.

Parallel Reading

A case tends to treat an unknown person but one whose situation or traits may be considered typical and therefore have applicability to others, whereas biography is generally written about a person who is already famous or interesting to the public. Many feature articles in magazines and newspapers are cases. The *New Yorker* is an excellent source, as it is for all kinds of reportage and research. In addition, there are many case books in various fields that should be scanned for accounts that are not too mature or technical for adolescents. In *The Seesaw Log,* playwright William Gibson presents his journal of what happened in getting a play produced on Broadway. It is a valuable document about the economics and hysterics of the American commercial theater, resembling on a larger scale the sort of journals students would keep. George Plimpton wrote up, in *Paper Lion,* his record of an extended stay with a professional football team. Classroom collections of biography* should include some case histories to provide a model for student composition. Many short stories—Willa Cather's "Paul's Case" and Conrad Aiken's "Silent Snow, Secret Snow," for example—are fictional equivalents of the personal case. As noted before, juxtaposition of real and invented accounts reveals the special qualities of each mode of reporting on human experience.

THIRD-PERSON TRUE STORY

Biography

Children can write simple true stories about relatives and friends just as they wrote a "Book About Me," illustrating them with snapshots and drawings. Older youngsters choose an interesting person in their school or community to go watch and talk to. A youngster might choose a craftsman with a special skill, the oldest person in the community, a political leader, a person in an interesting job, and so on. He can interview him to find out how he got to be the way he is. What experiences has he had? What does he most like to do? What does *he* think is his most significant achievement? Then he can interview others who know this person, asking them to describe him, telling all they know about his life and achievements. The student then decides on one event or place that would make a good true story about his chosen person and writes it up. He can read over this account with the person who is its subject, asking for suggestions for making it more accurate, interesting, or complete, and then rewrite it in light of this feedback and share it with his classmates.

Experienced students can write biographies of persons they don't know, basing their true stories on research. If they choose a relative or ancestor to write about, old photographs, letters, certificates, diaries, and other documents might be available as sources for the account. If they choose an important figure, they can draw on newspaper accounts, archives, letters, diaries, autobiography, and memoir. If the person is alive, students can write to him for material; they may want to send along a first draft of their biography for feedback. See page 372 for ways to shape this kind of material into a profile.

Chronicle

For chronicle the focus is on a group of people. Teenagers might decide to follow the actions of a school, neighborhood, or community group who have done something interesting—an athletic team, a club, a church organization, a political action group such as an antipollution citizen's committee, or a union organization. They choose one action this group has taken and research this event, interviewing as many members of the group as they can to find out about what the group has done. They can interview persons outside of the group itself who might have a different perception of what the group has done. The final chronicle would be a result of their pooling of observation, interviews, and research.

As with biography, the students may choose to write about a group of people they have only heard or read about, not one they have known. Then their source of material would be pieced together from different sources—reference books, journals, articles, documents, transcripts, responses to letters to members of the group, and so on. Emphasis has to be on the originality of the subject matter, however, so that students move away from the idea that book research is merely a glorified form of plagiarism. The difference is in whether the student is digesting original sources or whether he is copying somebody else's digestion.

Parallel Reading

Collections of both biography* and chronicle* make particularly appropriate reading matter for children and teenagers, providing an opportunity to identify with individuals pursuing a career or exhibiting a kind of behavior that the readers aspire to, such as excelling in sports, adventure, or public service.

Biography and chronicle provide students with an advantageous way to approach history since in the more personal focus historical figures are presented without the dry overcondensation of generalized history. Chronicle typically covers much of what is generally called history except that the degree of abstraction is not as great. When students read third-person narrative and autobiography and memoir, they are reading the source documents out of which more general histories are abstracted. It may often happen that some students will become interested in a whole period or country or phase of history as a result of reading a couple of biographies or chronicles from it, in which case they will be motivated to read the more abstract kind of history and will become more capable of understanding how it was written and what was necessarily left out. Thus it is that students reading source documents become more sophisticated about the necessary biases and emphases and distillations inherent in the writing of history.

Finally, because they are true, these nonfiction narratives contain much valuable factual information necessarily included to illumine the careers or the circumstances in which the main figures are involved. This way of acquiring geographical or scientific or historical background may be much easier for many students than reading more abstract or general articles on these subjects, yet at the same time it may encourage these students to turn next to just such nonnarrative articles.

Speaking generally now, the interweaving of true stories with fiction that poses as such should help sharpen the contrasts as well as the parallels between fiction and nonfiction. Though they borrow from each other, the artist and the real memoirist or chronicler may use different rhetorics, one appealing more to emotion, the other to reason, this difference being reflected in the language itself. Fiction suggests general significance in implicit ways, whereas cases are usually more explicit (though both achieve generality by the choice of *types* for subjects). As students will know very well from their own writing, when you are telling the actual truth, you cannot fill in what you don't know. The informant is limited by circumstance, and his information is incomplete. When you fictionalize, on the other hand, you imagine the whole world of the story and can permit the narrator to know as much as you wish him to. Not only can the truth then be whole, but the material can be controlled for harmony and climax. This too the student can learn from his own writing.

The capacity to give clear directions and follow those of others is one of our culture's most widely valued language competencies. The fact that this chapter is short does not imply that directions are less important than other kinds of discourse. It is rather that they are a part of almost every other kind of discourse and of each of the basic processes of this curriculum and thus cannot easily be separated out and treated in isolation.

This discourse goal is simply to give and take directions for how to do and make things. The mode is typically imperative, of course. Directions are usually utilitarian and most often occur as operating instructions affixed to or accompanying objects, as procedure manuals or memoranda, or how-to-do-it books and articles. Recipes are a notable form. Many directions are oral, such as instructions on how to get to a certain place or coaching during sports or music lessons. To establish a sequence of actions, directions are often put in chronological order like the events in a narrative, but the practical needs of the operation that is being directed may well require another ordering.

Directions constitute a difficult kind of exposition, important both for its own sake and for the effective checks on comprehension and composition that directions afford by the very fact that they are intended to be performed. Senders and receivers can find out more readily than with most other discourse whether they are getting across or receiving the message. They quickly discover problems of communication, many of which originate in egocentricity. Directions then serve as a mirror for the sender because they are translated into actions and provide immediate feedback of successful or unsuccessful communication. Receiving directions develops the ability to convert language into actions. The ability to follow written directions is perhaps the most direct index of reading comprehension. See page 417. There is little chance for misreading to remain unnoticed as it often does in other kinds of discourse.

Directions do not have to be in words, of course. Gesture and body language communicate as well; we have treated this kind of direction-giving in games such as charades and mirror exercises in Chapter 5, Dramatic Inventing.

Oral activities

Any activity that calls for isolating words from gesture and body language poses a valuable problem for children who are used to communicating largely nonverbally. Directions for movements such as those for a walk in a circle (see page 90) are a good way to ease young children into listening attentively and translating the word to the act. Here is an activity that can begin in the upper elementary grades and continue through junior high.

BACK TO BACK

Give each of two players the same number of paper shapes. Or, you might give each one identical sets of solid pieces from the "Talk and Take" game* or an attribute game. Then give the children these directions:

- Sit back to back with your materials in front of you. One of you is the sender; the other, the receiver. A few others can watch, but they are not to talk or otherwise help you.

355

- If you are the sender, assemble your pieces into a certain pattern, telling the person behind you what you are doing.
- If you are the receiver, listen to the other person and assemble your pieces into the same pattern. You cannot look around or ask questions.
- Compare what you have done and ask the observers how it went and what you might have done to make the directions clearer.

The point of not letting the two players see each other is to enforce a total reliance on words. A barrier between the two will work as well as having them sit back to back. In such situations most children will still try to express directions egocentrically, by gesturing even though they should know that their receiver cannot see their signals. However, giving and following verbal directions for any process that is essentially nonverbal is never easy.

For the first time or two, the communication is restricted to one-way talk. The players may decide to role-play a boss giving a worker directions over a one-way intercom. Then the "worker" is finally allowed to ask questions. Withholding conversation for a while demonstrates its great advantage, which is the receiver's feedback in the form of questions of clarification and requests for omitted information. The onlookers of the groups may need to be reminded that kibitzing spoils the game and that they should watch silently so that they can observe the causes of miscommunication and try to avoid these mistakes when their turns come to give directions. Depending on the difficulty of the puzzle, a number of students may have to act as sender before the receiver can assemble it successfully. Sets of puzzles are exchanged and players rotate roles.

Using common geometrical shapes gives students an opportunity to put into play the vocabulary of geometry. However, if odd shapes rather than conventional ones are cut out and used, players have to stretch their imagination for ways of describing.

A graded difficulty in puzzles can be achieved by gradually increasing the number of pieces (starting with three) and by making the component shapes harder to describe and to position. It is good to have the completed puzzle sometimes form a familiar figure in order that the sender, if he thinks of doing so, may state at the outset, "We're going to put the pieces together so that they look like a house." This way, if he omits this general framework, he can create the same kind of communication problems that can be created in a piece of written exposition,

since in either case the receiver lacks context for relating particulars to each other.

OTHER VARIATIONS

After students have become aware of at least some of the factors that make for success and failure in the game, variations are introduced. The goal is still to match senders' and receivers' materials by means of verbal directions, but, to vary and generalize the communication issues, puzzles are replaced by other things. Someone who has learned how to do some origami creations (paper-folding) talks a partner, or perhaps his group, through the procedure, still back to back or with a barrier between. The success the sender has with his directions when he is speaking from memory can be compared with his success when he is folding as he speaks. Or, the sender can look at an abstract picture composed especially for this purpose and tell how to draw it; or draw a simple picture as he tells the receiver how to do it; or cut out a shape with scissors and tell what he is doing; or perform a certain action, finger play, or exercise such as "Cross your legs and fingers and lean over with your chest touching your knees" and have the receiver do the same. Direct students to bring or suggest other materials to use.

A variation in the game situation is to let one student give directions to the whole class. What is lost here is that there are no onlookers who get good insights from observing, simultaneously, what the sender intended and how the receiver took the message.

Older youngsters might respond well to a competitive game for two teams of five or so members. Each team chooses a "describer" who looks at a pattern, puzzle shape, picture, or whatever and tells about it to the rest of his team, each member of which will draw the design as best he can from the description. Drawers cannot look at the model that the two describers can look at. Finished drawings are shown to a team member appointed to act as judge. He chooses the diagram most like the one described, which everyone can now look at, and gives it to you or a student to judge against his opponent's. The team with the most accurate drawing wins.

BUILDING BLITZ

- The game leader builds a simple model out of construction material such as Tinker Toys or

Lego and does not show it to the other players. He puts it into another classroom or a closet. Then he puts out on two separate tables exactly the same number and type of building pieces that he used to build the model.

- Divide a large group into two teams; each team divides itself into three groups—observers, runners, and builders. The leader tells each team that they will have twenty to thirty minutes to build a model out of the materials set out on each table. Only builders may touch the materials. The runners run from the building table to a spot where they can meet the observers but not see the model. The observers must run to meet the runners at that spot, but they cannot see the tables where the builders are working. The observers are the only ones who can see the model built by the game leader. They describe it to the runners, who relay the message to the builders.
- The leader says, "Go." Any observer who goes beyond his designated spot and sees the builders, or any runner who sees the model or touches the building materials is out of the game.
- The two groups of builders may copy each other, but they do not know if the other builders are doing the right thing, of course.
- After twenty to thirty minutes, the leader calls, "Time." The team which has built a model most like the original one wins.

How to do and make

Most classroom processes are first introduced to students in the form of directions, oral or written, the former predominating in the early grades. Children who have made something can give their own directions to others in small groups.[1] This specialized kind of show-and-tell is valuable because as the group members ask questions they help the speaker become aware of the audience's need for more detail and more precise diction. Afterward, they can tape their directions for others to follow later, revising these as they see the need.

Older elementary-school and junior high youngsters can engage in this process in a variety of ways. They might set up an "I'll Tell You How" service whereby they share skills. They can advertise on a poster or on a dittoed handout telling what they know how to do and are willing to teach—for example, how to make a God's-eye, to type, to play chess, to run a machine such as a Thermofax or a ditto, to do square roots, to baby-sit. They can set up a "teaching center" where they show anyone interested how they do what they are skilled in doing. The teaching can be oral with a demonstration. After one group of interested classmates has followed his oral directions, the "teacher" can write up the directions, taking account of the questions the "learners" had, adding diagrams or drawings, if appropriate, and attaching the final version to the machine or next to assembled materials.

READING ACTIVITY CARDS

Each activity card of the sort described in Chapter 3, Organization and Materials, poses a direction-receiving task. So do books that tell how to do and make things*; these comprise an important part of the classroom library for students of any age.

Elementary-school children can read and follow directions for making a wide range of art products—specialized card decks with pictures, mobiles, models and dioramas, dollhouse furniture, sculptures including those of papier-mâché, puppets, paper foldings, toothpick constructions, rubbings, soap carvings, collages, stitching, greeting cards, kites, and so on. They can follow written directions for making math props—such as clocks, graphs, and play money—or furniture and other objects for a playhouse or play store. In short, *anything* you want the children to have as an optional activity in the class can be introduced in the form of written directions. Questions or disputes about procedure can be settled by referring back to the written directions. Youngsters who read directions on activity cards or in books can follow them and then explain what they have done to others, thereby moving from the written to the nonverbal and finally to the oral translation of directions.

WRITING DIRECTIONS [2]

Students can play direction games like this one:

- Each child should write out on an oaktag strip,

---

[1] See the elementary level *English Through Interaction* film "Do and Talk."

[2] See the elementary level *English Through Interaction* film "Small Group Writing."

approximately three inches by twelve inches, three directions, such as:

> Walk to the door.
> Open and close it twice, leaving it open.
> Hop back to your chair.

Or:

> Walk backward to the blackboard.
> Turn and write on it "4 × 4 = 16."
> Erase what you have written and clap your hands four times.

- Divide into two teams.
- The first player of team one gives the first player of team two a card. That player reads the directions aloud and then puts the card down. He must follow the directions *exactly;* if he cannot do so, he is out of the game. If he does follow correctly, his team has a point.
- Then the player who has just had a turn calls on any player on the other team and asks him to tell him exactly what his directions said. If that player can do so, his team gets a point.
- Then it is the first player of team one's turn to do what the directions of the first member of team two say to do. The game is played as before.
- The team with the most points after all directions have been followed wins.

Another thing to do is have each student think of something he knows how to make from common materials, write the directions as clearly as he can, and exchange them with another pupil. They all follow out the directions as homework, and bring to school what they have made. Any problems or uncertainties about the directions are noted down on the paper, which is returned to the author. The performer and author can then discuss where the directions might need to be changed. Revised directions might be compiled into a class "Things to Do and Make" booklet, or filed in an accordion file folder with appropriate headings. A secondary benefit of this whole process is that students learn from each other how to make things.

Another way to write directions is to imagine that you are writing an explanation to someone on another planet or in a very different culture who has never been here to see how we do things. Write out in detail the steps involved in tying a shoe for someone who has never seen a shoe, for example, or how we use a knife and fork, put on a coat, use a pen to write, and so on. Then exchange papers and follow

the set of directions exactly as written, pretending to know no more about the process described than what is on the paper.

Students can write step-by-step directions for working machinery, including such useful tools as tape recorders; slide, overhead, and movie projectors; cameras; and auditorium and stage lights. Others can try out these directions and trouble-shoot any problems, which can then be corrected in a revision. The directions can be posted at appropriate spots or attached to the machines.

Teenagers might enjoy dreaming up needed inventions, describing their operation and directing their construction. They might write craft or hobby manuals to exchange with one another. They can write up detailed instructions for the essential steps in making such things as lampshades out of large tin cans, bird feeders, macrame, origami birds, mobiles, ship models, soapbox-derby cars, wax imprints from comics, decorative mosaics from pebbles, pressed wildflowers, cornhusk dolls. Adding drawings and diagrams with captions may clarify the instructions, as will revision based on feedback from a friend who has followed the directions.

After students of any age have had some experience reading and working with activity cards, they can try their hand at thinking up projects that call for talking, listening, acting, reading, or writing and can put these and their appropriate illustrations onto activity cards of their own to add to the classroom collection.

GAMES

Receiving and giving game directions exercises social interplay, language, strategic decision-making, attention, and memory. If game booklets* are a part of the classroom library and games are available, youngsters go to them for high-interest reading matter. Game directions can also be given orally, taped and played later, or written onto charts or activity cards and illustrated with diagrams. If children read directions for games they already know how to play, they encounter in written form something they can easily translate back into action. Collections of jump-rope jingles* and game songs* can be read and taught to classmates in the same way games are. Games children know how to play as part of their oral culture can be taught to others. Questions the group asks check egocentricity and push the leader to revise misleading directions. Some game directions are in the form of songs, so a book of game songs should be handy.

Most board and card games call for attentive direction-reading. A game like "Talk and Take" requires not only reading of initial rules but also reading of and listening carefully to the individual instruction cards throughout the game and discussing how to interpret each one.[3] If nonreaders are paired with readers, they gain a strong stimulus for learning to read as well as the help they need to understand the game. Once children have played this game a lot, they will enjoy making up new instruction cards and trying them out in games with their friends. Writing good, complicated instructions for "Talk and Take" requires considerable thought and experience with conditional adverbial clauses. This game gives players practice in using a variety of sentence types, such as those containing *if, unless,* and *when* clauses, that are frequently hard to comprehend because of semantic, syntactic, and logical complexity.

Youngsters can take turns inventing a board or a card game for their small group to play and then watch them playing it. They can make the materials for the game and put onto a tape or write out the goal, procedure, and rules, specifying the number of players, any penalties, how a person wins, and directions for scoring. An interesting feature of this activity is the likelihood that unforeseen situations will arise for which the directions do not allow. This fact builds in a frequent need for revision of the directions. Revised, these instructions can be affixed to the game, and the games exchanged and taken home, added to the classroom game collection, or exchanged with youngsters in another class or school. Generally, it is important that a direction writer either get back written comments or have a chance to talk with whoever played his game; sometimes both would be in order.

For making board games youngsters will need large pieces of heavy cardboard; porous-tipped pens in various colors; buttons, bottle caps, chips, or something else for markers; dice, a spinner (it can be homemade), or numbers written on cards; a ruler; and graph paper. Children who have played board games will know how to set up squares for the markers to advance along. Board games or a chess board might be drawn large on a sidewalk or basement floor in chalk; then the players can be their own playing pieces, wearing hats or captions to distinguish themselves. For a more permanent game, paint on an inexpensive plastic drop cloth from a paint store.

RECIPES

Booklets of recipes* that contain lists of ingredients in prescribed quantities and directions for cooking generally appeal to children. You don't have to sponsor this cooking in school, but youngsters can either take the books home or copy recipes they like to use at home with a parent or each other. The language arts goal is to focus on an interesting kind of written material that children can find easily in newspapers, magazines, and books at home. They can make collections of recipes they like in scrapbooks or recipe files to exchange, read, and take home to use. This way they have another opportunity to read action sequences and at the same time learn vocabulary for food, utensils, and units of measure. They also need to do arithmetical calculations.

If a committee plans to do some cooking at school, they will need to plan what ingredients, utensils, and equipment they will need and who will bring what. If some items need to be purchased, they need to determine the cost and how to divide it among them or raise money to pay for the supplies. All these are valuable problems. Relating cooking to health food, ethnic traditions, and consumer shopping gives it a depth that will no doubt increase interest. Do not let sex-role stereotypes prevent boys from showing their interest in cooking.

Youngsters can write their own recipes, illustrating each step in the process with a drawing, and post them on a recipe board or make them into a booklet. They can take down dictated recipes from other people or try out and write down an original of their own. A fine activity is to make up "recipes for life," usually humorous and aimed at particular things, such as "a recipe for getting along with girls." This eighth grader turned her recipe into witty word play:

RECIPE FOR MATH PIE

by the Cantering Cook

Stir three cotangents into one pan of boiling polygon juice. Gingerley add seven reciprocals and four multipli-

---

[3] Described on page 417.

cative inverses. Let cool for five days, and squeez ten ounces of cherry parallelogram and six ounces of liquid vertex into the pan. Sprinkle some radius' and hypotenuse' on top. Baste with a mixture of four medians, one circumberence and ½ teaspoonful of triginomic functions, for a few weeks. Serve with a nice selection of square roots and subsets and rays, in a good sized parabola. (serves 5–300, depending on how big the pieces are cut.) Tastes best on Ground Hog day.[4]

HOW-TO-GET-THERE DIRECTIONS

This is a kind of direction-giving most people use frequently to guide a person to a place he has never been before. Because this discourse demands allowing for the receiver in an especially perceptive way, making up directions for getting from one place to another is an excellent project. Very young children can make a plan for a walk around the classroom that calls for touching, say, five different places. This plan can either be presented in a drawing or written in words and given to a friend. The friend follows the directions, and if he does not do as the writer had planned, the directions may be revised. Then the two reverse roles.

Older children can write more detailed step-by-step directions, such as:

1. Start at . . .
2. Go right along the . . . ten steps.
3. Go left three squares on the floor tile to . . .
4. Turn right and step backward . . . and so on.

The children can direct each other to destinations outside the classroom, inside the school, and, later, out in the community. By this time, you can rule out maps or diagrams by pretending that the directions are coming over telephone or telegraph so the children have to make words do the job. In small towns, perhaps, where distances are short and buses not used, children might exchange directions and go to each other's houses. Directing each other to specific places on the playground or to places within the school block might be a next best possibility. The final destination should not be stated but rather discovered by the person who is following the direc-

tions. A "treasure" might be buried at that spot. If the traveler does not get to where the writer intended, the two can go over the route together and find out whether the problem is in the way the directions were written or the way they were followed. Older youngsters might give identical directions to two people instead of one, and the two race to see who reaches the destination first.

How-to-get-there directions work well on the day of a class outing or as part of an outdoor education project wherein students camp out together for two or more days and nights. Walks along nature trails or treasure hunts can be directed by picture maps first and later only by written words.

Some directions should be projected and discussed. One of us sat in once on a lively and interesting fifth-grade discussion of home directions. In every paper there were some directions the class felt sure it could not follow. For example, "then turn up Linden Street" indicated only a turn, not the direction of the turn, since *up* expressed nothing but the writer's subjective mental picture of aiming himself where he wanted to go (this kind of egocentricity is equivalent to the puzzle-director's saying, "Now pick up the next piece," or "Put the funny-looking piece against it"). Since the children frequently did not know the names of streets, locations were often identified by ambiguous descriptions that more accurate word choice or better vocabulary would have cleared up. "Store," for example, could have been one of several retail places, but there was only one supermarket on the street. Since improving directions often requires replacing some words by others, this is another important place to work on vocabulary. Then, later in the discussion, a paper referred to the Western Building, at which point it occurred to some of the children that only someone familiar with the town would know that landmark. Whom were these directions written for anyway? Suppose a stranger had to follow them. So they themselves brought up the issue of adapting directions to different receivers.

For another occasion a story situation based on the problem could be imagined: an out-of-town visitor is staying overnight at such and such hotel, and the next day he is coming out to the school to show a film. What directions should the principal give when he telephones him that evening? Will he be walking or driving? These directions are read and discussed in a small group. Ask them to look at their papers, check for directions that a stranger

---

[4] Written by a girl in an eighth-grade class at the Demonstration School of National College of Education, Evanston, Illinois.

would not understand, and change them so that he would.

STAGE DIRECTIONS

As noted before, directions are a part of almost all other kinds of discourse. A good example of this is the stage direction that is a part of a script. To put forth a blueprint for action, which is what a script is, one needs much accurate description of appearances. This type of description is highly functional, being related to and justified by accompanying action and the purpose of a given scene. Since writing isolated description for its own sake usually turns students off and is too artificial to defend, it is important to realize the fine experience in describing that scripting affords. Scripts include directions for costumes, intonation, gesture, and movement, thereby providing another valuable need for putting the nonverbal into words. Writing out a film script calls for an even greater detailing of directions as not only the actors but also the cameramen need to be advised. See page 298. Directions for a cameraman need to take account of not only the point of view of the receiver, but also the nature of his equipment. A bonus is that if a script is enacted, the accuracy of the description will be put to the test as students try to follow its directions, whether they are to paint flats and arrange furniture or to relate concurrent actions to each other. Description and direction-writing turn out to be closely related.

18

information

Although the term *information* is a broad one, we are limiting it as a goal to generalized fact, stated in the present tense, to distinguish it from the narrative fact of true stories. It comprises informative articles such as those printed in magazines, newspapers, professional journals, science textbooks, encyclopedias, and certain manuals and memorandums that mainly set forth facts. Precisely because it is generalized, the content of information will naturally tend to be from the physical or social sciences or, if not scientific, from utilitarian writing and everyday conversing. The charting, graphing, and mapping of information are treated in Chapter 13, Labels and Captions.

Creating information entails many fine learning tasks in observing, experimenting, thinking, and using language. It draws on work done in other kinds of discourse—actual dialogue, true stories, directions, ideas. Understanding information entails equally good learning experience in comprehension. Some of the classic problems of expository writing concern how to blend factual narrative, directions, general statements of fact, and general ideas in one or another combination. Sometimes one serves merely as evidence or illustration embedded in another. How one classifies mixed exposition depends on which kind of discourse predominates and frames the whole piece of writing.

A large part of task and topic talk, described in Chapter 4, Talking and Listening, concerns treatment of information. Oral experience in selecting, describing, and ordering facts develops that most crucial skill in the composition of informative articles—explaining one's material.

Generalizations of fact are based on assimilating data into a relationship between the raw material of experience and some verbalization of it. Data may be collected from four main sources: (1) what the environment shows, (2) what experiments reveal (manipulations of the environment for purposes of observation), (3) what other people know, and (4) what records store. We shall take these one at a time.

What the environment shows

Any environment is beaming information at the learner. The degree to which he is responsive to this stimulation and can perceive, assimilate, and make sense of it is the degree to which, at that moment at least, he is educable. The language arts goal is to put into language what one picks up from the environment and to understand others' verbalization of it. Practice in observing and accurately reporting information that an environment presents is one function of the sensory recording activities described on pages 160 to 170. Whenever one describes what he senses, he is practicing not only his language skill but his precision of observation and other sense response as well.

The easiest material to start with is that from a close and familiar environment—objects from home or pets in the classroom. All one has to do is observe and verbalize things with which one already has some personal relationship. To this can then be added the practice of visiting places less familiar for the express purpose of "reading" the environment there.

Familiar objects are the focus for show-and-tell oral composition as presented on pages 73 and 74. Some show-and-tell presentations can be taped and later transcribed. Others can be written up after sessions in which all members of a small group have spoken about and answered questions on the items they brought in, thereby benefiting from group interaction. Writing up might be most appropriate when the session is specialized in the direction of, say, explanation—"Bring in something of which the purpose, use, care, or operation can be explained." Having rehearsed while talking, and having received from their audience an idea of how to explain some things better and what emphasis might be most interesting, youngsters should be ready to write. The personal choice of the items and the intention of printing the papers as information booklets should ensure motivation.

Another way to go about this is to have the students write up their show-and-tell presentation in the first place. If this is done in the form of riddles, it has the same appeal as the sensory games described in Chapter 8, Writing.

GUESSING GAMES

"What Am I?"

These riddles, consisting of descriptions of familiar objects, can be exchanged orally, written on flash cards with the answer on the back, or compiled into booklets. Here's a sample:

> I am a flat, round metal disk shaped like a silver dollar to which are attached two long flexible tubes, each of which has a soft plastic end. (stethoscope)

Potato Game

You can pile together enough potatoes for each person in a group or class. Then each student takes one and writes a description that would help another person find that particular potato when it is back in the pile. Students then put all the potatoes back together; each gives his paper to another student to see if that person can find the potato after reading the description on the paper. When he thinks he has found it, he checks with the person who wrote the description to see if he is right. Of course, any cheap durable vegetable can be used for this game. So can photographs with similar characteristics such as pictures of TV sets or washing machines from sales brochures or catalogues. When all of the objects or pictures described are very similar, students will frequently resort to simile or metaphor in their descriptions because of the frustration of trying

to be precise about what have to be very fine distinctions. This frustration is a far more authentic stimulus for imaginative comparison than a teacher assignment to write similes and metaphors.

"Where Have I Been?"

Another guessing game is to figure out where a person has been by reading his record of the sounds, smells, textures, and temperatures, but not the sights he experienced. Two students take separate walks around the school, or block the school is on, and note on a pad what they sense. Then the two meet, trade sensory impressions with each other, and try to take one another's trip using only those notes. They might draw maps of this second journey to show each other so the two of them can see how well they did.

Observation Games

Two students stand facing one another and look for three minutes at everything about each other. Then they turn back to back and each takes a turn describing what the other looks like, what he is wearing, the color of his eyes, how his hair is parted, and so on. Another time, this game can be varied by having each partner, while standing back to back, change two (or later three or four) things about his personal appearance (unbuttoning a button, rolling up a cuff, removing beads, and so on), then turn back toward each other and take turns guessing what is different. Another variation of this is to let the class make a thorough survey of the classroom and then all walk out in the hall, leaving a leader in the room to make five changes and list them on a piece of paper. Then the other members of the class come back in and list on their own papers all the changes that they notice. Their lists are then compared with that of the leader.

RECORDING OBSERVATIONS

Even very young children can gather data and record it, making wall charts or reports for their classmates. Here are some of the types of directions you might give them for these reports:

- Measure anything in the classroom and report its dimensions.
- Guess which is the tallest thing in the room and which is the widest; then measure the height

and width of everything that's likely to be the highest or widest, and report your findings.

- Use yourself as a measuring stick and see how many times your length a bookcase or a wall is by lying down next to what you are measuring and marking the place on the floor the top of your head touches. Try again, but this time mark where your fingertips touch when stretched above your head. On a chart, record how many times as long as you are, the bookcase or wall is. Do this again using a foot, hand, or arm for a measure.
- Guess how many tiles are on the floor, bricks are on a section of wall, chairs are in the auditorium, books are on a shelf, crayons or pencils are in a box, or beans are in a jar. Then count them and see whose guess is closest.

A pair of students might make up separate lists of questions that call for careful observation and give them to each other to answer. For example, they might ask:

- Do the birds stop singing before or after sunset?
- Who is the fastest eater in your family?
- Who among your classmates talks the least in class?
- Do you put on your right or your left shoe first when you dress in the morning?
- When you lace your shoes, do you cross the right lace over the left, or vice versa?

After a day or two of observing, the children can report their answers. Answers to questions like these might be collected from various class members and presented on a chart or graph.

If more than one kind of animal is in the room, children can compare and contrast, making drawings to show the differences in the animals' feet, ears, noses, tails, and so on, thereby heightening their own observation of detail. For elementary-school children, the more the subject moves the better, although once involved in a project children do become motivated to observe small changes from day to day, if, say, they are growing certain plants, culture molds, or crystals. Since the foundation of science is observation, noting down sensations places students in the basic role of the scientist or naturalist. In fact, the children can be told that they are going to "be" scientists and do one of the things scientists do.

When children are new to the process of record-

ing what they observe, they can take notes as they watch for five or ten minutes and then meet with their small group. The function of the notes is, first, to remind each child of what he observed so he can "compare notes" with his colleagues and, second, to provide specific words, phrases, and observations for a group write-up of a collective recording. The children collate their individual notes in a small-group discussion and write together a dated entry for that day in a group journal. Since a lot of the same words are used over and over, these can be gradually added to a long-standing list on the board, which children can consult for vocabulary and spelling. One child writes down what the others decide should go into the report. There may be disagreements about what was actually seen and precisely what the color, shape, movement, and so on was which may have to be settled by returning to their subject for another look. The goal of this collaboration is to produce a full record of their observations, written in continuous prose.

Some observing sessions can be devoted to drawing pictures or taking photographs of the subject while watching it. These pictures can be dated and captioned to explain, for example, what the animal was doing at the time and can be added to the journal. After several days each group meets to read over its collective journal and then tell or write a summary of it. (See page 153.) Their drawings might be put together into a presentation for the class, using an opaque projector. If photos were taken, they can have a slide show.

Human as well as plant and animal behavior may be observed and generalizations reached. Youngsters can record the body language people use, noting greeting and good-by rituals and gestures, such as handshakes, back slaps, kisses, or louder voices; eating rituals; and typical stances of teachers, receptionists, or students, and so on. They may want to observe an individual and record his behavior or watch a group of peers interact and record the dynamics of their group behavior. They might gain insight about whether the appointed leader is the real leader, how final decisions are made, whose ideas are adopted and whose are rejected, and perhaps why. This kind of observation can easily be incorporated in a discussion session to evaluate the quality of a small-group discussion.

Elementary-school children can read books of observation, such as Olive Earle's *Paws, Hoofs, and Flippers,* which focus on distinctions among animals that children can then observe for themselves. Magazines such as *Ranger Rick's Nature Magazine, National Geographic, National Wildlife, Natural History,* and *Audubon* feature records of observation.

VISITING OTHER PLACES

Class Trips

An appropriate extension of classroom observation is a trip to a zoo or museum. If small groups have been responsible for recording specifics such as eating behavior or diet or have been describing and drawing particular parts of the bodies of classroom animals, they can take a sketch book to the zoo and make drawings of and write names of, say, all the animals they can find that have paws like a gerbil, ears like a mouse, a bill like a parakeet, or tail fins like a goldfish. The more specific the information each small group is seeking, the more likely they are to observe and record accurately. Their purpose for going on the trip then is related to an information-gathering project in the classroom.

Cemetery Research

Stones that present information can be researched —cornerstones marking public buildings, grave markers, and so on. Students can go to find out the date of the first burial in the local cemetery or the most common names or nationalities represented on the gravestones, or to make a comparison of the average length of life of persons buried in the first decade of burials with those buried in the last decade, or to discover the most common first name on gravestones or whether more men or more women are buried there, and so on. In some older graveyards students may find gravestones marked in languages other than English. Rubbings of epitaphs or carvings can be used to illustrate cemetery research reports. When trips to the cemetery are combined with research with documents in historical societies, students have a valuable opportunity to pose as historians. Think of other local sites that will yield similar raw information—bargain basements, junkyards, parking lots. Results of visits are graphed or written up as reportage or articles. Collateral reading is feature reportage in newspapers and magazines and other items in periodicals based on such visits.

What experiments show

When the environment is manipulated, new information emerges. Simple science experiments can be conducted to find out the answers to such questions as: What happens to the pupils of your eyes when you look at a bright light? Does your heart beat faster before or after exercise? Is mud or sand heavier? Does a gerbil eat more than a hamster? Does a guppy hatch from an egg or is it born live? Young children can take a thermometer to various spots such as near a radiator, in a snow pile, or in a refrigerator and record the various temperatures. Whenever measurements are called for, computations are appropriate; these can be presented graphically. Youngsters can teach animals to run a maze by a reinforcement schedule of feeding and can record their observations. The animals' movements may be traced on maps, diagrams, or charts. More mature students can set up experiments that incorporate a control. For example, they can compare animals whose environments are altered by such things as constant light, loud sounds, different colors or diets, with control animals. Students record observations and keep journals as described in the last section.

Topic-centered discussion of science experiments can focus on changes in appearance, behavior, feeding habits, weight, and so on, referring to the journal for evidence. If the journal is about an ant farm, one would not expect the topic to get at development but at generalities in behavior—the routine operations and labor divisions of the colony. One would expect such a journal to record similar behavior on different occasions, so that gradually a general picture builds up. Thus the topic might be "What different kinds of ants are there and what does each kind do?"

The combination of manipulating while observing and recording can develop important language skills. While visiting one third-grade class that was recording what happened to candle flames when various things were done to them, one of us noticed that several group papers contained sentences beginning with *if* and *when* clauses, which appear rather rarely in the writing of children this age. Then we noted that it was their physical manipulations of the candles that were causing these sentence constructions: "If I put a jar over the candle, the flame goes out," or "When we throw alum on the flame, it turns blue." This is typical of the organic way in which experiencing and thinking should lead to increased language complexity.

Mature students can set up a controlled sequence of events structured in advance and later written up either as a report or as a case study. See pages 351–352. The experimenter is also the reporter. The natural scientist who tries to isolate a compound or a social scientist who wants to determine how a problem-solving group evolves over a period of weeks does not simply observe naturalistically; he arranges what he will observe. He wants to know not just what happens of itself but what happens *if* conditions are such and such. He chooses the subject and situation and sets the occasions and duration. So a lot of what he reports is of his own making, usually in order to test a hypothesis. Although this control over the material creates some difficulties in allowing for one's own influence and for one's personal investment in the outcome—very real problems for all scientists—the reporter's task is essentially the same, to keep accurate records and digest these in some significant way. Recourse to documents may again be necessary in order to enlighten and orient the layman reader sufficiently for him to grasp the significance of what the experimenter is trying to do.

Following either a spontaneous or experimental sequence will lead to narrative and probably a final paper that combines chronological and thematic organizations. This is the main fact from which the writing issues will stem, because this kind of narrative is not a tale told just for its own sake; it is a case. The sequence, progression, growth, or change informs in a general way: this is what happens when rats fed extra calcium learn to run a maze. But how far the claim of typicality should go is an important matter for cross-commentary in a small group. Would statements from other documents prove that the case is an instance of a general truth? Is the case offered for the reader to verify for himself? Is the generality implied or stated? If stated, should it be qualified more exactly?

Some case studies of experiments will call for co-ordinated research as described on page 373. Whether the experiment deals with animals, things, or people, the writer frequently has to situate his material by referring to the findings of others or to the history of his subject. His case may be one more instance of a generality previously reported by other people; or perhaps it contradicts prior evidence. The case may be understandable only if the writer, for example, fills in a bit of welfare history, or sets forth some established facts about ducks or legislative routine. This is the optional secondhand information that must come from reading. The need for it can lead students to the library to use the card catalogue or indexes such as the *Reader's Guide to Periodical Literature.*

Reading articles reporting the results of experiments* written by adults along with those written by their peers enhances both. Not only science books but magazines like *Science Digest, Popular Science,* or *Psychology Today* report results of experiments of interest to students.

What other persons know

The most common way a young child finds out what he needs to know or is curious about is to ask questions. Once he is asking more than one person the same question, he is doing what more sophisticated pollsters call a survey. Asking honest questions and sharing what one finds out are appropriate activities for any age.

INTERVIEWS

One of the best ways for a young person to find out about something is to ask questions of a specialist who knows about the subject. Interviews can be part of many different kinds of information-gathering projects such as putting together a reporter-at-large story, a case study, a profile, a human-interest story, a chronicle of a group experience, and so on. Models for the process can be TV or radio interviews, like those of Studs Terkel, or collections of transcripts* of interviews. As students conduct interviews, they discover how to ask the right questions, how to ask further questions on the basis of responses to the first questions so the interviewee clarifies what he means, and how to find out in a dialogue what lies behind what they can see about a person and what they can infer about him from his surroundings.

The information about intangibles acquired by interview can be added to the sensory experience of an observational visit. An interviewer gets background, references to other times and places, sentiments of the interviewee, generalizations, and so on. Thus the material in an interview is more abstract and more secondhand than information that the environment shows. Person is at least as important as place in an observational visit that includes an interview, although in some cases the person may be important precisely because he represents a place. In an interview the reporter is not merely observing; by putting questions to his subject he is influencing the material he will report.

Procedure

A good way for youngsters to ease into the unfamiliar role of interviewer is to ask questions of peers, but the only honest motive for this activity exists early in the school year when learners do not yet know each other well. After that, if students are the subjects of interviews, they will need to be from another class or another school.

A get-acquainted game is to interview each other in groups of two or three, taking turns asking each other questions and answering those others ask. Then take turns telling each other a summary of what you heard each one say about himself, correct any misimpressions, and then take turns introducing each other to the class as a whole, telling as much as you can remember. Another thing to do is to have each person write up a report about another person after the interview and then read that to the class and see if they can guess who is the subject of the report.

The next step might be interviewing newsworthy subjects to gather material for a newspaper. A small group discusses which people in their school or community would be good to interview for any number of reasons—their involvement in newsworthy affairs of the moment, their representativeness, their kinds of occupation, or qualities of their personalities. In discussing why they want to interview these people, the reporters should help each other crystallize the kinds of questions they would ask. They may want to try these questions out on each other. Interviewing is an art, of course, and composition of the reportage begins with the selection of questions. Queries about date of birth, education, and so on will read later like a dossier or encyclopedic entry of a minor poet, though of course some such bare facts may be relevant if inserted into more promising material. Don't attempt to head off this problem, however, by admonishing. Emphasize, rather, the deriving of questions from their original intention in wanting to interview the subject they have chosen. The directions are to arrange the time and place for the interview, with the idea of catching the person in appropriate surroundings, take notes during the interview, and write it up afterward. (Students,

especially young ones, may feel that for some subjects a casual interview, not arranged in advance, would be more suitable.) The write-ups are exchanged and discussed by a group acting as editorial board for the newspaper or other medium for sharing.

Issues for Discussion

After their first interview, the small group can share any problems they may have had in interviewing and ask for suggestions for solutions. With mature students this discussion may range over matters of technique—how much to query, which sorts of questions are most productive, when to give the interviewee an opportunity to go ahead without questions, when to drop prepared questions and ask spontaneous ones. Help the group to examine a sample set of notes and ask the reporter to criticize his own interview. Then together look at the write-up of those notes and ask him to explain how he went about digesting the notes. Invite the class to say how they would handle some of the same problems. When is it best to quote and when to summarize? How much should you shuffle the actual order of remarks for the sake of better continuity of ideas? Should the reporter include his own questions? How much physical description should there be in relation to verbal matter? Are you going to play up surroundings, mannerisms, and dress, or sacrifice some of these for what was said? Do you describe at the beginning only, or return periodically to appearances? Let's note in passing that these are not only very real decisions that any reporter has to make but also some of the options the novelist has to play. The way these questions are answered is by referring them to the overall purpose that governs decision-making and that determined the choice of interviewee and setting in the first place. The focus may be on the person as personage, on his ideas, on his relation to setting, and so on.

Other Developments from Interviews

Interviews might be part of a process of finding out the answer to a question such as what school dropouts say about their experience. Each interview would then be a brief case history, written independently but compared later with others for possible generalizations about dropping out. Students might set out, as the authors of the *Foxfire* books did, seeking old people to interview as part of a gathering of folk knowledge and craftsmanship.[1] The anecdotes and memories can be pulled together for a chronicle of how it was in the old days.

Contrasts, generalities, and other ideas can arise as secondary effects of interviewing if the subjects are deliberately selected for oppositions, similarities, and other relationships. What do different dietitians say about a vegetarian diet? What do a retailer and a repairman say about the same product? When placed in the service of a project (but not merely reduced to opinion polling), interviewing can lead to further writing and to a special issue of a newspaper in which appear not only the related interviews centering on a certain subject, but also some articles of interpretation and generalization that refer to the interviews as testimony.

SURVEYS

Information gathered by interviewing a number of people or gathering information shown by the environment can be presented as a survey. Young children can poll their classmates to find out such things as what they do on Saturday morning, what TV shows they like best, what time of day they were born or what their birth weight was, what hobbies or collections they have. The results can be displayed on wall charts. Older students may prefer opinion polls on burning issues among their peer group—rationing to conserve energy, equal funds for women's athletic training, capital punishment, abortion, and so on; or on feelings—ambitions, fears, joys. They can start with interviews of students in the class, then go to others outside of class or school. For example, teenagers might take a survey of favorite movies, TV shows, or models of cars and then draw conclusions as to what the differences are between, say, the men and women respondents.

Information on language habits gathered in a survey may be compiled into a book such as a dictionary of local lingo* (expressions or word usages that are characteristic of a local subculture) or a report such as a summary of the dialects of a cross-section of people in an area. (A tape recording of

---

[1] *Foxfire* books, ed. Eliot Wigginton, Doubleday & Co., Inc., Garden City, N.Y., 1972. The genesis of these books was the very creative idea of this Georgia teacher, who sent his students out to record the rapidly disappearing lore of local old-timers.

each is helpful here.) See page 377 for more on making dictionaries.

Interviews conducted on paper are questionnaires. Some students may enjoy polling via this medium. A group might set up a "computer dating service" by using a questionnaire to inventory each classmate's personal likes and dislikes, hobbies, travels, physical condition, ambitions, and so on. Then they could match personalities to each other on the basis of what was revealed by each person's answers. They might also match people to jobs, making predictions, based on the questionnaire responses, for success in certain careers.

After some experience collecting information via questionnaires, students can solicit opinions on various subjects, learning in the process how to word questions so they are not "loaded." Unbiased and open-ended questions are often the most difficult for immature survey-takers to formulate, particularly if their own opinions on the subject are strong. Writing up a good questionnaire is a fine challenge to precision, clarify, and objectivity. See page 384 for a discussion of ways to present opinions.

If a real computer is available, students can have valuable experience working with a programmer to translate their information into computer language. No matter what the subject, the computer print-outs will be reading matter of high interest. Gradually accumulated data can be used to answer further questions.

What records store

Books, periodicals, films, recordings, archives, and documents of all sorts, including family records such as birth and marriage certificates, store information. Your job is to set in motion processes whereby this vast source of information becomes interesting and accessible to students. Collections of short informative articles* such as those that appear in magazines and newspapers can array a range of this type of information in a form that will not be overwhelming to inexperienced readers of expository prose. Students of all ages should have a large amount of reading matter centered on topics of proven interest. These can be part of the whole newspaper and magazine world of articles and useful information, such as maps*. Collections of the latter depict information of special interest and importance since mapping is basically a symbolizing experience. Like charts and graphs, maps are an alternate and supplementary way of saying something; for practical reasons, as well as for entertainment, students need to become acquainted with road maps and atlases. See pages 269–271.

Dictionary and encyclopedia entries are easily accessible information because they are alphabetized. By junior high most students can learn to look for information by using the *Reader's Guide to Periodical Literature* and other indexes. Almanacs and other collections of facts hold answers to student questions; the sooner students find this out, the better. Some information-gathering will lead to local historical society archives or microfilms of old newspapers. Information magazines like *Popular Mechanics, Mechanix Illustrated, Sky and Telescope,* or *Consumer Reports* are full of the kind of matter that students find practical.

A high proportion of information is of value only to the degree that it is up to date; this provides another reason for students to read newspapers, periodicals, and recently published almanacs, reports, and compilations, such as the know-your-town type of studies done by the League of Women Voters or Chamber of Commerce.

People go to informative matter for two reasons: (1) to get on with their tasks, as when they read newspaper listings of upcoming events in their communities, TV guides, or ads for things they want to buy or jobs they want to apply for; and (2) out of a restless curiosity to make sense of the world. When students want to know something, you should help them find out, but the last thing you should do is to assign vast amounts of highly abstract material before students have a context for processing information of that sort.

In short informative articles, students find models for writing in a wide range of nonliterature. For young children information about real animals holds as much fascination as fantasy featuring animals. Throughout the school years students can put together their own books of information on subjects of interest to them. Some of these will be in the form of specialized dictionaries such as a collection of ballet terms, others in the form of miniencyclopedias, still others as sets of generalized articles.

RESEARCH WITH DOCUMENTS

Mature teenagers may be able to pull together information from a variety of sources into a research paper. However, to cull, synthesize, and interpret the content of what others have written presupposes maturity, motivation, experience with abstracting one's own documents, and the capacity to organize a long piece of writing. Let us contrast the traditional "long paper" or "research paper" with the *original* research with *lower-order* documents that we have in mind.

When a student pieces together information and ideas from several books that are themselves high-level syntheses—encyclopedia entries, summary articles, or synoptic books—he really has little choice but to rearrange, reword, and regurgitate. The result is just a fancy book report. But if he sifts lower-order documents, many of them of the sort he has previously written himself—eyewitness accounts, journals and diaries, correspondence, fragments of autobiography and memoir, cases, and profiles—and some of them of a sort he has not been writing, such as municipal files, archives, and congressional records, then he can do a piece of honest research that no one has done before. This is the only kind of research a student should be asked to do. From having created most kinds of lower-order documents, he will know how they come into existence, what the nature and worth of their information is, and consequently how he should assess them. This approach leaves many more decisions up to the student—from selection of sources to drawing conclusions—but if this is not so, a research paper is not worth doing. Furthermore, he can have plenty of consultants. Subject matter teachers can give leads to sources, librarians and clerks can help in locating documents themselves, and the English teacher and the small groups can assist in methods of composition.

The key is personal interest. What kinds of information and ideas do students read for on their own? Any subject matter is fair game, since the learning is in the *process.* Different pursuits will lead to biography, chronicle, or exposition. That is, some student papers will be about a person whose life work relates to their interest; others will feature a group or movement; still others a state of affairs or state of knowledge. The research will usually be an extension of a subject the student already has some knowledge of because it attracts him. For example, a high school student who wrote about secessionist sentiment in northern Virginia during the months preceding the Civil War drew heavily on local newspapers, convention proceedings, and archives—

records written at the time in question and available in the author's locality. He was able to tie his interest in his home region to the broader national framework presented in the course. Any time you can, help a student follow out his interest in a question by going to community archives, historical societies, or records offices for real estate transactions, photos, newspapers, letters, and so on, as well as to library sources such as almanacs for census records.

Original research with higher-order documents is of course not impossible, but unless one is an authority in a subject area, the likelihood of originality, we would say, decreases as the abstraction level of the sources rises. Research at this high level of abstraction involves pulling together what different experts or researchers say on the same subject, or generalizing what recurs over a historical period. This kind of writing is very sophisticated compared to, say, doing a biography from letters, diaries, newspaper accounts, and so on. If a student chooses to write on a historical subject, help him find one that will lead him to an examination of primary sources. History is especially limiting because the further events are from the present, the more others have already assimilated them. The Virginia boy had some luck on his side. Recent events offer better opportunities. Several years ago, another student did research on the Black Muslim movement at a time when the movement was new and not much had been written about it.

The issues for class discussion, outside consultation, and small-group suggestions range over many phases of the project. The subject must be small enough to be treated significantly in around two thousand to thirty-five hundred words and must not have been so treated before. Help from adults, some quick reconnoitering, and airing of proposals in the small groups will help establish the subject and may also prompt better ideas about it. Then, during the gathering of information, students periodically tell their group what they have done so far and discuss problems they foresee. Periodicals are again the main source for models (like *American Heritage* for history). In reading these, students can pick up ideas for organizing and presenting their own material, having now a particular motivation both to read such discourse and to think about how it is put together. But most compositional problems will have to be handled by cross-commentary just before writing up and again before revision.

Like all other student writing, research papers are also classroom reading material.

Composites of information-gathering

After secondary-school students have had experience with two or more of the following—eyewitness reportage (see page 349), recording observations, interviewing, and researching with documents—they can try their hand at pulling some of these together into a composite, a summary of information gleaned in a variety of ways.

THE REPORTER-AT-LARGE

This is an omnibus activity in that it brings together several different kinds of writing that the student has been doing. It is a transitional kind of writing between true narrative and generalization. It involves re-creating some of the dialogue of the interview, recounting actions, describing appearances of things, and exposing facts. Having received some data directly through his senses, and having received other data in verbal form from his informant at the scene, the student is dealing with information of different orders from different sources. He must digest all this and fuse the different modes of drama, narrative, and exposition into a whole piece of reportage that makes a general point of some kind.

Here are the directions:

> Go visit some place of business or other enterprise, talk with people there, watch its operation, take notes, then write an account of the visit afterwards. Use your narrative to convey a lot of information about the enterprise, to catch the atmosphere of the place, and to show what the people there are like.

The *New Yorker*'s "A Reporter at Large" is the model for this activity. Some of these articles comprise many interviews and much book research, but a simpler kind is based, ostensibly at least, on the material of one visit. Many of the long pieces in "The Talk of the Town" run more nearly the length that students would write. While students are working on their reports, let them read examples of this kind of reportage* so they can see for themselves how professionals handle the assignment *with different subjects.*

Don't try to distill a formula. The best way to prepare students is to let them (1) garner techniques from the reading, and (2) try to foresee the problems that their particular subject is going to raise. An insurance office, for example, which offers nothing but desks and papers, is going to limit the reporter almost entirely to the relaying of conversation. The directions to the small groups are for individuals to take turns telling where they are going and why, to envision the problems, and to make suggestions for each by drawing on similarities they see between a proposed visit and one or more of the Reporters-at-Large they have read.

The hazard of models is that less confident students will imitate too directly, but one hopes that their being accustomed to writing from fresh experience will avert the hazard. Looking at professional selections while anticipating their own writing decisions gives students a motive to read more analytically, for technique, than they usually do. But to offset the other hazard of models—the intimidation of the novice, who may feel he is being made to compete out of his class—let students read some papers done by other students. While demonstrating that other people like themselves have done this kind of reporting and done it well, these can serve as inspiration.

Farms, stores, bakeries, factories, hospitals, and laboratories are among the many places that students have visited and written up. We remember funny, wry, and fascinating accounts of picturesque or rarely observed activities—at a Vermont country bookstore, on a Hudson River tugboat, and in an organ factory.

Generally, the narrative account of the reporter's visit provides a frame, but the stipulations about conveying information and characterizing the people and the place force the student to make a lot of decisions that will modify the narrative considerably. He may interrupt it to linger over description or to inject explanation he acquired at some other point in the visit. He may digest in his own way information received from the people and feed this in gradually or in blocks, the alternative being to quote everything his informants said at just the moment they said it. Dialogue is a good way to characterize people and a readable, but inefficient, way of conveying information; compromise is necessary. Narrative and description will convey automatically a lot of information about the physical aspects of the people and the operation they carry on but cannot convey generalities and other unseen facts such as background, purposes, and overall method, which must come from the people through dialogue.

Ideally, Reporters-at-Large would be balanced between information and characterization, and between firsthand reportage and secondhand reportage. Drama, narrative, description, and exposition would be interwoven, and none used to do what another might do better for the given situation. Some papers may never rise above miscellany, which represents a failure to find coherence either in the operation of the enterprise or in one's attitude toward it. This common difficulty usually means that the student got lost in the details and never let himself react to the totality of the enterprise. At some point in writing up the material he should survey it for general impressions and try to recall what things were salient about it. Perhaps the enterprise struck him as mechanistic, or money-grubbing, or old-fashioned, or quaintly casual, or typical of some modern trend. In other words, he could hardly not have distilled some *idea* of the operation, some essential characteristics. If he organizes around some such idea at the same time he follows chronology, he should produce a *pointed* narrative, which is by definition well on its way to being an essay. The problem of finding a good way to end the piece is then automatically solved: he strikes a note at the end—a keynote—that points up the idea or characteristic that was his dominant impression. Tell the students to have in mind a meaningful title as they are writing, one that keeps before them and the reader the unity of the paper. Have them bring a first draft of this paper to class, read it aloud in their group, and note the reactions of their colleagues.

The Reporter-at-Large technique opens the way to the covering of court sessions, legislative debates, hearings, neighborhood meetings, and other public dialogues. If at all possible, every student should have at least one chance to witness firsthand, and try to assimilate for himself, what goes on routinely in the official and unofficial bodies that run the affairs of society. Writing up such sessions, and reading the accounts by classmates, would give him a real grasp of social and governmental institutions that few students ever have and that it is almost impossible to convey in civics books.

When combined with research with documents and written up at length, Reporters-at-Large provide a very powerful kind of firsthand research that not only should reflect the student's private interest—there are people and places for all interests—but should also relate to his work in other subjects. For a project in science he could visit a laboratory, research center, observatory, or agricultural station. For government there are municipal operations and state agencies. For social studies, including economics, any business or other enterprise is germane.

Seeing for himself how a profession is conducted, and who goes into it, can also help a high-schooler deliberate about a career, and reading the printed reports of other students extends his knowledge of professions considerably. Perhaps the teachers of other subjects could help to steer students to places they might not otherwise think of.

THE PROFILE

A profile is a verbal sketch of someone or something, shorter and necessarily less complete than a full-length biography, but at the same time capturing a significant aspect of the subject, much as an artist's profile or quick sketch might. A profile may also be a sketch of a place or operation. Like a Reporter-at-Large article, a profile is a composite of one or more interviews, sensory observations, and sometimes research into documents as well, designed to give a substantial look at a person or an enterprise, showing what is typical. A profile, like those in the *New Yorker* magazine, is a distillation of information about some subject. It is more generalized than a case, contains more information from documents, and results in a logically rather than chronologically ordered essay. In doing a profile, students go across the frontier between eyewitness reportage and research. Also the tense shifts from *what happened*—narrative—to *what happens*—generalization. A profile is about recurring or typical things. Not progression, but pattern, will provide the shape of the material. Though abstracted to a higher level, the material is still concrete, as in case writing, and the generalities are exemplified with anecdotes.

Some students might enjoy making a relative or grandparent the subject of a profile, writing up their generalizations about this person based on interviews with the subject and other relatives or friends of the subject; on information gleaned from old photos, family documents, letters, and so on; and on observations of the subject's habits, friends, surroundings, manner, and style. The goal is a distinct, coherent impression of what the subject is like, not the story of his life.

Another kind of profile describes what goes on routinely in a place such as a courtroom, a welfare office, or a business. For either kind of subject, the procedure is this: Students do preliminary research on their subjects and then undertake a series of visits, keeping a journal as the basis for later writing-up. A student may go to different courtrooms,

visit several companies making the same product, or observe the person on a number of occasions, interviewing anyone he thinks can give him the information he wants. In addition to this material, he will most likely need some printed matter on the subject —official manuals, company brochures, newspaper files, local records, and so on—both to orient himself and to supply information that it would be inefficient to acquire through observation and interview. For example, rules of procedure or biographical data could be looked up, though an interviewee might tell him where to look or supply copies of what he needs.

Colleagues in the same group should keep up with each other's journal by exchanging them occasionally for reading and commentary. Some deficits and problems in the raw material may be headed off in this way and later writing issues raised. Encourage students to note down helpful ideas in the margin of the journal. Concurrent reading of similar research articles by both professionals and previous students should help the reporter become aware of the technical matters mentioned above.

When he comes to summarize his journal, a reporter will probably have to organize by generalized aspects of his subject—kinds of matters handled in court, differences in how several companies solve production problems, what so-and-so does and is like. When paragraphs do not follow the order of time, what succession shall enchain them? This would be a key question for discussion and cross-commentary while journals are running and during the writing-up. Which kinds of court matters, for example, or which comparisons of production methods, should precede which others? Although there are standard logical orders such as big to little, important to unimportant, and specific to general, discussion and suggestions should especially consider: (1) What is the best *organically* logical order for the subject—which succession of items or subtopics would allow earlier items to prepare for later ones and allow for the most meaningful juxtapositions and transitions? (2) What is the best *rhetorical* order—to begin anecdotally or with a general frame of reference, to feed in background gradually or to insert it once in a block, to build toward conclusions or assert conclusions first and then substantiate them? And for each item or subtopic, how much anecdotal illustration should one give? The same amount for all items? As for citing and footnoting, students are referred to examples in their reading and in classroom collections of informative articles.

COORDINATED RESEARCH

Many kinds of operations, notably newspapers, news broadcasts, or TV documentaries depend on a variety of information-gathering techniques and a coordinated presentation of the information.

Shop and Tell

For example, consumer surveys call for collecting data in more than one way. Elementary-school youngsters can take a product and divide into groups to make lists of the ingredients, record and compare the costs of different brands, and interview users respectively. Another group might run a taste test—if the product is edible—to see which brand the majority of the class prefers. Then all the groups can get together and share all they have learned about the product and write it down with a recommendation for their classmates regarding its purchase. Older students can make up more sophisticated consumers' guides, testing several brands of the same product, noting the cost per ounce or pound, ranking the items in terms of cost per unit and quality of performance, and interviewing regular users of each brand. The results of this cost analysis, quality testing, and opinion poll can be put onto a chart or into a report for the class. The group can include a recommendation for the product they think tastes the best or is the best buy for the money. They may want to find out which product has the most vitamins or the fewest additives. Consumer research can be part of a class project such as putting on an authentic colonial meal, furnishing a club room, going on a camping trip, or putting on a party for convalescent-home residents. In this case, the problem of fitting the purchases within a budget will demand comparative shopping and possibly following ads as well. For related reading, see *Consumer Reports* and similar periodicals.

Other Practical Problems

Any problem a class faces can be the focus of a discussion that leads to coordinated research, whereby each member of a group takes a different part in pulling together the facts they need to solve the problem. Building the equipment for classroom experiments, such as a hamster cage, a terrarium, or an animal maze, calls for a variety of information-seeking activities. Putting on a performance to mark a historical event such as the first opening of a school or a town's birthday will entail interviews, examination of documents, collecting photographs or slides, and seeking out old furniture or props for the stage. Another fine kind of coordinated research is to tape-record and analyze local dialects, comparing pronunciation, vocabulary, grammar, and so on.

To do any kind of coordinated research a large group divides into pairs or small groups and approaches the topic in a variety of ways. Some might go to documents, others to the library; others might do a case study, survey, interview, eyewitness report, experiments, or whatever. Then they meet together as a large group to report what they have found out. They can discuss areas of agreement or conflict; if important information is still missing, they can go out and get it. Then they can meet again as a large group and pull their efforts into one coordinated report to be shared in some way with each other and outsiders.

Ideas are either explicitly stated thought, cast usually in the present tense of generalization or implicitly stated thought, cast in metaphor or symbol. This goal includes aphorisms, essays, editorials, manifestoes, discussions of ideas, reflections, lyric poetry, and philosophical poetry. It is of course not easy to separate fact from thought, especially since, when explicit, both are asserted through the present tense of generalization, but still this difference in emphasis is what distinguishes ideas from information. Here we are concerned, then, with opinion, reflection, generalization, and argumentation. These are often supported by material from information and true stories as evidence or illustration of points. No matter how great the quantity of such documenting material, however, if the discourse predominantly and explicitly expresses thought and is organized around certain ideas, then it furthers the goal we aim at here.

Single statements

Some generalizations stated in a sentence or less constitute complete discourses in the realm of ideas. Thus sayings and slogans offer a legitimate opportunity to analyze and otherwise work or play authentically within the structure of a single sentence or less without having to wrench it out of some larger context. They can be looked at for refined work with construction without being divested of point and purpose as a group of words pulled out of context might be. Encourage students to read and test each other's generalizations and to rewrite them. Both the content and the form of a statement can be discussed and amended to qualify the idea by altering or adding words, phrases, and clauses; and to improve the rhetoric by adjusting diction and sentence structure for greater effect. The brevity encourages many students to spend much more time working on a single phrase or sentence than they would if it were part of a longer continuity. They can examine alternate ways of punctuating, ordering words, or constructing sentences to see which best suits their purpose.

Short statements have another great advantage in that they are small enough to post in the classroom, to show together, perhaps as the work of several students, or to serve as the basis for a semipermanent board that can be continuously added to and changed, prompting people simply to walk up and add or change statements already posted there. These also invite illustration and thus become captions. See page 271.

A good way to stimulate short discourse is to set up a graffiti board. Ideally, this board should be erased, painted over, or covered with clean newsprint or wrapping paper every night or very frequently so more students can have a chance to contribute to it, and so there is pressure for all to read it before it is gone, or to copy the best for a classroom graffiti collection. One teacher solved the problem of space for a board by propping a large pad of newsprint on a paint easel and flipping over a new page each day.

A badge-making kit is a popular stimulus for sharing values or insights in the form of short maxims. These may be nonverbal messages, of course, like the smile buttons. If you do not have a badge-making kit, use pop-bottle caps, removing the inside carefully, painting the cap, printing the message on it, and pushing the material of a shirt or blouse into the back of the cap and sealing it with the inside of the cap. Maxims can also be printed onto sweat shirts or made into bumper stickers.

Posters are another medium for presenting short idea statements. Students often enjoy adding a design or picture to emphasize the message. One class of students whose school was within a few blocks of the Mississippi River decided to erect a three-dimensional message. They had decided together that people were ignoring the pollution of the river, so they put together a raft. On it they erected a scaffold and hung a dummy labeled "Old Man River" from it. They wrote a sign on the raft: "Too Late?" and tied the whole thing in the middle of the Mississippi for the first three days of Earth Week.

Popular culture abounds in advice and maxims—short and snappy statements of ideas. Most are propaganda or advertisement of ideas, many are humor, and some are pure word play—all provide an entrée into short idea statement. They perpetuate in modern media the ancient tradition of epigram or moralistic aphorism.

Small children appreciate short environmental messages nearly a decade before they are able to make sense of a developed and supported essay.

EPITAPHS

Another type of environmental writing is inscriptions on tombstones or monuments in memory of the dead, or any short eulogies in prose or verse. They are a more ancient and respectable cultural form of what lives on as graffiti. Students can go to graveyards and look for epitaphs on the tombstones, making rubbings to show the class. The older the cemetery, the more likely they are to find epitaphs. Children might want to write epitaphs for pets who have died. They can also make up apt ones for famous persons whose biographies they have read. Some may find it intriguing to write an epitaph for their own gravestone.

Collections of epitaphs, such as *Over Their Dead Bodies* by Thomas C. Mann and Janet Greene (Stephen Greene Press, Brattleboro, Vermont), can be part of the classroom library. For example, on the day after the poet John Donne's burial in 1631 some unknown friend wrote this epitaph with a piece of coal on the wall over his grave:

> *Reader! I am to let thee know,*
> *Donne's body only lies below;*
> *For, could the grave his soul comprise,*
> *Earth would be richer than the skies.*

PROVERBS

These are pithy folk sayings in metaphor and often in alliterative form, like "Birds of a feather flock together." Part of a long tradition, they express generally accepted views of common human experience; it is understood that anyone can easily supply his own instances of these general truths from his own experience. Because proverbs are in the air, part of the oral literature passed down by word of mouth, they will be *recognized* by many children when they see them in print; they will know some as they do jokes and riddles that they can write down and collect. Because they are virtually always based on a metaphor, they provide an excellent way for students to work with metaphor as a complete discourse in itself. Far too many school efforts to have children focus on metaphor in longer kinds of discourse desecrate it in the very act of isolating it from context.

Encourage students to illustrate their proverbs because this is good experience in supplying anecdote for a generalization, albeit a visual and not a verbal one. Set up the activity in such a way that any tendency to illustrate the metaphor of the proverb literally will be noted and discussed by partners or at least challenged at some point. Illustrating a proverb by depicting some other *application* of the metaphor is an excellent way to head off literal-mindedness and to bring out the way in which the concrete image in the proverb is meant to serve merely as a representation of many other concrete instances: "A rolling stone gathers no moss."

Using proverbs as topics for small-group discussion also forces students to translate the metaphor into other applications. Encourage students to read proverbs aloud and talk about each one long enough to explore its meaning, implications, and potential truth. This amounts to testing each, trying it out on each other, and attempting to find instances that would support or refute it.

Another thing students can do is to write their ideas about a proverb individually and then come together afterward to read and discuss these and compare ideas. They can write why they think it is or is not true. This process entails supplying instances one way or the other. They can "prove" or test proverbs by choosing one they think is true and making up a story that shows that it is.

Collections of proverbs*, such as the *Book of English Proverbs* by V. H. Collins, the *Wit and Wisdom from West Africa* by Sir Richard Francis

Burton, or *Proverbs and Common Sayings from the Chinese* by A. H. Smith, provide one of the best entrées we know to metaphorical statement. Mature students may want to try writing original proverbs that distill general truths. In doing this they are creating their own metaphors, something not easy or natural for them to do. A good way to begin is to state a truth nonmetaphorically and then see if you can compare it to another kind of experience. A game like the metaphor game described on page 262 helps limber students up for proverb-making.

APHORISMS AND MAXIMS

These single-sentence sayings are concise statements of a principle, typically rules of conduct stated sententiously. Unlike proverbs, they are not metaphorical. They may be in verse, as in Benjamin Franklin's "Early to bed and early to rise/ Makes a man healthy, wealthy and wise." Their truths are of general import as in the Afro-American maxim, "You can't hurry up good times by waiting for them."

A good way to begin writing aphorisms is to write morals for tales from the folk tradition—fables (with their own morals covered up), folk tales, myths, or legends. See page 313. The moral of a tale, taken by itself, is much like a proverb or maxim in that it usually represents an extreme condensation of common experience. Hence, it can be used as a way into discussing, reading, and writing ideas.

There is a natural relationship between anecdote or incident on the one hand and generalization or idea on the other; students can see it in their own knowledge-building—namely, that out of a build-up of instances one distills generalizations or ideas or morals, and that, conversely, one's reflections are just that, a reflex or reaction to factual things, often to events, objects, places, or people, that directly stimulate certain ideas or generalizations. In fact, the close relation between instance and idea is the essence of knowledge-building and provides organic motives and means for reading and writing.

Students can pluck from magazines and newspapers or other reading matter certain statements that they think could stand alone as a saying and then illustrate each statement with a drawing or photograph or with an anecdote that fits it. Others might like to make a little booklet modeled on the UNESCO calendar, in which each page bears a saying and some illustration that may or may not go with it. A very popular activity may be for a small group to ransack different books of proverbs and aphorisms, especially from many different cultures, and put together their own anthology.

Aphorisms and maxims are very useful as ready-made topics both for group discussion and for idea writing. It is important, of course, that students choose or make up their own sayings to talk or write about, since success in treating a generalization depends a great deal upon interest in the idea.

Sometimes students can create their single statements as topics or as crystallizations of discussion points. At other times they may write them to restate a generalization that was implicit in or beginning to emerge from some previous writing, or to prestate their main idea for the next writing. Thus writing single-sentence generalizations ties into the writing of essays, presented at the end of this chapter. Working with these short idea statements is thus never outgrown; it can be one of the most mature kinds of abstraction that there is.

Steep students in literary examples of generalizations—those that are propositions and thus lend themselves well to discussion.[1] Conclusions based on experiences, observations, or experiments invite challenge from those whose experience does not support such a position. Students might enjoy amending, rewriting, or refuting literary generalizations. Here are some that invite response:

It is because of men that women dislike each other. (Jean de La Bruyere)

Nobody can misunderstand a boy like his own mother. (William O. Douglas)

Where ignorance is bliss, 'tis folly to be wise. (Alexander Pope)

Problems are difficult to solve when they require the use of the familiar in an unfamiliar way. (Bernard Berelson and Gary Steiner)

One is ordinarily more convinced of something by reasons he has found himself than by those that other people have thought up. (Blaise Pascal)

[1] Many suitable examples of discussable statements can be found in Blaise Pascal's *Pensées,* François de La Rochefoucauld's *Maxims,* and the poet-mathematician Paul Valéry's *Analects.*

There are people who would never have been in love if they had never heard of love. (Francois de La Rochefoucauld)

Among the many other uses of one-line sayings is the supplying of fodder—ready-made statements—that students can use in certain activities of making syllogisms and spotting illogical connections among statements. See page 398.

Collections of literary generalizations for the classroom library include: *Bartlett's Familiar Quotations* by John Bartlett, *Contemporary Quotations* by J. B. Simpson, *The Devil's Dictionary* by Ambrose Bierce, and the *Oxford Dictionary of Quotations.*

DICTIONARY DEFINITIONS

Defining is the process of arraying synonyms or explaining what something means. Some definitions present information; others, ideas. Obviously, students need repeated opportunity to use dictionaries and to make up their own operating definitions for words and concepts they use. Defining is composing single-statement generalizations in the present tense to show meaning.

One of the best ways for students to understand what a dictionary is, is to compile one of their own local or age-group lingo, omitting any words whose definitions correspond to those in a conventional dictionary. In the process of checking their usage with dictionary listings, they will become familiar with the format and imitate it as they compose their own entries. They will also find that meanings of words reside in human communities and that dictionaries merely record these meanings. Youngsters can make specialized dictionaries for their friends, defining terms associated with a special interest such as building model cars, skiing, cooking, or ballet. They can collect and collate index cards bearing their definitions. See pages 235 and 368.

Dictionary games such as that on page 254 can help students become familiar with dictionary format. So can the two below.

Small groups can be directed to look up and report on the origins of interesting words such as *sandwich*, which was the name of a gambler too busy to leave the gaming table to eat his roast, or *derrick*, the name of a London hangman. Books like Wilfred John Funk's *Word Origins and Their Romantic Stories* or one of Isaac Asimov's specialized dictionaries, such as *Words of Science and the History Behind Them*, interest some students.

Members of a small group can stage contests to see who can give the shortest and most accurate definition of words that they take turns springing on each other. Sometimes the words we use most commonly—such as *time, shadow, color, music, energy, speed, beauty*—are the most difficult to define. The winner is the one who can give the shortest and best definition for the most words.

Students can write imaginative definitions in the style of the popular "Happiness is . . ." books. Concepts such as "life" or "hate," various colors, or objects can be defined metaphorically, or operationally as in the well-known picture book *A Hole Is to Dig* by Ruth Krauss, so they come up with such definitions as "Sisters are to be jealous of." "Daffynitions" are funny or witty ways of defining that can be thought up in groups and made into booklets. Sometimes the humor is in the wording ("picnic" as an "eating outing"), sometimes in a point of view, ("risk" as defined by people in different walks of life or professions). Imaginative and witty definition leads naturally into epigrams, many of which are just that.

EPIGRAMS *

These are witty, brief, pointed remarks or observations typically marked by antithesis, like this:

War is for the sake of peace, but peace is not for the sake of war.   (Menander)

Sometimes epigrams are memorable definitions, as:

White is calling Africa the Dark Continent. (Preston Wilcox)

Work is the curse of the drinking class. (Oscar Wilde)

A *cynic* is a man who knows the price of everything, and the value of nothing.   (Oscar Wilde)

Radicalism is the conservatism of tomorrow injected into the affairs of today.   (Ambrose Bierce)

Other epigrams are verses:

A Robin Red Breast in a Cage
Puts all Heaven in Rage.
(William Blake)

OF EPIGRAMS

Short epigrams relish both sweet and sour
Like fritters of sour apples and sweet flour.
(Robert Hayman)

In trying to write haiku (see page 379), some students will come up with philosophical epigrams. Often these will be hand-me-downs, but many times they will be fairly original expressions of an idea as in this remarkably compact expression of a generality through imagery:

The stone axe falls,
Discarded beside a rusted musket
And Bikini vanishes beneath the waves.[2]

The author has written a three-line history of war delineated by the weapons used.

Loaded description

Sometimes a description is not *intended* as an objective recording; it is rather a description infused with opinion or response. There is no neat dividing line between the two, however, as we showed in the samples of sensory recording in Chapter 8, Writing. Subjective elements are always present, of course, but here we are considering that type of description that is *deliberately* loaded with opinion —either for a rhetorical end as in an advertisement, or for the expression of personal response as in poetry of observation. Loaded description often does not take the form of *explicit* statement, but we deal with it here because it leads into it.

ADVERTISEMENTS *

The composition of ads can begin orally in the elementary years. To pose in the role of an advertiser is to engage in a specialized type of show-and-tell, the aim not only to inform or entertain your listeners but to stir them to change their opinion on a matter or to want what you have to sell. Improvising and writing up sales pitches are activities that are easy for most youngsters because of the immersion in this medium that our culture affords. Anything can be advertised—services students are willing to perform for each other in exchange for other services, invented products that meet a need as yet unmet by things now on the market, or items one no longer needs. These last items may be wrapped up and sold at a class white-elephant auction for fake money. Each student can hold up his white-elephant package and, without telling what it is, make a case for its purchase. The amount of the bids on it will depend on his ability to describe it in appealing terms, for no one can see it prior to its "sale."

Some classes may want to hold contests for the most unusual or effective advertisements. They can be oral, like TV commercials, or written, as on posters or in magazines. In either case, they must have audience appeal, clear focus, succinct presentation, and visual attraction.

Students might be directed to take an object and describe it objectively. Then they can describe it again as if they were trying to sell it, in the process experiencing what happens to facts when they are used for a specific rhetorical end. For example, a student might tell exactly what his room at home looks like and how he feels about it. The next day he might try to look at it differently, describing it from the point of view of someone who is going to put it up for rent, or one who is going to redecorate it, for example.

MAKING IT STRANGE

Another way to load description is to look at the real world through the eyes of someone else. This can best begin as role-play and then lead to a report written to send back to peers who have not experienced what the writer has. For example, a student might be directed to describe the classroom as if he were a visitor from another planet, or a twenty-first century archaeologist who had just come upon this room inside a cave, or an ant crawling over the doorsill, or Gulliver in Lilliput. This kind of description is likely to evoke information about the real environment that has hitherto not been noticed or assimilated, as well as imaginative description. See *Making It Strange* (Harper and Row, New York, 1968) for a series of creativity activities for putting ideas about familiar things into metaphor.

---

[2] Tenth grader at Phillips Exeter Academy, Exeter, New Hampshire.

HAIKU *

This Japanese form of poetry is partly information in the form of sensory recording and partly idea in the reflection that charges the observation with insight. Like much other poetry and advertisement, it is loaded description. Although short, this poetic form is actually rather sophisticated.

Work with haiku will probably heighten perception and influence student prose in the direction of greater precision and better style. An emphasis on the concrete helps readers understand how much the statement of poetry is made through sensuous things weighted with insight instead of through explicit statement.

Because haiku offer a number of special advantages for learning how language can be used, we shall dwell on this form at some length here. This does not mean that other poetic forms should receive less treatment in the classroom but simply that haiku characterizes the best poetry and yet is short enough for the concentrated focus on a whole discourse that we advocated earlier in this chapter. In a haiku every word counts. As students work with haiku they learn to refine observation down to particulars, to express feeling in the concrete terms of what evokes it, to look at language and composition microscopically, and to gain special entrance into the whole world of poetry.

As poems of observation haiku relate rather directly to eyewitness reportage. But while focusing on things, the poet infuses his response into the description; feeling is expressed through the exact rendering of a physical moment. A haiku is at once about observer and observed. Its fidelity to things gives it a certain objectivity, but things are always registered by some sensibility. The object one senses is usually something in the natural world that the poet presents in an unexpected way.

Since the original haiku form is defined to a great extent by qualities peculiar to the Japanese language and not present in English, it is useless to try to define it too precisely by form. The Japanese original has no rhyme and no punctuation, uses a stock of "cut-words," or particle words, that serve for expressive punctuation, and contains a much smaller number of syllables than an English poem possibly could. All we can say about the haiku form in English is that it usually consists of one sentence, often broken in the middle by a dash or colon, set typographically into two or three lines. We prefer the three-line form because it gives more opportunity for making use of line-breaking, which is a unique feature of poetry. Because the form cannot be defined technically in terms of English prosody, the matter of line length, rhyme, and metrical dimension must be left open. The student's attention is on focus and intention rather than on technical form. The best definition is probably not by form but by substance—the fixed moment. In any case, you begin not by defining but by letting students infer a definition from reading instances of haiku and trying to write their own.

Activity card directions can suggest that students either make sensory notes for a few moments each day for a few days or lift a moment from some of their sensory or memory writings. See pages 160 and 328. One second will do, some moment when a sound, sight, smell, taste, or touch triggers a strong response or sets a mood, releasing a feeling. There may be many such moments in their previous writing. Directions need only indicate that they use a moment to write a haiku or three-line poem; rhyme is optional; and no mention is made of meter.

After a small group of students have written haiku, they pass them around and each member of the group writes on and around the haiku of the others, with the understanding that this is for suggestive value to the writer, who may perfectly well prefer his version to the revisions. In comparing and discussing different versions, the students can see very well how almost every change of vocabulary, sentence structure, and punctuation alters image and impact, sound and sense.[3] Booklets of student haiku, we have found, are eagerly read and often discussed.

The Problem of Overabstracting

Haiku is an implicit rather than explicit statement of an idea. Like proverbs, haiku let metaphor state; they are ideas in the form of perception and feeling. The difficulties students encounter trying to write haiku are the difficulties they encounter trying to write most kinds of poetry. The biggest, most consistent problem—which we observed many times as various teachers, including ourselves, have proposed haiku writing—is that students overabstract. They see macroscopically, grossly; instead of caterpillar hairs they observe:

[3] See this process with haiku in the secondary-level *English Through Interaction* film "The Writing Workshop."

A warm silent lake.
On a calm summer day . . .
Wake up, back to work[4]

This ninth-grade boy's haiku is very typical of many efforts. First, he has generalized an entire day, instead of registering what could be perceived only within a very brief compass of time and space (it is fine calibrations of time and space that define concreteness). Second, he has named, instead of rendered, the sensations—"warm," "silent," "calm." Likewise, he has stated, instead of implied, the season and the time—"summer day"—and all but flatly asserted his feeling—"Wake up," "back to work." This overabstracton of both outer things and inner experience is the mark of amateur poetry and of much nondescript, ineffectual prose as well.

Why should such writing be the spontaneous tendency of a person this age? We are not sure, but we think two very important learning factors are involved. One is developmental: youngsters grow gradually away from crude lumping toward finer and finer discriminations of perception and thought. The other is conventional: most expressions of perception and thought that youngsters hear and read are hasty, inexact verbalizations of the real things people want to express. Familiar general phrases like "summer day" come out of us automatically and indiscriminately in response to very different moments of experience.

Some masking of particularity is learned from reading bad, vague poetry, and some is learned from thoughtlessly diffuse categories that adults hand down:

SNOW STORMS

Window's shuttered white
Children showing sheer delight
Oh, what loveliness.

This seventh-grade girl does not depict how the children showed delight, nor does she evoke the feeling she had. She simply labels both feelings. The fact that the title is plural betrays the abstract atti-

[4] Weeks Junior High School, Newton, Massachusetts.

tude. We are not criticizing the children (or the teaching), for the problem epitomizes the lifelong struggle we all undergo to make language match experience.

For contrast, let us offer what we consider to be a very good haiku, which truly notes reality. A tenth-grade boy wrote this:

Breath on the window-pane—
remnants of someone watching
others play.

That breath did not linger as a remnant on that windowpane for more than a few seconds—and that is the chief reason for the poem's success. But a lot of sophistication lies behind such specificity and behind the restrained expression of feeling in the last two lines. Because the writer puts us in the moment, we feel the poignancy of it, as we could not if he merely named a feeling we were supposed to feel. To help students as much as possible to zero in on a moment and to render it as they really perceive it, the most useful thing you can do is to say, "Catch a feeling that you could not have had several minutes afterward or several minutes before." The more students read of each other's poems, the more impatient they become with imitation; this peer pressure exerts a strong force in favor of originality. Students can help each other to sort the fake from the real.

But borrowing is also necessary; from a common stock of phrases the individual gradually forms new combinations of words. This need for slow metamorphosis was brought home to us by the following haiku, which was far more popular among the author's tenth-grade Exeter classmates than we thought it should be.

Green shoots take breath
and bathe in tears for
winter's death.

Whereas advanced students probably would have scorned its clichés, the tenth-grade boys liked it tremendously for its slick play of sounds, the regular meter of the last two lines, and the rephrased but essentially familiar imagery. Without judging their judgment, we thought about their reasons for enjoying it and realized that the poem had the same winning way that so many hackneyed but pretty Elizabethan lyrics have, the kind that are moving when set to music but are distinguishable one from another only by variant wording when examined as texts. Still, a student recombining old stuff in his somewhat new way is enjoying language, exploring it, and getting ready to make it do his will.

The breakaway from clichés occurs most often with fresh subject matter, for familiar subjects come replete by association with the language that others have cast them into. That is the kernel of the matter and a powerful reason for tying writing to fresh perception.

Here are two poems by tenth-grade boys at Exeter, both of whom began with their own sensory experience, not generalization:

> *Towels hung up to dry*
> *Across the road—*
> *It's raining now.*

> *Through the cracked planks*
> *of an unfinished house,*
> *one violet opens.*

These poems illustrate how the subtlety of haiku teaches the reporter's art of making an indirect statement by sheer juxtaposition—an implication by the conjunction of two physical facts. It reminds us of how powerfully focus alone speaks. The simple singling out of a detail immediately invests that detail with meaning, even when the diction is neutral and no attitude is otherwise detectable. Many photographs demonstrate this power of sheer selection.

Generalizing in poetry is not in itself bad. Abstract statement can sometimes spring feeling in a startling way. Shakespeare's phrase, "uncertain glory of an April day," for example, evokes fleeting cloud shadows and passing showers, because the reader fills in the abstraction with concrete details he remembers; as he does so, he feels the way he has felt on experiencing such weather. What makes this work is the unusual yoking of "uncertain" with "glory," plus a skillful prediction of the reader's associations. So students may sometimes come off

well using this sort of generalized wording. The test is in reader response, which cross-commentary can furnish. Class discussion and small-group reading should help students sort out mere vagueness from happy phrasing that is abstract but evocative. On page 378 is a sample of a student's philosophical epigram in which concrete objects are used symbolically.

Haiku is a form that lends itself to imparting a state of mind without departing from the physical facts. A ninth-grade boy wrote:

> *From the darkened heavens,*
> *Striking all around,*
> *Rain.*

By suspending the subject "rain" until the last line, he lets us be struck from the dark without knowing at first what is striking. The pattern of words conveys as much as their meanings.

Here is another by an Exeter tenth-grader; although it is focused outward, it symbolizes the inward experience, as in so much of good concrete writing:

> *A flash; and*
> *Thunder stops the*
> *Cricket's song.*

A number of students in one of our classes became especially involved in haiku writing because it gave them a chance to fix in words cherished moments of some activity they loved very much and knew a lot about. This high school boy was a bird watcher and very knowledgeable naturalist:

> *Emphatic song*
> *ascending through the woods,*
> *the oven bird.*

> *With bulbous eyes,*
> *soar above the pond*
> *the Dragonflies.*

When young people write, they work intuitively with rhythm, especially if they have experienced a lot of poetry. Unable to render the birdsong itself, in the first haiku, this boy captured the ascension (of the bird and the song with it) by sustaining a regular iambic meter, thereby illustrating what a text on prosody might explain in vain, that lines beginning on an unstressed syllable and ending on a stressed produce a swelling, lifting effect if the lines are relatively unbroken. His second haiku combines a stunningly salient detail with precise diction ("bulbous," "soar"), natural rhyme, and a tight, suspended sentence structure.

How to break the lines and whether to rhyme are important decisions student writers of haiku will have to make, along with any consideration about meter and rhythm. Most haiku tend to break, or pause, at the end of the first or second line or in the middle, a fact that students may be left to observe themselves. Using this kind of caesura in composing haiku will usefully influence their choices about sentence construction, punctuation, and development of image and idea.

Some students might enjoy following the "answering" haiku pattern, in which one poet writes a three-line haiku and another writes a variation of it or a response in two additional lines, having a caesura between.

Drawing Haiku

Another way to gain a perspective on what haiku can do is to draw, paint, or photograph the image in a particularly visual haiku and then compare this with others' pictures. Then discuss which aspects of the poem *no one* succeeded in conveying visually. The drawings might be done on transparencies, shown one after another with an overhead projector, and discussed. Collecting and posting favorite haiku with illustrations lead to a discussion of what can be rendered visually and what must remain in the words of the poem. This tends to show how much is word play or idea.

Comparing Translations

Students can look at two translations* of the same haiku side by side, read them aloud, and discuss which they prefer. This can be especially worthwhile because the translations of haiku differ so markedly in image, tone, and feeling as well as in the use of rhyme, pattern, and number of lines (two to four).

Matters of form and effect arise from the comparison; students may decide why they prefer one poem over the other and share their reactions with each other.

OTHER POEMS OF OBSERVATION

The comparison approach can also help bridge from haiku to other poetry. Being careful not to preinterpret too much, pair off a haiku with some other fairly short and concrete poem that seems to treat a similar subject. For example, one of us often paired Carl Sandberg's "Grass"* with a remarkably similar haiku, and Emily Dickenson's "Snake"* with a snake haiku, and asked students which they preferred. But pairs should be dramatized or given thoughtful class readings first. ("Grass" is a kind of soliloquy spoken by the grass itself.)

According to the poems the haikus are paired with, a number of interesting issues come up. Sheer length, for example, involves these differences: the moment versus time sequence, subtle suggestion versus descriptive elaboration, intrasentence versus intersentence relations, the single and sudden impact versus progression and development, the isolated verse unit versus multiple stanzas. What are the gains and losses of brevity? of length? Several times students have pointed out that Dickenson's "Snake" contains several possible haiku embedded in it, and that the climax is really a haiku. What these juxtaposed pairs do is set off the particular qualities of each poem; they induce discriminations valuable for understanding and appreciating many kinds of poems.

Like haiku, many concrete poems consist of only a few lines, some of them only a single sentence, like Robert Frost's "Dust of Snow," or Francis Frost's "Skaters," Samuel Hazo's "The Parachutist," and Anna Engleman's "In a Vacant Lot."[5] The principle of approaching them is the same as with haiku. The manner of presentation includes line-by-line revelation (see page 138), dramatized reading, juxtaposition, depiction, and so on. As with any poems, students are asked to *do* something with the poems, which should not be merely read silently, or rapidly in great numbers, but savored slowly and really attended to.

[5] See an excellent paperback anthology for older junior high school students: George Bennett and Paul Molloy, *Cavalcade of Poems,* Scholastic Book Services, New York, 1965. It contains these poems.

One of the things students can do with poems is to write short poems of their own inspired by the ones they read. They simply pin down in four to eight lines a scene or action they have experienced that one of the poems they read brings to mind. Encourage them to try out forms from the professionals. An inspiration might come from a striking pattern, like the one in William Carlos Williams's "The Red Wheelbarrow"—four stanzas of two lines each, the second line being always a single word— or from a subject, such as sports, animals, or weather. When students read other classmates' writing, they should acquire the habit of writing "poem" in the margin when they see something they think the writer ought to make into a poem.

Dialogue of ideas

A dialogue focusing on a topic or problem can be stimulated in a variety of ways and finally written up as a single-statement generalization, advice-column letter, scale, script, essay, and so on. Improvisations such as "Play the Problem" described on page 99 help students explore ways to deal with difficulties in their own lives. Because they are in role, they are able to examine the problem and explore solutions more imaginatively. After an improvisation they can write their own generalized statement of how to deal with such a problem; this might be a topic for a discussion, an advice-column letter, or an essay.

TOPIC TALK

Discussion not only in role but in one's own person as well is one of the best ways to explore ideas. Burning issues of interest to students, problems, and single-statement generalizations like those presented earlier in this chapter evoke discussion. They can be examined from a variety of viewpoints, as noted in Chapter 4, Talking and Listening.

Talk about problems or ideas develops thinking skills. One can learn to think logically entirely by talking. We would even venture to say that one could learn to *write* logically, for the most part, by talking. Small-group discussions and panels are critical for growth in the more abstract forms of verbalization. First of all, the very existence in the classroom of topic-centered talk implies that language can be used to think and to solve problems, which is a discovery for those young people living in an environment that employs language only for emotional expression and social traffic. Second, the interactions that occur during more abstract conversation help people to adjust and refine their thought and language. Discussion consists, in fact, of constant adjustment: words are substituted, sentences qualified, ideas amended.

You can facilitate this process of adjustment. Suppose the topic is "Getting Along in Families." Opinions are piling up on all sides, but no idea is fastened and examined for a moment. Students are agreeing or disagreeing too quickly, without knowing what the statements of others mean or imply. They are lining up sides, identifying with or opposing other students. Word meanings are loose and statements unqualified. You suggest that they linger over one statement: "Ellen just said, 'Younger children of a family get their way more often than the older children.' From what Bill just said it is clear that he disagrees. But look at her statement a moment. Is it *never* true? Is it always? Instead of just accepting or rejecting it, see to what extent you can accept it and to what extent you cannot."

In other words, suggest a *strategy of amending a statement until it becomes acceptable*—that is, of *quantifying* it and *qualifying* it. In regard to how many people is the statement true—all, most, some, a few? For what kind of people, background, circumstances? The qualifying leads to linguistic amendments. One adds: limiting adjectives and adverbs; phrases of time, place, manner, and condition; clauses of condition, concession, exception (introduced by *if*, *although*, *unless* and so on). Qualification of thought and elaboration of sentence structure tend to go together. Show that the group can correctly tailor a statement to fit what the majority thinks is true: "In America today a younger child is more likely to get his way with parents than an older child but is no freer because the older child restrains him in turn."

But disagreement may well continue. "Bill, what evidence would Ellen need to convince you?" The piling of opinions represents not only a failure to consider closely what others have said but also a tendency to stop short at assertions instead of supporting them. For a given assertion, ask them what evidence *could* support it. Is it supportable at all? If so, with what? Firsthand examples? Citations from authorities? Statistics? Help them to distinguish between disagreements that cannot be resolved by documentation and those that can. Often a discussion falters because none of the participants can support a stand. Tell them to bring evidence to the next session. If each can base his case only on personal experience, then what is that experience? Anecdotes may be appropriate for homespun subjects but very inadequate for supporting generalities of a more scientific sort. "How could you find out which of you is more nearly right?"

The best strategy for discussing a certain topic might well be exactly the strategy that students should adopt in *writing* about that topic. And this is the point: through discussion, students can learn together about handling some of the problems of abstract idea writing, from how to assert single statements to how to phase an attack on a subject.

Involved idea writing often results when a spirited but unresolved small-group discussion is taken to paper. The topic is whatever the unresolved issue is about. Such writing gives everyone a chance to rebut or get the last word. The main things to avoid are the "old chestnut" topic that invites cliché and the loaded or narrow topic that dictates content or position. Ideally, the writing of opinions and personal views arises from the classroom drama of ideas and comes at moments of light and heat. Papers can be fed back into discussion by projecting and distributing them. Rather than thinking of a topic in advance and prescheduling it, teachers would do better to seize the moment when a topic does not have to be thought of: it is staring you in the face.

Interaction between discussion and writing is essential. Generalizations plucked from student papers such as the essays presented at the end of this chapter should become topics for small groups. Many of the activities in the previous chapter will produce good subjects for idea discussion. When students in a writing workshop discuss the writing issues of each other's papers, they usually discuss the ideas as well.

ADVICE LETTERS

An advice column modeled after *Dear Abby* in a class newspaper or on a bulletin board is another stimulus to a dialogue of ideas. Students with real or pretend problems can write for advice, using fictitious signatures if they like, to avoid exposure. Other students can answer the letter and post or distribute both the request and advice letter. Students may be directed by activity to explore a problem, such as a littered playground or the limitations of the school cafeteria menu, and to write advice letters to school authorities, public officials, or editors of newspapers or periodicals. Wording these so they are appropriately formal, tactful, and at the same time forceful can be a challenging exercise in rhetoric.

SCALES

After a small group has discussed a problem, they might arrange their opinions along a *scale,* which is a graphic display of a continuum. For example, group members might range in opinions on how a parent should deal with a child's misbehavior. At the ends of the scale would be the most extreme positions on the subject they could think of, and along the line between these extremes could be arranged the opinions of the group members. Thus a scale might look like Figure 19.1. Scales may also be used as a way of displaying the results of an opinion survey. See page 368. After discussing a problem and making a scale to display the positions

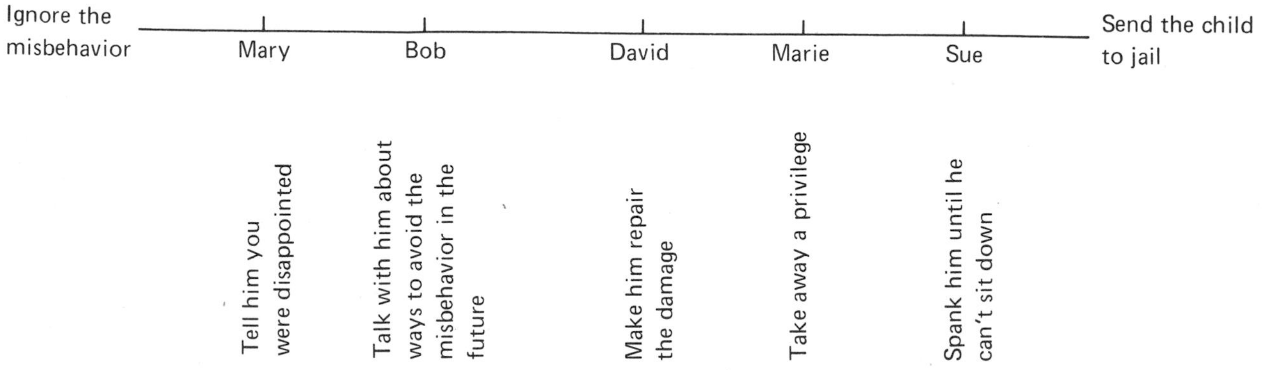

Ignore the misbehavior ——————— Mary — Bob — David — Marie — Sue ——— Send the child to jail

Mary: Tell him you were disappointed

Bob: Talk with him about ways to avoid the misbehavior in the future

David: Make him repair the damage

Marie: Take away a privilege

Sue: Spank him until he can't sit down

FIGURE 19.1 SCALE OF GROUP OPINION

of the group members, each person could write out his own position stating his reasons for holding that opinion.

SCRIPTS

Experience with dramatic inventing (Chapter 5), invented dialogue (Chapter 14), and topic talk (Chapter 4) should build students' confidence in speaking and sharpen their responses to one another's utterances to the point where they can develop in writing the intellectual, discursive aspect of dialogue. Drama and discussion are really just different wave lengths on the same band. Drama has a higher proportion of emotion, a lower one of thought; discussion has a higher proportion of thought, a lower one of emotion. To accomplish the shift from drama to a discussion of ideas start with a minimal situation that centers the action on a conversational topic, eliminate stage directions, and let the characters become less individual (approaching types) while the setting and topic become general.

When students choose their own topic or issue, they themselves set the abstraction level of the subject matter, in which case you might set the abstraction of the situation by stipulating that stage directions be dispensed with. Under these conditions a ninth grader wrote about teenage drinking:

PATTIE: Listen Rick what am I gonna do? Everytime Bill comes to a dance hes smashed. All he thinks of is drimking.

RICK: And just what else is there to do Pattie? If I found Bill tonite you could bet anything I would too.

PATTIE: But why? What's the sence of it? What if you get caught and taken to your parents than what?? You're grounded, can't do a thing. And on top of that your father is madder than . . . well you know.

RICK: It's one way to get away form everything. Everybody drinks anyway. My father drinks and I'd like to asked him how old he was when he started. Bet he was younger than I am now. In two more months I can get served in New York or maybe I'll be drafted. It's alright for me to fight or even die but when I'm on leave I can't even got a lousy beer. You just try and understand. I have my own

feelings and you have yours. So what if you believe it's no good?

PATTIE: Rick I didn't say it's not good, but there are places. Go out with the boys so you all get drunk at the same time and don't make fools of yourselves. In fact you wreck it for the rest of the kids. "NO MORE DANCES UNTIL . . ." Why do you think they say that? I'll tell you because kids like you get drunk, get rowdy and start wreckin' the place.

RICK: Listen I can't stop boys from drinkin'! I wouldn't want to because I enjoy it myself. So stop bothering me. Why don't you tell Bill yourself?? Maybe, *just maybe* he'll quit or something. But I know him and if I were you I wouldn't get my hopes up that he will! [6]

Personal interaction is rather strong here, but, despite the proper names, the characters essentially just represent two positions on drinking. Designating types such as Boy-Girl, Mother-Daughter, Adult-Teenager, and Student-Teacher shifts dramatic dialogue to a more abstract plane and parallels role-playing improvisations and mock panels. Also, in both the preceding and following dialogues, one can see how the absence of stage directions emphasizes a topic by reducing setting and action.

SHOULD DRIVING AGE BE RAISED

ADULTS: The driving age should be raised to around 18.

TEENAGERS: Why what good would it do?

ADULTS: It would put decrease in the number of accidents.

TEENAGERS: It wouldn't make that much difference because most accidents occur with kids 18 and 21.

ADULTS: That may be true but there are still a lot of accidents that could be avoided with kids 16–17.

TEENAGERS: In that case raise the age to 21 or 25 and stop almost all accidents.

ADULTS: Now thats going to far.

TEENAGERS: Its about as ridiculous as raising it to 18. Besides its easy for you to say because

[6] Lexington High School, Lexington, Massachusetts.

your'e over 18 and youv'e got your license. But you wouldn't say it if you were 16 or 17.

ADULTS: That isn't the reason its just that teenagers lack esperiance.

TEENAGERS: Everybody lacks experiance just starting out, Even if we don't drive until were 30 we will still lack experiance.

ADULTS: Another reason is that teenagers lack pride and respect.

TEENAGERS: We have just as much pride as anyone else and why have respect, we are always being put down, by the way we dress, and things we do etc.

ADULTS: Where is the pride and the way you dress is bad.

TEENAGERS: Kids take better care of their cars than adults. As for the way we dress, why is it bad, because you didn't dress that way? We think the way you dressed when you were kids was stupid too. Just because you didn't do it doesn't mean its bad or wrong.[7]

Giving the speakers generic names, or neutral names like A and B or One and Two is a device that may help students disembody the dialogue and thus to shift to ideas. One tenth grader put his dialogue, below, into the mouths of two personality types—the idealist and the practicalist. He chose the narrative way of quoting speakers.

I had been watching him writing for five minutes. "What's your idea?" I asked.

"It's about this guy writing an English composition," he replied without altering his activity.

"What do you think you'll get?" I asked laughing.

"Well, it follows the assignment and I know what I'm talking about firsthand—about a "B"—There, all finished."

"That's nice; I haven't even started yet," I said wryly.

"The trouble with you is that you want to stun the world with a measley English composition. Your chances of stunning even the teacher are only about fifty-fifty at best. Why risk it? Why not play it safe like me? Why lose?"

[7] A ninth grader at Lexington High School, Lexington, Massachusetts.

"Because It's worth it to lose for that one hope that you might win." It sounded trite, but I felt oddly inspired.

"So what if you 'win'. You get an "A" and that's it."

"You also get the personal satisfaction of knowing you had a good idea and succeeded. Less important but also present is the admiration you get from your friends. The infrequent gain is certainly worth the frequent loss. You also know that at least for a few weeks that composition is going to be remembered as something special and that you were the author of it. Even if it is rejected by your teacher and by your colleagues, if you think you have succeeded, then you have."

"What an idealist," he said disgustedly.

"On the basis just of my attitude towards English compositions, I don't think you can make an accurate conclusion. But I would like to think of myself as some sort of idealist. But everyone is an idealist to some extent."

"Not me," he said casually. "I'm a practicalist."

"If you are what you say you are, you're doomed to oblivion."

"How so?" he asked more interested.

"Take three examples: past, present, and future of the idealist and of a 'practicalist'. First, consider the past. I'm certain that you've heard of Miguel de Cervantes, author of Don Quixote."

"Yea, Look where his idealism got him—In trouble with the Spanish Inquisition for the greater part of his life." He thought he had me.

"You agree then that Cervantes was an idealist."

"Well, yes he had to be to write a book like Don Quixote," he said warily.

"Admittedly, Cervantes had a hard life in physical terms but we're discussing the question of oblivion, and even you are quite familiar with Cervantes."

"But what about scientists," he said trying to recover

"Galileo," I replied quickly. "Take Galileo. Everybody was sure that the sun moved around the earth, so he suggested that it was the other way around and was right. That's idealism for you in that he disregarded practical considerations in pursuance of what seemed an obsurdity, and I'm sure that you remember him."

"What was his ideal?"

"I suppose the ideal of every good scientist, the quest for truth. Then take the practical scientist of that age. He did the practical thing and read Aristotle. Everybody 'knew' that Aristotle was right so the guy made it through life pretty easily. But do you ever hear about some guy who did something like that? No."

"But things aren't like that today," he said desperately.

"Alright, take the present. You who claim not to be

an idealist will never be remembered. Sure, you can come up with practical ideas for slight betterment of your business that, if you're smart, will improve it through the years. But you're not going to do anything which you will be remembered for because any great ideas or inspirations have to transcend practical considerations. Your problem is that the details will guide your ideas whereas your ideas should guide the details."

"An example?" he said stubbornly.

"The Wright brothers," I replied. "The lightest engine made at the time was much too heavy for any of their aircraft and they couldn't afford one anyway. Notice the results."

"O.K., O.K., what about the future."

"Say that sometime in the future there should happen to be an atomic war and there were only a few survivors."

"Ha!" he exclaimed triumphantly, "where would your idealist be then."

"I agree that alone the full-fledged idealist could not survive. But as long as the others keep him alive, he will base that life on ideals and formulate the beginning of a perfect civilization. When that civilization has reached its peak, it will remember that man as the father of that civilization and will not remember the man who brought him water or food every morning."

"But what is so important about being remembered," he said flustered. The important thing is to have a happy life while you're alive. Once you're dead, you're dead, and you're not going to know whether you were remembered or not."

"No, the important thing is to die knowing that you have lived for something. Many idealists are not remembered. But they die knowing that they have spent their lives striving for that ideal of whatever their pursuits may be. Whether they reach it or not, they know that in their striving their lives had some purpose and that they were not just vegetables. For the idealist who is not remembered, he knows to himself that his life has had some worthwhile purpose. For the one who is remembered, the world knows that his life has had some worthwhile purpose but the important thing is the individual. Either way he can't lose. Hey, what are you doing?"

"Ripping up my first composition so that I can start a new one. Now to think of a good idea . . ." [8]

This mode of discourse allows the student to present in an entertaining way a dialectic of ideas

[8] Brooks Academy, North Andover, Massachusetts.

that is also, undoubtedly, an expression of his two selves in conflict. Certain dialogic poems do this: "Dialogue of Self and Soul" * by W. B. Yeats, "The Leaden Echo and the Golden Echo" * by G. M. Hopkins, "Ulysses and the Siren" * by Samuel Daniel, "Two Voices in a Meadow" * by Richard Wilbur, and "The Clod and the Pebble" * by William Blake. As these last titles indicate, the two points of view can be represented by objects as well as personages.

You might ask students to take two people who hold very different values and have them face the same problem together, or to give voice to two parts of oneself. See page 295 for more on interior monologue.

Writing dialogues of ideas should be interwoven with small-group and panel discussions. That is, sometimes students talk with others about a topic and sometimes they write an imaginary discussion alone. The dialogues are read aloud in small groups as scripts and expanded through oral discussion. This gives purpose to the writing and also reveals in a paper the rigged arguments, misinformation, omitted points or points of view, and so on, without necessarily impugning the author, who can claim not to be represented in his dialogue but will wear the shoe if it fits.

Values

Above all, writing this kind of dialogue should help a student proliferate ideas, examine matters from all sides without fear of contradicting himself, activate points of view he already has, and try out new ones. It provides a casual, expansive form for writing down thoughts before attempting to trim and organize ideas into an essay. It opens a face-saving way to abandon dogmatism and egocentricity.

We think that requiring students to shape thoughts into a consistent, logically continuous essay and then picking holes in their arguments retards idea writing more than it advances it. The important development for a while should be the exploring of ideas, not the constructing of watertight arguments. The fear of being illogical and inconsistent is very inhibiting when you are trying to find out what you think and when you still are only flexing your newfound logical muscles (at least in verbally explicit form). Monologic essays of ideas will be better later —more thoughtful, qualified, rich, and complex—if a period of dialogic writing is allowed as preparation. To buy a neat organizational job at the price of simple-mindedness is no educational bargain.

Transcripts* of public dialogues such as legislative deliberations, panels, or trials (see page 276) make good parallel reading for writers of dialogue of ideas. Sometimes students might find that a good way to write an editorial opinion for the class newspaper or a statement for part of a Readers Theater presentation is to begin by summarizing the ideas recorded in a transcript they have read. At other times they might summarize a recording of their own discussions. In either case, they are making a transition from dialogical to monological continuity.

Reflection

At almost any given moment, thoughts are running through your head—a spontaneous mixture of wonderings, wishes, conjecture, generalities, opinions, and other mental productions equally difficult to name accurately. It is this mixture that we will call, for convenience, reflections. By using this term, we would like to emphasize the reflexiveness of these mental productions; they are ongoing reactions to what is happening and to what has happened. As such, they flow in and out of sensations and memories, by which they are stimulated and to which they are linked by associations of either public or private logic.

But a part of what is happening now is this flow of inner events itself; reflections prompt other reflections and thus create what we call trains of thought. In unfocused moments our thoughts wander freely as we let various sorts of inner and outer stimuli draw our minds one way, then another. This spontaneous mental life is a rich source of material for student writing.

As Kenneth Koch demonstrated, wishes and dreams can stimulate children to some fine expressive composition.[9] The explicit assertion of wishes, opinions, attitudes, and ideas are neither fact nor fiction. Whether cast in prose or poetry, they constitute what is really personal essay, though the appellation seems stuffy and certainly need not be used in class.

Here is an activity for children or teenagers who

are not yet ready for the interior focus of the stream-of-consciousness writing suggested below but can benefit from small group experiences that help them become aware of their inner spontaneous associations, mental activity, and feelings:

- Start with a painting, photograph, or an object of the natural world. Hold a "concentration session" during which you focus your attention on your chosen starting stimulus, thinking together only about that one thing. Let nothing distract you. As you concentrate you may begin to see things you did not notice before and become conscious of the group around you, for all of you are focused on the same thing.
- Follow your feelings; keep track of them, for they are your natural response to the situation. Experience the picture or object and your group completely.
- Then make up a poem line by line, the first person writing the first line and passing it on to the next person, who reads that line, contributes another line, and passes it on. Do not break the intense concentration; this is all done silently. The last person adds his line and then reads all the lines aloud in the order written. Then discuss the best arrangement or rewording; add other lines or words as needed for the group poem. You may choose to write individual poems rather than one group poem.

STREAM-OF-CONSCIOUSNESS WRITING

We recommend this kind of writing for secondary-school students. The goal is to capture, on paper, chains of reflection. It is important for students to realize how some of the best thought and writing are prompted by stimuli one does not plan himself. By risking to write everything that is in one's head, a writer is more likely than not to get out bits of the very best writing he has ever done amid the pages of "garbage" as Peter Elbow calls it.[10]

Procedure

Stream-of-consciousness writing can best be preceded by writing invented interior monologue (see

---

[9] Kenneth Koch, *Wishes, Lies, and Dreams,* Chelsea House Publishers, New York, 1970.

[10] For free-writing exercises see Peter Elbow, *Writing Without Teachers,* Oxford University Press, Inc., New York, 1973.

page 288) because most students may need to project this flow onto someone else *before* they confront it in themselves. This way they can distance personal material, putting it into their invented persona rather than acknowledging it. Reading and writing interior monologues will, we think, make it easier for students to accept them as normal, safe, and meaningful. The mental set of students influences enormously how they react to any activity, of course.

These directions can be put on an activity card:

> Go alone to some quiet place and write down, for fifteen minutes, pell-mell, everything that comes into your head, using the first words that occur to you and without concerning yourself about grammar, spelling, form, and continuity. This should be a kind of fast note-taking to get down as much as you can of what you think, feel, and sense during those fifteen minutes. Keep the focus on the "right now" so you concentrate on what you are actually experiencing. No one else will ever see this, but it will be important for later work.

The point of quietness is to reduce the sensory stimuli and encourage an awareness of inner things —emotions and backaches as well as thoughts. Perhaps the students' own rooms would be good for the first attempt. Some may need to be convinced that they cannot possibly go wrong when recording; whatever happens is spontaneous, even when they write with one eye cocked toward the write-up. Peter Elbow suggests that the best thing you can do when a small group is writing a stream of consciousness is to join them and write your own along with them. Then you can share your writing along with the others.

After a group has written two or three thought streams they can select one of the papers and use it for a composition. The *emphasis*—and that is all it is—on reflection comes now in selecting from and shaping the spontaneous papers in the way described on page 334 for memories. The students can pick out trains of thought but without disrupting the setting or necessarily eliminating the sensations that triggered them, the emotions stirred by them, or the memories that may have occurred (some of which may exemplify the general reflections).

In other words, reflections are not simply sorted out, but the weight of the writing is thrown on them

by lowering sensory stimuli at the time of recording the stream, and by focusing on reflections when selecting for revision. The point is to act as secretary to oneself, not consciously selecting at all, and then only later, when acting as editor, to select. The reshaping and rewriting may result in a poem or a reflective essay.

One purpose of writing out the stream of consciousness is to provide each student with a sampling of his own verbalization that he can examine afterward in order to learn about putting things into words. For this purpose set up discussion with a list of questions that a small group can answer as they look at their own papers. With these questions as starters and the students volunteering short quotations from their writing, discussion can move into several important areas of language, semantics, and rhetoric. Here are some of the types of questions you might put onto an activity card:

> What did it feel like to do this kind of writing? Was it difficult? Is your mind ever blank? How did you decide which thoughts and feelings to put down and which to leave out? What standard of "important" or "interesting" did you go by since the directions indicated no topics or values or audience? Did you find yourself, despite the directions, trying to stay on a subject, find a continuity, or move toward a goal? If so, why? Did you use whole sentences or fragments? What kinds of words were most dispensable? Did you paragraph? If so, why? (What kind of logic determined new paragraphs?) Did you punctuate? Since no one else was going to read this, what purpose could it serve? What did you use dashes and commas for? Does your paper jump; that is, could someone follow from one part to the next? What would prevent them? In a month, would you be able to follow it yourself? Does it have any particular beginning or end?

Beginning in a private verbal chaos has the great advantage of letting the students discover for themselves the reasons and ways for moving toward form, communication, and a public universe of discourse. They might be directed to mark the different verb tenses they have used and to say which tense, if any, dominated. Distinguishing between the progressive form of the present, which records ongoing action, and the present tense of generalization, is an effective way of distinguishing sensory data from ideas. See the discussion of tenses on page 449. Students can be directed to label the contents of their paper by writing "sensation," "memories," "emotion," "fantasy," "reflection," and whatever other labels they think appropriate over the top of the original writing. Such distinctions may make them aware of the mixture of levels of abstraction in a discourse and of their different sources. The dominant tense is an index to the focus of their thoughts when they were writing; some students might have been fastened on the surroundings, some on the past, some on a dream world, and some on anticipation of coming events. They might ask themselves how characteristic this sampling is of their thinking all the time and how much it reflects present circumstances. This kind of awareness may be personally helpful to many students, and they are generally interested in this analysis because it is of their own text, although it obviously touches on universal issues.

Then comes the crucial question that pulls many of the previous questions together and that gets to the heart of rhetoric: What would you have to do to this paper to make it, first, *comprehensible*, and second, *interesting* to someone in particular you know (get a definite person in mind)? After they have thought this over and given some answers aloud, they may decide to make this paper comprehensible and interesting to a larger audience, in which case they should consider everything from word choice and punctuation to complete reorganization and reformulation of the content.

Sample

Here is a stream of consciousness written by a tenth grader who had difficulty writing, claiming she never knew how to begin. Compared to her self-conscious and awkward language production on other occasions when she spent much more time, her stream-of-consciousness efforts flowed more naturally.

I want to write for the next 30 minutes straight. It's really hard to begin. I'm scared, I haven't handed in hardly any writing assignments. I'm overdue 3. (My project is going to be a writing thing. It's got to be. I can't begin. It seems like I'd go nowhere, *if* I started. I've got lots of things important to me. I put those in my journal, far and few, they're important nonetheless. But how do I mold them into a story with a plot, developed character, and a universal conflict and them, symbolism backing the whole thing up. Where do I begin?)

I'm babysitting now and this has been a steady job, now in 2 weeks they'll be gone, it's kind of good, lately I get busier and busier on the weekends and schedules have been conflicting. I'm so glad I lost that weight before they moved. Everything, 3 yrs. is a long time. I remember the first time I was here, rocking Alexandria, then a blond 18 mo. old in green feety pajamas; in a wicker chair and that was the first time I sang what later evolved into "The Song; Our Song." Froggy Went A-Courting, and this year I made her a fluffy soft frog, so she'd never, ever forget. That one summer I babysat everyday for 2 weeks — she loved grapes and she'd stand by the frig. and say "bapes" which turned into "gbapes" and finally "grapes." One of the first signs of really growing up. What is really growing up? We're never finished, but people talk of it like it happened. Slam-bam-thank you ma-am. I'm grown up. Not quite, who or how could we think that? Mistake.

And now at most babysitting jobs after 5 times of babysitting the food begins to taste alike, the furniture and air get monotonous. Not here. Rare. And I remember thinking I hope I sit here again. On that first time when Bram was born, how exciting those last mos. 7–9 were. Bram was born naturally and they let me in on the whole process, everything that happened, was happening and would happen. I was fascinated. I guess my first real understanding of the miraculous complexity yet simple idea of a baby.

He was so ugly. Big ears, saggy eyes, have you seen a 3 week old kid with big purplish-black bags under his eyes? Bram looked just like he had a hangover all the time.

Now he grows up (more!) every time I see him, calls me "Kerner" [her name is Karen] just like Alexandra did.

They have a real Christmas tree. Ours is fake.

I have three brothers (no sisters). Sometimes my parents have 4 sons. Ken, 21, Harold, 18, Bobby, 13 (but he's a *real*, real jock, and is a whole lot bigger than me—he can press 150 lbs.) Harold is a frosh at college—Purdue. He hasn't spent the night at our house this vacation. Hestays with Mike (a 28 yr. old bachelor—who went to New Trier and his track record is still up at E.T.H.S. in the field house).

Well I was sitting in the living room and I noticed Harold's stocking was turned the other way. Face forward to the back. And I thought how perfect. He really isn't a part of the Xmas. Well he ate Christmas Eve dinner with us, a grand total of 23 mins., but I thought some more and decided the stocking symbolized his being in college, "growing up" and away from the "fold." Keep going. He never was an actual part of us, *too* freaky, messed up, easily influenced, funny and handsome, to be one of us. All this saddened me but I left the stocking the way it was, the way it honestly had to be.[11]

This student begins with a complaint, reflects on "growing up" as she faces the end of a baby-sitting job with its memories, and finally is reminded of the Christmas stockings in her living room at home which leads to her final reflection on "growing up" triggered by a concrete object. Her stream-of-consciousness writing can provide this student with material for memoir, reflective poem, or personal essay.

As we noted earlier in this chapter, some of the most valuable and interesting thoughts occur in association with other things, passing objects and momentary circumstances to which they are reactions. The connection in which thoughts arise is as important sometimes as the thoughts themselves. Consider a skylark or a Grecian urn, for example. In fact, it is often impossible to separate profound thought from the sight or sound that sets it off.

Lying on my bureau is my pay envelope. By the standards of the American economy it is very little. However, to me . . . .

So begins the paper of a girl looking meditatively around her room. How much more interesting an opening than the pompous generalities that students dredge up for the teacher's benefit to introduce topic-tailored material.

REFLECTIVE POETRY

Encourage students to write poetry based on their stream-of-consciousness writing because most poetry depends on the kinds of personal and idiosyncratic thought and feeling that characterize a stream of consciousness rather than on the logically developed thought of dialogue of idea and impersonal essay.

[11] From George Seidenbecker's class, Evanston Township High School, Evanston, Illinois.

Most poetry is loaded with response, significance, or reflection. It is multileveled. The surface structure of many poems is narrative or description, but its deep structure is idea. See page 316 for ballads and story poems—both invented story. We noted in Chapter 16 that true stories could be written in poetry as well as prose. Some invented dialogue is poetry.

Lyric poetry fuses the thing described with the reflection on it. This kind of simultaneous expression contrasts with personal essay, which takes off from objects or events and reflects on them. In an essay, thought and feeling are more separately stated. In lyric poetry description itself is loaded by spare use of some explicit naming or phrasing; even if the stating remains merely descriptive it is implicitly about ideas. See pages 440–442, 446, and 458.

Beginners might try writing one of the shorter poetic forms such as the cinquain to shape the comparatively formless material of stream-of-consciousness notes. This cinquain by Mabel Meadows Staats is the kind that might crystallize out of reflection:

SPRING THAW

If birds
Return to build
Each spring when winter goes
Must you recall cold words and stay
Away? [12]

Mature students might appreciate a specific form such as the sonnet at this point to provide just the amount of technical constraint needed to shape the stream of consciousness. Let the students read and try writing sonnets that consist of reflections inspired by an object, like Keats's "On Seeing the Elgin Marbles," or pure reflection, like Wordsworth's "The World is Too Much with Us." * (Many of Wordsworth's poems have the quality of spontaneous reflection and are often entitled according to the time and place in which they were composed.) Students might want to try a sonnet in dialogue such as the

[12] Mabel Meadows Staats, "Spring Thaw," from her book *Bright Quarry* and reprinted in Thomas E. Sanders, *The Discovery of Poetry*, Scott, Foresman and Co., Glenview, Ill., 1969.

sonnet* from act 1, scene 5, of *Romeo and Juliet* by William Shakespeare.

Help students see that lyric poems are largely thought trains prompted by something seen or heard, or by the mood of a place. Keats's "Ode to a Nightingale" is a beautiful example, though not the best to begin with. For students who have worked with haiku (see page 379), reflection on an object will not seem strange. Keats's poem is actually an interior monologue, but meditative rather than dramatic, except in the sense that the inner life can be very dramatic. The poetry follows moment by moment the movements of a man's sensibility as he stands in the odorous dark of summer shrubbery and hears a nightingale pass. Many poems conform to the immediate concatenation of sensation, fancy, and reflection. Others, like Robert Burns's "To a Mouse" and Robert Frost's "Departmental" talk to and about an animal or object that sets off thoughts, wishes, and wonderings, or perhaps broad generalizations (Truth is Beauty). This freer association of sensations, memories, fantasies, and reflections can produce very good writing.

As a vehicle for ideas, a poem may be written as:

an invitation
a vision of hell
a vision of heaven
an invocation to a spirit or force
an address to a public figure
a response to a news item
an epitaph or elegy
a eulogy
a celebration of an occasion
a farewell to something or someone
a blessing or prayer
a prophecy or warning
a blues or lament
a lullaby
a letter of advice or thanks

One of these might be just the right vehicle for a certain student to say what he has to say. Be sure that your students read around in good mixed anthologies of poems that offer interesting instances of these and other similar ways of writing a poem*. Help them to become aware of this array of uses of poetry and of what opportunities this offers them for expressing their own ideas. See also page 261 and following in Chapter 12, Word Play.

The "cloudy symbols of high romance" of Keats's "When I Have Fears That I May Cease to Be" are like the concerns and wishes for the future that adolescents want to express. And expressed as a poem, such feelings are less embarrassing. Juxtaposing disparate things along an emotional continuity is licensed, and the structures of poetry help fix this personal continuity in the public medium of language.

PERSONAL ESSAY

This is the prose counterpart of reflective poetry. Much of the student stream-of-consciousness sample on page 390 is actually reflective essay—the expression of personal thought and sentiment. Students can occasionally recast a short essay, or a main idea or feeling from an essay, into a poem, or vice versa. As they work to express the same idea or feeling in both prose and poetry and other media as well—letters, diaries, proverbs, slide shows, collages, dances, songs, and so on—they test the potential of each form.

Reflective essays should help students get a greater feeling for the difference between informal personal essay that remains closer to the objects or circumstances that stimulated the thought and that bears more of the author's personal feeling and statement, and those essays that become more impersonal in tone and more formal in the formulation and ordering of the ideas. See below.

Students can read personal essays in which thoughts remain embedded in the setting that inspired them. After doing their own stream-of-consciousness writing, they will recognize it in the expression of reflections they read—sometimes whimsical, sometimes very serious chains of thought that are not meant to be proved or documented. They can read essays by syndicated columnists in the newspapers or special departments or sections in magazines such as the "American Notes" section of *Time.* Mature students can read books like Barry Commoner's *Science and Survival,* Paul Goodman's *Growing Up Absurd*, Leslie B. Tanner's collection *Voices from Women's Liberation*, or Henry David Thoreau's *A Week on the Concord and Merrimack Rivers.*

Impersonal essay

We are using the word *essay* in the original sense that Montaigne gave it of an effort or trial to understand something or to render an idea. Students who have had experience with the other types of generalization outlined in this chapter can then move to essay—first to the personal and less formally organized essay and finally to the more intellectually structured essay, increasingly removed from the personal circumstances that prompted the ideas. There is a continuity between personal and impersonal essay, of course. Poems like Tennyson's "In Memoriam" illustrate each at different points throughout the work. Students will be better able to recognize this if they have spotted it in their own writing.

The language issue in an impersonal essay is how to assert, support, and connect generalizations. This process is both logical and rhetorical, for while the writer is classifying and syllogizing, he is also patterning and phrasing his ideas for maximum effect on a reader. The past tense of narrative will sometimes remain important for purposes of illustration and documentation. But such lower-order discourse is embedded in higher-order discourse through the relation of instance to generality. The following series of activities does not begin in impersonal essay but leads into it. It follows abstraction levels as discussed in Chapter 1, Basic Concepts, and detailed in the section on tenses in Chapter 22, Detecting Growth, (page 449) and in the section on discourse there (page 454).

THEMATIC COLLECTION OF INCIDENTS

The series of reading and writing we shall now present attempts to push up the abstraction ladder from instances to single generalizations to logically combined generalizations. Topic talk in which students match memories or add anecdotes to illustrate the truth of an assertion help prepare them for this type of writing.

Tell briefly several different incidents that seem to you to have something in common, that are joined in your mind by some theme or idea. Perhaps they all show the same thing. You may draw these incidents both from your personal knowledge and from your reading. State the theme only as much as you think you need to.

In order to illustrate the process most clearly we have chosen as an example a very successful paper written by an eleventh-grade boy in a class one of us taught at Exeter.

NOISE IS A TOLL OF THE DEVIL, OR QUIETNESS IS NEXT TO GODLINESS

It's well before eight; the tremendous hall is absolutely vacant; the students haven't started filling it yet. I'm on a bench way off in a corner, quiet because I'm occupied with watching and recording what goes on. Someone comes up the stairs towards chapel, snapping his fingers in the emptiness of the hallway. He comes through an entrance, still snapping his fingers and whistling between his teeth softly and tunelessly. He sits down, and as the squeak of the bench fades into deep silence, he gazes uneasily about, then begins pounding out a rhythm on the bench and on his hymnal. This sustains him until some friends come slowly in; he calls to them, then converses.

In church Sunday the guest minister sits back, then at the end of the sermon hymn, gets up and goes to the podium. For a long minute and a half he stands there looking down, saying nothing. The congregation shifts uneasily in seats, wondering "What's the matter? Doesn't he knew he's supposed to start talking? Doesn't he have a sermon prepared?" At last someone coughs, then many others. A whispering starts, each boy turning to his neighbor and discussing the situation. The time draws to a close, and the minister explains that the silence was calculated to produce a reaction, as it did, of uneasy noise.

Uncle Screwtape, a shade high in the hierarchy of hell, writes to his nephew Wormwood, whom he has been advising on Wormwood's work on his patient on earth. "Music and silence," he says, "How I detest them both! How thankful we should be that ever since our Father entered Hell . . . no square inch of infernal space and no moment of infernal time has been surrendered to either of those abominable forces, but all has been occupied by Noise—Noise, the grand dynamism, the audible expression of all that is exultant, ruthless, and virile. Noise which alone defends us from silly qualms, despairing scruples, and impossible desires . . . The melodies and silences of Heaven will be shouted down in the end!"

In Orwell's 1984 there is a gathering of all the adults in an area to a hate meeting—where established symbols of their hate are flashed on the screen, and the people looking at these symbols shout and rant and threaten and become bleating sheep. A chant rises from the group, a chant in which everyone participates with fervor, helplessly, and screams at the images. After a long time, they are lulled and leave, united and feeling fulfilled after their experiences together, better citizens for their society.

A few nights ago I had a tremendous amount of things to do—I was despondent and worried. From across the hall there was coming a large volume of sound —a record player blasting out surf guitar music, and eight guys shouting and laughing, two on the floor wrestling. For a few desperate minutes I sat at my desk trying to work, banging my fist on the desk and kicking the wall. Then, my always low power of concentration snapped, and I went in to join the fun. It was deafening, but I got so wrapped up and produced so much sound myself that I passed an hour, admittedly a carefree one, without even thinking of my work.

With all these examples I'm not trying to preach and show everyone how their time should be spent—singing celestial anthems or sitting in silent meditation. But I do always notice, when I'm asked to bow my head in silent prayer, how my thoughts wander frantically until they fasten on something I can day-dream easily about. I notice how embarrassing any silence is, and I wonder how long I could sit in an empty church and keep my mind free from earthly thoughts. I know how infectious noise is at a football game, and I've seen films of crowds watching Hitler and caught up in the chant. Noise is attractive, as Screwtape says, because it is distracting. Silence is embarrassing because there is no protection against oneself, no barrier that prevents trespassing into realms of forbidden soul-searching.

This is a crucial kind of writing, because it weans the student from organization by chronology to some other organization. He can follow a time order only when he is telling one of the incidents; since the next incident will be a new beginning, he must bridge by means of the idea. Doing this entails collecting several items that are similar in some way and putting them under the same heading, the items in this case being the incidents. Chronologic will not hold them together; some other logic must, some categorization of experience. If the incidents are summarized in a pointed enough way, so that the similarity they share is apparent, and if the author's classification is objective enough, the paper should be successful, at least logically.

For many students, narrative is a kind of haven that they are reluctant to leave because chains of events have a ready-made organization whereas exposition requires that the student create and assert a new order. This assignment is transitional: the order in which the student places the several inci-

dents may not be important, but they all illustrate the same theme and he needs to find some way of getting from one incident to the next.

Issues for the Writing Workshop

Group discussion of the first drafts should test an author's classification against the understanding of the group. Further: Is there one incident that does not fit the theme or classification as well as the others do? Are some of the incidents summarized in such a way that their relevance is not clear? Does the order of the incidents make any difference? Would the paper be more effective if they were placed in another order? Does the author make transitions between incidents? If not, does he need transitions? (Would juxtaposition alone make the point?) Does the author state the main idea in the title or in a sentence or paragraph? Where does the statement come—at the outset, at the end, or during transitions? Sometimes withholding the statement until the end creates suspense and permits the reader to make up the classification along the way. He may even have to change his classification midway as he encounters new incidents, and this could be very thought-provoking. However, if the connections among incidents are too difficult to make without guidance, then the author should probably make his statement early in the paper or use transitions to guide the reader. Some discussion about how well the examples from real life and the examples from reading go together might be profitable also.

Purposes

A student who masters this kind of writing should not have trouble with that classic problem of coordinating example and statement, of illustrating generalizations. In general, examples are always drawn from a level of abstraction lower than that of the statement being illustrated. Frequently the examples are narrative. The difficulties are (1) summarizing the bit of narrative so that it will fit under a heading containing other bits of summarized narrative, and (2) finding an apt and accurate heading that can logically contain the examples assigned to it. The narrative summaries must be trimmed of irrelevance and worded abstractly enough to stand clearly as items sharing similarities with other items in their class. This is precisely what is required when illustrating generalizations in a piece of exposition.

Writing morals for fables and other highly pointed stories should help establish this relationship.

This project, furthermore, relates concept formation to composition. As in the freer kind of logical card games (page 472) the student creates a class concept of his own by clumping items that he sees as instances of one generality.

Writing About Reading Selections

A variation of this project is to have the student draw *all* the incidents from reading selections, possibly mixing poems, plays, and fiction. The purpose, of course, is for him to put the reading together according to categories of his own, but this experience will also serve him well when answering essay questions on examinations in other courses, now and in college. In fact, this and the following two sets of directions ask students to do essentially what examination essays require; it is not necessary for the teacher to imitate such questions as preparation for them. Students who can write from their own categories will certainly be able to write from the categories of others. And many examination essays are so open as to approximate this assignment very closely. Of course, some students will create categories that are too simple and shallow, but if their papers are read and criticized, they can have a chance to see this and to revise them before the final draft. When students do tie together the reading in their own way, the papers usually are more interesting—and certainly more educational—than when the students have to write on an assigned topic, unless that topic is one they have set up themselves.

Drawing Writing Material from Previous Writing

This activity holds the important possibility for students of drawing some of their incidents from their own previous writing. If they have been following this program and keeping papers in their folders, they should have a stock of narratives, some of which, in fact, would have implied or stated a generalization. These previously told incidents would need to be summarized and retold in order to fit clearly the category that would contain them. One advantage of further abstracting material they have already abstracted to a lower level is that students can then understand as they never would any other way how the raw material of life is processed by

stages into higher and higher symbolizations. Another is that they can get ideas for this present paper by building on previous ones. At the same time, finally, they are building their own knowledge structures by combining firsthand experience and observation with material from other sources and thence distilling a truth from them. Whenever possible, the basing of later writing on earlier writing should be encouraged. Activity cards can direct students to look over old diaries and reportage, research, autobiography, and memoir (any sensory and memory material) and cull generalizations they made, then try some of these out in their minds. Are there other incidents from reading or real life that illustrate or substantiate the generalization?

Perhaps you noticed that the process we just described is demonstrated in "Noise Is a Toll of the Devil." The first paragraph was drawn from a sensory recording, as he indicates in the paper. In fact, the special attention he paid to what happened in the interlude before chapel began gave him an insight to which he could later assimilate his reading and other experiences.

Published equivalents of these thematic collections are apt to be personal essays, whether called that or not. A simple example is de Maupassant's "Fear."

GENERALIZATION SUPPORTED BY INSTANCES

A *generalization* is a statement cast into the present tense. It summarizes instances into an abstract deduction or postulate, something the speaker or writer asserts to be true. To generate such a statement and evidence to support it, an activity card can direct students to:

> Make a general statement about some aspect of people's behavior that from your own observations seems true to you. Use a number of examples to illustrate your generalization. Draw your examples from among the things you have observed and read about that led you to this generalization in the first place.

This process essentially just shifts the ratio between instance and generality. The main purpose of it is to throw the emphasis definitely on ideas. Illustrations are distinctly subordinated, and paragraphing follows a logic inherent in the generalization. Although the task calls mainly for an assertion and examples, most generalizations break down in some way into lesser ideas or into variations of the main statement. Thus a typical pattern would be for the first paragraph to assert the generalization and for the lead sentences of the following paragraphs to make the substatements, with follow-up sentences illustrating them. But of course there should be no formula for such a paper. The first paragraph might consist of an arresting example that is to be explained later, or the substatements might lead inductively up to the generalization as the conclusion of the paper.

Issues for the Writing Workshop

Each student paper will embrace a certain segment of the abstraction hierarchy. Some generalizations will be on a very high level of abstraction, encompassing a wide range of time and space. If a paper contains no past tense, this means that the illustrations are also generalizations, though presumably of a lower order than the main statement. The issue for the writing workshop, then, is whether such illustrations *illustrate* well enough or whether they themselves are so abstract as to require examples. The highest point on the abstraction hierarchy in any paper will be the main assertion, and the lowest point will be the most concrete example. If the main assertion is high, such as "Men have a strong need for exploration and adventure," one would expect the secondary assertions and the illustrations to run high also, though they should still be well below the main assertion. But if the main assertion is something like "Older brothers are more confident than younger brothers"—a much more specific generalization—one would expect all the other statements in the paper not only to run below this one but to dip down into past-tense, narrative sentences, which are near the bottom of the hierarchy. *Concrete* and *abstract*, *specific* and *general* are entirely *relative* terms, relative to the master statement that provides the context for the whole paper. Illustrating is translating a statement down the hierarchy. What is a generalization in one paper might be an illustration in another. But if the illustration is not very much farther down, it cannot illustrate well. If it is too far down, it may be too trivial, relatively, to be persuasive ("My friend so-and-so joined the Peace Corps last year because he was restless" to illustrate "Men have a strong need for exploration and adventure"). The student must play up and down the abstraction ladder according to

the situation, jumping further down for illustrations, and then jumping back up occasionally for transitions or other restatements of the main idea.

As students explore these matters in discussion of their own first drafts, direct them to amend statement X, if they think it is exaggerated or "overgeneralized" or simply not true. What words, phrases, or clauses could be added that would make the statement truer in their view? Then: Do the examples fit? Are they specific enough, or are they themselves too general? Where did the author place his main assertion? Where did he place his examples? What determined the order of his paragraphs? If the order were changed, would it make any difference? Does each paragraph consist of an illustration, or are the paragraphs based on substatements? (So-called development is the breaking down of the main generalization into its variations or substatements.)

Some common faults are: letting an illustration run away into irrelevance (usually a narrative for its own sake); piling on examples that all show the same point; stringing the examples with weak transitions such as "Another example is . . ."; repeating the first paragraph as the last paragraph; and repeating the main generalization instead of developing it. Almost all of them stem from too simple a generalization. Developing the main statement through qualification and variation would solve most of them. Bear in mind that this activity does not necessarily invite development, and that illustrating a generalization naturally tends toward a string-of-beads organization. With help from each other, however, students can find a way of stringing the illustrations artfully and with as much development as the assignment accommodates.

Sample

An eleventh-grade boy at Exeter wrote this:

CHEATERS

Some of the golfers cheat all of the time, and all of the golfers cheat some of the time. That is an axiom that usually holds true. In the five years that I have been playing the game, I doubt if I've met an honest golfer. I don't care how scrupulous a man is in his daily life; put him on the golf course, and I guarantee his golfing companions will corrupt him.

Not all golfers cheat with the same regularity, nor do

they employ the same methods. For example, the seventy shooter could not use the crude methods to which the duffer, striving to break 100, must resort. Nor would the duffer profit by using only the more refined techniches of the par shooter.

As my golfing companions represent various degrees of skill, a description of their methods of deception should include most of the deceitful practices seen on the golf course.

Mick is the best of my golfing partners. He usually shoots around par and occasionally breaks it. For a golfer of Mick's caliber, the opportunities for cheating are few and far between. As he usually takes only four or five strokes per hole, he cannot rely on poor memory to reduce his score. If he is to cut even a single stroke, he must employ the most subtle techniches.

One of Mick's favorite tricks involves a shot hit out of bounds or a lost ball. The penalty in each case is two strokes. Mick rarely loses a ball, but often another member of his party will. When this happens, Mick will say, "Toss another ball out in the fairway. You'll be lying two, hitting three" (assuming that the ball was lost on the tee shot.) Mick know's the rules of golf, and he's fully aware that the boy is actually lying three, hitting four. Mick gives him this break because he expects the same treatment should he hit an errant shot. In the club house, when Mick is bragging about breaking par, his opponent cannot bring up that forgotten stroke, as he was guilty of the same sin.

Mick, also, is able to gain an occasional stroke through use of the "double putt." Any putt of three feet or less he deftly backhands in. If he misses, he says, "Guess I'd better putt that one. Thus, he gives himself two chances to make the short putt.

Most golfers who play regularly score somewhere between eighty and one hundred. Tom is a good representative of this class of average golfers. When it comes to cheating, he employs the same methods as Mick, but is also able to make use of a few others. Occasionally Tom will have a disastorous hole. If this hole is any worse than a triple bogey, you can bet that arithmatical error will eliminate at least one stroke.

The best way to distinguish the average golfer from the expert is that the average player rerely plays the ball as it lies. Tom, for example, always plays winter rules (winter rules allow the golfer to give himself a preferred lie by moving the ball with his club-head for a distance of no more than six inches). Tom not only uses these rules in midsummer, but also frequently improves his lie when in the rough. This is something winter rules strictly forbid.

Mike is the member of our foursome who represents the biggest class of golfers—the duffers. For him each round is a frantic struggle to break 100, usually ending in dismal failure. Mike has been playing for over five years, but still has not mastered the fundamentals of the game. However, when it comes to cheating Mike is a pro.

One of his favorite techniches is pencil pushing. This can be employed only by the scorekeeper and Mike is quick to volunteer to undertake this task. The pencil pusher simply reduces his score a stroke or two before marking it on the card. I would estimate Mike plays five to ten strokes better when he is keeping score than when he is not.

Mike is a master of the foot mashie. This shot is used chiefly when the ball is behind a tree or in a bad lie in the rough. It is of special advantage because it is never recorded on the scorecard. The shot consists of a light glancing blow by the side of the foot, which causes the ball to roll a short distance and out of trouble.

When a greater distance is to be covered, Mike finds the "pitch and run" effective. This should not be confused with another shot of the same name often used around the greens. Mike's pitch and run ressembles the foot mashie in that it is never counted on the scorecard. The shot is especially effective when Mike finds himself in deep rough, and none of his playing partners are looking. He simply picks up the ball and, with a flick of the wrist, tosses it ten to twenty years nearer the fairway. This is usually enough to give him a clear shot; if not, a couple foot mashies can be applied.

Cheating in golf is not limited to casual play. In my hometown, the city tournament is played under winter rules. One reporter, covering the tournament, recorded over twenty violations in which a player had given himself a preferred lie while in the rough.

A story I read a couple years ago in "Golf Digest" is the classic example of cheating. It involves two men, Sam and Joe, who were playing a match for the rather high stakes of ten dollars a hole. On the first hole Sam banged a 250 yard drive down the middle of the fairway. Joe sliced his tee shot into the trees and thick rough on the right. Previously, they had agreed to take only ten minutes in hunting for lost balls. At the end of the allotted time, Sam said, "I'll go ahead and play out the hole. If you find your ball before I finish, go ahead and play it. If you don't, you'll have to forfeit the hole." Sam hit his second shot into the middle of the green and was lining up his birdie putt when Joe's ball came plopping down two feet from the pin. Sam missed his putt and lost the hole to Joe's birdie. Completely unnerved, Sam dropped the next three holes. Who could blame him for being upset. After all, he had Joe's ball in his pocket.

The only group of golfers who play the game entirely honestly are the professionals. Of course, these men cannot afford to have their reputations ruined by dishonesty, but it is deeper than that. For these men, golf is a livlihood, and they have great respect for the game. Just as the banker, businessman, or lawyer is honest with his clients; so is the professional golfer with his scorecard. I have heard of several instances in which a professional has accidentally touched his ball, moving it not more than a fraction of an inch. No one saw this, yet the golfer reported it and added an additional stroke.

All this points out a basic facet of human nature. People rarely cheat in things which they regard especially important, such as earning a living; however in relatively minor things dishonesty is rampant.

One can see here the overlaying of one organization upon another. The larger one is based on development. The author moves from good golfers to average ones to duffers; then he shifts from amateur play to tournament to professional contest, the last of which allows him to end with a new version of his generalization—that cheating at golf is a particular case of the broader truth that people cheat at play, not at work. The significance of this order—the fact that shuffling the sequence of topics would make a great difference—is what we mean by "developing an idea."

Within each category of golfer the order of examples is not significant: whether pencil-pushing or foot-mashie comes first makes no difference except for ease of transition between them. Thus the string-of-beads organization is embedded within a meaningful progression. But in many papers it will be dominant, perhaps because the subject truly provides no development, perhaps not. Cross-commentary can help determine which is true.

The stipulation in the directions about human behavior is not necessary; people are simply the handiest subject to generalize about. Students can repeat this kind of writing with different subjects. At bottom, it is precisely the one that is most often given in school and college for practice in exposition and to "cover the reading." Our approach is different only in that *it stipulates the conceptual task rather than what the generalization is to be about.* Also, we have tried to distinguish this task from the next, which would build on it. If you would like to use this activity as a means of getting students to write about the reading, you could simply ask them to draw all their illustrations from the reading selections in question.

Collateral reading, generalizations on contemporary issues and other matters can be found in periodicals such as *Commentary*, the *Black Scholar*, the *New York Times Magazine*, the *Rican Journal*, and the *Atlantic*; and books like Eric Berne's *Games People Play* or Alvin Toffler's *Future Shock*.

COMBINING GENERALIZATIONS INTO A THEORY

We are using the term theory here in a somewhat double sense, the most important meaning being that the essays do not merely state generalizations but combine them in some syllogistic way, and the secondary meaning being that sometimes the ideas are also speculative, that is, extrapolated somewhat far from fact.

Procedure

In skeletal form, the main process underlying this final project can be demonstrated and carried out orally. Basically, the task is to write a paper conceived like a syllogism.

Take a generalization from a previous paper or a saying such as a proverb, aphorism, or epigram and combine it with two or more generalizations from other sources so as to conclude a further statement not evident in the original ones. Illustrate or document the generalizations.

To prepare for this kind of advanced essay writing students can hold several small-group sessions on working out syllogisms, that is, series of generalizations consisting of at least two premises and a conclusion. See page 452. For example, they might look at syllogisms* such as these and come up with their own, modeled on the same pattern:

All who are anxious to learn work hard.
Some of these boys work hard.
Some of these boys are anxious to learn.

Improbable stories are not easily believed.
None of his stories are probable.
None of his stories are easily believed.

They can begin with a single-statement generalization they have heard, read, or written in one of their own papers, come up with another one or two on the same subject and write them under the first one. Suppose they came up with:

Conforming is an unconscious part of growing up.
Conformity is necessary to society.
Conformity leads to harmful excesses such as intolerance and artificial behavior.

Activity card directions can then ask them to pretend for a moment that they all accept these propositions as true. Then they can write the following additions so they have this:

If it is true that

Conforming is an unconscious part of growing up,

And if it is true that

Conformity is necessary to society,

And if it is true that

Conformity leads to harmful excesses such as intolerance and artificial behavior,

Then it must also be true that
(Blank).

Fill in the blank. What is the fourth statement that you conclude from the first three? Propose several possibilities and discuss which seem to follow logically. Write these down too. Are several equally valid conclusions possible? Do you think that such and such a conclusion is a true statement? Narrow down the proposed conclusions to one that some of you think is false. Does it follow from the premises? If you think it does not, go to another conclusion that you consider false but admit is logically derived. Why then is it false? Now return to the three premises you pretended to accept earlier. Which one is false and therefore falsifies the conclusion?

Students continue to work backward and downward. That is, when an unacceptable premise has been identified, those who think it is false try to qualify and rephrase it. If others disagree with their changes they decide what sort of evidence they would need to settle the matter. Do enough of these

sessions to make clear the process of syllogizing and its continuity with their previous work in asserting and supporting individual generalizations.

Next they can write down and bring to their discussion groups other unconcluded syllogisms consisting of two or three premises about the same subject. The groups select one of these sets, amend the premises until they agree on them, and then discuss what conclusions might logically follow. Afterward, a spokesman for the group might describe what happened during the process and read the premises and conclusions to the class. Some premises will have been too unrelated to each other to conclude anything from, some will have yielded several tenable conclusions, and some will have yielded only one logical possibility.

The next directions on activity cards can be to combine generalizations into a theory. First, students draw as many starting generalizations as possible from their previous writing, reading, and discussion. The purpose of this is to let them continue to build their own thought structures on the foundation of their lower abstractions. Make it clear that syllogizing is to be the heart of the paper but that it does not imply any particular organization.

Issues for the Writing Workshop

The following compositional issues will probably arise for commentary during revision: Should the premises be announced all at once in the beginning or fed in at intervals? Should or can they be documented simultaneously? Each in turn? In what order should they be taken up? Is the order indifferent, or can one generalization be developed in some way from another? Do some premises need more documenting than others? Should the conclusion(s) be suspended until the end for climactic effect or posted at the outset to make the thread of argument easier to follow? Of course, a very complex paper might contain subsidiary syllogisms and thus two or three secondary conclusions in addition to the main one.

Project for classroom discussion at least one legible first draft or paper by a student. Read it aloud as the class follows visually, and stop for comment en route. When the audience feels that something is unclear, help them to determine whether the difficulty is in *the syllogistic drawing of conclusions, the statement of single generalizations,* or, farther down still, *the concepts contained in a generalization* (definition of a word, for example; but often the premises are themselves definitions).

Both these logical problems and the compositional problems described above should be touched on enough in class discussion to enable students at least to identify them when they encounter them in the writing workshop groups. *As usual, this raising of issues is achieved by asking the class to propose solutions for the difficulties they encounter as reader*, *restating their diagnosis for them when necessary.*

Sample

A STUDY OF CONFORMITY

It is often assumed that people consciously conform. This is seldom true. Conformity is either a process of maturing, or a subconscious development. In either case, it is the essence of society.

Conformity as a process of growing up occurs generally at an early age. For a small child it is natural to try to emulate grown-ups. The child attempts to speak as they speak, walk as they walk, and act as they act. Children often pretend to be grown-ups because of the natural desire to conform to the adult world.

This force decreases as age increases. It disappears simultaneously with the "loss of innocence." When a child, or even a teen-ager is exposed to derision or disillusion, his dream world crumbles. This, however, is often a gradual process. The natural instinct to conform, therefore, gradually fades away as the child becomes more and more exposed to the world.

It is very hard to say when loss of innocence occurs. Certainly, vestiges of it carry on well into the teens in many people. This may seem incredible, but it is true. The average senior high school American History textbook is still concerned with Alvin York single-handedly winning World War I and George Washington chopping down the cherry tree. The United States is always moral, always right. This unreality shows the extent that even high school seniors are protected from unpleasant truths.

When the illusionary world of innocence is destroyed, a replacement must be made. These replacements come in many different forms. Charlie Gray in *Point of No Return* finds himself in an artificial world of conformity. He dresses like everyone else, works in a bank like everyone else, rides the right train and belongs to the right country club. Many will say that Charlie must conform in order to keep his job. This is not entirely the case. Conformity is a replacement for his lost naivete, a means of keeping himself from falling apart. Only by conforming to his artificial world can he tolerate it.

Conformity at Exeter is obvious. The greatest objection to it, however, is the form it takes. To adults, the sight of a bored, lazy, apathetic boy is repelling. To them it seems a waste of what should be a happy, exciting time of life.

What these adults fail to understand is why the "innocent scared little prep" becomes a nego. The answer is glaring. If a prep comes to Exeter scared and innocent, his situation is soon exploited by his fellow students. He is baited beyond his ability to tolerate abuse. His self-respect and innocent values are destroyed. To attain any sort of security, these values must be replaced.

At Exeter there is only one possible replacement— negoism. To protect himself from being baited a boy must assume an air of indifference. If he shows that he is hurt, the smell of blood will make the sharks all the more vicious. But this is not enough. To prevent being baited a boy also has to destroy his individuality.

Superficially, most Exonians are the same. Their dress, general vocabulary and actions are almost identical. Even their values are the same. High school is great, Exeter is bad, parents and faculty are not reasonable or human, the Dean is a sadist, sports cars and liquor are good, and finally the purpose of life is the fulfillment of animal desires.

This behavior is condemned by the adult world. To them, conformity to the extent of loss of individuality is wrong. The paradox of the situation is never observed. It is the adults who have to belong to the right country club.

There is a rule in chemistry called Le Chatelier's principle. In essence it states that when a stress is applied to a system in equilibrium, the system must adjust to counteract the stress. This is also very applicable in explaining human behaviour. The world of the innocent is a system in equilibrium. When an outside force upsets the system, it is the system itself that must change. Whether or not the system changes to life in a grey-flannel suit or negoism is immaterial.

This argument should not be taken to mean that a person willfully and consciously conforms. That is ridiculous. No person can be objective enough in examining himself to be able to state exactly what steps he should take in order to become more popular, or less vulnerable to baiting. Similarly, nobody can control his actions sufficiently to truly fit the image he has set for himself.

Instead, conformity is a sub-conscious attempt to gain security. It is an adjustment to the demands of society. For most people, it is a natural reaction. Because of this, there are very few non-conformists in the world.

Due to the variance in the extent of the stress on different people, conformity comes in varying degrees. In cases of great stress, there exists a case of over-conformity. Over-conformity is a concept, not a scientifically defined segment of behavior. The symptoms of over-conformity are easily detectable. Artificiality of emotion, behavior and speech are the most apparent signs of the disease. Others such as inability to think independently are also prevalent.

It is customary for many writers and thinkers to repudiate over-conformity. *Point of No Return* is such a repudiation. Many of Sinclair Lewis' works reflect this too. In fact, the whole expatriate culture of the 1920's was against the over-conformity of American society.

Over-conformity is not attacked for the sake of attacking it. It is the result of over-conformity which is repelling. At Exeter the natural tendency is for a student to write a "nego"-style theme. This is not because the student really wants to write about Exeter negoism—most students try to avoid it. The intellectual sterility of the Exeter climate is so great, however, that this form of expression completely dominates the style of student writing.

Conformity is an inevitable product of society. To oppose it is to defy the universe. This does not mean, however, that conformity can not be controlled. Indeed, it is vital to the interests of society that conformity be restrained.

The danger of conformity is intolerance, as intolerance leads to a stagnant society. For society to be fruitful, intolerance must be suppressed. Conformity must be allowed only as long as it is tolerant. Unfortunately, this distinction is very difficult to make.

In the past, conformity has followed a cycle. A mode of behavior and expression is accepted, and gradually becomes the model for a society, to the exclusion of all others. The society soon ceases to become intellectually productive. A small group of individuals will revolt, but for a long time society does not tolerate them. Eventually, tolerance does increase until the new order replaces the old. This order, in turn, wears out to be replaced by another.

This cycle explains the various literary, musical and artistic movements of Western Civilization. To us, looking back, the cycle seems the best way of keeping our culture fresh. This does not mean, however, that society recognizes that the cycle is necessary in the future for the continuation of our civilization.

Many people dislike "modern art," "modern music," or "modern writing." They can not understand how it can be meaningful expression. They support the changes of the past, recognizing them as a vital part of our heritage. Furthermore, they know that at the beginning many of these movements were not tolerated. But at the same time, they oppose any future change. Intolerance is typical of society.

I predict that within twenty years, the styles of expression that are beginning to be accepted now will become a materialized movement, very possibly past its prime. It, in return, will be gradually replaced. The present movement, like all others, will appear well-defined with recognized advantages and disadvantages. When it is worn out, the advantages growing thin and the disadvantages becoming more evident, a new movement will be started as a reaction to the accepted style. When this happens, there again will be people who want to freeze progress.

Conformity is a paradox in itself. It is recognized as inevitable, yet it is never accepted. It is based on intolerance, and at the same time its very intolerance is both criticized and praised. It is a function of the complexity of society—the more complex the society the greater the demands of conformity.

Without conformity our civilization would have no foundation. Yet without non-conformity we would still be in the stone ages. Perhaps our complex, contradictory system of conformity is the only workable form of progressive civilization[13]

The three generalizations about conformity that we presented earlier as examples were, of course, drawn from this paper, and the reader can see for himself which conclusion the boy drew and where he placed it in relation to the premises. Cross-commentary would probably have helped him to improve the continuity in some places and also the balance among illustrations.

The frame of the paper is syllogistic, multipropositional, but this boy quite spontaneously embeds within this frame several orders of discourse of lower abstraction levels, through which he has already worked in previous papers. That is, after announcing two of his premises in the first paragraph, he narrows down to one in the second paragraph and for a long sequence of following paragraphs

[13] One of Exeter's main contributions to the intellectual growth of its students is in permitting them to write about its "intellectual sterility."

proceeds to substantiate and develop that generalization exactly as if he were doing the preceding paper in this sequence, paragraphs three and four dealing with substatements about conformity as a process of growing up, and the other paragraphs in the sequence dipping down nearly to the narrative levei for the instance of Charlie Gray, and then back up slightly for the more generalized (and digressive) example of Exeter behavior. Then he surfaces later for his third premise—that conformity is dangerous —without signaling it very well, and launches into another documented generalization that lasts nearly to the end and contains the digressive example of art vogues. The second premise—that conformity is the essence of society—is treated in undocumented and scattered fashion, reappearing in connection with the conclusion. This paper did not receive the benefit of any commentary before the second draft (except perhaps from a roommate).

Parallel Reading

Mature students can read books that present theory, such as Ruth Benedict's *Patterns of Culture*, Henry Adams's *The Education of Henry Adams*, Charles Beard's *An Economic Interpretation of the Constitution*, William F. Buckley, Jr.'s *The Jeweler's Eye*, or Arnold Toynbee's abridged *A Study of History*.

The *Interaction* booklets called *Essays in Reflection* and *Essays in Generalization* (levels 3 and 4) contain selections especially chosen to fit some of the kinds of writing and writing issues described in this chapter.

aims & assessment

S tating aims is a very important process, because statements of aims become the touchstones to which everything is referred. Means are chosen to fit aims. Materials, methods, plant, personnel, evaluation—all follow from key decisions about what people want. But people are Tweedledums and Tweedledees—alike and different. They agree to set up and pay for certain institutions such as schools because they want something in common. But how do you get consensus about exactly what kind of education everybody wants, especially when the people are both numerous and various, as they are in American school districts?

Two main issues

WHO SHOULD SET GOALS?

In a democracy, the answer to who should set goals is easy. Everybody. Everybody means all the stakeholders—parents, educators, other taxpayers, and students. Too often educators assume that they know best and should set aims by themselves. For its part, too often the public takes goals for granted, leaving educators to infer what it wants from negative reactions it makes to what schools have been doing—outcries, defeated bond issues, and so on. Their children make their wants known in inarticulate and even more negative fashion—by misbehaving inside school, by breaking windows outside, by "underachieving," dropping out, or withdrawing. Many problems of schooling could be much better solved if school and home worked out understandings in advance about goals. The best way, cumbersome as it seems, is to engage the community in a forum about what it wants. This is what the California legislature required all its school districts to do.[1] But the forum must be long and honest, perhaps perpetual, for the first results will almost certainly be shallow and will risk legitimizing those very malpractices that cause schools to be criticized in the first place.

Differences Among Stakeholders

How do stakeholders differ? A fundamental tension exists, for one thing, between parents, who have spent considerable time making their children the way they are, and educators, who have a professional investment in changing children as a measure of learning. But educators disagree of course among themselves about what should be taught. Warring factions in reading circles, for example, or competing schools of thought on teaching literature and writing, make consensus hard among teachers. At a famous prep school, English teachers could agree on teaching the classics but couldn't agree on what the classics were! Parents of different ethnic or economic groups seem to want different results from schools. Everybody can agree on the aim of survival, but to the poor, survival usually means the three Rs, for jobs, whereas to the affluent, it means personality integration, for sanity. Parents and children differ too. Youngsters generally want access to the world and

[1] See *Education for the People,* Vol. II: *A Resource Book for School-Community Decision-Making,* and other documents obtainable from the Joint Committee on Educational Goals and Evaluation, Assembly Post Office Box 83—State Capitol, Sacramento, California 95814.

outlets in it for their driving energies, whereas their elders fear this liberation of green energy and want to limit accesses and outlets. Students, finally, differ enormously from each other in their previous learning experience and educational needs.

The Community Double Bind

Even the same people ask contradictory things of schools without being able to see the bind they are placing teachers in. Many parents, for example, say, "Teach my child to read, but I don't want him to read that, or that, or that." "Teach my child to write, but make him spend his composition time labeling parts of speech, as I did in school." Sometimes citizens' notions of what schools should do betray ignorance and superficiality because their own education was not very good. So at the very root of public education is a dilemma that every teacher must understand. What you can do, or perhaps even conceive of doing, with students always depends on what the community will let you do with its children and its money. You are accountable to it for both. But if the community's knowledge is not equal to its power. . . . That is exactly the dilemma. Good public education requires good education of the public.

Far from being a reason to bar the public from goal-setting, community ignorance argues for an ongoing forum about goals so that while affording children a more enlightened education, school can continue the education of their elders. Conflicting values, self-contradictory demands, ignorant imperatives—these take time and good will to bring out and acknowledge, and doing so will further the learning of those adults who did not get enough from schools when they attended them.

WHAT IS THE LEVEL OF GENERALITY FOR STATING GOALS?

Eventually all stakeholders can agree on goals because they share universal human needs—if people state their goals as generally as what they share. Disagreement occurs when we translate our universal human needs more specifically than we are alike. One family, for example, may want school to teach exactly what's on College Board exams because it believes college is the key to success in life, whereas another family may feel that college does not ensure success because minority discrimination washes out the advantages, or still another

family may have an ideal of spiritual success that they feel conflicts with what colleges do. The Amish won a Supreme Court decision which ruled that their children do not have to attend public school because what public schools do works against the religious values they are trying to instill in their children.

If it is easy to say *who* should set aims, it is very difficult to say *how* they should be set. Traditions of democracy require that goals do justice to *all*, but traditions of individual rights require that goals do justice to all *differently*. Here again arises the dilemma of unity versus plurality. The conflicts and confusions of goal-setting come down to this: *at what level of generality shall aims be stated?*

Since some goals have to be assumed in order to discuss curriculum and methods, we have assumed those on page 23 according to our understanding of what will do justice to all stakeholders and to the nature of learning. Good goal-writing must move downward from the most comprehensive and cut off at a point of specificity that covers family aims, whether to master basic skills or to fulfill oneself creatively, to make out in this world or to make one's way out of this world. Our list of goals and objectives stops at a cutoff point that will also leave teachers leeway to use whichever methods and materials work with their students on an individual basis. It allows youngsters to make choices according to need, interest, and readiness and thus to practice decision-making in their own education.

Why objectives should remain general

Stating language arts objectives more specifically than the objectives stated for discourse and literacy in Chapter 1, Basic Concepts, is very dangerous, because it works against effective practice in speaking, listening, reading, and writing. We will array here the main reasons why we think this is true. But opposing specific *objectives* is not opposing specific *thinking* about how to teach, of which we hope we have done our share in this book. In fact we feel that having to think in terms of specific objectives puts blinders on the mind. *First* think through how to teach language arts; *then* think through how to evaluate it.

CONFUSING ENDS WITH MEANS

Goals and objectives describe activities. The activities we described as discourse and literacy goals stop short of being specific enough to be carried out by a student on a given day. What we will call "specific objectives" are activities specific enough to be assignments, exercises, or test items.

Here is an example of an assignment:

> The student will write directions for making something that a peer can carry out successfully.

This describes an activity that can be carried out on one occasion. As we will use the term, an assignment refers to such a whole, authentic discourse, in contrast to an exercise. The assignment above is still general enough to be repeated profitably several times. We can imagine one more specific, however, that students most likely would not repeat, such as to write directions to younger children for how to make a puppet. This assignment we would recommend, but not in the form of an objective. It contrasts with an exercise, which we wouldn't recommend in any form.

Here is an example of an exercise:

> The student will write a paragraph using comparison and contrast as the method of exposition.

An exercise does not stipulate a whole, authentic discourse but rather a substructure of the language like the paragraph or some process like comparing that does not ordinarily achieve any communication purpose in isolation. Unlike discourses, exercises occur only in school. They too can vary in specificity. One might, for example, say that the student should label the parts of speech of given sentences or make up sentences containing certain subordinate conjunctions.

Here is an example of a test item:

> Given a passage containing a simile, the student will underline the simile.

Frequently it is difficult to distinguish an exercise from a test item:

> Given a pair of kernel sentences with a common adjective in the predicate, the student will apply the appropriate transformational comparative rule to form a result sentence which shows comparison, and diagram the transform. ("James was helpful." "Bob was

helpful." "Bob was more helpful than James.") [2]

This activity could be asked of students either as an exercise to prepare for a future test or as an item on the test itself. In either case we do not recommend it.

Defining What an Objective Is

If any activity at all can be called an objective, as these typical examples indicate, then the notion of an objective loses meaning and utility. Objectives should express purpose and intention. They are breakdowns, it is true, of main aims, because organizing curriculum requires *some* kind of breakdowns, but to convert assignments, exercises, and test items into objectives by a wave of a wand, as some educators have done, creates tremendous confusion and disservice. Only by a misnomer can the exercises and test items above be called objectives, and even the more specific form of assignment—the once-only sort—comes closer to being means than end. And this is the chief issue. The more concretely objectives are stated, the more they say *how* to teach, not merely *what* to teach.

Real aims don't have to be warranted by anything but people's wishes, whereas methods must be validated by experience. Calling exercises objectives allows some interest group's preferred method to become locked into the curriculum on the same footing as true goals for which consensus exists.

Activities in a middle range of generality are admittedly hard to classify as either aims only or means only. Many goals are means to other, higher goals. To write well may seem like a goal in itself when viewed within the field of English teaching, but it is also a means to earning a living or expressing oneself, which goals are in turn means of surviving and enjoying life. How are we to distinguish aims from means in dealing with such activities?

One way is to filter out those activities that are clearly done *only* to further higher activities, like sentence exercises. Similarly, we can filter out all those activities done *only* to test other activities, like underlining similes. An objective must be done for its own sake, whether or not it is also done for

[2] *Objectives Collection, Language Arts, Grades 7–9,* Instructional Objectives Exchange, University of California, Los Angeles, undated, p. 127. This book was also an inspiration for other examples in this chapter of too specific objectives.

another reason. Another way to distinguish is to accept as objectives only those activities that *must* be done and to consider as methods those activities that are optional or alternative. Giving directions for how to make something should be required, but whether the directions are oral or written might be optional, at least for a certain age. Writing directions to younger children for making a puppet seems definitely an alternative to some other specific assignment aiming at the same goal.

When definition runs out on us, we can decide where to draw the line on the basis of the practical effects of converting an activity into an objective, since many activities of medium generality can be fairly considered either aims or means according to strategy. What happens when classroom activities are stated as objectives? Certainly it changes the way students and teachers behave toward the activity, because it changes how the activity is organized and processed in the routines of classroom management. To know the effects of objectives we have to know what will be done with them. This in turn depends on whether the curriculum is organized into one lesson plan for all each day and one sequence for all each year or organized by processes of individualization. Let's assume the first for a moment.

SWAMPING THE CLASSROOM WITH OBJECTIVES

The more specific the objectives, the more numerous they must necessarily be. If objectives stipulate exercises and test items, the sheer quantity of them so bureaucratizes a classroom that actual learning is seriously crowded out. Imagine the number of objectives it takes to cover all aspects of the language arts if they are stated as specifically as the eight subactivities of literacy on page 246 or the objectives to identify simile and to embed one kernel sentence within another. The number of sentence transformations alone that students might be asked to do runs very high. Many schools' objectives include each of the forty-odd sounds of English, the twenty-six letter shapes, and the punctuation marks as separate objectives for literacy. This amounts to splintering skills number five and number two on page 246 into nearly a hundred subobjectives. Remember that an objective is pointless if each student is not tested out on it. Not only does testing have to be administered for this vast quantity of objectives but results have to be recorded and re-

ported. The curriculum becomes one vast scoreboard as students get checked out on every subactivity.

Biasing to Offset the Quantity

By Narrowing Language Arts

There are three ways by which educators can fool themselves into believing that specific objectives need not be so numerous as to stall the classroom's real function. One way is to restrict language arts, however unconsciously, to the narrow range of language activities and kinds of discourse that we discussed in Chapter 1. If students talk, read, and write across the whole range of discourse, producing as well as receiving, the absurdity of trying to specify objectives to lower levels becomes rather quickly apparent.

By Not Individualizing

Another way is to ignore individual variation and make all students do the same things. Students can do only so many assignments in a given period of time. If they all do the same ones, the school does not have to produce nearly so many objectives as it would if different students were doing different assignments, that is, fulfilling different specific objectives by way of fulfilling common general objectives. At the more specific level of exercises, the quantity of objectives is kept down by preferring one method or medium of learning instead of including all methods and media that work. This biasing prevents matching student to method, individually.

By Resorting to Programmed Materials

The third way is to deliver education over to materials of programmed learning in which the distinction between teaching and testing is simply obliterated. Every activity becomes like the objective on page 406 for embedding one kernel sentence into another or for matching the long *e* sound with the spelling *ea* in single-syllable words. Teachers do not have to test out and report on students themselves, because the students do all that automatically as they are inched along the line of itsy-bitsy steps by the instructions. The price paid for this pseudosolution is a drastically reduced education, because any learning activities specific enough to be doled out in such small, teach-test units are themselves trivial compared to the main mission of a language arts program, even as conventionally conceived. Like the other two escapes from the dilemma, programmed materials solve the problem of too many specific objectives simply by limiting, to suit itself, what can be learned and how learning can occur.

UNREAL LEARNING UNITS IN UNREAL ORDER

A truism of education is that testing acts backward to determine the curriculum. Intended or not, national examinations dictate much of what local schools teach and much of how they teach. "Teaching to the test" expresses this truth. The way the objective is stated is the way teachers will try to meet it. If specific objectives break down learning on the basis of what is easily measurable rather than of how people function, then we can be sure that learning units will follow suit. The more specific an objective the more nearly it becomes a test question. The final effect is that learning units approximate small test questions. The assumption behind specific objectives is that if educators can break down learning into little bits, then surely students can put them back together again.

The Fallacy of Parts and Wholes

The fallacy is that a whole in composition or comprehension, or even in literacy, is the sum of its parts. A whole is the sum of its parts only in certain domains of inert matter, not of organic, living processes such as those of thought and speech going on in people's nervous systems. Composition is not the sum of topic sentences, transitions, subordinated sentence structures, and so on. Nor is reading comprehension the sum of vocabulary, organizational headings, and inferences. For a whole to be the sum of its parts the parts have to be fixed and discrete. The "parts" of comprehending and composing are relative and interactive.

Transitions and topic sentences, decoding and making inferences, are *variable functions* of each other. That is, the more one is a certain way the more the other has to be a certain way. A good topic sentence, for example, must often serve as a transition from the preceding paragraph as well as announce the upcoming topic; how much it can afford to serve one function depends on how much it must serve the other, and this is all relative in turn to word choice, because sometimes an adverb like *nevertheless* will effect a transition quite well alone, whereas other transitions may not be effected in

less than a sentence or two or even a whole paragraph. How much to spell out transitions versus how much to assume them is a major issue of composition and relates in turn to the kind of audience one has and how directly or indirectly one wishes to talk to it.

Similarly, comprehension depends on any number of elusive and intuitive processes interacting with each other at lightning speed as one listens or reads. One makes inferences on the basis of phonetic interpretations of words, but in order to interpret words phonetically one has to make inferences constantly about what the word sequences mean. People do not hear or see each word separately but rather skim the peaks of significance and assume the valleys of the obvious, all the time corroborating both the phonetic interpretations and the actual meanings by means of each other and other cues.

No Learning Units So Small

The crude truth is that *nobody knows how to specify learning units as small as those required by objectives specific enough to be exercises and test items*. Learning units must be practical, decision-making units. Decomposing composition into analytical units does not yield learning units. Nor can we teach comprehension by filtering out and teaching separately to those processes that work only when they work together. Objectives specific enough to yield tidy exercises and precise test items for easy scoring force us to fabricate unreal learning units. What looks efficient on paper is incoherent to the learner, who, when reading and writing, has to operate on all three levels of coding at once, in all substructures of the language at once, and in an enormously intricate network of decision-making that has to keep parts integrated within the wholes they function in. Furthermore, there is no way we can sequence artificial learning units into a series of experiences in the growth of thought and speech. Unreal units in unreal sequence is unreality squared.

Unscientific and Irrational Method

Though clothed in scientific principles, the curricula that have been created by lining up such specific objectives have no scientific backing in the research of language acquisition or of developmental psychology or, certainly, in classroom experimentation. If breaking composition, comprehension, and literacy down into small learning units worked, we would know so by now, God knows, for that has been conventional practice. The units of composition and comprehension that we *know* work and that *do* fit the practical learning facts, because they most resemble the goals themselves, are whole, authentic discourses. The further we get from these—and the more specific, the further away—the more we get into fantasy and the heavier becomes the burden of proof that advocates of specific objectives must bear. The only scientific curriculum is one based on how people learn. The logical atomizing gives a rational look to a specific-objectives curriculum but, because it forces educators to specify more than is true, creates a wildly irrational learning environment. Specific objectives create a manager's heaven and a learner's hell. This is not science but a science fiction.

Wholes Not Testable by Parts

Unreal units in unreal sequence, moreover, not only fail to teach the wholes that they do not add up to, but they also fail even to *test* the wholes, for the assumption that testing out parts one at a time will evaluate the target activities merely turns around the fallacy of parts and wholes and works it in the other direction. If learners cannot put the analytical pieces together to comprehend and compose, neither will evaluators be able to build up a realistic assessment of comprehending and composing by totting up the little test scores. But meaningless evaluation can go unnoticed a long time in a humming bureaucracy.

The difference in evaluating wholes versus their parts is essentially a matter of patience. Assessing general objectives requires many occasions over a long period of time and judgments by more than one person. But it is for that very reason a more objective evaluation.

Fragmentation Not Necessary

A very ironic self-contradiction runs through the whole mistaken line of thought. If a subactivity does in fact constitute a vital part of a large target activity, then logically any student who accomplished the larger activity that entails the smaller would automatically have learned the smaller. Hence evaluating the whole activity would serve to check out its constituent parts or subactivities, and specific objectives would not be necessary for evaluating. Suppose the subactivity is looking items up in the encyclopedia, a so-called library skill. A corresponding specific objective may look something like this:

> The student will look up an author's name in three encyclopedias and list three facts about the author from each.

Now, a number of good discourse assignments will ensure that students learn to look up items in the encyclopedia. One is for students to make a mini-encyclopedia on a subject they already know a lot about, because they have to familiarize themselves with the form of encyclopedias in order to make their own. Another assignment is to do a consumer's report on some item like flashlight batteries that requires in addition to the consumer shopping and surveying some technical information that can be found in encyclopedias. Both assignments *entail* use of the encyclopedia, and students will learn to use the encyclopedia without use of it ever being made into an objective. The specific objective, in other words, is covered automatically anyway in the general goal (page 23) of gaining access to all sources of information and in the discourse objective of sending and receiving Information (page 24). All that making this activity into an objective does is to wrench it from a discourse context that gives it meaning.

Limiting Learning to Partialities

The presence of a whole hierarchy of goals and objectives falsely suggests that objectives of all levels are all being taught to and tested out at their own levels, so that, for example, at the same time students are rearranging sentences in a dummy paragraph for better coherence they are also writing original compositions from the ground up, or that at the same time they are identifying the long vowel spellings and various punctuation usages they are also transcribing whole blocks of actual speech. Literacy, composition, and comprehension would be evaluated according to general as well as specific objectives. But if the main impetus behind specificity is to measure more precisely, why bother with the "fuzzy" assessment of whole acts of composing and comprehending? All the little subactivities are thought to be better measures and have to be tested out anyway. The curriculum shrinks to fit facile testing instruments, because if the small parts are what is actually assessed—the naming of sentence parts and the spellings of the long vowels—a teacher is safer teaching to those and letting real reading and writing go hang. Why not?

In actuality, the main target activities themselves are practiced little if at all. The specific objectives are assumed to express, only in more detail, the higher goals. Doing the little things will teach the big ones. The net effect is that the most important aims do not get fulfilled, and trivia take over. Since only the small activities are actually being taught, the hierarchy of general-to-specific objectives amounts to mere window-dressing and deceives all parties into thinking they are doing more than they are. The chief reason so many youngsters can't write today is that despite years of schooling they have seldom actually been assigned any real writing.

No one knows how to state specific objectives that will start at the "bottom" and lead up to such broad and deep goals as critical thinking or effective writing. The consequence is inevitably that such goals get shunted aside in favor of naming parts of speech or giving a dictionary definition of satire, which can be demonstrated on one occasion and ticked off the objectives list. The tail truly wags the dog.

Testifying in a hearing before an educational committee of the California legislature in November, 1970, Sheldon Myers, at that time Chairman of the Mathematics Department of Educational Testing Services, stated (we quote from a memorandum of that date):

> The current statements of behavioral objectives in mathematics for grades K–6 reveal a number of serious defects which would rightly prevent them from being accepted by the mathematics community. The first of these defects seems to result from the energetic attempt to achieve great specificity. The unfortunate consequence of this atomization is that the interrelatedness of mathematical concepts is lost and the statement is a tedious list of very trivial low-level skills.

SPECIFICITY VERSUS INDIVIDUALIZATION

Objectives for democratic schooling must be either general enough to apply to all students together or specific enough to fit all students individually. If general enough, they will have to cut off just above the level of once-only assignments, as we have in-

dicated with our own list of objectives. If specific enough, they have to specify so many particular assignments that different students may take on different specific objectives to the same general goals.

So far in arguing for general objectives only, we have assumed that all students would be doing the same activities and in the same order. Let's assume now a curriculum individualized so that different students are doing different activities at the same time and reaching the same general discourse and literacy objectives by doing different assignments. So far we have focused on objectives specific enough to be exercises or test items. Let's focus now on activities general enough to be good discourse assignments. What happens when the writing of a limerick or a recipe, the transcribing of an improvisation, the reading of a fable or diary are cast into the form of objectives for an individualized curriculum?

Different Assignments for Different Students

The number of good assignments for sending and receiving directions alone, orally and in writing, could easily run to hundreds. Think of only a few examples as diverse as carrying out oral directions for making paper origami constructions, talking someone else through the drawing of a figure you are looking at, making a puppet following written instructions, writing card-game directions for peers, writing other game directions for younger children, and so on. Surely, parents, teachers, and students can all agree on Directions, Invented Stories, and True Stories as general objectives that all students should aim at, but we wouldn't expect every student necessarily to write some biography or to read some fiction written in diary form. We have to expect, rather, that students will follow different specific paths to the same general goals. Traveling instructions, recipes, game rules, and the others all teach Directions.

Below the level of generality at which we stopped stating objectives, people have to specialize, because they are alike only that far down. This is the real point of individualization. Even when people are learning basic skills that are alike for all, as with literacy, they have to do so by different means and media. If students specialize by doing different assignments, and if assignments are to be cast as alternative objectives, then we need to write objectives for the thousands of worthwhile assignments in speaking, reading, and writing that would be right for different students.

Variation in Timing

Right for different students *when?* If committed to individualization, we need not order all these objectives into a single sequence, and indeed *cannot* if individual variation in timing is allowed for, because people vary greatly in their readiness even if they eventually do the same activities. The more general an objective the longer the time span in which it can be met. Over a span of many years, most students will have done many of the same assignments as other students but at different times. They will have repeated certain general assignments. They will have done a number of assignments that teach toward the same general objective and will have accumulated varying amounts of experience in the nine discourse areas and in the target activities of listening, speaking, reading, and writing.

Individualized Classroom Management

What individualization requires, then, is a classroom management that (1) makes available in any year all alternative assignments that any student might benefit from; (2) logs which assignments each student does over a span of at least several years; and (3) subsumes his specific activities under objectives common to all so that a teacher can counsel him in his choice of future assignments on the basis of his past work. Such a logging and counseling system is described on page 29. Recall that many of our goals for communication and language, on pages 23–24, aimed to expand each individual's range as far as possible. The point of such formulation is to take students where they are and carry them as far as they can go. This assumes a system whereby students log what they have covered and the teacher counsels them about what they might cover next.

If objectives are to be individualized, why state them in advance without the students? The realistic psychological fact is that youngsters do not choose activities in the way that schools write objectives for evaluation purposes. They choose actions they want to do or some materials or people they want to work with. Their objectives will be very specific indeed—like finding out how baby turtles are born!—not cast in the learning terms that schools need to use to monitor their operation. The youngster with this aim has none of the school's objectives above as his objective, and yet he may end by consulting an encyclopedia, observing nature, or interviewing someone who knows. If we settle for the general objective of gaining access to all channels of information, and if we let the student pursue the spontaneous objectives generated by his inclinations and all the ongoing influences of a yeasty classroom environment, then individualization can take place and we can translate his activities into our learning goals for purposes of evaluation. No conflict can or should exist between school and student goals, but we must expect the terms to differ and must plan to mediate between what educators see themselves as trying to accomplish and the truly bottomless specificity of individual objectives.

Charting what students have done and ought to do, and matching them off with the right activities at the right time—this is a formidable enough job without converting learning activities to objectives. Why prestate assignments as objectives when you don't want to require them of all students, when you cannot sequence them without being wrong for most students, and when you need another bookkeeping system? Once you admit that you have to match assignments to students individually by counseling and that evaluation must be long-range and cumulative, then specific objectives come as a harassment.

What you really want to do is check each student's literacy experience against the literacy objectives and his discourse experience against the nine areas of discourse and the four language arts that may be practiced in each area. You are not trying to determine if each student did certain required specific activities, because what is required are not *certain* specific activities but *some* specific activities toward each general objective—as many as each student can do, given where he started from and how long he has worked within this sort of logging and counseling system. A student learns far more this way than when forced to meet the same miniobjectives year after year but seldom allowed to do anything more important or at least to do as much as he might. However teachers proceed, evaluating still has to be figured out, and making objectives out of assignments does not help that.

Management by specific objectives competes with the logging and counseling system needed for individualization and keeps reasserting the very standardizing procedures that it was originally created to serve. Real individualization requires flexibility and the minimization of bureaucratic rites. All the traits of specific objectives—the quantity, the pre-statement in school terms, the fragmenting, the separate reporting—make insurmountable the necessarily difficult feat of meshing individual actions with the workings of a mass institution.

We have made the point here about specificity conflicting with individualization only with the example of objectives still general enough to stipulate authentic discourse assignments. But a system of specific objectives usually proliferates all the way down through exercises and test questions, because they are its logical extreme. At these lower levels the possibility of individualization is no more than ludicrous wishful thinking. A contradiction inheres in trying to *generalize* the treatment of people at *specific* levels of action.

Politics and economics of objectives

The public wants better schools for nothing more than what it is already paying in taxes. Public officials charged with education—such as legislators, administrators of state education departments, and board members and superintendents of local districts—want to promise to do this. Getting more for the same money means tougher accountability, it seems. And out of Detroit and Pentagon think-tanks has come a "systems approach" to accountability based on making aims into actual categories of a budget and on spelling out these aims in "behavioral" or "performance" objectives measurable within a very small compass of time and space. Only too eager to implement such a system are programmed-learning manufacturers to teach this way, testing manufacturers to assess this way, accounting businesses to budget this way, and computer manufacturers to report this way. Industry is ready to go because it invented the system for itself and lobbied to extend it into education on a false analogy between making machines and educating people. Pressured in this direction anyway by funding sources higher up in government and by industry, it is small wonder that education officials embrace specific objectives as a way to solve their problems and, often in good faith, the problems of schools too.

BETTER EDUCATION AND ACCOUNTABILITY

Heading in from the opposite side, on a collision course, is real individualization. For both the public

and the profession it represents the "better education" that the public will get out of the more efficient schools resulting from tougher accountability. Nobody is against individualization and nobody is against accountability. When the public official promises better education for no more money, he is usually filling in the ambiguous terms *individualization* and *accountability* with what government and industry have surrounded him with—programmed instruction and performance objectives, which are indeed compatible. Confusion about the meaning of *individualization* and *accountability* make it possible for both educational manufacturers and high-level public officials, sincerely or not, to propose what looks like the answer to public demand.

But what parents mean by *individualization* is roughly what it should mean—that their child does something different from many other children because the teacher has perceived that he has different needs and interests and readiness from many other children. Taxpayers don't mean the mechanical, ministepped programmed materials flying banners today of "individualization." And what taxpayers mean by *accountability* is also roughly what it should mean—not some systems approach with computer breakdowns fetched up from strongholds of technocratic esoterica but clear and simple evidence that continuing to stoke schools with high taxes is worth it when right now it doesn't appear so. Parents cannot see that what they're asking is not really what is being lined up for them. Nor are they in a position to understand that even when a school aims exactly at the real individualization they have in mind this aim is incompatible with the specific-objectives approach to accountability that some school may be committed to. Their officials may truly believe that their promise makes sense. Chances are that they haven't thought through to the fundamental contradiction between individualizing and stating specific objectives any more than the public has—or than most teachers.

HOLDING TEACHERS ACCOUNTABLE

As a teacher you have to understand this political issue, because those sitting in the hot seat of accountability will pass on to your classroom, usually quite innocently, this impossible bind. If so, you will be expected to implement a human-rights definition of individualization with a hopelessly ill-fitting technological device for cost-benefiting. Since this conflict may turn out to be your main professional problem, it is worth a great deal of thought. What leaves the door open for serious difficulties is that a community or administration can tell its teachers how to teach, right down to step-by-step details, and yet claim that it is merely expressing what parents want for their children. All it has to do is call a method an objective. In the name of accountability, legislators, school boards, administrators, and parents can hold teachers responsible for results in reading and writing and at the same time reserve to themselves the right to force on teachers certain methods and materials to achieve these results. This is intolerable. Even in the business world you're not supposed to tell somebody how to do his job and at the same time threaten his job if he fails. Being accountable means having power commensurate with the results for which one is accountable.

A Curriculum of "Your Own Choosing"

But what if teachers are told to write their own objectives? Isn't that fair? Not if they are forced to make them too specific. At first glance it may seem fair to require a teacher to say what he is trying to accomplish, then to hold him to his own objectives. It also seems fair to make him be specific. But again, there is a built-in trap to being specific that this line of thinking never seems to allow for. If you spell out your "objectives" down to the level of assignments, exercises, and test items, you will disagree, for one thing, with other teachers. No teacher wants to be held accountable for reaching objectives that some other teachers wrote, not without at least ratifying them. Consensus is very difficult, can occur only after long and honest forums, and must remain as general as what teachers think in common.

In actual practice, what has happened over and over when teachers have been asked to "write their own objectives" is that either a very few write them for all the rest, after paying lip service to consensus, or that the whole institution borrows objectives from an "objective bank," that is, from a repository of past practices where one district takes in another's dirty laundry. If hurried and harried, teachers send up to the office some objectives they have inherited rather than thought out. If new or timid, they merely convert into objectives the teaching conventions they think they are paid to perpetuate. Drowning already in institutionalism, most teachers assume that objectives writing is just one more bureaucratic hassle to shrug off as soon as possible in order to

get back to that stack of papers or that lesson plan for tomorrow. Without time and resources enough to grapple seriously with the many important issues of writing goals, the task force falls back on what is lying at hand—old curriculum guides, publishers' materials, the objectives banks, and pet assignments of their own.[3] Typically, the result is a compendium of error to the extent that the whole educational-industrial complex they are drawing from is precisely what tougher accountability is supposed to reform.

Whether biased unconsciously by spontaneous tendencies, or biased deliberately by some priority policy, any set of *specific* objectives that eventually gets put into total operation in a school will be skewed, in violation of both individual rights and fair representation, because only severe selectivity can prevent the proliferation of huge quantities that specific objectives bring on otherwise. In addition to inclining toward the past and the institution, specific objectives will favor some particular interest group or another—some administrators trying to tidy up learning for greater ease of handling, some teachers writing in pet assignments or a specialty they shone in once in a college course, some parents or other citizens asserting or repressing ethnic differences or just riding personal hobbyhorses, or some educational manufacturers influencing school purchasing.

The ironic futility of accountability by specific objectives is that by trying to nail down teachers so tightly it makes it impossible to hold any teacher responsible for classroom outcomes! Teachers should be told, "Teach my kid to read," and held accountable for that. Finding the means to do it is the teacher's job, and he had better sweat it out successfully. But if the community tells a teacher how to teach under the guise of objectives, then it thereby releases him from responsibility.

Too often administrators do not inform teachers at the time of writing behavioral or performance objectives that these objectives will become part of a district-wide or state-wide fiscal accountability

---

[3] For corroboration of this statement see Ernest R. House, Wendell Rivers, and Daniel L. Stufflebeam, "An Assessment of the Michigan Accountability System," *Phi Delta Kappan*, 55 (June 1974), 664. They also say "Perhaps our most unexpected finding was that the assessment program has little apparent value for any major group" (page 668). Michigan was the first state to install an accountability system based on specific objectives. See also page 433 of this book for these assessors' conclusions on tests.

system in which their worth on the job will be assessed by matching their students' performance against the objectives. Too late you may realize that you have to make good with a bad curriculum "of your own choosing." These issues of good or bad faith are complicated by the fact that a subordinate usually finds it hard to object to a superior's order. If the order unfairly threatens his job security, so may criticizing the order! If the order has come down from the state legislature or the district governing board, teachers must either give in, cheat, or organize an extraordinary lobbying effort.

Good Accountability

The public has a right to expect schools to pay off plentifully for the twelve years or so their children are supposedly being educated in them. Very rare indeed is the educational institution worth the student's time and the parents' money. Drastic reform must take place, and teachers will have to know more clearly what they are about. But it is simply not that difficult to evaluate speaking, listening, reading, and writing. These whole-target activities are what the public wants teachers to account for, and they should be assessed as such, not indirectly and falsely as sums of bits. The management of individualization proposed in this book should make daily observation and long-range evaluation feasible enough to provide realistic accountability for those large targets the public is concerned about.

Summary

Unavoidable contradictions exist between specific objectives and some fundamentals of democracy, individual rights, and learning that schools have not generally been able to face up to under all the pressure. The use of force has obscured what the use of reason makes fairly obvious. Goals have to accommodate the basic fact of life in learning—that people are alike only to a point and then are very different. The more you *get specific* the more you bring out their variation. Youngsters learn the same things in different ways and in different orders. Their parents can agree *down* to a point, then want specifically different things. Parents and teachers differ—but only *up* to a point. Leeway has to be left between main aims and the means of fulfilling them. Atomizing learning into meaningless and unmotivated steps is the final turning of the screw, not deliverance. It adds more institutionalism when schools are already dying of institutionalism.

What is needed is not more objectives but more thought. To some extent, specific objectives are a misplaced effort to educate teachers in the details of their job. Much of what is written into specific objectives is simply facts, ideas, and possibilities about language learning that someone believes, maybe rightly, teachers should know. Saying more clearly and specifically what one is trying to do does indeed help, not always in the form of objectives but, as we attempt in this book, in the form of specific suggestions about how to make individualized learning work.

Trends toward fascism by well-meaning people in a democracy originate, classically, in impatience with the processes of consensus and individual rights. It seems much easier to spell out to schools with the force of job insecurity the details of how teachers are to act than to state goals flexibly enough to gather in all differences or to educate teachers up to the demands of their very demanding jobs. The unwillingness to tolerate the frustrations of assessing high goals and to accept the necessity of patient, daily human judgments causes the curriculum to shrink to fit testing instruments unequal to the breadth, depth, and complexity of human learning.

The best way to reach a goal is never to take your eyes off it for a minute, to keep aiming straight at it all the time. Bad drivers peer down over the top of the hood at the pavement right in front of the car—and are forever seesawing rather dangerously back and forth, because the perspective is too small and they lose sight of where they are going. A good driver keeps his eyes fastened into the distance, which allows him to see at once both the far goal and the immediate way to it.

E valuating is a staple classroom process, but it must be done very thoughtfully. Much waste and much harm occur when evaluation is run off mechanically without considering its exact function and the possibility of negative side effects.

> Knowing a child's reading level or his competence in pronouncing initial consonant clusters or his ability to select the main point of a story from four options is of little value unless these data are collected as an aid to a particular decision. Collecting periodic data on reading ability, as many schools and school districts do today, merely for "knowing" what is happening is a monstrous waste of time and money and serves no purpose other than to create suspicion among politicians and parents.[1]

This chapter deals with processes of evaluation in relation to purposes. Be sure to read first Chapter 20, Setting Goals, which treats goal-setting and accountability, and to read, before or after this chapter, Chapter 22, Detecting Growth, which describes the kinds of growth in thought and speech that evaluation should detect.

Different functions

Language arts evaluation usually serves about five functions. It should indicate

- to the individual student how effectively he is communicating,
- to the parent how much the student is learning in school,
- to the teacher the needs of the student, for diagnosing and advising,
- to the administrator how good a job the teacher is doing, and
- to all parties how effectively the curriculum and materials reach their goals.

Too often educators expect a few standardized test scores to fulfill all five functions at once, and yet it is obvious that one type of evaluation cannot serve such different purposes. Students want to know if they are making themselves clear to others and understanding what others are saying or writing. They care of course sometimes for test scores or grades but only because adults do. Otherwise, they do not need the blanket judgments of themselves, comparing one with others, that parents seem to want. Teachers must have specific information to trouble-shoot and guide students, especially in an individualized situation. And if the teacher is assessed by the very same test scores that assess the student, this puts the teacher in an impossible position of conflicting interest. No one turns in a bad report on himself; if salary and job security rest directly on these test scores, teachers may teach to the test and precious little else, or simply cheat, or try to drive out of their class those students who score low. This sort of evaluation explains some teacher hostility to disadvantaged children, some of the recent proliferation of separate classes for the so-called handicapped, undue pressure on counselors to classify some children as mentally retarded, and large

---

[1] Richard L. Venezky, *Testing in Reading,* National Council of Teachers of English, Champaign, Ill., 1974, pp. 5–6.

numbers of "force-outs" from school. Far from guaranteeing students good teaching, tying teachers' jobs to their students' test scores creates a me-or-them atmosphere hardly conducive to learning. Finally, these same test scores cannot assess the curriculum and materials because they do not tie learning results to causes. If every activity or piece of material is pre- and post-tested—the only way to find out is by testing which parts of the curriculum are working well—then learning becomes so dominated by evaluation that little is left to learn and to evaluate!

How is it possible to do justice to all five functions, indeed, without letting evaluation take over the classroom? And how may different parties be furnished the right sort of evaluation for their purpose without crossing up the sort the others need? The best answer may be to follow strictly two cardinal principles.

The first principle is: *Each party should do his own evaluating*. Each party should evaluate himself for himself, and if he wishes to know how well another party is doing, evaluate that other independently and yet take account of that other person's self-evaluation. No one should evaluate himself for another person. Some teachers feel that letting students grade themselves is fair and "liberal," but actually it shifts unfairly the teacher's burden to the student and merely finesses an important issue of internal versus external assessment. These teachers exclaim that students usually rate themselves too low rather than take advantage of the self-grading, but that is not a good sign, and the student should no more be put in the position of evaluating himself for another's purpose than the teacher should. If good reason exists for others to have an evaluation of students, then those others should do it, availing themselves of the students' self-evaluation as *part* of their own. A dual inside-outside view makes for excellent assessment. But a student should evaluate his work only for his own reasons and by his own means.

Likewise, the administrator must size up a teacher's ability and effectiveness by more means than just such evidence as the teacher collects and passes up to him. This can be too self-serving when job security is at stake. Observations and talks with the teacher may be weighed in with the pattern of the teacher's activities and attitudes, with broad, consensual assessments of the teacher by parents and students, with student performance as measured by outsiders, and with student performance as measured by the teacher. Nor should the school or the system be judged by its officially promulgated results, which could cover up, intentionally or not, a low quality of education. Parents judge schools, in fact, not just by grades and scores but by what learning they can see for themselves when they observe and talk with their children. This is right and healthy.

The second cardinal principle is: *Evaluation should not dictate, distort, or displace what it measures*. It is difficult but essential to follow this rule, for to the extent that the institution breaks it, it defeats itself. Learning is the mission. The only goal of evaluation is to further learning. If evaluation ends by determining what is taught and how it is taught, by grossly or subtly turning learning from one thing into another not originally intended, or by simply appropriating to itself the time and energy that could be used for more learning, it is bad evaluation. Most traditional assessment breaks this rule.

Though tremendously overrated, the biannual standardized tests do not hurt so much as the daily and weekly tasks that are assigned only or mostly to get a grade off of students or to get a glimpse of what is going on in their heads—the quizzes, oral questioning, "reports," and so on. As we explained on page 22, school writing has been perverted into a testing instrument of the reading. The "marking" of papers in the name of evaluation has made generations of students hate to write even so much as a personal letter later in life and probably accounts, more than any factors of intrinsic difficulty, for the poor writing ability of most high school graduates. Writing is hard to assess, but the solution cannot be to replace it with mechanical exercises called composition just to simplify the evaluation. For example, dropping the writing sample from the College Board exams in the 1960s contributed no doubt to the decline in writing ability currently being deplored by college instructors. Constant testing for reading comprehension by oral or written questions makes students feel punished for reading. So long as educators give reading such negative associations, it is pointless to rail about the abominations of television and to blame such other factors. Until reading and writing become divested of the stunningly negative effects caused by breaking this second cardinal rule of evaluation, no one will ever *know* how well they can fare in competition with other media. Testing virtually kills off the very two Rs everyone is most worried about; then, under pressure from the public, schools frantically increase testing! The more score-keeping, the lower the score.

So we seem to face this dilemma: a lot of evaluation is needed, because a number of different parties and purposes must be served, and yet a lot of evaluation destroys the very learning it is supposed to facilitate. The two cardinal rules above have too much common sense to dispute, but they may appear to be unworkable. Indeed, many educators take the view that no way out exists except to compromise the learning for the sake of evaluation, on grounds that evaluation cannot be dispensed with, that doing without it will hurt learning more because then it cannot be controlled for quality. A narrowly programmed curriculum that teaches small things in small steps seems to solve the problem because of the claim that all the items are taught and tested at virtually the same time, but the kind of items that can be so taught and tested do not rise to a high enough level of mental organization to constitute significant education.

Evaluating without special testing activities

A solution does exist to this dilemma. The secret is to evaluate by means of valid learning activities themselves without making students do additional activities only for the purpose of evaluation. The most efficient curriculum allows students to spend all their time learning. It is perfectly possible to evaluate learning without winding up in the position of accounting for something that is of little account. The dilemma is unreal. The same passivity, paucity, and poverty of traditional classroom dynamics that make learning to read and write seem harder than they really are make evaluation seem like an inevitable parasite. The brute fact is that *ordinarily students don't do enough to provide the evaluator something to see.* But if students are constantly producing and receiving discourse in great volume and variety, and if the teacher is freed from emceeing to circulate and observe, then good evaluation becomes possible without resorting to special activities that detract from learning and make students hate reading and writing.

To understand this point well, consider the difference between assessing receptive as opposed to productive activities. If a student says or writes or performs something, an observer can see or hear it and make a judgment about it. There is overt behavior or a tangible product. No need to make the student do something further to yield wherewithal for evaluating. When a student listens or reads or witnesses, however, there is ordinarily nothing to show for it. In order to turn his head inside out to look at his comprehension, the evaluator has to make him do an additional, unnecessary activity that produces something—traditionally, answering oral or written questions. The more the curriculum is oriented toward the receptive language arts, the more serious looms this problem of evaluation.

Now, listening, reading, and witnessing may be followed up by productive activities that while secondarily permitting the evaluator to see and hear a student's comprehension are, foremost, valid learning activities that a teacher might assign anyway for their own sake. Performing, discussing, and acting out texts externalize reading comprehension. A teacher or other evaluator witnessing performances or sitting in on rehearsals and other small-group discussions of common reading may not only note well the points of incomprehension but have a chance to hear incomprehension itself discussed in some detail. Chapter 5, Dramatic Inventing, 6, Performing Texts and 7, Reading, contain numerous productive activities that follow up reading and are valuable for their own sake. Translating texts into other media, such as illustrations or film, demonstrates comprehension also.

Among other virtues, oral and written directions are by nature meant to be carried out and hence naturally lend themselves to translating comprehension into visible action. Enacting words, in fact, is the chief way that truly scientific researchers—psycholinguists, for example—employ to ascertain comprehension. It is for no small interest to us here that they do not measure comprehension the way schools do, by pencil-and-paper tests that translate words into other words; they go from verbal to nonverbal and thereby rule out the ambiguities involved in matching language to thought. They have subjects point to pictures or move game tokens according to verbal directions, and they watch what they do.[2]

[2] For example, see the *Interaction* game "Talk and Take," which Henry F. Olds, Jr. developed for a Harvard Ph.D. thesis in psycholinguistics. Each card that players draw directs the player to move a board piece, and each direction represents a type of sentence of a certain difficulty: "Move a circle to any orange space, but do not capture a

Simply including Directions as a category of discourse in the curriculum—how to do and make things—enlarges greatly the means of evaluation by increasing occasions for translating words into deeds. Using activity cards helps considerably also, because every time a student attempts to carry out their directions, he provides an observer an opportunity to assess his comprehension. In sum, evaluate comprehension mainly by seeing how students translate what they understand into either action, other media, or other words.

The same curricular changes needed to put individualization, interaction, and integration into the classroom will change utterly the picture of evaluation. Not only do they free you to observe constantly but they ensure the volume and variety that make daily observation the ideal means of evaluating. Even productive activities can be hard to assess if quantity is too limited. You may be uncertain how to judge learning from what a student says or writes or performs on only a few occasions but not from numerous samples. Similarly, if discourse is restricted to only a few types, you have no way of knowing what a student might do with other types and have insufficient data on which to base general evaluations about language strengths and weaknesses. Interweaving all of the language arts naturally alternates receptive and productive activities and allows one valid learning task to display what was learned in another. Consider, for example, a working party reading, discussing, acting out, and writing fables.

Finally, the pattern of decisions a student makes shows a lot about him. True individualization lets a student sift himself into those methods, media, and modalities he needs or prefers. You may decide, for your part, to intervene in this pattern, and that is part of counseling, but the point here is that by picking up on the spontaneous patterns, you can assess tendencies you would not be able to see if students were all following a standard, prescribed course. Much so-called diagnostic testing will tell you no more than this self-screening. Teachers who have worked with the curriculum described in this book say that they know their students as they never knew them under a traditional curriculum. This knowledge forms the basis of the most realistic and useful evaluation possible in the classroom, alongside of which standardized tests and quizzing seem slipshod and shallow.

Student self-evaluation

Let's go back now to the different functions evaluation must serve for different parties. How does the student evaluate himself? The very essence of the action-feedback model of learning is self-evaluation. A person talks or writes or performs for a reason and for a known audience that responds to his production. Partner work, small-group discussion and improvisation, the writing workshop, rehearsal and performance, coaching from the teacher—all these reflect back to the learner the effects of his language actions. If that action is receptive, it is linked to further action that is productive and hence can be evaluated by feedback. There is no other way, in fact, that people can ever know if they understand something than to take further action with it and see the results.

The curriculum presented in this book is so thoroughly committed to learning by doing, trial and error, interactive processes, and receiver-sender feedback that student self-evaluation is a foregone conclusion and takes care of itself without need of any more setting up than the activities and materials already built in. We are saying, in fact, that only by continual self-evaluation can practice make perfect, and that language arts methods consist mostly of human feedback systems. The effects of action should be reflected back by as many different people as possible, by peers, teacher, aides, and whenever possible by outsiders and students of other ages.

Teacher evaluation of student work

You the teacher have to assess student work not only for yourself, in order to diagnose and counsel, but to some extent also for students, as part of their feedback, and for parents, and for administrators. That is, what you perceive about students' work will naturally be of great value to all the other parties, because of your special, close observer position, even though they should also assess independently of what you perceive. But you do not need to do separate evaluations for each party. All you have to do is transmit the same perceptions to each in different forms.

---

piece unless it is a square." A player who moves correctly according to this direction has to understand both the logic and the language in it.

Follow the principle that evaluation is an organic part of your everyday role, not a separate function done on special occasions. Detailed, composite pictures build up before your eyes of what each student can and cannot do, needs and doesn't need. The beauty of what you see when free to circulate and observe in your own classroom is that it gives you a slice-of-life view of the truth, because students are not thinking about being tested.

You stand near a group discussing a story they have read together and hear a student defending an interpretation that shows the same literal-mindedness you have noticed in the way he responds to others' figures of speech in conversation. You sit in on a group helping each other to revise some limericks they have written individually and note what they are able to help each other with and what they are not, who shows confidence in his writing, who has trouble taking constructive criticism, and what aspects of poetry—meter, original fancy—this activity is helping different students in the group to understand and create. You coach a student as he reads to you alone a selection he wants to work up to perform for others; while using you for rehearsal he is letting you assess his decoding and comprehension skills. You join a group in playing a card game and can easily tell from the way each member plays how much he knows about long-vowel spellings, or how well he can classify items or manipulate sentence construction, or how strong is his memory or understanding of directions or social cooperation. Watching a group perform a rehearsed reading of a poem, you note when the interpretation shows insight or incomprehension. You stop for a moment to watch a trio improvising and see how well they listen to and pick up on each other's words and body English, how inventively they exploit the situation, the range of language and role they take on that is not ordinarily their own. You cruise by the bulletin board and check some new fables for old morals that a group has written, illustrated, and posted. And so on. There is hardly anything you do to facilitate the learning itself that will not help you evaluate, for in order to coach, counsel, and consult, you must observe constantly anyway. The same information you act on you can selectively communicate to student, parent, or administrator when you need to.

Active, involved students produce so much to judge that it is not hard to remember your judgments, and less bookkeeping is needed. Immersed daily in this richness, you have stronger, deeper judgments that you will not easily forget. You probably should carry around a little notebook, however, in which you can jot down specific observations. Gradually you'll find out how many such notes you need actually to write down. Involve aides too in evaluation. Ask them what they notice about different students and use their commentary to corroborate or complement your own observation.

Oral work particularly requires this ambulatory observation. Although many improvisations, discussions, rehearsed readings may get taped so that you can hear them out of class, many of them pass forever, and since you can catch only a certain fraction of what is going on at any one time, you need to overhear or sit in a lot. A major reason oral work usually gets so little emphasis in the curriculum is that it leaves no record for evaluation. Encourage students to tape-record often so that they can evaluate themselves and so that you may listen later if you were not present. It is critical not to slight, or let students slight, the many valuable speech activities simply because they do not leave marks on paper. Let all parties know that *all activities* are assessed *all the time*.

For help with evaluation of

Decoding, see "Coaching and Diagnosis," starting on page 219.

Spelling, see "Self-Diagnosis," starting on page 229.

Punctuation, see "Sequencing," starting on page 237, and "Reading Aloud," starting on page 244.

Writing, see page 246 and many sections of Chapter 22.

Vocabulary, see "Naming" and "Phrasing," starting on pages 443 and 447, and page 468 of Appendix A.

Grammar, see "The Case of Grammar," starting on page 19, "Stating" on page 448, and page 464 of Appendix A.

Performing Texts, see "Teacher Role" and "The Value of Performing Texts," starting on pages 106 and 120.

Thinking Skills, see Chapter 19, Ideas, and Appendix A.

The specialized chapters in Part Five provide many indications of what to look for in the writing and reading of various kinds of discourse. The whole of the following chapter is devoted to detecting signs of growth in thought and language.

INTERACTION ANALYSIS

Since students must interact a great deal to facilitate individualization, work out for yourself or with other teachers some ways of analyzing what happens in groups so that you can assess the worth of the exchanges. In doing so, you can evaluate both individuals and the curriculum. For many years, people working with group process inside and outside education have been developing various ways of doing "interaction analysis" of groups according to their emphasis—on the content of the task, the dynamics among members, the emergence of leaders, the roles that various individuals take, or the differences that changes in size or purpose or organization make. You can draw up a list of things you want to look for, then invent a convenient form for noting down observations. For example, some teachers working with this sort of curriculum adapted the form in Figure 21.1 from one of the experts.[3]

Some key questions for group discussion by which either individuals or groups could be evaluated:

1. Are students involved in various types of discussion—enumeration, brainstorming, comparing, planning, explaining how to do something?
2. Do students hear each other out and take turns without having to resort to mechanical means like holding up a hand?
3. Are students growing in their ability to elaborate on, refer to, question, or amend what other members of the group say?
4. Do students support their assertions by giving evidence based on firsthand experience, empirical proof, authority, or logic?
5. Are different questioning strategies suggested to help students catch on to their role as participants in a discussion? For example, students can learn to ask the

[3] See Robert F. Bales, *Interaction Process Analysis: A Method for the Study of Small Groups*, Addison-Wesley, Reading, Mass., 1950.

C. Group Discussion: Analysis of the Roles of the Discussants
As you observe a discussion or listen to a taped discussion, identify the role that each participant assumed, and record the appropriate number in the box.

Shows TASK orientation:

1 — Gives information, ideas, or opinions about the subject.
2 — Asks for information, others' ideas or opinions, or constructive critical questioning.

Shows MAINTENANCE:

3 — Supports, helps, agrees, jokes, to relieve tension.

DISTRACTS from discussion:

4 — Argues, inserts irrelevant information, shows antagonism, is sarcastic.

Example: Mary may assume several roles during a single instance of dialogue. She might, for instance, give information (1), express sarcasm (4), and ask for information (2), before the next person speaks.

Mary	1, 4, 2					
Tom		1		1, 3		
John			4			
Sue				2		
Jane						

FIGURE 21.1 A FORMAT FOR INTERACTION ANALYSIS

Source: Bess Osburn and Jeanne Shane, "Evaluation Guide" *Interaction,* Houghton Mifflin Co., Boston, 1974, p. 10.

kinds of questions mentioned on page 79.
6. Do students evaluate their own discussions—sometimes by taping them and listening to them later?[4]

See page 82 in "Topic Talk" of Chapter 4, Talking and Listening, for other criteria.

Again, for both individuals and groups, this set of questions for evaluating a writing workshop can merely guide your observations, as a mental check list, or be formalized on paper as a chart or table.

1. Are students responding to and revising each other's writing ideas, collaborating rather than competing?
2. Does the cross-commentary make students aware of their reader's vantage point and of alternative ways of expressing their material?

[4] Bess Osburn and Jeanne Shane, "Evaluation Guide," *Interaction,* Houghton Mifflin Co., Boston, 1974, pp. 7–8.

3. Do students sometimes compose together as well as critique each other's work?
4. Is the quality of student comments and suggestions improving?
5. Do students help each other make the content of their compositions more interesting and the structure more comprehensible?
6. Do students help each other catch faulty sentence structure and punctuation, but without concentrating solely on mechanics?
7. Do students make suggestions to help overcome sentence monotony, confusion of tenses, unnecessary repetition, obscure phrasing?
8. Can some students suggest sentence expansion, joining or disjoining sentences, using subordinate clauses, rewording phrases?
9. Do workshop discussions center on issues pertinent to the form of discourse as well as on issues common to all writing? [5]

See "The Writing Workshop" on page 154.

These samples merely illustrate the kinds of questions you might formulate for your own interaction analysis. The chapters in Part Two, Basic Processes, and Part Four, Developmental Reading, Speaking, and Writing, contain or imply more things to look for, and you will find yourself crystalizing your own questions. For some criteria of dramatic interaction see "The Value of Dramatic Inventing" in Chapter 5, Dramatic Inventing.

For other ideas on interaction analysis, see the work of N. A. Flanders.[6] From such experts you may borrow ideas, but we suggest you practice analyzing group process with a small group of other teachers. Listen together to an audio tape or watch together a video tape of some student exchanges, discuss afterward what you perceived, and develop criteria for assessing the *processes* of improvising, small-group discussion, writing workshop—what students are doing for each and what each is getting out of it. If each teacher supplies some material from his class, and if you critique these together periodically, you will generate for yourselves about the best kind of staff development possible. Pool insights, trouble-shoot together, and share the burden of formulating what to look for and how to evaluate these difficult but vital processes.[7]

WORK PORTFOLIOS

You should judge a student's writing by generalizing as many instances of it as you can have access to. Ask each student to keep a folder into which all paperwork eventually goes after it has been posted, printed, performed, or whatever. Besides compositions, this folder should contain drawings, tracings (in the case, for example, of younger children working on handwriting), punctuations of unpunctuated passages, crossword puzzles, and consumable booklets of the read-and-write or "Comics-to-Fill" sort. Actually, a box will replace a folder very soon if students are very active at all. Ideally, written work would be passed on from one year to another, or at least some selection of it, not only so that teachers can counsel on a more informed basis, but also so that students can look back over their work and sometimes use an old composition as a starter for a new one.

Review this folder or box periodically, before a conference or when you have to make reports. Some of the compositions you will know already from having seen them performed, from reading them posted, from hearing them discussed in a writing workshop, or from simply having read them alone for a conference. Other of the compositions you will encounter for the first time during your review. Students need to write more than you can process, and papers should not be simply gathered and "marked" or "corrected." They should be used first, as intended, then accumulated in the folder, sometimes after dittoing. Most commentary written on papers is wasted. It is better to confer periodically with individuals about their writing, at which time you can talk about both particular papers and general tendencies. We recommend a mixed approach. Give some of your feedback during writing workshops, some during conferences, and some via written comments on papers.

---

[5] Osburn and Shane, pp 11–12.

[6] For example: N. A. Flanders, *Teacher Influence, Pupil Attitudes, and Achievement: Studies in Interaction Analysis,* Final Report, Cooperative Research Bureau Project No. 397, University of Minnesota, Minneapolis, 1960.

[7] The *English Through Interaction* series of classroom documentary films—nine for elementary, nine for secondary—were shot in various schools around the country just to provide discussion pieces for teacher pre-service and in-service and to serve as models for schools to make their own films or video tapes for the same purpose.

Even if your school gives letter grades, you do not have to write letter grades on papers. Make comments on papers mostly descriptive and functional; pass judgment only to the extent that it serves a really good psychological purpose. Then for a grade make a blanket judgment on the whole of a student's written work for the marking period. This is easy to do when you look it all over at once, because then you can spot traits and trends in a student's writing that might well escape you marking one paper at a time, especially if you had less writing to judge by. In this way you can allow plentiful writing and still assess it. Bookkeeping is minimal. This assessment of writing would then of course be added in to assessments you make of oral work and reading.

Grades may be made up independently of any particular curriculum and may be done in myriad ways. The best way is not to give a grade to individual activities but only to the totality of a student's work. Students unused to purely utilitarian feedback may experience some frustration for a while, but they will get used to it. Once a school has operated this way beyond the memory of its current student body, most students will not even require adjustment. Utilitarian feedback implies value judgments anyway, but if value judgment is minimized in favor of relating a learner's intents to his effects, the learner stays focused on the intrinsic learning issues instead of on grades. You can distill value judgments to satisfy parents and the institution from the evaluation you do anyway for purposes of diagnosis and counseling. Reporting that permits descriptive statements about a student's strengths, weaknesses, needs, natural tendencies, and so on (qualitative evaluation) will do more good than a letter or number on a report card, since it informs parents better and better facilitates administrative decisions within and between schools, including those about college admission.

Teachers should work toward the elimination of grades. Both students and parents must and do evaluate for themselves anyway. Grades maintain a competitive atmosphere that militates against learning. Students who receive low grades develop a low self-concept that often makes them perform worse than they would have if no one had labeled them. Students who get high grades often think they know more than they do, especially if the grades are based on just a couple of things like reading-comprehension scores and grammar tests. So long as grades must be turned in on students, collaboration tends to be viewed as cheating and discouraged because individual marks become harder to make up. Thus a powerful learning force is stymied. Further, growing up in an atmosphere that favors competition over collaboration produces adults unable to cope with world problems of today, which require collaboration. Surely the argument that school competition prepares for life must stick in the throat today, when all evidence indicates that far from helping people in life, competition is itself one of the major causes of both personal and international difficulties.

Grades distract students from the actual goals of effective communication. While competing and comparing themselves, they are also aiming to please adults, which is not a school goal. Youngsters allowed to keep a pure learning focus will naturally please adults by becoming powerful learners. Methods and materials that cannot engage students without grades, candy, coercion, or other irrelevant and artificial motivation do not belong in schools. It is not at all idealistic to assume that communication has its own rewards. If this has not appeared so in schooling, that is only because purposeless exercises have too often reigned in place of communication. Social reinforcement naturally plays a part in communicating and hence will always play a part in learning the language arts. Precisely because it is built in, however, it does not need to be reintroduced by a reward-punishment system, part of which pits student against student, endangering self-esteem. Sender-receiver relations are broad and various and must never be simply boiled down to commands from a superior. Much of the ineffectuality of traditional language teaching stems from such a confusion. Students should not communicate because big people make them, but that is the message implied by grades. A major goal of education is, precisely, self-evaluation. Grades constantly orient a learner toward what an outside observer thinks of his performance and encourage him not to judge for himself the effects of what he is doing. One judges communication, it is true, by its effects on others, but the "other" must be an authentic receiver, not a wielder of power over the sender.

Grades determine advancement to the next station, including eventually college and graduate school and hence careers. To the younger child, grades indicate acceptance or rejection of him as a person. To the older student they represent control of his destiny. Both feelings about grades play havoc with the learning process. In fact, the time must come when the society removes from schools entirely this misplaced function of *certifying*. It is not the business of schools to certify people for jobs. Employers should do their own screening. So should colleges and graduate schools. Again, each party should do his own evaluating. Too long have private universities and private businesses been allowed, in effect, to have their admissions and employment selection partially done for them by public institutions at public expense. The job of schools is to take each student as far as they can in the time they have responsibility for his education. For this no grades or value judgments of *individuals* are necessary. (We're not forgetting the *teacher*'s need to evaluate individuals for diagnosis and counseling, however, which is specific and descriptive.) Grades do not really serve the student, the parent, the teacher, or the administrator, each of whom must do his own evaluating. The mission of schools is learning, and that mission is impaired so long as schools continue to act as screening agencies for employers.

CHARTING EXPERIENCE

On page 29 we described generally the logging and counseling system necessary for individualizing. Let's detail this. The student needs to keep some kind of record of what he is doing, and the teacher needs to translate this into coverage of general language arts goals by keeping some experience chart for each student. This is the logging part. Then on the basis of the cumulative experience charts, which should be passed on from one year to another, you can advise a student about which areas of discourse and kinds of activities to stress next. This is the counseling part. Both parts come together during conferences that you may arrange for regularly or irregularly, often or occasionally, depending on need. In fact, you may handle conferences themselves differently for different individuals. The backbone of classroom management for individualized learning, a logging and counseling system serves by its very nature to evaluate student work for in-class purposes. It allows the learner to evaluate himself and the teacher to diagnose. It charts past and future together.

The form of these has to balance simplicity against utility. Don't overburden students with bookkeeping. All one can expect from primary students is probably a checking or coloring or circling or dating of materials worked with. Whenever possible, it is very valuable to know the titles of activity cards, reading selections, games, recordings, and so on, but less mature students may do well just to check or date an activity card *category*, such as "Making Up Stories," a whole book from which they have read only a part, or "games" or "recordings" without indicating titles. A listing of all the classroom materials will boggle the mind and be hard for younger children to scan for certain titles. Some may not be able to read the titles in the list. And besides, new materials are being brought in or created all the time. So any chart must simplify. The question is how much. Part of the point of conferences, after all, is to elicit more detail from the student, such as specific titles.

A simple tracking chart for discourse goals might look like Figure 21.2 (page 424). For older students it might look like the one in Figure 21.3 (page 425), which could be a long fold-out, repeating the form. The tracking chart for games and manipulable materials could be separate. Distribute the items in that list of materials and activities over enough chart space so that students can easily find items and have room to check, fill, or date some squares or circles next to each item. A pictogram, emblem, or miniature picture of items will help nonreaders to identify what they have worked with (Figure 21.4, page 425). Make squares large enough so that less mature children can color in and more mature can enter the date. Punching, stamping, and other ways of keeping up the chart may be more fun and better ensure that the bookkeeping gets done. Try to find out during conferences how complete a student has kept his chart and ask for omissions. Say very strongly—more than once—that these are not scoreboards on which they are to try for large numbers of items. Children who get the wrong idea may feel they should win your approval by racing through a lot of materials and activities or simply by lying.

The Teacher's Experience Chart

We recommend that you keep an individual experience chart for each student that relates his activities

Aims and Assessment

Your name _____ Activities from _____ to _____

To keep track of the cards you do,
fill in the box with a crayon, ☐

or you can make an X in the box, ☐

or you can put the date you
finished the card in the box. ☐

ACTIVITY CARD GROUPS

BOOKS TO MAKE

PLAY-ACTING

SHARING BOOKS

FINDING OUT

TELL IT/WRITE IT

THINGS TO MAKE

GAMES

(Note: The shaded
boxes should be
color-coded to
activity card.)

WHAT I HAVE READ AND LISTENED TO

Name _____   Year _____

Date Finished	Book Title	Heard Recording	Read Part Only

FIGURE 21.2 SIMPLE TRACKING CHART FOR STUDENTS (FRONT AND BACK)
Source: From *Interaction* Evaluation Guide, Level 1.

Name _____ Teacher _____ Year Used _____

read this before you begin.

On this chart keep track of the things you do. Keep it handy so you and your teacher can use it in talking about what you are doing, how you feel about it, and what you plan to do next. When you complete an activity or change to another one, write briefly and honestly under each of these headings:

WHEN — Write the date you began an activity and the date you completed it or dropped it.

MATERIALS — List the titles of books, stories from the books, activity cards, recordings, or other items you used, either INTERACTION materials or other materials.

WHAT — Write down the kinds of things you did, such as interviewed people, read, wrote poetry, made up signs, wrote or directed a play, or produced a newspaper.

WHO — List others with whom you worked or note that you worked alone.

VALUE — Write how you felt about the activity. If you worked with others, talk with them before deciding what to write, but keep in mind that an activity can have a very different value for each group member. Tell whether or not you felt satisfied with how well you did the work.

WHEN	MATERIALS	WHAT	WHO	VALUE
Beginning:				
Completed:				
Beginning:				
Completed:				
Beginning:				
Completed:				
Beginning:				
Completed:				
Beginning:				
Completed:				

FIGURE 21.3 TRACKING CHART FOR OLDER STUDENTS

Source: From *Interaction* Evaluation Guide, Levels 1–4.

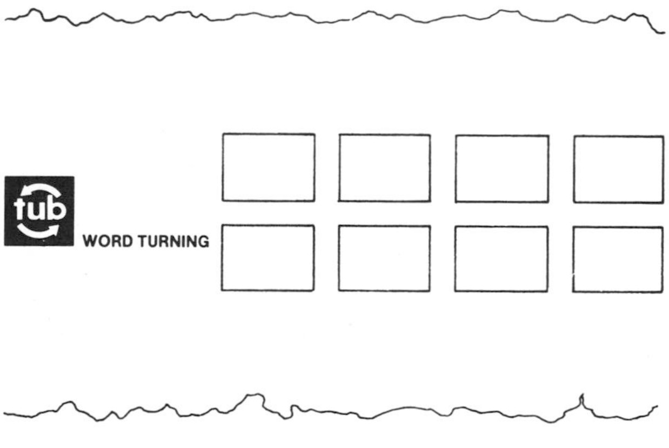

tub WORD TURNING

to the general goals. Basically it consists of some layout of the goals, permitting you to log under each goal the amount of experience a student has so far accumulated. Since the discourse goals are to be attained orally and in writing, as sender and receiver, you should log not only the experience accumulated toward each goal but also indicate which language art—listening, speaking, reading, or writing—the experience was gained by. It is useful to add performing as a fifth activity. See Figure 21.5, page 426.

FIGURE 21.4 SECTION OF TRACKING CHART WITH IDENTIFICATION DEVICE

Source: From *Interaction* Literacy Kit.

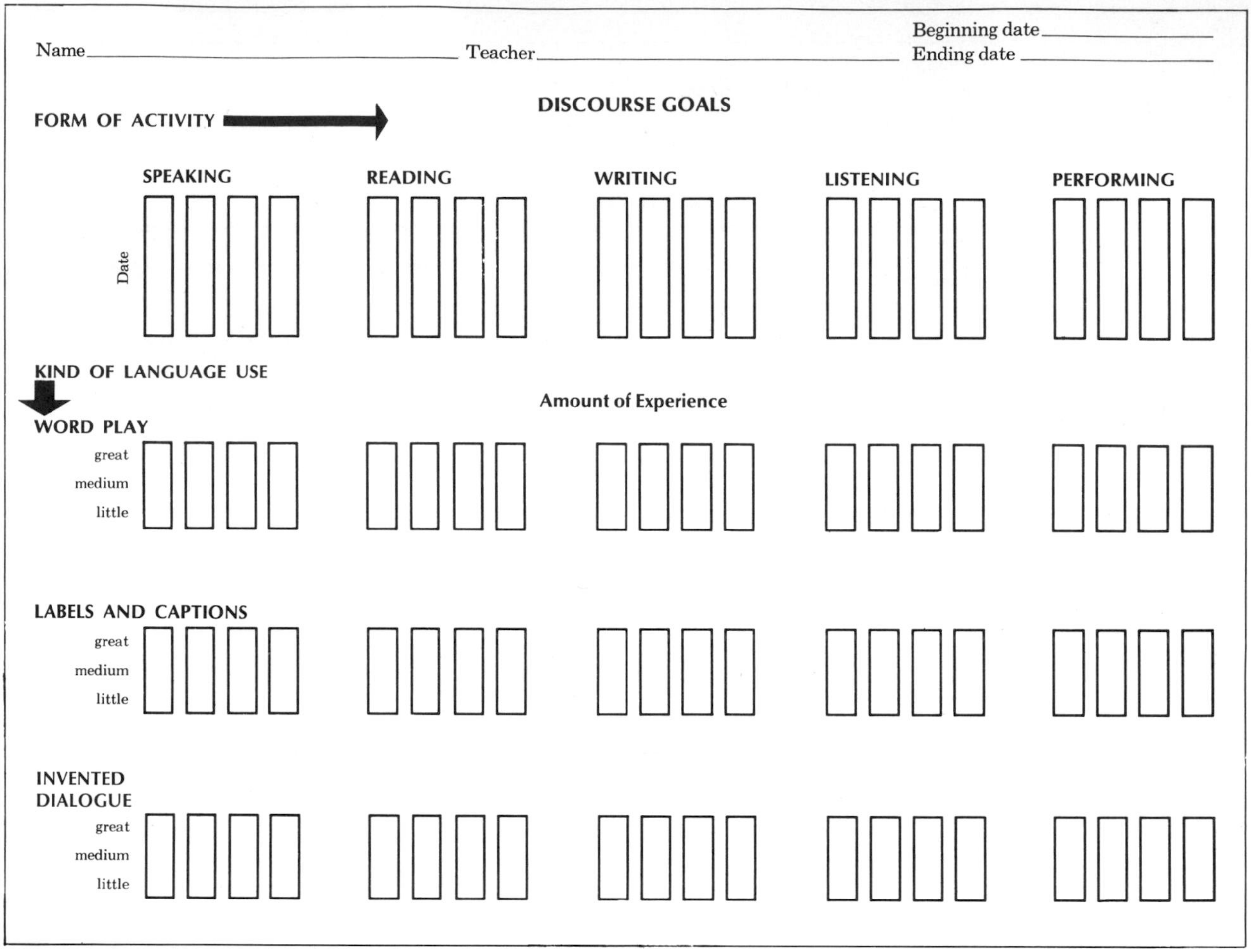

Name_____ Teacher_____ Beginning date_____
Ending date _____

FORM OF ACTIVITY ➡

DISCOURSE GOALS

| SPEAKING | READING | WRITING | LISTENING | PERFORMING |

Date

KIND OF LANGUAGE USE

⬇

Amount of Experience

WORD PLAY
great
medium
little

LABELS AND CAPTIONS
great
medium
little

INVENTED DIALOGUE
great
medium
little

FIGURE 21.5 DISCOURSE EXPERIENCE CHART

Source: From *Interaction* Evaluation Guide, Levels 1–4.

Since SPEAKING is defined here as conversing and orally improvising, any entry under SPEAKING would imply experience under LISTENING, so reserve LISTENING for purely receptive experience. Similarly, since PERFORMING is defined as rehearsed reading or enactment of a text, it implies the necessary silent reading that performance entails, so reserve READING for silent reading. An improvisation later performed for others should be just counted under SPEAKING.

Spaces are provided for making four entries a year for each goal. Write in the date and shade in the box up to an appropriate point on the scale of little-medium-great, as in the example in Figure 21.6.

These three terms refer to the amount of experience accumulated so far this year.

This chart registers "how much," not "how well." That is, it does not attempt to measure *quality* of achievement. But because experience consists of direct practice of the target language activities, the charting of work with recommended materials and activities should in large measure indicate higher achievement in each goal area. Comparison with other measures such as direct observation may show that experience is high and achievement low in some areas. This may yield valuable knowledge about a student's learning efficiency. Other measures may indicate that a student is already so

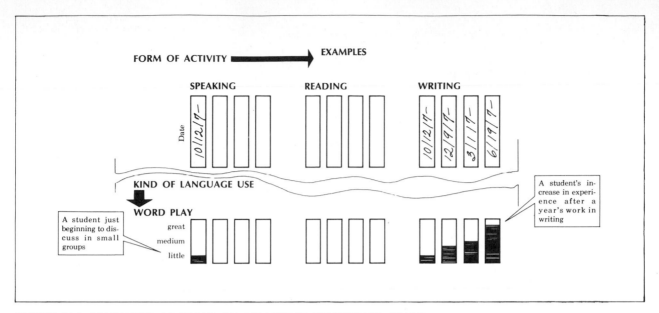

FIGURE 21.6 COMPLETED SECTIONS OF DISCOURSE EXPERIENCE CHART

Source: From *Interaction* Evaluation Guide, Levels 1–4.

proficient in a certain goal area that he does not need any more experience in it, even though this chart shows he has not yet spent much time in that area.

It can be useful to maintain a check list of the nine literacy subskills, so long as these are not separately tested out but are merely noted for counseling purposes. In fact, keeping track of experience accumulated in these subskills is an alternative to such testing, which is often justified on diagnostic grounds. A literacy experience chart might look like Figure 21.7 (page 428).

Somewhere on your chart of the student you will probably want an overall profile that summarizes both literacy and discourse experience. See Figure 21.8, page 428.

Converting from Student Chart to Teacher Chart

Translating an individual's particular selection of materials and activities into general learning terms is hard, but because the very feasibility of individualizing depends on it, the difficulty must be faced. For basic literacy skills the problem is not so difficult, because the materials and activities that teach them do not number many. The table at the end of Chapter 11, Decoding and Encoding Separated, (page 246) will do the trick alone if you keep in mind that all speaking, listening, reading, writing, and performing contribute to literacy. Whereas literacy is finite, discourse is infinite, so that a purely tabular approach to conversion cannot work alone. Many activities and materials teach toward a dozen discourse and literacy goals at once. If the curriculum array comprises the rich variety that we advocate and that effective teaching requires, and if students themselves are constantly making and bringing in other materials, any correlated listing of goals to materials and activities would not only constitute a staggering compilation job but would be mind-boggling and time-consuming for you to consult if you had to keep looking up items in order to connect them to goals.

Computers

Such a job fits a computer perfectly, of course, and we should consider this possibility. Computers can, in fact, do both the student's and the teacher's record-keeping, including correlating an individual's work with general goals for all. Technically, there is no serious problem except for the great expense, which might conceivably decline in the future. But computers have a way of becoming the tail that

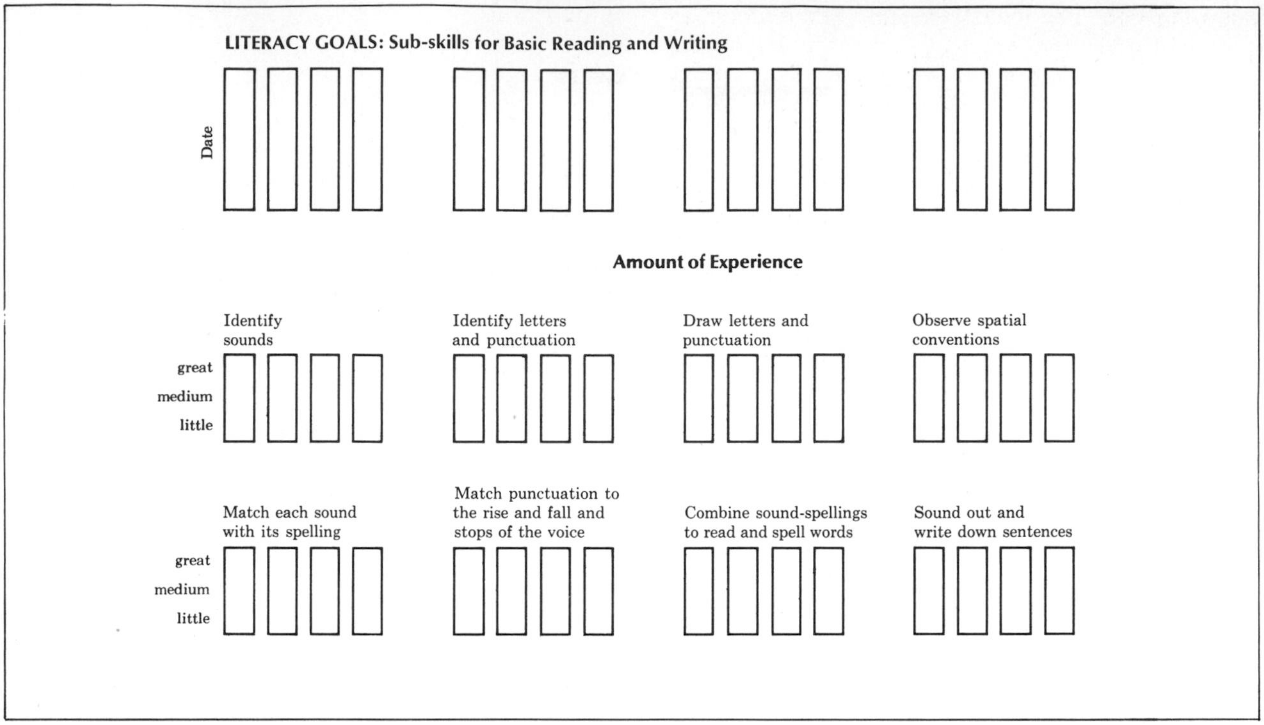

LITERACY GOALS: Sub-skills for Basic Reading and Writing

Date

Amount of Experience

Identify sounds

Identify letters and punctuation

Draw letters and punctuation

Observe spatial conventions

great
medium
little

Match each sound with its spelling

Match punctuation to the rise and fall and stops of the voice

Combine sound-spellings to read and spell words

Sound out and write down sentences

great
medium
little

FIGURE 21.7 LITERACY EXPERIENCE CHART

Source: From *Interaction* Evaluation Guide, Levels 1–4.

OVERALL PROFILE

LITERACY GOALS

DECODING (WORD ATTACK): Sound out new texts with normal intonation

TRANSCRIBING (SPELLING AND PUNCTUATION): Transcribe speech to paper according to conventions of spelling and punctuation

great
medium
little

DISCOURSE GOALS

SPEAKING

READING

WRITING

LISTENING

PERFORMING

great
medium
little

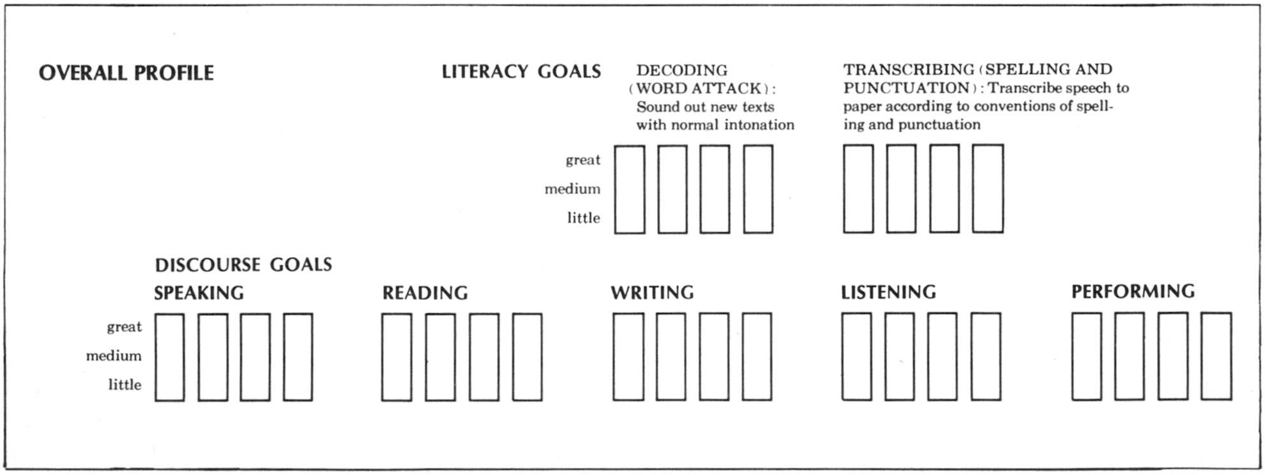

FIGURE 21.8 OVERALL STUDENT PROFILE

Source: From *Interaction* Evaluation Guide, Levels 1–4.

wags the dog. The investment and commitment required for their use are so great that everyone involved feels obliged or pressured to fit human needs to the computer's needs. Also, the programs that are made to work with such a computerized logging system tend to be made by the computer company itself, or an allied one, and tend toward small-step programming and a closed, standardized curriculum although their advertising describes them as "individualized." There is danger of the program existing to sell the computers and the programmed learning hardware. This is a very dangerous bias. Students must make decisions under teacher counseling, and there is no way that higher learning can be preprogrammed into small-step sequences. (See pages 407–412 for further reasons to doubt this approach.) A great risk exists that computers for record-keeping will lead to programmed materials and that both will squeeze out any real student choice and teacher counseling, which may then seem unnecessary. If computerization could be limited just to logging student activities and correlating them to goals, without altering the curriculum or interfering with the student-teacher relation, it could be a strong help in solving a difficult problem, but the learning price as well as the dollar price may well be too high—and may be discovered too late.

Goal Check Sheets

You or a teacher team can make Goal Check Sheets as one aid for reference if nothing else. The list in Figure 21.9, for example, arrays the materials in one elementary program that teach the goal of sending and receiving information. (One virtue of activity cards is that they name and catalogue, in effect, most of the activities offered in a classroom.)

Surely, this may be useful, once compiled, but if you have nine goal sheets for each student and have to check off "Touchy Riddles," for example, on every goal sheet that it appears on, and thus have to look for each title across all nine goal sheets—well, there's a chance you won't do this. And what about adding new materials to the list all the time? You could, of course, make a list by title and enumerate after each title the goals that it teaches toward. Unless you know the materials so well that you need not search much for titles, you will be grossly overburdened and, if forced to operate this way will simply have to cut back on the amount of materials and student options.

Goal Check Sheet: Sending and Receiving INFORMATION

BOOKLETS AND RECORDINGS	SPEAKING	HEARING	READING	WRITING	PERFORMING
Animals, Sports, Adventure					
Adventure Stories 1 and 2					
Animal Stories (True)					
Animal Stories (Fiction)					
Sports Stories					
Facts and Ideas					
Information 1 and 2					
True Stories 1 and 2					
Science Encyclopedia					
Dictionary of Local Lingo					
Pictures					
Charts and Graphs					
Maps					
Photos with Captions					
GAMES					
Messages					
North American Plants					
Life in the Sea					
READ 'N WRITE BOOKLETS					
All About Me					
ACTIVITY CARDS					
Acting Out					
Create a Contraption					
Guess My Song					
Playing Opposites					
Talking with the Body					
The Game of Charades					
TV Commercial					
Two to Do					
Where Am I?					
Doing					
Animal Blames and Praises					
Building Blitz					
Class Newspaper					
Reading Minds					
Send Secret Messages					
Touchy Riddles					
What's for Dinner?					
Writer's Workshop					
You're on the Air					
Finding Out					
Charts					
Classify					

ACTIVITY CARDS	SPEAKING	HEARING	READING	WRITING	PERFORMING
Eating Habits Compared					
Finding Out Outside					
Getting to Know Each Other					
Graphs					
Hobby Research					
How's Your Touch					
Interviews					
Keep an Animal Log					
Keep It . . . It May Be Useful					
Log Along					
Run an Experiment					
Shop and Tell					
The Masked Letter Writer					
Vital Statistics					
What Did You Hear?					
Making Things					
Badges and Bumper Stickers					
Begin a Scrapbook					
Capture with Captions					
Dictionary of Local Lingo					
Group Cooking					
Make an Ad					
Making a Special Dictionary					
Map a Zoo or Park					
Map Your Room					
Say It on a Poster					
Slide Show Story					
Treasure Map					
You Make It Move					
Your Own Encyclopedia					
Making Up					
A New Planet					
If the Shoe Fits—					
What's Going On?					
Telling About					
Are All Stories the Same?					
Be a Salesman					
Epithets					
Find the Picture					
Found Objects					
How Does It Work?					
Keeping in Touch					
Show It Off					
Talk Spin-Off					
Tell a Dream					
Topic Talk					
What I Think About—					

FIGURE 21.9 SAMPLE GOAL CHECK SHEET

Source: From *Interaction* Evaluation Guide, Level 3.

A Combination

Another alternative is less systematic but more practical. You have several ways of finding out what goal(s) an activity teaches toward. Just combine these in a sensible way for each case. You will know already the goals of some common or obvious activities. If the student notes down more than a title, as he is asked to do on the form in Figure 21.3, under "What," then you may be able to tell from his description what the activity teaches. If lists have been made correlating activities with goals—Goal Check Sheets or Tables—you can consult those for some items. Perhaps the best way of all is to talk over unknown activities during conferences. Chances are that not too many such items will require explaining at any one conference. Besides, asking a student to tell more about an activity is a good opportunity to help you both assess his work. Part of the point of conferences is for you to get a better picture of his work than records can provide.

Conferences

Meet with work portfolio, Student Tracking Chart, and Teacher Experience Chart. If you are familiar enough with all materials and activities to know which Goal Check Sheets to check them off on, you may want to maintain those and bring them along also. Other useful materials are notes you may have made observing the student at work, doing miscue analysis of his oral reading to you, and examining his products. Look over his chart and note patterns such as emphasis on one language art or type of activity, sameness or variety in both the materials and the people he chooses to work with, and so on. Glancing down the columns of the form in Figure 2.3 will tell you a lot fast—which materials and people he has been working with.

Then encourage the student to elaborate for you. The more you can get him to level with you, the more you can help, and the more he will learn, but he must feel that frankness will not be used against him. This is how grades make counseling difficult. To encourage him to break ground in new activities, assure him you will protect his grade by allowing for temporarily reduced success as he grapples with new challenges.

Be sure to give reasons for recommending new tacks, shifts of emphasis, and particular activities and materials. This is part of the student's education, and the more he understands the kinds of discourse that exist to become acquainted with and the ways you are trying to open for him toward both literacy and discourse goals, the more he can successfully take over this decision-making. Say what you see in his writing and other products. Try to describe more than judge. Mention what you notice when he reads aloud to you, which kinds of spelling and punctuation errors he makes, the roles he takes in groups, the sort of reading and writing he gravitates toward, and so on. Generally focus on *traits* and *trends*. Although these often imply a value judgment, they emphasize fact and act as a useful reflection of the student to stimulate and guide growth. This makes you an ally instead of a menace.

Evaluation by those outside the classroom

The best way for parents to evaluate results is to see and hear what their children have done. Again, the typical slice of life most convinces, because it does not depend on rare, special occasions, as do standardized tests, which have the further disadvantage that parents don't know what to make of them. The same variety and volume that provide you with plenty to judge also display for parents the evidence of learning. They should see many of the papers from the folders, hear audio tapes, and whenever possible see routine performances, live or video-taped. Compositions and transcriptions will show the literacy skills of handwriting, spelling, and punctuation and the creative abilities to think and imagine. An audio tape can catch an improvisation or rehearsed reading. If a curriculum enables students to reproduce for themselves the kinds of materials they find—learning games, recordings, books, photos, films, and so on—then you will have no problem rounding up something for parents to examine.

The problem is how to bring parents and products together. The old "parents' night" and parent conferences are fine to the extent that you can succeed in getting parents to come to the school. Alternating the two is a good idea. Many parents will not come to an open house but will come when appointments are made systematically. For conferences, arrange time so that they may look over their child's portfolio of work, sample tapes they may have made, and examine other of his creations. Then you can talk together.

You can describe traits of their child's work as it appears to you. Global value judgments mean less than specific comments about which kinds of talking, reading, writing, and performing their child tends to choose on his own, or has most and least experience in, which skills come easiest or need more work, habits and patterns, areas of recent progress. If you think you see why a learner is having trouble in spelling or in comprehending literature, explain this and say what you will be recommending that he emphasize next. If you think both the spelling and the literary comprehension will progress better from reading while listening with recordings, then you could explain the connection to parents who might not understand how this practice can teach these two skills.

PARENT INVOLVEMENT

Try to involve parents as much as possible in helping as aides. The more they work with your students, the more they will understand how the curriculum should function and will be able to assess results the same way you can, by observing while facilitating. These aides can help other parents to understand how much their children are learning. It would be very good if a parent committee undertook to study standardized tests and alternative ways for the community to evaluate your classroom. Once parents actually look at standardized tests, read what testing experts say about them, and think about them in relation to their own goals, they can see their limitations and the need for other measures. The more people know about tests, the less eager they are to rely on them. Explain the idea of interaction analysis and let parents devise criteria and apply them when listening to tapes. Invite parents to come up with their own means of evaluating for themselves. If they suggest means that seem misguided, explain why you think so, but cooperate with them, at the same time making clear that beyond an open-door policy permitting them to look at student work, you and the school have to leave it to them to judge for themselves.

Opening the classroom to parents not only shows confidence in yourself; it actually can head off unduly negative criticism of you. It often happens, for example, that parents concerned about basic skills will not understand why basic skills are not isolated into drills and will fail to see how the skills are being taught by ways other than those they are expecting. Such parents may believe that their child is just having fun and not learning anything. The more contact you have, one way or another, with parents, the more chance you have of correcting this misunderstanding by explaining to such parents how the skills are taught within larger contexts and by showing where in their child's work the basic skills are being practiced and perhaps improved.

STANDARDIZED TESTS

One conventional way for those outside the classroom to evaluate what happens inside is to institute periodic testing with instruments sanitized supposedly against any bias of the teacher or the school. For this purpose many commercial tests are put out both independently and as part of a curriculum package. They are not of course sanitized, because teachers whose job security is linked to their students' test scores may teach so closely to the test as to bias results heavily toward favorable scores. The only advantage of such evaluation is that student performances may be compared with those of other times and places—if that is an advantage.

Norm-Referencing

For most well-known standardized tests, this comparison occurs in two ways. First, they are usually *norm-referenced,* which means that the score of anyone taking the test now is compared to the scores of some original "normal" student population. So a student obtaining today a reading score indicating "third grade, fourth month" is simply being scaled by the norms of that first population. Second, a student today may be compared with his contemporaries throughout a school district or, in most cases, the nation. The great weakness of norm-referencing, of course, lies buried back in the original "normal" population. How was *its* normality determined? Is it normal for today also or only for then? But most of all, do norms established by performance of *any* population in public schools as we have known them do anything but set low standards? Norm-referencing reposes on what some student *did* do, under all the usual handicaps of conventional language teaching, not on what students *could* do under improved learning conditions. Teachers, parents, and administrators happy with "third grade, fourth month" may be accepting a meaningless standard, possibly a very low standard that holds back many youngsters.

Furthermore, comparison itself should be challenged. It serves, of course, the immediate practical purpose of selecting out students for this group or that class or certifying some for admission and employment. In other words, the more schools operate by *limiting* membership or admission, by segregating and screening for their own or others' purposes, the more comparative evaluation seems to make sense. Parents need comparison only to the extent they are using their child to keep up with the Joneses. The student does not need comparison to "know where he stands" because good learning processes always show him by feedback how well he is performing, so that his only reason for comparing his performance with others' would be to know where he stands in the eyes of adults manipulating his destiny. For your own diagnosing and counseling purpose, comparison among students has no value.

Criterion-Referencing

To ensure meeting minimums, schools are choosing more and more another type of test called *criterion-referenced,* which measures students absolutely, against a fixed standard rather than relatively, against each other. The idea of it is by no means new. A Civil Service test to screen applicants for a certain job simply tests for certain skills necessary to do the job with little regard for how many applicants are likely to fall above or below the passing point, so long as enough pass to fill the job vacancies. If you give a test to your students and grade it afterward "on the curve," that is, by setting the passing point only after seeing how students do, you are setting up a kind of norm-referencing, because although you have no prior set of scores to go by, still you are scoring each individual according to norms that the class as a body provides. If, on the other hand, you decided in advance how many errors constituted a passing grade, how many an A, and so on, without knowing how well students would do, then you would be criterion-referencing the test, because you are setting standards according to a certain desired performance, not according to comparison of student scores.

Is there, then, any more use for criterion-referenced testing than for norm-referenced? Is its specific performance a virtue? Consider the main purpose of criterion-referencing. It is not to distribute students against each other on a curve. It is to find out which students or how many students can do certain tasks. The tasks tested for tend to set a floor, because they are selected as indicators that students and teachers are achieving *at least* such and such. Any test tasks have to gear themselves somehow to realistic expectations of what students may achieve. If this gearing is not built in by some kind of averaging of what students do in fact achieve —by norming—then it has to be accommodated another way, because schools can't administer tests on which too many students fail—for political reasons if for no other.

Criterion-referenced tests ensure that too many do not fail by including mostly very safe items. They focus on *minimal* standards. They are a pass-fail kind of test and assume that the large majority of students will pass. But how can they assume this without a prior score group? Obviously there is a kind of score group in the minds of the test-makers, only it is not a particular population actually run through a particular test but rather a general notion of what most students have done, and can do, based on common school experience. Most children learn to master the long-vowel spellings—at least long enough to pass such a test, even if they never really read.

The only value of criterion-referenced tests is to cover one teacher for one year. It came to the fore in an age of mechanical accountability. It aims to get masses over a minimal threshold. Since each teacher must cover himself for each student, students are tested again each year for virtually the same material, and hence taught the material again each year, so that they do not rise far but rather circle over the same minimums, getting checked out again and again, hovering over a required floor but under a low ceiling. In short, criterion-referencing differs not so much from norm-referencing as might appear at first blush, because both set low standards based on moving large masses a short way. This low center of gravity owes to the misguided practice of treating all students at once in the same way, of standardizing.

For true individualizing the only relevant measure is the student against himself. If schools take each individual as far as he can go, charting experience year to year, they will accomplish manyfold what they do by standardizing. So long, however, as student achievement is measured by student-to-student comparison and by minimal thresholds, school achievement will remain low, perpetuating low standards and further low achievement. It might be argued, however, that a student can be measured against himself if he takes a standardized test periodically, because scores of the same student at different times will vary.

This takes us back to other general inadequacies of standardized tests; they are simply not the best way to measure a student against himself. Direct observation and direct examination of student products are the best ways to measure individual student progress. Standardized tests do not measure nearly a broad enough range of language activities or over a broad enough range of difficulty to be useful in individualized learning, which requires the same breadth of possibility in evaluation that it does in curriculum array. Tests covering all learning by all individuals would be impossible and obviously contradict the whole idea of *standardized* testing.

Criterion-referenced tests can be used as only one, inadequate sort of evaluation—just to reassure everybody that students are getting over a threshold, but the major evaluation would have to go far beyond these tests. Standardized testing overfocuses on a few, easily testable skills and ignores what is hardest to teach and learn and ultimately most important. The alleged strength of criterion-referenced tests is the concrete specification of the behavior to be evinced by a student on that special occasion of the testing twice a year. To fit the tight time compass, the test catches only the most specific, not the larger, more complex behaviors that cannot be seen or heard on one occasion but can only be built up into a composite picture by continual observation. Furthermore, even when the behavior is fairly specific, such as comprehending a certain short statement or command, standardized tests go about this in a crude, cheap way—by quick pencil-and-paper means—that do not test well. To translate from verbal to nonverbal is, as we said, the best test of comprehension, but it is expensive because it often requires a live tester to observe or administer. You can do this daily while going about your regular business. So as a measure of the student against himself, standardized testing offers little but drawbacks.

Let's take as a significant example of the evils of standardized paper-and-pencil tests the case of reading scores. If a student scores low, one does not know what to make of the score. Without an oral component there is no way to distinguish between decoding ability and comprehension. If a student does not know certain vocabulary—that is, does not have certain words in his oral repertory—or does not understand certain concepts, he will score low on standardized reading tests regardless of whether he can read or not. He would also score low if asked comprehension questions after merely *hearing* the same text. Since the test is called a *reading* test, school people usually assume that a low score means the student cannot decode rather than he lacks yet certain oral vocabulary and concepts. So such a student is shunted to phonics program to drill more on sound-spellings when in fact that is not his problem at all. The result is that the student gets an increasingly negative notion of what "reading" is and gets no opportunity to learn more vocabulary and concepts, which he could acquire only from general language experience, including much oral activity and audiovisual intake. In short, standardized reading tests have set up a national pattern designed, perversely enough, to perpetuate and proliferate rather than solve problems associated with reading.

If you really want to know how well a student decodes, ask him to read aloud to you from a text that you can see and that he has not seen before. If the passage contains a fair sampling of English sound-spellings and if sentence constructions are roughly similar to those the student could understand orally, only a minute or so of this will show you very clearly how well he decodes word strings. If you want to know, on the other hand, how well the student comprehends, *you* read to *him,* then talk with him about what he understands. Your judgment of results when testing with an oral component will not be standardized, allowing you to compare the student with so-called norms, but it will be far more useful otherwise. Reading aloud permits you to test for one variable at a time. Your homespun testing of this sort, believe it or not, will therefore be more scientific than standardized tests, which blur decoding and comprehension hopelessly and hence, to some extent do not test reading at all but oral language development. It is a cruel irony that results should then be used to channel some low scorers into narrow "reading instruction" or "remedial reading" labs and away from what they need most— more oral language and conceptual experience. The chief reason for this appalling situation is the mistaken desire for a cheap way of comparing. It would be far cheaper in the long run of reading education to institute oral reading testing. As for the comparing, it serves only an institutional convenience, not a diagnostic function.

Apparently it doesn't even serve the institutional function very well. After saying, "Test results are not good measures of what is taught in school, strange as it may seem," the assessors of the Michigan accountability system continue, "Even if the tests were completely valid and reliable, it would not be possible to attribute achievement gains to the school or teacher." [8]

---

[8] Ernest R. House, Wendell Rivers, and Daniel L. Stufflebeam, "An Assessment of the Michigan Accountability System," *Phi Delta Kappan,* 55 (June 1974), 668–669.

Granted that continual observation measures best, how can outsiders like parents and administrators avail themselves of this way? Don't they have to send standardized tests into the classroom as a kind of reporter on their behalf? A reporter who can detect only a few limited things and who eventually causes those he is observing to do only what he can see is no reporter at all. Except to the extent that parents and administrators can actually visit the classroom, they are indeed handicapped for live observation, but they can certainly examine products, and machine recorders make it possible to let outsiders observe outside, since audio tapes and video tapes can be sampled at the convenience of the outsider. Still, however true it may be that outsiders to the classroom have to devise their own evaluation anyway, independently of the teacher's, will they really look for themselves?

The matter comes down to this, that though standardized tests are very inadequate to measure what good schooling would attempt and though they create negative side effects that impair learning, still any alternative seems to take too much time or money. At this point we need to differentiate again the purposes of the outsider's evaluation. The parent is interested first in his child and second in the efficiency of the whole curriculum. What's my child getting, and how much does the system deliver for what it costs us? The parent can evaluate the child at home by both observation and examination of products. As for the administrator, he need not be interested in individuals as such but in their aggregate welfare—in how many children are faring well, not which ones (except as subgroups or types). He wants to know how well the teacher and the curriculum are functioning. All this means that outsider evaluation can focus on groups.

Now, if the outsider needs only to evaluate the total class functioning, as a means to judge the efficiency of the teacher or the curriculum, then examining students' written and oral products becomes a realistic alternative, because random slice-of-life samplings can be periodically made of a class by principals, language arts coordinators, department heads, other school officials, and by rotating parent committees. Parents and officials doing this sort of evaluation together might find the collaboration and contact useful to both.

The products examined should not be especially selected by the teacher but should be pulled out by the outsider evaluators in the classroom, though the teacher can cooperate by helping them find samples that show this or that sort of activity. Outsiders may easily sample decoding skills if you routinely record the sessions of coaching and diagnosis reading described as miscue analysis on page 220. At the same time, evaluators can assess the methodology, as they can likewise with most other products and recordings. Reading student reportage, for example, will allow them to connect composition with assignments that entail gathering raw material by visiting and interviewing. Hearing a taped improvisation while looking at the students' own transcription of it will show perhaps not only how improvisation may teach thinking and theater but also spelling and punctuation. Unlike standardized tests, this kind of evaluation permits relating cause to effect, in many cases at least—important for curriculum assessment. The more materials you and your students produce the less you need worry about how any one of them may strike outside evaluators and the more confidently can you trust the total impact of it all. If evaluators have an embarrassment of riches to choose from, that's their problem, and the quantity itself will surely count in favor of you and the curriculum.

When students learn by doing and by getting feedback on what they have done, the curriculum and the teacher can be evaluated by monitoring both *products* and *processes*. Outsiders should examine products and do their own interaction analysis of processes. Classroom assessment should be based on how well the learners' self-assessment systems are working. To the extent that the small-group processes and your coaching and counseling function as intended, students will be learning. So both you and outsiders should look for signs of strength and weakness in the quality of interactions and the utility of the feedback. These have to involve subjective judgments, but all evaluation—make no mistake about it, "objective" tests or whatever—always comes back down anyway to someone's subjective judgments, however hidden. The more consensus, however, the more impartial. A curriculum or a classroom operation can be very effectively evaluated by combining judgments of different human raters. These can in turn be combined with test scores, but it is essential that all parties understand the limitations of testing a few isolated skills with paper and pencil on rare special occasions and of comparing the resulting student scores against one another. If you and the curriculum are to be judged by these *alone,* then make sure outsiders understand that (1) they will either gain data about only a fraction of what you are trying to do, or (2) they may force you to teach to the tests and hence to teach only a fraction of what you should, in order to cover yourself. In return for broader evaluation, you must willingly open your classroom and its products to inspection. You can do so with confidence if you set in motion the practices recommended herein.

Summary

Tolerate standardized tests if required, but don't count on them much for evaluation. Only daily slice-of-life observation carried on without distracting students from honest language tasks will really tell you what you need to know and avoid negative side effects. Students taught by this curriculum should score well on standardized tests and do much more besides. Tolerate grades if required but depend on student products and parent conferences to convey progress and problems. Encourage all outsiders to evaluate as you do, by observing processes and examining products on a random basis. Assess the curriculum mainly by how well it enables students to assess themselves, that is, to get useful feedback about their efforts to comprehend and compose.

S ince students achieve the same general objectives in specifically differ-ent ways, you need to be able to detect signs of language growth by yourself in order to evaluate your students' work and to counsel them about future work. For the most part, you must be able to do this without testing, by cumulative daily observation. One reason is that you cannot find or buy evaluation measures adequate for individualizing and worthy of higher learning. Also, specific testing cannot often be done for groups in an individ-ualized system, and to test individuals separately would take too much time. To help each student make good choices about building his own sequences of activities you have to interpret his ongoing work by your personal judg-ment. This chapter is meant to help inform this judgment but can do so only as a supplement to your direct experience and native intuition. All that we can describe here, of course, is behavior so general as to be common to all people. You apply it to individuals.

Literacy is not dealt with in this chapter because progress in learning it does not partake of growth in thought and speech. As explained on page 174, literacy learning is virtually nondevelopmental, being essentially a matter of acquiring some information, the spellings and punctuation marks that render vocal sounds. It is absurd to check off these spellings and punctuation marks in a certain order and to call that evaluation. Any sequence is as good as another (spellings and punctuation usages being learned as much simulta-neously as sequentially anyway). The only sensible way to evaluate whether they have been learned is by listening to a student read aloud or by observ-ing him write down dictation. See page 419 in the last chapter for references to places in this book that describe literacy evaluation.

In contrast to the matching of speech with print, the matching of thought with speech cannot be done by acquiring some information, because ideas and words do not match off in a single, fixed correspondence. The idea of causality, for example, may be expressed in a discourse without the word *because* appearing in it. Concepts of relations especially are often conveyed "between the lines" by context. Juxtaposition and punctuation may convey the cause-and-effect relation: "He decided to leave; he knew they wanted to be alone." Omitting *because* makes the logic more implicit and gains the rhetorical advantage of understatement. If we were to measure growth by counting this author's logical conjunctions we would score him low because of his more sophisticated composing! Nothing is harder to explain than an absence, for it may mean many very different things. Any researcher who has tried to measure the effect of some teaching treatment on the growth of thought and speech knows what easy-scoring standardized tests ignore—that the presence or absence of a certain word or sentence structure does not necessarily indicate the presence or absence of certain thinking. The fact that someone uses the word *because* does not mean that he understands causality, for many small children use the word before they grasp the con-cept. A chief issue, in fact, is distinguishing between true growth and hollow verbalism. *To judge language growth you have to sample a learner's speech on many different occasions and make a composite judgment.*

Thought is invisible until it is translated into deeds or words. So while in-tellectual growth is more important, language existing only to convey thought, still you most often have to detect intellectual growth as manifested in lan-guage, precisely because language incarnates thought. Since the language half is all we can *see*, we are much tempted to forget this invisible thought that it is being matched off with and even forget the whole process of matching. Too often teachers just focus on language forms as if these existed alone.

There are several reasons why thought and language cannot be matched off in predictable, standard ways. First of all, thought is more various; it is too big for words. The possibilities of what many individual human minds can conceive and combine are greater than the permutations possible with a single lexicon and grammar. Creative use of language, as in poetry, bends language to fit the mind but also risks obscuring communication and is not available to all.

Second, before less-developed learners have learned how to use all the resources of language, they must make shift to cast their thought into language by any means they can. So they will express their thinking in more ambiguous, less differentiated forms of language than if they knew how to employ all its resources.

Third, language does not exist merely to convey thought; besides its logical function it has a rhetorical function, to exert some kind of force on other people. So many of the choices speakers and writers make in composing aim to have an effect on other people, not just to express ideas. This is of course one great difference between *abstracting from* and *abstracting for,* as developed in Chapter 1, Basic Concepts.

Fourth, any shift of thought from one medium to another necessitates loss and slippage. Language can only do certain things. Like any medium, it has its limits. In fact, it is most likely true that language can never do complete justice to thought, especially the subtlest, deepest, most original thought. Mathematical language and symbolic logic were developed, in fact, to offset some of the logical deficiencies of ordinary language. Other media may be more successful sometimes in rendering certain kinds of nonlinear and intuitive thought. Language is a flexible mold, however, and growth consists of finding out just how much, and which kinds of, thought language can indeed render.

Finally, language arts are arts, and many of the options about how to put thought into speech are aesthetic choices for the sake of wit, economy, beauty, and so on. At the same time one puts his thinking into words he is often also playing games with the medium somewhat for game's sake, as in painting, photography, dance, and other arts. Practitioners "make statements" in those media but also just use the media as wherewithal with which to compose form. You have to think of language as

both means and end and look for growth at once in communication effectiveness and in what we have called word play.

While discussing abstraction in Chapter 1, Basic Concepts, we implied several lines of growth that we will state now in a form to be used throughout the rest of this chapter to sum up periodically the sorts of growth to look for.

GROWTH SEQUENCE 1: Toward generalizing more broadly while elaborating more finely. See page 6.

The formulation above aims directly at heading off the mistaken notion that either generality alone or detail alone is good of itself. An *overgeneralization* is a statement based on too few instances and hence lacks underpinning. Endless inventory of details, on the other hand, comes to no more than laundry and grocery lists until organized under some generality that relates particulars to each other and to elements in a discourse. This statement of growth along the logical dimension of *abstracting from* should be paired off with the following statement of growth along the rhetorical dimension of *abstracting for.* Together, the two very general kinds of growth frame the more specific sorts formulated throughout this chapter.

GROWTH SEQUENCE 2: Sending toward more general and more differentiated audiences.

Also in Chapter 1, page 7–8, we implied an elemental growth progression about awareness of abstracting that later growth sequences in this chapter will further specify.

GROWTH SEQUENCE 3: Toward increasing awareness that one creates what he knows and that this knowledge is partial.

The main way a learner grows verbally is toward increasing his number of options about how to compose thought into language and how to interpret language into thought. This enables him to send and receive messages with people increasingly different and distant from himself. These options are played in four main language actions—the naming, phrasing, stating, and chaining of ideas. That is, individual words are assigned to stand for concepts, concepts are elaborated by clustering words into phrases, the clusters are related by predicates to make clauses, the clauses are related in turn by logical connectives, and sentences are organized into sequences and patterns to make whole discourses. For the developed speaker choices exist about how to name, phrase, state, and chain his own ideas, and about how to interpret the way others have named, phrased, stated, and chained their ideas. But for the undeveloped speaker, the way speech comes out seems to be the only way the ideas could have been cast into language. Indeed, he doesn't really distinguish thought from speech at all and attributes to words a kind of magical absoluteness. Unable to envision alternatives, he cannot appreciate what is artful and cannot know how some utterance that does not work could have been better.

Egocentricity

To be egocentric is to assume too much. Egocentricity is the main cause of communication difficulties in comprehending and composing. People assume at first that minds match, that the other fellow sees the world as he does, thinks about it the same way, means the same thing when he uses the same words, and fills in the gaps of language as he does. Thinking that something couldn't be any other way is the very essence of egocentricity. The writer is sure that what he said can be taken only one way, and the reader is sure he understands the text in the only way it can be understood. The assumptions, furthermore, are hidden. One doesn't know what it is he doesn't know. People overcome egocentricity only very slowly, and so it is developmental, a lifelong process requiring much verbal and social experience to discover that minds do not match as specifically as we thought but rather have to *be* matched in many particulars.

Examples of egocentricity in reading are "subjective interpretation," omitting cues to meaning, skewing the selection of points or details, "reading in" what is not there, and failing to get in the author's point of view to follow his intent. Examples in writing are missing punctuation, "poor transitions," "illogicality," "lack of focus," "incoherence," overexplaining or underexplaining, and "weak organization." In other words, take almost any serious problem that teachers agree occurs universally in comprehension and composition and you will find, if you examine it closely, that it is caused by unawareness of one's limited point of view. One way to put the matter is that a successful reader must be able to role-play

the author if he is to comprehend what he is trying to say and how he is going about it. The writer must role-play ("allow for") his audience.

Egocentricity is the smallest of several concentric circles that fence in the mind of the individual. He is also ethnocentric—inclined to view life from within a set of ethnic, racial, cultural, and linguistic assumptions that are hard for him to see because, like his private assumptions, they are taken for granted. We can "be subjective" collectively, sharing with some people a mental set not shared by people outside our group. Individuals differ in their thought and perception and values partly just as a result of being born into different groups. Every culture and every language are biased. Although some aspects of all languages are universal, the assumptions built into each language are not the same for all, and often the difference can be startling. We are also geocentric, sexcentric, and so on. Most of humanity's breakthroughs in thinking are *removals* of ideas—unthinking something that was not so or was partial. Children growing are becoming increasingly aware of cognitive options in how things can be thought about. More and more they unthink ideas they took for granted. This is the real meaning of *open-minded*. It does not deprive the thinker of a position. The key, again, is awareness. He knows where he stands. This awareness not only liberates his mind; it makes it possible for him to use language judiciously.

GROWTH SEQUENCE 4: Toward increasing awareness that meaning resides in minds, not in words, and that different people may see the same things differently, verbalize the same ideas differently, and interpret the same words differently.

Explicit and implicit

A listener or reader who doesn't understand a communication does not know if the failure is his or the sender's. If the communication is oral, however, sender and receiver can talk together and find out, in effect, whose hidden assumptions impede the message. But if the communication is written, the reader cannot let the author know what he does not understand so that the author can cast his ideas another way or make more explicit his intent and content. Such a situation puts a premium on the sender's judging right *the first time* around. He has to be aware enough of his possible egocentricity to *predict* the problems his reader may have in understanding what he is trying to say. It puts a premium on the reader's getting the meaning *on one attempt* by the author.

Both efforts require awareness of similarity and difference between sender and receiver. If the receiver knew everything the sender plans to tell him, the communication wouldn't be needed in the first place. So some discrepancy must be assumed. Yet, both have to assume they already share a great deal, or else the author would have to fill in a whole culture's worth of background before he could begin to make his particular points. Here is the crux of the verbalization issues. How much detail people need to make explicit in communicating depends on how much they can assume the receiver shares with them certain factual knowledge, frameworks of understanding, and values. The less the difference between the speaker and listener, the less detail is needed. Tolstoi said that lovers talk in mumbled fragments because they know so well already what's on each other's mind that they need to convey very little.

One of the indications of maturity is the ability of a speaker to predict what different receivers will need to have made explicit for them and what they will understand without elaboration. The small child will expect you to know who Charlie is when he refers to him, whereas an older person will throw in an appositive like "Charlie, my wife's brother . . . ." This is how sentence structure and other language forms grow as a result of growth in awareness of differences. For his part, the receiver must anticipate that some parts of the communication he is getting are omitted and assumed, and he must be prepared to fill them in.

An eighteen-month-old child may have to use the single word "Juice" to say "Give me some juice," "Is that my juice?" or "I'm drinking juice." An adult too may utter "Juice" as a whole sentence, in response to the question, for example, "What are you going to serve to drink?" His answer is really, "I am going to serve juice." For both infant and adult in these cases, the subject and the predicate of the unfinished sentence are implied and have to be "understood." The adult's "Juice" can indeed be understood from the context the conversation creates, but the context for the infant's "Juice" resides only in his mind, and his utterance remains obscure or ambiguous unless the listener can infer his meaning from the context of the child's action toward the juice as he speaks.

The adult could, if pressed, replace "Juice" with the whole statement it stands for, but the infant has no choice, because (1) he cannot yet sort out his global states of mind into parts that fit the parts of speech used to make sentences, (2) he has not yet figured out the different parts of speech and how to put them together to make statements, and (3) he is unaware of the ambiguity and of the listener's need for elaboration. It is likely that all three grow along together, if unevenly, and that any differentiating of one sort—parts of thought, parts of speech, or speaker from listener—will bring along differentiating of another.

In verbalizing his experience for a listener, a speaker is making explicit for himself as well as his listener what until then was a cloudy impression made up of many details he had not singled out in his mind. In uttering the experience he differentiates it into aspects that *fit language*—subjects, actions, objects, time, place, manner, and so on. Eventually he becomes more expert at expressing similar experiences, because language breaks experience down into only so many classes and relations, but even as a very mature speaker later in life he will have trouble making some new experiences explicit because he has not yet tried to parcel them into language. Experience that is especially hard to shape into language may get ignored even by the experiencer, since not making it explicit for others in speech may cause him to remain unaware of it also. So growth in explicitness is relative to the nature of the experience—the less common, the harder to verbalize.

All this is not to say that making thought explicit is always and automatically a good thing. In the first place, as we said, it is impossible in any one communication situation to make *everything* explicit. Some things must be assumed—either some frameworks, on the one hand, or some details, on the other. The receiver has to draw some conclusions and supply some illustrations himself. Furthermore, besides being unavoidable to some degree, implicitness is the main mode of the highest language expression—literature. So in an exact parallel to the simultaneous growth toward generalization and elaboration, people develop at once along the reversed directions of explicitness and implicitness.

GROWTH SEQUENCE 5: Toward increasingly sensitive judgment about when explicitness or implicitness is more appropriate in composing and comprehending.

Both modes of knowing

There is another reason why growth must be toward greater implicitness as well as explicitness, and this may be the real reason for literature. Language must do justice to the two main ways by which, we said earlier, the hemispheres of the brain abstract experience. French, German, and other languages have two different verbs for these two modes of knowing (*savoir* and *connaître, wissen* and *können*), so well were they recognized centuries before modern brain research—intuitively at least! The one associated with the analytic hemisphere is the intellect, and the one associated with the synthesizing hemisphere is intuition. Interestingly, all cultures consider intuitive knowing "direct." The one emphasizes parts and differences; the other, wholes and similarities. The analytic hemisphere sequences separate items in linear, cumulative fashion, moving in a time progression. It is digital and specializes in seriation. It is called the verbal hemisphere because language too is linear and analytic and seems to be essentially controlled by this half of the brain. But the two halves do work in tandem, after all, so that verbalization is significantly influenced by the mode of operation of the synthesizing hemisphere, even though that half is regarded as nonverbal. This hemisphere processes items simultaneously instead of sequentially and therefore is associated with space rather than time. It is analogical and specializes in classification. In holistic fashion, it fuses information coming from different sources at the same time. Because of its spatial orienting, it is associated with arts, sports, and crafts. It works by collecting diverse items together into a constellation based on some intuition of affinity among them. It is metaphorical. It links experience *implicitly,* whereas the other hemisphere names and states explicitly.

If language is to render thought effectively, it must somehow capture both of these modes of knowing—even though its own functioning is governed by the analytic/linear hemisphere alone. Since growth occurs in both modes, and since language tries to do justice to both, we have to look at how it pulls off this feat.

To be explicit is to verbalize, to put into words rather than merely to imply. This difference between what is actually stated and what is left unstated strikes at the heart of our matter here, the rendering of thought into speech. The working of the analytic hemisphere naturally tends to make thought explicit in language, because it breaks thinking down into the kinds of items and relations that characterize language—the grammatical parts of speech, the types of sentence structures, and the kinds of discourse. Indeed, the fact that only humans have specialized hemispheres has prompted a hypothesis that specialization evolved to facilitate speech. But how does language render the thought that characterizes the synthesizing hemisphere?

Literal and figurative

The dimension going from explicit to implicit, upon which the learner grows in both directions, corresponds to another, parallel dimension running from literal to figurative. *Literal* refers to letters, *figurative* to figures of speech. When a gardener talks about how to prune roses, he speaks literally in using their name; he does not, like a poet, refer to roses only as a way of referring to love or intellectual beauty or the house of Tudor. The difference here is between single and multiple levels of meaning. The gardener, like the scientist, does not intend for *the referent to refer in turn* to something else. He means nothing but a rose. Wishing to strip the poor overloaded rose of all its culturally accumulated burden of symbolism, Gertrude Stein said, somewhat testily perhaps in her rebellion against the philosophical poetry of the preceding generations, "A rose is a rose is a rose," that is, nothing but a rose.

A word used literally denotes one and only one thing. If the word normally has several possible meanings, like the word *interest,* only one of those is intended. Used figuratively, a word connotes more than its common meaning or any one of its meanings alone. It implies more than it says. So to speak literally is to be more explicit, to narrow down meaning precisely, whereas to speak figuratively is to refer simultaneously to several things at once. *Equivocal* means exactly this (equi-vocal, several-voiced), and the useful counterterm is *univocal* (single-voiced). James Joyce tried to create a whole language of words such as "gracehoper" that would have meaning at two or more levels. But ordinary language is virtually like this, since the etymology of most words shows that they have or had a primal, concrete meaning upon which the more familiar one is overlaid. In this way Joyce's language is like any other, but his also makes new connections among things as original metaphor always does. The root meaning of *metaphor* itself, for example, is to carry over.

Any metaphor links together two otherwise unconnected items. If someone speaks of a politician put at bay, he is referring by one term to two referents—some politician and some game animal that hunting hounds have closed in on and backed into an impasse. The term bridges two domains, synthesizes two items within some similarity. The receiver has to fill in some of the meaning from his own imagination, because metaphors work implicitly. He must decide for himself how far the comparison goes—perhaps even of what the comparison consists. There is not one term for each referent but one term for both. That is how metaphors operate implicitly. The same concepts that are serially conveyed over time, one concept per word in literal usage, can be conveyed in a single figure of speech, metaphor, or representative token. The term *condensation* has been used to denote this sort of multilevel expression when it occurs in dreams. It applies equally well to figurative language, which *compresses several levels of thought into one language term.*

The same is true for the symbolic figures and actions abounding in folk literature, novels, and other imaginative stories. Ostensibly, *Beowulf* or *Moby Dick* or *Alice in Wonderland* has a single level of meaning, since only one thread of language spins out the cumulative sequence, and, taken at face value, these works are productions of the analytic hemisphere. Items and actions are explicitly designated, and the subject matter is broken down and spread over parts of speech and sentence structures that dutifully dole it out according to conventional public categories. But what an extraordinary, original rendering of experience and thought! The authors have *embodied* their ideas in representative figures and deeds that stand for more than themselves. So a whale and a sea chase manage to carry along several levels of meaning simultaneously—psychological, physical, sociological, anthropological, theological—in exactly the way that the synthesizing hemisphere asserts simultaneously and implicitly a complex of different things.

The verbal work does not have to be fictional, however. Most case histories are such because the central figure or group or experience is *typical,* that is, acts not just as referent of the words but refers in turn to other things in the common experience of reader and writer. A token represents a type, so that referring to the token automatically refers to the type as well and hence to all the other members of it. A chronicle of a Depression family, for example, has double meaning, somewhat like a metaphor or Melville's white whale, in that what is said about it applies elsewhere as well.

This amounts to compressing generality and illustration into one. To the extent that it is literal, standing only for itself, a case at hand is only an instance that might be used to illustrate a general point; but to the extent that it is figurative, standing for others of a class, the case states a generality and illustrates it at once, though the generality, like the symbolism of the white whale, may never be stated *in so many word*s. Literal discourse works by *embedding* generalities as particular sentences, strategically positioned in a discourse, which are supported by examples separately stated. Figurative discourse works by *embodying* generalities throughout the whole in recurring tokens invested with extra meaning by a web of suggestive detail.

Compare literal meaning to melody, in which one note is struck at a time sequentially, and figurative meaning to chords, in which several related notes are struck simultaneously. Figurative language has "overtones" and "undertones" precisely because several things are being referred to *at once*. Neither use of language is good or bad but has its own function. Both must be practiced. When people speak literally, they take one meaning at a time and build some kind of linear, cumulative abstraction, the way they play a tune by sounding one note at a time. When people speak figuratively, they express several meanings together in a complex, the way they strike a chord.

Literal language parcels out thought into speech in such a way that each concept is assigned its own term. In making language commensurate with the thought it conveys, this mode takes longer and allows only one connection among concepts at a time but makes each concept stand out separately, as the notes do in a melody. Figurative language is more economical and emphasizes the kinship and the totality of the concepts considered at once but makes it hard to single out any one of them from the rest and to make explicit what the relations are among them. A chord is like a fundamental, general idea in that it contains many possible melodies, as an idea contains implications and ramifications that can be spun out separately. Each melody is an elaboration of a chord, and each chord is a complex of potential melodies united by some intuition of vibrational affinity. Such is the *resonance* of the experiences Moby Dick stands for.

Figurative use of language answers the question how language can manage to serve at once both modes of knowing though controlled itself essentially by the linear/analytic hemisphere. The secret seems to lie in a certain kind of close collaboration between halves: intuition synthesizes experience into metaphorical complexes and feeds them to the intellect, which processes them in explicit sequences. It's as if the analogical half, specializing in classification, makes up the collections or categories of experiences, while the digital half, specializing in seriation, names and chains these categories. The digital half processes literal and figurative names the same way, so that it can be fooled if the names are equivocal, not univocal. It is not concerned with what isn't said.

The analogical halves of sender and receiver have to conspire, in a sense, to put in and take out of the words what isn't said. This is why shared experience must be assumed. Assuming is dangerous, as we have implied, but the only alternative is to limit communication to one mode of knowing. At any rate, communicating the analogical perceptions through the digital mode is like sending a coded message by means of an unwitting messenger.

The linear half performs its work not on raw material but on material as abstracted already by the holistic half. This same coordination occurs in music when melody is played out a note at a time as the harmony sounds with and includes these notes in chord *progressions,* which are sequenced complexes. (See Table 22.1.)

Ambiguity

Language loaded with multiple meaning is called *ambiguous,* a term like *equivocal* that more often than not suggests that the sender has failed to communicate clearly by not stipulating which of several possible meanings is the one the receiver should select. But it is equally clear that the story of Moby Dick is meant to be ambiguous and that when people speak of the "rich meaning" of much great literature they are praising its ambiguity. Puns and double-entendres are *supposed* to mean more than one thing. So whether ambiguity is desirable or not depends on whether intended or not

TABLE 22.1 THE SPECIALIZED HALVES OF THE BRAIN IN MOST RIGHT-HANDED PEOPLE

Source: This table owes a lot to Robert Ornstein, *The Psychology of Consciousness,* W. H. Freeman and Company, San Francisco, 1972. This is a good book for the lay person and one that we recommend highly.

Left Hemisphere	*Right Hemisphere*
Intellectual	Intuitive
Analytic	Synthetic
Linear	Holistic
Verbal	Nonverbal
Sequential	Simultaneous
Temporal	Spatial
Digital	Analogical
Explicit	Implicit
Literal	Metaphorical

and whether, if intended, it is appropriate or not. Who wants manuals for Strategic Air Command missions to be rich in ambiguity? Most composing problems stem from unintended ambiguity, stemming in turn from egocentricity. Most comprehending problems result from not expecting ambiguity in what one is hearing or reading, so that one is misled by others' unintended ambiguity or interprets figurative language literally.

GROWTH SEQUENCE 6: Toward increasing ability to verbalize literally, when unintended and pointless ambiguity will otherwise result, and to verbalize figuratively when multiple meaning is desirable.

To grow is to become aware of ambiguity, whether engendered by design or by default. This awareness relates directly to the decline of egocentricity, since it is egocentricity that prevents the learner from knowing when a verbalization is ambiguous. As composer, he must know what he has not made explicit that his receiver needs to know. As comprehender he must know when a talk or text should be taken literally and when it aims for multileveled meaning of metaphor and pun and representative token. Further, he needs to understand when a speaker or writer is creating unintended ambiguity through egocentricity. What teachers call literal-minded is a tendency to interpret all discourse on a single level even when the language is figurative and the discourse allegoric or symbolic. Likewise, some learners seem "tone-deaf" or insensitive to connotations and overtones, the subtler effects of holistic simultaneity, for the similar reason that they are over-fastened in the linear, literal, denotative mode.

This kind of incapacity sounds suspiciously school-induced, however, rather than native to childhood, because children are coming from a global state of mind in which the synthesizing mode is most natural, as we can see from their love of far-fetched and highly symbolic stories in which "incongruity" is permitted. Since they can't be identifying with such unrealistic figures and events, they must be attached to what those things represent. Teachers often err in forcing students to paraphrase deliberately ambiguous works in an unambiguous, literal statement—an endeavor that is bound to fail, that makes students detest literature, because it makes them look stupid, and that thwarts the whole point of such works, which is to communicate to the analogical hemisphere of the mind.

Tolerating ambiguity is a mark of maturity, for it is often useful and, even when not, must be expected and dealt with. There is no way to avoid it, but as a person grows he learns increasingly how to exploit it when he wants and minimize it when he wants. But literal-minded people fear ambiguity. They do not want to believe that things may not be what they seem. They insist rigidly on literal meanings in language as they do on physical appearance in life. The absurd lengths to which some English teachers push symbol-chasing and the hunt for hidden meanings make such people feel justified in reading both books and reality as flat and single-leveled. If not pushed constantly to translate figurative into literal, they would respond fearlessly to ambiguity and thus handle it appropriately. So growth here amounts to really undoing a culturally induced problem, the child certainly not being born to reject metaphor.

Many children have experienced disturbingly mixed messages from parents or other adults and fear plural meanings because these have been contradictory. Beaming contradictory messages to someone at the same time places the receiver in a double bind—unless that person can become aware that precisely that is happening to him. Classically, a child hears others say one thing and do another, or say with words something that their voice or gesture contradicts. If he responds to the signal in one channel, he is wrong by the other. The underdeveloped person just tunes out altogether.

Such a student misses both metaphor and irony. Irony scares him, because it is saying the opposite of what you mean in order to say better what you do mean. A Housman poem about death skips nim-bly along in a lively meter. When you know this is deliberate and can accept multiple signals for their richness, you appreciate this consonance between form and content under the apparent dissonance. Understanding the reason for the ambiguity of dissonance—the confusion or the artfulness of other people, as the case may be—releases the fearful person from the double bind. This requires "standing in the other's shoes." The learner needs to know that he can respond to mixed signals at once and does not have to select only one to respond to. Only awareness and a larger perspective will permit him to make some whole in his mind of the mixed signals. Then he can respond to the whole at once.

GROWTH SEQUENCE 7: Toward increasing ability to attune to multiple meaning levels in discourse and to discriminate between egocentric and intended ambiguity in messages one receives.

Next let's look at growth more specifically in four successively larger forms of verbalizing—naming, phrasing, stating, and chaining ideas.

Naming

Words stand for concepts, and concepts grow as youngsters grow. Learning new words and learning new meanings for old words go together. The size of a person's vocabulary may well indicate growth, but we cannot take quantity at face value. Everything depends on how maturely a learner understands the word he "has." He can acquire vocabulary only as he can grasp the concepts denoted, and this understanding will depend on worldly experience and logical development.

As things in the environment become increasingly singled out for a learner by his physically engaging with them, by his seeing other people behaving toward them and pointing them out, or by his comparing them by means of his own sensorimotor equipment, he forms increasingly separated concepts of these things. Finer conceptualizing of anything—colors, musical tones, feelings, political positions—depends partly on experience in the area of the particular subject matter (Eskimos distinguish more kinds of snow than people usually do in temperate climates) and partly on the sensitivity of a person's overall mental and physical development. Differentiating the environment leads to differentiating concepts, which in turn leads to differentiating names.

Concepts develop in the same direction as the rest of mental growth—toward broader generalization and finer elaboration. Concepts will extend further over time and space. A child may at first understand the concept of duty as household or classroom chores he is asked to do, then perhaps as some local allegiance or patriotism, then much later as giving every part of creation its due. Similarly, he will gradually expand the concept of trading from swapping baseball pictures with friends to barter among tribes to the complex of tariffs and balance of payments that comprise international trade.

At the same time, the number of members in a class concept swells, spreading also over time and space, because the learner discovers from his refining discrimination that his classes have subclasses. At first the concept of water-going vessels is limited to the few boats a person has had experience with—a rowboat with outboard motor, let's say, a simple sailboat, and pictures of ocean liners. The concept is vague and global, failing to distinguish less visible traits such as the purpose or the power source and not even distinguishing much about silhouette and structure. Gradually the learner distinguishes yacht from tanker, motor-powered from sail-powered, river-plying from ocean-going, and so on. Discriminating catamaran from schooner from clipper makes him realize that a whole subclass of sailing boats exists having in turn its own membership of subclasses and unique instances.

A less physical concept may not break down into such a definite and systematic branching of particulars but may nevertheless comprise specialized submeanings, as the general concept of duty eventually comprises, as one grows, the concept of a customs tax. As with all abstracting, the combined power of generalizing and elaborating creates hierarchical knowledge of increasing internal complexity.

GROWTH SEQUENCE 8: Toward concepts of broader applicability, of larger membership, and of greater internal complexity of subclasses.

In some cases children learn a more general word first, and in some cases a more specific. Surely most children learn *boat* before *dinghy* and call every water-navigating vessel a boat. Many children call every quadruped *dog* at first, whether the animal is a horse, goat, or tiger. By contrast with *boat, dog* represents the case of learning first the more con-

crete word and moving upward to the more abstract (*quadruped,* or perhaps *mammal*). How specific or general are the words children first learn depends on what is most practical, so that you can expect vocabulary to begin with both concrete and abstract words. What you can count on for consistency is that both will be somewhat misused until the concept fills out in the other direction. Calling all quadrupeds *dog* is overgeneralizing the word (which designates only some quadrupeds) and calling all water-navigating vessels *boat* is overconcretizing (since for any one instance that a person has in mind, a more specific word exists).

GROWTH SEQUENCE 9: Toward vocabulary that more precisely fits the generality level of the concept the user actually has in mind.

NAMING BY PARTS OF SPEECH

The most explicit way to verbalize a concept is to name it with a word especially assigned to it. If a concept is conventional enough to be assigned its own word, and if the speaker knows that word, he may affix the word to the concept. Tradition recognizes nine kinds of words, the grammatical parts of speech—nouns, verbs, adjectives, adverbs, pronouns, articles or determiners, prepositions, conjunctions, and interjections (the last of which we will not consider, since they do not name things but vent feeling). A crude sort of growth order may be plotted among these parts of speech, of some value in the early years, but longer-range growth centers on *alternatives* about how to name things. Naming with single words is itself only one alternative.

Concepts of objects are easier than concepts of relations, and concepts of time-space relations are easier than concepts of logical relations. Because some parts of speech name one of these sorts of concepts and some another, parts of speech vary in degree of learning difficulty. So growth in use of the different parts of speech is linked with abstractive growth of concepts. The hardest parts of speech of all are those that do not refer to the subject matter but refer rather to the communication about the subject matter (*however,* for example). Let's call this communicating about the communication itself *meta*-communication, *meta* meaning on a higher plane. Whatever is meta in respect to something else governs it and is necessarily more abstract and hence more difficult.

Varying Abstractive Difficulty

Proper nouns, common nouns, and pronouns represent a definite abstraction hierarchy corresponding to a growth sequence in the preschool years. A proper noun like *Michigan* refers to only one particular item—something literally in a class by itself. A common noun like *state* refers to a whole class of like items, each of which alone might, like Michigan, have a proper name. Children find proper nouns easier to learn because a singular referent requires little abstracting and because virtually no choice exists for how to refer.

One alternative does exist always, however, for proper nouns as well as for common nouns: a speaker may substitute a pronoun for the original noun and refer to Michigan, for example as "it" or Mommy as "she." Pronouns are comparatively sophisticated because they are relatively meta-communicative. Who "It" or "she" designates depends on context, on a double reference, first from "it" to "Michigan" then from "Michigan" to the concept or image of Michigan.

I, you, and *it* are the algebraic *x, y,* and *z* of ordinary language. They serve exactly the same purpose in speech that "unknowns" serve in math—to act as a variable function in a system so that a particular value may be assigned to each, relative to values assigned other functions in the system. For example, of three people talking together about each other any one may be *I, you,* or *it* from one moment to the next depending on who is sender, receiver, and referent of the talk at that moment. Tom, Dick, and Harry are like numbers, or particular values, that may be plugged into *x, y,* and *z* (*I, you* and *it*) such that if two are known, the other is known. In other words, pronouns are to proper and common nouns what algebra is to arithmetic, a further abstraction. This is why children learn how to use pronouns last.

Whereas nouns, verbs, adjectives, and some adverbs tend to name concepts of *things,* articles, prepositions, conjunctions, and some adverbs tend to name concepts of *relations.*

Adjectives name the traits by which class concepts are formed. Let's replace "articles" with the more modern grammatical notion of "determiners," which includes not only *a, an,* and *the* but *some, any, all, a few,* and any other expressions of quantity, including numbers themselves. Whereas adjectives express quality, determiners express quantity. Concepts of quantity overlap with concepts of logical relations, for *the, any, all,* and *some* also say how broadly a statement is to apply. So determiners are harder than nouns, verbs, and adjectives, quantity being generally more abstract than quality and more directly tied to logical relations.

Prepositions and conjunctions express only concepts of relations—spatial (*in, above, through*), temporal (*after, during, until*), and logical (*if, unless, because, despite*). In this way, they are fairly specialized, like determiners. Relations of time, space, and logic may also be expressed by adverbs (*now, later, farther, downward, therefore, nevertheless*). So the so-called functor words—determiners, prepositions, and conjunctions—may as a class be assumed to belong to a later stage of growth than the other parts of speech, as samples of small children's speech show. Older learners will have "acquired" all the parts of speech but will vary according to how often they use the more relational and meta-communicative words, that is, how explicitly they can *name* the connections among their concepts as opposed to egocentrically assuming them when explicitness is intended and desirable.

Reading the lists from left to right, we can summarize the increasing abstractive difficulty of parts of speech as follows:

proper nouns	common nouns	pronouns
verbs	prepositions	conjunctions
adjectives	determiners	adverbs of relations
time-space adverbs		

GROWTH SEQUENCE 10: From the use of words naming *things* to words naming *time-space relations,* then to words naming *logical relations,* when explicitness is intended and desirable.

GRAMMATICAL OPTIONS IN NAMING

Parts of speech differ only secondarily in the kind of concepts they refer to; they differ first of all in the specialized grammatical role each plays in a sentence. It is not the case that nouns name only things, verbs only actions, and adjectives only qualities. The noun *descent* refers to an action, the verb *encase* to an object (casing), and the adjective *lumpy* refers to an object. In keeping with the truth that thought may be cast into alternative language forms, we could say that the pudding is lumpy or that lumps float in the pudding, depending on the desired emphasis and effect. So a certain kind of concept may take one of several parts of speech when translated into language. This is why it is misleading to define *nouns* for students only as names of a person, place, or thing, and *verbs* only as actions. All parts of speech name, and they name concepts, and several may name the same concept. The difference between the adjective *helpless* and the adverb *helplessly* is not a difference in concept but in *how one wants to get the concept into the sentence.*

To some extent, then, the language form into which a speaker casts a concept merely reflects his choice about how to cast a more complex idea of which the concept is only a part. That is, one has options about how to get the concept of encasing or of helplessness into a statement of a larger idea. One may choose to place the concept in a subject or object role (noun) or into a modifying role (adjective or adverb), or to predicate a statement by means of it (verb). One may choose to convey causality by saying that such and such was the *cause* (noun) of the effect, that such and such *caused* the effect (verb), that the effect happened *because* such and such (conjunction), or that the effect happened *because of* such and such (preposition). The grammatical specializations of vocabulary that we call parts of speech exist to offer options about how to relate a concept to fellow concepts interacting in the same statement. Thus it is that naming depends in turn on the more inclusive process of stating.

GROWTH SEQUENCE 11: Toward increasing ability to name a concept by a part of speech befitting the role of that concept within a statement.

RHETORICAL OPTIONS IN NAMING

Something may be named by more than one word. Diction, in the sense of word choice, concerns alternative naming. This goes beyond mere synonyms, which are different words for the same concept (imitate, emulate). You may point to your car and call it a vehicle, a sedan, a chariot, a lemon, a liability, or a relic. In your discourse these all refer to the same thing—what you are pointing to. The physical referent of all is the same, but each word applies a different conceptualization to it. So be-

sides a choice among synonyms for the same concept, a sender has choices about how to verbally ticket nonverbal things, with the result that the receiver is influenced to regard the nonverbal item from only one of many possible viewpoints. The idea that a rose by any other name may not smell so sweet reminds us that naming guides response.

Maturity in naming relates of course to increasing size of vocabulary, but much more is required— some detachment from language and some liberation of mind, some wit. Beginners tend to fuse word with thing and only gradually differentiate symbol from symbolized to the point where they can detach a word they have associated with a thing and replace it by another name. Studying foreign languages certainly enhances this detachment, precisely by forcing the mind to accept alternative naming of the same concepts. Seeing clearly the independence of matter from mind is a prerequisite for virtuosity in naming, and this is a factor of general egocentricity, because such detachment is tantamount to separating self from world (*I* from *it*).

Figurative Names

Naming may be literal or figurative. Calling policemen *centurions* overlays on the concept of modern policemen the concept of Roman military officers and thus makes a double reference. Such metaphorical naming opens up limitless possibilities for wit and imagination, since virtually any two items in the universe may be classed alike by some attribute or other. In this way *naming can be a way of stating.* Calling policemen centurions states, in effect, that they have the professional dedication, self-discipline, and inherited esprit de corps that characterized these Roman officers. Naming figuratively is an *implicit* way of stating. In fact, the more any name departs from the most commonly used label for something, the more it tends to make an implicit statement while, or under the guise of, merely naming.

Distinguish this deliberate originality, however, from the naïve speaker's use of a single word to make a statement, exemplified in the extreme by a small child's tendency to say, "Hat," for example, when he means, "I see a hat lying over there." This way of making a word do duty as a sentence is very different of course. In both cases, a word is not only naming a concept but is relating that concept to one or more other concepts. An adult too might say, "A sail!" meaning, "I see a ship," in which case he is using the figure of speech called synecdoche (letting a part stand for a whole). The difference lies in awareness, or lack of egocentricity. In a sense, the child is merely using synecdoche too, but he has no choice, and unless the receiver is especially close to him both in the moment and physically in general, he will not understand, because no public convention supplies the missing elaboration.

GROWTH SEQUENCE 12: Toward increasing versatility and originality in naming.

Phrasing

A phrase may name also. Some phrases name, whereas some relate concepts in ways akin to stating. So phrasing overlaps the functions of naming and stating, by expanding one and compressing the other. A phrase is a word cluster relating the concepts that the individual words stand for. The result is a conceptual complex. Phrases add to naming the very important language operation of modifying. *Man in the moon, gesture of contempt, separate peace, delightful old coot, behind the curtain, during the war* are words brought to bear on each other so that the meaning of one is modified by the meaning of the other. This joining of concepts may create an original notion or may be so standard (*man in the moon*) as to have the force of a single concept and single word only.

Phrases modify either a noun or a verb and hence function in a sentence as an adjective or an adverb. This means they express both concepts of things and concepts of relations. Prepositional phrases treat relations directly because prepositions name relations (*near, during*). Phrasing increases enormously the variety of ways things can be named. The lexicon of a language is finite, but the permutations of this lexicon by phrasing are virtually infinite.

Suppose a speaker does not know the name for a public concept. If he does not know the word *nave* he will have to resort to talking around the concept—to a circumlocution—such as "the part of the church running lengthwise." In this case, phrasing indicates lack of growth in vocabulary. Often youngsters' concepts outstrip their vocabulary and force them to invent. Phrasing of this sort shows clearly the disparity in growth between thought and speech and also shows how the presence or ab-

sence of a certain word is no accurate index to the presence or absence of certain concepts.

Phrasing from necessity spurs invention, however, and some of it has the virtue of originality. A fourth grader writing about his trip to New York City referred to the Statue of Liberty as "that big metal girl," having forgotten the name. Fresh phrasing like this re-creates the world. It can amuse us, make us see old things a new way, and understate. The power of poetry depends tremendously on originality of phrasing, to name anew and relate the normally unrelated.

In a kind of parody of their future growth, the fourth grader's phrase and the preschooler's "Hat" do out of necessity and naiveté what the best users of language do. Once again, the surface form of the language does not show this difference. Growth of phrasing consists of doing with foreknowledge of effect what the fourth grader did as makeshift. In the play *Cyrano de Bergerac*, Cyrano reels off a fanciful catalogue of the ways in which his detractor might have referred to Cyrano's nose had he the wit to make his insults imaginative. Though not executed in phrases only, his tour de force exemplifies the high art of versatile and original referring that extends beyond the word and that learners grow toward. The skilled language-user does not always *want* to use the conventional term for a concept, because he can get various rhetorical effects by a creative circumlocution.

Furthermore, words do not exist for everything that can be conceived. Any trait whatsoever, visible or invisible, can be the defining characteristic of a class. Concept formation can be very personal. People classify other people, for example, into those who are safe or dangerous, useful or useless, attractive or repulsive, stable or flighty, and so on. Anyone can form a class concept any time merely by designating the trait or traits that would identify instances of the collection, just as anyone could decide to form a club whose members would all be left-handed Bach-loving expatriates. The more original the thinking, the more original will have to be the naming and phrasing of it. Vocabulary alone tends to stereotype thought. The only way to offset this is to combine vocabulary in unusual ways by making up phrases.

GROWTH SEQUENCE 13: Metaphor and circumlocution enter more and more into the learner's language as a way not to substitute for lack of vocabulary but to express a greater range of thought in a greater range of styles for a greater range of effects.

By bringing parts of speech to bear on each other, phrases explicitly relate one concept to another and hence approach the role of stating. Many a clause could in fact be a phrase (". . . after the show was over . . ." or ". . . at the end of the show . . ."). Reduced clauses or potential clauses will be treated below as statement, but it's important to keep in mind that an option nearly always exists to relate concepts as a phrase or as a clause. One chooses whether to assert the relation as a statement, thereby giving it more importance, or to subordinate the relation within a statement asserting something else.

Stating

Stating is saying that something is so. Like a phrase, a statement relates concepts, but a statement does more. It *predicates*. By means of a predicate, the speaker asserts a proposition. So verbs are the key, and the nature of the predicate determines the kind of statement. Grammatically, a statement corresponds to a clause, not to a sentence necessarily, since a sentence may contain many clauses. The clause corresponds in language to a proposition in logic. It is the fundamental arena of grammar, which is the sum of ways that words and phrases may be related to make statements.

The first issue of growth in stating is whether the speaker can parcel his thought out into at least a subject and a predicate and perhaps some modifiers of each. If he makes a statement through a single word or through a phrase, he is obviously leaving out elements and therefore making his statement implicitly. As we said, the immature speaker lets a part stand egocentrically for the whole he has in his mind—by default—whereas the poet compresses thought into figures of speech that—by design—imply whole statements.

MODIFICATION

Once capable of stating in clauses, the learner faces the second and very long-range issue of whether his clauses explicitly elaborate in language forms, to the extent he thinks they do and to the extent his receiver needs, just what he has in mind. Consider language as a kind of adjustable rack to fit thought onto. The more people spell out just what they mean, the more they do what we called earlier elaborating. The way to make ideas explicit is to put into words enough details about the subject and the predicate to connect up with shared assumptions in the receiver. This means adding modifiers—qualification, quantification, time, place, manner. This is the function of determiners, adjectives, and adverbs—whether in the form of a word or a word cluster.

The amount of modification is the key to innumerable composition and comprehension matters. Overgeneralizing, for example, results from failing to quantify (to say how many people or things are covered by one's statement), to qualify (to limit the subject or object by more detailed description and limit the conditions under which the statement is true). Both narrative and generalization may suffer if the time and space are indicated too vaguely. Paucity of vivifying detail and unclear concepts require more, or more precise, modification. Above all, the predicate itself must become as complex as the thought is complex. Compare:

> The middle child in the family has the best deal.

> A middle child may enjoy the advantages of having the elder fray a path for him and shoulder the most responsibility and yet not be treated as the "baby" of the family.

The first statement may imply the second, but does the receiver know that? At the grammatical level, explicitness entails more words and more interaction of words—verbal complexity.

GROWTH SEQUENCE 14: Toward increasing modification as required by the complexity of ideas and the needs of the receiver.

THE SPECIAL CASE OF *TO BE*

The verb *to be* requires special attention. It means several different things logically and hence tends to be widely used and ambiguous. It is the most important predicate. The notation of symbolic logic differentiates the various logical meanings of *to be,* by assigning to each its own symbol. For the best explanation of this important problem of translating thought into speech, we quote from logician Suzanne Langer:

> Few people are aware that they use so common and important a word as "is" in half a dozen different senses. Consider, for instance, the following propositions:

1. The rose is red.
2. Rome is greater than Athens.
3. Barbarossa is Frederick I.
4. Barbarossa is a legendary hero.
5. To sleep is to dream.
6. God is.

In each of these sentences we find the verb "is." But each sentence expresses a differently constructed proposition: (1) ascribes a *property* to a term; in (2) "is" has logically only an auxiliary value of *asserting* the dyadic relation, "greater than"; in (3) "is" expresses *identity;* in (4) it indicates *membership* in a class (the class of legendary heroes); in (5) *entailment* (sleeping entails dreaming); in (6) *existence.*

So we see that in (1) and (2) it is only part of the logical verb—it serves only to assert the relation, which is otherwise expressed—and in the remaining four cases, where "is" does function as the whole logical verb, it expresses a different relation in every case. It has at least four different meanings besides its use as auxiliary. Our linguistic means of conveying relations are highly ambiguous. But the expression of relations is the chief purpose of language. If we were interested only in *things* and not in their arrangement and connection, we could express ourselves with our forefingers. . . . the study of relations is necessarily bound up with a study of discourse. But if the latter obscures and disguises relations, as it often does, there is no escape from error, except by adopting another sort of discourse altogether. Such a new medium of expression is the symbolism of logic. In this ideography, the four propositions wherein "is" really names a relation would not appear to have a common form, but would wear the badge of their distinctions plainly in view:

3. Barbarossa = Frederick I
4. Barbarossa ∈ legendary hero
5. To sleep ⊂ to dream
6. E! God [1]

GROWTH SEQUENCE 15: Toward increasing ability to differentiate, as sender and receiver, the various meanings of *to be.*

[1] Suzanne Langer, *Introduction to Symbolic Logic,* Dover Publications, Inc., New York, 1953, p. 56–57. Reprinted by permission of the publisher.

If modifying *elaborates* statements, what *generalizes* them? The answer is, the tense of the verb that predicates the statement. What people generally call time differences are really degrees of abstraction. As we said in Chapter 1, Basic Concepts, distances between sender, receiver, and message amount to differences in levels of abstraction. Tenses describe when events occurred in relation to when the speaker is referring to them. Hence they denote point of view or the distance between the speaker and the original raw material that he has abstracted from. Besides, it is clear that people predicate about a lot besides events and that time is not an issue except in narrative.

One way the learner grows in the skill of stating is to assert explicitly more general statements. He may learn how to form all the tenses fairly early, but he will actually compose and comprehend statements in certain ones only as he grows into the abstraction levels they exist to convey.

The present tense of generalization predicates explicitly, as its name says, the analogizing of experiences of different times. It is an utterly different tense from the present progressive. *What happens* can only be recurring—that is, mental—events. "He eats catsup on his scrambled eggs" expresses a higher generalization than "He is eating catsup on his eggs," "He was eating catsup on his eggs," "He ate catsup on his eggs," or "He will eat catsup on his eggs." "He *eats* catsup on his eggs" *summarizes* all the other statements. Each statement in order summarizes, in fact, a bit more than the preceding one. Each tense applies more broadly over time and space until the sequence culminates in that tense that specializes in stating generalities as such.

GROWTH SEQUENCE 16: Toward increasingly general statement as indicated by the tense sequence below:

what is happening—progressive present
what has happened—perfect

what happened—past
what will happen—future

what happens—present tense of generalization
what might or could happen or be true—conditional

The boxed tenses above show most clearly the main expansion from the present to the past to the timeless, the other tenses fitting between these. Further generalizing the past leads to *what will happen*. The future is only an extrapolation of the past. Extrapolation is a mental extension over time and space of existing circumstances. Convinced by his analogies between past events that life has stability and consistency, the learner predicts that certain objects will reappear or events recur. But *nothing* ever recurs, of course. Establishing parallels between *what has happened* and *what will happen* is a matter of generalizing experience further: "The sun has always risen, and the sun will continue to rise." The next logical step is to generalize that "The sun always rises."

The shift from past to potential truth is a shift from fact in the Latin sense of *factus*—the "done," the deed or event—toward opinion. The growth sequence is that people record experience via perception, then report it via memory, then generalize it via reflection.[2] Not only are these stages by which anyone processes experience all the time, they are stages of growth accumulated by every youngster. As perception, memory, and reason successively develop, he makes and understands increasingly more statements in the corresponding tense.

GROWTH SEQUENCE 17: From emphasis on the present (sensorimotor abstracting) to past (memory abstracting) to timelessness (abstracting by reason).

If we look at the conditional tenses, we can see that further reasoning will take us beyond statement to the *relations among* statements. "If this happens, that will happen" (or will have happened). "If this happened, that would happen." "If this had happened, that would have happened." These tenses are coordinated as a function of each other. The reasoning resides not in one tense but in the relation of tenses. The truth of one statement is conditional on the other statement being true. The conditional tense breaks the bounds of the clause and forces us to consider how statements are connected to each other.

[2] To see how improvisation can be shifted to reflection see Betty Jane Wagner, Chapter 8, "Dropping to the Universal," in *Dorothy Heathcote: Drama as a Learning Medium,* National College of Education Association, Evanston, Ill., 1976.

Chaining

The clause, not the sentence, is the basic verbal form of statement. When teachers define a sentence as subject plus predicate, they are really defining a clause, and when they say a sentence expresses a complete thought, they mean an independent clause asserts a proposition. They are thinking of a single clause as a sentence, whereas a sentence may comprise several clauses. Indeed, a sentence is the main way clauses are chained.

SENTENCES

A set of clause-statements may be connected in three ways:

1. By making each a separate sentence and stringing them:
   I saw Bobby's hat. It was in a tree. The wind blew it there. Then it rained.

2. By joining several into one sentence by conjunctions, relative pronouns, or punctuation:
   I saw Bobby's hat and it was in a tree, and the wind blew it there, and then it rained. (The famous run-on sentence of the immature speaker.)
   I saw Bobby's hat, which was in a tree, where the wind blew it before it rained.

3. By reducing some clauses to phrases and embedding them in others:
   In a tree I saw Bobby's hat, blown there by the wind before the rain.

First, the learner predicates ideas separately, then he joins them with the easier conjunctions, then sometimes he joins them with more difficult conjunctions and relative pronouns, and sometimes he embeds some within others. So 1, 2, and 3 above represent a growth order if you keep in mind that the difficulty of conjoining (2) depends on the difficulty of the connector word (its concept, that is), and the difficulty of embedding varies considerably with the kind of clause reduction.

To demonstrate further the issues of 2 and 3, let's take another series having a more abstract topic:

1. Goodsayer was elected. He adopted the policies advocated by his opponent. He had harshly criticized them when he was running for office.

Notice the repetition of subject and object so clangingly present in children's clause strings but muted here by the pronouns. Strings are uneconomical because they keep predicating the same nominals. Personal pronouns disguise this, but of pronouns only the relative can solve this, not the personal (*he* above). The next sentence represents maturer development by conjoining the clauses:

2. After he was elected, Goodsayer adopted the policies that his opponent was advocating, which he had harshly criticized when he was running for office.

But the following version, which reduces and embeds four clauses from the first, requires substantially more development:

3. Once elected, Goodsayer adopted the policies advocated by his opponent—the very policies he had harshly criticized during the campaign.

It is worth the trouble to study these three sentences and compare the changes, because the differences exemplify a great deal about growth in sentence development. Though shorter, the last sentence above is harder than the second because students have to develop clauses first before they can learn to reduce them. Of course, a speaker or writer does not normally compare alternatives, as we are doing here. Most composition is more spontaneous than that, and even hard revision would not produce the shorter version until the author had logged considerable composing experience. Compactness comes harder, and when length is a sign of looseness, as in run-on sentences, it shows immaturity.

This is not to say the compacter version is always better. It has a different emphasis, partly because it leaves more implicit. It might not therefore suit as well a given intent. The point here is that to be *able* to reduce clauses and embed them in each other, when this relates concepts appropriately, indicates fairly advanced growth. Of course, "reducing and embedding clauses" is only a manner of speaking, since no one sees people do this except occasionally perhaps in written revision, but to infer some such inner process occurring gradually seems reasonable since language-users of different maturity levels differ by just such sample sentences. Inserting links between clauses is easier than reducing and fusing clauses, but the conceptual difficulty of individual linking words—spatial-temporal versus logical, for example—must be allowed for.

As clauses are conjoined and embedded, they require certain meta-communicative words—conjunctions like *but, or, although, because, unless* or relative pronouns like *who, which,* and *where.* The statements are the communication, and these connectors meta-communicate about how to take and relate the statements. As we said, such words are harder just as concepts, but they are also hard because they relate statements to form more complex ideas. Conjunctions name explicitly the relation, whereas relative pronouns merely plug one nominal into two predicates, naming nothing and relating implicitly instead. See preceding examples.

GROWTH SEQUENCE 18: Expanding the repertory of clause-connecting options as follows:

- String of separate clauses, each a sentence
- Clauses conjoined by coordinating conjunctions (*and, but, or*) and time-space conjunctions
- Clauses conjoined by logical subordinating conjunctions and fused by relative pronouns

Two things are important to the formulation above. One is to emphasize that the maturer learner not only can do these things but uses them *appropriately*, according to the place of the statements in a total discourse. Complexity for its own sake is no mark of maturity. Complexity is necessary but not sufficient for fullest growth. A string of single-clause sentences can be very effective for making an image or idea dawn gradually on the receiver. It understates and it also stretches out the reader's assimilation time. The more developed student would for these reasons employ such a string even though he was capable of fashioning very intricate sentence structures.

The second matter is the critical one of subordinating concepts one to another so that they are related with the proper emphasis. Stringing makes all statements equal, besides not making explicit the relations among them. The only connection is the primitive one of first-to-last, which says nothing unless the statements are about events, in which case the order of stringing them is assumed to be the order of their occurrence. Coordinating conjunctions say that the statements are equal in rank (*co*-ordinate) in addition to being, say, alternative (or) or adversative (but). More properly speaking, the statements are equal and the conjunctions are coordinating because equality is in the nature of the logical relationships *and, or,* and *but,* if you think about it, whereas the subordinating conjunctions, such as proviso (*unless*), concession (*although*), condition (*if*), and the time-space conjunctions require that the clause they introduce be subordinate to the one to which it is conjoined. (Time-space clauses are always adverbial modifiers, of course, and hence subordinated to the sentence predicate.)

Now let's bring in the conventional terms:

- Single-clause sentence—"simple sentence"
- Clauses conjoined by coordinating conjunctions —"compound sentence"
- Clauses conjoined by subordinating conjunctions—"complex sentence"
- Clauses conjoined by both coordinating and subordinating conjunctions—"compound-complex sentence"

Although this progression roughly parallels our growth sequence, it allows neither for the embedding of reduced clauses nor for variation in the difficulty among conjunctions and between conjunctions and relative pronouns. This old classification of sentences does bring out, however, subordination and emphasis, two critical factors of growth in making sentences and sentence sequences out of basic statements.

From his research with children's writing Kellogg Hunt concluded that sentence growth is marked by (1) increasing modification of nouns by large clusters of adjectives, relative clauses, and reduced relative clauses, (2) increasing use of nominalizations other than nouns and pronouns for subjects and objects (clauses, infinitival and gerundive constructions) and (3) embedding of sentences to an increasing depth (entailed by 1 and 2).[3] On page 20 we gave examples of degrees of nominalization; it is one form of embedding clauses and reducing clauses.

GROWTH SEQUENCE 19: Toward increasing versatility in constructing sentences, exploiting more nearly the total resources inherent in *modifying, conjoining, reducing,* and *embedding* clauses.

[3] Kellogg Hunt, *Grammatical Structures Written at Three Grade Levels,* National Council of Teachers of English, Champaign, Ill., 1965.

SYLLOGISMS

A special case of conjoining clauses was touched on when we spoke of conditional tenses joined by *if.* When two or more conditional clauses are linked to each other and to a conclusion clause, a syllogism is created. "If high spending contributes to inflation, and if advertising and credit stimulate high spending, then advertising and credit contribute to inflation."

At the material level, such a conjunction of conditions may be stated in a sentence like this: "*If* heavy rain falls a long time on loose dirt, and *if* the terrain is steeply tilted, a mudslide will occur." Note that this logical relationship may be expressed by other conjunctions and by adverbs: "A mudslide occurs *because* heavy rain falls a long time on loose dirt and *because* the terrain is steeply tilted." Or: "The rain falls a long time on loose dirt, and the terrain is steeply tilted; so [*therefore*] a mudslide occurs." The point is that underneath these various conjunctions and adverbs there lies a single logical relationship. This relationship is called entailment: certain things being so entail other things being so. (See on page 449 Suzanne Langer's mention of entailment.) It is important to realize that what is the same at the conceptual level—entailment—may be expressed at the verbal level as causality, conditionality, or something else.

Syllogizing may be, first of all, implicit or explicit and, second, may take several forms. It is an important sort of logical growth to look for, but the teacher can expect it to be revealed in more than one verbal way, if made explicit at all. A syllogism may perfectly well exist in a discourse without being verbalized in a single sentence. It may be embodied in another kind of linguistic linking than conjoined clauses—in one of the other kinds of chaining discussed in the rest of this chapter.

TRANSITIONAL WORDS

Besides conjunctions and relative pronouns, certain adverbs connect clauses and do so as explicitly as conjunctions (*moreover, however, nevertheless, so, therefore, accordingly,* and others referring to ideas in previous clauses), but these differ in being situated *within* a clause, not between clauses, so that they tie clauses together only by throwing an idea bridge, not by connecting grammatically. These are what we might call transition words, because they are added to a clause to relate statements explicitly in the same way that whole sentences may be stuck into a discourse to effect transitions from one main idea or part of the organization to another ("Leaving aside for the moment the objections to this idea, let's turn now to . . .").

Transitions too constitute meta-communication and hence do not occur to speakers too egocentric to realize that a receiver might not know how to connect his clauses unless guided. On the other hand, a mature speaker may choose to omit some transitions as being unnecessary, heavy, or verbose for the ideas and the audience involved, or he may wish to speak implicitly to make his audience think more and work out connections for itself— obviously a sophisticated stance, indeed a very confident one. And once again, the presence of the words—*hence* or *so*, say—does not guarantee the presence of the concepts they stand for. A trick of weak writers is to plaster their composition together with *therefore*s and *moreover*s in *lieu* of thought.

PUNCTUATION

Colons, semicolons, and sometimes commas also connect statements. They are much less explicit than word connectors, but they have some meaning. A colon tends to act as an equation mark and hence assumes one meaning of *to be* (identity), and a semicolon or comma implies unusual closeness between clause-statements. See page 239 for examples. Without indicating the nature of the relation, this binding nevertheless invites the reader to supply for himself a conjunction of time, causality, contradiction, and so on, according to context.

PARAGRAPHING

Paragraphing is another way of implying relations between statements. A paragraph break, for example, between one statement and another means that the thought takes a bigger jump than is usual between sentences or that thought is shifting to another time or plane or domain. Placing one statement at the beginning of a paragraph and another within may mean that the first is superordinate or more general and that the next one is subordinate or more concrete. The first sentence might state a generality and the second state an instance or consequence of it. The relative positioning may obviate the need of "for example" or "so." The sheer order in which statements are chained means something

of course, since juggling the order would usually make considerable difference in the intelligibility of the message. Paragraphing imposes upon this sequence other patterns of significance by clumping together statements so that distance, salience, and subordination vary among them and hence imply certain interrelations. The ways of chaining sentences that comprise paragraphs can comprise the organization of an entire discourse.

ORGANIZATION

The possibilities of paragraphing are the possibilities of organizing a whole discourse. The continuity may vary in length, but once beyond the sentence (with its special grammatical rules of relating) the ways of chaining statements are the same as for composing the units of any other linear medium— serial order, juxtaposition, and pattern. These are universal factors of form and constitute what English teachers mean by "organization" in a composition. Form establishes relations by sheer selection and arrangement, without naming relations. Form speaks —but implicitly. So clause-connecting throughout an entire continuity of statements is nothing less than the overall form of a complete discourse, and the forms with which people compose discourses are general forms common to many other media.

Ascending and Descending Forms

In music, we speak of the first statement of a theme and of its later variations. This form compares to an opening statement of the main idea of a discourse followed by the elaborating of its implications in substatements. Either a whole discourse, a subdivision of it, a paragraph, or even a sentence could be organized this way—from higher to lower abstraction. It is the deductive form exemplified by the famous "topic sentence," which sets a frame within which details, implications, consequences, evidence, and so on are expounded. Within a sentence this works out as a main clause followed by subordinate clauses and by modifiers:

> They just had to peer over the rim, although the canyon terrified them, leaning far forward over planted feet, heads tipped back for balance, eyes turned down their cheeks.

Within a whole discourse, paragraphs would so descend.

The opposite form may be equally right, depending on intent and content. It is the inductive order, by which a theme is gradually built up through partial statements until arrived at climactically. Within a sentence, modifiers and subordinate clauses would prepare for the main clause, which would come at the end as climax (the so-called periodic sentence).

> Whenever someone asked her to sing once again, perhaps at tea time in the old sunroom, perhaps at a garden gathering in the morning, imploring, saying she had no right to withhold that gift, her plump hand would go to her throat, and her head would slowly wag no.

Following the same model on larger scales, a paragraph or a whole discourse would start low and build high, suspensefully, revealing only enough per statement to carry the receiver to the next, broader view, whether the increments are physical details of a complex object, causes of some effect, or arguments leading toward a conclusion.

The direction that the chaining moves between low and high abstraction, whole and part, generality and instance, is of great significance for composition and comprehension, for the opposed approaches orient the receiver very differently. The growing learner has to understand that these options exist and what effect they have. Chaining need not follow the order in which events, images, or thoughts originally or logically occur, because rhetorical ends must be served. A reader may see a scene more clearly if the writer starts with a "panoramic shot" and then "zooms" in on details, but like William Faulkner and Stephen Crane on occasion, the writer may want the reader to experience with the character the feeling, precisely, of *not* being "on top of" a situation. An effect of dawning, produced by many poems, comes from forcing the receiver to orient himself by minimal cues that imply perhaps several possibilities that he must consider and check out as the statement continuity proceeds. A logical conclusion might go either at the beginning or at the end of a discourse, depending on whether the reader's knowing the conclusion first makes following the arguments much easier or on whether the writer wishes the reader to work through in his own mind the steps by which the conclusion was reached.

It may be better to derange the order in which events occurred and start in the middle, as Homer did with the *Iliad,* then flash back to the beginning, or to cut back and forth among different periods, as Marcel Proust and Kurt Vonnegut do, in order to juxtapose events in a new, mental relation. Inductive and deductive orders may be combined as when a main statement is built up by evidence then, once established and warranted, applied to various domains to see what it will turn up. Repetition is also an important formal device common to both writing and music as the "motif."

GROWTH SEQUENCE 20: Toward using and responding to the full rhetorical possibilities for chaining statements by grammar, transitional words, punctuation, paragraphing, and organizational form, according to the commitment of the whole discourse.

Emphasis must be on good judgment in playing options. No particular sentence construction, paragraph structure, or organizational form is better than another except relative to the communication needs of the content and intent. Growth does not consist of merely acquiring the tools of meta-communication to name or state connections explicitly. These tools constitute the technical prerequisite but alone are not enough. Always, the learner must learn to judge, as either sender or receiver, if meta-communication is desirable. Too often teachers incline to value only the explicit, because they can see it and *know* what a student's thought is, but explicitness is definitely only half of the matter. Since not all can ever be said, discoursing is always a matter of ascertaining how much will do the trick properly.

A concept may play different roles in a complex of concepts, may be more or less conscious in the speaker, may be more or less explicit in a discourse, and so may for these reasons be conveyed by a single word, a phrase, a simple sentence, a complex sentence, a continuity of sentences, a metaphor, a motif, or a formal pattern in the organization of the total work. A learner grows in mastery of composing and comprehending these alternatives for matching thought with speech.

Growth in kinds of discourses

Discourse begins in dialogue. Children first learn to speak from conversing. Dialogue is verbal collaboration, which means that utterances are chained by the reciprocal prompting of each speaker by the other. Sender and receiver constantly reverse roles. Feedback and correction are plentiful and fast.

Statements are mixed with questions, because speakers can get immediate answers, and mixed with commands, because speakers are localized together in the same space-time and hence more personally related. The *I-you* relation dominates the discourse, in fact, so that the organization is determined by a succession of social exchanges even when the dialogue is an earnest intellectual discussion sticking close to a topic. Dialogue may of course vary tremendously in maturity, but the less developed a speaker the more he is *limited* to dialogue. *Growth consists of extending one's range of kinds of discourse by learning to monologue at different abstraction levels.*

Monologue arises from dialogue. One speaker solos for a while within the context of a conversation to tell an anecdote, describe something he saw, explain a point of view, give a set of directions, or otherwise *sustain some continuity.* Thus are narrative, exposition, and argumentation born. Most kinds of discourse are monologue and, in self-contained form, are written. To compose and to comprehend most discourse, then, the learner must learn to spin out from within himself some mono-logical continuities based on the kinds of logical and rhetorical chaining that we have described. He must forgo at times the give-and-take prompting and fast feedback of dia-logical succession.

It takes emotional as well as conceptual and verbal maturity to compose alone, even just orally (though once able, a person may verbalize compulsively as a defense!). To shift from collaborating to soloing is only one case of the general law that external activity becomes internalized. (See page 32.) As mind digests matter, so personality incorporates sociality. Furthermore, composing monologues requires a certain inner attention to the ordering of thoughts and an understanding of the receiver's need for some elaboration. Comprehending monologues requires an ability to focus steadily on one thing and to hold in the mind a stream of accumulating statements until they can be assimilated.

GROWTH SEQUENCE 21: From mixing various kinds of discourse within dialogue to singling out and sustaining each kind of discourse separately in monologue.

At first, children talk rather indiscriminately to themselves and to their toys and to their partners at play. Even if you teach senior high students, it is important to understand this play prattle, because it is a base line from which all later growth can be better perceived. The first monologuing is very egocentric in that it does not allow much at all for an audience other than the speaker. (Adults accuse each other of talking only to themselves when they feel discourse is not "objective" enough.) Also, the subject is something present in front of the child—something he is watching or playing with. Actually, the subject is the child's feelings about what is present. Invoking our communication triangle, prattle represents speaker, listener, and subject at a point where egocentricity makes them barely separate. A lot of prattle does not, in fact, even attempt to communicate but represents sheer vocal exercise and sound games related to what we have called Word Play.

Gradually this egocentric monologuing begins to divide into external speech aimed at other people and internal speech for oneself that goes underground and becomes merely thought as the child begins to discriminate between himself and others. Verbal thinking then goes inward and merges with nonverbal thinking. Once more socially aware, there is seldom point to "thinking out loud."

In the same way that he begins to discriminate between talking to himself and talking to others, the child begins to discriminate between talking about himself and talking about other things. From prattle focused entirely on his involvement with things facing him here and now, he turns to subjects out of sight but not out of mind and thence gradually extends for the rest of his life the space-time compass of what he discourses about. He talks about absent people and objects, events he remembers, and things to do later. This movement of growth away from self occurs over both physical and psychological distance and results in increasingly clearer separation of speaker from subject. The three-way fission of verbalization into distinct "persons," schematized in Figure 22.1 (page 456), describes in one way the decline of egocentricity and the rise of impartiality, because another way of viewing composition and comprehension problems is as blurring of one's mind with the world and with other minds. But true growth merely *enables* a person to achieve this analytical clarity; it does not enforce it.

VARIETIES OF MONOLOGUE

Once launched into monologuing and the differentiation of sender, message, and receiver, the learner

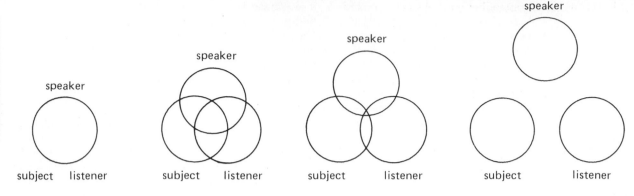

FIGURE 22.1 GROWTH OF COMMUNICATION TRIAD

then begins to differentiate among the various kinds of discourse so that he can match them to his gradually diversifying thought. Prattle about play objects leads directly to Labels and Captions, a kind of discourse in which one says what one sees, or comments on what one sees, and which consists often of single words and sentence fragments like a child's disjointed speech. Word Play clearly derives from and extends to more sophisticated levels the creative experimentation with sound and sense, the playful vocal exercising, that characterizes so much of prattle. Invented Dialogue and Actual Dialogue are of course a direct outgrowth of child-family conversation and ultimately cover the greatest range of subject matter. Though Word Play, Labels and Captions, and Actual and Invented Dialogue spin off directly from a child's first oral speech, they all exist also in written form, so that growth is partly a matter of carrying these kinds of discourse over into writing and reading.

Invented Stories, True Stories, Directions, Information, and Ideas are first done orally as fragments of dialogue—an anecdote here, a scrap of fact here—but as whole discourses unto themselves, they are most likely done in writing. True Stories take off from the here-and-now of prattle, other running commentary, and such sense-bound discourse as Labels and Captions and provide a fitting language form for memory, either that of the author or of someone he is drawing from as a source. Narrative shifts discourse up the abstraction scale, in other words, to accord on the one hand with whatever higher conceptualization memory represents over the senses, and on the other hand with whatever higher verbali-

zation sustained monologue represents over the partnering of dialogue.

IN THE LITERAL MODE

We have said that the learner expands from the present to the past to the future and then to the timeless so that the tense of his predicates is an index to his relative emphasis among sensation, memory, and reason. It is one thing to predicate one sentence in a certain tense but quite another to make that tense predominate throughout a whole discourse. The dominant tense of a discourse establishes the abstraction level—if the discourse is in the literal mode. A preschooler can state a generality in the present tense of generalization, but he will have to grow considerably before he *monologues*—chains a string of statements—in that tense. Actually, the predominance of a higher tense does not mean that it appears quantitatively more than another; the bulk of many an essay of generalization consists of past-tense documentation of only a few generalities, but the essay exists for the generalities, which dominate by forming the superstructure of the discourse, whereas the necessarily longer narrative elements only support.

So entire discourses may be scaled in composing and comprehending difficulty according to the abstraction level of the dominant tense. A blow-by-blow sportscast runs entirely in the present progressive (half-time generalizations are another matter!), and a novel runs off almost entirely in the past tense. A highly theoretical work will consist, on the other hand, entirely of the present tense of generalization led by conditionals. Here is one way of representing lower and higher discourse continuities:

now . . . now	present
then . . . then	past
if . . . then	general

A common mixture, however, interweaves timeless generality with narrative documentation or illustration:

then . . . then . . . . if . . . then . . . .

GROWTH SEQUENCE 22: Toward discourse of higher abstraction:

MONOLOGUES IN THE LITERAL MODE

What is happening	Prattle Interior mono- logue Blow-by-blow ac- counts Captions Field and lab notes	Recording
	Letters Journals	(Point of view from within events not yet ended)
What happened	Autobiography Memoir Biography Reportage Chronicle History	Reporting
What happens	Articles of factual generalization Essays of idea generalization Essays of theory Science, philoso- phy, and mathe- matics	Generalization

The order from letters and journals through chronicle and history is a whole progression within itself based on a shift from present to past and from author to other(s) as subject (first to third person, singular then plural). This is a growth order in the sense too that higher orders depend on and subsume lower ones. Generalizations about humanity, for example, may be based on history, which is based on source documents like memoirs and archives. Biography digests letters and diaries, and reportage abstracts ongoing notes. A student working at higher levels will have to draw on his own or others' work at lower levels. This absorption of lower by higher discourses corresponds to the hierarchical abstracting that takes place in the nervous system as people make information internally. Surely, being able to do this intuitively with raw material must be some kind of prerequisite for doing it consciously with discourse.

Let's look now at the nine discourse goals that we listed in Chapter 1, Basic Concepts:

Word Play*	Leaving aside for the moment figurative discourse (marked by asterisks), we have a crude growth progression in that Dialogue comes early, Labels and Captions are directly bound to sensory objects or images, and the last four follow the order of narrative to generalization. True Stories and Directions are bracketed together because they both follow chronological order, for the most part, and so are roughly on a par, as are Information and Ideas at their level of *what happens.*
Labels and Captions	
Invented Dialogue*	
Actual Dialogue	
Invented Stories*	
{ **True Stories**	
Directions	
{ **Information**	
Ideas	

Younger learners will find later discourse areas hard to work in, but even primary children may practice language in all nine areas concurrently, either by speaking some kinds before they can write them, or reading them before they can speak them, or by sending and receiving very short instead of long continuities. So this list indicates developmental sequence only in a very rough way: students may be expected to cover the lower areas sooner than the higher.

It is essential to understand, however, that all students will be working in all areas all the time. Although some higher areas build, in a sense, on some lower ones, it is definitely not necessary to hold off work in higher ones pending "completion" of lower ones. No one kind of discourse ever gets completed because these are lifelong learning categories. Not only is it true that less developed learners should be given credit for what they are able to comprehend and compose orally in an area of discourse, but by practicing orally they are learning the bulk of what they need to know in order to read and write in that area.

If one understands well the way in which naming, phrasing, stating, and chaining are nested within each other so that larger governs smaller, then it should be clear why it is undesirable and unnecessary to rig separate instructional sequences for vocabulary, grammar, paragraphing, and organization. Working within discourses of different abstractive levels ensures that students will come to grips with all the issues of diction, sentence construction, and organization. If students spread their work from easier to harder discourse areas in the directions we have indicated, this will of itself automatically program sequences at all language levels. Shifting, say, from narrative discourse to that of explicit generalization necessarily entails shifts in language and rhetoric and thus tends to bring successively to the fore different language structures and compositional issues.

Tense, as we have indicated, is one thing that changes. But so do other things. Adverbial phrases and clauses of time, place, and manner that abound in recording and reporting give way, in generalization and theory, to phrases and clauses of qualification; temporal connectives, transitions, and organization perforce yield to logical ones. The kinds of paragraph structure one uses tend to shift. Labeling and captioning naturally focus on names, phrases, and single sentences. Things named in fables *must* be figurative. If you counsel your students well about which sort of discourse to tackle next, you will also be sequencing work in the substructures of discourse. The detail with which we have treated naming, phrasing, stating, and chaining aims to show how you can detect growth in these substructures, not how to sequence them in isolation. Assess growth of substructures as one way of helping you to evaluate and to recommend whole discourses.

IN THE FIGURATIVE MODE

Invented Dialogue and Invented Stories cover plays and fiction, of course, in which characters, settings, and actions are themselves figures of speech, standing, as they do, for aspects of experience. Word Play covers the juggling of meaning for its own sake, but figurative language occurs obviously in any kind of discourse. It's just that in Word Play it may be the whole discourse, as in a pun.

Poetry, plays, and fiction are not just what they seem. On the surface, script and transcript, novel and biography look exactly alike, and judging from the language forms only, we would often not be able to tell real from invented. The difference is the other dimension or so of meaning given these works by the kind of ricocheting of reference among items inside and outside the text that we discussed as the figurative use of language. Taken literally, factually, a poem, novel, or play seems to represent no higher skill to read or write than the prattle, true story, or actual dialogue that each respectively simulates. But of course in simulating rather than factually abstracting, an author is in fact abstracting at a much higher level than the form he simulates. *In telling what happened, a novelist is also telling what happens*. The difference between *Hamlet* and a transcript of a local hearing, which as written dialogue it resembles, lies in the nature of artful, multileveled composition.

The author of imaginative literature is not just abstracting directly up from the ground in the manner we described for *abstracting from*. To some extent he is composing, over that sort of abstracting, another sort. His people, places, actions, and objects are already themselves abstractions of others they stand for. Putting these into play creates a much higher abstraction, in fact, than merely reporting or dramatizing what some real people actually did, unless, as we said with case histories, the real personages and actions have been especially chosen because they will be taken figuratively as tokens of a type. The more meaningful in this way is a case history or biography the more it must be selectively composed like a play or novel. Art is a double editing of reality, once by the holistic mode and once by the linear, and selectivity is the key to making a literary work operate both literally and figuratively at once.

Put it this way. Characters in literature, including children's literature, are concepts. The Wizard of Oz, the Three Billy Goats Gruff with Troll, Alice and the Red Queen and White Knight are concepts. So are Hamlet, Oedipus, and the Man in the Gray Flannel Suit. So too are the settings and key physical objects of literature—the church tower in *The*

Master Builder, the ring in the Tolkien trilogy, West Egg in *The Great Gatsby,* the way stations in *Heart of Darkness,* and the moldering wedding cake in *Great Expectations.* These concepts are not explicitly stated and can be grasped only by means of everything else in the work. The ultimate referents are in us, the readers, but we understand what these items stand for, though meaning is only implied, because they are significantly bound to other equally well-selected items, all of which are reciprocally defining. In literature, what relates concepts are story actions; the plot predicates personages and objects into statements, as verbs do literal concepts. Thus we apply the term *conclusion* to both a syllogism and a story and speak of the "logic of the events." The chaining of events in a plot corresponds to the linking of literal statements by logical conjunctions.

People project into invented stories those unobjectified forces of the psychic life that are hard to name or even recognize. At any time of life we have some inner material that we cannot express directly and explicitly; we have to say it indirectly and often unconsciously, through metaphorical fiction. Usually, the older we grow the more we can objectify and talk explicitly about feelings and ideas, but a child must for a long time talk and read about these things through a sort of allegory. There are two reasons for this. One is that he is not ready to acknowledge to himself a lot of his thoughts and feelings because he must defend against them. Another is that his abstractive powers are not developed enough to enable him to conceptualize, name, and interrelate these intangible things. As regards their deepest inner material, adults are in the same boat, and so we have art. In other words, students progressively push back the frontier of the unknown by converting the implicit into the explicit.

Whereas adults differentiate their thought into specialized kinds of discourse such as narrative, generalization, and theory, children must for a long time make narrative do for all. They utter themselves almost entirely through stories—real or invented—and they apprehend what others say through story. The young learner, that is, does not talk and read explicitly about categories and theories of experience; he talks and reads about characters, events, and settings, but these are charged with symbolic meaning because they are tokens standing for unconscious classes and postulations of experience. The good and bad fairies are categories of experience, and the triumph of the good fairy is a reassuring generalization about overcoming danger. In *The Wizard of Oz* the wizard is a humbug, and the bad fairy can be destroyed by water; Dorothy is stronger than she thought, and the adults are weaker than they appear at first. *Alice in Wonderland* makes a similar statement. A tremendous amount of thought—and intricate, at that—underrides these plots. So a youngster understands that *what happened* is *what happens,* but he grows toward a differentiation of kinds of discourse to match the differentiation in abstraction levels of thought.

Growth along the fictional dimension can be described by Northrop Frye's five kinds of heroes—the supernatural or divine figure, the mortal but miraculous man, the king or exceptional leader, the average man, and the ironic antihero. This progressive scaling down of the hero not only traces the history of literature, with its shifts in dominant literary modes from epic and myth to legend and romance, to tragedy, to bourgeois novel and play, to a very inner and underground fiction, but it also corresponds to the withdrawal of projection, to movement from the far-fetched there-then to the actual here-now.

Every child recapitulates the history of the species to this extent: he first embodies his wishes for power in fantasies of omnipotence akin to the myths and epics of divine and supernatural heroes. The figures, actions, and settings he likes to read about and create are as remote as possible from himself and the circumstances of his own life. Gradually settling for less, though, he shrinks his fantasies increasingly toward figures like himself dwelling in his own time and place, thus passing through legend and romance, tragedy, and realistic fiction. This passage comes about partly because he is gaining real power as he grows up and consequently needs less and less to fantasize about power, partly because he is becoming more aware of and explicit about his wishes and fears and thus wants to read and write about them for what they are, and partly because he is yielding his unlimited reality to the adults' official version of reality. All this, however, does not mean that in the beginning he cannot already appreciate familiar realism in some conscious areas of experience, or that later he will not still need the far-fetched modes for unconscious areas of experience.

Growth in Invented Stories and Invented Dialogue runs somewhat the reverse of growth in the literal mode. Whereas the symbolizing of recognizable, objectified experience does proceed up the ladder from the here-now to the there-then, it is in the nature of disguised psychic material that one symbolizes it first in the there-then and only gradually comes to represent it in explicitly personal terms. In other words, as regards his external observation and his acknowledged feelings, a person moves, in his speaking and writing, from the firsthand, first-person concrete levels of abstraction toward the second-hand, third-person timeless realms of abstraction. But as regards his unconscious psychic life, he moves along a continuum that begins in the far-fetched, with things remote from him in time and space, and works backward toward himself. As children we project ourselves first into animals, fantastic creatures, folk heroes, and legendary figures. Slowly, the bell tolls us back to our sole self. Gradually we withdraw projection as we become willing to recognize the personal meaning symbolized in our myths, and able to objectify inner experience to the point of treating it explicitly.

GROWTH SEQUENCE 23: From there-then settings and far-fetched characters and actions to the here-now of contemporary realism.

Realistic fiction represents a return toward the literal, at least in the domain of figurative narrative. But another kind of figurative discourse may arise as narrative declines—lyric and dramatic poetry, both of which contain some of a culture's highest thought, couched in metaphor. Poetic drama tends toward the lyrical or philosophical not only in soliloquies and external monologues but even in the dialogue, which is freed from the conventions of realism by the poetry of the speech itself.

The most valued poetry of a culture reaches the top of the abstraction hierarchy in *thought* but may do so in the most concrete *language.* That is, the figures make, by means of metaphor, "statements" of the most universal truth, but this truth is unparaphrasable because the depth so valued consists precisely in saying more than could ever be said in the literal mode. Great poetry breaks the bounds of language, says things it ought not to be able to say, breaches the unspeakable, which is the goal of it all.

GROWTH SEQUENCE 24: Toward poetry of increasing distillation.

The very highest growth in discourse ultimately carries a person through language entirely and back out into the wordless world, just as the story journey returns one to the here-now. If the story-lover keeps on growing far enough, he may *realize* in actuality the marvelous powers he admired in epic and supernatural figures. The final twist is that tales of power can be converted from metaphorical to literal reality. This happens at about the same stage of growth as when the poetry-lover so bends language back upon itself that he springs his mind free from his lifelong verbal cage and lives liberated beyond thought and speech.

Conclusion

To describe how people change as they grow older is to mix inevitable and universal genetic unfolding with the relative conditioning of local culture. We do not know and may never know which changes must take place because internally programmed, and which merely depend on the time and place into which one is born. So a description of growth as known in our culture can mislead in grave ways. It can imply that some trends are good just because they happen and look like the work of nature. It can imply that some trends cannot be changed. What is biological is probably good and unchangeable except by slow evolution, but it's most likely that people's biological endowment is very open and that much of the change we see as people grow older is culturally induced. The more general, the more biological; the more specific, the more cultural, for biology governs culture as context does text.

A lot of evidence supports the idea that many changes accepted as necessary growth are cultural and that in some respects it would be better for the culture than for the child to change. Jean Piaget has said, for example, that what he regards as the highest kind of thinking prevails commonly among younger children but very little among adults—the ability to consider any state in a continuum of states as equally valid and yet to return to the point of departure. This defines *open-minded* in a way. Until about school age, children can also use either brain hemisphere to process language and to do other things. Some, perhaps many, children seem to be able to see naturally the "auras" around other people (probably just certain bands of the electromagnetic spectrum) until their perception is made to

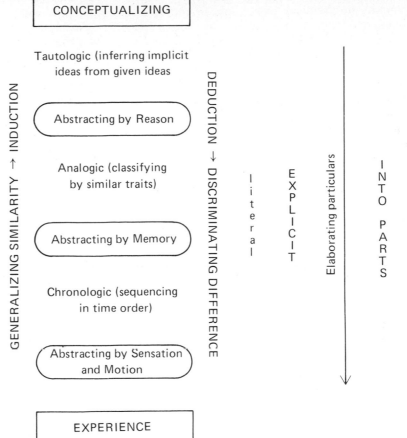

Mental growth moves in both directions at once.

FIGURE 22.2 THE FORMS OF THOUGHT

conform. Many lose musical aptitude and other skills associated with the nonverbal half of the brain.

Probably the most dismal evidence of negative growth comes out of school performance itself in the form of a virtually never-failing slump starting around fourth grade, when many children suddenly don't seem to be able to read and do other things well that teachers thought they had mastered. Scores drop, attitudes become negative, and students begin dropping out either mentally or physically. It's at about this time—around eight or nine —that the full force of acculturation in and out of the home really hits the child. The reason this can influence growth so negatively sometimes is that culture tries to preserve itself by making everybody perceive and think and act alike, even though this ends by so starving out creativity that it dooms the culture itself.

An overemphasis of the verbal/analytic half of the brain in our own culture is endangering the culture, because it drives out the integrative, analogical thinking desperately needed to coordinate action within the vast intricacies of both individual and international life in this era of modern technology. Balance is the key, and the grand paradox is that people reason and verbalize better if they stop sometimes in favor of intuition and metaphor.

Although it is necessary to examine the problems egocentricity causes in discoursing, don't regard egocentricity as just a bad thing. Failure to separate oneself from the object—not being objective—is at bottom the self's oneness with the world. It is a problem at the practical level, because getting and spending and fending and begetting all require making distinctions and then reordering the pieces of the world in some utilitarian way once you've broken it down. Jogging the child out of the oneness of the world surely does him a mixed service. If it is true that for survival he simply must learn sooner or later to think and talk in analytic and linear ways, it is also true that every culture has always upheld this global feeling we call egocentricity as the basis of spirituality, and children forced out of it too soon or too far look for it again later through drugs or other ways to release their psyche from the isolating fragmentation of the analytic lesson too well learned.

The final stage of growth, though, is having the best of the mystical world of unity and the practical world of plurality—being able to play the whole abstraction scale with virtuosity and still be able in a moment to fuse self with world, one thing with another. In fact, the abstractive process carries within it the means to regain paradise. Pursuing differentiation and integration far enough leads out the other side, back into the nonverbal world. The more people interrelate the things of experience by one logic or another, the more they are rebuilding the world within.

Abstracting is "converting" matter to mind, a kind of alchemy. The more people at the same time make unconsciousness conscious, the more they identify with the world they are incorporating. In total fulfillment of communication's goal—to remove a differential—the inner and outer worlds equalize. This return to the newborn's unity with people and things is not, of course, mere regression. Consciousness makes the difference. The ego that arose to negotiate between the organism and the world has expanded from a point to an area. In a sense egocentricity is not at all reduced; the secret has been to expand it over the community and then over the cosmos—to overdo it extravagantly so that ego feels identified with all it encompasses by mind. The highest abstractions cover all time and space and in fact expose time and space as mental blocks. Instead of merely "projecting" himself unconsciously into what he sees or reads, the fulfilled individual deliberately reflects the world in his mind. Consciousness makes the difference between confusion of mind with world, and fusion of mind with world, and that difference is the most important thing a teacher needs to know about growth in discourse.

appendixes

Certain topics that teachers may especially want to look up directly have not been allotted a section of their own in the organization of this book, either because—like thinking, grammar, vocabulary—they are language elements that crop up in all discourse, or because—like media and English as a second language—they are concerns applying throughout a whole curriculum. Here we wish to indicate how these topics are treated at different points within the text and at the same time mention some additional learning practices, mostly in the form of games.

Grammar

First, be sure to read in Chapter 1, Basic Concepts, the sections called "The Sentence" (page 16), "Language Arts as Mere Information" (page 18), and "The Case of Grammar" (page 19), which define grammar and place it in its proper role for this curriculum. Then be sure to read in Chapter 22, Detecting Growth, the sections called "Naming by Parts of Speech" (page 444), "Grammatical Options in Naming" (page 445), "Phrasing" (page 447), "Stating" (page 448), and "Chaining" (page 450), all of which describe grammatical parts and the growth of grammar. See also pages 383 and 458.

Grammar is learned and practiced orally. Reading and writing fasten it and develop it further. Any act of comprehending or composing is a grammatical exercise. So the best way to improve grammar is to practice discourse in all its forms. Below are listed particular activities to teach grammar in three senses of the term as used in schools—adding standard dialect, expanding sentence versatility, and naming parts of speech and analyzing sentences.

ADDING STANDARD DIALECT

- *Conversing constantly with speakers of standard dialect.* (See all of Chapter 4, Talking and Listening.)
- *Role-playing speakers of standard dialect,* a way of practicing another speech community's dialect without renouncing one's own. (See page 95 in Chapter 5, Dramatic Inventing.)
- *Listening to readings of standard-dialect texts while following the text with the eyes.* (See "The Lap Method" on page 201, in Chapter 10, An Integrated Literacy Program.)
- *Participating in choral reading of standard texts.* (See "Choral Reading" on page 110.)
- *Performing and witnessing others' performances of standard-dialect texts.* (See Chapter 6, Performing Texts.)
- *Hearing and seeing phonemes presented and blended into words, as described for the sound shows in "An Audiovisual Presentation" on page 191 in Chapter 10, An Integrated Literacy Program.* This word building and word transforming help teach the word endings of standard dialect that are often dropped in some other dialects.

Certain illogicalities of construction, having nothing to do with dialectical difference, will result in failure to make agreement between subject and predicate or to connect elements into a complete statement. These should be pointed out by both classmates and teacher as they arise in practice. It is important to realize that these mistakes are basically *logical* and that although they cause grammatical mistakes, they are not committed in ignorance of grammar but through some breakdown in the thinking. However, if lack of agreement characterizes the speech of whole community (as "they is," for example) and is not a personal error, then the deviation is dialectical, and the practices above apply.

EXPANDING SENTENCE VERSATILITY

• *Imitating sentence constructions heard and read.* This is where the intake of varied and voluminous discourse influences considerably what a learner will produce. Total immersion in a language-rich environment is a great teacher of grammar because it exposes the young to the many possibilities of English grammar beyond the basic, uncombined forms they learned before entering school. Hearing a text while reading it, or performing a text imprints constructions strongly indeed.

• *Collaborating in dialogue to build sentences more complicated than original utterances.* In accordance with the explanation of internalization of dialogue on page 32, a speaker tends to assimilate the give-and-take of exchanges and on the basis of this generate more mature sentences that synthesize, in effect, the kinds of utterances all speakers previously made.

For example, one such operation is question-and-answer. A makes a statement and B asks for more information. The answer to B's question may be a sentence or a potential sentence that if fused with A's original statement would result in a conjoining, an embedding, or some simpler expansion. At the same time, the original statement is qualified by the further information or different point of view.

A: I saw the dog again.　　I saw that dog again
B: Where?　　　　　　　　*down along the river.*
A: Down along the river.
　　(Verb modification with a locative phrase)

A: I saw that dog again.　　I saw that *shaggy* dog
B: Which one?　　　　　　　again *that we found in*
A: That shaggy one we　　　*the barn yesterday.*
　　found in the barn
　　yesterday.
　　(Embedding—adjective and relative clause)

A: The bill will never
　　pass.

B: Why not?　　　　　　　The bill will never pass
A: It's too close to elec-　　*because it's too close to*
　　tions.　　　　　　　　　*elections.*
　　(Subordinate conjoining—causal)

A: The bill will never　　　The bill can't pass *until*
　　pass.　　　　　　　　　*after elections.*
B: Never?
A: Well, I mean it can't
　　until after elections.
　　(Subordinate conjoining—temporal)

A: I just talked with Mr.　　I just talked with Mr.
　　Anaheim.　　　　　　　Anaheim, *the assistant*
B: Who's he?　　　　　　　*director of the pro-*
A: The assistant director　　*gram.*
　　of the program.
　　(Embedding—appositive)

In the following operation B directly embeds A's utterance:

A: He won't talk to them.
B: Whether he talks to them or not makes no difference.
　　(Embedding—noun clause)

A: Who's going to help him get out of that mess?
B: His getting out of that mess is no business of ours.
　　(Embedding—gerundive nominalization)

B may incorporate or annex the main idea of A's utterance by referring to it, but may not directly embed the utterance. Needing to refer and not wishing to repeat, B finds a linguistic structure accommodating both A's idea and his own overlying idea.

A: Who's going to help him get out of that mess?
B: That's not our business.
　　　　　　or
Regardless of his mess, we have to go ahead.
A: I think the price is too high for them.
B: They'll pay despite the price (whatever the price) (nevertheless).

Another operation consists simply of appending a qualifying clause to the original statement:

A: He'll make it, don't
　　worry.

B: If he finds the key in time.
(Subordinate conjoining—conditional)

He'll make it *if he finds the key in time.*

A: These angles will always be equal, then.
B: So long as these lines are parallel.
(Correlative conjoining)

These angles will always be equal *so long as these lines are parallel.*

Perhaps the most important operation occurs when B adds to A's statement another fact, point of view, or argument that (he implies) A should allow for. The conjunctive or embedding relation between the two statements is only implied in the conversation but would be supplied by A in a future discourse:

A: Government ownership of railroads would not work in the United States.
B: It has worked in England and France.
(Subordinate conjoining—concessive)

Although government ownership of railroads has worked in England and France, it would not work in the United States.

or

The fact that government ownership of railroads has worked in England and France does not mean it will work in the United States.
(Embedding—noun clause)

A: Miss Leary scowls all the time and makes you stand outside the door.
B: I've heard that she gives the lowest grades in the whole school.
(Coordinate conjoining—additive)

Miss Leary scowls all the time, makes you stand outside the door, and gives the lowest grades in the whole school.

or

Miss Leary not only scowls all the time and makes you stand outside the door, she also gives the lowest grades in school.
(Correlative conjoining)

A: King Alfred voluntarily abdicated.
B: But that was after the assembly had already stripped him of his power.

Already stripped of his power by the assembly, King Alfred voluntarily abdicated.
(Embedding—participial phrase)

These examples are crude compared to the dynamics of continuous dialogue, where this process of questioning, appending, and amending may continue across many utterances, and sometimes with A further elaborating B's contributions. Also, the reader will have to extrapolate from these examples to more complicated dialogues involving multiple speakers.[1]

This tremendously important process of expatiation extends parent-child exchanges of the same nature into peer relations, where it is not a matter of directly filling out language forms, as when a mother paraphrases or expands a child's statement, but rather of filling out the *thought*. The effect, however, is still to elaborate sentences, because this is implied in alteration of the thought. Dialogical development of grammatical versatility can go on by virtue of improvisation and task talk as well as of topic talk. This development will come out in writing as the writer transcribes inner speech influenced by such exchanges.

• *Revising written sentences.* See pages 154–156, 163, 166–167, and 379 for examples and discussion of writing-workshop members altering each other's sentences to improve effectiveness or to change effect. This playing with and working with sentence alternatives shows learners what different grammatical forms their ideas may take. This pools group knowledge of possibilities and stimulates writers to revise sentences alone. Some sentence revision is actually sentence-combining.

More than anything else, intellectual activity teaches sentence construction. See the example on page 365 of how the effort to fit sentences to physical and then mental operations naturally evokes a certain fitting complexity of grammatical construc-

---

[1] These examples are taken from James Moffett, *Teaching the Universe of Discourse,* Houghton Mifflin Co., Boston, 1968, pp. 79–82.

tion. The more youngsters have to think about, and the more reasons they have to say and write what they think, the more they have to explore the possibilities of English syntax.

• *Reading and writing single-sentence discourses.* See "Single Statements" on page 374 for activities with proverbs, epithets, aphorisms, epigrams, and definitions, all of which place grammar under a microscope and make students conscious of construction because each constitutes the whole discourse one is reading or writing. See also "Haiku" on page 379. Effect is as important as message, and the effort to get it right inspires much rewording and hence grammatical recasting. See also tongue twisters, labels, and captions, in Chapter 12, Word Play, and Chapter 13, Labels and Captions.

• *Playing sentence games.* This is playing with the medium for its own sake but proves a good secondary approach to grammatical versatility, since the sentence-building experience no doubt carries over to the other language-production activities of speaking and writing.

Scrambled Sentences* One student cuts up into words a sentence that he has found or written, scrambles the pieces, and gives them to a partner to reconstruct. To challenge each other more, partners come up with harder sentences (and may find that some can be put together more than one way).

Sentence Building* Again playing in pairs, one player makes up a sentence by writing words or placing word cards in a sequence; then his partner attempts to add to that sentence with other words; then the first tries to build further; and so on, the object being to make as long a sentence as they can. Thus:

Bobby plays ball.
After school Bobby plays ball.
Every day after school Bobby plays ball with his friends.
Every day after school Bobby plays football with his new friends.
Every day after school Bobby plays football with his new friends until his mother calls him.
Every day after school Bobby plays football with his new friends until his mother calls him to come eat supper.

Telegram Writing* Players make up messages as economically worded as possible on the pretense

that these have to be sent by telegraph. Situations are invented from which the message is sent and about which it says something. This is really a sentence-reduction activity that shows which parts of speech and grammatical elements are most redundant and hence more dispensable. Do different people interpret these telegraphic sentences in the same way, or are they ambiguous? See page 259.

Silly Syntax* This game was produced as part of the *Interaction* program and consists of eight sub-games in an order of easy to difficult that are played in the same general way but with different card decks and by somewhat varying rules. The main idea is to build sentences by putting together a "hand" of word cards.

Playing cards are color-coded to indicate the function of different sentence elements. A single word or group of words have the same color if they perform the same function. Thus, in the process of playing the "Silly Syntax" games a student learns by deduction, for example, that an adjectival element (pink) of a sentence may be a single word as in "*gruesome* spiders kicked"; a phrase as in "doctors *with fat stomachs* hurried"; or a relative clause as in "vampires *who have bad breath* are screaming." Color coding according to function emphasizes what the word or group of words does in the sentence.

Students who play "Silly Syntax" develop a sentence sense, becoming more aware of word order as they face the problem of rearranging sentence elements to produce meaning. The first thing players learn in the primary games is that without a noun and a verb, they cannot make a hand, for they haven't the basics of a simple declarative sentence. They deduce that certain parts of speech have a regular position in relation to the other words in the sentence. For example, a noun determiner has to precede a noun or an adjective word and a noun; an adjective phrase or relative clause must follow a noun. Students also learn by manipulation that the adverbial element in a sentence—be it word, phrase, or clause—is the most flexible in terms of position. Players develop a feeling for the logic of word order as they compare the subtle difference in meaning when an element is placed in a different position in the sentence as in these two placements of the same participial phrase: "Lance, *eating candy bars,* wants to be inside an unidentified flying object"; and, "Lance wants to be *eating candy bars* inside an unidentified flying object." Certain sentences imply certain punctuation. Most of all, from "Silly Syntax" students learn to expand modifiers, shift moveable elements, and embed whole clauses or reduced clauses into the noun slots.

NAMING PARTS OF SPEECH AND ANALYZING SENTENCES

We do not think it is important to learn to analyze and identify by name the grammatical parts, but many other school people do, or say they do, and in any case enough of this can be taught painlessly and incidentally through games to get students through tests on formal grammar and to satisfy those who insist on it. The best solution is for this kind of learning to occur as a secondary effect of more important learning. Such is the case with the game just described.

• *Playing "Silly Syntax."* In addition to being color-coded for grammatical parts of speech (which means several colors sometimes for one word or phrase), the playing cards bear the name of the grammatical element represented by the word or word group on the card. In the more advanced games, students must supply their own examples of the various sentence elements in order to win. They must be able to generate examples of units such as nouns; verbs; prepositional, infinitive, and participial phrases; or adverbial clauses; all that is printed on the card is the grammatical term for these elements. Furthermore, to play some games, one must ask for cards from other players having the part of speech one needs to complete a certain sentence.

• *Playing "Blankety Blanks"* * This is a very popular game outside as well as inside school and goes under several names. One player reads a story from which certain words or word groups have been removed and asks listening players to supply these sentence elements, naming for them the part of speech or element needed: "In [a place] on a particularly [adjective] evening, [a noun] was sitting [adverb] on the couch when there was a [adjective] knock on the door." Parts of speech are conveyed as part of the game directions by exemplifying them in sample sentences, where verbs can be circled, nouns boxed, adjectives underlined, and so on, or colors used. The game can be made as sophisticated as desired by asking for sentence elements that are more than single words. When the story is read back results are very amusing because of the nonsensical but grammatically correct mixture of the original story with the random elements supplied: "Wildly the striped man coughed into an embarrassed rose."

• *Making Dictionaries.* See pages 235 and 377. Since dictionaries identify words by parts of speech, students who make their own have to learn what the parts are and apply the terms for them to their own words.

Vocabulary

Be sure to read first the sections "Naming," and "Phrasing" on pages 443 and 447 in Chapter 22, Detecting Growth.

Mouthing new words for which a learner has no referents in his experience is not increasing vocabulary. Some research does indicate, however, that exposure to words for certain distinctions, like *aquamarine* and *fuchsia* for shades of color, speeds along the experiential discrimination itself, as if the awareness of finer color vocabulary impels the learner to look for the differences being referred to. In this way language acts on the very experience to which it refers. So a handy dictum may be: "Surround students with new words, but don't be fooled by the rattling off of new words."

Acquiring vocabulary from dictionary definitions rather than from context risks hollow verbalism. Sheer memorization can allow someone to parrot back a word and its definition and hence to get high scores on tests without ever knowing what the words mean. The only real test, of course, is being able to comprehend and compose discourse containing the words. All that a dictionary can do is refer the reader to other words. If he doesn't understand the words used in the definition he is like a six-year-old who has memorized a Hamlet soliloquy. One-word definitions, or synonyms, usually are of the same level of generality (*disparage* and *denigrate*) and thus may be of no help at all. The phrase or sentence definition usually explains meaning in more concrete terms than the word being defined— *malleable* has the entry, "that can be hammered, pounded, or pressed"—but often this is not so: *to disparage,* for example, is "to lower in esteem." A student who writes or circles "to lower in esteem" for *disparage* on a vocabulary test still does not understand *disparage* if he doesn't understand *esteem.* Meaning has to break out of purely verbal circles into some continuity of thought or action before learning is assured.

The best way to learn new words is to listen and read a lot. Youngsters figure out for themselves the meanings of newly met words by means of the same inborn capacity to generalize and draw conclusions that enabled them to learn to speak and then to read. Until reading has become a strongly established habit, people learn most new words orally, from conversation, television, films, and radio. A good classroom can offer, besides these, other aural opportunities. If it is individualized, students are reading different texts, and if it is stocked with the unusual variety of reading matter that we have advocated, the class pool of vocabulary should be very big and rich. If the classroom is also interactive, students can exchange vocabulary as they talk, act, and write together in small groups.

To really stick, new words must be *used*—in talk and in writing. The volume and variety of language-using situations must be great enough to draw constantly on the range of words the students are being exposed to. This curriculum converts passive vocabulary to active by creating many activities that call for kids to produce language. At the same time, student interaction in discussion, improvisation, and writing workshops constantly checks this active vocabulary to alert the user to misuse or imprecision.

A couple of activities are especially helpful for imprinting both the sound and meaning of new words.

• *Listening to a text while following it with the eyes.* A professional or good amateur reading of a text should enable a listener to figure out new words more easily from context than when reading silently alone. Combining the sound and the sight of new words also makes them more memorable, especially if the rendition is absorbing anyway. Hearing pronunciation encourages students to *use* new words. See pages 130 and 201.

• *Rehearsing and performing texts.* Student performers have to find out the pronunciation and meaning of new words. And going over the text in rehearsals fixes the new words tightly in memory.

• *Playing card games in which items are depicted and named on the card faces.* See page 471 and the accompanying card games. Some card games teach vocabulary in a special way—as interrelated sets of words; that is, as nomenclature. Card decks having science or math or social studies material, for example, depict and name items that form a system—classes of animals, say, or kinds of vehicles or media. In these games, the total deck creates a context for learning the vocabulary given on each card. Thus, the new words are defined not just by the pictures or symbols shown on the cards but also by the system within which the cards are played. Furthermore, in playing the game, players usually have to utter the new words and therefore have to find out how to pronounce them.

• *Revising and discussing word choice in writing.* See page 162 for examples of how sensory recording creates special occasions to work on vocabulary and page 360 for the same with direction writing. The writing-workshop practice of suggesting alternative wording for ideas and images helps to make students aware of distinctions among words they already know, or think they know, as well as to add new words to their repertory.

• *Making dictionaries.* See pages 235 and 377. Students can make dictionaries for specialized vocabularies of certain hobbies, sports, trades, cultural communities, and so on, and can exchange these. As makers, they round out mastery of the specialized vocabulary; as readers, they become acquainted with a new vocabulary. As either, they become more interested in word acquisition and dictionaries and more aware of the whole range of specialized subcultural languages.

• *Labeling and captioning.* See Chapter 13, Labels and Captions.

• *Playing word games such as crossword puzzles, Scrabble, and anagrams.* For these and others see Chapter 12, Word Play. Many such games require consulting the dictionary or other people and provide a way of acquiring new words supplementary to learning from context.

Thinking Skills

Logical thinking is sometimes likened to traditional school-taught skills such as reading, writing, and counting. But the analogy is misleading.

If a child is not taught one of the basic skills—by teachers or parents or someone—he simply will not have the skill. We can, in other words, imagine a child who is illiterate.

But logical thinking is something everybody does. It is something that every normal human being learns to do just by living. In fact, logical thinking is a major component in the definition of a human being.

Thus, this program doesn't *teach* logical thinking but, by encouraging youngsters to act, react and interact, the program creates an environment in which they can exercise their intellect. The analogy here would be to a body-building program. Such a program doesn't literally build a body from scratch but fosters activities which help the body to grow stronger.

The opportunity for logical thinking is so much a part of this program that it cannot be isolated. There isn't a special unit or a special time to do logical thinking, just as the adult doesn't set aside a certain time each day to be logical. The very conception of activities and of reading breakdowns we recommend is founded on how people think. So if learners are doing the activities in this book they will be exercising their logical faculties constantly and across the whole range of the thought spectrum.

Be sure to read all of Chapter 22, Detecting Growth, if you are concerned about thinking skills, because in it we attempt to show how all authentic comprehending and composing are forms of conceptualizing. See also pages 3 to 9 on mental growth and abstracting. Pages 127–129 treat thinking skills generally associated with reading. See also "Cooperation to Operation" on page 32 and the discussion of grammar earlier in this appendix for examples of the internalization process so important to the growth of thought. See page 383 for a discussion of how topic talk develops thinking skills.

It's useful to distinguish two main kinds of logical thinking—the logic of classes and the logic of operations (*classifying* and *inferring*). These correspond to "concept formation" and "drawing conclusions."

CLASSIFYING

All the vocabulary activities just described in the preceding section involve classifying since words designate classes of either things or relations. Any activity of comparing also involves classifying, because to compare is to establish similarity and difference, as in discussing or writing about many topics.

- *Sorting objects or ideas.* One activity is to collect or encounter a variety of objects or photos of objects, then to sort these in any way at all and ask classmates to say what the piles represent. Different people can sort the same miscellaneous collections

and compare categories afterward, or the same people can classify the same collection as many ways as they can think of, trying to move toward more original categories and still have others guess what they are. Distinguish conventional categories from unique ones. Sort actions as well as objects. Another activity is to sort one's memories (page 329 in Chapter 16, True Stories) or one's mixed thoughts and perceptions (page 368 in Chapter 19, Ideas).

- *Making figures of speech.* Metaphor and simile are forms of classification, again based on comparison. Two things said to resemble each other fall into some category together, no matter how much they may differ in other respects. One frequent concern of language arts teachers is how to teach metaphor. But again, metaphor isn't something you need to introduce kids to. Language is so full of buried metaphor that it is impossible for the youngest child to speak and understand language and not use metaphor. The real issue in "teaching metaphor" is helping youngsters to create and respond to *original* comparisons, whether in the form of metaphor and simile or just in the form of a classification. Natural occasions to work with metaphor arise in some sensory recording (page 163), riddles (page 251), proverbs (page 375), comparison poems (page 262), and of course all poetry and other discourse that are figurative. See the section "Literal and Figurative" on page 440. Some work coordinating words and graphics creates visual metaphors—mapping, charting, graphing, and so on.

- *Playing card games.* See page 471.

INFERRING

Inferring is drawing conclusions, putting two and two together. The logical relating of ideas is of course a regular feature of most discussion, role-playing, and writing-workshop exchange. It is vital to interpreting. (See page 8 for *making sense.*) In explicit form it is syllogizing, discussed in "Syllogisms" on page 452.

- *Reading and writing detective stories.* Detective stories are really deductive stories about drawing conclusions logically from some given clues. As further evidence is fed into the story the reader progressively eliminates possibilities. Much of the appeal of murder and mystery stories of the who-done-it sort is the challenge to the mind.

- *Making syllogisms.* See "Combining Generalizations into a Theory" in Chapter 19, Ideas (page 398), for activities in which students plug propositions into each other to create further ones and then base writing on this.

• *Reading and writing brain teasers.* Brain teasers are thinking games cast in the form of problems or puzzles to figure out. See page 259 in Chapter 12, Word Play.

• *Playing twenty questions.* A popular process-of-elimination game, this is played by asking a strategic series of yes-or-no questions designed to narrow down and finally zero in on what someone has in mind.

• *Playing checkers, chess, and other board games of strategy.*

• *Playing Wiff 'n Proof and other games based on formal and symbolic logic.* Especially developed for elementary children at a Yale project supported by Carnegie Corporation, *Wiff 'n Proof: The Game of Modern Logic* (Layman E. Allen, Box 71, New Haven, Conn.) is a kit of twenty-one graduated games intended to "encourage a favorable attitude towards symbol-manipulating activities in general, and, incidentally, to teach something about mathematical logic and provide practice in abstract thinking." Players learn how to "recognize 'well formulated formulas' (Wiff's) and how to construct proofs of theorems in propositional calculus." Essentially, these games further the growth of logical analysis and deduction of the sort one needs in order to draw correct conclusions from complicated verbal problems. We strongly recommend trial of this kit because it provides the possibility of joining mathematics and English. Look for other logical games in game stores.

CARD GAMES FOR LOGIC AND VOCABULARY

For our general position on games, please read "Acceptable Cases of Focusing on Substructures" on page 41 and "Games" on page 58. See also "Games for Active Practice," especially the subsection "Card Games" on page 216.

Card games are fun. They also have built into them some very important and natural kinds of learning. While enjoying games, students will learn:

Social interaction
    the give and take of winning and losing
    discussing directions
    heeding each other's behavior
    arbitrating differences
Attention, concentration, and recall
Strategic decision-making
Vocabulary, systematic and interrelated
Coordination of words and illustrations
Reading and following of directions
Classifying
    seeing similarities and differences
    conjoining and disjoining attributes
Sequencing
    serial relations of lesser and greater
    syntactic relations of mathematical as well as verbal sentences
Logical deduction
    drawing inferences from available clues
    calculating possibilities
Factual information from science or social studies
Making own games

Sentence-making card games teach grammar. A deck of cards bearing labeled pictures is really a kind of movable, modular chart, and relates to booklets and activity cards for charting, labeling, captioning, and vocabulary building.

Cards bearing new factual information about nature and machines relate to booklets of information and to fact-finding activity cards.

The kinds of card games that can teach vocabulary, classifying, and inferring are exemplified by the *interaction* games listed below. We urge you to look at these games to get the details about decks and rules of this type. One main idea is to substitute for the now meaningless categories of conventional decks—clubs, diamonds, hearts, and spades—some categories from science and social studies, like kinds of animal life or kinds of transportation and communication. Then the decks can be played by familiar rules of rummy, concentration, war, old maid, poker, and other games based on putting like items together ("melding" a "book") or on ranking items by some order (animal hierarchy for example, instead of ten, jack, queen, and so on). Most well-known card games are played by classifying or serializing, that is, by making "flushes" or "straights" or by making both at once.

What can be taught of biology through print—that does not require laboratory work and observation—is essentially its system of classification, which reaches upward into such abstract things as classes of vertebrates and downward into discriminations among species of canines. It also introduces new designations, such as *arachnids* and *crustaceans,* that subsume the familiar spiders and lobsters according to scientific criterial attributes that are not always obvious. Part of the learning problem is to conceive spiders and lobsters as similar enough to be lumped together as arthropods and as different enough to part company into arachnids and crustaceans. The logical principle of multiple membership in successively included classes is difficult for children to grasp because of its relativity: whether one calls the ant an arthropod, insect, or hymenopteran depends on the level of abstraction at which one is making distinctions. The other part of the problem is not conceptual, but informative: before you can place a spider in the class of arachnids you have to know whether it has the four sets of jointed legs, the sac or breathing tube, and the segmented exoskeleton that qualify it for membership. Of course, students can memorize the fact that spiders, scorpions, and mites are all arachnids, but the true test of having learned a class concept is to be able to identify new instances of it.

Games Fostering Original Concept Formation

Some card games, however, should invite free and original categorizing. The games above would help a student *attain* concepts established by convention. But the taxonomy of biology has changed considerably over the years, and the classifications of some plants and animals are still very controversial. The issue, there and elsewhere, concerns which of the many attributes of a thing shall be deemed criterial for the classification. Color, shape, structure, function, behavior, are only a few possible kinds of criteria. The increasing ability to categorize an item in different ways, to create fresh categories, and to make explicit one's hidden categories is a major dimension of mental and verbal growth.

Though limited of course to pictorial things, a deck of very mixed and unlabeled pictures has one advantage that characterizes all card games—a random hand. (Such a deck can be made from cutouts by students.) Let us say that four players are dealt a meaningless mixture of three cards each. The rules say to think of some way in which the three items pictured are all alike—any way at all. Some categories might in fact have to be "mineral" or "manufactured" or "can't be seen through" or "has moving parts." But the object of the game is to tailor the category as specifically to the three items

as possible. This is done, first, by allowing eight or ten rounds of drawing and discarding during which the players attempt to narrow down their hand so that others would have the most difficulty playing on it. Each time they draw, they try to replace one of their three previous cards by one that will permit a more specific category. After the eight or ten rounds, they place their hands down and declare their category. The rest of the game, in effect, is spent determining who has the narrowest or most specific category by drawing from the rest of the deck and trying to add cards to the others' hands according to the categories they declared. (Cards they cannot place are simply laid aside.) When the deck is used up, the player whose tabled hand is smallest—whose category is most specific—wins. The idea is that the rules should cause players to create original categories and to classify the same items in different ways.

Inferring

It is important to keep in mind that in many games, the exercise of logic may occur more in the *strategy* of play—deciding what to do on the basis of play so far and of what moves others will make—than in the classifying and relating of the cards to each other. A strategy is a chain of moves based on "If he does this, then I'll do this." The essence of inferring is "If this is true and that is true, then this too is true." In games, this chaining is embodied in a series of moves that have to be "thought out" to be successful. Thus inferring makes up a good part of any play with card and board games.

A kind of card game that beautifully combines classifying and inferring was suggested by research in psychology.[2] It differs from familiar card games by emphasizing how categories are made by some and figured out by others. If someone points to a pen and says, "That's an example of what I have in mind," we do not know whether he means writing instruments, metal objects, a shade of blue, careless mislaying of items, or any number of other things. If he continues to point out instances, or if we ask him whether various other objects are instances, we can gradually figure out the concept he has in mind. This kind of inferring goes on all the time as people learn individual and cultural concepts by isolating out those attributes of an object or a situation

[2] Jerome Bruner, Jacqueline Goodnow, and George Austin, *A Study of Thinking,* Science Editions, New York, 1962.

that are criterial for the concept. The strategies we use may be more or less systematic or random, cautious or hasty. The game in question here consists of some players' efforts to guess the category one player has in mind by presenting to him one at a time certain cards chosen for him to identify as positive or negative instances of his category. On the basis of his response to one instance, fellow players choose next whichever card to present that they think will yield the most information about the category. High-risk guesses may lead to quick victory but if unsuccessful will take longer than a conservative, systematic varying of one attribute at a time, the latter being a logical procedure for checking out and keeping track of the various combinatorial possibilities.

Some decks and rules can be based on conjunctive classification—making a category, for example, of things *both* blue *and* circular—or on disjunctive classification—making a category of things *either* blue *or* circular. Inference strategies vary a great deal for one and the other, because negative instances of conjunctive classes yield less information than negative instances of disjunctive classes.

Another kind of card game consists of making

hands that are math-English classes or sentences, that is, alternative symbolizations for the same number or for the same equation. A number can be said many ways in mathematical notation, and each of these ways has a corresponding English sentence. Such games help students translate between the two languages and to see the underlying logic common to both.

For models of the various card games mentioned in this appendix see the *Interaction* card games in Table 1.

BILINGUAL EDUCATION OR ENGLISH AS A SECOND LANGUAGE

Some of the same features of this program that permit some students to add standard dialect to their own help others to add English to their native language. Any new language is acquired by conversing with native speakers of it. The biggest way in which this program helps non-English speakers acquire English is by providing plentiful oral experience from which they can learn pronunciation, vocabulary, and sentence formation. Naturally, this oral acquisition may be speeded up by special practice

TABLE 1 INTERACTION CARD GAMES

English *Sentence-making*	Math *Sentence-making*	Science *Classification and Seriation, Vocabulary*	Social Studies *Classification and Seriation, Vocabulary*	Logic *Conjunctive and Disjunctive Classification*
LEVEL I				
Silly Syntax 1 Silly Syntax 2	Clock Wise, Add On, Take Away	North American Animals	On the Move (transportation)	
LEVEL II				
Silly Syntax 1 Silly Syntax 2 Silly Syntax 3	Connect	North American Plants, Life in the Sea	Messages (communi- cation)	Dragon Pack
LEVEL III AND LEVEL IV				
Silly Syntax 1 Silly Syntax 2 Silly Syntax 3	Equivalents	Animal World, Arthropods		Who's Who

in a language laboratory and by special coaching from someone who understands the so-called interference that the old language generates. Usually a student for whom English is a second language knows *some* oral English, though he may not if the locality has no bilingual environment nor special classes in English as a second language. In any case, the following activities should help a non-English speaking student build up an oral base and lay English literacy over it.

Help such students make up a special program, permitted by the individualization, that allows for inexperience with English. This means that students can be counseled to emphasize the following activities and others they especially need without segregating them from native speakers of English, with whom they need interaction.

• *Improvising and role-playing.* Teachers charged with teaching English as a second language within a regular classroom with native speakers have consistently found improvisation to be about the most useful single activity—after casting about for some time among many activities. Small-group improvisation encourages students not confident of their little English to use it until it develops enough to enable them to discuss, read, and write.

• *Seeing and hearing the audiovisual presentation described for literacy in Chapter 10,* An Integrated Literacy Program. The isolating and blending of English phonemes should especially help such students to grasp both the sounds and spellings of English with minimal interference from the old language. Small units help segment English speech, but word-building and sentence-building restore the flow.

• *The lap method* (page 201) *and choral reading* (page 110). Both of these also allow students to hear and see English words at once and thus to use the look to help learn the sound and vice versa. The voices of native speakers provide the audio to match with the spellings.

• *Playing word games.* The games described in "Games for Active Practice" on page 206, as well as some card games described in this appendix will help students learn English spelling patterns, memorize some words by sight, and learn the meanings of some words from accompanying pictures.

• *Playing sentence games.* Teachers using "Talk and Take," * for example, described on page 417 in

a footnote, find that working with one sentence at a time in relation to game-board movements helps students a great deal to improve their comprehension of certain English sentence types that would be too difficult in a prose continuity. Other games can be made like this that vary sentence types in ways somewhat akin to pattern drills but that make a more entertaining activity than working out in a language laboratory.

• *Discussing and making up stories about photos.* See "Pictures" on page 157. Pictures in any form—photo, illustration, film strip—allow a second-language learner to pick up and practice vocabulary without translating. Hearing native speakers refer to items in the pictures furnishes vocabulary that he can then use as he takes part. Many of the materials and activities in Chapter 13, Labels and Captions, should prove useful also in tying things to English words without the intermediary of the native language. This "direct method" permits translation later but doesn't count on it as a teaching aid.

MEDIA

Both the goals of this curriculum (page 23) and the communication definition (page 16) take account of a variety of media. Be sure to read "Integrating Language Arts with Other Arts and Media" on page 40 for the general position of media in this program. They are constantly interwoven with language use, as the following list of activities shows.

GRAPHICS

• Make original drawings and title and caption
• Draw comics and cartoons, illustrations for stories
• Create roll-a-stories on scrolls or strips of paper or plastic
• Design posters, bulletin board displays, greeting cards, letterheads, stamps
• Make word and picture collages, dioramas of scenes from stories
• Create classroom museums
• Make signs, practical and entertaining
• Create ads, badges and bumper stickers, money
• Write concrete poems, rebuses
• Invent codes, picture symbols, brain teasers
• Draw charts and diagrams, graphs and scales
• Make maps, objective and subjective

- Create math-English problems and equations
- Make up card and board games

PHOTOGRAPHICS
- Take own photos and title, caption, or collage them
- Tell true stories about photos one has made or found
- Make up stories about any photos—singles, sequences—action, dialogue, inner speech, setting
- Make animated moving pictures
- Adapt a story or poem to screen
- Discuss photos, referring to internal evidence
- Make live motion picture

LIVE PERFORMING
- Make statements through body movements alone—pantomime, charades, dance
- Write or improvise puppet shows
- Do choral reading or voice chorus of texts
- Sing texts
- Combine voice, gesture, and stance in Readers Theater, Chamber Theater, Story Theater, and other rehearsed reading of texts
- Memorize, rehearse, and perform scripts/transcripts
- Put together multimedia shows combining slides, films, light, music, dance, pantomime, reading, and improvising
- Make up action and dialogue from a given situation
- Write songs and musicals to perform

AUDIO RECORDING
- Make a sound story of nothing but sound effects in sequence and ask others to verbalize a story for it. Or make their own narration and weave into the tape
- Tape something they have to say, then transcribe it later as a composition, revising if needed
- Tape a group discussion, then play it back and critique themselves
- Record a rehearsed reading of a text and put in the listening library for others to hear
- Write a radio script and tape it to play to others
- Record a blow-by-blow account of a game or other physical event. Play as is or transcribe later
- Record interviews to present directly for others

- Record interviews as part of a research project to use as notes
- Record a telephone improvisation and play back or transcribe
- Record school announcements and ads
- Listen to recordings while following text with eyes

VIDEO RECORDING
- Tape improvisations, performances, and discussions to play back and critique afterwards
- Do a talk show
- Make up and perform commercials and newscasts
- Do a TV documentary on location, with interviews

MEDIA MATERIALS OFFERED AS BOTH MEANS AND MODELS

- Booklets that combine words with graphics (found in *Interaction*):

Photos	*Jokes*
Photos with Captions	*Charts and Graphs*
Comics	*Maps*
Comics to Fill	*Signs*
Codes	*Things to Make*
Rebuses	*Songs*
Brain Teasers	

- The audiovisual presentation for literacy (page 191)
- Decks of photo cards for story making
- Card games combining words with pictures and other symbols, on cards and charts
- Books containing scripts for different media
- Listening library permitting seeing and hearing a text simultaneously
- Combination of recorded text with unpunctuated printed text to teach punctuation
- Manipulable materials and letter-moving devices for word making—spelling and phonics
- Activity cards combining graphics with words
- Films and videotapes, fictional and documentary, for discussion and stimulation of writing and other creativity.[3]

The magazine *Media and Methods,* published in Philadelphia, carries articles on the use of media.

[3] For a book about different media written to teachers of K–12, see Murray Suid and James Morrow, *Media and Kids,* Hayden Book Company, New York, 1975.

See also *Learning,* published in Palo Alto, California. For reviews of media materials, see *Media Mix,* a newsletter on ideas and resources for educational change, published by Jeffrey Schrank, 221 W. Madison, Chicago.

A good book written to explain still photography to elementary-school children is Murray Suid's *Painting with the Sun,* Dynamic Learning, 60 Wharf St., Boston, 1970.

A good book written for high school students about moving pictures is *Moviemaking Illustrated: The Comicbook Filmbook* by Murray Suid and James Morrow, Hayden Book Company, Rochelle Park, N.J., 1973.

Session	Vowels	Consonants
1	a (at)	
	i (it)	
2		t (tat)
3		p (pip)
4		s (sits)
5		s (is)
		z (zip)
6	e (set)	
	schwa (a pest)	
7		m (miss, am)
8	o (mop)	
9	u (must)	
10		n (nut, pen)
11		h (ham)
		b (Bob)
12		
13		c (can)
		k (kit)
14		
15		f (fan, if)
		g (gag)
16		d (dad)
17		r (rob)
		w (wish)
18	silent e (simple)	l (lip, apple)
19	a_e (cake)	
	ai (rain)	
	ay (way)	
20	i_e (kite)	
	ie (tie)	
	y (fly)	
	igh (fight)	
21	o_e (hope)	
	o (go)	
	oe (goes)	
	oa (coal)	
	ow (row)	
22	ee (keep)	
	ea (wheat)	
	e (me)	

Phoneme sequence chart B

[1] This sequence corresponds to that presented in the *Interaction* series of cassette films "Sound Out," except for the last two phonemes here, which were deemed easy enough to omit from the films.

Appendix B

Session	Vowels	Consonants	Session	Vowels	Consonants
23	u_e (cute) u (music) ew (few)		29	u(r) (blur) i(r) (stir) e(r) (her, batter)	
	ew (grew) u_e (dude)		30	a(r) (far)	
24	oo (pool)			a(r)e (care) ai (r) (hair)	
	oo (hook)			ea(r) (near) ee(r) (steer)	
25	e (rested)		31	au (cause, taught) aw (straw) a (call, talk) o (dog)	
	e (hopped)				
26		c (cent, Grace) v (vent, shave)	32	o(r) (for)	z (azure)
27	y (daddy)	j (jam) g (Gene, stage)			
		x (six)			
28	ou (mouse) ow (down)				
	oy (boy) oi (point)